standard catalog of®

LIONEL TRAIN SETS

1945-1969

ELECTRIC TRAIN SET

TRACK

SANTA FE

NEL CTRIC AINS

LIONEL

3419 LIONEL

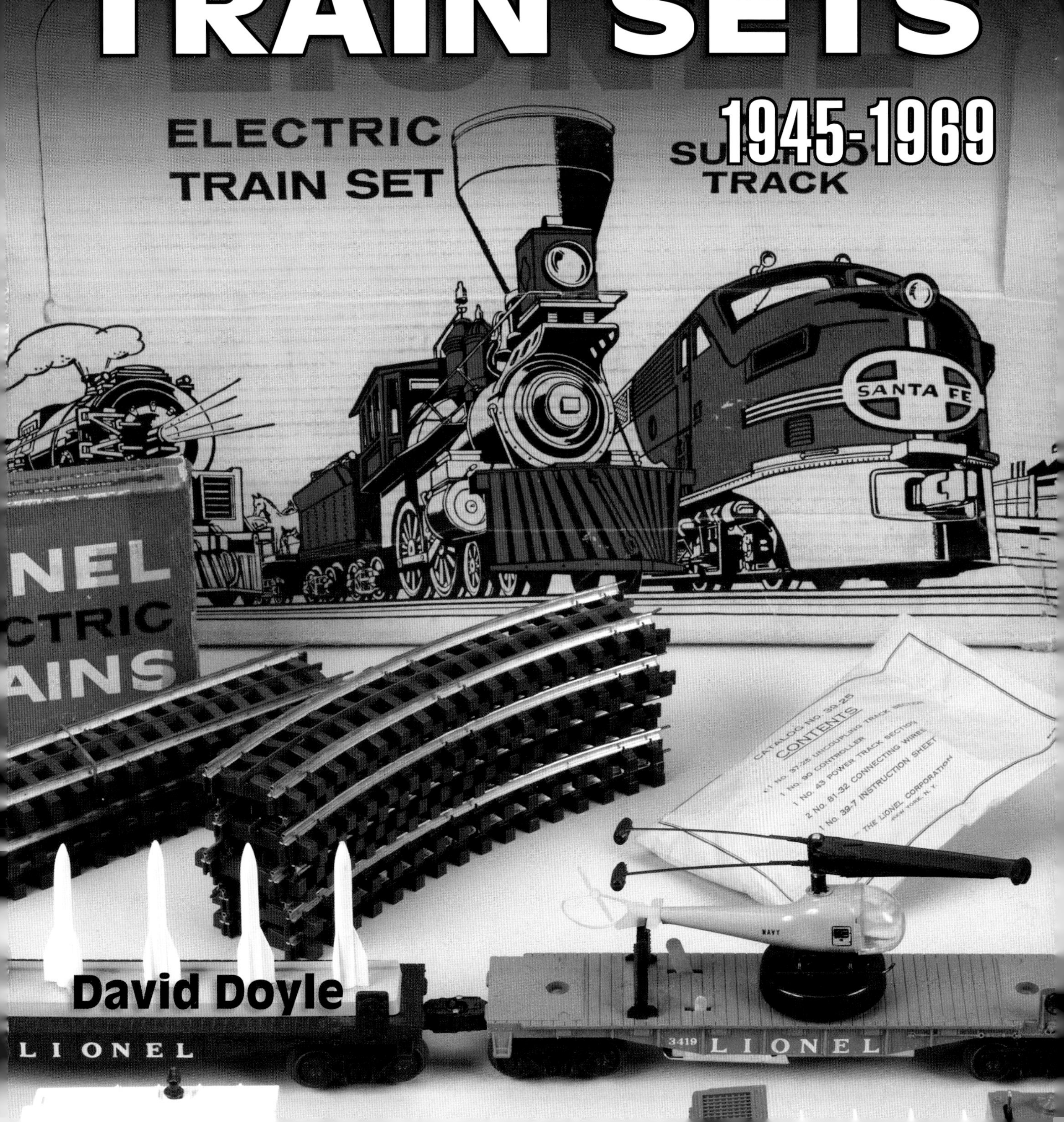

David Doyle

Published by

700 East State Street • Iola, WI 54990-0001
715-445-2214 • 888-457-2873
www.krausebooks.com

Our toll-free number to place an order or obtain a free catalog is (800) 258-0929.

Library of Congress Control Number: 2006925056

ISBN-13: 978-0-89689-444-0
ISBN-10: 0-89689-444-4

Designed by Kay Sanders
Edited by Justin Moen

Printed in China

ACKNOWLEDGMENTS

Once again, many long time friends, as well as new ones, generously allowed me to photograph their trains. A widespread group of collectors offered correction, criticism and commentary on subjects ranging from value and scarcity to fraudulent pieces. Every effort has been made to present complete and factual information, and any errors herein are purely my own.

The items included in this volume are by and large "normal production" items – trains likely to be encountered by the typical collector. Omitted were the occasional factory error, prototype and paint sample which even the most advanced collector is likely to encounter, and even fewer are interested in.

Once again, brothers Bill and John Autry graciously allowed me to photograph their extensive collection of fine postwar pieces – and even allowed me to bring select pieces to the publisher's photo studio. There, Krause's skilled photographers Bob Best and Kris Kandler shot the covers, as well as the chapter opening photos – most of which feature John and Bill's trains. But most of all, I'd like to thank John and Bill for their many years of friendship, which stretches beyond trains.

The contribution of Greg Stout to this volume cannot be overstated. Greg's firm, Stout Auctions, is one of the nation's premier sellers of collectable Lionel trains. Not only did Greg provide open access to the prices realized at these auctions through the years – which were taken into account in this volume, along with other factors – but Greg also graciously allowed us to reproduce many photos from his color auction catalogs.

Bob and John Tschopp opened their collection for photography and shared their knowledge. Bob's son, Bobby—a knowledgeable collector in his own right—was a tremendous help during the many days of photography.

Parts with Character shared much knowledge and experience with me, as well as allowing needed photographs to be taken.

My old friend, Jeff Kane of www.ttender.com, sent needed component photos of many individual items from his extensive inventory of postwar Lionel repair parts.

Special thanks to Greg Nicholas at www.NicksTrains.com for use of some of his photos. Special thanks are due as well to the auction firms of New England Toy and Train Exchange and Lloyd Ralston Gallery. A thank you to Dennis Waldron for generously providing the 1967 Winternitz auction catalog.

While some contributing to this volume have chosen to remain anonymous, there are three who obscurity is not deliberate. Paul Kennedy, who persuaded the publisher to make this edition a reality; Justin Moen, whose careful editing saves my former schoolteachers much embarrassment; and Kay Sanders, the skilled designer to who not only put it all together, but also endured countless phone calls and emails to incorporate last minute changes. Thank you all.

This book would not have been possible without the groundbreaking efforts of Paul V. Ambrose. Paul began gathering and publishing information about Lionel's postwar cataloged sets long before most collectors gave them a glance, making him truly a pioneer of postwar collecting and one of the foremost experts on postwar cataloged sets.

INTRODUCTION

While the Lionel train sets—or outfits as Lionel often termed them—shown in this book were created as playthings, today they are collector's items. While Lionel trains themselves have been collected for decades, only in the last 10 years or so have complete postwar sets become collectibles.

This in large part is a result of the maturing of the hobby. Initially, most collectors sought one of "everything"—everything being defined as each catalog number. Then came the collection of major variations, such as color, and then the criteria for variations grew, and included such minutia as the number of molded-in rivets, or the color of the plastic under the paint. At all times condition is paramount, with the presence of the original box or packaging being tied to the condition, or completeness of the item. Not surprisingly, as more and more enthusiasts' collections met these criteria, the bar was raised. Enter the set. As late as the mid 1980s, postwar set boxes were being discarded as unnecessary and bulky. Today they are recognized as yet another layer in the elusive "completeness" of a collection.

Today these sets or outfits, when still with the original individual item boxes and the original outfit carton, are prized collector's items.

The same components, without the outer outfit carton, are just a group of trains and lose their outfit or set, distinction and much of the value listed in this book. For a comprehensive listing of the values of such components, consult "The Standard Catalog of® Lionel Trains, 1945-69," or for a summary, refer to "Warman's® Lionel Train Field Guide, 1945-69."

The sets described in this book are those offered by Lionel in their regular consumer catalogs from 1945 through 1969. During this same time period, Lionel produced many uncataloged outfits as well; some were offered through the normal dealer network, others through mass merchandisers such as Sears and J.C. Penney, and others were used as premiums by firms such as Wix and Swift. These uncataloged outfits, some quite collectable, are not listed here. Collectors tend to gravitate toward those sets shown in Lionel's annual catalogs. Perhaps this is a result of the tremendous merchandising effort Lionel put into these sets. The Lionel catalog was lavishly illustrated, frequently by top-quality artists renderings, and the catalogs extensively circulated. The catalogs themselves have become collectibles, and are as poured over today as they were in our days of youth—continuing to fuel desire. By comparison, many uncataloged sets had only local or regional promotion, and few as elaborate as Lionel's marketing efforts. This is compounded by the lack of accurate documentation, until recently, as to exactly what sets were made when and for whom.

In addition to the locomotives and rolling stock, outfits typically came with instruction books and sheets, wire, lockon, accessory catalogs, brochures, smoke pellets and tampers (if applicable), and miniature billboards. All of these items must be present to realize the full value shown. Traditionally, O-Gauge and Super 0 outfits did not include a transformer, which was sold separately, while 027 outfits included a transformer. This situation changed in 1964, when a transformer was supplied with Super 0 outfit 13150. From that point on, transformers began to be supplied with more and more 0 and Super 0 outfits. One item that normally can be missing from outfits today without affecting the value is standard 027 and O-Gauge track. Unlike Super 0 track, 0 and 027 track is so common it is almost worthless, and most collectors feel that the damage caused to the boxes by the track rubbing on it exceeds the value of the track. In part because sets were ignored for so long by collectors, many were "dismantled"—their contents removed and displayed separately or sold. Today, some of these outfit boxes are being refilled—sometimes with the wrong item. Likewise, dealers or collectors wishing to upgrade their set sometimes replace worn or damaged locomotives, cars, or boxes with "better" examples. Too often these are not the correct variations for the "set."

This book will aid the collector in determining the originality of a set. A caveat to the above, Lionel was a profitable manufacturing company, and accordingly discarded little in the way of useable material. If a new design of rivet was introduced, the old one continued to be used until exhausted, leading to an apparent miss-match of components. Today collectors refer to these items as "transition" pieces. Further, period dealers were known to "swap" cars in outfits to suit customers' needs, a practice encouraged by the factory. Presence of "wrong" cars in sets today is not inherently proof of larcenous intent on the part of the seller, or of a rare factory variation, but in some cases merely a long-forgotten effort to make a customer happy. Likewise, Lionel's extensive network of factory authorized service centers endeavored to repair trains as quickly as possible, and at a maximum profit. Trucks, couplers and other components that failed were replaced with whatever workable parts were in stock, without regard to minute details so critical to collectors today.

CONTENTS

COLLECTING

Toy train collectors are their own fraternity, eagerly welcoming new buffs with a sincere interest in toy trains. Avail yourself of this knowledge base and friendship, whether you are an experienced collector or a rookie, and something can always be learned. There is no substitute for experience in this hobby, as in any other. No book, no matter how complete, contains all the answers. Thousands of words and the best illustrations cannot equal the experience gained by holding a piece in your own hands. There is no finer place for an enthusiast than in the home of a friend and fellow collector. The piece that is not for sale can be examined unhurried and questions answered honestly. It is excellent preparation for seeking an item in the marketplace.

The advent of Internet auctions has been a boon for collectors in remote areas. But for those in more populous areas, there is no substitute for shopping in the company of fellow collectors in hobby shops and train shows. Examining an item personally, with the counsel of more experienced collectors, is especially important when purchasing expensive, often repaired, or forged items.

Enthusiasts have been collecting toy trains perhaps as long as the trains have been produced. In the United States, the largest and oldest collectors group is the Train Collectors Association, or TCA. Founded in 1954 in Yardley, Pa., the group has grown to more than 31,000 members. An annual convention is held at various locations around the country each summer. Smaller, regional divisions and chapters dot the nation. Twice each year, one such group, the Eastern Division, hosts the largest toy train show in the world. The York Fairgrounds, in York, Pa., becomes a veritable Mecca for the toy train buff, with several buildings encompassing tens of thousands of square feet are full of toy trains for sale or trade. Members of the TCA agree to abide by a code of conduct, assuring fair and honest dealings between members. The nationally recognized grading standards were developed by the TCA.

The TCA headquarters is located in its Toy Train Museum and can be reached at:

The Train Collectors Association
P.O. Box 248
300 Paradise Lane
Strasburg, PA 17579
(717) 687-8623

The second-oldest organization is the Toy Train Operating Society, formed on the West Coast in 1966. It is similar in style and purpose to the TCA. Traditionally, the bulk of the TTOS members and events have been in the West, but the group has been gradually spreading eastward. The TTOS can be contacted at:

Toy Train Operating Society
25 W. Walnut Street, Suite 308
Pasadena, CA 91103
(626) 578-0673

One of the first, and certainly the largest, Lionel-specific clubs is the Lionel Collector's Club of America. Founded Aug. 1, 1970, by Jim Gates of Des Moines, Iowa, the organization has grown steadily since. The club was founded on the idea that collectors and operators of Lionel trains need an organization of their own. The clubs' mailing address is:

LCCA Business Office
P.O. Box 479
La Salle, IL 61301-0479

The youngster of these groups is the Lionel Operating Train Society, or LOTS. Founded in 1979 by Larry Keller of Cincinnati, this club's purpose is to provide a national train club for operators of Lionel trains and accessories. Like the others, it publishes magazines, swap lists, and a membership directory. LOTS can be reached at:

LOTS Business Office
6376 West Fork Road
Cincinnati, OH 45247-5704

Chapter 1

HOW TO USE THIS CATALOG

Because the value of an outfit is so dependent on the presence and condition of the outfit and component boxes, values are listed only for Excellent and Like New examples. In order for the set to grade in a specific condition, each and every component of the set: locomotive, cars and packaging, must be in the listed condition. The initial listing is done in numeric order; a chronological listing of cataloged outfit numbers follows the main listing. The outfit number, year, catalog name, and the catalog numbers of major components, beginning with locomotives, are shown below. A final note: A "W" suffix on an outfit number indicated that the train whistled, or had an operating horn; a "B" indicated an operating bell; "S" indicated the locomotive smoked.

To the collector, condition is everything. Many years ago the Train Collector's Association, the world's oldest and largest train collector group, established grading standards, which have recently been refined. This terminology is used by all reputable dealers and collectors when describing items offered for sale, and protects both parties from potential misunderstandings. Failure to properly use these terms in transactions between members can result in expulsion from the organization. These grading standards are as follows:

Fair, or C4: Well-scratched, chipped, dented, rusted, warped.

Good, or C5: Small dents, scratches, dirty.

Very Good, or C6: Few scratches, exceptionally clean, no major dents or rust.

Excellent, or C7: Minute scratches or nicks, no dents or rust, all original, less than average wear.

Like New, or C8: Only the slightest signs of handling and wheel wear, brilliant colors and crisp markings; literally like new. As a rule, trains must have their original boxes in comparable condition to realize the prices listed in the grade.

Mint, or C10: Brand new, absolutely unmarred, all original and unused. Items dusty or faded from display, or with fingerprints from handling, cannot be considered mint. Although Lionel test ran their locomotives briefly at the factory, items "test run" by consumers cannot be considered mint. Most collectors expect mint items to come with all associated packaging with which they were originally supplied.

As one can imagine, Mint pieces command premium prices. The supply is extremely limited, and the demand among collectors is great. Often it is the billfold of the buyer, rather than a more natural supply and demand situation, that dictates the price of such pieces.

Demand is one of the key factors influencing values. The Santa Fe F-3 diesel was the most-produced locomotive in Lionel's history, yet clean examples still command premium prices due to demand. Its classic beauty endures, and essentially every enthusiast or collector wants one.

Scarcity is also a factor influencing the value of trains. Low production quantities or extreme fragility make some items substantially more difficult to find than others. When scarcity is coupled with demand the result is a premium price, while other items, though extremely scarce, command only moderate prices due to lack of demand, or appreciation, on the part of collectors. In this guide we have rated each item on a scale of 1 to 8 for rarity. One represents the most common items, such as the 6017 caboose, while 8 is assigned to those items hardest to find, such as the gray 3562-1 barrel car with red lettering. It is hoped that this rarity rating will help the collector when they are faced with the proverbial "How likely am I to get this chance again?" question. The scarcity ratings given in this volume are relative only to each other, not to the individual items listed in *"The Standard Catalog of® Lionel Trains, 1945-1969."* This is because any boxed set is inherently scarcer than an individual component.

Supply is related to rarity and also affects price. If only one sought-after item is at a given show, the seller is unlikely to negotiate or reduce his price. If, however, multiple sellers at a given event have identical items, no matter how rare, the temporary market glut can bring about temporarily reduced prices.

Lastly, the **buyer's intent** will affect what they are willing to pay. A collector who intends to add a piece to their permanent collection will normally be willing to pay more for an item than a dealer who is intending to resell the item.

Prices are given in this guide for trains in Excellent and Like New conditions. Trains in less than Very Good condition are not generally considered collectable, and as mentioned earlier, Mint condition trains are too uncommon to establish pricing on. Among set collectors, the most sought after and traded items are in the Excellent and Like New categories.

The prices listed are what a group of collectors would consider a reasonable market value—a price they would be willing to pay to add that piece to their collection. When contemplating a sale to a dealer, you should expect to receive 30 to 50 percent less, with the poorer condition of the trains, the greater the amount of discount, due to the greater difficulty the dealer will have selling them. Remember that these prices are only a guideline. When you are spending your money, what an item is worth to you is of greater importance than what it is worth to the author. Conversely, the publisher of this book does not sell trains, this is not a mail-order catalog, and you should not expect a dealer or collector to "price match."

Unlike certain other collectibles, the age of a Lionel train is not a factor in its value. That is, an older train is not inherently more valuable than a newer train. It is rather the variations in construction throughout an item's production run that affect its scarcity, and thus its collector value. Many Lionel trains are marked on the sides with "New" or "Built" dates. These dates are totally irrelevant to when a piece was actually produced, and are decorative only. During the mid-1950s, Lionel added the year introduced as a prefix or suffix to the stock number of some cars, such as the 336155 markings on the log dump cars introduced in 1955, or the 546446 N & W hopper car from 1954, but this was not universally done.

Although a few collectors specialize in a specific year or two of Lionel production, they are the exception as opposed to the rule. The production dates of individual set components, however, are important in establishing the authenticity of a set. Keeping in mind that Lionel was first and foremost a profitable manufacturing concern—it was inherent that there was a period of transition among features. That is to say, pieces produced in early 1951 are likely to have characteristics of late 1950 production. There are, however certain limits to this. That is, a 1966 dated set won't include features last normally used in 1948 production. Similarly, a 1948 set can't possibly have features not introduced until 1952. When such circumstances do arise, they are most often the result of repairs done to the train, or the improper substitution of a component by a dealer or collector seeking to improve the condition of the set, or, in rare instances it can be the result of fraud.

Among the key aids to dating trains are the construction techniques used in the manufacture of the trucks and couplers, and the type of original packaging used. Throughout this book these features will be highlighted at the beginning of each chapter—and occasionally additional information will be given within the chapter. A brief overview of the key changes is given here for reference.

Aids to Dating Trains

Unlike certain other collectibles, the age of a postwar Lionel train is not a factor in its value. That is, an older train is not inherently more valuable than a newer train. It is rather the variations in construction throughout an item's production run that affect its scarcity, and thus its collector value. Many Lionel trains are marked on the sides with "New" or "Built" dates. These dates are totally irrelevant to when a piece was actually produced, and are decorative only. During the mid-1950s, Lionel added the year introduced as a prefix or suffix to the stock number of some cars, such as the 336155 markings on the log dump cars introduced in 1955, or the 546446 N & W hopper car from 1954, but this was not universally done.

Establishing the production dates of these trains is usually done more out of curiosity for most collectors, or when they are trying to properly and precisely recreate a given train set.

Among the key aids to dating trains are the construction techniques used in the manufacture of the trucks and couplers, and the type of original packaging used, if it's still present.

Lionel Couplers and Trucks

For the greatest part of the 20th century, Lionel trains were produced as toys, not as collectibles. Thus, there were manufacturing variations induced by supply shortages and the company's continuing efforts to reduce costs. These variations, having been carefully studied, can today be used as an aid in dating given pieces. No components are more universally used than trucks and couplers. In railroading terms, a truck is the assembly of wheels, axles and suspension components. In most instances, each truck has two axles and four wheels, though in some cases there were three axles and six wheels. In real railroad practice, occasionally trucks were found with four axles and eight wheels.

The most startling innovation in Lionel trains when production resumed after WWII was the knuckle coupler. The first type, known to collectors as the "coil coupler," had a solenoid on each coupler, which was used to release the knuckle. Part of the copper windings on this example are visible (indicated by an arrow). In 1948, Lionel began to wrap the distinctive copper windings of the coupler coil in black friction tape, which helped conceal them.

Lionel used the interruption of toy production during World War II to design a more realistic appearing truck and coupler assembly than it previously used. When train production resumed very late in 1945, pieces were equipped with operating couplers and trucks of a much more realistic (albeit oversized) style than used previously. Period advertising flaunted Lionel's "Real Knuckle Couplers." The first couplers had a built-in solenoid, which was activated by current passing through a steel pin surrounded by a plastic shoe.

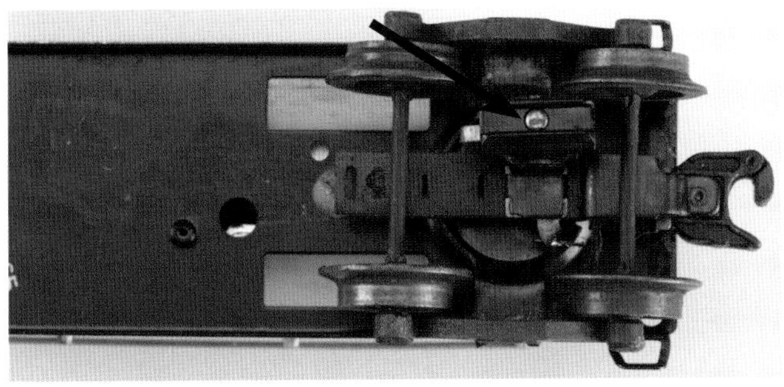

The very earliest coil couplers, those produced in 1945, were of a style known to collectors as the "flying shoe" type. These couplers had their pickup shoes suspended from a fiber strip. The shoe itself merely guides a rivet (indicated by an arrow), the head of which is exposed and served as an electrical contact to allow current to pass from the special uncoupling track mechanism to the solenoid coil. After 1945, a steel baseplate was used to mount the shoe, the basic design of which would be carried over into magnetic coupler production.

The six-wheel truck, shown here, was used with various coupler and drawbar configuration on Lionel's better tenders, passenger cars and cranes from 1946 through 1951.

"Staple-end" is a term used by collectors for Lionel's common postwar metal trucks produced prior to 1951. The name stems from the appearance of the swedging on the end of the bolster in order to secure it to the diecast sideframe. This resembles a staple (arrow 1). Notice the top center of the sideframe as flat (arrow 2). These so-called "staple-end" trucks were used from 1945 until 1951.

The magnetic coupler was introduced in 1949. From Lionel's standpoint it was much less expensive to produce. Rather than having a copper-wound solenoid coil on each coupler, a single copper-wound electromagnet was imbedded into the uncoupling track section. A simple spring-loaded steel plate with locking pin held the knuckle closed on this type coupler (see arrow 1). The benefit to the customer was that the trains could now be uncoupled manually anywhere on the track, rather than only on special track sections. The flying shoe was retained on some examples, such as this one (see arrow 2), but now it provided an electrical path to actuate operating mechanism on certain rolling stock such as the log and milk cars. Initially, this later coupler was used on 027 cars, but by 1950 it was also being used on 0-Gauge trains.

Scale vs. Gauge, And What Is Super O?

In miniature railroading there is much confusion over the use of the terms "scale" and "gauge," even amongst experienced model railroaders. Unfortunately, Lionel's usage of the terms adds to the confusion.

Scale is a numeric ratio describing the relative size of a miniature to an original. An example would be 1/48th scale. A 1/48th scale model occupies 1/48th the volume of the real article, so 48 model boxcars in 1/48th scale placed end to end would equal the length of the real railroad car duplicated.

Gauge is the distance between the tops of the rails. On most real U.S. railroads, this is 4 feet 8-1/2 inches. For Lionel's most popular size of trains, this width is 1-1/4 inches. In miniature railroading, most of the various gauges are named by number or letter. A toy train track with a rail-to-rail width of 1-1/4 inches is named with the numeral 0. Other popular early train gauges and their rail-to-rail widths were: Number 1-Gauge, 1-3/4 inches; Number 2-Gauge, two inches; Number 3-Gauge, 2-1/2 inches; Number 4-Gauge, 3-1/4 inches. Many of these sizes, though popular in Europe, were not widely accepted in the United States.

"Standard Gauge," a popular size for U.S. toy train makers prior to World War II, had a rail-to-rail width of 2-1/8 inches. The relative newcomer HO has a width of 5/8 inches—half that of O-Gauge, and that is where the name comes from; HO means half-0.

Most trains running on O-Gauge track are scaled 1/48th the size of the original, but keep in mind that Lionel, despite its occasional claims otherwise, largely was manufacturing toy trains, not scale models. Great liberties were often taken in size and detail to meet the demands of practical production and operation.

In 1951, Lionel introduced what came to be known as the "bar-end" truck in order to rectify a problem with sideframes loosening. With this type of construction the sideframe was crimped rather than the bolster. Notice now the end of the bolster is smooth, like a steel bar—hence the name (arrow 1), while the top of the bolster is cupped (arrow 2). This truck was the mainstay of Lionel's freight car production until 1961, when it was largely phased out until 1969, when it reappeared on selected better items.

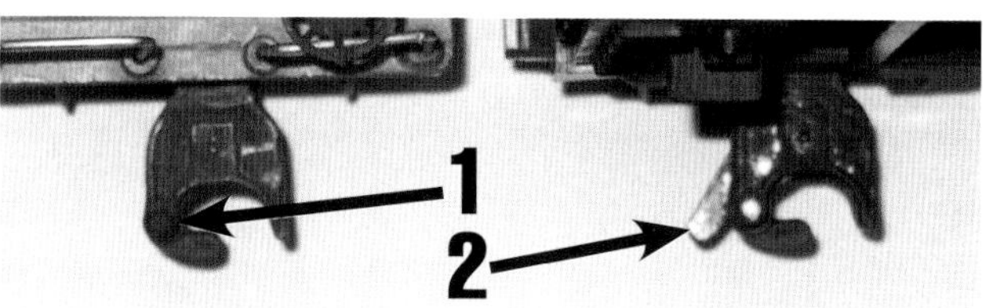

The knuckle on the coupler on the left was attached with a black rivet (arrow 1). This was used prior to 1955. During 1955, Lionel began to use a shiny rivet as seen on the right, and it was used exclusively by 1956. Also in 1955, a tab was added (arrow 2) to the coupler release plate, making it easier to manually uncouple cars.

Introduced in 1948 for use on the least-expensive sets, the "Scout" truck had a one-piece sheet metal bolster and sideframe. Decorative plastic panels were attached to the side frame. Today these panels are often found covered with a gray mold-like discoloration. This discoloration can be removed by gently heating them with a blow drier on the low setting.

The Scout trucks originally were equipped with the "Scout coupler" seen here. The coupler was discontinued in 1951 because it was not compatible with any of Lionel's standard couplers, but the trucks continued to be used on inexpensive items through 1953.

A circle of Lionel's traditional O-Gauge curved track measured 31 inches in outside diameter, and a section of track was 11/16 inches tall. Other types of trackage were produced by Lionel to accommodate its O-Gauge trains. Wide-radius curved track, called 072, which had the same cross section as regular 0, but formed a circle 72 inches in diameter center to center (74 inches overall), was introduced just prior to WWII, and produced briefly afterwards.

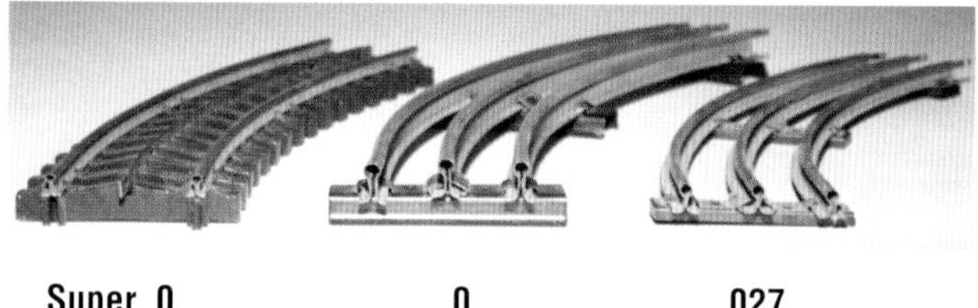

Super 0   0   027

Much more common was 027 track. It had the same 1-1/4-inch gauge as 0, but used less and lighter-weight material. It stood only 7/16 inches tall and formed a circle 27 inches in outside diameter. (Notice the name of 027 was based on outside dimension, whereas 072 was based on the center-to-center measurement.)

Super 0, introduced in 1957, was Lionel's first attempt at realistic-looking track since WWII. (Prior to WWII Lionel had briefly produced what it called T-rail track, with an accurate rail cross section.) Rather than the sparse three sheet-metal crossties of 0 and 027, Super 0 had many smaller, closely spaced plastic ties. The center rail, necessary for electrical pickup on a Lionel system, was replaced by a less-visible narrow copper blade, and the outside rails had a much more realistic shape than did the tubular rails of 0 and 027.

Both 0 and Super 0 track-equipped sets were discontinued in the mid-1960s as Lionel found itself with an ever-smaller, and increasingly cost-conscious, customer base.

Lionel introduced the truck, primarily of plastic construction, in 1957. Molded of Delrin, a self-lubricating plastic, the detailed trucks were styled after a real railroad truck developed by the Association of American Railroads (AAR), and bore the tiny raised word "Timken" on the ends of the simulated journals.

Another feature of the new trucks was an integral coupler, which produced further cost savings.

On trucks made from 1957 through 1963, the ends of the axles are not visible when viewed from the bottom. Beginning in 1963 and until the end of production in 1969, the design was changed, and when turned over the ends of the axles are visible.

Initially, the AAR truck used a metal coupler knuckle that was retained by a silver-colored pin, part number 480-16. In late 1961, Lionel began to form the coupler knuckle from Delrin, which was less expensive than the previously used metal. The plastic knuckle was retained with the same type silver pin used with the metal knuckle.

Sometime in 1962 Lionel introduced a redesigned Delrin knuckle with integral "tits," which engaged the holes of the coupler casting and acted as pivot points for the knuckle. This style knuckle was used from 1962 through 1969.

However, with the company seeking even greater cost reductions, lower-end items were assembled with either one or both trucks having molded, fixed non-operating couplers.

The other plastic truck of the postwar era was the archbar truck. Originally created in 1959 for use on cars pulled by the Civil War-era "General" steam locomotive, ultimately it was used on a variety of other cars as well even though real railroads had long since stopped using this style truck.

The trucks themselves had either no coupler, as used on tender fronts and passenger cars (which had separate body-mounted couplers), or non-operating couplers, as used on tender rears and the General set flatcar. In the later desperate years of Lionel's production, these trucks came to be used across the product line, regardless of whether they were correct for the period of the prototype railcar.

This truck, with its die-cast side frames and coil-type coupler, was used on 2400-series sreamlined passenger cars from 1948 through 1953.

In 1954, the 2400-series passenger car trucks were equipped with magnetic couplers as seen here. This considerably lowered manufacturing costs as compared to the coil coupler style. This coupler continued to be used until the end of passenger car construction in 1966, with only a 1955 change in 480-16 pivot pin color from black to silver.

The 2500 series truck was an upsized version of the 2400 series truck, with increased axle spacing and larger die-cast side frames. The long overhang of the car body from the truck pivot point necessitated a very long articulated drawbar and coupler operating linkage. The early 1952 production trucks used wire electrical leads from the pickup rollers to supply current for the interior lighting of the cars, but by 1953 these were replaced by a simpler-to-manufacture rivet and wiper system. In 1955, there was a change in 480-16 pivot pin color from black to silver, and beyond that the truck ran without change until the 2500 series cars were discontinued in 1966.

072 Super 0 0-Gauge 027

Chapter 2

1945

THE LIONEL LINE for Christmas 1945

Flash! This is a quick picture of available LIONEL merchandise for Christmas 1945. It's only the beginning, of course! Some sensational suprises on the way for 1946.

FEATURING THE *NEW* REMOTE CONTROL REAL RAILROAD KNUCKLE COUPLERS, DIE CAST TRUCKS, AND *SOLID* STEEL WHEELS

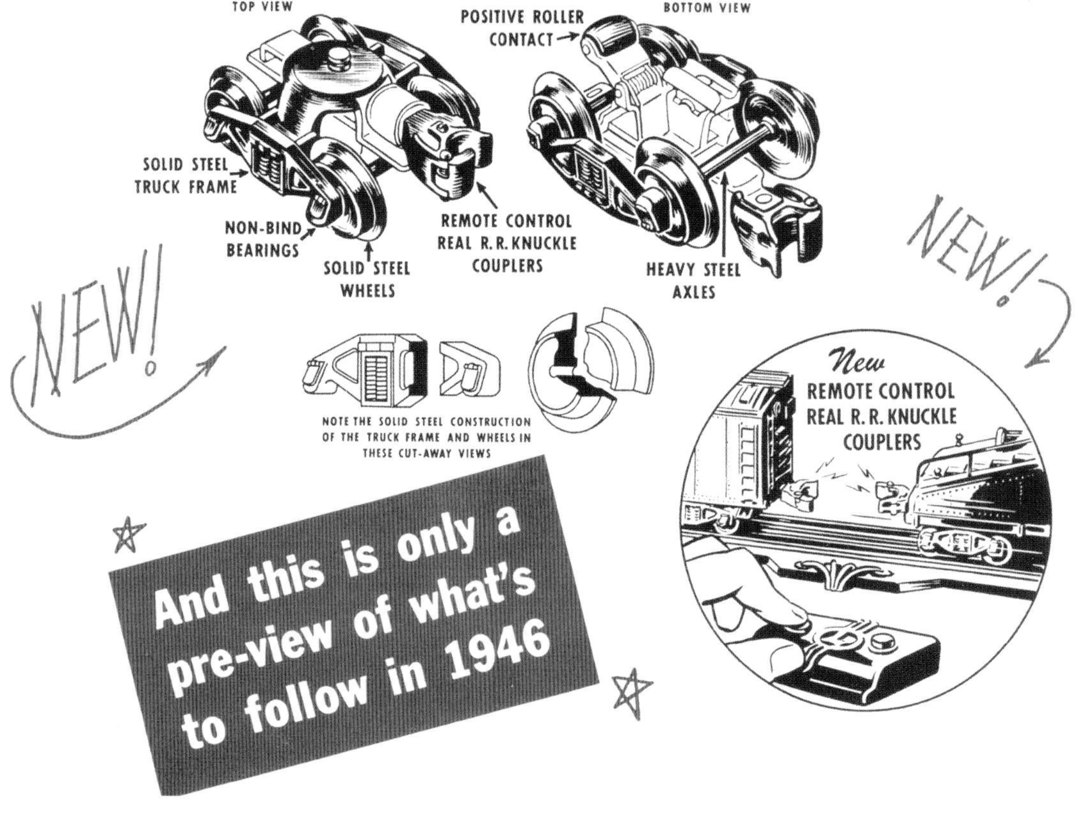

The Second World War changed the routine of the nation. Toy trains were frivolous commodities, consuming both critical raw materials and skilled labor, and their production ceased. In their place, Lionel churned out telegraph keys, as well as compasses and other navigational instruments for the nation's defense. Eagerly anticipating the end of the war and the return to normalcy, executives at Lionel met on Saturdays, making plans for resuming toy train production as soon as the war ended.

The complete halt in production, carried through three Christmas selling seasons, provided the firm an opportunity to completely revamp its line. The biggest planned change was the introduction of a realistic, albeit oversized, knuckle coupler. These couplers were to be mounted on newly designed trucks with die-cast side frames and solid metal wheels. Also significant was the planned-for increased use of plastics in toy train production.

Immediately after the August 1945 end of WWII, Lionel began implementing its plans and introducing the new features. In addition to the knuckle coupler, production of a gondola car with a molded plastic body and stamped sheet-metal frame, the 2452, began as well.

Rushed into production, the knuckle coupler design was not finely refined, and underwent several revisions.

To promote Lionel's products for the Christmas 1945 season, a simple brochure was hurriedly produced. Printed on both sides of an 11 x 17 piece of paper, which was then folded to create a four-page flyer, it announced the new coupler, and illustrated the only outfit offered in 1945: the 463W.

Though the 2452 gondola car was new, the balance of the outfit was made up of reintroduced prewar items. Many of these items were even packaged in boxes left over from prewar production, with their new product numbers rubber stamped on the boxes. The component boxes were packed in a set box made of tan corrugated pasteboard, which was marked with "463W-2" printed in black directly on the carton; further identification was provided by an orange, blue and white label that was pasted on one side of the box.

463W **$33.50 retail**

Contents: 224 2-6-2 steam locomotive with headlight; 2466W early coal tender with whistle; 2458 automobile car; 2452 gondola with barrels; 2555 Sunoco single-dome tank car; 2457 Pennsylvania N5 illuminated caboose; eight curved and three straight sections of O-Gauge track; RCS remote control section; 167 whistle controller, instruction book.

The 224 locomotive included in this set was carried over from the prewar era. The rear of the locomotive's cab floor was square, and its handrails were blackened (as opposed to the shiny rails used in other years. A long drawbar coupled the locomotive with its tender. This coupling was unique among postwar steamers, with the tender having no drawbar. The extra-long locomotive drawbar was hooked into an oval hole stamped out of the tender frame.

In addition to its unique frame, blackened handrails also distinguish the 1945 2466W tender. The tender had white heat-stamped lettering.

In tow behind the locomotive was a 2458 Pennsylvania automobile boxcar. Except for the trucks, the brown boxcar was identical to the prewar model, including the number stamped on its side, 2758, not the cataloged number of 2458. In the rush to get an outfit on the market for Christmas 1945, Lionel reused the prewar heat-stamp tooling, or, more likely, assembled these cars with leftover prewar bodies.

Also carried forward and included in the set was a steel and die-cast tank car. Like the boxcar, the number

463W

Shown here is the unique 1945 locomotive-tender coupling system.

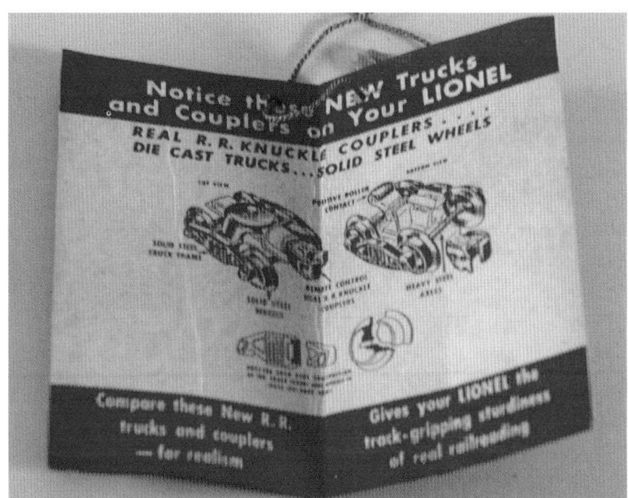

Set 453W included a red tag with red braided string describing the new coupler.

The earliest postwar trucks had patterns embossed on the rear of the wheels.

Even after the wheel rears were plain the axles remained thick.

Ultimately wire axles began to be used.

on the car body, 2755, was a carryover from the similar prewar car; presumably the old decals were used to both expedite production and utilize existing inventory. Its box, however, was marked "2555." The cars had all the trim details: steps on all corners, brake stands, brake cylinders, ladders, placards and handrails of their prewar predecessor. The car was marked with the Sun Oil Co. "Sunoco" logo, with the word "GAS" above and "OILS" below the "SUNOCO" on the herald. There were two varieties of the "Sunoco" decal used. In one version, the decal film around the data beneath the logo was rectangular; in the other version, the decal film was cut to fit the text of the data. The lettering of the word "SUNOCO" was much heavier on this version than on the rectangular-cut decal. Likewise, there were two versions of decals with the S.U.N.X. weight and capacity markings—one being in a much larger typeface than the other, the smaller-lettered decal being cut square, while the larger-lettered decals were cut to follow the shape of the text. The tank, or car body, was painted silver.

The 2452 gondola was the first all-new car of the postwar era. Painted black with white heat-stamped lettering, the car had the number "347000" on the side, along with the PRR keystone logo. There are four lines of technical data on the car, with the last line ending in "G27." This "G27" was notably smaller on 1945 cars than it was on later cars. On the right corner of each side of the car was an ornamental brake wheel. These cars were loaded with four 0209 two-part turned wooden barrels that could be opened. The number 2452 was sometimes rubber-stamped on the underside of the car's steel frame.

The all-steel 2457 was a carryover from prewar days; indeed, some of the bodies used were likely produced prior to WWII. Initially using a brown body with red window frames, the later cars had red bodies and black window frames and celluoid glazing. The white rubber-stamped lettering included "EASTERN DIV." on most examples. All were numbered "477618" on their sides. On some of the brown-bodied 1945 cabooses the lettering was not properly centered on the car. The number "2457" was rubber-stamped only on the bottom of the black-painted frame, but not all examples got the frame numbering.

Although shown in the brochure as a stripped-down model without window inserts, smokestack or rear coupler, that is not how it was produced. The caboose had interior illumination, steps, end rails, ladders, and a simulated battery box. In most cases, the front and rear windows of the cupola were stamped open.

Excellent	Like New	Scarcity
850	1,550	8

CHAPTER 3

1946

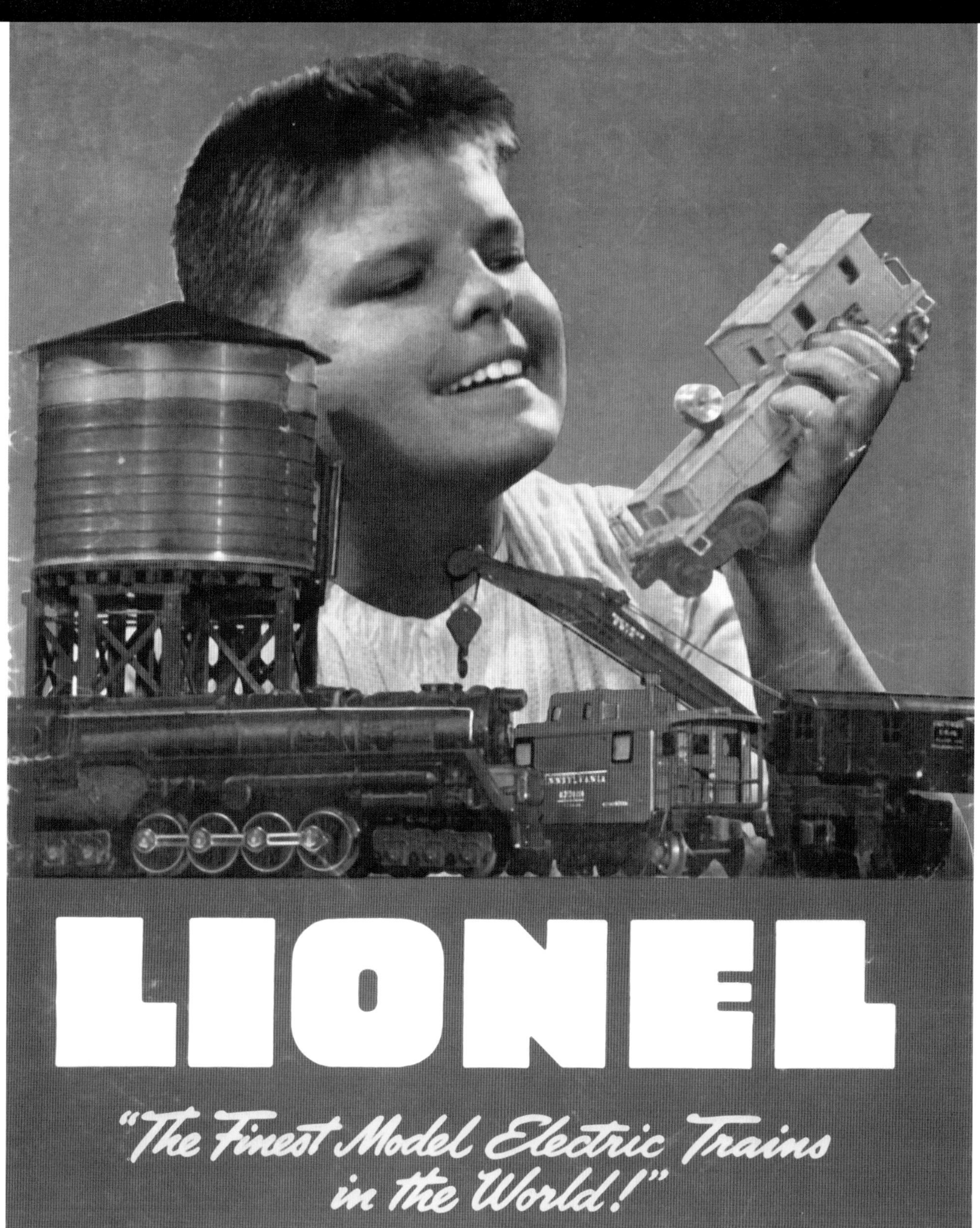
LIONEL
"The Finest Model Electric Trains in the World!"

Selling trains in 1945 was not a challenge. The nation, rejoicing over the end of World War II, was also flush with money from returning veterans and the upsurge in employment due to war production. The next year would be more challenging. Anticipating this, Lionel produced an array of goods similar to those from prewar catalogs. Among these offerings were 23 sets. This broad spectrum of sets allowed outfits for any price point, with the least expensive outfit retailing for only $24.95, while the deluxe outfit was $85.

Whereas the 1945 lineup was, with the exception of the gondola, a rehash of previously produced products, 1946 was the debut year of many new designs. New motive power included the O-Gauge 726 Berkshire—produced by installing a 2-8-4 mechanism in a boiler based on the prewar 226E—and the all-new 6-8-6 Pennsylvania turbine. The latter was offered in O-Gauge outfits as catalog number 671, while those included in 027 outfits were numbered 2020. Nearer to the low end of the line was a streamlined 2-6-4 with the catalog number of 221.

New freight cars were introduced as well. The 2411 "big inch" flatcar shared its die-cast frame with the 2419 and 2420 work cabooses. Also using die-cast frames were sophisticated new dump cars: 3451 for logs and 3459 for coal. The new 2460 crane also had a die-cast frame, and rode on a pair of six-wheel trucks. These trucks shared many components with similar six-wheel trucks used on Bakelite-bodied 2625 passenger cars and the die-cast-bodied 2426W tender used by the 726.

The engineering having been proven with the 1945 2452 gondola, the design element of an injection-molded plastic body mounted on a stamped steel frame was expanded. The 2454 boxcar, 2465 Sunoco tank car and 3454 operating merchandise cars included plastic bodies mounted on steel frames. The 2452 was continued, and joined by a second gondola, the 2452X, which lacked the brake wheels and barrels that adorned the 2452.

The low-end 027 sets contained many cars that were reworked from prewar designs, but as more of the year passed, increasing numbers of new products were produced, which were included in more expensive outfits.

Following up on the success of the 1945 knuckle couplers was a spectacular new feature included in the better sets—smoke. Even more spectacular, but much less widespread, was Electronic Control—the latter available only in set 4109WS.

As was the case in 1945, the 1946 outfit boxes were simple corrugated cartons with pasted-on labels to identify the set they contained. Typically the trains, in their individual component boxes, were packed into these cartons in two layers.

027-Gauge Outfits

1400 Lionel 027 Passenger Set $30 retail

Included: 221 2-6-4 steam locomotive with operating headlight; 221T sheet-metal tender; two 2430 blue Pullman cars; 2431 blue observation; eight 1013 curved and three 1018 straight track; 1019 027 remote control track section; UTC Lockon, 926-5 instruction booklet; 1037 40-watt transformer.

The 1946 Lionel catalog showed the locomotive and tender painted green, as were a few pre-production samples. However, the production models were gray—initially with aluminum wheels and later with black wheels.

The non-illuminated passenger cars were based on prewar 1630 series cars, and the silver lettering stamped on their blue flanks matched their silver roofs.

Excellent	Like New	Scarcity
550	1,250	6

1400W Lionel 027 Passenger Set $35.95 retail

Included: 221 2-6-4 steam locomotive with operating headlight; 221W sheet-metal tender; two 2430 blue Pullman cars; 2431 blue observation; eight 1013 curved and three 1018 straight track; 1019 027 remote control track section; UTC Lockon, 926-5 instruction booklet; 1041 60-watt transformer.

This set was a slightly more expensive version of the 1400 outfit. For the $5.95 premium over the 1400, a 221W whistling tender replaced the 221T, and the transformer was upgraded to a 1041 60-watt unit. The balance of the outfit, including locomotive, passenger cars and track, was unchanged.

Excellent	Like New	Scarcity
650	1,400	7

1401 Lionel 027 Freight Outfit $24.95 retail

Included: 1654 2-4-2 steam locomotive with operating headlight; 1654T sheet-metal tender; 2452X gondola; 2465 Sunoco double-dome tank car; 2472 red non-illuminated Pennsylvania N5 caboose; eight 1013 curved and one 1018 straight track; 1019 027 remote control track section; UTC Lockon, 926-5 instruction booklet; 1037 40-watt transformer.

Like the caboose, the locomotive in this outfit was derived from a prewar item. The 2452 gondola, introduced in 1945, was cheapened for inclusion in this outfit. Shorn of its brake wheels and its cargo of barrels, the revised version was given a new number—2452X.

Debuting in this set was a car that would become a mainstay of Lionel freight outfits through the remainder of the 1940s and into the 1950s—the Sunoco double-dome tank car. As first produced, and included in this set, the car was given catalog number 2465. Some of the early cars had only a single decal centered on each side, this decal being the Sunoco "diamond" logo. The bulk of the cars had this decal near the left-hand end of the car, with a second decal of reporting marks near the right-hand end of the car.

This outfit had the dubious distinction of having the lowest retail price of any set offered in 1946.

Excellent	Like New	Scarcity
150	275	4

1401W Lionel 027 Freight Outfit $30.95 retail

Included: 1654 2-4-2 steam locomotive with operating headlight; 1654W sheet-metal tender with whistle; 2452X gondola; 2465 Sunoco double-dome tank car; 2472 red non-illuminated Pennsylvania N5 caboose; eight 1013 curved and one 1018 straight track; 1019 027 remote control track section; UTC Lockon, 926-5 instruction booklet; 1041 60-watt transformer.

This set was a slightly more expensive version of the 1401 outfit. For the $6 additional cost over the 1401, a 1654W whistling tender replaced the 1654T, and the transformer was upgraded to a 1041 60-watt unit. The balance of the outfit, including locomotive, freight cars and track, was unchanged.

Excellent	Like New	Scarcity
250	450	6

1402 Lionel 027 Freight Outfit $30 retail

Included: 1666 2-6-2 steam locomotive with operating headlight; 2466T early coal tender; two 2440 Pullmans; 2441 observation; eight 1013 curved and three 1018 straight track; 1019 027 remote control track section; UTC Lockon, 926-5 instruction booklet; 1037 40-watt transformer.

Though the catalog showed this set with blue and silver passenger cars, those actually packaged with the outfit were green with silver rubber-stamped lettering. The locomotive differed from the prewar model in that its cab floor was rounded at the rear, in contrast to the earlier squared-off version.

Excellent	Like New	Scarcity
500	750	6

1401, 1400, 1403, 1402, 1405, 1407B, 1409, 1411W

1402W Lionel 027 Freight Outfit $35.95 retail

Included: 1666 2-6-2 steam locomotive with operating headlight; 2466W early coal tender with whistle; two 2440 Pullmans; 2441 observation; eight 1013 curved and three 1018 straight track; 1019 027 remote control track section; UTC Lockon, 926-5 instruction booklet; 1041 60-watt transformer.

As was the case for many outfits in the early postwar era, this number merely reflected the inclusion of a whistle and associated controls in a standard set.

Excellent	Like New	Scarcity
600	900	6

1403 Lionel 027 Freight Train $30 retail

Included: 221 2-6-4 steam locomotive with operating headlight; 221T sheet-metal tender; 2411 flatcar with pipes; 2465 Sunoco double-dome tank car; 2472 non-illuminated red Pennsylvania N5 caboose; eight 1013 curved and three 1018 straight track; 1019 027 remote control track section; UTC Lockon; 926-5 instruction booklet; 1037 40-watt transformer.

As was the case with the passenger set, the catalog indicated this outfit was headed by a green 221 locomotive. This was not the case in actuality, as the streamlined 221 was painted gray with black wheels.

The die-cast 2411 flatcar was loaded with three metal pipes. The pipes, as well as the 2411-4 stakes, have been reproduced. Absence of original pipes significantly reduces the value of this car. The internal ridges running lengthwise in the pipes can distinguish original pipes.

Excellent	Like New	Scarcity
425	650	5

1403W Lionel 027 Freight Train $35.95 retail

Included: 221 2-6-4 steam locomotive with operating headlight; 221W sheet-metal tender; 2411 flatcar with pipes; 2465 Sunoco double-dome tank car; 2472 non-illuminated red Pennsylvania N5 caboose; eight 1013 curved and three 1018 straight track; 1019 027 remote control track section; UTC Lockon; 926-5 instruction booklet; 1041 60-watt transformer.

This set was a duplicate of the 1403, with the addition of a whistle and inclusion of a more powerful transformer.

Excellent	Like New	Scarcity
525	775	6

1405 Lionel 027 Freight Train $30 retail

Included: 1666 2-6-2 steam locomotive with operating headlight; 2466T early coal tender; 2452X gondola; 2465 Sunoco double-dome tank car; 2472 non-illuminated red Pennsylvania N5 caboose; eight 1013 curved and three 1018 straight track; 1019 027 remote control track section; UTC Lockon; 926-5 instruction booklet; 1037 40-watt transformer.

This set was an upgraded and more expensive version of outfit 1401. Replacing outfit 1401's model 1654 2-4-2 was a much more impressive-looking 1666 2-6-2. The 1666 was equipped with prewar-style metal number plates. Like the other sets produced early in the 1946 model year, many of the 1405 outfit's cars ride on trucks equipped with "flying shoe" couplers.

Excellent	Like New	Scarcity
175	300	4

1405W Lionel 027 Freight Train $35.95 retail

Included: 1666 2-6-2 steam locomotive with operating headlight; 2466W early coal tender; 2452X gondola; 2465 Sunoco double-dome tank car; 2472 non-illuminated red Pennsylvania N5 caboose; eight 1013 curved and three 1018 straight track; 1019 027 remote control track section; UTC Lockon; 926-5 instruction booklet; 1041 60-watt transformer.

A further upgrade—including a whistle and larger transformer with whistle control—to the 1405 resulted in the 1405W.

Excellent	Like New	Scarcity
225	400	7

1407B Lionel 027 Switcher Bell Outfit $37.50 retail

Included: 1665 0-4-0 steam switcher with operating headlight; 2403B slope-back tender with ringing bell; 2560 crane; 2452X gondola; 2419 work caboose; eight 1013 curved and five 1018 straight track; 1019 027 remote control track section; UTC Lockon; 926-5 instruction booklet; 1037 40-watt transformer.

This work train was powered by a 1665 0-4-0 switcher, which was a revamped prewar 1662 switcher. Among the changes made to the locomotive were the installation of the new postwar trucks on the tender, and mounting Lionel's new knuckle couplers on the rear of the tender and pilot of the locomotive.

Mounting an injection-molded plastic cab and two injection-molded plastic toolboxes onto the die-cast body casting created for the 2411 flatcar created the 2419 work caboose. A die-cast smokejack was installed on the caboose cab.

The sheet metal 2560 crane car was carried over from the prewar line in its original colors of yellow cab with red roof. The 1946 production of these cranes included two-piece booms that were riveted together, and had the Lionel name molded in.

Excellent	Like New	Scarcity
900	1,500	7

1409 Lionel 027 Freight Train $40 retail

Included: 1666 2-6-2 steam locomotive with operating headlight; 2466T early coal tender; 3559 automatic dump car; 2465 Sunoco double-dome tank car; 3454 operating merchandise car; 2472 non-illuminated Pennsylvania N5 red caboose; eight 1013 curved and five 1018 straight track; 1019 027 remote control track section; UTC Lockon; 926-5 instruction booklet; 1037 40-watt transformer.

Joshua Cowen believed that in order to maintain a child's interest in a toy train, the child needed to be directly involved with the train, rather than merely watching it circle. Set 1409 was born out of that philosophy, featuring not one but two operating cars.

One of these was the new 3454 operating merchandise car. The body and doors were painted silver and usually its markings, including PRR logo, were heat stamped in blue. The car had opening die-cast metal doors and a black-painted sheet-metal frame with steps on all four corners. It rode on staple-end trucks with coil couplers. It came with six plastic "crates" (actually cubes) engraved "BABY RUTH." The cubes came in black, brown and red, with brown being the most common. The operating mechanism ejected these by remote control after it first opened a door. The cubes were reloaded manually through a roof hatch. True 1946 cars were built using a design that hid the brass hinge pin for the rooftop hatch from view, and the wires to operating shoes were blue. Later production cars, overall more common when post-1946 production is considered, used black wires and the end of the aluminum roof hatch hinge pin is visible on the car end.

The other operating car, the 3559 dump car, was merely the prewar sheet metal car fitted with postwar trucks and couplers. It had a black Bakelite mechanism housing and blue-insulated wiring.

Excellent	Like New	Scarcity
400	550	5

1409W Lionel 027 Freight Train $45.95 retail

Included: 1666 2-6-2 steam locomotive with operating headlight; 2466W early coal tender; 3559 automatic dump car; 2465 Sunoco double-dome tank car; 3454 operating merchandise car; 2472 non-illuminated Pennsylvania N5 red caboose; eight 1013 curved and five 1018 straight track; 1019 027 remote control track section; UTC Lockon; 926-5 instruction booklet; 1041 60-watt transformer.

But for the inclusion of the 2466W whistle tender in lieu of the 2466T, and corresponding upgrade from 1037 to 1041 transformer, this set was identical to the 1409.

Excellent	Like New	Scarcity
450	650	6

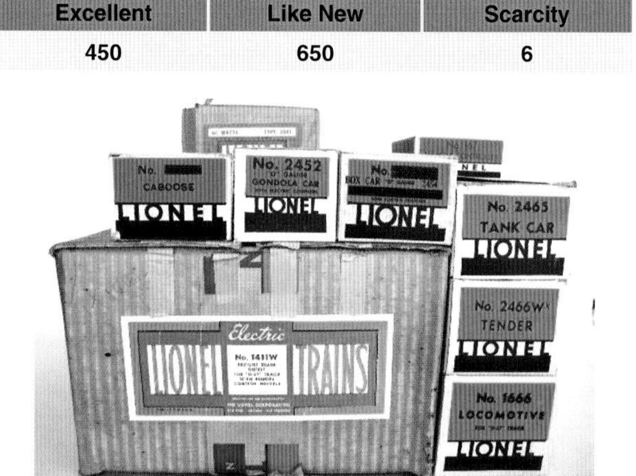

1411W Freight Outfit $42.50 retail

Included: 1666 2-6-2 steam locomotive with operating headlight; 2466WX early coal whistle tender; 2452X gondola; 2465 Sunoco double-dome tank car; 2454 boxcar; 2472 non-illuminated Pennsylvania N5 caboose; eight 1013 curved and three 1018 straight track; 1019 027 remote control track section; UTC Lockon; 926-5 instruction booklet; 1041 60-watt transformer.

The gradual improvements in 027 outfits continued with this set. Outfit 1411W was based on the 1405W (which in turn was based on the 1401W), but the train was lengthened with the addition of a boxcar. Less visible was the inclusion of the handrail-adorned 2466WX in lieu of the rather plain 2466W.

The boxcar added to the train was the new 2454. This car consisted of a plastic body with die-cast doors mounted on a sheet metal frame. The early sets included the very desirable 2454 Pennsylvania boxcar. This car came in two variations—one version had doors painted the same orange color as the body, the other version had doors painted brown. Later 1411W outfits were supplied with the much more common 2454 Baby Ruth boxcar. This car has Pennsylvania markings to the left of the door and Baby Ruth markings to the right of the door.

With Baby Ruth boxcar.

Excellent	Like New	Scarcity
225	375	5

With Pennsylvania boxcar.

Excellent	Like New	Scarcity
375	625	7

1413WS Lionel 027 Freight Train $55 retail

Included: 2020 6-8-6 steam turbine locomotive with operating headlight and smoke; 2466WX early coal whistle tender; 2452X gondola; 2465 Sunoco double-dome tank car; 2454 Baby Ruth boxcar; 2472 non-illuminated Pennsylvania N5 caboose; eight 1013 curved and three 1018 straight track; 1019 027 remote control track section; UTC Lockon; 926-5 instruction booklet; 1041 60-watt transformer.

Just up the 027 product line from the 1411W was the nearly identical 1413WS. The difference was the replacement of the venerable 1666 with the powerful new 2020 6-8-6 steam turbine, which unveiled Lionel's newest innovation—smoke!

The smoke generator in the 1946 locomotives amounted to an oversized bulb with a depression formed in it that held the smoke compound as it melted. A retrofit kit was produced in 1947 to convert these locomotives to the newer heater-type smoke unit. The motor in the 1946 models was mounted horizontally.

Excellent	Like New	Scarcity
350	550	4

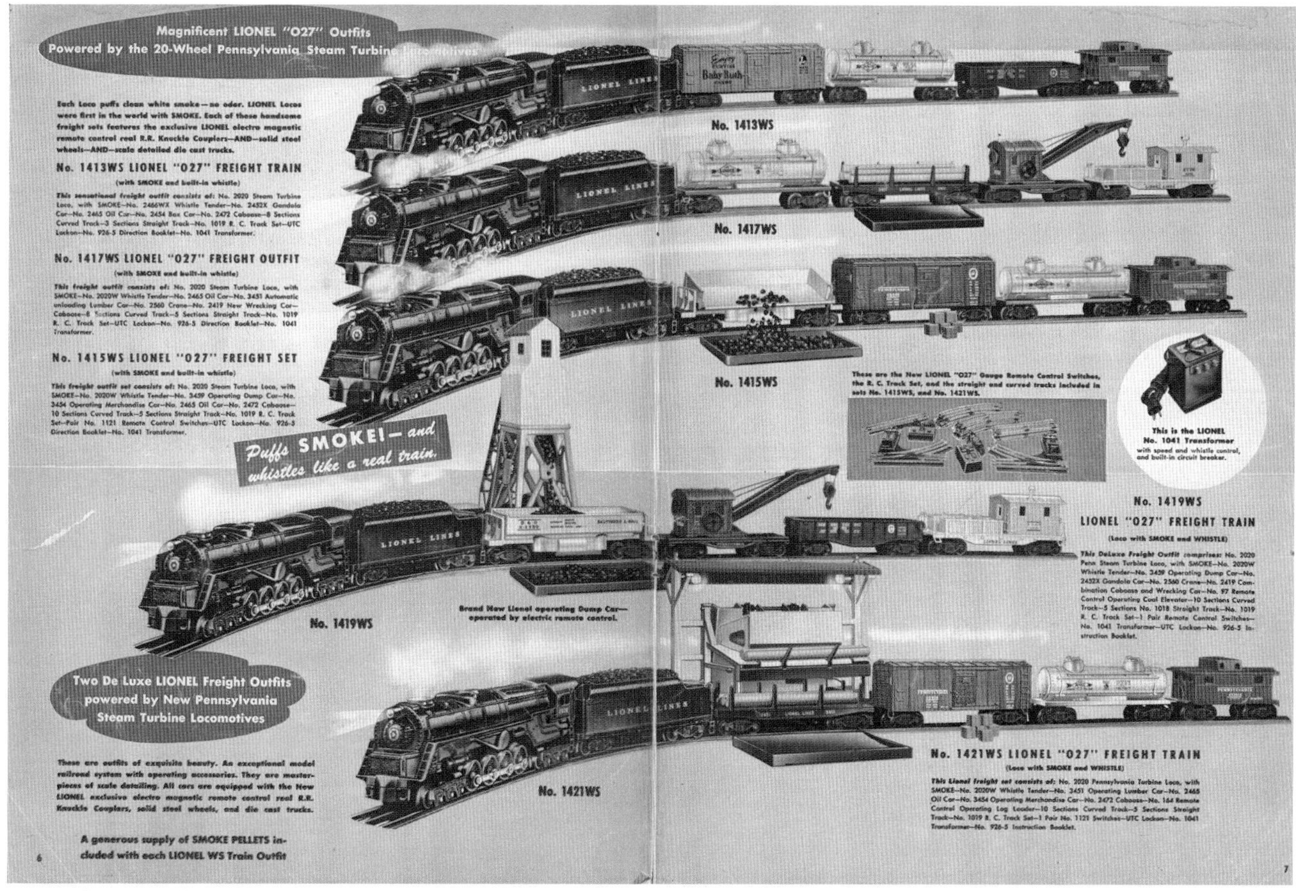

Magnificent LIONEL "027" Outfits
Powered by the 20-Wheel Pennsylvania Steam Turbine Locomotives
No. 1413WS LIONEL "027" FREIGHT TRAIN
No. 1417WS LIONEL "027" FREIGHT OUTFIT
No. 1415WS LIONEL "027" FREIGHT SET
Puffs SMOKE!—and whistles like a real train.
No. 1413WS
No. 1417WS
No. 1415WS
No. 1419WS
No. 1419WS
LIONEL "027" FREIGHT TRAIN
Two De Luxe LIONEL Freight Outfits powered by New Pennsylvania Steam Turbine Locomotives
No. 1421WS
No. 1421WS LIONEL "027" FREIGHT TRAIN
A generous supply of SMOKE PELLETS included with each LIONEL WS Train Outfit

1413WS, 1417WS, 1415WS, 1419WS, 1421WS

1415WS Lionel 027 Freight Set $67.50 retail

Included: 2020 6-8-6 steam turbine locomotive with operating headlight and smoke; 2020W early coal whistle tender; 3459 automatic dumping ore car; 3454 operating merchandise car; 2465 Sunoco double-dome tank car; 2472 non-illuminated Pennsylvania N5 caboose; ten 1013 curved and five 1018 straight track; 1019 027 remote control track section; pair remote-control switches; UTC Lockon; 926-5 instruction booklet; 1041 60-watt transformer.

This set was essentially a premium version of the 1409, featuring the new 20-wheel steam turbine and new die-cast coal dump car. The 3459 coal dump included in this set was the hard to find version with the unpainted aluminum bin. As delivered, the outfit did not match the catalog illustration. The merchandise car was not brown as shown, but rather silver, just like the rest of the freight cars in the set.

Excellent	Like New	Scarcity
525	1,000	5

1417WS Lionel 027 Freight Outfit $60 retail

Included: 2020 6-8-6 steam turbine locomotive with operating headlight and smoke; 2020W early coal whistle tender; 2465 Sunoco double-dome tank car; 3451 operating log car; 2560 crane; 2419 work caboose; eight 1013 curved and five 1018 straight track; 1019 027 remote control track section; UTC Lockon; 926-5 instruction booklet; 1041 60-watt transformer.

This set included the new die-cast frame-equipped 3451 operating log car, along with a 2560 crane, providing it with two operating cars. The 3451 was rubber stamped in silver, its wiring was blue and its cargo was five unstained logs.

Though shown in the catalog with a brown cab, the crane was actually produced with a yellow cab and red roof. Bringing up the rear of the train was a 2419 work caboose, which was based on the die-cast 2411 flatcar. The new, smoke-equipped 20-wheel steam turbine number 2020 provided motive power.

Excellent	Like New	Scarcity
750	1,100	6

1419WS Lionel 027 Freight Train $85 retail

Included: 2020 6-8-6 steam turbine locomotive with operating headlight and smoke; 2020W early coal whistle tender; 3459 automatic dumping ore car; 2452X gondola; 2560 crane; 2419 work caboose; 97 operating coal elevator; ten 1013 curved and five 1018 straight track; 1019 027 remote control track section; pair of 1121 remote-control turnouts; UTC Lockon; 926-5 instruction booklet; 1041 60-watt transformer.

At $85, this outfit was more expensive than any of the 1946 O-Gauge sets. But what an outfit it was! Not only did the set come with the new 2020 turbine, but it also included the new 3459 die-cast ore car. To load the 3459, as well as provide it a destination, the massive metal 97 operating coal loader was included. Since the 97 required two parallel tracks to function, a pair of 1121 turnouts was included in the set.

Many examples of this set have been found with a 75-watt 1042 transformer rather than the listed 60-watt 1041.

Excellent	Like New	Scarcity
900	1,300	7

1421WS Lionel 027 Freight Train $85 retail

Included: 2020 6-8-6 steam turbine locomotive with operating headlight and smoke; 2020W early coal whistle tender; 3451 operating log car; 2465 Sunoco double-dome tank car; 3454 merchandise car; 2472 non-illuminated Pennsylvania N5 caboose; 164 operating log loader; ten 1013 curved and five 1018 straight track; 1019 027 remote control track section; pair of 1121 remote-control turnouts; UTC Lockon; 926-5 instruction booklet; 1041 60-watt transformer.

While the 1419WS provided the owner with a coal empire, the 1421WS, also priced at $85, created a lumber empire. Trailing the 2020 steam turbine in the set was a die-cast 3451 log dump car to be used in conjunction with the 164 log loader. The 1946 log car carried five unstained logs and was rubber stamped in silver. The pickup shoes were wired with blue wire. Of course, a pair of 1121 remote-control turnouts was included in order to incorporate the 164 in the track layout. A silver 3454 operating merchandise car added even more action to the train, which was surprisingly finished with a plain red, non-illuminated 2472 caboose.

Like the 1419WS, many examples of this set have been found with a 75-watt 1042 transformer rather than the listed 60-watt 1041.

Excellent	Like New	Scarcity
1,000	1,500	7

O-Gauge Outfits

2100 O-Gauge Three-Car Passenger $37.50 retail

Included: 224 2-6-2 steam locomotive with operating headlight; 2466T early coal tender; two 2442 illuminated Pullmans; 2443 illuminated observation car; eight OC curved and three OS straight track; RCS uncoupling/operating section; UTC Lockon; 926-5 instruction booklet.

The motive power for this set was the 224 2-6-2 steam locomotive, with the earliest outfits coming with engines carrying over 1945 features such as black handrails and locomotive-only tender couplings. Though the catalog illustrated green passenger cars, some sets actually came with 2442 and 2443 brown cars. Green cars were also produced, which were numbered 2440 and 2441, and some sets included these cars. Regardless of color, the cars were marked with silver rubber-stamped lettering.

As was the case with all O-Gauge outfits of this time, a transformer was not included.

Excellent	Like New	Scarcity
550	950	7

2100W 📷 O-Gauge Three-Car Passenger $43.50 retail

Included: 224 2-6-2 steam locomotive with operating headlight; 2466W early coal tender with whistle; two 2442 illuminated Pullmans; 2443 illuminated observation car; eight OC curved and three OS straight track; RCS uncoupling/operating section; 167 whistle controller; UTC Lockon; 926-5 instruction booklet.

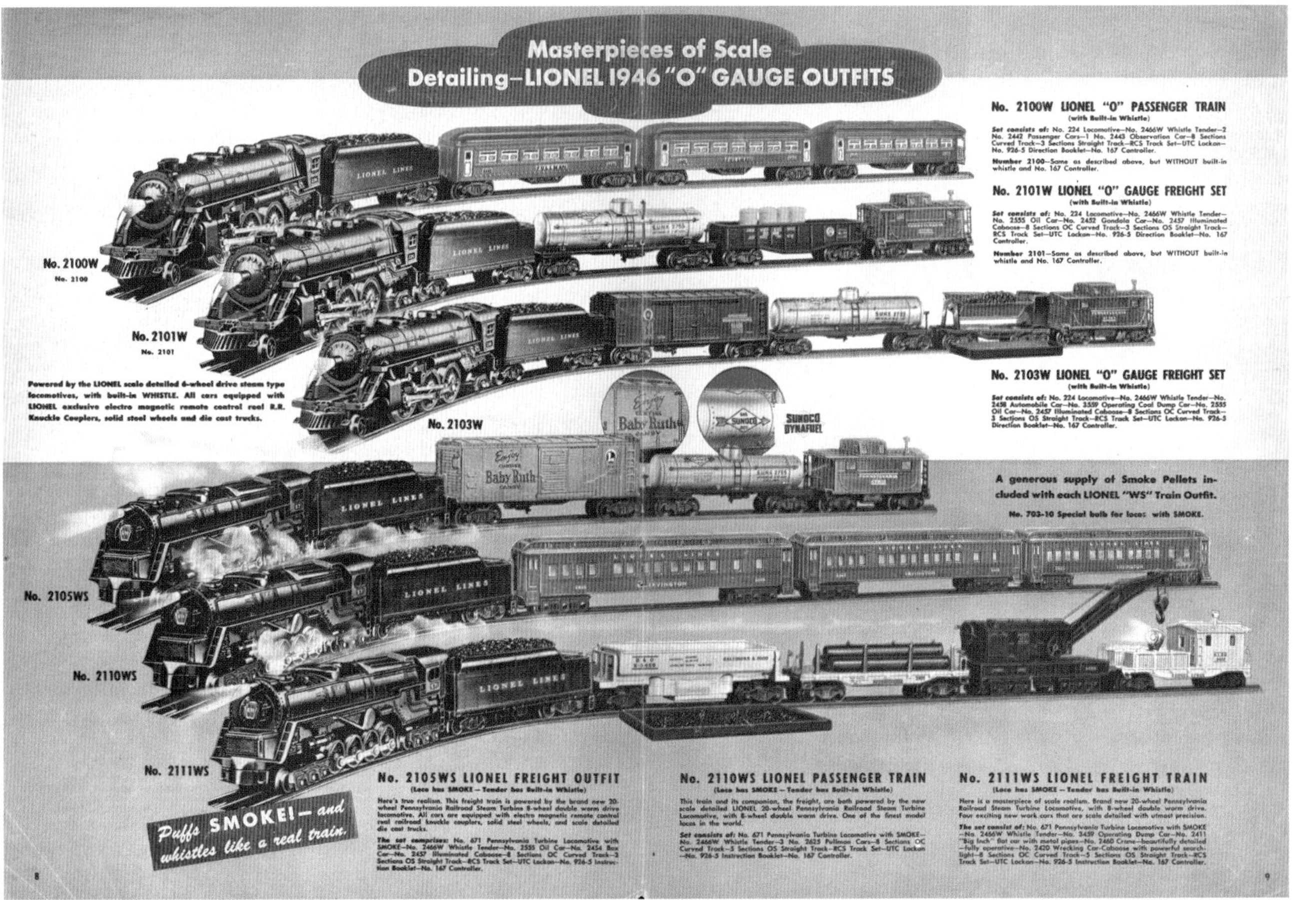

2100W, 2101W, 2103W, 2105WS, 2110WS, 2111WS

This set was a duplicate of outfit 2100 except for the inclusion of a whistle and related control.

Excellent	Like New	Scarcity
500	800	5

2101 0-Gauge Three-Car Freight $37.50 retail

Included: 224 2-6-2 steam locomotive with operating headlight; 2466T early coal tender; 2452 gondola; 2555 Sunoco single-dome tank car; 2457 illuminated Pennsylvania N5 caboose; eight OC curved and three OS straight track; RCS uncoupling/operating section; UTC Lockon; 926-5 instruction booklet.

Like the 2100, this set was powered by a 224 2-6-2 steam locomotive. However, unlike in the passenger set, the locomotives in this set always came with the typical 1946 features of shiny handrails and rounded rear cab floor. Its tender, too, had shiny handrails and now included its own drawbar to mate with that of the locomotive. It was lettered in silver.

The 2452 gondola, while retaining its brake wheels (unlike its 027 cousin), now carried barrels that were solid woodturnings, unlike 1945 gondolas that carried two-part hollow wooden barrels. Similarly, with the supply of surplus 2755 decals exhausted, the tank car in this outfit now displayed its actual number, 2555. Lionel lowered its cost on this set by equipping the caboose with only a single coupler.

Excellent	Like New	Scarcity
400	675	6

2101W 0-Gauge Three-Car Freight $43.50 retail

Included: 224 2-6-2 steam locomotive with operating headlight; 2466W early coal tender with whistle; 2452 gondola; 2555 Sunoco single-dome tank car; 2457 illuminated Pennsylvania N5 caboose; eight OC curved and three OS straight track; RCS uncoupling/operating section; 167 whistle controller; UTC Lockon; 926-5 instruction booklet.

This set was a duplicate of outfit 2101 except for the inclusion of a whistle and related control.

Excellent	Like New	Scarcity
300	500	5

2103W 0-Gauge Four-Car Freight $45 retail

Included: 224 2-6-2 steam locomotive with operating headlight; 2466W early coal whistle tender; 2458 automobile car; 3559 automatic dump car; 2555 Sunoco single-dome tank car; 2457 illuminated Pennsylvania N5 caboose; eight OC curved and three OS straight track; RCS uncoupling/operating section; 167 whistle controller; UTC Lockon; 926-5 instruction booklet.

The final outfit to be headed by the venerable 224 was the 2103W. Like the locomotive, the cars in this set were all updated versions of pre-World War II equipment.

The 3559 was essentially the prewar 3659 equipped with the new trucks and operating couplers. The operating mechanism was protected by a black Bakelite housing and connected to the truck-mounted pickup shoes by wire with blue insulation.

Excellent	Like New	Scarcity
425	1,000	5

2105WS Three-Car Freight Outfit $50 retail

Included: 671 6-8-6 steam turbine locomotive with operating headlight and smoke; 2466W early coal whistle tender; 2454 Baby Ruth boxcar; 2555 Sunoco single-dome tank car; 2457 illuminated Pennsylvania N5 caboose; eight OC curved and three OS straight track; RCS uncoupling/operating section; 167 whistle controller; UTC Lockon; 926-5 instruction booklet.

This popular set was the first O-Gauge outfit to include smoke. It was powered by a smoking 20-wheel steam turbine, identical to the 027 2020 except for the catalog and cab numbers.

Being produced later in the year than the comparable 027 meant that the 2454 in this set was never the "Pennsylvania" version, but rather always the "Baby Ruth."

Excellent	Like New	Scarcity
400	1,000	5

2110WS Three-Car Passenger $75 retail

Included: 671 6-8-6 steam turbine locomotive with operating headlight and smoke; 2466W early coal whistle tender; three 2625 heavyweight Pullmans; eight OC curved and five OS straight track; RCS uncoupling/operating section; 167 whistle controller; UTC Lockon; 926-5 instruction booklet.

To create a premium O-Gauge passenger set, Lionel revived its prewar Bakelite "Irvington" passenger car. The postwar incarnation of this car included newly designed six-wheel trucks with knuckle couplers—derivatives of these trucks were used on the 2460 crane and 2426W tender as well. The car bodies were painted maroon or reddish-brown in contrast to the prewar color of medium brown. To tow this passenger train, Lionel used its replica of the Pennsylvania 20-wheel steam turbine, the 671.

Excellent	Like New	Scarcity
1,750	2,975	7

2111WS Four-Car Freight $60 retail

Included: 671 6-8-6 steam turbine locomotive with operating headlight and smoke; 2466W early coal whistle tender; 2460 crane; 2411 flatcar with pipes; 3459 automatic dumping ore car; 2420 work caboose with searchlight; eight OC curved and five OS straight track; RCS uncoupling/operating section; 167 whistle controller; UTC Lockon; 926-5 instruction booklet.

This outfit was a true heavyweight. Not only was the locomotive die-cast, but all of the freight cars featured die-cast frames as well. Included in some examples of this set were some of the most desirable cars from 1946—the gray cab 2460 12-wheel crane and the 3459 ore dump car with unpainted aluminum bin.

Excellent	Like New	Scarcity
825	1,400	7

2113WS O-Gauge Three-Car Freight Outfit $67.50 retail

Included: 726 2-8-4 Berkshire steam locomotive with operating headlight and smoke; 2426W die-cast whistle tender; 2855 black Sunoco single dome tank car; 3854 operating merchandise car; 2457 illuminated caboose; eight OC curved and seven OS straight track; RCS uncoupling/operating section; 167 whistle controller; UTC Lockon; 926-5 instruction booklet.

Premiering in outfit 2113WS was the new 2-8-4 Berkshire steam locomotive. Though a 2-8-4 would be a staple of Lionel's O-Gauge sets into the 1960s, the 1946 model was unique. The smoke unit was based on a light bulb, the motor and reversing E-unit was mounted horizontally, and the handrails mounted with turned stanchions. The earliest versions of the 726 were equipped with what collectors refer to as the "large stack" motor. Later, the number of field laminations was reduced, resulting in what is known as a "short stack" motor.

The corrugated component box was unique to the 1946 locomotive. Sealed with prewar-style orange and blue sealing tape, the carton was marked with a manufacturer's seal reading, "GAIR BOGOTA CORR. & FIBRE BOX CORP." The ends of the box were stamped with "No. 726" in small lettering.

The cars in tow were no less unique or spectacular. Though cataloged as the common silver 2755, the tank car included was actually the scarce black 2855. The prewar semi-scale boxcar tooling was revived and modified with the addition of a roof hatch and internal mechanism to create a spectacular operating merchandise car—the 3854. This car is one of the most difficult to find items from the postwar era.

Though the catalog illustrated a semi-scale caboose, the set contents were something of a disappointment, containing only the sheet metal 2457 illuminated caboose.

Excellent	Like New	Scarcity
2,000	3,200	7

2114WS O-Gauge Three-Car Passenger Outfit $77.50 retail

Included: 726 2-8-4 Berkshire steam locomotive with operating headlight and smoke; 2426W whistle tender; three 2625 heavyweight Pullmans; eight OC curved and five OS straight track; RCS uncoupling/operating section; 167 controller; UTC Lockon; 926-5 instruction booklet.

This was the most expense passenger outfit offered in 1946. The three Bakelite 2625 Irvington passenger cars presented the 726 with a formidable load, especially those locomotives equipped with the later "short stack" motor. The magnificent die-cast tenders of 1946 were equipped with die-cast whistle housings and, though initially stamped in white, ultimately were lettered in silver.

Excellent	Like New	Scarcity
2,500	4,000	7

2115WS O-Gauge Four-Car Work Train with Smoke $72.50 ($87.50) retail

Included: 726 2-8-4 Berkshire steam locomotive with operating headlight and smoke; 2426W whistle tender; 2458 automobile car; 3451 operating log car; 2460 12-wheel crane; 2420 work caboose with searchlight; eight OC curved and three OS straight track; RCS uncoupling/operating section; 167 whistle controller; UTC Lockon, 926-5 instruction booklet.

If one looks only at the catalog, it appears that this is the most expensive outfit offered in 1946. However, the catalog price of $87.50 was an error, and the outfit boxes were plastered with a red-lettered, white label correcting the price to $72.50.

While the 2458 was based on a prewar design, all the other cars were new designs. Accompanying the crane was the 2420 work caboose with operating searchlight. Most often the car was overall dark gray, but scarce examples with a light gray frame have surfaced as a component of this set.

The black log dump car was lettered with silver rubber-stamping and carried five unstained logs. Its pickup shoes were wired with blue-insulated wire.

Excellent	Like New	Scarcity
1,350	2,400	7

4109WS Electronic Control Set $75 retail

Included: 671R 6-8-6 steam turbine locomotive with operating headlight and smoke; 4424W early coal whistle tender; 4452 gondola; 4454 Baby Ruth boxcar; 5459 ore dump car; 4457 illuminated Pennsylvania N5 caboose; eight OC curved and four OS straight track; ECU-1 electronic control unit, UTC Lockon; 926-5 instruction booklet, Electronic Control Instruction booklet.

The 4109 WS Electronic Control Set was such a revolutionary product that it was given the distinction of being the first set listed in the 1946 catalog. With conventional Lionel trains, direction control was achieved by sequencing the E-unit by interrupting the power to the track; with electronic control, a receiver mounted in the tender interrupted the power only to the reversing unit, causing it to cycle. Uncoupling and unloading functions were similarly controlled by receivers rather than by special track sections.

Despite its prestigious position in the catalog, the illustrations of the Electronic Control items were not accurate. Rather than brown, the boxcar was orange and featured Baby Ruth markings. The ore dump car was black rather than silver, and like all the items in the set, had special round color-coded decals on its flank, which corresponded to the colors on the control buttons on the Electronic Control Unit (ECU). The ECU served as a transmitter, and controlled all functions of the train except speed. All the cars in the set were equipped with center rail pickup rollers, but uncoupling "shoes" were not needed, and were hence absent. Finally, the axles of all the freight car trucks were stainless steel.

The electronic control receiver housed in the tender was coupled to the locomotive by means of plug and jack assembles, the latter attached to the brush plate of the locomotive. In 1946, this required no change to the locomotive due to the use of an identical arrangement with the leverless E-unit used in 1946 turbines and Berkshires. To distinguish the Electronic Control turbine from regular production locomotives, a circular black Electronic Control decal was affixed to its side.

Excellent	Like New	Scarcity
1,000	1,800	5

4109WS - *Electronic Control Set*

Chapter 4

1947

The big news in the 1947 catalog was the introduction of Lionel's first post World War II electric—the magnificent GG-1. With a die-cast body and trucks, the model captured the lines of prototype. The replica, given catalog number 2332, was prominently featured in the catalog.

At the other end of the spectrum, in more ways than one, was the introduction of a new caboose style. The body of the new caboose, loosely based on a Southern Pacific prototype, was injection-molded plastic. Although this style caboose was to be a staple of Lionel outfits through the remainder of the postwar era, the caboose was not shown in the 1947 consumer catalog and was only mentioned in the year's advance catalog. Perhaps a delay in the design or tooling occurred between the printings of the two catalogs—but in any event, few 1947 sets included the new caboose. The bulk instead came with cabooses that were continuations of 1946 offerings.

Several outfits were headed by sister locomotives, the O-Gauge 675 and 027 2025. Both 2-6-2's, identical except for cab numbers, were based on the prewar 225E, with the boiler modified to resemble the Belpair firebox favored by the Pennsylvania railroad—fittingly that railroad's Keystone emblem adorned the newly designed smokebox (boiler) front.

Most of the carried-over steam locomotives were revised as well. The previously gray 221 was now produced in black, and was produced from modified tooling, which produced a stronger pilot. Its drive wheels now featured shiny rims like those on the larger steamers. At the same time, the 726 Berkshire, as well as the Turbines, got new boilers. Counter to Lionel's usual practice, the amount of detail formed into the 671 and 2020 turbines' shells actually increased over that found in 1946 examples. However, this was somewhat offset by the marring of the boiler by a slot to accommodate the lever of a conventional E-unit. The 1947 and subsequent Berkshire also had a slotted boiler for the same reason—the 1946 versions of all three locomotives had been equipped with special lever-less horizontal E-units. Only the 1654 2-4-2 was unchanged from the previous year's production.

Despite the massive investment Lionel made to introduce the new products and revamp the old ones previously listed, the most memorable and successful new product of 1947 was the 3462 operating milk car. An instant best seller, tens of thousands were produced.

With Standard-Gauge trains not being produced for a number of years, there was no need to continue production of the complex UTC Lockon. A simpler, cheaper 0- and 027-only Lockon was introduced. With a lockon being included in each of the thousands of outfits sold by Lionel, the potential cost savings by the adoption of the CTC Lockon as standard was enormous.

Other cost-saving moves include the elimination of the welded-on steps from the 2457 caboose, and deletion of the rivet detail from the roofwalks of the 2457 and 2472 cabooses. The die-cast frame used by both the 2411 flatcar, as well as the 2419 and 2420 work cabooses, was strengthened, reducing damage both in the factory and by consumers.

Though the outfit boxes themselves were unchanged from 1946, in 1947 the component boxes were changed. Though the Early Postwar box continued to be used, the American Toy Manufacturers Association logo was now printed on one side.The knuckle coupler was redesigned, with additional staking securing the coupler head to mounting plate. Other sweeping changes included the addition of an automatic circuit breaker to the 167 whistle controller—which brought about that unit being identified as a 167C in corporate documents. A new transformer, the Type S, was introduced in 1947. Though cataloged as a 75-watt unit, the transformer itself was marked with an 80-watt rating. This transformer was included in the better 027 outfits.

027-Gauge

1431 Lionel Freight Train $22.50 retail
Included: 1654 2-4-2 steam locomotive with operating headlight; 1654T sheet-metal tender; 2452X gondola; 2465 Sunoco double-dome tank car; 2472 non-illuminated Pennsylvania N5 caboose; eight 1013 curved and one 1018 straight track; 1019 uncoupling/operating section; 1035 60-watt transformer; CTC Lockon; tube of Lionel lubricant; 926-5 instruction booklet.

Outfit 1401 was a success during the 1946 selling season, so Lionel revamped it slightly by including the new CTC Lockon and 1035 transformer, and gave it the new number of 1431.

Excellent	Like New	Scarcity
150	250	5

1431W Lionel Freight Train $27.50 retail
Included: 1654 2-4-2 steam locomotive with operating headlight; 1654W sheet-metal whistle tender; 2452X gondola; 2465 Sunoco double-dome tank car; 2472 non-illuminated Pennsylvania N5 caboose; eight 1013 curved and one 1018 straight track; 1019 uncoupling/operating section; 1042 75-watt transformer; CTC Lockon; tube of Lionel lubricant; 926-5 instruction booklet.

This set was an upgrade of outfit 1431 to include a whistle, with an associated upgrade in the transformer to accommodate the whistle.

Excellent	Like New	Scarcity
175	275	5

1432 Lionel Passenger Set $27.50 retail
Included: 221 2-6-4 steam locomotive with operating headlight; 221T sheet-metal tender; two 2430 blue and silver Pullmans; 2431 blue and silver observation; eight 1013 curved and three 1018 straight track; 1019 uncoupling/operating section; 1035 60-watt transformer; CTC Lockon; tube of Lionel lubricant; 926-5 instruction booklet.

Economy-priced passenger outfit 1400 from 1946 was updated for 1947 and given a new number. The 221 and its tender were now painted black, the loco body casting was strengthened and its black drive wheels had shiny rims. Trailing the revamped locomotive were three blue and silver passenger cars, which were marked with white heat stamping.

Excellent	Like New	Scarcity
900	1,500	5

1432W Lionel Passenger Set $33.50 retail
Included: 221 2-6-4 steam locomotive with operating headlight; 221W sheet-metal whistle tender; two 2430 blue and silver Pullmans; 2431 blue and silver observation; eight 1013 curved and three 1018 straight track; 1019 uncoupling/operating section; 1042 75-watt transformer; CTC Lockon; tube of Lionel lubricant; 926-5 instruction booklet.

For a $6 premium over outfit 1432, consumers could purchase this virtually identical outfit, which included a whistle in the locomotive tender and a more powerful transformer with integral whistle control.

Excellent	Like New	Scarcity
900	1,500	5

1433 Lionel Freight Train $27.50 retail
Included: 221 2-6-4 steam locomotive with operating headlight; 221T sheet-metal tender; 2411 flatcar with logs; 2465 Sunoco double-dome tank car; 2472 non-illuminated Pennsylvania N5 caboose; eight 1013 curved and three 1018 straight track; 1019 uncoupling/operating section; 1035 60-watt transformer; CTC Lockon; tube of Lionel lubricant; 926-5 instruction booklet.

For a second year Lionel chose to head a freight outfit with a streamlined steam locomotive. Outfit 1433 was a revision of 1946's set 1403. Most visible of the changes was a switch in locomotive color from gray to black, with the associated change in casting and drive wheels. Less noticeable was the replacement of the 2411 flatcar's steel pipe load with wooden "logs"—actually 5/8 x 7-inch unstained dowels, and the

1434WS, 1435WS, & 1439WS

strengthening of its die-cast frame. Though advertised as containing an illuminated 2457 caboose, the set was in fact produced with the non-illuminated 2472 instead.

Excellent	Like New	Scarcity
400	700	5

1433W Lionel Freight Train $33.50 retail

Included: 221 2-6-4 steam locomotive with operating headlight; 221W sheet-metal tender; 2411 flatcar with logs; 2465 Sunoco double-dome tank car; 2472 non-illuminated Pennsylvania N5 caboose; eight 1013 curved and three 1018 straight track; 1019 uncoupling/operating section; 1042 75-watt transformer; CTC Lockon; tube of Lionel lubricant; 926-5 instruction booklet.

For a $6 premium over outfit 1433, consumers could purchase this virtually identical outfit, which included a whistle in the locomotive tender and a more powerful transformer with integral whistle control.

Excellent	Like New	Scarcity
400	725	5

1434WS Passenger Train $42.50 retail

Included: 2025 2-6-2 steam locomotive with operating headlight and smoke; 2466WX early coal whistle tender; two 2440 green Pullmans; 2441 green observation; eight 1013 curved and three 1018 straight track; 1019 uncoupling/operating section; Type S transformer; CTC Lockon; tube of Lionel lubricant; 926-5 instruction booklet.

The midrange passenger outfit from 1946, the 1402, was upgraded in 1947 as the 1434WS, which included the handsome new 2025 steam locomotive rather than the smaller 1666 used the previous year. The pilot of this locomotive did not include a simulated coupler, and oftentimes the locomotive's smokestack was unpainted aluminum. Three illuminated passenger cars, painted green, were in tow behind the big steamer, their markings applied with white heat-stamped lettering.

Excellent	Like New	Scarcity
400	725	5

1435WS Lionel Freight Train $42.50 retail

Included: 2025 2-6-2 steam locomotive with operating headlight and smoke; 2466WX early coal whistle tender; 2452X gondola; 2454 Baby Ruth boxcar; 2472 non-illuminated Pennsylvania N5 caboose, or 2257 or 2357 SP-style caboose; eight 1013 curved and three 1018 straight track; 1019 uncoupling/operating section; Type S transformer; CTC Lockon; tube of Lionel lubricant; 926-5 instruction booklet.

Though common, this set is a classic. The big 2-6-2 pulled a gondola—minus brake wheels and load—a boxcar and a caboose; just which caboose varied considerably throughout the outfit's production. It was cataloged with an illuminated 2457 caboose, but was never supplied with this model. Instead a succession of cabooses was used, starting with the non-illuminated 2472 sheet metal caboose. The new plastic SP-style 2257 caboose and, occasionally, the scarce red 2357 with matching stack replaced this.

Like the 1434WS, this set was headed by a 2025 that did not include a simulated coupler, but often had an unpainted aluminum stack.

With 2472 or 2257

Excellent	Like New	Scarcity
250	375	3

1437WS, 1441WS, 1443WS

1437WS Lionel Freight Train $47.50 retail

Included: 2025 2-6-2 steam locomotive with operating headlight and smoke; 2466WX early coal whistle tender; 2452X gondola; 2465 Sunoco double-dome tank car; 2454 Baby Ruth boxcar; 2472 non-illuminated Pennsylvania N5 caboose or 2257 SP-style caboose; eight 1013 curved and five 1018 straight track; 1019 uncoupling/operating section; Type S transformer; CTC Lockon; tube of Lionel lubricant; 926-5 instruction booklet.

Essentially the same set as the previously listed 1435WS, this outfit added a 2465 tank car to the train. To accommodate the longer train, two more sections of 1018 straight track were added to the set.

The locomotives in this set lacked simulated front couplers, and their stacks could be either black or unpainted aluminum.

Excellent	Like New	Scarcity
275	450	4

1439WS Lionel Freight Outfit $52.50 retail

Included: 2025 2-6-2 steam locomotive with operating headlight and smoke; 2466WX early coal whistle tender; 3559 automatic dump car; 2465 Sunoco double-dome tank car; 3454 merchandise car; 2472 non-illuminated Pennsylvania N5 caboose; eight 1013 curved and five 1018 straight track; 1019 uncoupling/operating section; Type S transformer; CTC Lockon; tube of Lionel lubricant; 926-5 instruction booklet.

The 1946 outfit 1409W, powered by a 1666 2-6-2, was updated for 1947 by the inclusion of a smoking 2-6-2 locomotive, specifically the 2025. The 2025 included in the 1439WS lacked simulated front couplers, and its stacks could be either black or unpainted aluminum.

The 3559, originally a prewar design that was revived in 1946, returned again in 1947. Its wiring was now black and, at least in this outfit, the mechanism housing was black Bakelite.

The catalog indicated that the caboose for this outfit would be the illuminated 2457, but the 2472 was included instead.

Excellent	Like New	Scarcity
425	750	5

1441WS De Luxe Work Outfit $57.50 retail

Included: 2020 6-8-6 steam locomotive with operating headlight and smoke; 2020W early coal whistle tender; 2560 crane; 2461 transformer car with red transformer; 3451 operating log car; 2419 work caboose; eight 1013 curved and five 1018 straight track; 1019 uncoupling/operating section; Type S transformer; CTC Lockon; tube of Lionel lubricant; 926-5 instruction booklet.

The 20-wheel steam turbine, introduced the year before, was extensively redesigned in 1947. Mechanically, the motor was now mounted at an angle and drove only the rear axle via a worm and wheel. The previous year's design had a horizontally mounted motor that drove the front and rear main axles through a long worm shaft. The locomotive now used a vertically mounted E-unit, and the old bulb-type smoke unit gave way to the improved resistance-element smoke unit.

The 3451 log dump car returned this year, now with black wiring and white heat-stamped lettering.

A new piece of rolling stock was introduced with this set—the 2461 depressed center flatcar with transformer load. This nicely detailed die-cast car would later form the basis for a variety of cars. The plastic transformer cargo was painted red and was topped by four relatively fragile, though now reproduced, insulators.

Excellent	Like New	Scarcity
550	900	6

1443WS Four-Car Freight $70 retail

Included: 2020 6-8-6 steam locomotive with operating headlight and smoke; 2020W early coal whistle tender; 3459 automatic dumping ore car; 3462 operating milk car; 2465 Sunoco double-dome tank car; 2472 non-illuminated Pennsylvania N5 caboose; ten 1013 curved and five 1018 straight track; 1019 uncoupling/operating section; pair remote-control switches; Type S transformer; CTC Lockon; tube of Lionel lubricant; 926-5 instruction booklet.

Outfit 1443WS was the ultimate 027 set in 1947, and it also introduced the most successful of all Lionel operating cars—the operating milk car. As first produced, the base plate of internal operating mechanism was brass and visible through various holes in the black sheet metal frame of the car. Some of these early cars were painted a distinctly glossy white. The accompanying platform of the earliest cars had an irregularly shaped opening in the area beneath the track.

The end of the train was somewhat confusing, as the catalog listed the inclusion of a 2457 illuminated caboose, when in fact the packaging contained a non-illuminated 2472. The balance of the outfit was relatively straightforward, being headed with the redesigned-for-1947 turbine.

Excellent	Like New	Scarcity
425	750	5

3105W Advance catalog. No retail price listed.

Included: 1666 2-6-2 steam locomotive with operating headlight; 2466WX early coal whistle tender; 2452X gondola; 2465 Sunoco double-dome tank car; 2472 non-illuminated Pennsylvania N5 caboose; eight 1013 curved and three 1018 straight track; 1019 uncoupling/operating section; 1042 75-watt transformer; CTC Lock-on; tube of Lionel lubricant; 926-5 instruction booklet.

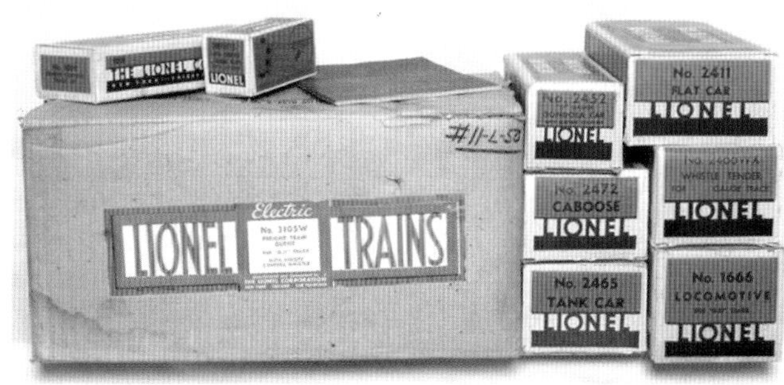

Though not found in the 1947 consumer catalog, this outfit was included in the 1948 advance catalog. There it was heralded as a "Spring Promotional Set"—designed to give retailers something new to carry them through the lean spring and summer months.

The outfit was a continuation of the 1946 1405W set, assigned a new number, and now equipped with a 1042 75-watt transformer. The motive power for this set was a hard-to-find variation of the 1666, which was rubber stamped rather than having separately installed number plates.

Though the illustration in the 1947 advance catalog showed a 2472 sheet metal caboose with this set, the description accurately listed the new plastic-bodied 2257 SP-type caboose.

Excellent	Like New	Scarcity
400	750	6

O-Gauge

2120S Three-Car De Luxe Passenger $37.50 retail

Included: 675 2-6-2 steam locomotive with operating headlight and smoke; 2466T early coal tender; two 2442 brown Pullmans; 2443 brown observation; eight OC curved and three OS straight track; RCS uncoupling/operating section; 88 reversing controller; CTC Lockon; tube of Lionel lubricant; 926-5 instruction booklet.

Like this loco's contemporary twin, the 027 2025, the early production of the 675 lacked a simulated coupler on the pilot. The locomotive's stack can be found in black or unpainted aluminum. The keystone on its smokebox front could be decorated with the white-stamped number "675" or a red and gold Pennsylvania keystone decal bearing the number 5690.

The brown 2442 and 2443 passenger cars were lettered with white heat-stamped lettering; as opposed to 1946's silver rubber-stamped lettering.

Excellent	Like New	Scarcity
500	875	6

2120WS Three-Car De Luxe Passenger $43.50 retail

Included: 675 2-6-2 steam locomotive with operating headlight and smoke; 2466WX early coal tender; two 2442 brown Pullmans; 2443 brown observation; eight OC curved and three OS straight track; RCS uncoupling/operating section; 167c whistle controller; CTC Lockon; tube of Lionel lubricant; 926-5 instruction booklet.

This set was a duplicate of 2120S, with the addition of a whistle. To activate the 2466WX whistle tender, a 167 whistle controller was included. This was the new, improved "c" version, with integral circuit breaker.

Excellent	Like New	Scarcity
525	900	4

2121S Three-Car Freight $35 retail

Included: 675 2-6-2 steam locomotive with operating headlight and smoke; 2466T early coal tender; 2555 Sunoco single-dome tank car; 2452 gondola with barrels; 2457 illuminated Pennsylvania N5 caboose; eight OC curved and three OS straight track; RCS uncoupling/operating section; 88 reversing controller; CTC Lockon; tube of Lionel lubricant; 926-5 instruction booklet.

This was the lowest-priced O-Gauge outfit cataloged in 1947. The 675 2-6-2 locomotive can be found in the same variations as described in set 2120S. The 1947 issue of the 2457 caboose lacked the "Eastern Division" lettering found on earlier production and oftentimes the welded-on steps were omitted from the caboose, as well.

Excellent	Like New	Scarcity
375	550	6

2121WS Three-Car Freight $41 retail

Included: 675 2-6-2 steam locomotive with operating headlight and smoke; 2466WX early coal tender; 2555 Sunoco single-dome tank car; 2452 gondola with barrels; 2457 illuminated Pennsylvania N5 caboose; eight OC curved and three OS straight track; RCS uncoupling/operating section; 167 whistle controller; CTC Lockon; tube Lionel lubricant; 926-5 instruction booklet.

This set was a duplicate of 2121S, with the addition of a whistle. To activate the 2466WX whistle tender, a 167 whistle controller was included. This was the new, improved "c" version, with integral circuit breaker.

Excellent	Like New	Scarcity
400	575	5

2123WS Four-Car Freight $47.50 retail

Included: 675 2-6-2 steam locomotive with operating headlight and smoke; 2466WX early coal whistle tender; 2458 automobile car; 3559 automatic dump car; 2555 Sunoco single-dome tank car; 2457 illuminated Pennsylvania N5 caboose; eight OC curved and three OS straight track; RCS uncoupling/operating section; 167 whistle controller; CTC Lockon; tube of Lionel lubricant; 926-5 instruction booklet.

The early production of the 675 lacked a simulated coupler on the pilot, though one is found on later issues. The locomotive's stack can be found in black or unpainted aluminum. The keystone on its smokebox front could be decorated with the white-stamped number "675" or a red and gold Pennsylvania keystone decal bearing the number 5690. The 1947 issue of the 2457 caboose lacked the "Eastern Division" lettering found on earlier productions, and oftentimes the welded-on steps were omitted from the caboose as well.

Oftentimes the 3559 automatic dump car included in this outfit featured a brown Bakelite mechanism housing rather than the more common black. The pricing presumes the housing is brown; if black the values should be reduced $25.

Excellent	Like New	Scarcity
450	800	5

2124W Three-Car Passenger $62.50 retail

Included: 2332 Pennsylvania five-stripe GG-1; three 2625 Pullmans (with different names); eight OC curved and five OS straight track; RCS uncoupling/operating section; 167 controller; CTC Lockon; tube of Lionel lubricant; 926-5 instruction booklet.

Lionel's first post-World War II electric, the magnificent GG1, headed this spectacular set. Representing the famed GG1 locomotives of the Pennsy, the 2332 had a die-cast metal body painted Brunswick green with five rubber-stamped stripes and gold rubber-stamped lettering on its flanks. (The Pennsylvania Railroad referred to this color on the GG-1 drawings as "dark green locomotive enamel." The term "Brunswick green" was not in the Pennsy's vocabulary until well into the diesel era.) A PRR keystone decal was centered on the upper sides between the windows, and smaller keystones with the number 2332 were placed on the end doors. Detailed pantographs, which could be wired to actually work, were mounted on the top near either end. A single motor powered the engine. Inside the body were a three-position E-unit and a unique, realistic-sounding horn.

The earliest of Lionel's GG-1 locomotives had the motor attached to a thin die-cast post. These locomotives were painted black. Rubber stamped on each side of the locomotive was a PRR keystone with red background and gold lettering. The gold of this lettering, as well as that of the stripes, has frequently changed color to silver due to application problems or aging.

Very early in production, the red background of the keystone was eliminated, leaving the black body color as the background for the gold cum silver PRR keystone. Ultimately the red background for the keystone returned to the black GG-1, now in the form of a decal. Sometime during the first year of production, the color of the locomotive bodies was changed to a dark green known as Brunswick green. These locomotives had their keystones applied with rubber stamping, as were their gold stripes.

Regardless of paint color or keystone type, the locomotive came packaged in a Standard carton with protective liner, held the box manufacturer's information. Of note is the fact that the 1947 box was somewhat smaller than those used in later years.

Also new with this set were individual names for the passenger cars. Madison and Manhattan joined the long-running Irvington. Some of the component boxes were overstamped 2627 and 2628, although all three cars continued to wear a single catalog number: 2625. The 1948 catalog would later reflect the individual product numbers.

With green GG-1.

Excellent	Like New	Scarcity
3,000	5,000	5

With black GG-1.

Excellent	Like New	Scarcity
4,000	7,300	7

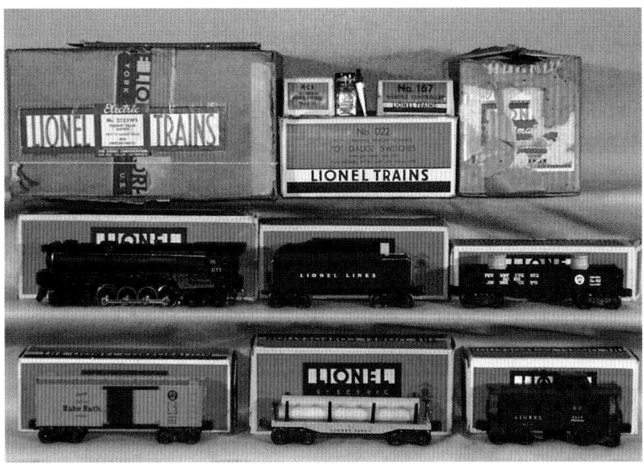

2125WS Four-Car Freight **$50 retail**

Included: 671 6-8-6 steam turbine locomotive with operating headlight and smoke; 671W early coal whistle tender; 2411 flatcar with logs; 2454 Baby Ruth boxcar; 2452 gondola with barrels; 2457 illuminated Pennsylvania N5 caboose; eight OC curved and five OS straight track; RCS uncoupling/operating section; 167 whistle controller; CTC Lockon; tube of Lionel lubricant; 926-5 instruction booklet.

This outfit was one of the first O-Gauge sets produced for 1947. All indications are that two production runs were made: one to fill orders in spring, the later for fall sales.

The initial outfits were packaged with 1946-design, if not indeed 1946 production items, including the double-worm, smoke bulb-equipped version of the 671. Naturally the whistle controller for these outfits was the 167S—and the "S" suffix was stamped on the box. Unlike most boxes from 1947, the packaging for these did not include the logo of the American Toy Manufacturers Association.

Those 2125WS outfits furnished with the newly redesigned single-worm drive 671 locomotives came with the revised 167C whistle controller. These whistle controllers were packed in boxes labeled 167. The component boxes in these outfits bore the American Toy Manufacturers Association logo.

The gondola came with solid barrels, brake wheels and steps. The flatcar was manufactured with the later style reinforced frame and carried large 5/8 x 7-inch unstained logs. The caboose usually did not have steps or Eastern Division lettering.

Excellent	Like New	Scarcity
575	975	5

2126WS Three-Car Passenger **$65 retail**

Included: 671 6-8-6 steam turbine locomotive with operating headlight and smoke; 671W early coal whistle tender; three 2625 Pullmans (with different names); eight OC curved and five OS straight track; RCS uncoupling/operating section; 167 whistle controller; CTC Lockon; tube of Lionel lubricant; 926-5 instruction booklet.

This 2126WS outfit was purchased by its original owner in this configuration, three Irvingtons—just as the 2110WS of 1946. In fact, the outfit included a 671 with 1946 features—all evidence of model year transitions not being as smooth as the catalog would have one believe.

Outfit 2110WS had been successful in 1946 and, with minor changes, it was offered again in 1947. However, the 1947 edition carried a new number, 2126WS, and included the redesigned 6-8-6 turbine with vertical E-unit.

Included in the 1947 set were passenger cars with individual names—the long-running Irvington was joined by Madison and Manhattan. Some of the component boxes were overstamped 2627 and 2628, although all three cars continued to wear a single catalog number: 2625.

Excellent	Like New	Scarcity
1,700	3,000	5

2127WS Lionel Work Train $60 retail

Included: 671 6-8-6 steam locomotive with operating headlight and smoke; 671W early coal whistle tender; 3459 automatic dumping ore car; 2461 transformer car; 2460 12-wheel crane; 2420 work caboose with searchlight; eight OC curved and five OS straight track; RCS uncoupling/operating section; 167 whistle controller; CTC Lockon; tube of Lionel lubricant; 926-5 instruction booklet.

The redesigned O-Gauge turbine was selected to head this elaborate work train. Included in it was a 12-wheel 2460 crane with black cab, accompanied by a dark gray 2420 work caboose with searchlight. The 2461 transformer car initially came with a red-painted transformer, though in later production the paint on the transformer was changed to black. The 3459 automatic dumping ore car was black as well, resulting in a rather drab consist.

Excellent	Like New	Scarcity
750	1,250	5

2129WS Four-Car Freight $67.50 retail

Included: 726 2-8-4 Berkshire steam locomotive with operating headlight and smoke; 2426W whistle tender; 3854 scale merchandise car; 2411 flatcar with logs; 2855 Sunoco single-dome tank car; 2457 illuminated Pennsylvania N5 caboose; eight OC curved and seven OS straight track; RCS uncoupling/operating section; 167 whistle controller; CTC Lockon; tube of Lionel lubricant; 926-5 instruction booklet.

Like the turbine, the Berkshire was redesigned for 1947 to eliminate the double worm drive. At the same time, a vertical E-unit—with a corresponding slot in the boiler casting—was introduced, and cotter pins replaced the turned stanchions in supporting the handrails on the boiler. The locomotive was packaged in a brown corrugated engine box marked with a manufacturer's seal reading "GAIR BOGOTA CORR. & FIBRE BOX CORP." On the end of the box was rubber stamped "726" in large print. This box was slightly smaller than similar ones used in subsequent years.

Trailing the loco was the die-cast 2426W tender with die-cast whistle housing. In tow was one of the most desirable of all postwar pieces of rolling stock, the 3854 operating merchandise car. The 3854 version packaged in this outfit had chemically blackened doors and, like all components of this set except the locomotive, came packaged in a box that bore the American Toy Manufacturers Association logo.

Not as scarce as the 3854, but still sought after, was the tank car included in this outfit. The 1947 2855 had a gray-painted sheet metal body mounted on a die-cast frame. The underside of the frame was rubber stamped "2855" in white. The die-cast flatcar was typical 1947 production, with reinforced frame and cargo of unstained logs.

Some of the 2129WS outfits came with a red caboose.

The caboose, however, was not as straightforward. Though some outfits have been reported with the sheet metal 2457 Pennsylvania caboose, most came with the new plastic-bodied 2357 SP-style caboose. The 2357s packed in these outfits were the early production versions with brake wheels mounted on the inboard side of the caboose end rails.

Excellent	Like New	Scarcity
2,100	3,500	6

2131WS Four-Car De Luxe Work Train $75 retail

Included: 726 2-8-4 Berkshire steam locomotive with operating headlight and smoke; 2426W whistle tender; 3462 operating milk car; 3451 operating log car; 2460 12-wheel crane; 2420 work caboose with searchlight; eight OC curved and seven OS straight track; RCS uncoupling/operating section; 167 whistle controller; CTC Lockon; tube of Lionel lubricant; 926-5 instruction booklet.

This outfit tied the Electronic Control set for the honor of being the most expensive set offered in 1947. Every car included in the set operated, either by remote control or as in the case of the 2460 and 2420, manually. All the cars in the outfit were packaged in Early Postwar boxes with the American Toy Manufacturer's Association emblem.

The 12-wheel 2460 crane was equipped with a black cab, and the 3451 log dump car was lettered in white and carried five unstained birch "logs." The 3451, like the 3462, had pickup shoes wired with black insulated wire. This outfit has not been observed with the super-glossy white version of the 3462. However, the milk cars packed in 2131WS did have brass mechanism bases and came with a small box containing seven magnetic milk cans.

Excellent	Like New	Scarcity
1,100	1,900	5

4109WS Electronic Control Set $75 retail

Included: 671 6-8-6R steam turbine locomotive with operating headlight and smoke; 4671W early coal whistle tender; 4452 gondola; 4454 Baby Ruth boxcar; 5459 ore dump car; 4457 illuminated Pennsylvania N5 caboose; eight OC curved and six OS straight track; ECU-1 electronic control unit; CTC Lockon; tube of Lionel lubricant; 926-5 instruction booklet.

The revolutionary Electronic Control set entered its second year in 1947. Perhaps because unsold 1946 inventory of this outfit remained in stock at Lionel or throughout its distribution network, the 1947 release used the same outfit number as had been used in 1946, even though the catalog now listed the inclusion of two additional sections of straight track.

However, demand was sufficient to warrant additional production of outfit 4109WS, apparently in two different lots. Those sets first packaged in 1947 used locomotives with 1946 features such as double worm drive and smoke bulb—interestingly these locomotives were not factory retrofitted with the 671S conversion kit. Because the plug and socket brush plate used on 1946 turbines were also required by the electronic control, this may have been an effort on the part of Lionel to dispose of otherwise obsolete locomotives or assemble more from then obsolete parts.

Once the supply of double-worm locomotives was exhausted, the 4109WS outfit was provided with the new single-worm, heater smoke unit turbine. In order to use this style locomotive with the tender-mounted electronic controls, the 1946-style socket-type brush plate had to be installed. The additional detailing present on the 1947 and later boiler casting forced the relocation of the decals to a position near the cab.

The balance of these sets, including rolling stock and component boxes, all exhibited 1947 characteristics.

Excellent	Like New	Scarcity
1,000	1,500	5

Chapter 5

1948

The big news for 1948 was the introduction of Lionel's first post-World War II diesel locomotives—replicas of EMD's famous F-3 locomotives. As a rule, the bodies were molded in black plastic, although extremely rare unpainted clear examples exist.

Though the Santa Fe locomotive was poorly rendered in the catalog illustration—the illustrator relying on a photo taken in bright sun, which made the shiny stainless panels of the actual locomotive appear black—the Lionel replica went on to be a best seller.

The red and silver Santa Fe "warbonnet" and New York Central two-tone gray "lightning stripe" paint schemes were painted on; and the white, red, yellow and black delineating stripes were rubber stamped on. The nose heralds were applied using a water-release decal, and decals were used for the GM logo on the rear sides of the units. A battery-operated, transformer-controlled horn, based on a bicycle horn, was installed in the powered A-unit, along with a lever-down three-position E-unit, operating headlight and dual horizontally mounted motors. The dummy, or non-powered A-unit also had an operating headlight. Both units featured fixed rear couplers and operating coil front couplers.

Externally, on the roof of the units were ventilators with actual wire-cloth detailing, and a pair of two-piece ornamental horns. A clear window casting was installed in the cab windows and a clear operating headlight lens was used as well. The clear, illuminated number boards were molded with the number "2333" recessed into the casting, regardless of road name worn by the locomotive. Separate black plastic grab handles were installed on the nose, and separately cast black plastic ladders led from the cab doors down to stamped steel steps that were attached to the side frames. Identical blued steel steps were mounted on the rear truck side frames, and led to access doors molded into the body. Four clear plastic conical porthole windows, often missing today, were mounted in openings in the body. Per an agreement whereby General Motors paid for a portion of the tooling cost of this model, a "GM" logo decal was applied to each side of the model. These decals were intended to be red and white on Santa Fe locos, and black and white on New York Central units, but occasionally examples will surface with the "wrong" decals installed.

Less dramatic, but nonetheless noteworthy, was the introduction of a new component box as the First Traditional box made its debut, although some of the holdover items continued to be packaged in Early Postwar boxes. Unfortunately, at this time, the heavy corrugated liners used in conjunction with earlier orange and blue boxes were eliminated except for a handful. Those boxes continuing to use liners were primarily locomotives, tenders and passenger cars. The balance of the cars used new boxes with integral coupler protection flaps. The outfit boxes themselves were unchanged from the type used in 1946 and 1947, with labels pasted on one end of the set box.

A new component box was introduced in 1948. Known as the First Traditional, this box can be distinguished from the Early Postwar by its "The Lionel Corporation" lettering, which no longer touches orange and blue surfaces.

A new steam locomotive was introduced to the mid-range 027 line—indicative of the increased demand for smoking steam locos. The new steamer, designated 2026, took the place of the venerable 1666 on the Lionel roster. Also returning to the steam roster was a switcher. The 1656 was a 0-4-0 based on the 1665 design of 1946, and included an operating bell-equipped 2403B tender.

In addition to the 2403B tender, another new tender was introduced in 1948. Styled loosely after the actual tender the Pennsylvania Railroad used behind its 6-8-6 S2 steam turbine number 6200, this new tender rode on a pair of six-wheel trucks similar to those used on the 2426W (the actual tender rode on a pair of eight-wheel trucks). Inside the tender, designated 2671W, was mounted a new whistle assembly that used a plastic acoustic chamber and a motor with a vertical armature shaft.

The very first of these tenders was equipped with a light in the rear of the body that replicated the internally mounted backup lights of the prototype. This lamp shone through a Lucite lens that was inserted through three "portholes" in the rear of the tender body shell. Apparently the benefit of this feature was lost on the buying public, and Lionel first discontinued the operating light, and soon thereafter the separately installed lens. Today such tenders are coveted by collectors, but widely forged.

Brand New! LIONEL "Scout" LINE
The biggest model railroad news in years! Just look at the super scale-detailing! Presenting two richly-colored freight sets, with sensational "Manumatic" control for uncoupling cars. Powerful four-wheel drive locomotive!
"Manumatic" Control—one of the new 1948 Lionel features, found only in the colorful "Scout" line! Cars uncouple going forward or in reverse at the pressure of the "Manumatic" button. Track section to which control unit is affixed can be placed anywhere on layout.
"Scout" freight set realism is enhanced by authentic "Baby Ruth" lettering on side of Box Car. Like real rolling stock, two "Scout" cars carry famous trade emblems.
Enjoy CURTISS Baby Ruth CANDY
LIONEL SCOUT
LIONEL
LIONEL LINES
Each "Scout" train includes new No. 1011 Transformer, with a power output of 25 Watts. Transformer uses A.C. current only.
No. 1111 LIONEL "SCOUT" SET
With "Manumatic" Control
This speedy freight train is one of the newest additions to the Lionel fleet. Cars have railroad type Knuckle Couplers and are uncoupled by means of amazing new "Manumatic" device. Locomotive is modified 2-4-2 "Columbia" type and goes forward or reverses by Remote Control. Accurately-designed freight cars are bright and colorful. Train set is 41½ inches. Track forms oval 17⅝" x 27⅜".
Train set consists of: 1 No. 1001 steam-type Locomotive—1 No. 1001T Tender—1 No. 1002 Gondola Car—1 No. 1005 Oil Car—1 No. 1007 Caboose—8 sections No. 1013 Curved Track—1 section No. 1018 Straight Track—1 No. 1009 Uncoupling Track Section—1 No. 1011 Transformer—1 CTC-10 Lockon—1 Tube of Lionel Lubricant—Instruction Booklet.
$15.95
No. 1112 LIONEL "SCOUT" FREIGHT
With "Manumatic" Control
Brand new four-car freight train, built to roll at high speeds. Brilliantly colored cars include a Gondola, for carrying barrels, pipes or other cargo; a Box Car, with realistic detail; a Southern Pacific Caboose and an authentic single dome Oil Car. Locomotive has four powerful drivers and is patterned after famous "Columbia" type. Extraordinary "Manumatic" control uncouples cars. Set is 50¾ inches. Track forms oval 42½" x 27⅜".
Outfit includes: 1 No. 1001 steam-type Locomotive—1 No. 1001T Tender—1 No. 1002 Gondola Car—1 No. 1004 Box Car—1 No. 1005 Oil Car—1 No. 1007 Caboose—8 sections No. 1013 Curved Track—3 sections No. 1018 Straight Track—1 No. 1009 Uncoupling Track Section—1 CTC-10 Lockon—1 No. 1011 Transformer—1 Tube of Lionel Lubricant—1 No. 926-5 Instruction Booklet.
$18.95
No. 1656LT "027" AND "O" GAUGE SWITCHER
With Built-in AUTOMATIC BELL
This powerful, realistic Switcher Locomotive and Tender may be purchased separately. A perfectly-proportioned model of the "yard goats" seen in the vast Pennsylvania Railroad terminals. Just the thing for shunting your Lionel cars from sidings to mainlines. Has powerful headlamp and pilot coupler. Ladder-back Tender features rear light. Built-in Bell clangs in life-like tones. Motor has double reduction gearing. Locomotive is 15¼" long. $25.00
Switcher train set illustrated on opposite page
4

1111, 1112

027

1111 Lionel Scout Set **$15.95 retail**

Contents: 1001 Scout 2-4-2 steam locomotive with operating headlight; 1001T sheet-metal tender; 1002 blue gondola; 1005 Sunoco tank car; 1007 SP-type caboose; eight sections 1013 curved and one section 1018 straight track; 1009 Manumatic uncoupling section; 1011 25-watt transformer; CTC Lockon; tube of Lionel lubricant; 926-5 instruction booklet.

Lionel executives had long realized that customers were likely to have great brand loyalty once they started to purchase trains, if for no other reasons than control and track compatibility. Faced with mounting competition for entry-level trains—particularly from Marx—Lionel set out to develop a competitive line. The result was the Scout line. The locomotive for this series had an injection-molded plastic boiler—in fact, plastic was even the principal material for the motor—which soon developed a reputation for poor reliability and serviceability. However, such measures, combined with the special plastic and metal composite trucks and couplers, allowed the base set to carry a retail price of only $15.95. An equally inexpensive uncoupler, known as the Manumatic, operated the new economy couplers.

The contents of this outfit were component boxed in First Traditional boxes, the locomotive box with a liner. These were placed in the typical corrugated outfit box of the period.

Excellent	Like New	Scarcity
125	225	2

1112 Lionel Scout Set **$18.95 retail**

Included: 1001 or 1101 Scout 2-4-2 steam locomotive with operating headlight; 1001T sheet-metal tender; 1002 blue gondola; 1004 Baby Ruth boxcar; 1005 Sunoco tank car; 1007 SP-type caboose; eight sections 1013 curved and one section 1018 straight track; 1009 Manumatic uncoupling section; 1011 25-watt transformer; CTC Lockon; tube of Lionel lubricant; 926-5 instruction booklet.

The second Scout set outfit cataloged had the same rolling stock as the first, with the addition of a 1004 Baby Ruth boxcar. Some of these sets were powered by a die-cast 1101 2-4-2, but some used the plastic 1001 2-4-2. Both locos used the plastic Scout-type motor.

With 1001.

Excellent	Like New	Scarcity
100	250	4

With 1101.

Excellent	Like New	Scarcity
125	300	5

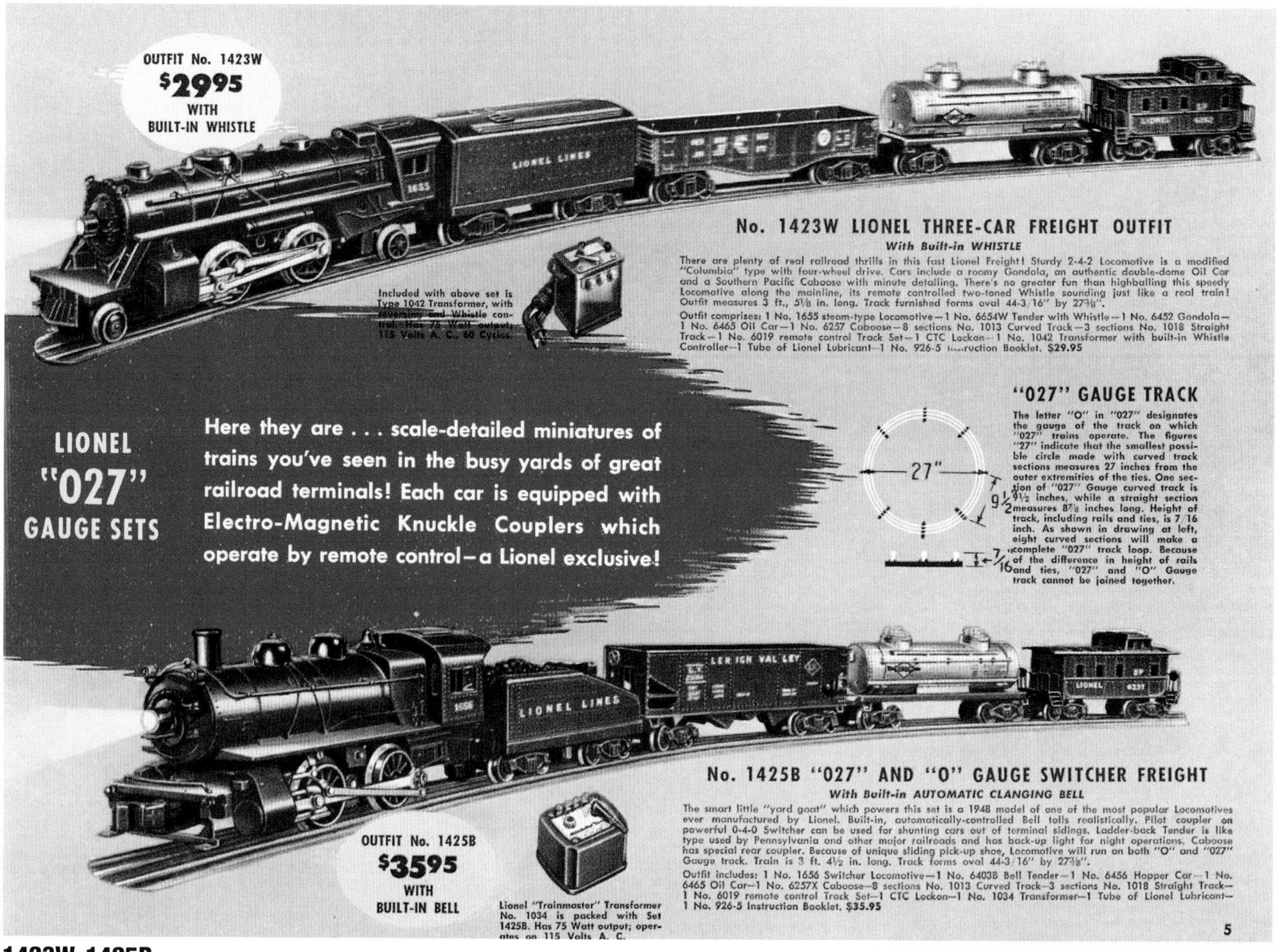

OUTFIT No. 1423W
$29.95
WITH
BUILT-IN WHISTLE

Included with above set is Type 1042 Transformer, with reversing and Whistle control. Has 75 Watt output; 115 Volts A. C., 60 Cycles.

No. 1423W LIONEL THREE-CAR FREIGHT OUTFIT

With Built-in WHISTLE

There are plenty of real railroad thrills in this fast Lionel Freight! Sturdy 2-4-2 Locomotive is a modified "Columbia" type with four-wheel drive. Cars include a roomy Gondola, an authentic double-dome Oil Car and a Southern Pacific Caboose with minute detailing. There's no greater fun than highballing this speedy Locomotive along the mainline, its remote controlled two-toned Whistle sounding just like a real train! Outfit measures 3 ft., 5⅛ in. long. Track furnished forms oval 44-3/16" by 27⅜".

Outfit comprises: 1 No. 1655 steam-type Locomotive—1 No. 6654W Tender with Whistle—1 No. 6452 Gondola—1 No. 6465 Oil Car—1 No. 6257 Caboose—8 sections No. 1013 Curved Track—3 sections No. 1018 Straight Track—1 No. 6019 remote control Track Set—1 CTC Lockon—1 No. 1042 Transformer with built-in Whistle Controller—1 Tube of Lionel Lubricant—1 No. 926-5 Instruction Booklet. $29.95

LIONEL "027" GAUGE SETS

Here they are . . . scale-detailed miniatures of trains you've seen in the busy yards of great railroad terminals! Each car is equipped with Electro-Magnetic Knuckle Couplers which operate by remote control—a Lionel exclusive!

"027" GAUGE TRACK

27"
9½
7/16

The letter "O" in "027" designates the gauge of the track on which "027" trains operate. The figures "27" indicate that the smallest possible circle made with curved track sections measures 27 inches from the outer extremities of the ties. One section of "027" Gauge curved track is 9½ inches, while a straight section measures 8⅞ inches long. Height of track, including rails and ties, is 7/16 inch. As shown in drawing at left, eight curved sections will make a complete "027" track loop. Because of the difference in height of rails and ties, "027" and "O" Gauge track cannot be joined together.

No. 1425B "027" AND "O" GAUGE SWITCHER FREIGHT

With Built-in AUTOMATIC CLANGING BELL

The smart little "yard goat" which powers this set is a 1948 model of one of the most popular Locomotives ever manufactured by Lionel. Built-in, automatically-controlled Bell tolls realistically. Pilot coupler on powerful 0-4-0 Switcher can be used for shunting cars out of terminal sidings. Ladder-back Tender is like type used by Pennsylvania and other major railroads and has back-up light for night operations. Caboose has special rear coupler. Because of unique sliding pick-up shoe, Locomotive will run on both "O" and "027" Gauge track. Train is 3 ft. 4½ in. long. Track forms oval 44-3/16" by 27⅜".

Outfit includes: 1 No. 1656 Switcher Locomotive—1 No. 6403B Bell Tender—1 No. 6456 Hopper Car—1 No. 6465 Oil Car—1 No. 6257X Caboose—8 sections No. 1013 Curved Track—3 sections No. 1018 Straight Track—1 No. 6019 remote control Track Set—1 CTC Lockon—1 No. 1034 Transformer—1 Tube of Lionel Lubricant—1 No. 926-5 Instruction Booklet. $35.95

OUTFIT No. 1425B
$35.95
WITH
BUILT-IN BELL

Lionel "Trainmaster" Transformer No. 1034 is packed with Set 1425B. Has 75 Watt output; operates on 115 Volts A. C.

5

1423W, 1425B

1423W **Lionel Three-Car Outfit** **$29.95 retail**

Included: 1655 2-4-2 steam locomotive with operating headlight; 6654W sheet-metal whistle tender; 6452 gondola; 6465 Sunoco double-dome tank car; 6257 SP-type caboose; eight sections 1013 curved and three sections 1018 straight track; 6019 uncoupling/operating section; 1042 75-watt transformer; CTC Lockon; tube of Lionel lubricant; 926-5 instruction booklet.

The old favorite 1654 was redesigned to incorporate an improved two-gear motor for 1948 and given the new catalog number of 1655. Perhaps more notable, however, was the use of a newly designed coupling system on the cars of this outfit. The complicated, expensive to produce coil couplers used previously were replaced with "magnetic" couplers, which relied on a single track-mounted electromagnet to actuate the mechanical couplers mounted on the cars. This considerably reduced the amount of labor and materials required to produce a given train set.

Excellent	Like New	Scarcity
150	225	3

1425B **Switcher Freight** **$35.95 retail**

Included: 1656 0-4-0 steam switcher with operating headlight; 2403B slope-back bell-ringing tender; 6456 Lehigh Valley hopper; 6465 Sunoco double-dome tank car; 6257X SP-type caboose; eight sections 1013 curved and three sections 1018 straight track; 6019 uncoupling/operating section; 1034 75-watt transformer; CTC Lockon; tube of Lionel lubricant; 926-5 instruction booklet.

The locomotive and caboose are the key pieces to this outfit. The 1656 0-4-0 switcher was essentially a re-motored 1665 from 1946 with the boiler shell modified to allow the E-unit lever to protrude. While the die-cast boiler shell carried

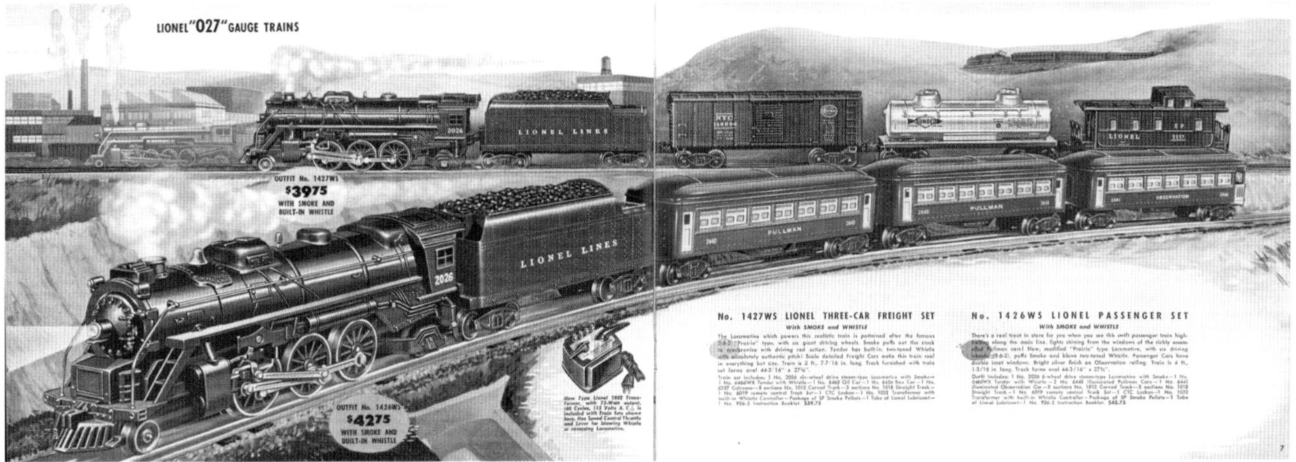

1427WS, 1426WS

the "B6" medallion, this was merely a result of the reuse of the prewar switcher die. The actual Pennsylvania Railroad B6 switchers were 0-6-0; all of Lionel's postwar switchers were 0-4-0. Nevertheless, this was an attractive little unit with its ornamental bell, sheet metal front step and wire handrails. There were coil couplers on the front of the engine and on the back of the die-cast tender, which housed an electrically operated bell. Both the locomotive and tender had operating headlights. Earliest production used the remaining stock of 2403B-type die-cast tender bodies with separate Bakelite coal pile and widely spaced Lionel Lines lettering. This tender is often found in the Early Postwar box, although the rest of the set components were packaged in First Traditional boxes.

The 6257 caboose, which had couplers on both ends, was packed in a special box marked 6257X. Because an additional coupler can easily be added to any 6257, it is the box that makes this truly unique. The coupler on the rear facilitated its use with the switcher that, unlike most Lionel steam locomotives, had an operating coupler on each end.

Excellent	Like New	Scarcity
850	1,250	3

1426WS Lionel Passenger Set **$42.75 retail**

Included: 2026 2-6-2 steam locomotive with operating headlight and smoke; 6466WX early coal whistle tender; two 6440 green Pullmans; 6441 green observation; eight sections 1013 curved and three sections 1018 straight track; 6019 uncoupling/operating section; 1032 75-watt transformer; CTC Lockon; SP smoke pellets; tube of Lionel lubricant; 926-5 instruction booklet.

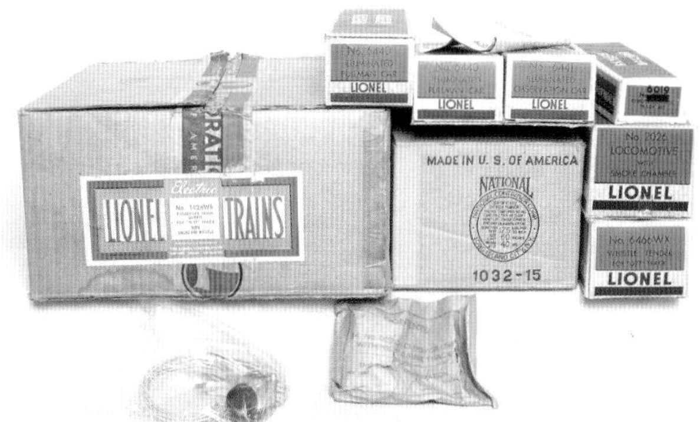

This outfit may frustrate collectors trying to match their sets to the catalog illustrations. As shown in the catalog illustration, the passenger cars were in the 2440-series—as in fact a handful of sets were. However, the bulk of the sets contained the listed 6440 and 6441 green sheet metal passenger cars.

A further anomaly may occur in this outfit, as the Lionel Service Manual states that some of the new 2026 locomotives produced in 1948 were equipped with Baldwin disc drive wheels. The locomotive and its matching coil coupler-equipped 6466WX whistle tender were packed in the new First Traditional boxes, as were the 6440 and 6441 passenger cars. Not surprisingly, the leftover 2440-series cars sometimes used were packaged in leftover Early Postwar boxes.

Excellent	Like New	Scarcity
600	1,000	5

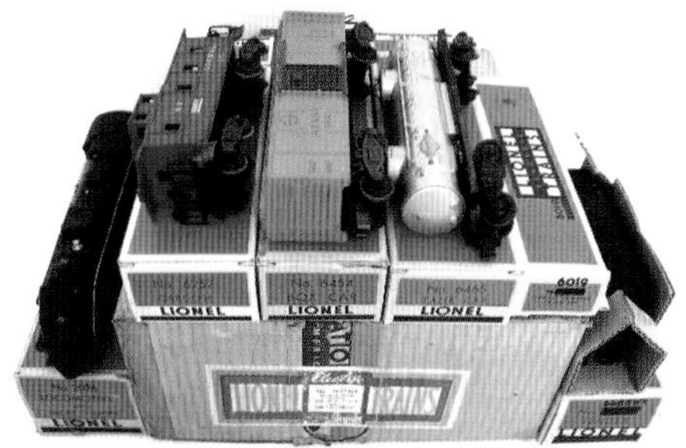

1427WS **Lionel Three-Car Freight** **$39.75 retail**

Included: 2026 2-6-2 steam locomotive with operating headlight and smoke; 6466WX early coal whistle tender; 6454 boxcar; 6465 Sunoco double-dome tank car; 6257 SP-type caboose; eight sections 1013 curved and three sections 1018 straight track; 6019 uncoupling/operating section; 1032 75-watt transformer; CTC Lockon; SP smoke pellets; tube of Lionel lubricant; 926-5 instruction booklet.

This freight outfit was also powered by the new 2026. The freight cars were essentially reissues of 1947 products, updated with the new mechanical couplers. The 6454 boxcar was produced in three road names—Baby Ruth, New York Central and Santa Fe—and any of these were apt to be used in this outfit. These cars all were equipped with stamped steel steps integral with their frames.

The components of this outfit were packaged in First Traditional boxes, with the locomotive and tender boxes including liners. Occasionally a 2466WX was substituted for the prescribed 6466WX tender.

Excellent	Like New	Scarcity
250	450	3

1429WS Four-Car Freight Set **$47.95 retail**

Included: 2026 2-6-2 steam locomotive with operating headlight and smoke; 6466WX early coal whistle tender; 3451 operating log car; 6454 boxcar; 6465 Sunoco double-dome tank car; 6357 illuminated SP-type caboose; eight sections 1013 curved and five sections 1018 straight track; 6019 uncoupling/operating section; 1033 90-watt transformer; CTC Lockon; SP smoke pellets; tube of Lionel lubricant; 926-5 instruction booklet.

The $8 increase in price of this outfit over the 1427WS covered the inclusion of an illuminated 6357 SP-type caboose and a 3451 operating log car. The 3451 came packed in an Early Postwar box, along with its unstained logs and 160 receiving bin. The wiring on the car was black.

The correct 2026 for this outfit, as well as other 1948 2026 outfits, can be distinguished by the routing of the headlight wire, which should be visible.

Excellent	Like New	Scarcity
200	325	3

1430WS Passenger Train **$59.75 retail**

Included: 2025 2-6-2 steam locomotive with operating headlight and smoke; 6466WX early coal whistle tender; 2400 Maplewood Pullman, 2401 Hillside observation, and 2402 Chatham Pullman eight sections 1013 curved and seven sections 1018 straight track; 6019 uncoupling/operating section; 1033 90-watt transformer; CTC Lockon; SP smoke pellets; tube of Lionel lubricant; 926-5 instruction booklet.

Though the 2025 2-6-2 locomotive had been introduced in 1947, the cars in tow behind it in this outfit were all new. Featuring molded plastic bodies mounted on sheet metal frames, these handsome cars are often thought of as 027-Gauge passenger cars. But, as can be seen from their inclusion in outfit 2140WS later in this chapter, the 2400-series passenger cars were neither 027- nor O-Gauge specific. The separately molded roofs were retained by aluminum thumbscrews, which were styled to resemble ventilators. The cars rode on newly designed trucks with articulated coil couplers.

A new truck was created especially for the new 2400-series passenger cars.

Excellent	Like New	Scarcity
800	1,500	5

1445WS Four-Car 027 Freight **$52.50 retail**

Included: 2025 2-6-2 steam locomotive with operating headlight and smoke; 6466WX early coal whistle tender; 6454 boxcar; 3559 automatic dump car; 6465 Sunoco double-dome tank car; 6357 illuminated SP-type caboose; eight sections 1013 curved and five sections 1018 straight track; 6019 uncoupling/operating section; 1033 90-watt transformer; CTC Lockon; SP smoke pellets; tube of Lionel lubricant; 926-5 instruction booklet.

This outfit was powered by the 2025 2-6-2, now in its second year of production. The locomotive and tender were packed in First Traditional boxes with liners. Included in an outfit for the last time was the prewar carry-over 3559 automatic dump car, packaged in a lined Early Postwar box

1449WS

with American Toy Manufacturers Association logo. This car had black wiring and black Bakelite mechanism housing.

The 6454 boxcar in this outfit—which could have been any of the three road names: Baby Ruth, New York Central or ATSF—was equipped with stamped frame steps and came in a First Traditional box.

Excellent	Like New	Scarcity
325	550	5

1447WS De Luxe Work Train **$59.50 retail**

Included: 2020 6-8-6 steam turbine locomotive with operating headlight and smoke; 6020W early coal whistle tender; 3451 operating log car; 2461 transformer; 2460 12-wheel crane; 6419 work caboose; eight sections 1013 curved and five sections 1018 straight track; 6019 uncoupling/operating section; 1033 90-watt transformer; CTC Lockon; SP smoke pellets; tube of Lionel lubricant; 926-5 instruction booklet.

Though cataloged as including a 6020W tender, some of the earliest of these outfits instead included the earlier 2020W tender. The locomotive itself lacked the thick nickel drive wheel rims used on all previous turbines. They were replaced with much thinner rims that were blackened and installed only on the first and fourth driver wheels. The tender number was changed to 6020W, reflecting the conversion to magnetic couplers. As with all the other components of this set, the locomotive and tender were packaged in Early Postwar boxes with liners.

With an operating log car and a 12-wheel crane car, outfit 1447WS was loaded with play value for young railroaders. Both the crane and log car were all black, as was the transformer load of the 2461.

Excellent	Like New	Scarcity
525	950	5

1449WS **$65 retail**

Included: 2020 6-8-6 steam turbine locomotive with operating headlight and smoke; 6020W early coal whistle tender; 3462 operating milk car; 3459 automatic dumping ore car; 6411 flatcar with logs; 6465 Sunoco double-dome tank car; 6357 illuminated SP-type caboose; eight sections 1013 curved and 11 sections 1018 straight track; 6019 uncoupling/operating section; 1033 90-watt transformer; CTC Lockon; SP smoke pellets; tube of Lionel lubricant; 926-5 instruction booklet.

The 1449WS was the top-of-the-line 027 set for 1948 and, except for the track, was the equal of many of that year's O-Gauge outfits. Although the new magnetic coupler had been introduced as the standard coupler for the 027 line, two cars in this outfit, the 3462 milk car and 3459 dump car, used instead the more expensive coil couplers. These two cars came in Early Postwar boxes, as sometimes did the locomotive and tender. The rest of the cars, as well as the bulk of the locomotives and tenders, were packed in First Traditional component boxes.

Despite the retention of coil couplers on the dump and milk cars, the log and tank cars used the new magnetic couplers, and the number change of these cars from the 2000-series to the 6000-series reflected this change.

Excellent	Like New	Scarcity
450	800	5

O-Gauge

2133W Twin Diesel O-Gauge Freight $65 retail

Included: 2333P/2333T Santa Fe or New York Central A-A F3 units; 2458 automobile boxcar; 3459 operating log car; 2555 Sunoco single-dome tank car; 2357 illuminated SP-type caboose; eight sections OC curved and seven sections OS straight; RCS track set; CTC Lockon; tube of Lionel lubricant; 926-5 instruction booklet.

Lionel's postwar diesel age was ushered in with this outfit. Before World War II, Lionel had offered replicas of diesel-powered articulated streamlined trains, the F-3s powering this set were the first "stand alone" diesel locomotives. Tooling for these new miniature diesels was jointly financed by Lionel, General Motors and the New York Central and Santa Fe railways. Thus, the locos were offered in NYC and Santa Fe paint schemes, and adorned with GM logo decals. GM of course built the full-sized units.

Though poorly illustrated in the catalog, as mentioned earlier, the locomotives and outfits containing them sold very well. However, paint adhesion was problematic on the molded plastic body, thus making excellent or better examples of the 1948 production locomotives difficult to find. The locomotive side lettering was typically rubber stamped, and the GM logo was applied with a decal—red and white for Santa Fe, and black and white for the New York Central. This decal was positioned above the "Built by Lionel" lettering on the locomotives' sides. The original, conical porthole lenses used on these locomotives, part number 2333-14, were easily lost and have been often replaced with the snap-in plastic lens 2343-133, which was introduced in the 1950s. Sometimes these sets are found with dealers or collectors having replaced the entire locomotive with a 1949 issue, which can be distinguished by its flat, celluloid porthole 2333-167.

Though the number boards read the same for both road names—2333—in reality only the Santa Fe was assigned that stock number; the stock number of the New York Central was 2334. The powered unit, or "P" unit in Lionel nomenclature, was packaged in a standard lined corrugated carton, while the dummy, or "T" unit was packaged in a lined First Traditional box.

The set carton itself was typical for the era, and the set box label was rubber-stamped indicating the road name of the locomotive within. The remaining components of the set were packaged in Early Postwar boxes.

New York Central rubber-stamped:

Excellent	Like New	Scarcity
1,000	2,500	7

New York Central heat-stamped:

Excellent	Like New	Scarcity
700	2,000	5

Santa Fe:

Excellent	Like New	Scarcity
800	2,200	5

2135WS Three-Car Freight $39.95 retail

Included: 675 2-6-2 steam locomotive with operating headlight and smoke; 2466WX early coal whistle tender; 2456 Lehigh Valley hopper; 2411 flatcar with logs, 2357 illuminated SP-type caboose; eight sections OC curved and three sections OS straight; RCS track set; CTC Lock-on; SP smoke pellets; tube of lubricant; instruction booklet.

This O-Gauge outfit came packaged in Lionel's typical 1948 corrugated set carton, but the components inside were packaged in Early Postwar boxes with liners of the style characteristic of 1947. This was true for even the newly introduced 2456 Lehigh Valley hopper car. As was the case with all 1948 O-Gauge sets, this outfit included an RCS uncoupling track and cars equipped with coil-type couplers.

The 675 towing this set was equipped with Baldwin Disc wheels, and featured a red and gold keystone on the boiler front. Its smokestack was painted black, and the newly redesigned pilot casting included a rigidly cast simulated coupler.

Excellent	Like New	Scarcity
325	525	4

2136WS Three-Car Passenger $42.50 retail

Included: 675 2-6-2 steam locomotive with operating headlight and smoke; 2466WX early coal whistle tender; two 2442 brown Pullmans; 2443 brown observation; eight sections OC curved and three sections OS straight; RCS track set; CTC Lockon; SP smoke pellets; tube of lubricant, instruction booklet.

The 675 was used to lead this outfit—just as it had in 1947 when the set carried the catalog number 2120WS. Other than the catalog number and retail price, strangely $1 lower in 1948 than in 1947, the two years' outfits were identical. Even the Early Postwar component boxes and the characteristics of the cars were in the previous year's style.

Excellent	Like New	Scarcity
550	900	5

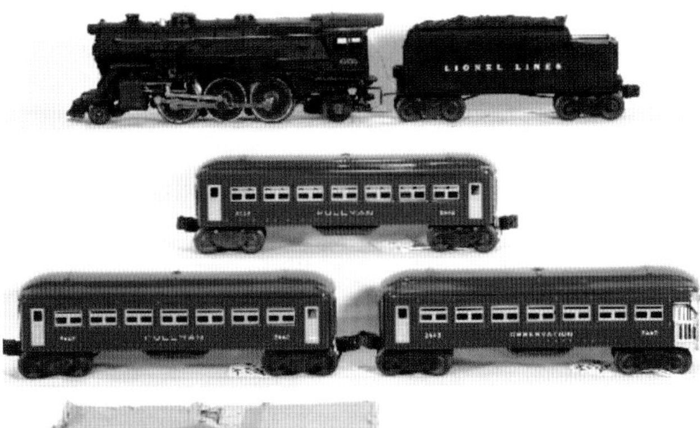

2136WS

2137WS Four-Car De Luxe Freight $47.50 retail

Included: 675 2-6-2 steam locomotive with operating headlight and smoke; 2466WX early coal whistle tender; 2458 automobile boxcar; 3459 automatic dumping ore car; 2456 Lehigh Valley hopper; 2357 illuminated SP-type caboose; eight sections OC curved and three sections OS straight; RCS track set; CTC Lockon; SP smoke pellets; tube of lubricant; instruction booklet.

This is another outfit headed by the 675, which is one reason these locomotives are so abundant today. In tow behind the 2-6-2 and tender were three freight cars and a caboose. The locomotive, tender and cars were all packaged in 1947-style Early Postwar boxes with liners. The outfit box itself was typical for 1948. The rolling stock was nondescript, however the 3459 automatic ore-dumping car in this outfit was often the somewhat desirable green version. As was the case with all 1948 O-Gauge sets, this outfit included an RCS uncoupling track and cars equipped with coil-type couplers.

Excellent	Like New	Scarcity
400	700	4

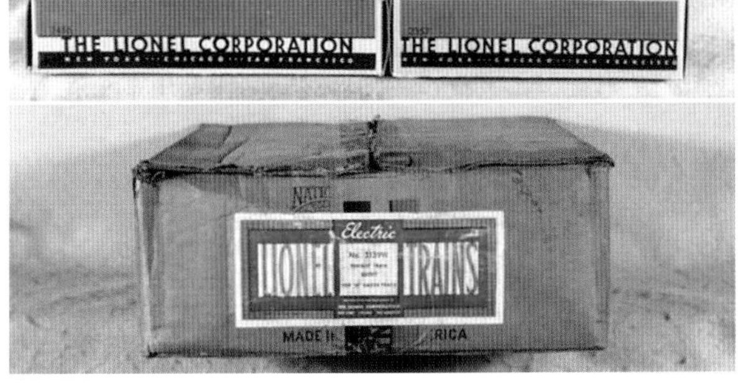

2139W Four-Car Freight $57.50 retail

Included: 2332 Pennsylvania five-stripe GG1; 2458 automobile boxcar; 3451 operating log car; 2456 Lehigh Valley hopper; 2357 illuminated SP-type caboose; eight sections OC curved and five sections OS straight; RCS track set; CTC Lockon; tube of lubricant; instruction booklet.

Packaged in a corrugated set box was a 2332 GG-1 and four freight cars. The box, though a standard brown carton, was ever so slightly larger than that used in the previous year. The locomotive had a corrugated wrap-around liner, and the cars were packaged in Early Postwar boxes with liners of the style characteristic of 1947. This was true for even the newly introduced 2456 Lehigh Valley hopper car. As was the case with all O-Gauge 1948 sets, this outfit included an RCS uncoupling track and cars equipped with coil-type couplers.

Excellent	Like New	Scarcity
1,500	2,500	4

1948

2140WS Three-Car De Luxe Passenger $57.75 retail

Included: 671 6-8-6 steam turbine locomotive with operating headlight and smoke; 2671W streamlined whistle tender; 2400 Maplewood Pullman, 2401 Hillside observation and 2402 Chatham Pullman in the new streamlined series with green-and-gray paint scheme; eight sections OC curved and five sections OS straight; RCS track set; CTC Lockon; SP smoke pellets; tube of lubricant; instruction booklet.

The 1948 edition of the 671 introduced an all-new tender, the streamlined 12-wheel 2671W. Stretching along the flanks of the tender in silver was "Pennsylvania" lettering. The very earliest of these tenders, and today quite coveted, featured operating backup lights.

This is an original backup lamp. Beware of other mountings.

The locomotive itself had thin black rims on the first and last drive wheels on each side and was packed in a First Traditional box with a liner. The same style of packaging was also used for the new tender as well as the passenger cars. Unique to this year, the tender box was marked with "2671W" printed on each end, as well as all four sides.

The consist was an all-new design of passenger car with molded plastic bodies and roofs mounted on a sheet-metal floor/frame combination and riding on die-cast trucks with coil couplers. The bodies of the cars were painted green, with yellow lettering and striping applied. The roof was dark gray and retained by a pair of thumbscrews, the heads of which were knurled to resemble ventilator housings.

Excellent	Like New	Scarcity
900	1,500	5

Original backup light lenses are curved not flat.

2141WS Four-Car Freight $58.75 retail

Included: 671 6-8-6 steam turbine locomotive with operating headlight and smoke; 2671W streamlined whistle tender; 3451 operating log car; 3462 operating milk car; 2456 Lehigh Valley hopper; 2357 illuminated SP-type caboose; eight sections OC curved and five sections OS straight; RCS track set; CTC Lockon; SP smoke pellets; tube of lubricant; instruction booklet.

The locomotive itself had thin black rims on the first and last drive wheels on each side and was packed in a First Traditional box with a liner. The same style of packaging was also used for the new tender. The 1948 edition of the 671 introduced an all-new tender, the streamlined 12-wheel 2671W. Stretching along the flanks of the tender in silver was "Pennsylvania" lettering. Unique to this year, the tender box was marked with "2671W" printed on each end, as well as all four sides. The locomotive and cars were all packaged in 1947-style Early Postwar boxes with liners. The outfit box itself was the typical corrugated carton used during this period.

An RCS uncoupling track was included in this set, as was the case with all O-Gauge 1948 sets, and the cars were equipped with coil-type couplers.

Excellent	Like New	Scarcity
500	775	4

2143WS Four-Car De Luxe Work Train $60 retail

Included: 671 6-8-6 steam turbine locomotive with operating headlight and smoke; 2671W streamlined whistle tender; 3459 automatic dumping ore car; 2461 transformer car; 2460 12-wheel crane; 2420 work caboose with searchlight;

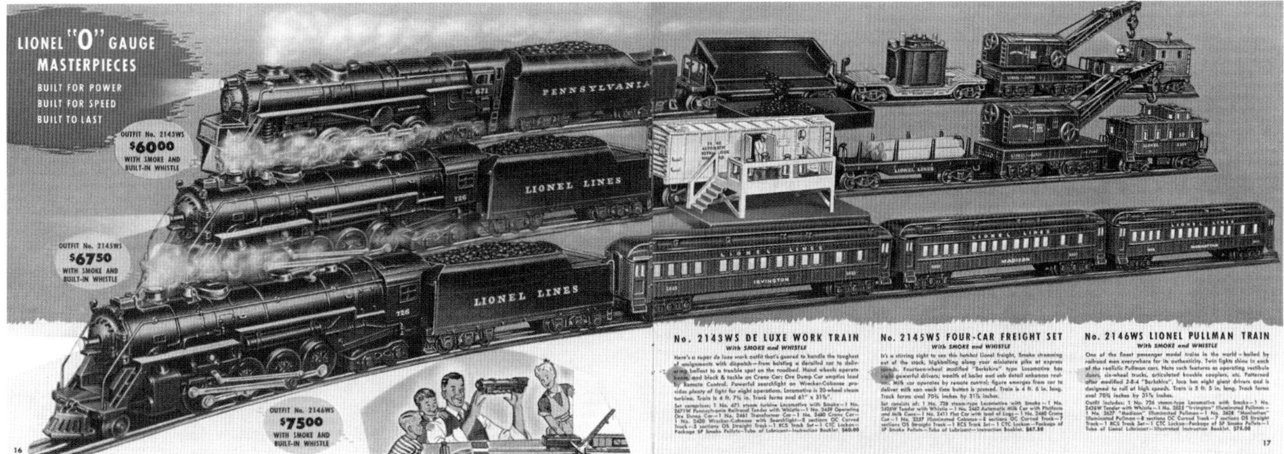

2143WS, 2145WS, 2146WS

eight sections OC curved and five sections OS straight; RCS track set; CTC Lockon; SP smoke pellets; tube of lubricant; instruction booklet.

Because of the success of outfit 2127WS in 1947, Lionel recreated it for 1948 with a new number, 2143WS. While the set continued to retail for $60, it now included the deluxe new 12-wheel 2671W tender. There have been reports of some instances of the tender included in this outfit being the scarce variation with operating backup lights.

Unlike 1947, when the cargo of the 2461 was red, the simulated transformer in 1948 was painted black. The locomotive came in an Early Postwar or First Traditional box with a liner, while the freight cars used 1947-style Early Postwar boxes. The tender was packaged in its unique-to-1948 box marked with "2671W" printed on each end, as well as all four sides. The set box itself was typical 1948 issue.

Excellent	Like New	Scarcity
700	1,200	5

2144W Three-Car De Luxe Passenger $67.50 retail

Included: 2332 Pennsylvania five-stripe GG-1; 2625 Irvington, 2627 Madison and 2628 Manhattan heavyweight Pullmans; eight sections OC curved and five sections OS straight; RCS track set; CTC Lockon; tube of lubricant; instruction booklet.

The magnificent 2332 GG-1 headed up this set, which was nearly a repeat of the previous year's outfit 2124W. This year, the locomotive came in a lined standard brown box that was slightly larger than that used previously. The deluxe passenger cars, which only the year before had gotten unique names, now also were given unique numbers as well. Oddly enough, some of these cars were packed in 1947-style Early Postwar boxes with liners, even though they were new in 1948.

The paint did not adhere well to the Bakelite from which the passenger car bodies were made, making it especially difficult today to find this set with blemish-free cars.

Excellent	Like New	Scarcity
2,400	4,000	5

2145WS Four-Car Freight $67.50 retail

Included: 726 2-8-4 Berkshire steam locomotive with operating headlight and smoke; 2426W whistle tender; 3462 operating milk car; 2411 flatcar with logs; 2460 12-wheel crane; 2357 illuminated SP-type caboose; eight sections OC curved and seven sections OS straight; RCS track set; CTC Lockon; SP smoke pellets; tube of lubricant; instruction booklet.

Returning for a third year, a 2-8-4 726 Berkshire was selected as the motive power for this set. A 2-8-4 in some form would appear in almost every catalog of the postwar era. Like the 1948 675, the 1948 726 had a new pilot and steam chest casting, which included a small simulated knuckle coupler. The locomotive's standard brown carton bore the maker's mark, "GAIR BOGOTA CORP" and was slightly larger than that used in previous years. The box included a liner. The spectacular die-cast 2426W tender was packed in a lined Early Postwar box. The remainder of the rolling stock also used this type of box.

With the die-cast tender, the die-cast frames of the crane and flatcar, and heavy operating mechanism of the milk car, the locomotive in this outfit certainly was in for a workout.

Excellent	Like New	Scarcity
850	1,400	5

2146WS Three-Car Pullman $75 retail

Included: 726 2-8-4 Berkshire steam locomotive with operating headlight and smoke; 2426W whistle tender; 2625 Irvington, 2627 Madison and 2628 Manhattan heavyweight Pullmans; eight sections OC curved and seven sections OS straight; RCS track set; CTC Lockon; SP smoke pellets; tube of lubricant; instruction booklet.

Similar to outfit 2144W, but appealing to customers living outside of the Pennsylvania Railroad's electrified northeastern territory, was this three-car passenger set towed by a big steam locomotive. New in 1948, the 726 had a new pilot and steam chest casting, which included a small-simulated knuckle coupler. The locomotive's standard brown carton bore the maker's mark, "GAIR BOGOTA CORP" and was slightly larger than that used in previous years. The box included a liner. The spectacular die-cast 2426W tender was packed in either a lined Early Postwar box or the new First Traditional boxes.

The Bakelite forming the bodies of the passenger cars did not take paint well. Thus, today it is difficult to locate these cars in pristine condition.

Excellent	Like New	Scarcity
2,400	4,000	7

4110WS Lionel Electronic Railroad $199.95 retail

Included: 671R steam turbine locomotive with operating headlight and smoke; 4671W early coal whistle tender; 4452 gondola; 4454 Baby Ruth boxcar; 5459 ore dump car; 4357 illuminated SP-type caboose; 10 sections OC curved, 18 straight and two half-sections OS straight; pair 022 remote-control switches; 151 semaphore; 97 operating coal elevator; ECU-1 electronic control unit; VW 150-watt transformer.

In what appears today to be a bizarre marketing strategy, Lionel responded to disappointing sales of the prior years' 4109WS Electronic Control outfit by adding items to the set and raising the price. What makes this strange is that the company took an already expensive outfit, added $67.25 (retail) worth of goods and raised the price almost $125!

For the collector, this made what would have already been no doubt a difficult set to find become extraordinarily difficult. Many dealers in 1948 had the previous 4109WS on the shelf and were unlikely to reorder an even more expensive version.

For consumers who did pay the princely sum of $199.95, they got to take home the basic electronic control train set, but also a 97 coal elevator, 151 semaphore and a pair of switches. A mighty VW 150-watt transformer powered this empire. The sheer mass of these goods makes it difficult today to find the huge outfit carton in collectible condition.

The train itself differed from previous models most notably by the inclusion of a plastic-bodied 4357 caboose rather than the sheet metal 4457 featured previously. The new caboose had ladder slots molded into the body casting, which was red plastic-painted brown.

The other notable change was the relocation of the locomotive's Electronic Control decal from a turbine casing to near the locomotive cab. This was due to a change in the boiler and cab casting, which now had additional details molded in, and the former location of the decal, which had been smooth, now featured cast-in detail. Strangely, the new 2671W tender, which was included with all the other O-Gauge turbines, was not produced in an electronic control version. Instead, the 671R continued to be paired with the smaller 4671W tender.

The balance of the rolling stock was unchanged from the previous year, but, like the locomotive and caboose, was packed in First Traditional boxes rather than the Early Postwar boxes of 1947.

Excellent	Like New	Scarcity
2,000	3,700	7

Chapter 6

1949

Perhaps built on the success of the 1948 F-3, a second diesel replica joined the Lionel roster in 1949. This second diesel, like the F-3, was also a representation of a General Motors diesel—this time an Electro-Motive NW-2 switcher. Significant, but uncelebrated in the catalog of the time, was the inclusion in these units of Magne-traction. This Lionel-exclusive feature increased locomotive adhesion to the rails by magnetizing the drive wheels and installing nearby magnets.

The new locomotive was offered in both 027- and O-Gauge versions as the 6220 and 622 respectively. The catalog illustrated these locomotives decorated in Lionel markings, but in reality all examples were produced with Santa Fe livery.

Magnet couplers, introduced on the 027 lines in 1948, were now used on the bulk of the O-Gauge lines as well. This move no doubt saved Lionel thousands of dollars annually in reduced materials and labor costs. Further cost savings were likely made by making a minor change to the set packaging, eliminating the pasted-on outfit label in favor of labeling information printed directly on the box. During the year, "San Francisco" was removed from the component boxes inside those set boxes. While the locomotives and premium tender boxes continued to have liners, they were eliminated from many of the rolling stock boxes. This reduced packaging labor as well as the shipping and storage volume required for these items.

A further change to outfit component packaging involved the log and ore dump cars. Previously the receiving trays for these cars were packed with the respective car and separated by a liner. Beginning in 1949 the trays were packaged loose in the outfit box itself. This allowed the cars in these outfits to be packaged in smaller, liner-less boxes, which were designated by an X suffix stamped on the box. Those items intended for separate sale, however, were packaged in conventional lined boxes along with their receiving bins.

Destined to become one of the mainstays of Lionel's postwar outfit, the 6462 gondola was introduced this year. The new car, 10-1/2 in. long, featured a stamped sheet metal frame with integral steps on each corner. A plastic body was mounted on this, with brake wheels on the right-hand corner of each side. These cars were laden with six turned wooden barrels.

Also new was an adaptation of the 2461 depressed center car for use as a searchlight car. Searchlight cars were not a new product to Lionel. The firm had produced numerous versions during the prewar era. For the new car, a simulated General Motors generator, made of injection-molded plastic, was installed on the well, while a die-cast searchlight housing was mounted via a yoke on one end deck. The mounting permitted the operator to aim the searchlight, and the simulated generator housed an off-on switch that could be controlled by the electromagnet of an uncoupling track section.

Hoping to capitalize on the success of the 1948 milk car, Lionel introduced the 3656 operating cattle car. The first year's production of this car and its corresponding corral differed from subsequent years and included notable variations—particularly the application of an "Armour" label to the car doors and the occasional stamping of the car in black rather than the common white.

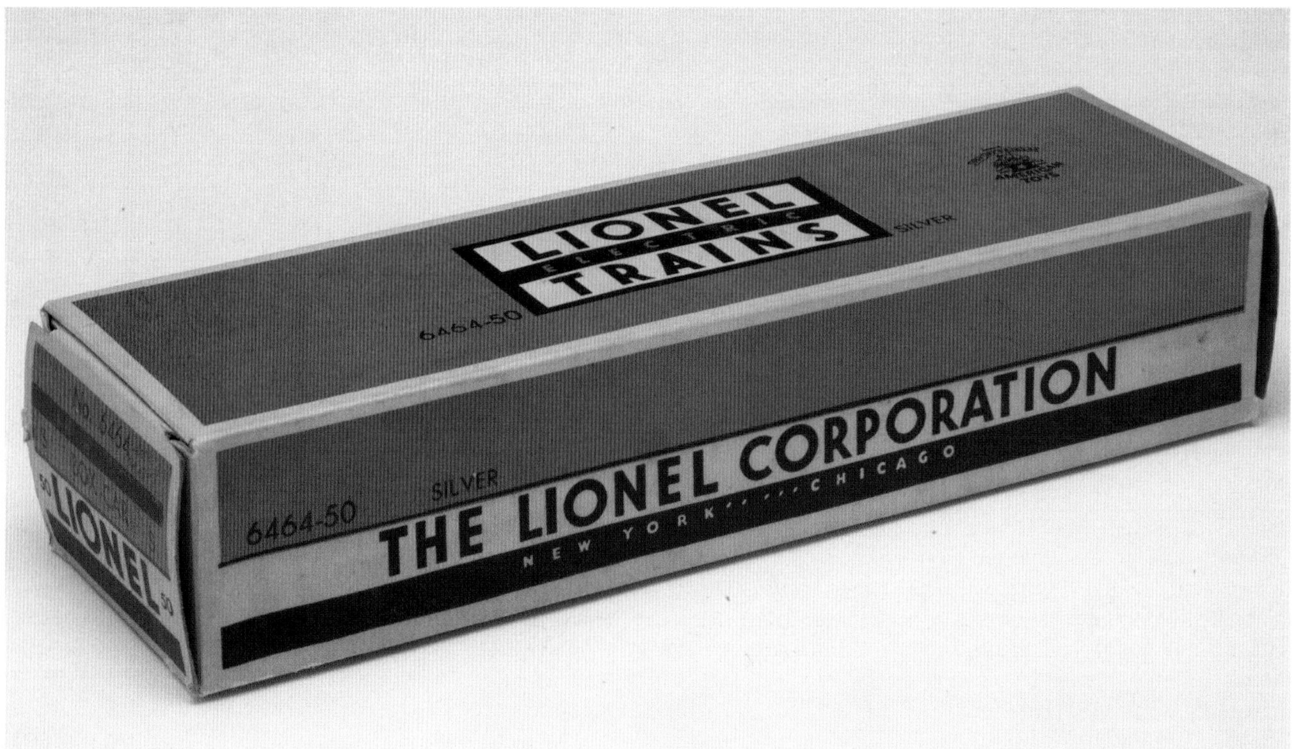

During 1949, "San Francisco" was removed from the outside of the component boxes, leaving only New York and Chicago listed.

1115, 1117

1949

027-Gauge

1115 📷 **Lionel Scout** **$15.95 retail**

Included: 1110 2-4-2 Scout steam locomotive with operating headlight; 1001T sheet-metal tender; 1002 gondola; 1005 tank car; 1007 SP-type caboose; eight 1013 curved and one 1018 straight track; 1009 Manumatic uncoupling section; 1011 25-watt transformer; CTC Lockon; tube of Lionel lubricant; instruction booklet.

Lionel pressed on with the second year of its economy-priced Scout series with this set. Patterned after outfit 1111 from 1948, this outfit was somewhat upgraded through the use of the 1110, which had a die-cast boiler and cab in lieu of the plastic-bodied 1001 from 1948. The earliest editions of this locomotive were equipped with Baldwin disc drive wheels, while the bulk of the production used spoked drive wheels. Unfortunately, the mechanical quality of the 1949 locomotive was not an improvement over the 1948 edition, though its heft and look were.

The rolling stock were largely duplicates of the 1948 item. However, the 1002 gondola, which had been blue in 1948, was black for 1949. The components of the box were packaged in either First or Middle Traditional boxes, with the locomotive box including a liner. These components were placed in the new 1949 pre-printed outfit box.

Excellent	Like New	Scarcity
150	250	4

1117 **Lionel Scout** **$18.95 retail**

Included: 1110 Scout 2-4-2 steam locomotive with operating headlight; 1001T sheet-metal tender; 1002 gondola; 1005 tank car; 1004 Baby Ruth boxcar; 1007 SP-type caboose; eight 1013 curved and one 1018 straight track; 1009 Manumatic uncoupling section; 1011 25-watt transformer; CTC Lockon; tube of Lionel lubricant; instruction booklet.

The four-car Scout outfit was re-powered in the same manner as the 1115 three-car outfit. Similar to the 1948 1112, 1949's 1117 added a Baby Ruth boxcar to the roster of outfit 1115. The die-cast boilered 1110 2-4-2 had charge of this consist, with the locomotive in most cases having spoked drive wheels.

The components of this outfit, including the locomotive that had a lined box, were packaged in either First or Middle Traditional boxes. In most instances, the gondola utilized the new black body, but a few collectors have examples of this set apparently assembled with leftover 1948 blue cars.

Excellent	Like New	Scarcity
150	250	4

1423W 📷 **Lionel Three-Car Outfit** **$29.95 retail**

Included: 1655 2-4-2 steam locomotive with operating headlight; 6654W sheet-metal whistle tender; 6452 gondola with barrel load; 6465 Sunoco double-dome tank car; 6257 SP-type caboose; eight sections 1013 curved and three sections 1018 straight track; 6019 uncoupling/operating section; 1033 90-watt transformer; CTC Lockon; tube of Lionel lubricant; 027C-1 track clips; instruction booklet.

1423W, 1425B, 1451WS

Essentially a repeat of a 1948 outfit with the same number, the 1949 offering was improved by a transformer upgrade. The 90-watt 1033 Trainmaster transformer replaced the previously used 1042 75-watt transformer in 1949. Most outfits were packaged in the new pre-printed 1949 boxes, but reportedly some used leftover 1948 boxes with separately applied labels.

Excellent	Like New	Scarcity
150	225	3

1425B Switcher Freight $35.95 retail

Included: 1656 0-4-0 steam switcher with operating headlight; 6403B slope-back bell-ringing tender; 6456 Lehigh Valley hopper; 6465 Sunoco double-dome tank car; 6257X SP-type caboose; eight sections 1013 curved and three sections 1018 straight track; 6019 uncoupling/operating section; 1034 75-watt transformer; CTC Lockon; 027C-1 track clips; tube of Lionel lubricant; instruction booklet.

Another of the successful 1948 outfits repeated was this—the 1425B. Identical to the earlier version except for the tender number, which was changed to 6403B, some of these outfits were even packaged in surplus 1948 boxes. Most of the 1949 1425Bs, however, came in the new boxes with preprinted labels.

Excellent	Like New	Scarcity
850	1,250	6

1426WS Lionel Passenger Set $42.75 retail

Included: 2026 2-6-2 steam locomotive with operating headlight and smoke; 6466WX early coal whistle tender; two 6440 green Pullmans; 6441 green observation; eight sections 1013 curved and three sections 1018 straight track; 6019 uncoupling/operating section; 1033 90-watt transformer; CTC Lockon; 027C-1 track clips; bottle of SP; smoke pellets; tube of Lionel lubricant; instruction booklet.

The prewar design-based sheet-metal passenger cars returned again in this repeat of a 1948 outfit. Painted green with cream window inserts, the cars' 6000-series numbers reflected their magnetic couplers, which had begun to be introduced the previous year.

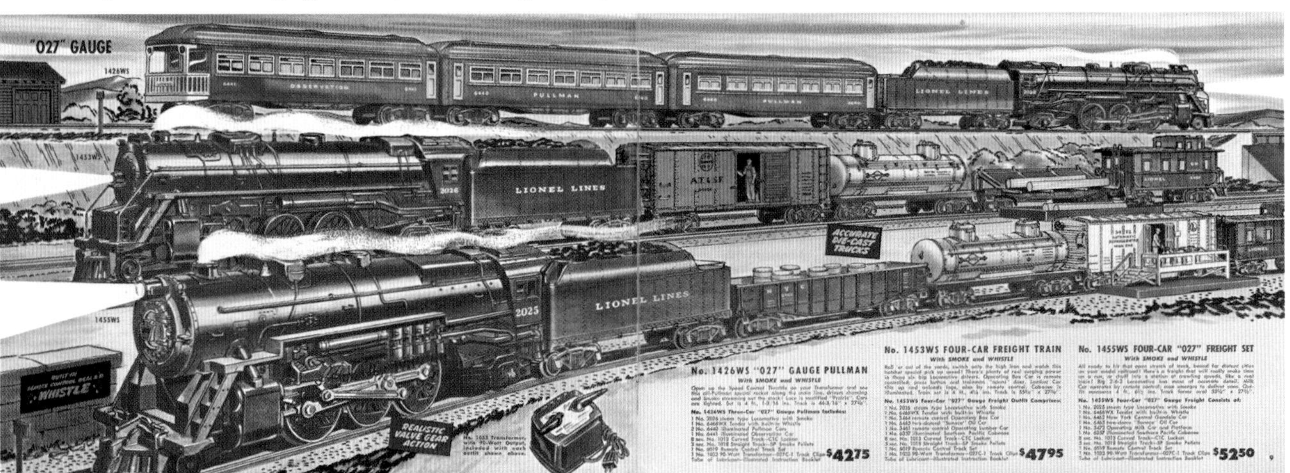

1426WS, 1453WS, 1455WS

1457B, 1430WS

Because this set was a repeat of a 1948 outfit, some could have been packaged in surplus 1948 outfit boxes, but most came in the 1949 set box with integral labeling.

Excellent	Like New	Scarcity
600	1,000	5

1430WS De Luxe Pullman $59.75 retail

Included: 2025 2-6-2 steam locomotive with operating headlight and smoke; 6466WX early coal whistle tender; 2400 Maplewood Pullman, 2401 Hillside observation and 2402 Chatham Pullman in the new green streamlined series; eight sections 1013 curved and seven sections 1018 straight track; 6019 uncoupling/operating section; 1033 90-watt transformer; CTC Lockon; 027C-1 track clips; bottle of SP; smoke pellets; tube of Lionel lubricant; instruction booklet.

The second 1949 027 passenger outfit included the somewhat newer streamlined 2400-series passenger cars. The attractive green cars, with yellow striping and lettering and dark gray roofs, were named Maplewood, Chatham and Hillside—all New Jersey towns with ties to Lionel.

This set was a continuation of a 1948 set with the same number. Therefore, it is possible some were packaged in leftover 1948 boxes, but all known 1949 examples observed in preparing this volume were contained in new for 1949 packaging.

Excellent	Like New	Scarcity
800	1,500	5

1447WS "027" Gauge Four-car De Luxe Work Train $59.50 retail

Included: 2020 6-8-6 steam turbine locomotive with operating headlight and smoke; 6020W early coal whistle tender; 3461 automatic lumber car; 6461 transformer; 2460 12-wheel crane; 6419 work caboose; eight sections 1013 curved and five sections 1018 straight track; 6019 uncoupling/operating section; 1033 90-watt transformer; CTC Lockon; 027C-1 track clips; bottle of SP; smoke pellets; tube of Lionel lubricant; instruction booklet.

This outfit was an updated repeat of a 1948 set with the same number. Included in the 1949 edition was a 6461 transformer car and 3461 log car—both equipped with magnetic couplers. These cars replaced similar coil coupler-equipped cars in the previous year's offering. The lumber car included in this, and apparently all 1949 outfits, was loaded with unstained logs, though a few of the separate sale cars produced late in the year may have had stained logs. All reported examples were packaged in preprinted 1949 boxes, but as a carryover item it is possible that some were shipped in surplus 1948 cartons.

The 1949 locomotive did not have rims on any of its drive wheels, and its brush plate was based on that of the 622, lacking the tubular brush holders used in previous years.

Excellent	Like New	Scarcity
525	950	5

1451WS Three-car Freight $39.75 retail

Included: 2026 2-6-2 steam locomotive with operating headlight and smoke; 6466WX early coal whistle tender; 6462 gondola; 3464 operating boxcar; 6257 SP-type caboose; eight sections 1013 curved and three sections 1018 straight track; 6019 uncoupling/operating section; 1033 90-watt transformer, CTC Lockon; 027C-1 track clips; bottle of SP; smoke pellets; tube of Lionel lubricant; instruction booklet.

One of the new outfits joining the 1949 line was the 1451WS. Though the locomotive and tender was carried over from 1948, the two freight cars in tow were new.

The 3464 operating boxcar, which was produced in both New York Central and Santa Fe liveries, was based on the then current 6454 boxcar. However, distinguishing the new cars was an operating mechanism that included a vinylite man who simulated the action of opening the car door from the inside when activated by the uncoupling track section. Of note to collectors is the fact that the 1949 edition of the "man" inside the boxcar had flesh-painted face and hands.

The 6462 gondola, as mentioned in the chapter introduction, was to become a mainstay of Lionel's freight outfits for years to come. Economical to produce, it was nonetheless ideal for such use, as its open top design allowed youthful railroaders to laden the car with Lincoln Logs, toy cars, American Bricks, etc.—increasing the play value of the outfit.

The spoke-wheel equipped locomotive and its accompanying tender were both packaged in boxes with liners, though both First and Middle Traditional boxes were used. Both styles of boxes were used interchangeably for the remainder of the rolling stock as well, though bereft of liners.

Excellent	Like New	Scarcity
275	450	4

1453WS Four-car Freight Train $47.95 retail

Included: 2026 2-6-2 steam locomotive with operating headlight and smoke; 6466WX early coal whistle tender; 3464 operating boxcar; 6465 Sunoco double-dome tank car; 3461 automatic lumber car; 6357 illuminated SP-type caboose; eight 1013 curved and five 1018 straight track; 6019 uncoupling/operating section; 1033 90-watt transformer, CTC Lockon, 027C-1 track clips; bottle of SP smoke pellets; tube of Lionel lubricant; instruction booklet.

The new animated 3464 boxcar was included in this outfit. It was a near duplicate of 1948's 1429WS, which had included a non-operating 6454 boxcar. As was the case with all 3464 boxcars produced in 1949, the face and outstretched hands of the vinylite figure were painted a flesh color. New York Central and Santa Fe boxcars were included indiscriminately in these outfits.

The operating lumber car included in this outfit was the 3461, which had magnetic couplers. The receiving bin was packaged separately from the car itself. The bulk of the lumber cars produced in 1949, and evidently all the ones included in outfits, were furnished with unstained logs, though a few of the separate sale cars produced late in the year may have had stained logs.

The outfit was packed in the new style 1949 carton, which included label information printed directly on the box. Inside, the locomotive and tender component boxes included liners, and the other components were packed in either First or Middle Traditional boxes.

Excellent	Like New	Scarcity
325	525	4

1455WS Four-car Freight Set $52.50 retail

Included: 2025 2-6-2 steam locomotive with operating headlight and smoke; 6466WX early coal whistle tender; 6462 gondola; 6465 Sunoco double-dome tank car; 3472 operating milk car; 6357 illuminated Southern Pacific caboose; eight 1012 curved track, five 1018 straight track; 6019 remote control track set; 1033 90-watt transformer; CTC Lockon; 027C-1 track clips; bottle of SP smoke pellets; tube of Lionel lubricant; instruction booklet.

The 2025 leading this set is indistinguishable from those produced the year prior. Once again it had in tow the 6466WX early coal tender, which in the catalog illustration was followed by two cars destined to be among the most common of all Lionel freight cars, the 6462 New York Central gondola and the 6465 Sunoco two-dome tank car. Notably included was the common but very popular 3472 operating milk car with platform. Bringing up the rear was an illuminated 6357 Southern Pacific caboose.

These items were packed in a mixture of First and Middle Traditional boxes, with the locomotive and tender boxes including liners. The outfit box itself could either have been a surplus 1948 box or the new-for-1949 pre-printed carton.

Excellent	Like New	Scarcity
400	750	4

1457B Diesel Freight $49.50

Included: 6220 Santa Fe bell-ringing NW-2 diesel switcher; 3464 operating boxcar; 6462 gondola; 6520 searchlight car; 6419 work caboose; eight 1012 curved track, five 1018 straight track; 6019 remote control track set; 1034 75-watt transformer; CTC Lockon; 027C-1 track clips; tube of lubricant; instruction book.

Keeping with Lionel's policy of assigning four digit numbers to 027 locomotives, the new switcher heading this outfit was numbered 6220, though for all intents and purposes it was identical to its 622 O-Gauge sibling. The "B" in the outfit number denoted the operating bell feature of the switcher.

Unlike the bell-equipped steam switchers, which rang the bell electrically and included an on-off switch, the bell of the diesel switchers was rung mechanically. With no "off" switch, it is not surprising that many are found today with the bell removed—no doubt by parents who grew quickly weary of the constant clanging. Though the catalog showed this locomotive in "Lionel" markings, it was in fact produced in Santa Fe livery. Also marked for Santa Fe were the 3464 operating boxcars included in many of the sets, though New York Central 3464 cars were as often packaged in the outfits.

Though commonly featuring an orange plastic generator housing, some of the 6520 searchlight cars included in 1457B outfits were equipped with the scarce molded green plastic generator.

The preprinted box, typical of new 1949 items, strangely omitted the "B" from the product number of this outfit.

Excellent	Like New	Scarcity
625	950	5

1459WS **027-Gauge Five-car Freight Outfit**

$67.50 retail

Included: 2020 6-8-6 Steam Turbine with operating headlight and smoke; 6020W early coal tender; 3656 operating cattle car; 6411 die-cast flatcar with logs; 3469 automatic dumping ore car with 207 artificial coal; 6465 Sunoco double-dome tank car; 6357 illuminated caboose; eight 1012 curved track, eleven 1018 straight track; 6019 remote control track set; 1033 90-watt transformer; CTC Lockon; 027C-1 track clips; bottle of SP smoke pellets; tube of lubricant; instruction book.

Though the outfit carton was the typical unremarkable box of the year, the contents of set 1459WS were no doubt spectacular to the children receiving them in 1949. For inside outfit 1459WS was a spectacular 027 freight train featuring two operating cars, as well as a tank car, flatcar and caboose—headed by the impressive 20-wheel steam turbine.

The 2020 steam locomotive did not have the rims on any of the drive wheels, unlike previous years. It was furnished with the 6020W early steam tender, which, while not rare, seems to have often been replaced by similar-appearing tenders by latter-day dealers. The motor inside the locomotive utilized the new style brush plate most often associated with the 622. This brush plate used a spring somewhat resembling a safety pin, whereas earlier editions of the turbine used coil brush springs that were housed in protruding tubular holders.

The 3469 was packaged individually without its receiving bin, which was packed loose in the outfit box. Packed in the box with the car, however, was the bag of 207 artificial coal—actually ground Bakelite.

The other operating car included in the outfit was the new-for-1949 operating cattle car. As produced in 1949, the corral furnished with the car had orange gates, and the binding posts were on the end of the corral opposite the ramp.

Four rubber grommets surrounded tabs formed into the end of the corral deck, isolating the deck from the fence. The decks of the earliest corrals were painted yellow to match the fence. Appearing on more corrals than did the yellow deck, but nonetheless discontinued early on, was a tiny chain closing off the end-of-corral ramp from the deck.

The car itself was also produced in numerous variations during its debut year. Lettering was commonly stamped on the car in white, but scarce black-lettered versions of the car exist as well. Regardless of lettering color, the cars were produced both with and without "Armour" labels adhered to the doors. The entrance or right-hand side of the internal cattle runway measured 1-1/8 inches in 1949; it was narrower in later years.

The 6465 Sunoco tank car, 6357 caboose and 6411 flatcar with unstained logs were all standard issue items, but nonetheless rounded out a very nice 027 outfit. The locomotive and tender boxes were equipped with liners, though that was not the case for the other items. The components of this outfit were packaged in a combination of Early and Middle Traditional boxes.

Excellent	Like New	Scarcity
550	950	5

2135WS, 2136WS, 2147WS

O-Gauge

2135WS Three-car Freight $37.50

Included: 675 2-6-2 steam locomotive with operating headlight and smoke; 6466WX early coal whistle tender; 6456 Lehigh Valley hopper; 6411 flatcar with logs, 6457 illuminated Lionel Lines SP-type caboose; eight sections OC curved and three sections OS straight; UCS track set; CTC Lockon; SP smoke pellets; tube of lubricant; instruction booklet.

Though the number of this outfit was carried over from 1948, the sets were far from identical. The magnetic coupler-equipped 6000-series cars dominated the O-Gauge line in 1949, as they had 027 in 1948. Thus, the hopper and flatcars found in the 1949 sets differed from those used in 1948. Also, the caboose packed with this set was the top of the line crummy for 1949: the 6457. This caboose featured ladders and brake wheels at both ends, and a pair of stamped sheet metal toolboxes were suspended from the frame. A smokejack extended from the roof, which was plastic and painted to match the roof on the earliest production before changing to chemically blackened metal during later production.

Motive power for this consist was the reliable 675 2-6-2 with operating headlight and smoke. The 1949 edition had a painted smokestack, red-decaled keystone and a simulated knuckle coupler on the pilot. It was accompanied by the 6466WX tender.

Liners in their boxes protected the locomotive and tender, and these boxes, like those of the rolling stock, could be Early or Middle Traditional. The outfit box itself was normally the preprinted 1949 issue, although as a carryover item it is possible that some surplus 1948 boxes were used to package the early portion of the run.

Excellent	Like New	Scarcity
325	525	4

2136WS Three-car Passenger $39.95

Included: 675 2-6-2 steam locomotive with operating headlight and smoke; 2466WX early coal whistle tender; two 6442 brown Pullmans; 6443 brown observation; eight sections OC curved and three sections OS straight; UCS track set; CTC Lockon; SP smoke pellets; tube of lubricant; instruction booklet.

Though the catalog number of this outfit was a repeat of one used in 1948, the 1949 edition of this set utilized magnetic coupler-equipped 6000-series cars, and naturally included a UCS uncoupling track set to actuate them. The locomotive had a black smokestack, red-trimmed keystone and a simulated knuckle coupler on its pilot. While the locomotive and tender were packaged with liners, the boxes for the cars lacked liners. All the components of the set were contained in Middle Traditional boxes.

Excellent	Like New	Scarcity
500	850	4

2139WS O-Gauge Four-Car Freight $57.50

Included: 2332 Pennsylvania five-stripe GG-1; 3464 operating boxcar; 3461 automatic lumber car; 6456 Lehigh Valley hopper; 6457 illuminated SP-type caboose; eight sections OC curved and five sections OS straight; UCS track set; CTC Lockon; tube of lubricant; instruction booklet.

Another of the 1948 outfits to get a facelift for 1949 was this set headed by the famed 2332 GG-1. As a result of the adoption of the magnetic coupler throughout most of the product line, the hopper and log cars were renumbered, becoming 3461 and 6456. The caboose was upgraded to the fully trimmed 6457, and the boxcar was replaced entirely. The 1948 edition utilized the sheet-metal double door boxcar of prewar origin, while the 1949 edition featured the operating version of the new injection-molded boxcar. This car included a blue vinylite workman with flesh-painted face and hands. The arms of this man were spread. All of these cars were packaged in a mixture of Early and Middle Traditional boxes.

The locomotive charged with handling this freight was the rugged GG-1. The green locomotive was packed in a standard brown corrugated box made by the Union Bag and Paper Corp.

Excellent	Like New	Scarcity
1,400	2,400	4

2140WS Three-car De Luxe Passenger $57.75

Included: 671 6-8-6 steam turbine locomotive with operating headlight and smoke; 2671W streamlined whistle tender; 2400 Maplewood Pullman, 2401 Hillside observation, and 2402 Chatham Pullman in the new streamlined series with green-and-gray paint scheme; eight sections OC curved

2149B, 2139W

2140WS, 2141WS, 2153WS

and five sections OS straight; UCS track set; CTC Lockon; SP smoke pellets; tube of lubricant; instruction booklet.

Although, to the casual observer, this set is identical to one of the same number issued the year previously, the aficionado will notice many subtle differences. The locomotive lacks rims on any of the drive wheels and its motor incorporates the new 622-style brush plate that lacks the projecting tubular brush holders of earlier models.

The passenger cars were unchanged from the 1948 issue, however, the new UCS uncoupling track set was now included in the set in lieu of the RCS used previously.

Though it is possible that the early 1949 production was shipped in surplus 1948 boxes, the bulk of the production was placed in 1949 packaging.

Excellent	Like New	Scarcity
900	1,500	5

2141WS Four-Car Freight $57.50

Included: 671 6-8-6 steam turbine locomotive with operating headlight and smoke; 2671W streamlined whistle tender; 3461 automatic lumber car; 3472 operating milk car; 6456 Lehigh Valley hopper; 6457 illuminated SP-type caboose; eight sections OC curved and five sections OS straight; UCS track set; CTC Lockon; SP smoke pellets; tube of lubricant; instruction booklet.

This was one of many 1948 outfit numbers carried forward into 1949 with a price reduction. Typical for such continued sets, the rolling stock was equipped with magnetic couplers and their catalog numbers were changed to reflect this. Naturally, the new UCS universal uncoupling track section was included in the 1949 edition.

The automatic lumber car included in this set, now numbered 3461, was laden with five logs. Lionel no doubt had thousands of these 7/16 x 4-5/8-inch logs on hand at all times. Although the 1949 production of these logs were stained, either stained or unstained logs could be found on the cars in these outfits.

For 1949, the first year of production of the 3472, the cars continued to use the same type of aluminum doors as had the 3462. Initially the 3472 was painted white, but early on unpainted white plastic car bodies were used instead—no doubt with considerable savings to Lionel in material and labor.

The locomotive and its attractive 2671W tender were packed in boxes with liners, as was the milk car. The balance of the rolling stock came in unlined boxes of either Early or Middle Traditional styles. The outfit box was the preprinted 1949 style, though as a carryover set it is theoretically possible that some surplus 1948 outfit boxes were used early on.

Excellent	Like New	Scarcity
500	775	4

2144W, 2155WS, 2146WS

2144W Three-car De Luxe Passenger $67.50 retail

Included: 2332 Pennsylvania five-stripe GG-1; 2625 Irvington, 2627 Madison and 2628 Manhattan heavyweight Pullmans; eight sections OC curved and five sections OS straight; UCS track set; CTC Lockon; CO-1 track clips; tube of lubricant; instruction booklet.

The De Luxe GG-1 passenger set was another repeat of a 1948 outfit. The green locomotive was packed in a standard brown corrugated box made by the Union Bag and Paper Corp., while the passenger cars were packaged in First Traditional boxes.

The Irvington series passenger cars produced in 1949 can be distinguished by the black tape wrapping applied to the coupler coils, the routing of the wiring of the interior lights which was largely hidden and the positioning of the "Lionel Lines" markings. The "Lionel Lines" stamping now began directly over the leftmost of the center group of windows, whereas in earlier years the lettering began to the left of the center group of windows. Like 1949 production, the sets should have been packaged in the preprinted box introduced that year, but one 1949 outfit has been reported packaged in a 1948-style box with a separately applied label.

Excellent	Like New	Scarcity
2,400	4,000	5

2146WS Three-Car Pullman $75 retail

Included: 726 2-8-4 Berkshire steam locomotive with operating headlight and smoke; 2426W whistle tender; 2625 Irvington, 2627 Madison and 2628 Manhattan heavyweight Pullmans; eight sections OC curved and seven sections OS straight; UCS remote control track set; CTC Lockon; CO-1 track clips; SP smoke pellets; tube of lubricant; instruction booklet.

Just as the GG-1 headed passenger outfit was repeated, so was the Berkshire passenger set. Also like the GG-1 outfit, a UCS track set was included in the 1949 edition, rather than the RCS used earlier.

The Irvington series passenger cars produced in 1949 can be distinguished by the black tape wrapping applied to the coupler coils, the routing of the wiring of the interior lights which was largely hidden, and the positioning of the "Lionel Lines" markings. The "Lionel Lines" stamping now began directly over the leftmost of the center group of windows, whereas in earlier years the lettering began to the left of the center group of windows.

The locomotive was packaged in a standard brown corrugated carton with a liner, while the tender and passenger cars were packed in First Traditional boxes. The tender box came with a liner. The set box was the 1949 style with the preprinted label.

Excellent	Like New	Scarcity
2,400	4,000	7

2147WS Four-Car Freight Set $50 retail

Included: 675 steam locomotive with operating headlight and smoke; 6466WX early coal whistle tender; 3472 operating milk car; 6465 Sunoco double-dome tank car; 3469 automatic dumping ore car with 207 artificial coal; 6457 illuminated SP-type caboose; eight OC curved and three OS straight track; UCS remote control track set; CTC Lockon; CO-1 track clips; SP smoke pellets; tube of lubricant; instruction booklet.

Automatic dumping ore and milk cars ensured that loads of action was included in this outfit. The aluminum-door 3472 was packaged along with its platform and cans in a liner-equipped box. The earliest milk cars were painted white, while later production utilized unpainted white plastic bodies. The black 3469 was furnished with a small cloth bag of 207 artificial coal—in actuality, ground Bakelite. The 6457 caboose was lighted and featured two stamped sheet metal under slung toolboxes. Its smokejack could either have been plastic painted to match the body or chemically blackened metal.

The locomotive included in this outfit had the latter-style pilot and steam chest casting, which included a simulated knuckle coupler. The keystone on the boiler front was decorated with a red and gold decal, and its smokestack was painted to match the boiler. The locomotive was placed inside a lined box, and its tender in its own lined box. The rolling stock, except for the milk car, was packaged in unlined boxes. A mixture of First and Middle Traditional boxes were used in these sets. The outfit box was the new 1949 style with a preprinted integral label.

Excellent	Like New	Scarcity
350	600	3

2149B **O-Gauge Four-Car Diesel Work Train** **$52.50 retail**

Included: 622 Santa Fe bell-ringing diesel switcher; 6520 searchlight car; 3469 automatic dumping ore car with 207 artificial coal; 2460 12-wheel crane; 6419 work caboose; eight OC curved and five OS straight track; UCS uncoupling/operating section; UCS remote control track set; CTC Lockon; CO-1 track clips; tube of lubricant; instruction booklet.

Lionel selected its new replica of an NW-2 diesel switcher to head up this work train. In tow behind the locomotive was an array of operating cars sure to keep a young engineer occupied for hours and delight a collector today.

The 2460 12-wheel crane with die-cast base, painted black, was included in this outfit, along with its accompanying 6419 work caboose—the latter also had a die-cast frame.

The ore-dumping car came with its requisite 207 bag of artificial coal, while the new-for-1949 6520 searchlight car was included to allow imaginary miniature workers to labor through the night. In some instances it has been reported that this set has included the early production 6520 searchlight car with a green-molded generator.

The switcher itself featured a die-cast base with a mechanically ringing bell. The bell, which rang incessantly as the train moved around the track, is often found removed or disabled today. The earliest of these diesels had their catalog numbers stamped on the front of the hood as well as under the cab windows, but the front numbers were discontinued early on.

The locomotive was boxed in a lined Middle Traditional box, while the crane was packaged in a lined Early Postwar box. The other cars were packed in Middle Traditional boxes. The set box was naturally the preprinted 1949 style.

Excellent	Like New	Scarcity
700	1,100	5

2151W **O-Gauge Five-Car Diesel** **$67.50 retail**

Included: 2333P/2333T Santa Fe or New York Central A-A F3 units; 3464 operating boxcar; 6555 Sunoco single-dome tank car; 3469 automatic dumping ore car with 207 artificial coal; 6520 searchlight car; 6457 illuminated SP-type caboose; eight OC curved and nine OS straight track; UCS remote control track set; CTC Lockon; CO-1 track clips; tube of lubricant; instruction booklet.

The enormously popular F-3 sets from 1948 were unsurprisingly carried forward into 1949 with some updating. Foremost of these changes was the inclusion of the new-for-1949 6520 operating die-cast searchlight car. Less noticeable at a glance was the replacement of the dated sheet metal 2458 automobile boxcar with the new-operating 3464 boxcar.

Both New York Central and Santa Fe versions of the boxcar were packaged in these outfits without any correlation to the road names of the locomotives pulling them. These cars included a blue vinylite man with painted face and hands, and outstretched arms.

The deluxe sheet-metal tank car with die-cast frame was included in this set, but since it was now equipped with magnetic couplers its number was changed to 6555. Similarly, the 3459 from the 1948 outfit was replaced with the magnetic-coupler equipped 3469 in 1949. A 6457 caboose brought up the rear of the train.

At the front of the consist was an updated pair of EMD F-3 diesels. The 1949 issues can be distinguished from the 1948 models by the positioning of the GM decal. Whereas in 1948 such decals were applied above the "Built by Lionel" lettering, in 1949 they were moved to the side door just forward of Lionel's builder's mark. Once again the same 2333 number boards were installed in both the Santa Fe and New York Central locomotives, although Lionel knew the two types of units as 2333 and 2334 respectively.

The powered units were packed in standard brown corrugated cartons that were dated 1949. The dummy or T-unit, which, like the powered unit had a lined box, was packaged in a First or Middle Traditional box. The same style box was used for the rolling stock, though the freight car boxes did not include liners.

New York Central:

Excellent	Like New	Scarcity
1,100	1,900	4

Santa Fe:

Excellent	Like New	Scarcity
1,200	2,000	4

2153WS **Four-Car De Luxe Work Train** **$60 retail**

Included: 671 steam turbine locomotive with operating headlight and smoke; 2671W streamlined whistle tender; 3469 automatic dumping ore car with 207 artificial coal; 6520 searchlight car; 2460 12-wheel crane; 6419 work caboose; eight OC curved and five OS straight track; UCS remote control track set; CTC Lockon; CO-1 track clips; SP smoke pellets; tube of lubricant; instruction booklet.

The 20-wheel steam turbine with 2671W tender in this outfit pulled a train of all die-cast framed cars. The black-cab, 12-wheel crane car and 2671W tender were equipped with coil-type couplers, but the remainder of cars was fitted with magnetic couplers. Naturally, a UCS section was included to activate the couplers, as well as to control the 3469 dump car.

The work crane was packaged in a lined Early Postwar box, while the locomotive and tender came in lined First or Middle Traditional boxes. The rolling stock, other than the crane, was packaged in unlined First and Middle Traditional boxes. The outfit box itself was the new 1949 preprinted carton.

Excellent	Like New	Scarcity
600	1,000	4

2155WS **Four-Car Freight** **$67.50 retail**

Included: 726 2-8-4 Berkshire steam locomotive with operating headlight and smoke; 2426W whistle tender; 6411 flatcar with logs; 3656 operating cattle car; 2460 12-wheel crane; 6457 illuminated SP-type caboose; eight OC curved and seven OS straight track; UCS remote control track set; CTC Lockon; CO-1 track clips; SP smoke pellets; tube of lubricant; instruction booklet.

The magnificent Berkshire, updated with a 622-type brush plate, returned to head this four-car freight set. The locomotive was packed in a lined standard brown corrugated carton, while the spectacular die-cast 2426W tender was in either a First or Middle Traditional box with a liner.

The 12-wheel crane was packaged in a lined Early Postwar box. The crane and the 2426W tender were the only items in this set that had coil couplers; all the other rolling stock was equipped with magnetic couplers.

Included in the outfit was the new-for-1949 operating cattle car. As produced in 1949, the corral furnished with the car had orange gates, and the binding posts were on the end of the corral opposite the ramp.

Four rubber grommets surrounded tabs formed into the end of the corral deck, isolating the deck from the fence. The decks of the earliest corrals were painted yellow to match the fence. Appearing on more corrals than did the yellow deck, but nonetheless discontinued early on, was a tiny chain closing off the end-of-corral ramp from the deck.

The car itself was also produced in numerous variations during its debut year. Lettering was commonly stamped on the car in white, but scarce black-lettered versions of the car exist as well. Regardless of lettering color, the cars were produced both with and without "Armour" labels adhered to the doors. The entrance or right-hand side of the internal cattle runway measured 1-1/8 inches in 1949; it was narrower in later years.

The cattle car, as well as the flatcar and caboose, were packaged in unlined Middle Traditional boxes. The outfit box was the new 1949-style box with preprinted labeling.

Excellent	Like New	Scarcity
800	1,300	5

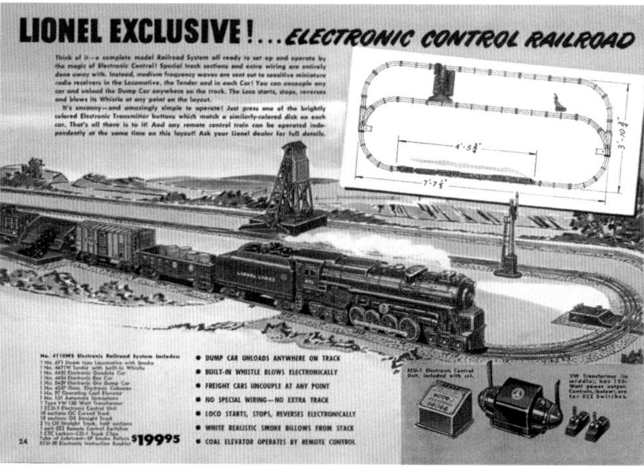

4110WS **Electronic Control Set** **$199.95 retail**

Included: 671R steam turbine locomotive with operating headlight and smoke; 4671W early coal whistle tender; 4452 gondola; 4454 Baby Ruth boxcar; 5459 ore dump car; 4357 illuminated SP-type caboose; 10 sections OC curved, 18 straight and two half-sections OS straight; pair of 022 remote-control switches; 151 semaphore; 97 operating coal elevator; ECU-1 Electronic Control unit; VW 150-watt transformer.

No doubt due in large part to its princely price, sales of the Electronic Control Sets in 1948 were disappointing. Thus, Lionel and its retailers were left with unsold inventory in 1949. Accordingly, Lionel merely re-cataloged the same outfit.

It is doubtful that additional Electronic Control sets were actually manufactured in 1949.

Excellent	Like New	Scarcity
2,000	3,700	7

Chapter 7

1950

Lionel's advertising from 1950 emphasized two things—the fact that this was Lionel's golden anniversary year and trumpeting the inclusion of Magne-traction in all of the year's locomotives. The set boxes were changed in 1950. Though the outfit boxes continued to be preprinted, now the labeling was blue print against an orange background. Inside those set cartons all the component items were individually boxed, except for the new-for-1950 Alco FA diesel replicas. These locomotives introduced the concept termed by collectors as "master cartons." The powered and dummy units were placed, without benefit of individual boxes, inside a single box, separated from each other by cardboard. This master carton could then be used for separate locomotive sales, or packed inside the set box as an outfit component.

As part of Lionel's continuing efforts to lower costs, many of the freight cars were redesigned for 1950. Steps, integral with the stamped sheet metal frames of many freight cars, were eliminated. This reduced the amount of raw material required to produce the frames. Perhaps even more significant, the stepless frames allowed the trucks of most cars to be rotated 180 degrees until the coupler head was under the car body. This significantly reduced the amount of space required for transport and storage of the cars and, by extension, the sets. It also permitted the elimination of the coupler protection flaps from many of the boxes, further reducing packaging costs. However, keep in mind that Lionel owned a considerable inventory of product, not only finished goods but component parts as well, that still had integral steps.

027-Gauge

1113 Lionel Scout Train $14.95 retail

Included: 1120 2-4-2 Scout steam locomotive with Magne-traction; 1001T sheet-metal tender; 1002 gondola; 1005 Sunoco tank car; 1007 SP-type caboose; eight 1013 curved and one 1018 straight track; 1009 Manumatic uncoupling section; 1011 25-watt transformer; CTC Lockon; tube of lubricant; instruction booklet.

Even the lowly Scout outfits were re-equipped with Magne-traction for 1950. The new locomotive, numbered 1120, was die-cast and rode on spoked drive wheels. It was not equipped with an operating headlight or smoke unit. The engine was packed in a lined Middle Traditional box, while the other outfit components were packaged in unlined Middle Traditional boxes. The outfit box was the new-for-1950 style.

Excellent	Like New	Scarcity
125	225	4

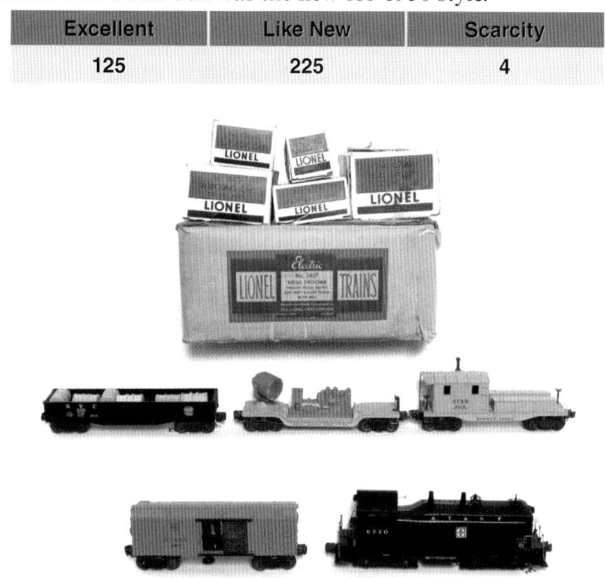

1457B Four-Car Diesel Freight $39.95 retail

Included: 6220 Santa Fe bell-ringing diesel switcher; 3464 operating boxcar; 6462 gondola; 6520 searchlight car; 6419 work caboose; eight 1013 curved and five 1018 straight track; 6019 remote control track set; 1034 75-watt transformer; CTC Lockon; tube of lubricant; instruction booklet.

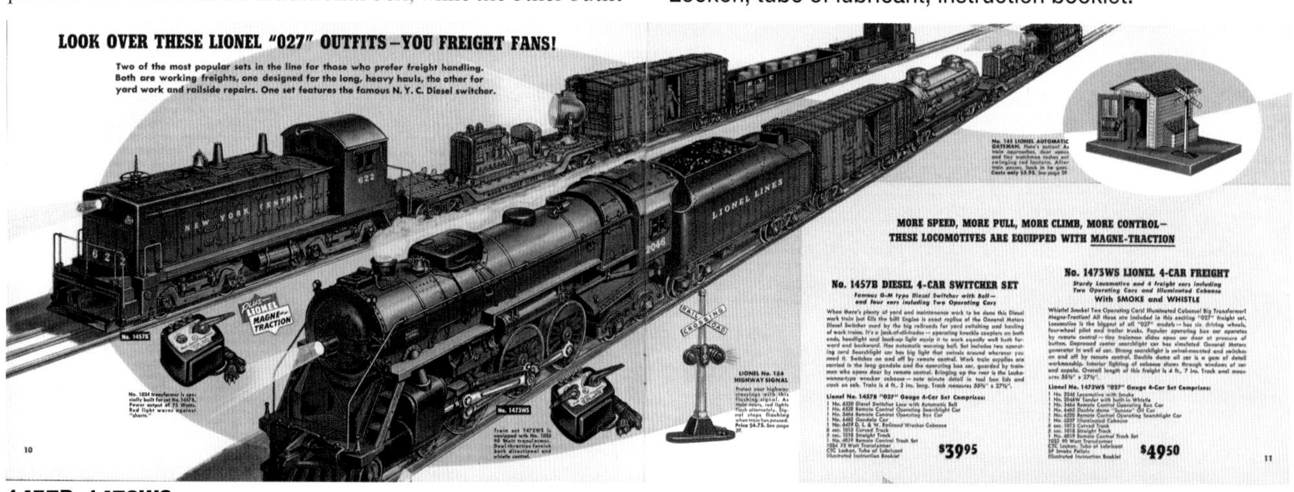

1457B, 1473WS

1461S, 1463W, 1469WS

This outfit was a near duplicate of a 1949 outfit with the same name—possible only because the 1949 issues of the 622 and 6220 had the then-unheralded feature of Magne-traction. Perhaps even more amazing was the almost $10 reduction in the outfit's retail price for 1950. Although shown with a "Lionel" road name in 1949 and New York Central in 1950, the 6220 was produced with only Santa Fe markings. The locomotive, as well as the caboose, were packaged in lined Middle Traditional boxes.

The generator mounted on the searchlight car was commonly orange, though the slightly more desirable maroon version was sometimes included. The 3464 boxcar, now without steps, was supplied in this set with either Santa Fe or New York Central markings. The wooden barrels previously furnished with the gondola cars were eliminated. The boxcar, gondola and searchlight were shipped in unlined Middle Traditional boxes.

Excellent	Like New	Scarcity
625	950	5

1461S 📷 **Three-Car Freight With Smoke $19.95 retail**

Included: 6110 2-4-2 steam locomotive with smoke and Magne-traction; 6001T early coal tender; 6004 Baby Ruth boxcar; 6002 gondola; 6007 SP-type caboose; eight 1013 curved and three 1018 straight track; 6019 remote control track set; 1012 35-watt transformer; CTC Lockon; tube of lubricant; instruction booklet.

Lionel's Scout program was not the success that the firm had hoped for. In large part, this was probably due to the unreliability of the early motors and the incompatibility of the Scout couplers with those used on the rest of Lionel's rolling stock. To address the second of these concerns, the company produced this style outfit, which collectors have dubbed semi-Scout. The stamped sheet metal with plastic decorative side frames composite trucks were now fitted with the 480-25 magnetic couplers rather than the plastic Scout couplers.

To power this set, Lionel created the 6110. This locomotive was essentially an 1120 fitted with a low-cost smoke unit; the 1120 was essentially an 1110 equipped with Magne-traction. The smoke unit of the 6110 did not have the piston and chuffer assembly of other Lionel steamers. Rather, the moving locomotive drew in air through a hole in the boiler face.

The tender pulled by the locomotive was the early coal tender, minus the whistle. Its lettering was a different, larger style than that used by the other early coal tenders. The rolling stock in this set was essentially the Scout cars, renumbered to indicate the new truck-coupler combination installed.

All the components were packaged in Middle Traditional boxes, with only the locomotive box including a liner. The set box was the new 1950 style.

Excellent	Like New	Scarcity
150	250	2

1463W Three-Car Freight $29.95 retail

Included: 2036 2-6-4 steam locomotive with operating headlight and Magne-traction; 6466W early coal whistle tender; 6462 gondola; 6465 Sunoco double-dome tank car; 6257 SP-type caboose; eight 1013 curved and three 1018 straight track; 6019 remote control track set; 1033 90-watt transformer; CTC Lockon; tube of lubricant; bottle of SP smoke pellets; instruction booklet.

The 2026 was extensively redesigned to become the 2036. The locomotive gained Magne-traction, but lost most of its valve gear and side rides. A somewhat plain, sheet metal-framed four-wheel trailing truck superceded the nicely detailed die-cast trailing truck used on the 2026.

The freight cars were updated versions of carryover items and the tank and gondola cars lost their sheet metal steps. The gondola also lost its wooden barrel load. All the components of the outfit came in Middle Traditional boxes and the locomotive and tender boxes even included liners.

Excellent	Like New	Scarcity
150	250	2

1464W Diesel Three-Car Pullman $55 retail

Included: 2023 Union Pacific Alco A-A units; 2481 Plainfield Pullman, 2482 Westfield Pullman and 2483 Livingston observation with yellow-and-gray paint scheme; eight 1013 curved and five 1018 straight track; 6019 remote control track set; 1033 90-watt transformer; CTC Lockon; tube of lubricant; instruction booklet.

1950

One of the most coveted of all postwar outfits is this passenger set, dubbed the "Anniversary Set" by collectors. Many variations of the new 2023 Alco diesels exist, with the most desirable (and most often forged) version having the top of its nose painted gray to match the rest of the locomotive roof. However, evidence suggests that this variation was not included in the passenger outfit, but instead in the 1467W freight set.

While most of the 2023 diesels had chemically blackened truck side frames, some of the passenger sets included locomotives with side frames painted the same shade of gray used on the die-cast loco frames. A battery-operated horn with actuating relay was housed inside the powered A-unit, and both units had operating headlights. The yellow 2023 locomotives have not aged well. Many appear today with a distinctly milky cast to the yellow paint and their red markings somewhat subdued.

The plastic-bodied 2400-series passenger cars were given a new paint scheme. While retaining their gray roofs and "Lionel Lines" lettering, the green bodies of their predecessors were now painted yellow and the markings, formerly yellow, were now red.

The cars were packed in Middle Traditional boxes, while the locomotives were placed loose inside their corrugated master carton. That master carton joined the other component boxes in the new-for-1950 outfit box.

Excellent	Like New	Scarcity
2,000	4,000	6

1467W Diesel Four-Car Freight $47.50 retail

Included: 2023 Union Pacific Alco A-A units; 6456 Lehigh Valley hopper; 6656 stock car; 6465 Sunoco double-dome tank car; 6357 illuminated SP-type caboose; eight 1013 curved and five 1018 straight track; 6019 remote control track set; 1033 90-watt transformer; CTC Lockon; tube of lubricant; instruction booklet.

The newly designed 2023 Alco units were used to head this otherwise unremarkable freight set. Of particular interest to collectors is the occasional inclusion of the scarce gray-nosed 2023 in this set.

New for 1950, and included in this outfit, was the non-operating 6656 stock car. Strangely, given Lionel's step-elimination policy, the frame of this car was equipped with integral steps. Despite the catalog illustration of a brown car, this car was always produced in yellow.

The set components, except for the master carton-packed locomotives, were packed in Middle Traditional boxes, then placed inside the outfit box, which naturally was of the new 1950-style.

Excellent	Like New	Scarcity
600	900	4

1469WS Four-Car Freight $39.95 retail

Included: 2035 2-6-4 steam locomotive with operating headlight, smoke and Magne-traction; 6466W early coal whistle tender; 6462 gondola; 6456 Lehigh Valley hopper; 6465 Sunoco double-dome tank car; 6257 SP-type caboose; eight 1013 curved and three 1018 straight track; 6019 remote control track set; 1033 90-watt transformer; CTC Lockon; bottle of SP smoke pellets; tube of lubricant; instruction booklet.

First cataloged in 1950, there is some evidence that production—or at least component production and procurement—of this set actually began in late 1949. This set carton could have been either a 1949 type or the new issue for 1950.

The locomotive was in essence a Magne-traction-equipped 2025. The die-cast Baldwin Disc wheels previously used giving way to sintered iron wheels, which promoted the magnetic flux. Simultaneously the detailed die-cast trailing truck was replaced with a four-wheel truck with a sheet metal frame, which was less costly to manufacture. The locomotive and tender were packed in Middle Traditional boxes with liners.

The rolling stock was unremarkable and was boxed in unlined Middle Traditional boxes. The gondola was not furnished with a wooden barrel load.

Excellent	Like New	Scarcity
225	425	3

1471WS Five-Car Freight $57.50 retail

Included: 2035 2-6-4 steam locomotive with operating headlight, smoke and Magne-traction; 6466W early coal whistle tender; 6454 boxcar; 3469 automatic dumping ore car; 6465 Sunoco double-dome tank car; 3461 automatic lumber car; 6357 illuminated SP-type caboose; eight 1013 curved and seven 1018 straight track; 6019 remote control track set;

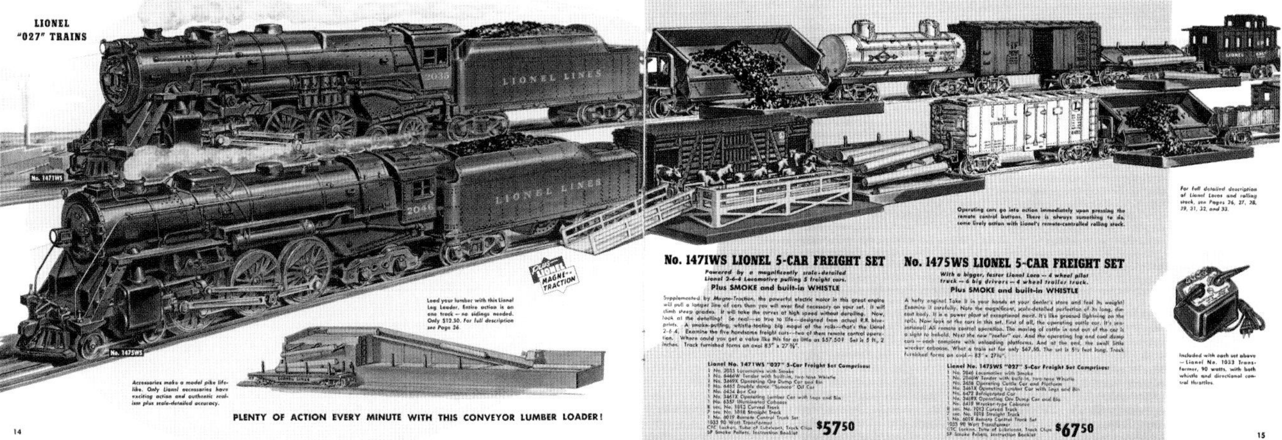

LIONEL
"027" TRAINS
LIONEL LINES
LIONEL LINES
No. 1471WS LIONEL 5-CAR FREIGHT SET
No. 1475WS LIONEL 5-CAR FREIGHT SET
PLENTY OF ACTION EVERY MINUTE WITH THIS CONVEYOR LUMBER LOADER!
$57.50
$67.50

1471WS, 1475WS

1033 90-watt transformer; CTC Lockon; bottle of SP smoke pellets; tube of lubricant; instruction booklet.

The 2035 was selected to head this freight set as well. With two operating cars in tow, it is not surprising that this outfit was 50 percent more expensive than the other 2035 set, the 1469WS. However, the money was well spent, as the ore and log dump car greatly increased the interaction that a child—or young adult—could have with the train. These two cars were packed in their own boxes, with their receiving bins placed loose in the outfit box. The ore car was provided with a bag of ground Bakelite "coal"—the cloth bag being marked "No. 207 Artificial Coal"—while the log car carried five matte-stained logs.

A non-operating boxcar was also included in the outfit. Numbered 6454, the car could have been decorated in the markings of the Erie, Pennsylvania or Southern Pacific railroads, although the catalog illustration showed a Southern Pacific car. Middle Traditional boxes were used for the components of this outfit, with the locomotive and tender boxes lined. The outfit box was the new 1950 style.

Excellent	Like New	Scarcity
350	575	3

1473WS Four-Car Freight $49.95 retail

Included: 2046 4-6-4 steam locomotive with operating headlight, smoke and Magne-traction; 2046W streamlined whistle tender; 3464 operating boxcar; 6520 searchlight car; 6465 Sunoco double-dome tank car; 6357 illuminated SP-type caboose; eight 1013 curved and five 1018 straight track; 6019 remote control track set; 1033 90-watt transformer; CTC Lockon; bottle of SP smoke pellets; tube of lubricant; instruction booklet.

Lionel combined the tried and true six-wheel drive mechanism from the 675 with the boiler of the Berkshire to create this new small Hudson (4-6-4) steam locomotive. As a companion for the new locomotive, a new tender was created, but it too was an adaptation of existing components. The new tender, appropriately numbered 2046W, was in essence a 2671W riding on four-wheel rather than six-wheel trucks. The lettering of the new tender read, "Lionel Lines" rather than the "Pennsylvania" of the 2671W. The Lionel Lines lettering used in 1950-51 was of a smaller and different typeface than that used in subsequent years. The 1950-51 tender was packaged in a lined Middle Traditional box lettered, "No. 2046/TENDER/WITH WHISTLE"—which was also different from the labeling used in later years.

In order to add just a slight amount of animation to the outfit, a 3464 operating boxcar was included in the set. Both New York Central and Santa Fe boxcars were supplied in the outfit during the course of its production. However, no one road name was predominant.

The locomotive was packed in a conventional brown corrugated carton with a liner, while the balance of the components were shipped in unlined Middle Traditional boxes. The outfit box was the new 1950 style.

Excellent	Like New	Scarcity
425	750	3

1475WS Five-Car Freight $67.50 retail

Included: 2046 4-6-4 steam locomotive with operating headlight, smoke and Magne-traction; 2046W streamlined whistle tender; 3656 operating cattle car; 3461X automatic lumber car; 6472 refrigerator car; 3469X automatic dumping ore car with 207 bag of artificial coal; 6419 work caboose; eight 1013 curved and seven 1018 straight track; 6019 remote control track set; 1033 90-watt transformer; CTC Lockon; bottle of SP smoke pellets; tube of lubricant; instruction booklet.

The best of the 1950 027 outfits was headed by the new 2046 Hudson steam locomotive. The outfit's three operating cars provided plenty of play value for junior engineers. The 3461 was supplied with five logs stained brown, while the 3469 came with a small cloth bag of artificial coal. At least one one-owner

Values for each condition are in U.S. dollars. | **Scarcity** = Scale from 1-8 with 8 being the hardest to find.

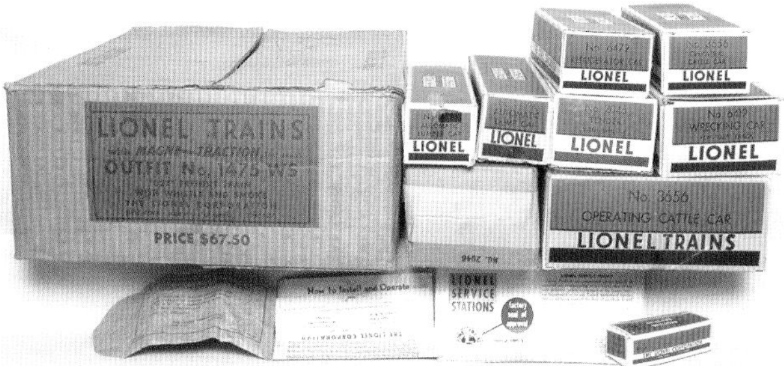

example of this outfit has been observed containing the black-lettered 3656 operating cattle car without "Armour" lettering.

The lettering of the new eight-wheel streamlined tender read "Lionel Lines" rather than the "Pennsylvania" of the 2671W. The Lionel Lines lettering used in 1950-51 was of a smaller and different typeface than that used in subsequent years. The 1950-51 tender was packaged in a Middle Traditional box lettered "No. 2046/TENDER/WITH WHISTLE"—which was also different from the labeling used in later years.

The locomotive was packaged in a conventional brown corrugated cardboard box, the tender and cattle car in liner-equipped Middle Traditional boxes, and the remainder of the rolling stock in unlined Middle Traditional boxes. The dumping ore and lumber cars were packed in boxes with X number suffixes and their receiving trays were packaged loose in the outfit boxes.

Excellent	Like New	Scarcity
575	975	6

O-Gauge

2148WS **Three-Car Pullman** **$85 retail**

Included: 773 4-6-4 Hudson steam locomotive with operating headlight, smoke and Magne-traction; 2426W whistle tender; 2625 Irvington, 2627 Madison and 2628 Manhattan heavyweight Pullmans with silhouettes; eight OC curved and seven OS straight track; UCS remote control track set; CTC Lockon; bottle of SP smoke pellets; tube of lubricant; instruction booklet.

Only one O-Gauge passenger train was offered in 1950, but it was spectacular. The venerable Irvington-series passenger cars, each with its own name and number, were given a minor facelift for Lionel's golden anniversary. The window strips of the cars were now printed with passengers' silhouettes—a feature unique to the final year of Irvington passenger car production. The "Lionel Lines" lettering on these cars began just to the right of the vertical line of rivets above the leftmost window of the center group. Like the 1949 cars, the coils of the couplers were wrapped in black tape.

2148WS, 2169WS

2148WS outfits came in both styles of outfit packaging shown here.

More remarkable than the Bakelite passenger cars was the motive power. Though not as detailed as the prewar 700E and 763 steamers, the 773 approximated their size. Notable changes included the introduction of smoke to the big steamer, along with Magne-traction. The latter required the use of solid sintered iron wheels with simulated spokes in lieu of the fabulous prewar drive wheels with open spokes. The semi scale steamer retained the prewar gearing, which yielded a scale-like speed range for the locomotive. Because of the rocket-like speeds attained by most Lionel locomotives, many operators wrongly believe that the performance of the 773 is sluggish. The locomotive was packaged in a black-lettered brown cardboard box made by Star.

Selected to accompany this engine was the 2426W Lionel Lines tender, which would be making its final appearance. Unique to this year's production of the 2426W was the use of a plastic whistle chamber rather than the die-cast whistle chamber used previously.

Excellent	Like New	Scarcity
4,700	8,500	6

1950

2150WS 📷 O-Gauge Deluxe Passenger $55 retail

Included: 681 6-8-6 steam turbine locomotive with operating headlight, smoke and Magne-traction; 2671W streamlined whistle tender; 2421 Maplewood Pullman, 2422 Chatham Pullman and 2423 Hillside observation with silver-and-gray paint scheme; eight OC curved and five OS straight track; UCS remote control track set; CTC Lockon; bottle of SP smoke pellets; tube of lubricant; instruction booklet.

The Maplewood, Chatham and Hillside car names continued in the 1950 product line, though the green and yellow color scheme worn since 1948 was supplanted by somewhat plainer silver with black trim scheme. The dark gray roof of previous issues was continued and was shared with the yellow and red cars of the 1464W set.

Powering the streamliner was a Magne-traction-equipped version of the 20-wheel steam turbine, numbered 681. In 1950 and 1951, the 681 was marked with silver rubber-stamped lettering and furnished with the 2671W tender.

All the components of the set were packaged in Middle Traditional boxes, which were then placed in the new-for-1950 style outfit boxes.

Excellent	Like New	Scarcity
800	1,300	5

2159W 📷 Five-Car Freight $52.50 retail

Included: 2330 Pennsylvania five-stripe GG-1; 3464 operating boxcar; 6462 gondola; 6456 Lehigh Valley hopper; 3461X automatic lumber car; 6457 illuminated SP-type caboose; eight OC curved and seven OS straight track; UCS remote control track set; CTC Lockon; tube of lubricant; instruction booklet.

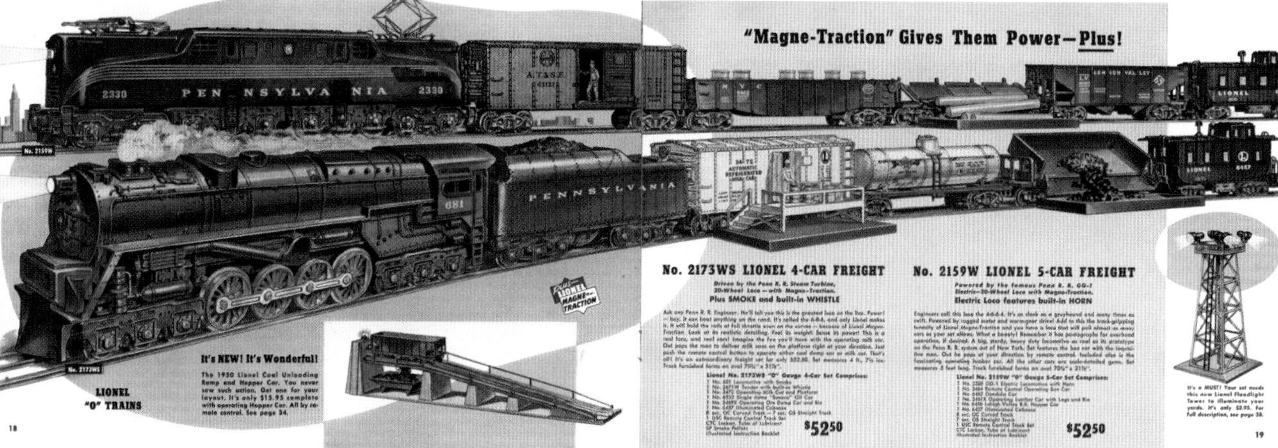

2159W, 2173WS

The GG-1 returned at the head of a freight set for the anniversary year, but with a new number and major improvements. In a real case of Lionel understating an item's features, no mention was made by the catalog of the inclusion of a second motor in the locomotive. Almost as if an afterthought, a tag packed with the outfit stated simply, "This Lionel electric locomotive No. 2330 is equipped with 2 motors." The locomotive was packaged in a conventional brown corrugated cardboard box with a liner.

As a payload for this behemoth, the outfit included a 3461 dump car with stained logs, a 3464 operating boxcar which could be either Santa Fe or New York Central, a maroon or black 6456 hopper car, the ubiquitous 6462 gondola and a 6457 caboose. Despite the die-cast chassis of the log car, this consist was hardly a burden for the dual-motored electric.

The blue vinylite figure riding in the boxcar had outstretched arms, but the hands and face were no longer painted. The gondola, which could have been either black or red, was laden with six turned wooden barrels. Bringing up the rear of the train was a 6457 Lionel Lines caboose with a blackened metal smokejack. All the rolling stock was packed in Middle Traditional boxes.

Excellent	Like New	Scarcity
2,000	3,500	6

2161W SF Twin Diesel Freight $67.50 retail

Included: 2343P/2343T Santa Fe A-A F-3 units; 3469 automatic dumping ore car; 3464 operating boxcar; 3461X automatic lumber car; 6520 searchlight car; 6457 illuminated SP-type caboose; eight OC curved and seven OS straight track; UCS remote control track set; CTC Lockon; tube of lubricant; instruction booklet.

Like the rest of the 1950-edition locomotives, the popular Santa Fe F-3 units were equipped with Magne-traction. To distinguish the new models with this feature, the stock number 2343 was assigned. Less important, but significant to collectors, was a change in the porthole lenses on the car body, which were now somewhat flatter and were assigned the part number 2333-167.

An impressive assortment of operating cars trailed the dual-motor equipped powered unit and its matching dummy. Die-cast dumping ore and log cars, with their cargoes of Bakelite artificial coal and five stained logs respectively, provided operator interaction. The operating boxcar, with its all-blue vinylite man with spread arms, was furnished in either New York Central or Santa Fe markings. A 6520 operating searchlight car was provided for nighttime operations. Bringing up the rear was a 6457 caboose with a die-cast smokejack. All the rolling stock, as well as the dummy or

2163WS, 2167WS

T F-3-unit, was packed in Middle Traditional boxes. The dummy unit box had a liner, as did the conventional tan corrugated carton of the powered F-3 diesel locomotive.

Excellent	Like New	Scarcity
1,500	2,500	4

2163WS Four-Car Freight $49.95 retail

Included: 736 2-8-4 Berkshire steam locomotive with operating headlight, smoke and Magne-traction; 2671WX streamlined whistle tender; 6462 gondola; 6472 refrigerator car; 6555 Sunoco single-dome tank car; 6457 illuminated SP-type caboose; eight OC curved and seven OS straight track; UCS remote control track set; CTC Lockon; bottle of SP smoke pellets; tube of lubricant; instruction booklet.

Lionel updated its 2-8-4 Berkshire to include Magne-traction, and its number changed to 736. This number was rubber-stamped in silver beneath the cab window. Unlike locomotives made later in the decade, the 1950 Berkshire continued to use a die-cast trailing truck. Rather than the spectacular die-cast bodied 2426W, which had been paired with Berkshires since 1946, a new tender was used. The 2671W tender, developed to accompany the 20-wheel steam turbine, was fitted with a body decorated with small "Lionel Lines" lettering—rather than the turbine tender's Pennsylvania lettering—and was mated with the Berkshire. The new tender, which was unique to 1950-51, was numbered 2671WX.

The balance of the outfit was made up of run of the mill freight cars, including a new non-operating version of the milk car and a sheet metal die-cast tank car of prewar origins. The rolling stock and tender was packaged in Middle Traditional boxes, while the locomotive came in a lined conventional tan corrugated box. All components were placed in a preprinted 1950-style box.

Excellent	Like New	Scarcity
575	900	4

2165WS O-Gauge Four-Car Freight $57.50 retail

Included: 736 2-8-4 Berkshire steam locomotive with operating headlight, smoke and Magne-traction; 2671WX streamlined whistle tender; 6456 Lehigh Valley hopper; 3461 automatic lumber car; 3472 operating milk car; 6457 illuminated SP-type caboose; eight OC curved and seven OS straight track; UCS remote control track set; CTC Lockon; bottle of SP smoke pellets; tube of lubricant; instruction booklet.

For only $7.05 more than the $49.95 price of the 2163WS, shoppers in 1950 could bring home this upgraded Berkshire set. Rather than the non-operating milk car of the lesser set, 2165WS got the automatic version. Not only that, but an operating 3461 log-dump car was also included.

The 1950 edition of the 3472 operating milk car differed from the earlier model in that the aluminum doors previously used were replaced with plastic doors, and the roof hatch was enlarged. Earlier models had a die-cast roof hatch extending about halfway across the car, whereas the 1950 and later models used a plastic hatch that spanned the roof.

The 3461 log car was furnished with five 4-5/8-inch-long stained logs made of 7/16-inch dowels. Rounding out the set was a 6456 hopper car in either black or maroon and a 6457 caboose with blackened die-cast smokejack.

The locomotive and tender were identical to that described above for the 2163WS outfit.

All the components, except the locomotive, were packaged in Middle Traditional boxes. The locomotive, not surprisingly, was packed in a conventional tan corrugated carton. The outfit box itself was the new 1950-style preprinted package.

Excellent	Like New	Scarcity
600	1,000	4

2167WS Three-Car Freight $39.95 retail

Included: 681 6-8-6 steam turbine locomotive with operating headlight, smoke and Magne-traction; 2671W streamlined whistle tender; 3464 operating boxcar; 6462 gondola; 6457 illuminated SP-type caboose; eight OC curved and five OS straight track; UCS remote control track set; CTC Lockon; bottle of SP smoke pellets; tube of lubricant; instruction booklet.

While the 027 version of the 20-wheel steam turbine was dropped after 1949, its O-Gauge brother was upgraded to include Magne-traction and renumbered 681. The new locomotive number was rubber stamped in silver in 1950 (and 1951), and the Pennsylvania tender of the late 671, the 2671W was carried forward into the golden anniversary year.

The rolling stock was an unremarkable assortment of cars that were the staples of the era. Included was a step-less gondola in either black or red, carrying six turned wooden barrels; a 3464, also step-less, decorated in New York Central or Santa Fe livery, with an unpainted blue vinylite figure with spread arms; and a 6457 Lionel Lines caboose with blackened metal smokejack.

The locomotive box was a standard tan corrugated carton with a liner. The other items were packed in Middle Traditional boxes, the tender box being lined. The outfit box was the typical 1950 edition.

Excellent	Like New	Scarcity
400	650	4

2169WS Five-Car Freight W/Smoke and Whistle $79.50 retail

1950

Values for each condition are in U.S. dollars. | **Scarity** = Scale from 1-8 with 8 being the hardest to find.

When existing 2169W inventory was offered for sale in 1951, the carton was relabeled with 1948-style labels, as seen here.

Included: 773 4-6-4 Hudson steam locomotive, with operating headlight, smoke and Magne-traction; 2426W whistle tender; 3656 operating cattle car; 6411 flatcar with logs; 6456 Lehigh Valley hopper; 3469 automatic dumping ore car with 207 artificial coal; 6457 illuminated SP-type caboose; eight OC curved and seven OS straight track; UCS remote control track set; CTC Lockon; bottle of SP smoke pellets; tube of lubricant; instruction booklet.

In addition to powering the previously listed 2148WS passenger set, the re-born semi scale Hudson was selected to head this otherwise mundane set. Differing from the prewar editions of the large Hudson, the 773 was equipped with a smoke unit and Magne-traction. In order to accommodate the installation of Magne-traction, the locomotive used solid sintered iron wheels with simulated spokes in lieu of the fabulous prewar drive wheels with open spokes. The semi scale steamer retained the prewar gearing, which yielded a scale-like speed range for the locomotive. Because of the rocket-like speeds attained by most Lionel locomotives, many operators wrongly believe that the performance of the 773 is sluggish. The locomotive was packaged in a black-lettered brown cardboard box made by Star.

Selected to accompany this engine was the 2426W Lionel Lines tender, which would be making its final appearance. Unique to this year's production of the 2426W was the use of a plastic whistle chamber rather than the die-cast whistle chamber used previously.

Two operating cars, an automatic ore-dumping car and a cattle car with corral were included in this outfit. The cattle car was the non-"Armour" version and, while most often lettered in white, it was sometimes lettered in black. The 1950 corral also differed from the earlier editions. Most easily distinguished by its yellow gates, other details of its construction were changed as well. Under-floor foam rubber pads replaced the rubber grommets on the ends of the platform.

Also supplied with the outfit was a 6456 Lehigh Valley hopper, 6411 flatcar with logs and 6457 caboose with blackened die-cast smokejack. All of these cars were packed in Middle Traditional boxes. The outfit box was the new 1950-style package, though in 1951 examples could be found on dealer shelves re-marked with 1948-style paste-on labels.

Excellent	Like New	Scarcity
2,700	4,500	6

2171W NYC Twin Diesel Freight $67.50 retail

Included: 2344P/2344T New York Central A-A F-3 units; 3464 operating boxcar; 3461 automatic lumber car; 3469 automatic dumping ore car; 6520 searchlight car; 6457 illuminated SP-type caboose; eight OC curved and seven OS straight track; UCS remote control track set; CTC Lockon; tube of lubricant; instruction booklet.

This outfit was in every detail identical to the 2161W, except for the inclusion of a pair of New York Central diesels rather than the Santa Fe units found in the 2161W.

Excellent	Like New	Scarcity
1,200	2,000	4

2173WS Four-Car Freight $52.50 retail

Included: 681 6-8-6 steam turbine locomotive with operating headlight, smoke and Magne-traction; 2671W streamlined whistle tender; 3472 operating milk car; 6555 Sunoco single-dome tank car; 3469 automatic dumping ore car with 207 bag of artificial coal; 6457 illuminated SP-type caboose; eight OC curved and seven OS straight track; UCS remote control track set; CTC Lockon; bottle of SP smoke pellets; tube of lubricant; instruction booklet.

The 20-wheel steam turbine was upgraded to include Magne-traction and renumbered 681. The new number was rubber stamped in silver in 1950 (and 1951) beneath the cab window, and the 2671W Pennsylvania tender of the late 671 was carried forward into the golden anniversary year. The revamped locomotive was selected to head this freight outfit.

Included with the set was the large sheet metal and die-cast 6555 Sunoco tank car, 6457 Lionel Lines caboose with blackened die-cast smokejack, and operating milk and ore cars.

The 1950 edition of the 3472 operating milk car differed from the earlier model in that the aluminum doors previously

2175W, 2185W

used were replaced with plastic doors, and the roof hatch was enlarged. Earlier models had a die-cast roof hatch extending about halfway across the car, whereas the 1950 and later models used a plastic hatch that spanned the roof.

The locomotive was packaged in a conventional brown corrugated cardboard box, the tender and cattle car in liner-equipped Middle Traditional boxes, and remainder of the rolling stock in unlined Middle Traditional boxes. The dumping ore car package was marked with an X number suffix and its receiving tray was packaged loose in the outfit box.

Excellent	Like New	Scarcity
500	775	4

2175W Five-Car Santa Fe Twin Diesel Freight $57.50 retail

Included: 2343P/2343T Santa Fe A-A F-3 units; 3464 operating boxcar; 6462 gondola; 6456 Lehigh Valley hopper; 6555 Sunoco single-dome tank car; 6457 illuminated SP-type caboose; eight OC curved and seven OS straight track; UCS remote control track set; CTC Lockon; tube of lubricant; instruction booklet.

One of the most popular O-Gauge outfits offered in 1950 was this set led by the new Magne-traction-equipped 2343 Santa Fe F-3 diesels. Featuring real screen-wire roof vents, separately installed front grab handles and cab side steps, these units represent Lionel's postwar toy trains at their finest. The porthole lenses differed from those used in the earlier 2333-series locomotives—the new lenses were flatter looking.

Behind this magnificent pair of details was a string of typical Lionel freight cars of the period. The operating boxcar with unpainted blue vinylite figure was included in the set, with both Santa Fe and New York Central cars being utilized equally and indiscriminately. Similarly, both black and maroon Lehigh Valley hoppers made their way into the set, as did red and black New York Central gondolas with barrel loads. A sheet metal-bodied Sunoco single-dome tank car with die-cast frame was included, as was a 6457 Lionel Lines caboose with chemically blackened die-cast smokejack.

The cars, as well as the dummy diesel unit, were packaged in Middle Traditional boxes—the dummy unit box included a liner. The powered unit was supplied in a typical tan corrugated box, and all the components were placed in the new 1950-style preprinted outfit box, minus retail price.

Excellent	Like New	Scarcity
1,200	2,000	3

2185W Five-Car NYC Twin Diesel Freight $57.50 retail

Included: 2344P/2344T New York Central A-A F-3 units; 3464 operating boxcar; 6462 gondola; 6456 Lehigh Valley hopper; 6555 Sunoco single-dome tank car; 6457 illuminated SP-type caboose; eight OC curved and seven OS straight track; UCS remote control track set; CTC Lockon; tube of lubricant; instruction booklet.

In an effort to appeal to customers in the Northeastern U.S., the 2175W was also offered with New York Central diesels, the NYC outfit carrying stock number 2185W. However, the colorful Santa Fe set outsold the somewhat drab NYC coast to coast.

Excellent	Like New	Scarcity
1,200	2,000	3

Chapter 8

1951

The Korean War is frequently described as the "Forgotten War," but for those who lived through this period, it is unlikely to be forgotten. Fearing that fighting in Korea would escalate into World War III, the government mobilized American industry. Numerous defense contracts were issued, which were often lucrative. Critical materials for munitions were rationed, including the nickel that was a component of the Alnico magnets that formed the heart of Lionel's Magne-traction. The result was the new feature so heralded the year before that it was dropped from many of the less expensive locomotives, including several that headed sets.

Inflation was skyrocketing, leading to the formation of the United States Economic Stabilization Agency, Office of Price Stabilization (OPS), which established pricing guidelines for consumer goods. But before this office had opened, retail prices had soared 20 percent. The OPS issued a series of "special orders" for various goods that established a maximum retail markup and, thus in the case of Lionel trains, price ceilings. Lionel trains were covered under special order No. 396, and special OPS pricing labels were created. The dealer to goods in stock printed separate labels for application on September 10, and such labels were also applied to products packaged, but not yet shipped by the factory. This pricing was also printed on future orders of component boxes.

It became illegal for dealers to sell new products not marked, and priced, in accordance with the OPS directive. In the big scheme of things, the goal was to cut inflation and, as the "PS" suggested, stabilize prices. In the case of other consumer goods, the creation of OPS price ceilings also created a thriving black market environment, but no evidence has surfaced to indicate that Lionel's trains had such a market.

Without internal Lionel documentation—if it exists—we are left to guess why Lionel pared down its offerings so dramatically in 1951. It could have been due to the rampant inflation, or it could have been that the 1950 offerings had been "pumped up" as part of the golden anniversary celebration, or merely that 1950 sales did not meet expectations. Or it could merely have been that the giant Hillside plant only had so much capacity and defense contracts were more profitable than manufacturing the trains. Most likely it was a combination of these factors but, in any event, only 13 different outfits were shown in the 1951 consumer catalog.

Lionel changed the assembly process used for the steel and die-cast trucks late in 1951. Originally, the sheet-metal bolster was staked to the truck side frames in such a way that the end of the bolster was distorted, resembling the backside of a used staple. This assembly process resulted in the possibility of the side frames loosening, and a new process was developed. In the case of the so-called bar-end trucks, the upper portion of the side frame was forced downward against the bolster. While that resulted in a cup on the upper surface of the side frame, the ends of the bolsters were undistorted and resembled a smooth metal bar.

Outfit boxes for the year included preprinted label information although, unlike the 1950 issue, the blue "label" lacked an orange background. Also, whereas most 1950 set boxes had preprinted retail prices, this was not the case in 1951.

1119

027-Gauge

1119 Scout Three-Car Freight $17.75 retail

Included: 1110 Scout 2-4-2 steam locomotive with operating headlight; 1001T sheet-metal tender; 1002 gondola; 1004 Baby Ruth boxcar; 1007 SP-type caboose; eight 1013 curved and one 1018 straight track; 1009 Manumatic uncoupling section; 1011 25-watt transformer; CTC Lockon; tube of lubricant; instruction booklet.

Although Lionel included Magne-traction in the 1950 Scout outfits, material shortages prevented this feature from being included in the 1951 Scout sets. Accordingly, the number of the locomotive at the front of this set reverted to 1110. However, the 1951 1110 was not a clone of the 1949 loco of the same number; rather, it incorporated a newer motor design.

The black gondola and red caboose were unchanged from the previous year. The orange boxcar, which had had "Baby Ruth" stamped in outlined lettering in 1948-49, was now stamped in solid lettering.

The locomotive and rolling stock was packed in Middle Traditional boxes, and the locomotive box came with a cardboard liner.

Excellent	Like New	Scarcity
125	225	3

1463WS 027 Three-Car Freight $35.75 retail

Included: 2026 2-6-4 steam locomotive with operating headlight and smoke; 6466W early coal whistle tender; 6462 gondola; 6465 Sunoco double-dome tank car; 6257 SP-type caboose; eight 1013 curved and three 1018 straight track; 6019 remote control track set; 1033 90-watt transformer.

The 2036, introduced only the year before as a Magne-traction-equipped successor to the 2026, was unceremoniously shorn of its magnets in 1951. Thus stripped, its numbered reverted to 2026, but like the 2036, this locomotive lacked the extensive detail and side rods of the pre-1950 version.

The locomotive and the tender were packed in lined Middle Traditional boxes. The run of the mill rolling stock also came in Middle Traditional boxes, though without liners. The gondola, which could have been black or red, did not come with barrels and, following the precedent set in 1950; neither it nor the tank car had steps.

The outfit came packed in a new-for-1951 outfit box that was similar to the 1950 edition, except for the lack of preprinted retail prices and orange background in the label panel.

Excellent	Like New	Scarcity
200	325	3

1464W 027 Diesel Three-Car Pullman $66.50 retail

Included: 2023 silver-and-gray Union Pacific Alco A-A units; 2421 Maplewood Pullman, 2422 Chatham Pullman and 2423 Hillside observation with silver-and-gray paint scheme; eight 1013 curved and five 1018 straight track; 6019 remote control track set; 1033 90-watt transformer; CTC Lockon; tube of lubricant; instruction booklet.

In a somewhat pitiful effort to replicate the gleaming streamliners crisscrossing the nation, Lionel produced this silver-painted outfit. While consisting of the same type of components as used in the 1950 outfit of the same number, the paint scheme was much more subdued.

Despite the drab paint scheme of the set, apparently Lionel completed two production runs. This conclusion is based on the reported existence of outfit boxes with and without preprinted prices.

The passenger cars were packaged in Middle Traditional boxes that included coupler-protection flaps, while the locomotives, without individual component boxes, came in a corrugated master carton.

Excellent	Like New	Scarcity
900	1,500	4

1467W 027 Diesel Four-Car Freight $57.50 retail

Included: 2023 silver-and-gray Union Pacific Alco A-A units; 6456 Lehigh Valley hopper; 6656 stock car; 6465 Sunoco double-dome tank car; 6357 illuminated SP-type caboose; eight 1013 curved and five 1018 straight track; 6019 remote control track set; 1033 90-watt transformer; CTC Lockon; tube of lubricant; instruction booklet.

The 1950 Alco freight set was reprised as well, though with the silver-and-gray diesels in lieu of the yellow-and-gray units of the anniversary year. The locomotive continued to be packed in a master carton, without individual unit boxes. The selection of cars included in the outfit was unchanged from its 1950 counterpart.

The cars were packed in Middle Traditional boxes, and this set apparently was produced early in the year, as its 1951-style outfit box did not come preprinted with an OPS stamp.

Excellent	Like New	Scarcity
575	875	4

1469WS 027 Four-Car Freight $48.50 retail

Included: 2035 2-6-4 steam locomotive with operating headlight, smoke and Magne-traction; 6466W early coal whistle tender; 6462 gondola; 6456 Lehigh Valley hopper; 6465 Sunoco double-dome tank car; 6257 SP-type caboose; eight 1013 curved and three 1018 straight track; 6019 remote control track set; 1033 90-watt transformer; CTC Lockon; bottle of SP smoke pellets; tube of lubricant; instruction booklet.

Outfit 1469WS must have been a good seller in 1950, for it was repeated in 1951 with a new carton. The 2035 locomotives produced in 1951 can be distinguished from their 1950 counterparts due to the "two-pin" mounting of their eccentric cranks, contrasted to the "half-moon" style, which was unique to this loco's 1950 production.

More obvious was the inclusion of a maroon hopper car, called red on the component box, in many sets, rather than the more mundane black.

The components of this set were packed in Middle Traditional boxes, with the locomotive and tender boxes having liners. The outfit box, at least as originally produced, was the new 1951 style without OPS pricing.

Excellent	Like New	Scarcity
225	425	3

1471WS Five-Car Freight $70 retail

Included: 2035 2-6-4 steam locomotive with operating headlight, smoke and Magne-traction; 6466W early coal whistle tender; 6454 boxcar; 3469 automatic dumping ore car; 6465 Sunoco double-dome tank car; 3461 automatic lumber car; 6357 illuminated SP-type caboose; eight 1013 curved and seven 1018 straight track; 6019 remote control track set; 1033 90-watt transformer; CTC Lockon; bottle of SP smoke pellets; tube of lubricant; instruction booklet.

Another of the 1950 outfits reissued in 1951 was this freight set. The locomotive was naturally the revised edition described above, but the rolling stock was unchanged from the previous year. It appeared Lionel had a winner on its hands with this action-packed set featuring two dump cars.

The packaging consisted of Middle Traditional component boxes and a 1951-style outfit box.

Excellent	Like New	Scarcity
350	575	3

1477S 027 Three-Car Freight $29.95 retail

Included: 2026 2-6-4 steam locomotive with operating headlight and smoke; 6466T early coal tender; 6012 gondola; 6014 Baby Ruth boxcar; 6017 SP-type caboose; eight 1013 curved and three 1018 straight track; 6019 remote control track set; 1034 75-watt transformer; CTC Lockon; bottle of SP smoke pellets; tube of lubricant; instruction booklet.

Another of the outfits to be led by the lackluster 2026 was set 1477S. The 2036, introduced only the year before as a Magne-traction-equipped successor to the earlier 2026, lost its Magne-traction in 1951 due to wartime materials shortages. Downgraded, its numbered reverted to 2026, but like the 2036 this locomotive lacked the extensive detail and side rods of the pre-1950 version.

In order to hold the retail price of the outfit down, Lionel took a number of economizing steps. The tender supplied with this outfit was not equipped with a whistle, which naturally meant that a less costly transformer could be used as well. A new series of economy rolling stock was introduced for this outfit. Based on the Scout-design freight cars, but fitted with conventional trucks and couplers, the 6012 gondola and white 6014 Baby Ruth boxcar were born. The unpainted red 6017 caboose was either a stripped-down version of the 6257 or an upgraded version of the 1007, depending on one's point of view.

All the wheeled components of this set were packed in lined Middle Traditional boxes. The set came packed in a new-for-1951 outfit box.

Excellent	Like New	Scarcity
200	375	3

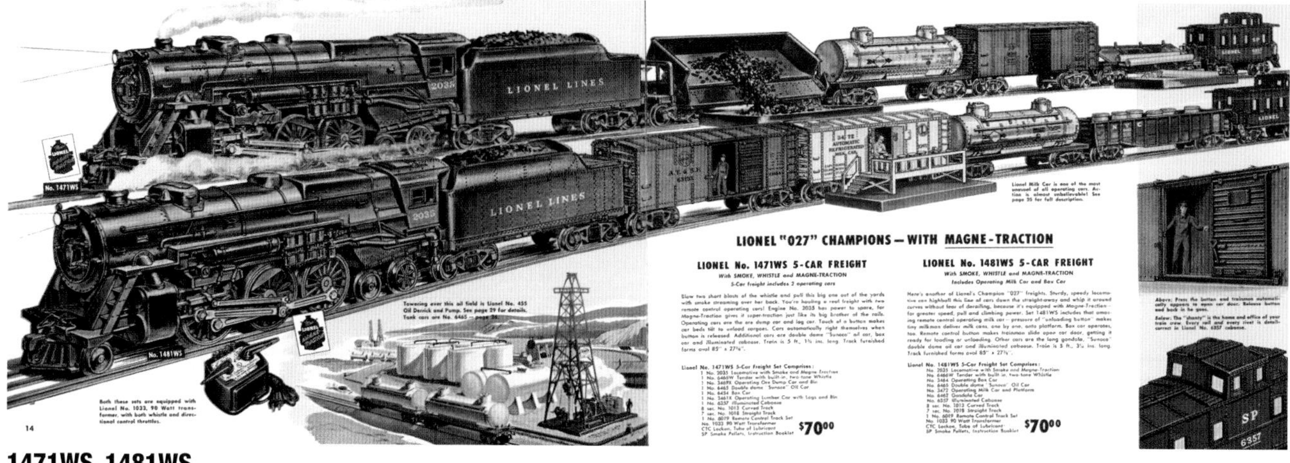

LIONEL "027" CHAMPIONS — WITH MAGNE-TRACTION
LIONEL No. 1471WS 5-CAR FREIGHT
LIONEL No. 1481WS 5-CAR FREIGHT
$70.00
$70.00
14

1471WS, 1481WS

1481WS Five-Car Freight **$70 retail**

Included: 2035 2-6-4 steam locomotive with operating headlight, smoke and Magne-traction; 6466W early coal whistle tender; 3464 operating boxcar; 6462 gondola; 3472 operating milk car; 6465 Sunoco double-dome tank car; 6357 illuminated SP-type caboose; eight 1013 curved and seven 1018 straight track; 6019 remote control track set; 1033 90-watt transformer; CTC Lockon; bottle of SP smoke pellets; tube of lubricant; instruction booklet.

It is strangely similar to outfit 1471WS, another 1951 set, and many people believe that this train was merely an effort by Lionel to deplete existing inventory of rolling stock. Included in the outfit was the celebrated operating milk car with platform. Milk cars produced in 1951 have frames with fewer openings stamped in them than in previous years. This was a result of separate frames being developed for the milk cars and boxcars. However, when placed on the track, they are indistinguishable from the plastic-door cars introduced the previous year.

The 3464 operating boxcar was mounted on a new style frame that, unlike previous issues, showed no evidence of mounting provisions for a milk car mechanism. During the course of the year, plastic doors began to be used on this car, rather than the 2458-style die-cast doors, and the trigger housing slung under the car changed from metal to plastic. The latter change required further modification of the frame stamping. The figure inside the car continued to have outstretched arms, but the hands and face were no longer painted.

All the components of this outfit, except the transformer, were packed in Middle Traditional boxes. The locomotive, tender and milk car boxes had liners, though the rest of the cars were packed in unlined boxes. The set box was the normal 1951-style.

Excellent	Like New	Scarcity
325	525	3

O-Gauge

2163WS **Four-Car Freight** **$60 retail**

Included: 736 2-8-4 Berkshire steam locomotive with operating headlight, smoke and Magne-traction; 2671WX streamlined whistle tender; 6462 gondola; 6472 refrigerator car; 6465 Sunoco double-dome tank car; 6457 illuminated

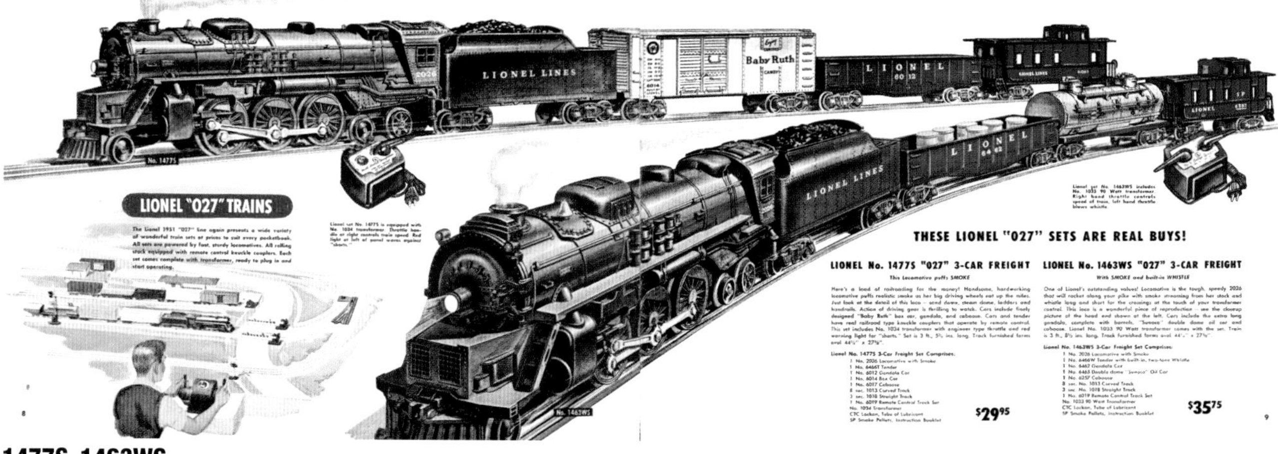

THESE LIONEL "027" SETS ARE REAL BUYS!

1477S, 1463WS

TWO GREAT LIONEL FREIGHTS–WITH MAGNE-TRACTION
LIONEL "O" GAUGE TRAINS
No. 2163WS LIONEL 4-CAR FREIGHT
No. 2167WS "O" 3-CAR FREIGHT
PENNSYLVANIA
LIONEL LINES
$60.00
$47.75

SP-type caboose; eight OC curved and seven OS straight track; UCS remote control track set; CTC Lockon; bottle of SP smoke pellets; tube of lubricant; instruction booklet.

Like all the O-Gauge outfits of 1951, this set was a repeat of a 1950 offering. However, though the catalog number and basic consist were repetitive, the specific contents varied slightly for the new year.

The sheet-metal-bodied, die-cast framed 6555 Sunoco tank car, whose lineage predates the Second World War, was replaced with the smaller, less costly plastic-bodied 6465 two-dome Sunoco tanker.

The locomotive continued to be the high-quality 736 with die-cast trailing truck and silver rubber-stamped lettering. The 12-wheeled 2671WX Lionel Lines tender was again paired with the big steamer.

The locomotive was boxed in a conventional tan corrugated carton with liner, while the remaining rolling stock was boxed in Middle Traditional packages. New boxes of the 1951 style were purchased for this set, although as a carryover item it is possible that some surplus 1950 boxes were used as well, with OPS stickers obliterating the 1950 price, which was more than $10 lower.

Excellent	Like New	Scarcity
575	900	4

2167WS Three-Car Freight $47.75 retail

Included: 681 6-8-6 steam turbine locomotive with operating headlight, smoke and Magne-traction; 2671W streamlined whistle tender; 3464 operating boxcar; 6462 gondola; 6457 illuminated SP-type caboose; eight OC curved and five OS straight track; UCS remote control track set; CTC Lockon; bottle of SP smoke pellets; tube of lubricant; instruction booklet.

The somewhat basic 2167WS outfit also returned for a second year in 1951. The Magne-traction-equipped 681 continued to be numbered with silver rubber-stamped markings and was supplied with a 2671W Pennsylvania tender.

The 3464 operating boxcar, which could be either the Santa Fe or New York Central version in this outfit, featured a new style frame that, unlike previous issues, showed no evidence of mounting provisions for a milk car mechanism. During the course of the year, plastic doors began to be used on this car, rather than the 2458-style die-cast doors, and during the year the trigger housing slung under the car changed from metal to plastic. The latter change required further modification of the frame stamping. The figure inside the car continued to have outstretched arms, but the hands and face were no longer painted.

The familiar 6462 gondola in this outfit could be either the red or the black version, and came with a load of six turned wooden unstained barrels. A 6457 caboose with chemically blackened die-cast smokejack brought up the rear of the train. All the rolling stock was packaged in Middle Traditional boxes, while a conventional tan corrugated carton with liner protected the locomotive. As a whole, the outfit was packaged in the new 1951 set box. As a carryover item, it is theoretically possible that some 1950-style boxes were used as well.

Excellent	Like New	Scarcity
400	650	4

2173WS Four-Car Freight $62.50 retail

Included: 681 6-8-6 steam turbine locomotive with operating headlight, smoke and Magne-traction; 2671W streamlined whistle tender; 3472 operating milk car; 6465 Sunoco double-dome tank car; 3469 automatic dumping ore car with 207 bag of artificial coal; 6457 illuminated SP-type caboose; eight OC curved and seven OS straight track; UCS remote control track set; CTC Lockon; bottle of SP smoke pellets; tube of lubricant; instruction booklet.

The second turbine-powered outfit carried over from 1950 was the operating car laden 2173WS. The 1951 edition was pulled by the same 681 with silver rubber-stamped numbers and 12-wheel tender as the previous year, but the large single-dome tank car of the earlier outfit was replaced by the ubiquitous 6465 two-dome Sunoco tanker.

The ever-popular milk car included in this outfit had fewer frame openings than prior years' cars. The ore dump car was packed in a box with an X suffix appended to the stock number, indicative of the receiving bin being placed separately in the outfit box.

The outfit box was the new 1951 edition, although as a carryover item, surplus 1950 sets could have been used in theory. The components, except the locomotive that was in a corrugated carton with liner, were packed in Middle Traditional boxes.

Excellent	Like New	Scarcity
500	775	4

2173WS

2175W Five-Car Santa Fe Twin Diesel Freight $70 retail

Included: 2343P/2343T Santa Fe A-A F-3 units; 3464 operating boxcar; 6462 gondola; 6456 Lehigh Valley hopper; 6465 Sunoco double-dome tank car; 6457 illuminated SP-type caboose; eight OC curved and seven OS straight track; UCS remote control track set; CTC Lockon; tube of lubricant; instruction booklet.

The Santa Fe double-diesel set was carried over, with the double-dome 6465 Sunoco tank car replacing a single-dome car of the same name that was found in the 1950 edition.

The 3464 operating boxcar—which could either match the Santa Fe locos or the New York Central version, featured a new style frame. Unlike previous issues, the 1951 versions showed no evidence of mounting provisions for a milk car mechanism. During the course of the year, plastic doors began to be used on this car rather than the 2458-style die-cast doors, and the trigger housing slung under the car changed from metal to plastic. The latter change required further modification of the frame stamping. The figure inside the car continued to have outstretched arms, but the hands and face were no longer painted.

Also included was a 6456 Lehigh Valley hopper, which can be found in this set in both black and maroon versions. At the rear was the familiar illuminated 6457 Lionel Lines caboose.

The twin 2343 Santa Fe F-3 locomotives heading the set were essentially unchanged from 1950. However, at some point during 1951, snap-in porthole lenses began to be used. The powered unit was packed in a tan cardboard carton, with liner, while the remainder of the set components came in Middle Traditional boxes, with only the dummy unit box having a liner. The outfit box was the new 1951 style.

Excellent	Like New	Scarcity
1,200	2,000	3

2185W Five-Car NYC Twin Diesel Freight $70 retail

Included: 2344P/2344T New York Central A-A F-3 units; 3464 operating boxcar; 6462 gondola; 6456 Lehigh Valley hopper; 6465 Sunoco single-dome tank car; 6457 illuminated SP-type caboose; eight OC curved and seven OS straight track; UCS remote control track set; CTC Lockon; tube of lubricant; instruction booklet.

Repeating the pattern set the year before by an outfit of the same number, this outfit was merely a 2175W powered by New York Central rather than Santa Fe locomotives. Beyond that, the description for the 1950 edition of 2175W is fully applicable to this outfit.

Excellent	Like New	Scarcity
1,200	2,000	3

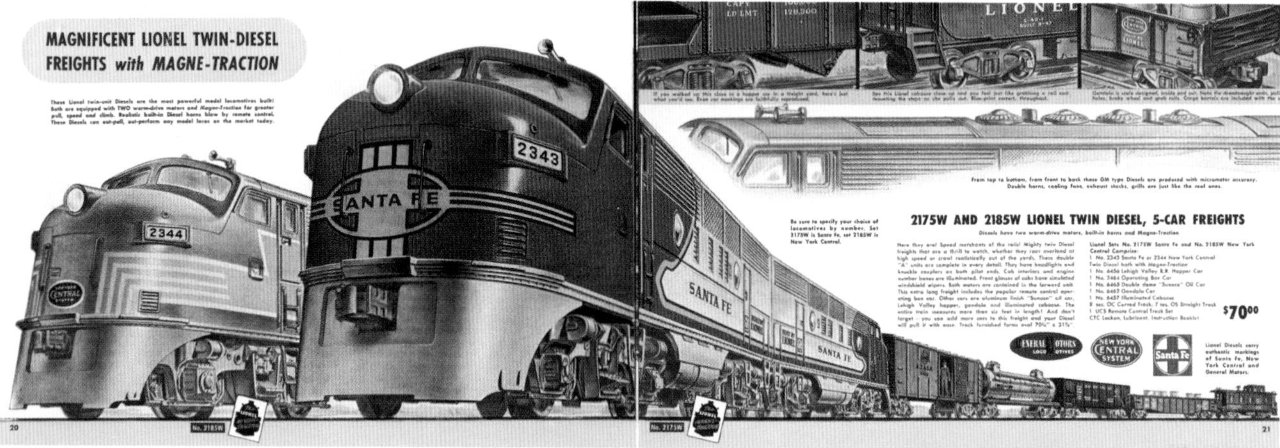

2185W, 2175W

Chapter 9

1952

The war on the Korean Peninsula continued to rage throughout 1952 and America's resources turned increasingly toward defense. Materials deemed critical for arms production, such as nickel and tin, were in extremely short supply for consumer goods.

For Lionel, this meant reducing the number of trains equipped with Magne-traction even below that of 1951. In fact, no steam locomotives cataloged in 1952 would be so equipped, although the diesels did retain the heralded feature. The brightly tin-plated track, familiar to Lionel's customers for decades, was replaced with a dull plating.

Spurred by competition from American Model Toys (AMT), Lionel created a series of extruded-aluminum passenger cars. (For more information about AMT's products, see *"O'Brien's Guide to Collecting Toy Trains, 6th edition."*)

Elsewhere, Lionel continued to cut costs: the die-cast based crane car lost its six-wheel trucks, now being fitted with conventional bar-end trucks. The NW-2 switchers lost their operating bell, which both lowered cost and spared parent's ears and patience.

Rather than applying OPS stickers, the bulk of the items were boxed in cartons preprinted with the OPS information. The text terms this box the OPS Traditional. However, a few components continued to be packaged in Middle Traditional boxes with separately applied stickers.

OPS TRADITIONAL: This box was the same as the Middle Traditional, but was factory printed with a Korean War-era OPS (Office of Price Stabilization) price. This box was used in 1952. As an aside, Lionel provided dealers with sheets of adhesive-backed white OPS stickers for application to older items already in stock.

LIONEL Scout TRAIN

LIONEL No. 1119 "SCOUT" 3-CAR FREIGHT

The Lionel 1952 "Scout" freight train is again the biggest dollar's worth in economical model railroading. At a price of only $17.75 you get a sturdy, Lionel-built 2-4-2 locomotive with headlight, three beautifully modelled cars, track and transformer. Set also includes Manumatic track section which permits uncoupling of cars. All cars are equipped with solid steel wheels. Transformer has 25 Watt capacity. Total length of set is 3 ft., 4½ ins. Track oval measures 37⅝" x 27⅜".

Lionel No. 1119 3-Car "Scout" Set Comprises:
1 No. 1110 Locomotive with Headlight
1 No. 1001T Tender
1 No. 1002 Gondola Car
1 No. 1004 Box Car
1 No. 1007 Caboose
8 sec. No. 1013 Curved Track
1 sec. No. 1018 Straight Track
1 No. 1009 Manumatic Track Section
1 No. 1011 25 Watt Transformer
CTC Lockon, Tube of Lubricant
Instruction Booklet

$17.75

BUILD A FULL-SIZE PIKE FOR YOUR "SCOUT"

For an additional $31.65 (which purchases the necessary track, switches and accessories) you can build a realistic pike like the one illustrated. The platform, landscaping, etc. are extra. This layout is only a suggestion — you may want to add more or less in the way of track and accessories. Of course you needn't build this whole setup at once — you can buy the additional items at your convenience. Consult your Lionel dealer for details.

CREATE THIS COMPLETE RAILROAD FOR A FEW DOLLARS MORE

LIONEL SCOUT

LIONEL 1002

LEFT: Here's a close view of the "Scout" Manumatic uncoupler.

RIGHT: "Scout" set includes this handsome, sturdy 25 Watt transformer.

3

1119

027-Gauge

1119 Scout Three-Car Freight $17.75 retail

Included: 1110 Scout 2-4-2 steam locomotive with operating headlight; 1001T sheet-metal tender; 1002 gondola; 1004 Baby Ruth boxcar; 1007 SP-type caboose; eight 1013 curved and one 1018 straight track; 1009 Manumatic uncoupling section; 1011 25-watt transformer; CTC Lockon; tube of lubricant; instruction booklet.

This was the final appearance of a true Scout outfit in the Lionel catalog. Though Scout-like locomotives and cars continued to be offered for many years, the 1952 edition of set 1119 was the final appearance of the Scout name and the incompatible Scout coupler.

The outfit itself was identical to the 1951 edition and may have been carried over inventory. A letter sent by Lionel to its dealers in early 1952 warning that only a limited number of these sets would be available reinforces this theory.

Excellent	Like New	Scarcity
125	225	3

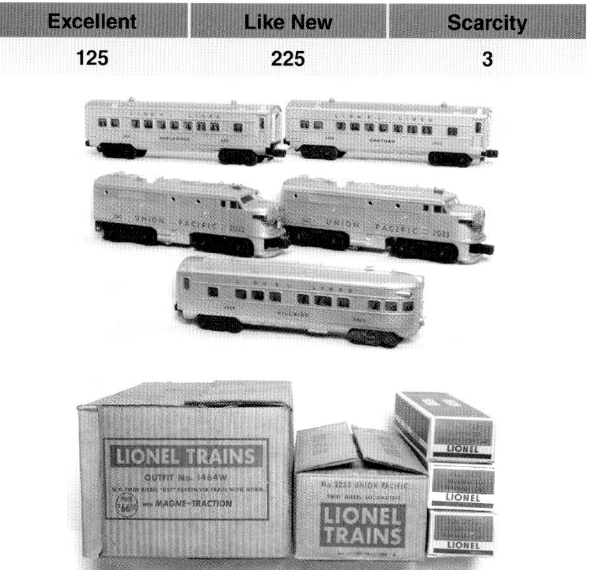

1464W 027 Diesel Three-Car Pullman $66.50 retail

Included: 2033 silver-and-gray Union Pacific Alco A-A units; 2421 Maplewood Pullman, 2422 Chatham Pullman and 2423 Hillside observation with silver-and-silver paint scheme; eight 1013 curved and five 1018 straight track; 6019 remote control track set; 1033 90-watt transformer; CTC Lockon; tube of lubricant; instruction booklet.

The degradation of outfit 1464W continued. In 1950, this was a beautiful yellow and gray consist with red trim, in 1951 it was silver and gray with black trim, and now it was overall silver with black trim. Perhaps Lionel adopted this paint scheme to entice buyers who would otherwise choose AMT's gleaming all-silver aluminum cars, Lionel's own versions of which were months away from production. The locomotives were renumbered from 2023 to 2033.

The passenger cars were packaged in OPS Traditional boxes that included coupler-protection flaps, while the locomotives, without individual component boxes, came in a corrugated master carton. The outfit box was the same as the 1951 version.

Excellent	Like New	Scarcity
850	1,400	3

1465 Three-car Freight $22.50 retail

Included: 2034 2-4-2 steam locomotive with operating headlight; 6066T early coal tender; 6032 gondola; 6035 Sunoco single-dome tank car; 6037 SP-type caboose; eight 1013 curved and three 1018 straight track; 6019 remote control track set; 1012 35-watt transformer; CTC Lockon; tube of lubricant; instruction booklet.

This apparently plain-Jane set likely has a somewhat interesting, though now hidden, story. The cars all have 1952 semi-Scout features—Scout trucks and conventional magnetic couplers—and semi-Scout numbers. The locomotive, though using a die-cast boiler similar to that of the 1110, had an all-new and significantly better mechanism, including a three-position reversing unit.

The puzzling part of the outfit is in its packaging and numbering. At this point in time, Lionel outfit numbers tended to follow a pattern of even numbers for passenger sets, odd numbers for freight. And they naturally tended to ascend with the passage of time: that is, 1950 numbers were bigger than those used in 1948.

This outfit's number is a throwback to 1950, where it is "missing." And further, its packaging followed the 1950 convention of an orange panel and blue lettering, a package that was two years out of date when this set was issued in 1952.

All the components were packed in Middle Traditional boxes and the locomotive box came with a liner.

Excellent	Like New	Scarcity
150	250	2

1467W Four-car Freight $57.50 retail

Included: 2032 Erie Alco A-A units; 6456 Lehigh Valley hopper; 6656 stock car; 6465 Sunoco double-dome tank car; 6357 illuminated SP-type caboose; eight 1013 curved and five 1018 straight track; 6019 remote control track set; 1033 90-watt transformer; CTC Lockon; tube of lubricant; instruction booklet.

This was the third year for an outfit assigned this number, but it was also the third change in motive power for the set. Except for model-year changes, the rolling stock was

1467W, 1464W

unchanged from the outfit's 1950 debut. The new-for-1952 2032 Erie Alco diesels headed the set in lieu of the previously used yellow (1950) or silver (1951) 2023 Union Pacific units.

The rolling stock was packaged in OPS Traditional boxes while the locomotives came in a two-unit master carton, typical of the die-cast base Alcos. The set box was the normal 1952 issue with preprinted OPS pricing.

Excellent	Like New	Scarcity
525	800	4

1477S **027 Three-Car Freight** **$29.95 retail**

Included: 2026 2-6-4 steam locomotive with operating headlight and smoke; 6466T early coal tender; 6012 gondola; 6014 Baby Ruth boxcar; 6017 SP-type caboose; eight 1013 curved and three 1018 straight track; 6019 remote control track set; 1034 75-watt transformer; CTC Lockon; bottle of SP smoke pellets; tube of lubricant; instruction booklet.

The Magne-traction-less 2026 headed outfit 1477S for a second year. Its assortment of cars, all derived from the Scout series, were unchanged from the previous year's edition.

Excellent	Like New	Scarcity
200	375	3

1479WS **027 Four-car Freight** **$49.95 retail**

Included: 2056 4-6-4 steam locomotive with operating headlight and smoke; 2046W streamlined whistle tender; 6462 gondola; 6465 Sunoco double-dome tank car; 6456 Lehigh Valley hopper; 6257 SP-type caboose; eight 1013 curved and three 1018 straight track; 6019 remote control track set; 1033 90-watt transformer; CTC Lockon; bottle of SP smoke pellets; tube of lubricant; instruction booklet.

The 2046 lost its Magne-traction in 1952, its number becoming 2056. Paired with the medium-sized Hudson was a 2046W tender. Behind the tender, one would find a black 6462 gondola, maroon 6456 hopper car and a Sunoco two-

1465, 1477S

dome tank car without steps. The final line of the tank cars reporting marks ends in "TANK." Bringing up the rear of the train was a 6257 non-illuminated caboose.

Inside the typical 1952 outfit carton, the locomotive was packaged in a conventional tan cardboard carton with a liner. The rolling stock came in OPS Traditional boxes without liners.

Excellent	Like New	Scarcity
425	700	3

1483WS Five-car Freight $65 retail

Included: 2056 4-6-4 steam locomotive with operating headlight and smoke; 2046W streamlined whistle tender; 3472 operating milk car; 6462 gondola; 6465 Sunoco double-dome tank car; 3474 operating Western Pacific boxcar; 6357 illuminated SP-type caboose; eight 1013 curved and seven 1018 straight track; 6019 remote control track set; 1033 90-watt transformer; CTC Lockon; bottle of SP smoke pellets; tube of lubricant; instruction booklet.

This set featuring two operating cars was headed by the non-Magne-traction medium-size Hudson number 2056. The operating milk car was the plastic door version, while the operating boxcar featured an all-new paint scheme; the correct car for this outfit has an unpainted 1-5/16-inch tall man, Western Pacific inside and packed in a box with OPS pricing preprinted on it. The 3474 boxcars dating from 1953 have unpainted 1-3/16-inch tall crewmen inside and their boxes do not include OPS pricing. The 1953 version is not correct for this outfit. None of the 3474 boxcars had steps and all had plastic plunger housings.

Routine 6462 gondola, 6465 Sunoco tank car and a 6357 lighted caboose completed the set. The rolling stock was packed in OPS Traditional boxes, while the locomotive was boxed in a lined conventional tan cardboard box. All of this was placed in a normal 1952 outfit carton.

Excellent	Like New	Scarcity
625	950	5

1484WS Four-car Pullman $70 retail

Included: 2056 4-6-4 steam locomotive with operating headlight and smoke; 2046W streamlined whistle tender; 2421 Maplewood Pullman, 2422 Chatham Pullman, 2423 Hillside observation and 2429 Livingston Pullman in the new silver-with-silver-roof color scheme; eight 1013 curved and seven 1018 straight track; 6019 remote control track set; 1033 90-watt transformer; CTC Lockon; bottle of SP smoke pellets; tube of lubricant; instruction booklet.

This was the third and final set to include the 2056 medium-sized Hudson locomotive. Four passenger cars trailed the steamer, the familiar 2421, 2422 and 2423 being joined by a new number, the 2429. While the three former cars carried the familiar Maplewood, Chatham and Hillside names, the fourth bore the name Livingston—itself having been previously used on the 2483 observation car of the yellow and gray "Anniversary Set." In this outfit, the passenger cars were silver with silver roofs and black trim. This was the only set to include the 2429 Livingston, no doubt accounting for the car's scarcity today.

The outfit was boxed in a normal set box for the day, with the locomotive in a conventional tan cardboard box with a liner, and tender and passenger cars in OPS Traditional boxes.

Excellent	Like New	Scarcity
950	1,500	6

1485WS 027 Three-Car Freight $39.95 retail

Included: 2025 2-6-4 steam locomotive with operating headlight and smoke; 6466W early coal whistle tender; 6462 gondola; 6465 Sunoco double-dome tank car; 6257 SP-type caboose; eight 1013 curved and three 1018 straight track; 6019 remote control track set; 1033 90-watt transformer; CTC Lockon; bottle of SP smoke pellets; tube of lubricant; instruction booklet.

1485WS, 1479WS

LIONEL TRAINS
OUTFIT No. 1485WS
"027" FREIGHT TRAIN
WITH WHISTLE and SMOKE
THE LIONEL CORPORATION
NEW YORK
CHICAGO
LIONEL
No. 6465
TANK CAR
LIONEL
LIONEL
LIONEL

The Korean War caused a shortage of magnetic material, resulting in all the steam locomotives in 1952 lacking Magne-traction. Model numbers were updated just two years previously to reflect the addition of this new feature reverted to their pre-1950 designation.

The 2025/2035 was an example of this. The 2025, cataloged from 1947 through 1949 with a 2-6-2-wheel arrangement, naturally lacked Magne-traction in its die-cast Baldwin Disc wheels. In 1950, Magne-traction was introduced, which meant that the wheels had to be made of sintered iron (to conduct the magnetic flux), and its number was changed to 2035. At the same time the wheel arrangement had been changed to 2-6-4, the sheet-metal frame of the four-wheel trailing truck being less expensive to produce that the die-cast two-wheel trailing truck frame used previously. The 1952 shortage of Magnetic material meant that the number reverted to 2025, yet the 1950-51 features of "spoke" sintered iron drive wheels and four-wheel trailing truck were retained.

The locomotive came with the long-running but unremarkable early coal tender, numbered 6466W in this case. The nondescript rolling stock included in this outfit included a 6462 New York Central gondola without brake wheels or steps, a Sunoco two-dome tank car without steps and a 6257 caboose, which was not illuminated.

OPS Traditional boxes were used throughout this outfit, with the locomotive and tender boxes having heavy cardboard liners. The components were then placed in the standard 1952-issue set carton.

Excellent	Like New	Scarcity
225	350	4

O-Gauge

2177WS 📷 Three-Car Freight $39.95 retail

Included: 675 2-6-4 steam locomotive with operating headlight and smoke; 2046W streamlined whistle tender; 6462 gondola; 6465 Sunoco double-dome tank car; 6457 illuminated SP-type caboose; eight OC curved and five OS straight track; UCS remote control track set; CTC Lockon; bottle of SP smoke pellets; tube of lubricant; instruction booklet.

Lionel did not have an inexpensive steamer in its 1951 line, a situation remedied in 1952. The revamped, Magne-traction-less 2025 2-6-4 was merely re-stamped with the number 675, which had been used on the same boiler and cab casting when offered in O-Gauge from 1947 through 1949. Only the number distinguished the 1952 675 from the 1952 2025 locomotives, but they were paired with very different tenders.

For the O-Gauge version of the 2-6-4, Lionel supplied the streamlined 2046W tender—the only time this style of tender was paired with the 675/2025/2035 style locomotive. The rolling stock included in this outfit was without exception unremarkable, yet it was the staple of the era for the firm's outfits. It included a 6462 New York Central gondola without steps or brake wheels, but including barrels, a Sunoco two-dome tank car without steps, and an illuminated 6457 caboose with chemically blackened die-cast smokejack.

The set box was typical for the period and all the components were packed in OPS traditional boxes. The locomotive had the benefit of a box with liner.

Excellent	Like New	Scarcity
300	500	5

2179WS **Four-Car Freight** **$47.75 retail**

Included: 671 6-8-6 steam turbine locomotive with operating headlight and smoke; 2046WX streamlined whistle tender; 3464 operating boxcar; 6462 gondola; 6465 Sunoco double-dome tank car; 6457 illuminated SP-type caboose; eight OC curved and five OS straight track; UCS remote control track set; CTC Lockon; bottle of SP smoke pellets; tube of lubricant; instruction booklet.

The O-Gauge 20-wheel steam turbine, like the rest of Lionel's steam locomotives, lost its Magne-traction in 1950, the number reverting to 671. It is possible that some of these locomotives were assembled using 671 boiler/cab castings that had been placed in storage or assigned for parts used when the 681 was unveiled in 1950. However, it is unlikely that Lionel's inventory control was so poor as to have a large stock of these "surplus." Most of the engines were marked with a small "RR" stamped below the "671" beneath the cab window. The large gap in the frame, normally housing the Magne-traction magnet and hidden by the steel flux plates of the 681, was revealed on the 671RR, which lacked these components. The locomotive was packed in a lined box. Some of these reportedly came packed in Middle Traditional boxes—likely surplus from late 1949 production—which is when this box was introduced, but the bulk of the 671RR production was packaged in OPS Traditional boxes.

The tender box, which came with a liner, was an OPS Traditional box marked "2046WX"—the X denoting the tender was stamped "PENNSYLVANIA" rather than "LIONEL LINES," which was the norm for the 2046W.

The rolling stock was also packaged in OPS Traditional boxes. The operating boxcar packed in this set could have either Santa Fe or New York Central markings. It lacked steps and had an unpainted 1-5/16-inch tall blue vinylite man inside. Both the doors and the trigger mechanism housing were plastic. The 6462 New York Central gondola included in this set included barrels, but came without steps. Some sets have been observed containing cars with brake wheels, while others have not.

The ubiquitous 6465 Sunoco tank car, sans steps and with the final data line ending in "TANK," was included. So too was the ever popular 6457 Lionel Lines SP-style caboose with interior lighting, sheet metal tool compartments and blackened die-cast smokejack.

All of these items were packed in a routine 1952-style corrugated outfit box.

Excellent	Like New	Scarcity
400	700	4

1952

2177WS

Values for each condition are in U.S. dollars. | **Scarity** = Scale from 1-8 with 8 being the hardest to find.

2183WS, 2187WS

2183WS Four-Car Freight $54.50 retail

Included: 726 2-8-4 Berkshire steam locomotive with operating headlight and smoke; 2046W streamlined whistle tender; 3464 operating boxcar; 6462 gondola; 6465 Sunoco double-dome tank car; 6457 illuminated SP-type caboose; eight OC curved and seven OS straight track; UCS remote control track set; CTC Lockon; bottle of SP smoke pellets; tube of lubricant; instruction booklet.

This outfit was the same as set 2179WS with the exception of a locomotive change. For this outfit, the 20-wheel steam turbine was replaced with the popular 2-8-4 Berkshire. Like the turbine, when the big Berkshire lost its Magne-traction, it reverted to its 1949 catalog number, in this case 726. Once again "RR" was stamped below the number on the cab side in most cases, though some engines could have been assembled with outdated 1949 cabs that were merely numbered 726. The locomotive was packed in a conventional tan box with a liner, which was dated "1952" below the manufacturer's crest. The locomotive was furnished with a 2046W Lionel Lines tender.

The rolling stock, including their boxes, was just as described earlier for set 2179WS. All the components came together in a typical 1952 outfit box.

Excellent	Like New	Scarcity
550	900	4

2187WS Five-Car Freight $62.50 retail

Included: 671 6-8-6 steam turbine locomotive with operating headlight and smoke; 2046WX streamlined whistle tender; 6462 gondola; 3472 operating milk car; 3469X automatic dumping ore car; 6456 Lehigh Valley hopper; 6457 illuminated SP-type caboose; eight OC curved and seven OS straight track; UCS remote control track set; CTC Lockon; bottle of SP smoke pellets; tube of lubricant; instruction booklet.

The steam turbine was also selected to head this set with two operating cars. The locomotive and tender in this set were identical to those in the 2179WS outfit listed earlier.

The 1952 3472 differed little from the 1951 edition, but came with bar end trucks. Also, beginning this year, Lionel included five milk cans in the milk car outfit. The 3469 ore car, as well as the balance of the rolling stock in this outfit, was equipped with bar end trucks as well. All the cars were packaged in OPS Traditional boxes, while the locomotive, tender and outfit itself were packaged as described in the 2179WS listing.

Excellent	Like New	Scarcity
500	850	5

2189WS Five-Car Transcontinental Fast Freight $69.50 retail

Included: 726 2-8-4 Berkshire steam locomotive with operating headlight and smoke; 2046W streamlined whistle tender; 3520 searchlight car; 3656 operating cattle car; 6462 gondola; 3461 automatic lumber car; 6457 illuminated SP-type caboose; eight OC curved and seven OS straight track; UCS remote control track set; CTC Lockon; bottle of SP smoke pellets; tube of lubricant; instruction booklet.

The Magne-traction-less 726RR with its accompanying 2046W tender had charge of this operating car-loaded freight outfit. With an operating cattle car, operating log dump car and operating searchlight car, this set offered the young engineer plenty to keep him occupied. The cattle car, with its nine black rubber cattle, came with a corral featuring yellow gates, and the log car transported a cargo of 7/16 x 4-5/8-inch stained birch logs.

The 3520 searchlight car was new for 1952. It was, in essence, an improved 6520. While the injection-molded generator of the 6520 was retained, the die-cast frame was modified to accommodate the 3520's new feature. Introduced on the 3520 was a vibrator-powered rotating mechanism for the searchlight. Along with the light, the mechanism was turned on and off with an uncoupling track-activated switch housed in the faux generator molding. A housing base assembly held a plastic searchlight housing. For the 3520 included in most of the 2189WS outfits, the base assembly had eight ventilation notches in the top and it was typically blackened as well, though a few of the eight-slit housings were cadmium-plated. Cars offered for separate sale, which were produced later in the year, typically were cadmium-plated and had only four slits.

The gondola and caboose were typical 1952 items riding on bar-end trucks, with the gondola lacking steps, but featuring brake wheels and a wooden barrel load.

All the rolling stock was packed in OPS Traditional boxes. The locomotive and tender, as well as their boxes, were just as described for outfit 2183WS. The outfit box was typical issue for 1952.

Excellent	Like New	Scarcity
600	1,000	5

2190W Four-Car Super Speedliner Passenger **$89.50 retail**

Included: 2343P/2343T Santa Fe A-A F-3 units; 2531 Silver Dawn observation, 2532 Silver Range Astra Dome; 2533 Silver Cloud Pullman and 2534 Silver Bluff Pullman extruded-aluminum passenger cars; eight OC curved and nine OS straight track; UCS remote control track set; CTC Lockon; tube of lubricant; instruction booklet.

One of the few sets that are still known by the name given to it by Lionel's marketing department is the Super Speedliner. The name was given to an outfit headed by a double-A pair of 2343 diesels towing four of Lionel's new extruded aluminum passenger cars. These cars, no doubt developed to compete with similar cars produced by Auburn, Ind.-based American Model Toys (AMT), apparently were rushed into production, as numerous variations exist in the first year's production.

These variations include wired and wireless interior lighting connections, as well as the method of attaching the cars' nameplates and those plates' decoration. While most collectors today prefer matched sets of cars, it is not certain that Lionel shipped the cars as matched sets. This is due to the vagaries of mass production, where outfit components—locomotives, cars, etc.—were stockpiled until all the components were complete. Then those components were packaged as a set. In a similar manner, subassemblies making up those components—such as trucks and pickups—were preassembled and staged for use on the assembly line. Once a car was completed, it was packaged in its OPS or Middle traditional box awaiting inclusion in a set, unseen.

It is understandable then how easily "mismatched" items were included in the same outfit. Once these trains became collectibles, owners tended to swap components to make "matching" trains, in reality often adding more confusion due to including boxes or items that don't date from 1952. One of the key areas of confusion is the box for the cars. Most of the 1952 cars came in OPS Traditional boxes, though it is possible some came in Middle Traditional boxes. All the passenger car boxes were lined and the cars were further wrapped in Lionel paper. The 2532 is handy in dating the boxes. To be correct for this outfit, the end of the box should read "Astra Dome," and all the other car boxes should be the same size as it.

The Santa Fe 2343 units had small black GM logo decals on their sides, which should not be confused with the large black GM logos created for the New York Central units and sometimes erroneously applied to Santa Fe units. The twin diesels featured the newly designed snap-in porthole lenses. The powered unit was packed in a conventional tan cardboard carton with a liner. The box vendor handily dated the box "1952"—a tremendous aid to hobbyists today. The non-powered unit, like the cars, came in a lined OPS Traditional box—though a Middle Traditional box is also possible.

The outfit box was typical for the period and is known to exist both with and without preprinted OPS pricing.

Excellent	Like New	Scarcity
1,800	3,000	3

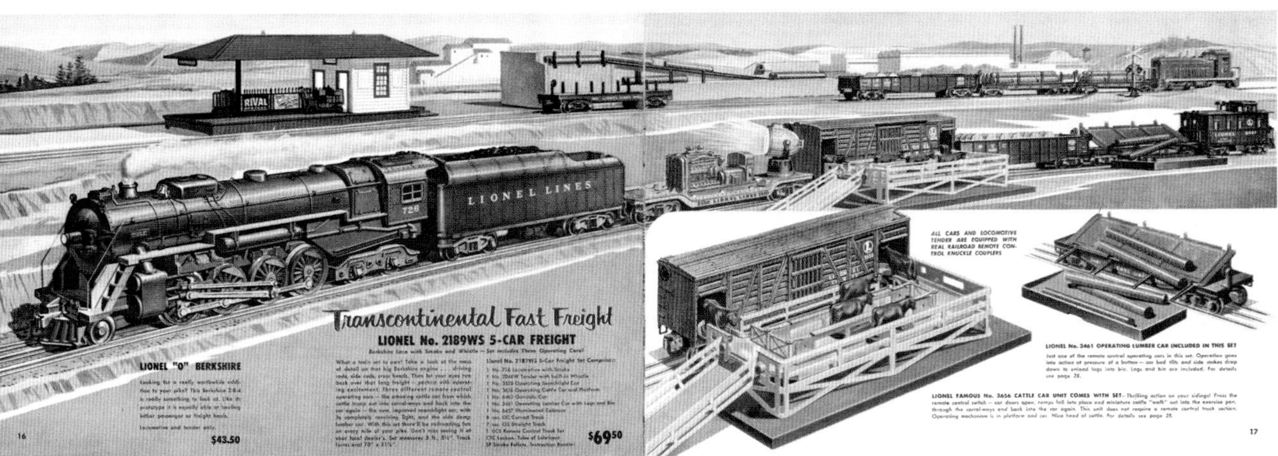

2189WS

2191W Four-Car Diesel Freight $70 retail

Included: 2343P/2343C/2343T Santa Fe A-B-A F3 units; 6462 gondola; 6456 Lehigh Valley hopper; 6656 stock car; 6457 illuminated SP-type caboose; eight OC curved and seven OS straight track; UCS remote control track set; CTC Lockon; tube of lubricant; instruction booklet.

The F-3 B, or booster unit—first produced by Lionel in 1950—was at last included in a set. The result of the addition of this unit, which Lionel cataloged as a C—for center—unit, was a three-unit locomotive stretching 40-inches. The downside of this is that the huge locomotive combination made the four-car freight train look somewhat ridiculous.

The four cars included were universally unremarkable, including a non-operating stock car, Lehigh Valley hopper and a 6462 gondola with wooden barrel load. All these cars lacked steps integral with their frames, but did include separately installed brake wheels. At the rear was a 6457 illuminated caboose with chemically blackened die-cast smokejack. All these cars rode on staple-end trucks.

The Santa Fe 2343 A-A units had small black GM logo decals on their sides, which should not be confused with the large black GM logos created for the New York Central units and sometimes erroneously applied to Santa Fe units. All three diesels featured the newly designed snap-in porthole lenses and screen-type rooftop vents. The powered unit was packed in a conventional tan cardboard carton with a liner. The box vendor handily dated the box "1952," a tremendous aid to hobbyists today. The non-powered A and B units, like the cars, came in lined OPS Traditional boxes, though a Middle Traditional box is also possible.

Excellent	Like New	Scarcity
1,500	2,500	4

2193W Four-Car Diesel Freight $70 retail

Included: 2344P/2344C/2344T New York Central A-B-A F3 units; 6462 gondola; 6456 Lehigh Valley hopper; 6656 stock car; 6457 illuminated SP-type caboose; eight OC curved and seven OS straight track; UCS remote control track set; CTC Lockon; tube of lubricant; instruction booklet.

Except for the substitution of New York Central diesels for Santa Fe units, this outfit was identical in content and packaging to the 2191W set described earlier. All three NYC diesels had screen-type roof vents and snap-in porthole lenses, as well as the new small-size GM decals.

Excellent	Like New	Scarcity
1,600	2,650	4

2193W

Chapter 10

1953

The year 1953 brought many new things from Lionel and the return of some old favorites. The improvement of the situation in Korea meant that strategic use of nickel had eased, hence Magne-traction returned to Lionel's steam locomotives.

The reintroduced steamers differed in detail from the earlier issues. Most visible were changes to markings and tenders. The previous heavy rubber-stamped silver numbering was replaced with white heat-stamped lettering. The turbine and Berkshire now were furnished with eight-wheel tenders, rather than the earlier 12-wheel models.

An expanded line of rolling stock was offered in 1953. Most notable of these were the new 6464-series boxcars. Responding to competitive pressure from American Model Toys—just as had been the case with extruded aluminum passenger cars—Lionel introduced these large boxcars, which in later years would wear increasingly colorful paint schemes. An operating version, numbered 3484, was introduced as well.

No less important to Lionel and collectors was another new car unveiled in 1953, the 6511 pipe car. While unassuming in its own right, the 11 1/8 inches long plastic flatcar was to become the foundation for Lionel's broadest range of freight cars during the postwar era.

Another indication of Lionel's shift from metal to plastic as a staple in rolling stock construction (the 6511's predecessor, the 6411, was die-cast) was the new 6415 triple-dome tank car. While all earlier tank cars had utilized metal frames, either stamped or die-cast, the new tank car had a molded plastic frame with only a small stamped sheet metal reinforcing channel.

With respect to motive power, a slight change was made in the body molding of the Alco diesel. Added was a small dome in the roof, which prevented warping. More significant was the creation of an all-new steam locomotive body style. The proven spur gear motor used in the 2046 powered the O-Gauge 685 and its 027 counterpart the 2055, with which it also shared pilot trucks. The totally new boiler and cab casting was loosely styled after 4-6-4 locomotives operated by the Santa Fe Railway. Paired with the new locomotive was a new tender, the 6026W.

Less noteworthy for us today, but important for the Lionel shareholders of the day, was the newly developed 6009 uncoupling section. Included in inexpensive 027 sets —the bulk of outfit sales—this section lacked the control rails needed to actuate most operating cars and uncouple older rolling stock. This modification resulted in significant savings in manufacturing costs—multiplied by the thousands of sets in which it was included, had a measurable effect on the company's profits.

Outfit boxes in 1953 were still two-tier with component boxes, but the graphics were revised again. The preprinted box label featured a red frame with blue printing and a large circle-L logo on its sides. Retail pricing was preprinted on the ends.

In 1953, orange returned to Lionel's outfit boxes in the form of an orange border around the labeling information and the distinctive circle-L logo. This type of box continued to be used through 1955.

Middle Traditional boxes were the norm for components of 1953 outfits, with only a few having liners.

First introduced in late 1951, the bar-end truck continued to be used on most rolling stock during 1953.

The 6066T, new in 1953, used the same basic body molding as did the 2466 and 6466 tenders, but was most often unpainted. The lettering was also a different style and typeface than that used by the whistle-equipped tenders.

027-Gauge

1464W 027 Diesel Three-Car Pullman $66.50 retail

Included: 2033 silver Union Pacific Alco A-A units; 2421 Maplewood Pullman, 2422 Chatham Pullman and 2423 Hillside observation with silver-and-silver paint scheme; eight 1013 curved and five 1018 straight track; 6019 remote control track set; 1033 90-watt transformer; CTC Lockon; tube of lubricant; instruction booklet.

Outfit 1464W was offered for the fourth time in 1953, essentially unchanged from the 1952 version. In fact, some collectors believe that early 1953 shipments were made with surplus 1952 packaging. However, some sets have surfaced in boxes of the 1953 style.

Excellent	Like New	Scarcity
700	1,600	3

1467W Four-Car Freight $57.50 retail

Included: 2032 Erie Alco A-A units; 6456 Lehigh Valley hopper; 6656 stock car; 6465 Sunoco double-dome tank car; 6357 illuminated SP-type caboose; eight 1013 curved and five 1018 straight track; 6019 remote control track set; 1033 90-watt transformer; CTC Lockon; tube of lubricant; instruction booklet.

The second 1952 set duplicated in 1953 was the Erie freight set. New style component and outfit boxes distinguish the newer production. Internally, as was the case with the 1464W, the new style Alco body was featured in 1953 production.

Excellent	Like New	Scarcity
250	600	6

1953

1500 027 Three-Car Freight $19.95 retail

Included: 1130 2-4-2 steam locomotive with operating headlight; 6066T early coal tender; 6034 Baby Ruth boxcar; 6032 gondola; 6037 SP-type caboose; eight 1013 straight and one 1018 straight track; 6009 uncoupling section; 1012 35-watt transformer; Lockon; lubricant; instruction booklet.

At $19.95 retail, this was the least expensive set Lionel cataloged in 1953. Not surprisingly, the Scout heritage of this outfit is readily apparent. Not only was the style of cars indicative of their predecessors, but also the trucks themselves were taken directly from the Scout line, albeit with magnetic rather than Scout couplers.

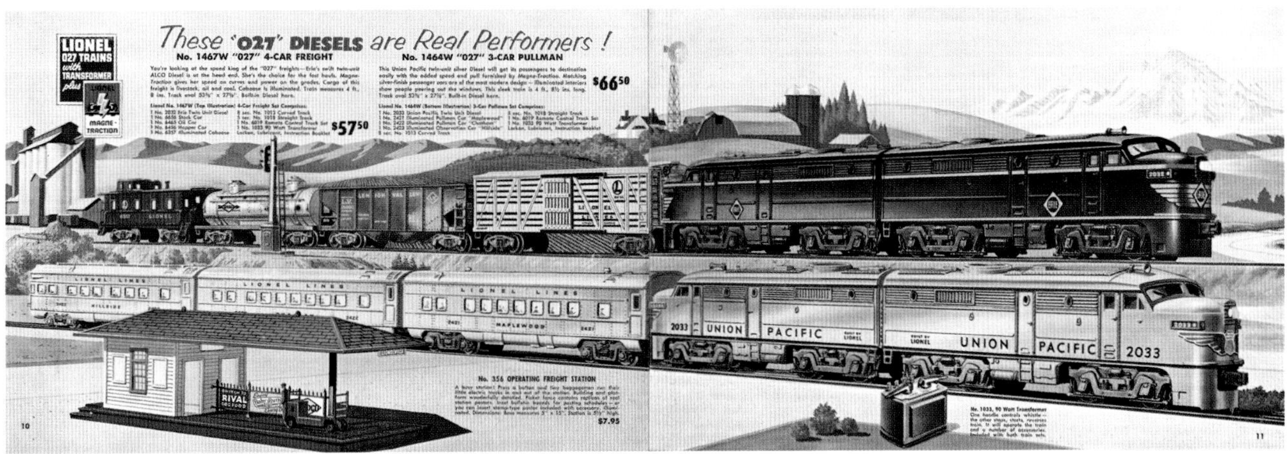

1467W, 1464W

The standard locomotive for this outfit was a plastic-bodied 1130, however the very earliest of these locomotives were manufactured using die-castings of the type produced for the 2034. Whether plastic or die-cast, the locomotives in this set were stamped 1130, with the rare die-cast version adding a considerable premium.

The 6066T tender, boxcar and gondola were all run of the mill items. There were, however, variations in the caboose production. A few were molded in red as shown in the catalog, but the bulk was molded in assorted shades of Tuscan plastic.

Middle Traditional boxes were used for all the components of this outfit, with only the locomotive box being equipped with a liner. Outfit boxes are known to exist in two types, some being packaged in the new 1953-style box, while others came in a box styled similarly to the 1950-type set box.

Even today, Lionel's basic starter outfits are produced with an early run for retailers to carry through the year and a larger, later run for the Christmas season, so two styles of packaging for this outfit is not surprising.

Excellent	Like New	Scarcity
100	150	1

1501S 027 Three-Car Freight $24.95 retail

Included: 2026 2-6-4 steam locomotive with operating headlight and smoke; 6066T early coal tender; 6032 gondola; 6035 Sunoco tank car; 6037 SP-type caboose; eight 1013 straight and three 1018 straight track; 6009 uncoupling section; 1043 50-watt transformer; Lockon; bottle of SP smoke pellets; lubricant; instruction booklet.

Given Lionel's promotion of Magne-traction and the introduction of the 2037, which was equipped with the exalted feature, it is somewhat surprising to see the Magne-traction-free 2026 appear in a 1953 set.

However, because this was a lower-end outfit, it was likely produced very early in 1953—perhaps Alnico magnets were not yet available or at least Lionel did not anticipate the material being available early in the year—leading to the decision to continue 2026 production. It is possible that the locomotives were unintentional surplus 1952 production, but given the company's production cycles and sales, this is unlikely.

The freight cars were of the style created for use in the earlier Scout line, and all the components, including the tender, rode on Scout-type trucks equipped with magnetic couplers.

The new-for-1953 style outfit box was used for this set and all the components came in Middle Traditional boxes. Only the locomotive box was furnished with a liner.

Excellent	Like New	Scarcity
125	200	2

1502WS Three-Car Pullman $57.50 retail

Included: 2055 4-6-4 steam locomotive with operating headlight, smoke and Magne-traction; 2046W streamlined whistle tender; 2421 Maplewood Pullman, 2422 Chatham Pullman and 2423 Hillside observation in silver-with-silver-roof color scheme; eight 1013 straight and five 1018 straight track; 6019 Remote Control Track Set; 1033 90-watt transformer; bottle of SP smoke pellets; Lockon; lubricant; instruction booklet.

The 027 steam passenger outfits for 1953 was powered by a newly designed steam locomotive. The die-cast steamer was styled after the six Hudsons of Santa Fe Railway's 3460-class. The 3460 was equipped with a blue-painted streamlined shroud (similar to that used by Norfolk and Western Class "J" 4-8-4 locomotives), but this was a feature unique to that engine. The remaining locomotives of the series were not streamlined.

Lionel's replica was based on the non-streamlined version, and featured a unitized boiler, cab and steam-chest casting. Its design permitted service technicians to remove only four screws to completely separate the running gear as an assembly from the locomotive body. The O-Gauge 685, also produced in 1953, as well as the succeeding 665 and 2065 locomotives also used the same casting.

The passenger cars were the same as those included in the 1952-53 edition of outfit 1464W and made their final appearance in this set. Because these cars were available in other sets as well as for separate sale, as was the locomotive, it is the outfit box that "makes" this set valuable.

The outfit box was the new 1953-style and inside all the components were packaged in Middle Traditional boxes. The locomotive and tender boxes were furnished with liners.

Excellent	Like New	Scarcity
675	1,100	5

1503WS Four-car Freight $39.95 retail

Included: 2055 4-6-4 steam locomotive with operating headlight, smoke and Magne-traction; 6026W square whistle tender; 6462 gondola; 6456 Lehigh Valley hopper; 6465 Sunoco double-dome tank car; 6257 SP-type caboose; eight 1013 straight and three 1018 straight track; 6019 Remote Control Track Set; 1033 90-watt transformer; bottle of SP smoke pellets; Lockon; lubricant; instruction booklet.

The new 2055 steam locomotive, described with outfit 1502WS, was equipped with an equally new tender for inclusion in this set. The new tender, numbered 6026W was of modern, no-nonsense design and housed Lionel's standard whistle equipment. The tender, as well as the locomotive, were packaged in Middle Traditional boxes with liners.

Outfit 1503WS was the first to include Lionel's new 6026W whistle tender. This basic style of tender would go on to be assigned a variety of numbers and would remain a part of the product line through the end of the postwar era.

The freight cars included in the set were nondescript and packed in unlined Middle Classic boxes. The outfit box itself was the 1953-style with the circled-L logo.

Excellent	Like New	Scarcity
300	500	2

1505WS Four-car Freight $49.95 retail

Included: 2046 4-6-4 steam locomotive with operating headlight, smoke and Magne-traction; 2046W streamlined whistle tender; 6464-1 Western Pacific boxcar; 6462 gondola; 6415 Sunoco three-dome tank car; 6357 illuminated SP-type caboose; eight 1013 straight and five 1018 straight track; 6019 Remote Control Track Set; 1033 90-watt transformer; bottle of SP smoke pellets; Lockon; lubricant; instruction booklet.

American Model Toys' line of colorful, scale-sized boxcars was making inroads into a marketplace traditionally dominated by Lionel. Lionel's response was to develop its own large boxcar style, known as the 6464-series, which first appeared in this outfit.

As included in this outfit, the 6464 was painted silver and wore the markings of Western Pacific. While the bulk of these cars were marked in blue, some of the earliest instead had red heat-stamped markings—today a scarce variation.

A second new car design was also included in the outfit: the 6415 triple-dome tank car. Like the previously standard 6465, the 6415 wore the "Sunoco" herald of the Sun Oil Co. The earliest, and most desirable, versions of this car did not have "6415" rubber stamped on the side of the tank.

1505WS

After an Alnico shortage caused discontinuation in 1952, the 2046 returned in 1953 to head this set. The 1951 model can be distinguished from the 1953 version by the silver rubber-stamped numbers on the former, versus the white heat-stamped numbers of the latter.

The locomotive was packed in a 1953-dated conventional corrugated carton with a liner. The other components were packaged in Middle Traditional boxes and all these items were then placed in the new-for-1953 circled-L set box.

Excellent	Like New	Scarcity
400	850	4

1507WS Five-Car Freight $65 retail

Included: 2046 4-6-4 steam locomotive with operating headlight, smoke and Magne-traction; 2046W streamlined whistle tender; 6415 Sunoco three-dome tank car; 6462 gondola; 3472 operating milk car; 6468 Baltimore & Ohio double-door automobile car; 6357 illuminated SP-type caboose; eight 1013 straight and five 1018 straight track; 6019 Remote Control Track Set; 1033 90-watt transformer; Lockon; bottle of SP smoke pellets; lubricant; instruction booklet.

With the 2046 back in the line, Lionel chose to head three freight outfits with the white-numbered locomotives. The second of these, the 1507WS, was also the second set to include the new 6415 triple-dome tank car. An additional new-for-1953 car included in the set was the blue 6468 Baltimore and Ohio automobile boxcar. The 6468 was similar in size and style to the new 6464 boxcar but had two doors per side rather than one.

Adding action to the outfit was the ever-popular automatic milk car. In this case, the car was the 3472, with plastic doors and bar-end trucks. This would be the final appearance of the 3472 in an outfit. The gondola and caboose were normal production with bar-end trucks.

The locomotive was packed in a 1953-dated conventional corrugated carton with a liner. The other components were packaged in Middle Traditional boxes and all these items were then placed in the new-for-1953 circled-L set box.

Excellent	Like New	Scarcity
425	900	4

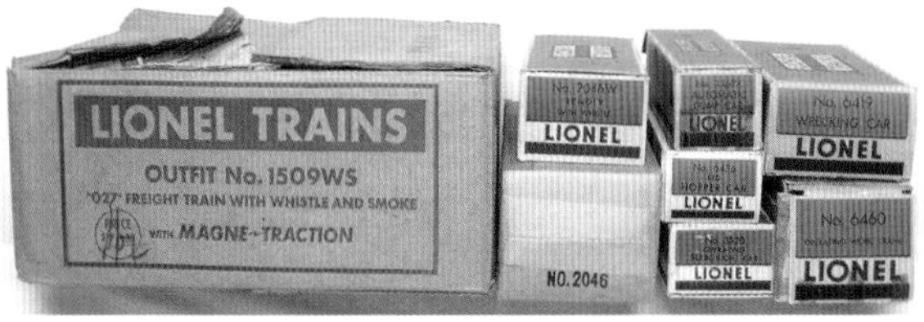

1509WS Five-Car Freight $70 retail

Contents: 2046 4-6-4 steam locomotive with operating headlight, smoke and Magne-traction; 2046W streamlined whistle tender; 6460 crane; 3469 automatic dumping ore car; 6456 Lehigh Valley hopper; 3520 searchlight car; 6419 work caboose; eight 1013 straight and five 1018 straight track; 6019 Remote Control Track Set; 1033 90-watt transformer; Lockon; bottle of SP smoke pellets; lubricant; instruction booklet.

This action-packed work train was the third outfit to be headed by the white heat-stamped numbered 2046 in 1953; behind the locomotive and tender were operating crane, searchlight and ore dump cars. The crane, dump and hopper cars were all black, while the searchlight car naturally had an orange generator. The work caboose featured a tall-blackened smokejack, which, like the rest of the rolling stock, rode on bar-end trucks.

The outfit box was the new circled-L type. The engine was packed in a Standard carton, dated to 1953, with a protective liner; the tender, also protected by a liner, and rolling stock came in Middle Traditional boxes.

Excellent	Like New	Scarcity
450	800	3

1511S Four-Car Freight $32.95 retail

Included: 2037 2-6-4 steam locomotive with operating headlight, smoke and Magne-traction; 6066T early coal tender; 6032 gondola; 3474 operating Western Pacific boxcar; 6035 Sunoco tank car; 6037 SP-type caboose; eight 1013 straight and three 1018 straight track; 6019 Remote Control Track Set;

1043 50-watt transformer; Lockon; bottle of SP smoke pellets; lubricant; instruction booklet.

The 2037 was a natural evolution of the 2026-2036 series. It used the same type of boiler/cab casting as the 2036, but included both smoke and Magne-traction. While the bulk of the locomotives were marked with heat-stamped lettering, rubber stamping numbered the early production units.

The locomotive was supplied with a 6066T rather plain non-whistling tender. The tender, as well as the gondola, tank car and caboose, were equipped with Scout-type trucks and magnetic couplers.

Opposite of this was the 3474 operating boxcar with bar-end trucks, which just the previous year had been the top of the line operating boxcar. The 1953 production of this car, which is much harder to find than the 1952 model, can be distinguished by its 1-3/16-inch height. The 1952 edition had a 1-5/16-inch figure aboard.

All the components of the outfit were packed in Middle Traditional boxes and the locomotive box was supplied with a liner. The outfit box was the new-for-1953 new circled-L type.

Excellent	Like New	Scarcity
300	500	4

O-Gauge

2190W Four-Car Super Speedliner Passenger
$89.50 retail

Included: 2353P/2353T Santa Fe A-A F-3 units; 2351 Silver Dawn observation, 2532 Silver Range Astra Dome, 2533 Silver Cloud Pullman and 2534 Silver Bluff Pullman extruded-aluminum passenger cars; eight OC curved and nine OS straight track; UCS Remote Control Track Set; Lockon; lubricant; instruction booklet.

The Super Speedliner outfit was continued in 1953, although with some changes. However, more significant was the new motive power at the front of the passenger consist. The most significant change in the outfit from the previous year's offering was the new motive power heading up the passenger consist.

Though to the consumer the change may have been hardly noticeable, the 1953 edition was powered by the 2353 Santa Fe A-A, which replaced the earlier, more detailed 2343 pair. The powered unit was packed in a conventional tan corrugated cardboard carton with a liner. The dummy or "T" unit, as well as each passenger car, was packed in its own Middle Traditional box with a liner.

Though collectors prefer matched sets of cars, when leaving the factory the outfits could contain an assortment of cars with glued- or riveted-on nameplates. Various methods of nameplate attachment were used and, once packaged, the cars' variations could not be distinguished. Lionel factory workers pulled cars from stock and indiscriminately packaged sets.

Excellent	Like New	Scarcity
1,800	3,000	3

The 685 was produced only in 1953, and the only set that included the new locomotive was the 2201WS. While some of these engines had rubber-stamped numbering, most, like this one, had heat-stamped numbers

2201WS Four-Car Freight $39.95 retail

Included: 685 4-6-4 steam locomotive with operating headlight, smoke and Magne-traction; 6026W square whistle tender; 6464-50 Minneapolis & St. Louis boxcar; 6462 gondola; 6465 Sunoco double-dome tank car; 6357 illuminated SP-type caboose; eight OC curved and five OS straight track; UCS Remote Control Track Set; bottle of SP smoke pellets; Lockon; lubricant; instruction booklet.

Lionel's new Santa Fe-style Hudson, cataloged as 2055 in 027, was offered in O-Gauge as well. Built without feedwater heater in O-Gauge only in 1953, it was assigned catalog number 685. Not only was the 685 a one-year only locomotive, this was the only outfit that included it.

The locomotive was paired with the new 6026W tender, which, like the locomotive, was packed in a Middle Traditional box with a liner.

The caboose, gondola and Sunoco tank car were all unremarkable, however the set did include one of the new 6464 boxcars. Though shown in the catalog as green, the 6464-50 M & St. L boxcar included in the outfit was always Tuscan.

The boxcar, as well as the rest of the rolling stock, rode on bar-end trucks and was boxed in Middle Traditional packaging.

Excellent	Like New	Scarcity
750	1,200	5

2203WS Four-car Freight $49.95 retail

Included: 681 6-8-6 steam turbine locomotive with operating headlight, smoke and Magne-traction; 2046WX streamlined whistle tender; 6464-25 Great Northern boxcar; 3520 searchlight car; 6415 Sunoco three-dome tank car; 6417 Pennsylvania porthole caboose; eight OC curved and five OS straight track; UCS Remote Control Track Set; Lockon; bottle of SP smoke pellets; lubricant; instruction booklet.

When Alnico magnet material became available in quantity again, Magne-traction returned to the 20-wheel steam turbine, and its number reverted to 681. However, the 1953 681 can be distinguished from the 1950-51 issue by virtue of its white heat-stamped numbers. The earlier models had been marked with heavy silver rubber-stamping. No less noticeable was the locomotive's pairing with the eight-wheel 2046WX "PENNSYLVANIA" tender, rather than the previously used 12-wheel 2671W.

Behind the locomotive and tender were four more cars, only one of which—the searchlight—was a carryover from previous years. The boxcar, tank car and caboose were all new-for-1953 items. The 6464-25 Great Northern boxcar provided a splash of orange color to the train, while a shiny new 6415 Sunoco tank car added sparkle. Bringing up the rear of the train was the newly designed replica of the Pennsylvania N5c caboose, known as a "cabin car" in Pennsylvania Railroad parlance. Though Lionel through the years has produced this body style in markings of several railroads, both real and fictitious. In reality only the Pennsylvania and its successor roads operated the 200 N5c the Pennsy produced in its own shops during 1942.

The new caboose, like the rest of the outfit components, was packed in a Middle Traditional box. Only the locomotive and tender boxes benefited from the presence of liners. All components were then packed in the new-style circle L set box.

Excellent	Like New	Scarcity
725	1,200	4

2205WS Five-car Freight $59.75 retail

Included: 736 2-8-4 Berkshire steam locomotive with operating headlight, smoke and Magne-traction; 2046W streamlined whistle tender; 3484 operating Pennsylvania boxcar; 6415 Sunoco three-dome tank car; 6468 Baltimore & Ohio double-door automobile car; 6456 Lehigh Valley hopper; 6417 Pennsylvania porthole caboose; eight OC curved and seven OS straight track; UCS Remote Control Track Set; bottle of SP smoke pellets; Lockon; lubricant; instruction booklet.

Like the O-Gauge turbine, the Berkshire began in 1946 without Magne-traction, gained this feature—and a new number—in 1950, then lost it during the height of the

Korean War buildup of 1952, with a number change to reflect this modification as well. In 1953, however, Magne-traction returned, as did the 736 product number. A die-cast framed trailing truck continued to be used.

Again paralleling the turbine, the Berkshire's number, rubber stamped in silver through 1952, was now heat stamped in white. Likewise, its 12-wheel tender had become a thing of the past during the Magne-traction-less 1952 season and did not return with the 1953 reversion to the 736 product number. The streamlined whistle-equipped tender was lettered "LIONEL LINES," and rode on bar-end trucks.

Though the locomotive was in essence an "old standard," all the rolling stock behind it, except the black Lehigh Valley hopper car, was new. Though the outfit did not include one of the new 6464 boxcars, it did include two of the series' sister cars: the 6468 Baltimore and Ohio double door automobile boxcar and the 3484 Pennsylvania operating boxcar.

Also included was the attractive new three-dome Sunoco tank car and 6417 Pennsylvania N5c porthole caboose. All rolling stock rode on bar-end trucks with magnetic couplers, without manual uncoupling tabs.

The heavy Berkshire was packed in a conventional tan corrugated carton with a liner, while the rest of the outfit came in Middle Traditional boxes. Of these, only the tender box had a liner. The outfit box was the new circle-L style.

Excellent	Like New	Scarcity
700	1,150	4

2207W Triple Diesel Freight **$70 retail**

Included: 2353P/2343C/2353T Santa Fe A-B-A F-3 units; 6462 gondola; 3484 operating Pennsylvania boxcar; 6415 Sunoco three-dome tank car; 6417 Pennsylvania porthole caboose; eight OC curved and seven OS straight track; UCS Remote Control Track Set; Lockon; lubricant; instruction booklet.

Like 1952's 2191W outfit, the 2207W included a three-unit Santa Fe F-3 diesel set. The booster unit, termed the "C" for center by Lionel, or "B" for booster by the actual railroad industry, continued to be assigned catalog number 2343C. However, the screen-type roof vents used previously were supplanted with louver-type vents. Lionel did this as a money saving measure, but it had the benefit of matching the redesigned A-units, the 2353P and T.

These powered and trailer units not only lacked the screen roof vents of the 2333 and 2343 series, but also were shorn of their separately installed front grab railings. Internally, the operating horn was moved from the powered unit to the dummy, or trailer, unit. The 2353P powered unit was packaged in a conventional tan corrugated box bearing a 1953 date. The center and dummy units came in Middle Traditional boxes with liners.

Middle Traditional boxes were used for the rolling stock as well. This rolling stock consisted of the new 3484 Pennsylvania operating boxcar, the new 6415 Sunoco triple-dome tanker, the new 6417 Pennsylvania N5c porthole caboose and the long-running 6462 New York Central gondola. Lionel's persistent mismatching of locomotive and caboose road names, as evidenced here, has been a source of consternation for both operators and collectors for decades.

Nevertheless, this overpowered set was handsome and appealing both in the catalog and on the shelf. The outfit components were packed in the new circle-L set carton.

Excellent	Like New	Scarcity
1,500	2,500	4

2209W Triple Diesel Freight **$70 retail**

Included: 2354P/2344C/2354T New York Central A-B-A F-3 units; 6462 gondola; 3484 operating Pennsylvania boxcar; 6415 Sunoco three-dome tank car; 6417 Pennsylvania porthole caboose; eight OC curved and seven OS straight track; UCS Remote Control Track Set; Lockon; lubricant; instruction booklet.

Identical to outfit 2207W except for motive power, this New York Central set provided an alternative to the Santa Fe for Eastern railroad fans.

Excellent	Like New	Scarcity
1,550	2,600	4

2211WS Four-Car Freight $62.50 retail

Included: 681 6-8-6 steam turbine locomotive with operating headlight, smoke and Magne-traction; 2046WX streamlined whistle tender; 3656 operating cattle car; 6464-75 Rock Island boxcar; 3461 automatic lumber car; 6417 Pennsylvania porthole caboose; eight OC curved and five OS straight track; UCS Remote Control Track Set; bottle of SP smoke pellets; Lockon; lubricant; instruction booklet.

The revived 681 with white heat-stamped lettering and eight-wheel "PENNSYLVANIA" tender was chosen to lead this four-car outfit. Included in the freight consist was one of the new 6464 boxcars—in this case the green 75 Rock Island version—and two operating cars, the 3461 log car and 3656 cattle car, as well as the 6417 illuminated caboose.

In contrast to outfits 2207W and 2209W, at least with this outfit the markings of the caboose matched not only the lettering on the tender, but also the prototype of the locomotive.

The 3656 was making its final appearance in an outfit with this set. Some of the cars produced in 1953 had a modified frame stamping to better accommodate the car's wiring. The 3461 lumber car was loaded with five 4-5/8-inch long, 7/16-inch diameter stained logs. It was packed, without its receiving bin, in a Middle Traditional box.

Middle Traditional boxes were used for all the components of this set, with the stock car outfit, locomotive and tender boxes having liners. The set box was the new circle-L type.

Excellent	Like New	Scarcity
700	1,200	5

The gold-lettered green 6464-75 Rock Island boxcar debuted in the 1953 outfit 2211WS.

2213WS Five-Car Freight $70 retail

Included: 736 2-8-4 Berkshire steam locomotive with operating headlight, smoke and Magne-traction; 2046W streamlined whistle tender; 6460 crane; 3520 searchlight car; 3469 automatic dumping car; 3461 automatic lumber car; 6419 work caboose, eight OC curved and seven OS straight track; UCS Remote Control Track Set; bottle of SP smoke pellets; Lockon; lubricant; instruction booklet.

The returning 736 Berkshire was placed in charge of the top of the line steam outfit for 1953, a position the popular 2-8-4 would hold for much of the postwar era. The steamer had die-cast framed trailing truck, and its numbers were applied with white heat stamping. The locomotive was paired with a "LIONEL LINES" 2046W eight-wheeled tender with whistle. The tender was packaged in a Middle Traditional box, while the locomotive used a conventional tan corrugated cardboard carton—both were furnished with liners.

The array of cars included four operating cars: the black log and coal dump cars, illuminated and rotating 3520 searchlight car, and the black 6460 crane car—the later being manually operated. Both the log and ore cars were the "X" versions, with their receiving bins being packed loose in the outfit box, rather than in their Middle Traditional component boxes. All the rolling stock in this set rode on bar-end trucks with magnetic couplers.

The searchlight car, as well as the 6419 die-cast framed work caboose, was also packed in Middle Traditional boxes.

Excellent	Like New	Scarcity
575	975	4

Chapter 11

1954

Although Lionel offered a dizzying array of new paint schemes on the boxcars and diesels offered in sets this year, there were few truly new items introduced.

One of these was the superb replica of a Fairbanks-Morse H24-66 Trainmaster diesel locomotive. This was to be the largest single-unit diesel offered in the postwar era, and all the versions of this loco are desirable collector's items.

New rolling stock joined the ranks with the introduction of a bi-level stock car; scale-proportioned refrigerator car, a covered hopper and an operating barrel unloading gondola.

Added to the Lionel Lines passenger fleet was the 2530 baggage car, made of extruded aluminum.

The 2046 4-6-4 steam locomotive was offered as an O-Gauge item as well in 1954. For this duty, it was given a new number—646. A new boiler front incorporating a protruding feedwater heater was installed on the new-for-1953 Santa Fe-type Hudson. The resulting "new" locomotives were numbered 665 and 2065 in O- and 027-Gauges respectively. The long-running Pennsylvania S-2 steam turbine got a facelift—a small linkage was added to the front drive wheel, an oversized rendering of a lubrication link on the actual engine, and at the same time a white stripe was added to the side of the running board. The locomotive was given a new number—682. Ironically, the only actual S-2 in the world, the Pennsy's 6200, had been scrapped in May 1953.

Related to steam locomotives, but far from sensational, was Lionel's introduction of a new tender for use with budget-priced locomotives. The 1130T was a non-whistling, miniaturized version of the 2046W, which became a staple of the Scout-like 2-4-2 locos through the 1960s, even occasionally being paired with some larger 2-6-4 steamers.

New road names were introduced on F-3 diesels and, for the first time, a single-motored unit was offered, paired not with a dummy A, but a dummy B-unit. The pairing was itself also a first.

A new tender was introduced in 1954 for inclusion in economy-priced outfits, the 1130T. Though styled along the same lines as the 2046W and earlier 2671W tenders, the 1130T was much smaller and lacked a whistle mechanism.

The "Circle-L" outfit box, introduced in 1953, continued to be used in 1954.

The trucks used on the plastic streamlined passenger cars were extensively revised in 1954. Coil couplers were eliminated, replaced instead with a magnetic coupler with articulated linkage.

On an actual steam locomotive, heat from the locomotive exhaust is used to warm the water being introduced into the firebox, increasing the efficiency of the locomotive. In Lionel's case, the only practical benefit (as opposed to aesthetics) was that the heavy die-cast feedwater heater casting would survive a derailment better than the somewhat fragile marker lights protruding above the tops of other boiler fronts.

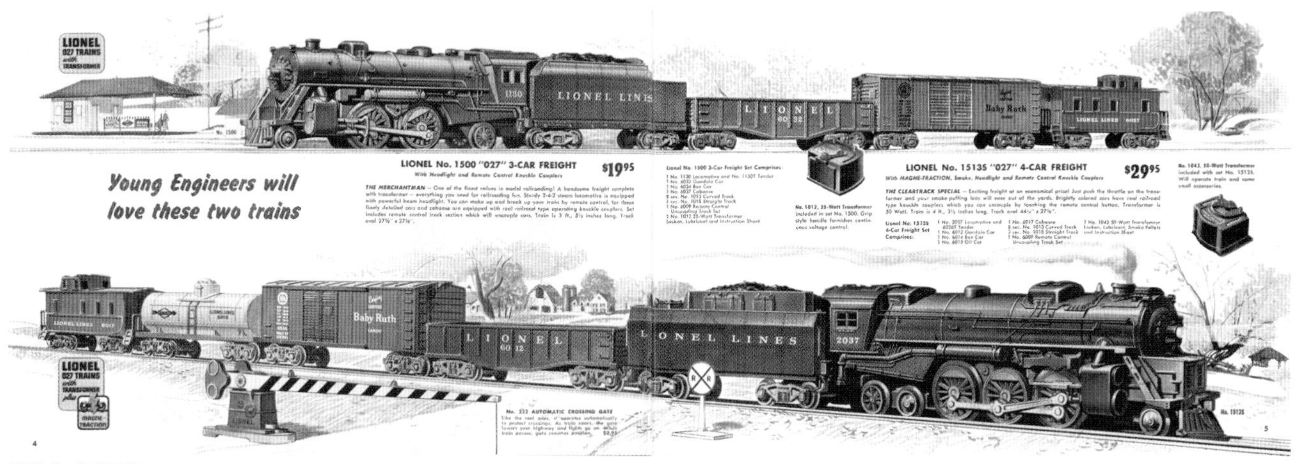

1500, 1513S

027-Gauge

1500 The Merchant Man **$19.95 retail**

Included: 1130 2-4-2 steam locomotive with operating headlight; 1130T small streamlined tender; 6034 Baby Ruth boxcar; 6032 gondola; 6037 SP-type caboose; eight 1013 curved and one 1018 straight track; 6009 uncoupling section; 1012 35-watt transformer; Lockon; lubricant; instruction booklet.

Though the catalog number was a carry over, the set contents differed from the previous year's set. Simultaneously, this outfit introduced something new—the 1130T tender—and was the end of something old—the final appearance of Scout-type trucks.

The 1130 locomotive included in the outfit was the standard plastic-bodied locomotive, now paired with the new 1130T tender. This tender was a smaller version of the 2046W-style tender, lacking a whistle and in this case riding on Scout-type trucks. The remainder of the outfit was unchanged from the 1953 edition, even including the component and outfit packaging.

Excellent	Like New	Scarcity
100	150	1

1503WS The Overlander **$39.95 retail**

Included: 2055 4-6-4 steam locomotive with operating headlight, smoke and Magne-traction; 6026W square whistle tender; 6462 gondola; 6456 Lehigh Valley hopper; 6465 Sunoco double-dome tank car; 6257 SP-type caboose; eight 1013 straight and three 1018 straight track; 6019 Remote Control Track Set; 1033 90-watt transformer; bottle of SP smoke pellets; Lockon; lubricant; instruction booklet.

Another of the 1953 outfits repeated in 1954 was outfit 1503WS. However, the new addition was a bit more colorful, with the black gondola and hopper cars of the previous year giving way to green and maroon versions respectively. The "N" of "NYC" was in the second panel of the car from the end. The car was loaded with six small stained barrels, originally designed for the 362 barrel loader.

Strangely, the 1954 gondola box was longer than the 1953 version, reverting to its 1949-50 size.

The markings of the 6257 changed, with a Lionel "L" logo inside a double circle replacing the "SP" initials previously used. This car had a brake wheel installed outside its platform.

Excellent	Like New	Scarcity
300	500	2

1513S Clear Track Special **$29.95 retail**

Included: 2037 2-6-4 steam locomotive with operating headlight, smoke and Magne-traction; 6026T square tender; 6012 gondola; 6014 Baby Ruth boxcar; 6015 Sunoco single-dome tank car; 6017 SP-type caboose; eight 1013 curved and three 1018 straight track; 6009 uncoupling section; 1043 50-watt transformer.

The locomotive included in this outfit is of distinctly higher caliber than the freight cars behind it. The robust smoke and Magne-traction-equipped die-cast 2037 was paired with a non-whistling version of the 6026 tender for inclusion in this economical set.

All the rolling stock was descended from Scout category items and looked somewhat out of place with the relatively large steamer. The Baby Ruth boxcar was red and the 6012 gondola, as always, was black. The 6015 tank car is worthy of special mention, however. While most are unpainted yellow plastic, the very earliest had gray molded tanks that were painted yellow. Paint adhesion on these cars was problematic, making what would already have been a scarce variation particularly difficult to locate in collectible condition.

All the rolling stock rode on bar-end trucks with magnetic couplers and, like the locomotive and tender, was packaged in Middle Traditional boxes. The locomotive and tender boxes were lined, and the outfit box was the style introduced in 1953.

The painted version of the 6015 is a scarce collectible in itself, worth at least $150 alone. Most often included in outfit 1513S was the common, unpainted yellow 6015, which has a markedly different shade and value.

This outfit was also available in 1955. To distinguish the two years of production, one just has to examine the box for

The 6026 tender included in outfit 1513S was the non-whistling version, arguably harder to find than the version with the whistle installed.

the gondola car. The box in 1954 had a 6012-10 inner flap number, while the –10 number was used in 1955.

Excellent	Like New	Scarcity
175	300	1

1515WS All-State Freight $49.95 retail

Included: 2065 4-6-4 steam locomotive with operating headlight, smoke and Magne-traction; 2046W streamlined whistle tender; 6464-25 Great Northern boxcar; 6462 gondola; 6456-25 Lehigh Valley hopper; 6415 Sunoco three-dome tank car; 6357 illuminated SP-type caboose; eight 1013 curved and three 1018 straight track; 6019 track set; Lockon; lubricant; instruction booklet; 1033 90-watt transformer.

By adding a feedwater heater to the boiler front used on the small Hudson, Lionel created a new look for the locomotive—and, of course, assigned it a new product number. Thus, Lionel created the 2065 heading this outfit from the previous years' 2055.

In tow behind the revamped locomotive was an orange 6464-25 Great Northern boxcar, a 6462 gondola in its enlarged-for-1954 box and a gray 6456-25 Lehigh Valley hopper—a new color for 1954.

The triple-dome Sunoco tank car and 6357 illuminated caboose rounded out the rolling stock of this attractive outfit. All the trains were packed in Middle Traditional boxes, but

1513S

only the locomotive and tender boxes included liners. The outfit carton was the normal 1953-54 circle-L style.

Excellent	Like New	Scarcity
450	750	4

1516WS Skylark Three-car Passenger $59.95 retail

Included: 2065 4-6-4 steam locomotive with operating headlight, smoke and Magne-traction; 2046W streamlined whistle tender; 2432 Clifton Astra Dome, 2434 Newark Pullman and 2436 Summit observation; eight 1013 curved and five 1018 straight track; 6019 track set; Lockon; lubricant; instruction booklet; 1033 90-watt transformer.

The 1954 027 steam passenger outfit was comprised of the new 2065 steam locomotive (as described under outfit 1515WS) and three plastic-bodied streamlined passenger cars. The passenger cars, newly renumbered and marked in red, would ultimately be included in 10 outfits before they were discontinued.

However, the correct edition for inclusion in 1954 sets such as this had some unique features, at least with respect to their packaging. First of all, the stock numbers were printed on all sides of the individual Middle Traditional boxes, rather than only on the ends as in later years. These boxes are also slightly longer than later generations. Finally, the 2432 dome car box is labeled "Astra Dome," rather than the "Vista Dome" terminology used in 1955. To further identify 1954 production 2432 cars in this and other sets, one should examine the number stamped on the car. In 1954, the "2432" was positioned so that it was centered between the second and third windows from the non-vestibule end.

The 2065 in this set is most often the difficult one to locate silver rubber-stamped versions. Unlike earlier rubber-stamped steamers, the numbers on this car are small, almost the same size as the white heat stamping usually associated with this locomotive.

Because the components of the outfit are relatively common, many collectors and dealers have erroneously tried to improve sets by replacing boxes, often with later editions.

The locomotive and tender were packed in Middle Traditional boxes with liners, while the outfit carton itself was the 1953-54 circle-L style.

Excellent	Like New	Scarcity
950	1,725	5

The Texas Special F-3 A-B combination included in outfit 1517W was the first appearance of the famed diesel in other than an A-A combination, and the first time the locomotive came with only one motor.

1517W Texas Fast Freight $59.95 retail

Included: 2245P/2245C Texas Special A-B F-3 units; 6464-225 Southern Pacific boxcar; 6561 depressed-center flatcar with cable reels; 6462-25 gondola; 6427 Lionel Lines porthole caboose; eight 1013 curved and five 1018 straight track; 6019 track set; Lockon; lubricant; instruction booklet; 1033 90-watt transformer.

Lionel began offering its popular F-3 in the 027 line as well in O-Gauge beginning in 1954. This outfit was the first to be cataloged with the new 027-type locomotive. In order to hold costs down, in line with customers' expectations for 027, the die-cast chassis-equipped dummy A-unit used with O-Gauge units was replaced with the non-illuminated, plastic-framed dummy B-unit. Only one motor was installed in the powered A-unit and it was of the horizontal type.

The porthole caboose, in reality developed and used exclusively by the Pennsylvania Railroad, was now offered with a new number, 6427, and named "Lionel Lines."

The 6561 flatcar was laden with molded orange cable reels wrapped with un-insulated aluminum wire. The 6462 gondola in the outfit was the green –25 variation, while the boxcar was the overall black 6464-225 Southern Pacific.

Values for each condition are in U.S. dollars. | **Scarity** = Scale from 1-8 with 8 being the hardest to find.

The powered unit was packaged in a lined conventional corrugated carton, with bold "MISSOURI-KANSAS-TEXAS" lettering running along the side of the box. The remaining outfit components were packaged in Middle Traditional boxes. The outfit box was the preprinted circle-L box of 1953-54.

Excellent	Like New	Scarcity
1,000	1,550	6

1519WS Five-car Freight **$65 retail**

Included: 2065 4-6-4 steam locomotive with operating headlight, smoke and Magne-traction; 6026W square whistle tender; 6462-75 gondola; 3461X-25 automatic lumber car; 3482 operating milk car; 6356 stock car; 6427 Lionel Lines porthole caboose; eight 1013 curved and five 1018 straight track; 6019 track set; Lockon; lubricant; instruction booklet; 1033 90-watt transformer.

This outfit included two operating cars: the 3482 automatic milk and 3461-25 automatic lumber car. Both of these cars were 1954 revisions of earlier items. The familiar 3461 log dump had its drab black frame replaced with a colorful green one, warranting the —25 suffix to its product number. That suffix, along with the X designator, appeared on the component box. The car was packaged along with its cargo of five 4-5/8-inch-long stained birch logs in a Middle Traditional box. Its receiving bin was packed loose in the outfit box.

The milk car, a descendent of the 3462-3472 series, included several changes to simplify construction while improving operation and lowering costs. Perhaps as a sign of the rush to produce outfits, some of the earliest of the 3482 were erroneously marked with both 3472 and 3482 numbers.

The 6356 stock car included in the set was an all-new item. Replicating a bi-level stock car, the bright yellow car was substantially larger than Lionel's earlier stock car and was a fitting companion to the company's 6464 series boxcars.

The gondola included in this outfit is also unusual, in that it is painted pure red, and the "N" of "NYC" is stamped in the second panel. Its box, which is slightly longer than 1953 gondola boxes, is marked with a –75 suffix.

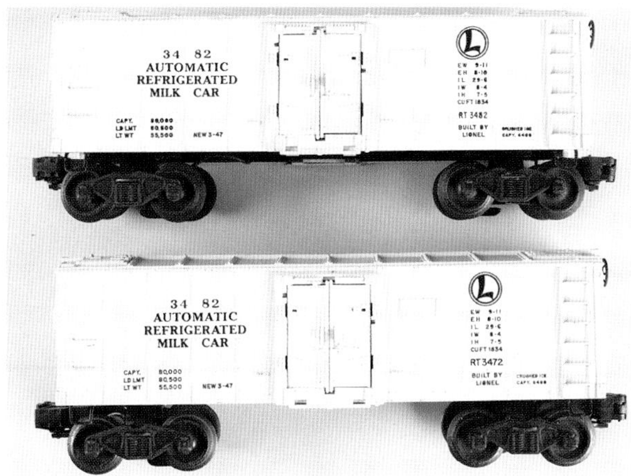

The dies used to mark the 3472 were modified for use making the new 3482. In the rush of production, someone failed to change the number on the bottom right of the car, resulting in the earliest cars being marked "3482" on the left of the door, and "3472" on the right of the door, as seen at bottom here.

The 6427 caboose, while new for the year, was typical production, as was the 2065 steam locomotive with 6026W tender. Both the tender and the caboose wore Lionel Lines markings, and all the rolling stock rolled on bar-end trucks with magnetic couplers.

Excellent	Like New	Scarcity
550	975	5

1520W Texas Special Three-Car Passenger $69.50 retail

Included: 2245P/2245C Texas Special A-B F-3 units; 2432 Clifton Astra Dome, 2435 Elizabeth Pullman and 2436 Summit observation in the new silver-with-red-letter color scheme; eight 1013 curved and five 1018 straight track; 6019 track set; Lockon; lubricant; instruction booklet; 1033 90-watt transformer.

This outfit combined the new-for-1954 single-motor Texas Special F-3 A-B diesel combo with the also-new-for-1954 red-lettered 2430-series passenger cars.

The diesel combination rode on trucks with silver side frames, and their bodies had clear portholes installed in both the A- and B-units. A horizontal motor powered the A-unit and came packed in a tan corrugated cardboard box, which was elaborately marked "No. 2245P MISSOURI-KANSAS-

TEXAS." The B-unit was packaged in a Middle Traditional box, and both the A- and B-unit boxes came with liners.

The passenger cars trailing behind the diesels were the red-lettered 2430-series new for 1954. Worthy of special mention was the inclusion in this set of the 2435 Pullman "Elizabeth"—a desirable car of the series. The stock numbers of all three passenger cars were printed on all sides of their individual Middle Traditional boxes, rather than only on the ends as in later years. The 1954 boxes are also slightly longer than those from later years. Finally, the 2432 dome car box is labeled "Astra Dome," rather than the "Vista Dome" terminology used in 1955. The 2432 dome cars built in 1954, and included in this and other sets, have the "2432" positioned such that it was centered between the second and third windows from the non-vestibule end.

Excellent	Like New	Scarcity
1,800	2,700	7

Outfit 1521WS included the sought-after black 3562 operating barrel car. Early production had the "conveyor" in the center of the car painted yellow to match the companion 362 accessory. Later cars had a black conveyor, which blended better with the black-painted plastic body.

1521WS **Five-car freight** **$69.50 retail**

Included: 2065 4-6-4 steam locomotive with operating headlight, smoke and Magne-traction; 2046W streamlined whistle tender; 6460 crane; 6561 depressed-center flatcar with cable reels; 3562 operating barrel car; 3620 searchlight car; 6419-25 work caboose; eight 1013 curved and five 1018 straight track; 6019 track set; Lockon; lubricant; instruction booklet; 1033 90-watt transformer.

The by-now-familiar 2065 steam locomotive, with accompanying 2046W Lionel Lines tender, was at the front of this set. The locomotive was followed by an array of top-quality rolling stock.

But for a single exception, all the rolling stock included in the outfit featured die-cast chassis and all rode on bar-end trucks with magnetic couplers. The black cab-equipped 6460 was, of course, an operating car—albeit requiring manual operation. The 3620 was a new-for-1954 version of the searchlight car. The on-off switch that had been present on the 3520 and 6520 was eliminated as an economy move. The bulk of the 3620 cars were equipped with gray molded nylon searchlight housings, although there is evidence that a few were produced with orange housings which were then painted gray. The simulated generator was always molded in orange plastic, with the 1954 version a paler color than that used in later years.

Like the 3620, the 6561 used a gray die-cast depressed center flatcar frame. An elastic band held in place two unpainted orange plastic cable reels, which were wrapped with bare aluminum wire.

The D.L. & W. work caboose with die-cast frame at the rear of the train was the single-coupler –25 version. Its Middle Traditional box bore the –25 marking, as well as the notation "For 027 track" on its end flaps.

The car within this set that attracts the most collector attention, however, is the 3562 operating barrel car. New for 1954, the car had a molded plastic body, which was painted black. Along the center of the car was a stamped sheet metal conveyor, or trough, which was originally painted yellow (the same color as used on the 362 barrel ramp) on these cars. But as production progressed, the color was changed to black.

1954

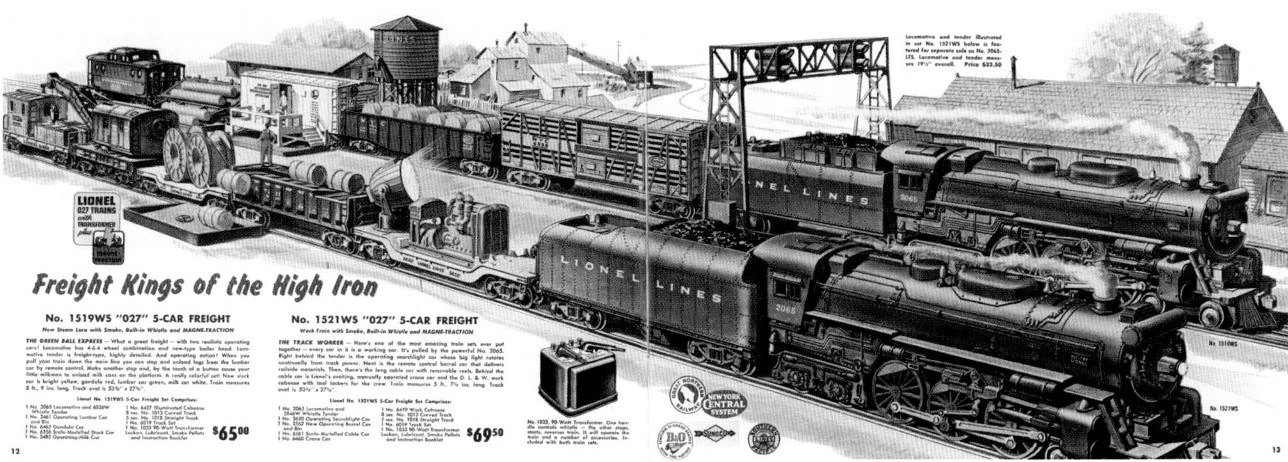

1521WS, 1519WS

The cargo for this car was six of the 362-78 wooden barrels. The black 3562 was cataloged only as a component of this outfit, accounting for its scarcity today.

All the rolling stock in the outfit, as well as the locomotive and tender, was packed in Middle Traditional boxes. The outfit box was the typical 1953-54 circle-L type.

Excellent	Like New	Scarcity
750	1,200	5

1523 Gandy Dancer Work Train **$49.95 retail**

Included: 6250 Seaboard NW-2 diesel switcher; 6511 pipe car; 6456-25 Lehigh Valley hopper; 6460-25 crane; 6419-25 work caboose; eight 1013 curved and five 1018 straight track; 6019 track set; Lockon; lubricant; instruction booklet; 1034 75-watt transformer.

The die-cast chassis-equipped switcher appeared in a new blue and orange paint scheme for this outfit, decorated with decaled "Seaboard" markings. In 1955, some of these locomotives had rubber-stamped "Seaboard" lettering. The Middle Traditional box of the locomotive came with a full wraparound corrugated liner.

At the other end of the train was a D.L. & W. work caboose with die-cast frame and single coupler. Its Middle Traditional box bore the –25 marking, as well as the notation, "For 027 track" on its end flaps.

Continuing the colorful theme set by the locomotive, rather than the common black crane and hopper cars, this outfit instead included a crane with a red painted cab and gray hopper. Boxes for each bore a –25 suffix.

Finally, completing the outfit was a 6511 pipe car, painted brick red and carrying five plastic pipes. The bar end trucks of this car were attached to detailed die-cast plates—the weight of these plates were used to help the car track properly. Were a train to contain a car markedly lighter than the others in the consist, that car would tend to derail.

Excellent	Like New	Scarcity
750	1,200	5

O-Gauge

2201WS Fireball Express **$39.95 retail**

Included: 665 4-6-4 steam locomotive with operating headlight, smoke and Magne-traction; 6026W square whistle tender; 6464-50 Minneapolis & St. Louis boxcar; 6462 gondola; 6465 Sunoco double-dome tank car; 6357 illuminated SP-type caboose; eight OC curved and five OS straight track; UCS Remote Control Track Set; bottle of SP smoke pellets; Lockon; lubricant; instruction booklet.

This outfit, popular the previous year, was continued unchanged except for the locomotive. Whereas the 685 powered the 1953 edition, for 1954 a feedwater heater-

1523

equipped boiler front was added to the locomotive and the number was changed to 665.

The box of the gondola was slightly longer than it had been during the previous year. The rest of the outfit was unchanged, including the Middle Traditional component boxes and the circle-L style outfit box.

Excellent	Like New	Scarcity
650	1,100	4

2217WS **Freight Master** **$49.95 retail**

Included: 682 6-8-6 steam turbine locomotive with operating headlight, smoke, Magne-traction and lubricator linkage; 2046WX streamlined whistle tender; 6464-175 Rock Island boxcar; 3562-25 operating barrel car; 6356 stock car; 6417 Pennsylvania porthole caboose; eight OC curved and five OS straight track; UCS track set; Lockon; lubricant; instruction booklet.

The long-time favorite replica of the Pennsylvania steam turbine was given a facelift and placed at the head of this freight train. A white rubber-stamped pinstripe was added along the running board edge of the locomotive, and an oversized replica of a lubricator linkage was added that connected the leading drive wheel with the boiler casting.

An eight-wheeled streamlined whistle tender lettered "PENNSYLVANIA" was paired with the locomotive. The tender had open portholes in the back and did not have number boards molded into its sides. On the underside, the tender was rubber stamped "2046W-50." The tender, like the locomotive, came in a Middle Traditional box with cardboard liner. The inner flap of the proper tender box for this outfit is marked 2046-85.

The new-for-1954 massive yellow bi-level stock car was included in this outfit, as was a 6464-175 silver Rock Island boxcar. Strangely, the correct box for this boxcar when included in this outfit is a 6464-50 Minneapolis & St. Louis boxcar box that has had the road name obliterated. It had the letter "S" stamped on the ends of the box, and the word "SILVER" added to the box sides. Some 2217WS outfits are known to contain 6464-175 cars lettered in black rather than the common blue. Such black-lettered cars warrant a substantial premium, easily exceeding the value of all the rest of the outfit.

Also included in the set was the new operating barrel car: 3562-25. Unlike the car in outfit 1521WS, the one included in this set was gray. Gray cars are today fairly common, however, all gray cars are not alike, and often the wrong car is found in sets that have passed through a number of collectors.

The 1954 version of the barrel car has a molded-in catch to hold the figure mounting plate in the retracted position when not in use. Thus, the motion of the train could cause

2217WS

the plate to swivel and the man to unload the car as it circled the track. The design flaw was corrected in later productions by the introduction of this catch. The correct car for this outfit lacks this catch.

A more significant variation has to do with the color of the lettering on the car. Though cataloged with red lettering in 1954, the bulk of the cars produced instead had blue ATSF lettering. A few of the very early production cars however were in fact produced with red lettering—and today these are quite sought after and valuable. Scarcer still is a gray car with red lettering erroneously numbered 35621 (the black car's number) rather than 356225.

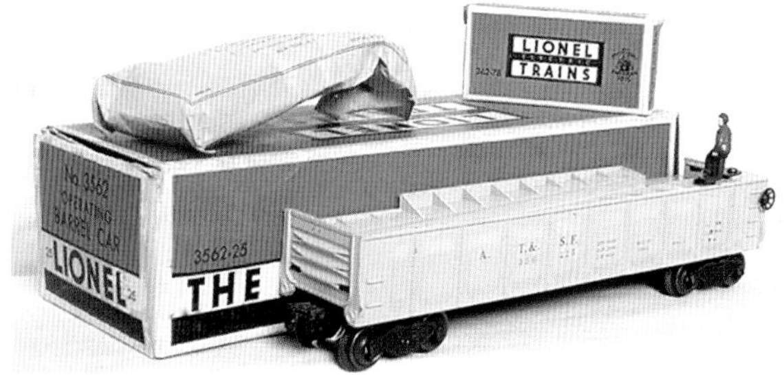

Barrel cars with red lettering were included in some of the 2217WS sets and are much more desirable than cars with blue markings. Particularly desirable are gray cars with red letters erroneously marked 35621, which are valued in the $3,000 range in Like New, or C9 condition.

Fittingly, the 6417 Pennsylvania porthole caboose was selected to complete this set.

All the components of this outfit came packed in Middle Traditional boxes, and the outfit box itself was the 1953-53 circle-L type.

Excellent	Like New	Scarcity
1,000	1,600	5

2219W **The Thunderbird** **$59.95 retail**

Included: 2321 Lackawanna Train Master; 6464-50 Minneapolis & St. Louis boxcar; 6462-25 gondola; 6456-25 Lehigh Valley hopper; 6415 Sunoco three-dome tank car; 6417 Pennsylvania porthole caboose; eight OC curved and five OS straight track; UCS track set; Lockon; lubricant; instruction booklet.

This outfit was headed by Lionel's new replica of the Fairbanks-Morse H24-66 "Trainmaster" diesel, the largest single-unit diesel produced by Lionel during the postwar era. This was a reasonably well-detailed, nearly scale-sized unit with two motors and battery-operated horn.

The FM, as collectors often term the locomotive, was to go on to be produced in numerous road names over the next dozen years, but the first year's production differed in several subtle ways. The plate on the bottom of the locomotive that retained the battery was etched with instructions. Stickers on later editions applied these instructions. Internally, the headlight mounting brackets were shaped like an inverted "L," unlike the vertical bracket of later years, and the windings of the motors were dark oxide color.

Although the catalog showed the locomotive with a gray roof, Lionel's earliest production of the locomotive is believed to have been the maroon roof version, and both types have been reported as components of this set. Incidentally, both roof colors were prototypical, as the Lackawanna first

2219W

painted its FM roofs gray, then later maroon, which better hid the discoloration caused by the diesel exhaust.

The rolling stock was all run of the mill. The boxcar was the brown Minneapolis and St. Louis 6464-50, while the green and gray -25 versions of the gondola and hopper cars (respectively) were welcome breaks from the routine black scheme typically worn by these items. The green gondola included in this outfit could have the "N" in either the second or third panel. A Sunoco triple dome tank car and 6417 Pennsylvania, like the rest of the rolling stock riding on bar-end trucks, completed the outfit.

The locomotive was packaged in a conventional tan corrugated carton with a liner and the remainder of the outfit components came in Middle Traditional boxes. The outfit box itself was the circle-L style typical of 1953-54 production.

Excellent	Like New	Scarcity
1,200	2,000	5

(A premium of about 15 percent can be added if the outfit includes a locomotive with maroon roof.)

2221WS **Diamond Express** **$59.95 retail**

Included: 646 4-6-4 steam locomotive with operating headlight, smoke and Magne-traction; 2046W streamlined whistle tender; 6468 Baltimore & Ohio double-door automobile car; 6456-25 Lehigh Valley hopper; 3469X automatic dump car; 3620 searchlight car; 6417-25 Lionel Lines porthole caboose; eight OC curved and seven OS straight track; UCS track set; Lockon; lubricant; instruction booklet.

A long-time staple of the 027 line, the 2046 was given a three-digit number (denoting O-Gauge status) and moved up in the line for 1954. The locomotive continued to have a trailing truck with die-cast frame and its number was typically stamped in white. Typical for such a large steamer, it was packed in a conventional corrugated carton with a liner, with the product number stamped on the box in blue. Its Lionel Lines tender, like the rest of the set components, was packed in a Middle Traditional box.

This was the only 1954 outfit to contain the black 3469X automatic dumping ore car. Most cars produced in 1954, including the ore car, had faint engraving on the top of the coupler knuckle "web," whereas in previous years this area was smooth. Keep in mind, however, that Lionel was a large manufacturing concern with extensive inventories of cars, couplers and knuckles, and such changes were made neither swiftly nor smoothly.

The 3620 searchlight car—in essence, a 3520 sans off-on switch—was new for 1954. Though cataloged with an orange searchlight housing, it was not known for production in that configuration. Most had searchlight housings molded of gray nylon, though some were molded in orange, which was then painted gray. Through the intervening years, the gray paint has been removed from some of these orange molded housings, making them resemble the cataloged orange hood variation. The knuckle pins on the 1954 production cars were black, whereas beginning sometime in 1955 they were silver.

The blue 6468 Baltimore and Ohio Automobile boxcar and gray 6456-25 Lehigh Valley hopper were typical production items, again with black knuckle pins and often with knuckle engraving.

At the rear of the train was a porthole caboose, but instead of the prototypical "PENNSYLVANIA" lettering, it was decorated with "LIONEL LINES" markings, thereby matching the locomotive and tender. The catalog number of the Lionel Lines version was 6417-25, and that number appeared on its Middle Traditional Box. On occasion, Lionel substituted the Pennsylvania caboose as a component of this set.

1954

Similarly, occasional shortages of the gray 6456-25 Lehigh Valley hopper led to its occasional replacement with a maroon version of the car.

The components of the outfit were all packed in the typical 1953-54 circle-L set box.

Excellent	Like New	Scarcity
600	1,000	4

2223W, 2221WS

2222WS The Mainliner **$65 retail**

Included: 646 4-6-4 steam locomotive with operating headlight, smoke and Magne-traction; 2046W streamlined whistle tender; 2530 Railway Express baggage car; 2531 Silver Dawn observation and 2532 Silver Range Astra Dome extruded-aluminum passenger cars; eight OC curved and seven OS straight track; UCS track set; Lockon; lubricant; instruction booklet.

The newly cataloged 646 Hudson was also selected to pull this passenger outfit, the first time Lionel had combined a steam locomotive with its extruded aluminum streamlined passenger cars. As was the case when this locomotive was a component of the 2221WS freight outfit, the locomotive was equipped with trailing truck with die-cast frame and had a rubber-stamped cab number. The locomotive was packaged in a conventional corrugated carton with a liner and the product number stamped on the box in blue.

A new addition to the extruded aluminum passenger car line-up debuting in this outfit was a baggage car. The earliest of these cars, and the one often found in this outfit, is what collectors refer to as the "large door" car. Due to the technical complexities of manufacturing cars with this size door, the baggage care was soon redesigned to include smaller doors.

Whether with a large or small door, the baggage car was the only style of extruded aluminum streamlined car that lacked interior illumination.

The large-door baggage car alone is valued in the $400-550 range in Excellent to Like New condition, leading to the frequent substitution of the small-door car in 2222WS outfits by dealers and collectors.

The 2531 Silver Dawn observation and 2532 Silver Range Astra Dome car were both typical production items. Like the baggage car and tender, they were packed in Middle Traditional boxes with corrugated liners. The outfit box was the typical 1953-54 circle-L box.

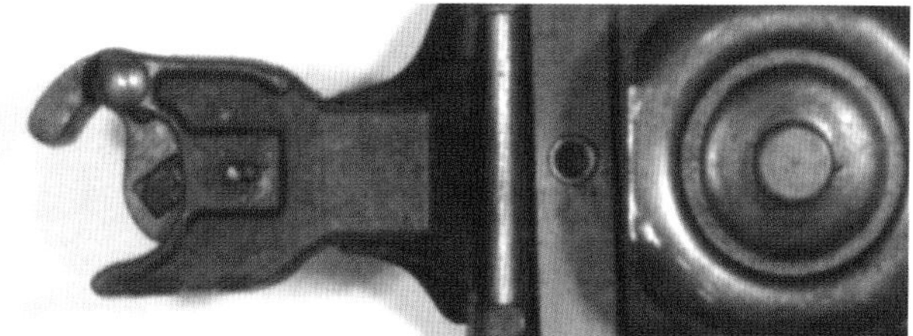

Engraving was added to the top of the "web" behind the knuckle during 1954. Such changes, however, took time to implement due to the enormous inventory Lionel had of such basic components.

The prices listed below are for the outfit with the common small-door baggage car, as this is how it is most often offered today. Increase values accordingly when the large-door car is present.

Excellent	Like New	Scarcity
1,600	2,700	5

2223W The Big Haul **$67.50 retail**

Included: 2321 Lackawanna Train Master; 6464-100 Western Pacific boxcar; 6462 red gondola; 3461-25X automatic lumber car; 3482 operating milk car; 6417-50 Lehigh Valley porthole caboose; eight OC curved and seven OS straight track; UCS track set; Lockon; lubricant; instruction booklet.

The spectacular Lackawanna Fairbanks-Morse Trainmaster, as described under outfit 2219W, was also the motive power for this set. As with the previously mentioned set, both maroon and gray roof versions have been reported as components of outfit 2223W.

LIONEL TRAINS
OUTFIT No. 2223W
LACKAWANNA DIESEL "O" GA. FREIGHT TRAIN WITH HORN
WITH MAGNE-TRACTION
LIONEL

However, the locomotive is not the only component of this set known to vary. More significant is the 6464 Western Pacific boxcar. Though the correct car for this set always is stamped with the number 6464-100, the car can be either silver with a yellow feather WP logo, or it could be the very scarce and valuable orange car with blue feather. Orange Western Pacific boxcars stamped 6464-250 are NOT correct for this outfit.

A known component of some 2223W outfits are the scarce orange with blue feather 6464-100 boxcar. This hard to find car should not be confused with the similar looking, but decade newer, 6464-250.

More common, but still attractive, was a silver Western Pacific boxcar with yellow feather decal. This car too is numbered 6464-100.

The familiar New York Central gondola was included in this outfit, with the "N" of the "NYC" name in the third panel from the end. Two versions of the red gondola are potentially included in this outfit. One version is painted red and comes in a box labeled 6462-100; the other version is unpainted and comes in a box marked 6462-125. Both came with a cargo of small 362-style stained barrels.

Also included in the outfit were two high quality, but unremarkable, operating cars: the green 3461-25X log dump car and the 3482 operating milk car. The 3461 was laden with a set of stained logs.

Bringing up the rear was a gray 6417-50 Lehigh Valley caboose. The caboose, as was the rest of the rolling stock, was packed in a Middle Traditional box. The locomotive was boxed in a typical tan corrugated cardboard box with a liner. All the components of the outfit were then packed inside a typical 1953-54 circle-L set box.

Valued here is the outfit with gray roof locomotive and silver boxcar. For maroon roof locomotives or orange boxcars, add $400 and $1200 respectively.

Excellent	Like New	Scarcity
2,400	4,200	6

2225WS The Troubleshooter $69.50 retail

Included: 736 2-8-4 Berkshire steam locomotive with operating headlight, smoke and Magne-traction; 2046W streamlined whistle tender; 3461-25X automatic lumber car; 3562-25 operating barrel car; 3620 searchlight car; 6460 crane; 6419 work caboose; eight OC curved and seven OS straight track; UCS track set; Lockon; lubricant; instruction booklet.

The venerable 736 was included in only one outfit in 1954, the 2225WS. All the components of this outfit, locomotive and cars, were better quality but unremarkable. The locomotive featured a trailing truck with a die-cast frame and white heat-stamped numbers. The green-based 3461-25X was included in the outfit, but naturally its 160 receiving bin was packed not in the component box with the car, but loose in the outfit box. A gray operating barrel car was always reported in this set with blue lettering, despite catalog illustrations showing red markings. The new, always-on 3620 searchlight car was also included in the outfit, presumably to illuminate nighttime recovery work performed by the 6460 crane that worked in conjunction with the 6419 work caboose.

The locomotive was packaged in a conventional tan corrugated carton with a liner. The remaining outfit components were boxed in Middle Traditional boxes, and all these components in turn were placed inside a 1953-54-style circle-L outfit box.

Excellent	Like New	Scarcity
750	1,200	5

2227W Golden West Special $69.50 retail

Included: 2353P/2353T Santa Fe A-A F-3 units; 6468 Baltimore & Ohio double-door automobile car; 3562-25 operating barrel car; 6456-75 Lehigh Valley hopper; 6356 stock car; 6417-25 Lionel Lines porthole caboose; eight OC curved and seven OS

Magnificent realism and Super-power
LIONEL Nos. 2227W AND 2229W "O" GAUGE 5-CAR FREIGHT
SANTA FE
NEW YORK CENTRAL
2354
LIONEL
No. 214 PLATE GIRDER BRIDGE

2227W, 2229W

straight track; UCS track set; Lockon; lubricant; instruction booklet.

The ever-popular Santa Fe F-3 A-A diesels, painted in red and silver passenger colors, were again selected by Lionel to head a freight outfit in 1954.

The operating barrel car included was new for 1954, and included in this set was the routine version painted gray with blue lettering. Production of this car in 1954 did not include a molded-in catch to hold the figure plate stationary while the train was in motion.

The yellow 6356 New York Central stock car and blue 6468 Baltimore and Ohio automobile boxcar were both routine production items, and both dwarfed the 6456-75 Lehigh Valley hopper—the scarcest item in the set. What makes this otherwise routine hopper desirable is the fact that the proper car for this set is painted in a glossy true red (not maroon) enamel. The lettering on the car is yellow (although it is suspected that the even scarcer –50 version of the car, red with white lettering, was also included in some of these sets), and the box is marked with the –75 suffix.

At the end of the train was a 6417-25 Lionel Lines porthole caboose with couplers on both ends. The caboose, as well as the entire outfit components of the powered unit, was packaged in a Middle Traditional box. The powered unit was packed inside a conventional tan corrugated carton. That box, as well as the dummy unit box, was provided with a liner. The outfit box itself was a standard 1953-54 circle-L carton.

Excellent	Like New	Scarcity
1,500	2,500	4

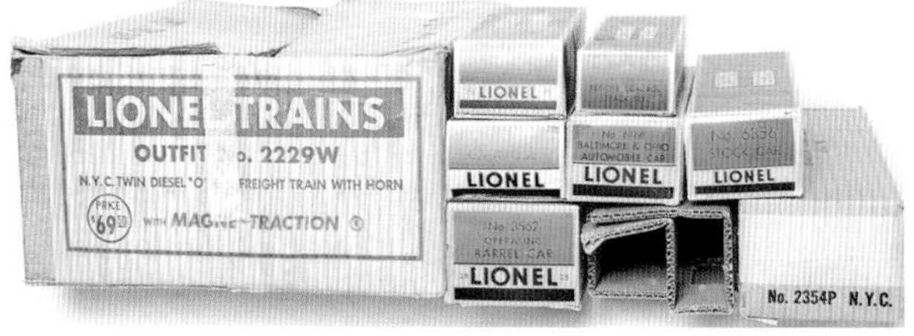

2229W Water Level Limited $69.50 retail

Included: 2354P/2354T New York Central A-A F-3 units; 6468 Baltimore & Ohio double-door automobile car; 3562-25 operating barrel car; 6456-75 Lehigh Valley hopper; 6356 stock car; 6417-25 Lionel Lines porthole caboose; eight OC curved and seven OS straight track; UCS track set; Lockon; lubricant; instruction booklet.

This outfit is a duplicate of outfit 2227W except for the replacement of the 2353 Santa Fe diesels with 2354 New York Central units.

Excellent	Like New	Scarcity
1,500	2,500	5

2231W Great Southern Freight $79.50 retail

Included: 2356P/2356C/2356T Southern A-B-A F-3 units; 6561 depressed-center flatcar with cable reels; 3482 operating milk car; 6511 pipe car; 6415 Sunoco three-dome tank car; 6417-25 Lionel Lines porthole caboose; eight OC curved and seven OS straight track; UCS track set; Lockon; lubricant; instruction booklet.

The top of the line freight outfit for 1954 was also arguably the most attractive outfit cataloged that year. At the front of the set was a triple unit A-B-A set of F-3 diesels wearing the brilliant green and white passenger paint scheme of the Southern Railway.

Stretched behind the twin-motored diesels were five top-quality freight cars. The 6561 depressed center flatcar featured a die-cast body and carried a pair of molded orange cable reels wrapped with un-insulated aluminum wire. The 6511 flatcar was the early painted version that was equipped with detailed die-cast weights to which the bar-end trucks were mounted. It was laden with five gray plastic pipes. Also included was the nicely proportioned and detailed Sunoco triple-dome tank car with its gleaming silver finish.

The sole operating car in the outfit was the ever-popular milk car, in this case the new-for-1954 3482 version. Because O-Gauge outfits were typically produced later in the year than were 027 sets, it is unlikely that the early version of the milk car was included in this set. The early version of the 3482 was stamped with that number prominently to the left of the door, and to the right of the door were much smaller "RT3472" markings. This mistake was soon corrected and "3482" appeared in both places.

In contrast to the brightly colored realistic-looking Southern F-3 units at the front of the set, at the rear was a rather drab Tuscan 6417-25 "LIONEL LINES" porthole caboose.

The outfit was packaged in a large circle-L type outfit box. The powered unit was packaged in a conventional tan corrugated carton with "No. 2356P SOUTHERN RAILWAY" stamped heavily on the box side. The remaining outfit components were packaged in Middle Traditional boxes. The powered unit, as well as the dummy A and B—or in Lionel lingo, T- and C-units—were protected inside their boxes by heavy corrugated cardboard liners.

Excellent	Like New	Scarcity
2,400	4,000	5

2234W Four-Car Super-Streamliner $89.50 retail

Included: 2353P/2353T Santa Fe A-A F-3 units; 2530 Railway Express baggage car; 2531 Silver Dawn observation, 2532 Silver Range Astra Dome and 2533 Silver Cloud Pullman extruded-aluminum passenger cars; eight OC curved and nine OS straight track; UCS track set; Lockon; lubricant; instruction booklet.

Once again Lionel's top streamliner included Santa Fe F-3 diesels with extruded aluminum passenger cars in tow. New to the consist this year was the addition of the 2350 baggage car, which replaced the 2534 Silver Bluff Pullman included in previous deluxe streamlined passenger sets.

None of the known original 2234W outfits examined during the preparation of this volume included the large door baggage car. The limited number of large door cars was likely exhausted by the time this set was packaged.

Though matched sets of cars are the preference for collectors, the outfits could contain an assortment of cars with glued- or riveted-on nameplates when leaving the factory. Various methods of nameplate attachment were used and, once packaged, the variations could not be distinguished. Lionel factory workers pulled cars from stock indiscriminately as they packaged sets.

The locomotive box was a conventional corrugated carton, while the remaining outfit components were packed in Middle Traditional boxes. All the component boxes of this outfit came with liners. The outfit box was a unique variation of the otherwise standard 1953-54 circle-L carton. Whereas the normal box of this type had a red border with a broad blue band showing the "Lionel Trains" logo, this color scheme was reversed for the 2234W outfit box.

Excellent	Like New	Scarcity
2,200	3,800	4

Chapter 12

1955

Several new products and features were introduced to the Lionel line in 1955. Among the new items were a new replica of a General Motors general-purpose diesel road switcher, the 6414 Evans Auto Loader, the 60 Trolley and the 41 Army motorized unit. A new innovation was the addition of a small tab to the coupler armature, to aid in the manual uncoupling of the cars. Another change made to the coupler assembly had to do with the coupler knuckle pivot pin, or rivet. Sometime during the year, the blackened part previously used was replaced with a bright plated pin.

But all the changes were not improvements. New values seem to have taken hold at the Lionel Corp. for 1955. Cost, while always a factor, had seemed of secondary importance to the company in previous years. But it clearly became a major factor in 1955's offerings. Many die-cast components were replaced with inexpensive sheet metal. These changes were apparent in both rolling stock and locomotives, returning items as well as new designs. Even the method of mounting trucks was changed to reduce material and labor costs. Rather than using a horseshoe clip crimped around a turned stud, Lionel introduced a push-in clip of spring steel.

The die-cast ore and lumber dump cars were replaced with similar units made of plastic and sheet metal. The NW-2 switchers were no longer heavy units with die-cast chassis, but now had stamped sheet-metal frames and substantially less detailed cabs.

Similarly, Lionel continued to cut costs in packaging. Liners, once present in all boxes, were eliminated across the board. However, the product number continued to appear on all sides of the Middle Traditional boxes used for set components, and 1955 was to be the last year this was the case.

The circle-L outfit box was revamped for the new year with the words "1955 OUTFIT" prominently displayed on the packaging.

More significant was the change made in the outfit packaging. Lionel continued to use traditional-type four-digit outfit numbers on those sets sold through its normal dealer network. Outfits destined for chain stores and other discounters were assigned three-digit numbers—a thinly veiled attempt to hide the identity of these sets. Regardless of distribution channel, the bold "1955 OUTFIT" slogan emblazoned on the box easily distinguishes all the sets from this year. Neither outfit numbers nor prices were included in the 1955 catalog. In fact, compared to prior and subsequent years, the 1955 catalog did an exceptionally poor job of illustrating outfits, and the advance catalogs were no better. Today's collectors must rely on what is known as an "executive catalog" and factory order forms for detailed information on set components.

027-Gauge

1000W or 506 Three-Car Set $39.95 retail

Included: 2016 2-6-4 steam locomotive with operating headlight; 6026W square whistle tender; 6014 Baby Ruth boxcar; 6012 gondola; 6017 SP-type caboose; eight 1013 curved and three 1018 straight track; 6029 uncoupling section; 1033 90-watt transformer; Lockon; lubricant; instructions.

In an effort to provide a low cost steam outfit headed by something other than a Scout-type locomotive, Lionel created this set. The specially created locomotive at the head of the consist was basically a 2037 stripped of its smoke and Magne-traction, and given the new number 2016. Surprisingly, the accompanying 6026 tender kept its whistle.

All the rolling stock was derived from Scout series freight cars, but they were equipped with bar-end metal trucks.

The locomotive was packaged in a tan cardboard carton without a liner. The rolling stock, including the tender, came in Middle Traditional boxes, also without liners. All the components were then packaged in a two-tier 1955 set box.

Excellent	Like New	Scarcity
200	350	4

1001 or 501 Three-Car Set $22.50 retail

Included: 610 Erie NW-2 diesel switcher; 6012 gondola; 6014 Baby Ruth boxcar; 6015 Sunoco single-dome tank car; 6017 SP-type caboose; eight 1013 curved and one 1018 straight track; 6029 uncoupling section; 1014 40-watt transformer; Lockon; lubricant; instructions.

Most of these outfits are considered wholly unremarkable. All the components of this low cost promotional outfit are

particularly commonplace, and in most cases the single-tier 1955 outfit box itself is the only item of interest in the set.

However, the 610 Erie switcher was produced in numerous variations. The most common version, and the one most often found in this set, has a blued steel frame as well as blued steel steps. Early and more desirable versions of the switcher had frames that were painted black with blued steel steps installed. The earliest and by far the most coveted version of the locomotive had blued steel steps, but the frame was painted yellow.

Some examples of outfit 1001 have surfaced containing the scarce yellow-frame variation of the 610 switcher.

The locomotive was packaged in a Middle Traditional box, but the other components of the outfit were unboxed, with only cardboard dividers protecting them from each other.

Excellent	Like New	Scarcity
250	475	4

1513S or 504 Four-Car Freight $35 retail

Included: 2037 2-6-4 steam locomotive with operating headlight, smoke and Magne-traction; 6026T square tender; 6012 gondola; 6014 Baby Ruth boxcar; 6015 Sunoco single-dome tank car; 6017 SP-type caboose; eight 1013 curved and three 1018 straight track; 6009 uncoupling section; 1043 50-watt transformer.

The outfit was poorly shown in the catalog, and it is likely the only reason it was shown at all was to help move 1954-surplus outfits already in the distribution network, with a minimal amount of new outfits packaged at the factory. This would account for the existence of 1954 outfits with paste-on labels reading "1955 OUTFIT" applied to their boxes.

Though the lineup of rolling stock was unchanged from the 1954, some outfits exist with rolling stock exhibiting only 1955 characteristics, such as coupler tabs, while others have only 1954 traits and still other outfits contain a mixture. It is likely that sales for this outfit, originally listed to deplete 1954 product, exceeded expectations, hence requiring further production.

One clue as to the age of an outfit can be found by examining the box for 6012, which had a 6012-11 inner flap number in 1955 as opposed to the –10 number used in 1954. Many, if not all, of the 1955 boxes had a pasted-on paper label, similar to that used in the late 1940s, rather than the printed-on labeling typical of 1955.

Excellent	Like New	Scarcity
200	350	4

1525 or 500 $19.95 retail

Included: 600 Missouri-Kansas-Texas NW-2 diesel switcher; 6014 Baby Ruth boxcar; (6111) flatcar with logs; 6017 SP-type caboose; eight 1013 curved and one 1018 straight track; 6029 uncoupling section; 1014 40-watt transformer; Lockon; lubricant; instructions.

This outfit is a superb example of the cost-cutting measures prevalent in 1955. The diesel switcher, rather than having the heavy die-cast frame and die-cast truck frames as in previous years, instead had a poorly detailed sheet metal frame and the truck frames were made of sheet metal and aluminum.

Also made of sheet metal stampings was the unnumbered flatcar. This car, though stamped with the "LIONEL" name, did not have its number appearing anywhere on the car. It came with a load of five stained wooden logs made of birch dowel.

The locomotive was packaged in a Middle Traditional box, but the other components of the outfit were unboxed, with only cardboard dividers protecting them from each other. All the components were packed inside a single-tier 1955-style outfit box.

While the bulk of these sets are of little to no collector interest, the earliest production sets are the exception to this rule. These early sets included the early runs of the 600 switcher, including the scarce gray frame versions, in both the yellow and black end rail variations. Either of these types of switcher arouses great collector interest. The values shown are for outfits containing the most common version of the locomotive.

Some of the earliest 1525 sets have been reported to contain this scarce locomotive variation with gray frame, black steps and yellow rails. This locomotive alone is valued at $600 in Excellent and $900 in Like New condition.

Also desirable, though not as valuable as the locomotive above, is this version with a gray frame and black steps and rails. Its value, while still substantial, is only about 75 percent of that of the yellow-rail version.

Most of the outfits naturally contain the common black-frame version of the switcher.

Excellent	Like New	Scarcity
200	500	3

1527 or 502 Three-Car Work Train $29.95 retail

Included: 1615 steam switcher with operating headlight; 1615T slope-back tender; 6462-125 gondola; 6560 crane; 6119 work caboose; eight 1013 curved and one 1018 straight track; 6029 uncoupling section; 1014 40-watt transformer; Lockon; lubricant; instructions.

This attractive little outfit contained several moderately desirable items. The 1615 steam switcher was easily damaged; its marker lights were particularly susceptible to damage. The tender paired with the loco, the 1615T, was somewhat disappointing because it had a plastic body. The locomotive was packed in a tan corrugated carton without a liner, while the tender, like the rest of the rolling stock, was packaged in its own Middle Traditional box.

The crane packaged with this outfit usually had a gray cab with lettering on the frame. Some of the cranes, however, had a reddish-orange cab and were mounted on an unlettered black frame. The red-cab cranes came in boxes with a –25 suffix included in the part number. Sometimes this suffix was separately rubber stamped, but in other cases it was preprinted on the box along with the normal markings. Some of these boxes also have an "X" suffix stamped behind "6560."

In either case, the crane was paired with a newly designed work caboose. The Lionel Service Manual also listed a black cab as being available on this crane.

This caboose had a black stamped sheet metal frame and was topped with an unpainted red plastic cab and oftentimes a gray open tool compartment. In some cases, however, the tool compartment was also molded in red. While the frame was stamped, "Lionel," the cab was marked, as had all previous Lionel work cabooses, with "D.L. & W."

The unpainted red gondola came in a Middle Traditional box with coupler protection flaps. The box was numbered 6462-125. The outfit box was a two-tier 1955 edition.

Excellent	Like New	Scarcity
400	750	5

1529 or 503 Three-Car Freight $29.95 retail

Included: 2028 Pennsylvania GP-7; 6311 pipe car; 6436 Lehigh Valley quad hopper; 6257-25 SP-type caboose; eight 1013 curved and one 1018 straight track; 6029 uncoupling section; 1014 40-watt transformer; Lockon; lubricant; instructions.

Lionel introduced a new style intermediate-priced locomotive replica during 1955. Styled along the lines of GM's Electro Motive Division's General Purpose locomotives, Lionel's GP diesels were assembled with construction methods similar to those introduced the same year with the economy-styled diesel switchers. The stamped sheet metal frame was exposed, forming the walkways at the ends and along the sides of the locomotive. An injection-molded plastic body was affixed to this.

However, the Magne-traction-equipped power train inside these road units was of better quality than that used in the economy switchers, being more along the lines of that used in the single-motor F-3 diesels.

The Pennsylvania GP-7 included in this outfit had only the features described above, as well as a headlight on the short-hood end. Other editions of the locomotive included an operating horn (with battery partially housed in a simulated fuel tank under the frame), wire cab handrails, headlights at each end, simulated horns and dynamic brake housing (which Lionel erroneously deemed to be the distinguishing feature between a GP-7 and a GP-9). Many of these features are sometimes found on 2028, installed by well-meaning dealers or consumers to dress up an otherwise very plain locomotive.

Several variations of the locomotive were produced, and all came in a liner-less tan corrugated carton. The values listed for the outfit presume the presence of the most common version of the loco.

The flatcar included in the outfit was derived—as would be dozens of later cars—from the 6511. The 6311 was a more economical version of the parent car, having stamped sheet metal weights rather than die-cast. It was loaded with only three pipes retained by seven stakes, versus the five and 13 respectively used on the 6511. A new 6436 hopper was based on the previous year's 6446 covered hopper, except that the 6436 was without a roof and was decorated in Lehigh Valley markings. Both black (-1) and maroon (-25) versions were produced, and either can be found in this set. The box for the maroon version bears the –25 suffix, as does the car.

When the body casting for these large hoppers was used in the manner for which they were originally designed, that is, as a covered hopper, the roof of the car provided support for the large side and retained their shape. However, when adapted for use as a large open top hopper as in this outfit, the unsupported sides had a certain tendency to distort. Upon discovering this problem, Lionel engineers added a metal "spreader bar," with a tiny hole in either side of the body that accepted this bar. A few scarce examples of these cars exist without the small holes for a spreader bar and occasionally these cars are found in this outfit.

At the rear of the train was a 6257 caboose decorated with the circle-L Lionel logo. A brake wheel was mounted on the railing of the caboose. The caboose, like the rest of the rolling stock, was packaged in a Middle Traditional box. The proper box for this caboose in this particular outfit has a small "s" suffix stamped behind the catalog number. The outfit box itself was a two-tier version of the new 1955 box.

Excellent	Like New	Scarcity
675	1,000	6

1531W or 505 Four-Car Freight $39.95 retail

Included: 2328 Burlington GP-7; 6462-125 gondola; 6465 Sunoco two-dome tank car; 6456 or 6456-25 Lehigh Valley hopper; 6257 SP-type caboose; eight 1013 curved and three 1018 straight track; 6019 remote control track set; 1033 90-watt transformer; Lockon; lubricant; instructions.

A more elaborate version of the new GP-7 diesel was included in this outfit. The gleaming silver Burlington unit had operating headlights on each end, and its body had decorative horns and wire handrails installed. Inside, Lionel's typical battery-operated diesel horn was installed. This engine can be found in this set packed in either a Middle Traditional box or in an unlined tan corrugated carton.

The locomotive was the only new item included in the outfit. All the rolling stock were carry over items, and unremarkable at that. Naturally, to be proper for this set, all these pieces must have the appropriate 1955 characteristics, though late 1954 features would be appropriate due to work-in-progress situations at the factory. Among the 1955 characteristics is the unpainted red body on the –125 New York Central gondola, which came in a similarly marked Middle Traditional box that had coupler-protection flaps.

An otherwise common car, the double-dome tank in this set was an unusual variation. Rather than having the number 6465 rubber-stamped on the bottom of the frame, the number appears below the reporting marks on the right side of the car. Like most 1955 cars, it also had a tab on the coupler armature to ease manual uncoupling.

The 6257 caboose included a brake wheel attached to its railing.

The outfit components were packed in a two-tier 1955 issue set box.

Excellent	Like New	Scarcity
575	975	6

1533WS or 507 Freight Hauler $49.95 retail

Included: 2055 4-6-4 steam locomotive with operating headlight, smoke and Magne-traction; 6026W whistle tender; 3562-50 operating barrel car; 6436 Lehigh Valley quad hopper; 6465 Sunoco two-dome tank car; 6357 illuminated SP-type caboose; eight 1013 curved and three 1018 straight track; 6019 remote control track set; 1033 90-watt transformer; Lockon; lubricant; instructions.

The familiar 2055 "baby" Hudson powered this outfit. The proper box for the locomotive in this box was the new-for-

1955, slightly smaller unlined tan corrugated carton. The 6026W was packed in a Middle Traditional box without a liner; the same type of box was used for all the rolling stock items in the outfit as well.

Like outfit 1529, both black and maroon hoppers, with and without spreader bars, were packaged in this set during the course of its production.

The operating barrel car in this outfit was usually yellow, although some outfits have been reported with gray cars. The yellow cars were initially painted, but the vast majority of the cars were unpainted yellow plastic. To be correct for this outfit, the barrel car must have black knuckle pins.

The Sunoco tanker and the SP caboose were routine issue items. All these components were packed, naturally enough, in a 1955 outfit box.

Excellent	Like New	Scarcity
425	725	5

1534W or 508 Three-Car Passenger $49.95 retail

Included: 2328 Burlington GP-7; 2432 Clifton Vista Dome, 2434 Newark Pullman and 2436 Summit observation; eight 1013 curved and three 1018 straight track; 6019 remote control track set; 1033 90-watt transformer; Lockon; lubricant; instructions.

Yet again the new 2328 Burlington diesel was paired with returning rolling stock, in this instance 2400-series plastic-bodied passenger cars. The red lettering of the passenger cars matched nicely with the red frame of the locomotive.

The 2432 box was revised for 1955 by changing the labeling from "Astra Dome" to "Vista Dome." Although the catalog illustration showed an Elizabeth Pullman, the outfit actually contained a Newark Pullman. Middle Traditional boxes were used for all the passenger cars. The 1955 boxes were slightly shorter and wider than the 1954 boxes for the same cars, but continued to have the stock number printed on all sides. Some of the locomotives were even packaged in Middle Traditional boxes, although some were known to have come in liner-less tan corrugated cartons. The outfit box was a two-tier 1955-style carton.

Excellent	Like New	Scarcity
950	1600	6

1535W or 509 $49.95 retail

Included: 2243P/2243C Santa Fe A-B F-3 units; 6468X Baltimore & Ohio double-door automobile car; 6462-25 gondola; 6436-1 Lehigh Valley quad hopper; 6257-25 SP-type caboose; eight 1013 curved and five 1018 straight track; 6019 remote control track set; 1033 90-watt transformer; Lockon; lubricant; instructions.

Not shown in the consumer catalog but nonetheless offered to dealers in 1955, this outfit is subject to considerable collector interest and, in many cases, substitution of components by dealers and collectors. One of the substitutions was the locomotive, which was the new-for-1955 2243 A-B combination of Santa Fe F-3 diesels. Though produced in later years as well, the 1955 production differed in detail. Ladders leading to the side doors were molded into the cab sides; in 1955 these were raised and reasonably well detailed. In later years, these ladders had a lower profile and less detail. The knuckle rivet on the front coupler was black in 1955, but shiny pins were used for the bulk of the production in later years. Unusually, the 2243 in this set had a plastic front coupler-centering plunger on the A-unit, a feature normally associated with 1956.

More noticeable, and certainly having a greater effect on the outfit's value, is the boxcar included in the set. Although the executive catalog indicated the outfit would contain the relatively common 6464-50 Minneapolis & St. Louis boxcar, it in fact contained a much scarcer and more desirable car—the 6468 Baltimore and Ohio Automobile boxcar—in a unique Tuscan color rather than the common blue. The number on the Middle Traditional box of this car was appended with a rubber-stamped "X" to denote its unique color.

A black 6436 Lehigh Valley hopper was included. This car did not include a top but did have a spreader bar to help it hold its shape. The ubiquitous New York Central gondola

Values for each condition are in U.S. dollars. | **Scarity** = Scale from 1-8 with 8 being the hardest to find.

was also included in this set, and the proper one for this outfit comes in a box with inner flap number 6462-31. Completing the train was a red 6257-25 caboose. Lacking illumination, the car was decorated with the double-circle Lionel "L" marks and included a brake wheel.

The locomotive was packed in a tan corrugated carton without a liner, while all the other rolling stock came in Middle Traditional boxes, with the stock numbers printed on all sides. The components were packaged in 1955-style two-tier outfit box.

Excellent	Like New	Scarcity
800	2,200	6

1536W or 510 Three-Car Passenger Set $59.95 retail

Included: 2245P/2245C Texas Special A-B F-3 units; two 2432 Clifton Vista Domes and 2436 Summit observation in the silver-with-red-letter color scheme; eight 1013 curved and three 1018 straight track; 6019 remote control track set; 1033 90-watt transformer; Lockon; lubricant; instructions.

No doubt as a result of good sales for outfit 1520W the previous year, Lionel created this near duplicate. However, instead of the previous year's Clifton, Elizabeth, Summit consist, for 1955 the company chose to eliminate the Elizabeth Pullman and add a second Clifton Vista Dome. The Middle Traditional boxes for the passenger cars were a bit wider and shorter in 1955 as well, though it is possible some of these outfits contained cars, or at least boxes, produced the year previously.

The 2432 of 1955 was slightly different from the one built in 1954. The number on the non-vestibule end of the car was positioned directly under the second window. The previous year this number was between the second and third windows.

The 1955 edition of the locomotive had trucks with black-oxide coated truck side frames rather than the silver side frames used in 1954. The pilot casting, which had been red in 1954, was now painted silver—the 1955 chassis was in fact the same as the one used on the 2243. Finally, the 1954 locomotive had a horizontal motor, whereas the new 1955 model had a vertically mounted motor.

The B-unit was produced in two variations. The early variation had portholes, as had all previous B-units, while the later productions used a body casting with the porthole openings molded shut.

The outfit was packaged in a typical 1955-style box. The values listed assume that the B-unit has portholes. If the B-unit has molded-closed portholes the values should be increased $500-600.

Excellent	Like New	Scarcity
1,900	3,000	6

Early 1955 production continued to use the same A- and B-unit bodies as 1954, but with a new A-unit frame and chassis. The new chassis included a rear vertically mounted motor. The trucks now had chemically blackened side frames without steps, and the pilot casting was painted silver rather than red, as it had been in 1954.

Later 1955 production of the 2245 included a B-unit with closed portholes, but the A-units always had portholes with lenses. Despite its comparative unattractive appearance, this locomotive variation is valued at about 50 percent more than the porthole-equipped version.

1537WS or 511 $59.95 retail

Included: 2065 steam locomotive with operating headlight, smoke and Magne-traction; 6026W square whistle tender; 6464-275 State of Maine boxcar; 3562-50 operating barrel car; 3469X automatic dump car; 6357 illuminated SP-type caboose; eight 1013 curved and five 1018 straight track; 6019 remote control track set; 1033 90-watt transformer; bottle of SP smoke pellets; Lockon; lubricant; instructions.

Old met new in this outfit as the 3469 operating ore car made its final appearance and was joined by the 6464-275 State of Maine boxcar, making its first run. These two cars, like the rest of the rolling stock in the outfit, were packaged in Middle Traditional boxes.

The State of Maine boxcars produced in 1955 came in three variations. All had grooves molded into their sides to aid in masking the tri-color paint scheme. Some cars had bodies molded of white, with the red and blue colors sprayed on. Others used the white body mold, with all three colors painted. The third version was molded in royal blue, with the white and red colors painted on. The white molded cars with unpainted white stripes had doors molded of red unpainted plastic without any stripes, while the blue molded cars used white doors with red and blue stripes painted on. The red-door cars are considered more desirable than the other variations.

The yellow barrel cars were initially painted and some came in 3562-25 boxes with a "Y" stamped on the end to denote yellow. Some of the early cars even lack the molded-in catches to secure the figure swivel plate, but the vast majority of the cars were unpainted yellow plastic with the molded-in catch. In any event, to be correct for this outfit, the barrel car must have black knuckle pins. Lionel is known to have substituted gray 3562-25 barrel cars for the yellow in this outfit.

The locomotive, tender and caboose were all unremarkable standard issue items. The locomotive was packaged in a tan corrugated carton without a liner, while the outfit box was the typical 1955-edition two-tier package.

Excellent	Like New	Scarcity
575	975	5

1538WS or 512 Four-car Passenger $65 retail

Included: 2065 4-6-4 steam locomotive with operating headlight, smoke and Magne-traction; 2046W streamlined whistle tender; 2432 Clifton Vista Dome, 2434 Newark Pullman, 2435 Elizabeth Pullman and 2436 Summit observation in the silver-with-red-letter color scheme; eight 1013 curved and five 1018 straight track; 6019 remote control track set; 1033 90-watt transformer; bottle of SP smoke pellets; Lockon; lubricant; instructions.

This attractive outfit contained one of each number of the 2430-series red-letter passenger cars, and was headed by a baby Hudson paired with a streamlined 2046W tender. In sum, this made for quite a handsome set. Middle Traditional boxes were used for the passenger cars and tender, while the locomotive came in a tan corrugated carton sans liner. The outfit box, of course, was the typical 1955 edition.

While the bulk of the locomotives included in this outfit had white numbers, some have surfaced with silver rubber-stamped lettering. The observation car for this set had some distinguishing characteristics in 1955. The car's number, 2436, was stamped under the third window from the observation end and under the last window on the vestibule end. In 1954, the number had been positioned below and between the third and fourth windows from the observation end, and preceded the last window on the vestibule end.

Excellent	Like New	Scarcity
900	1,500	6

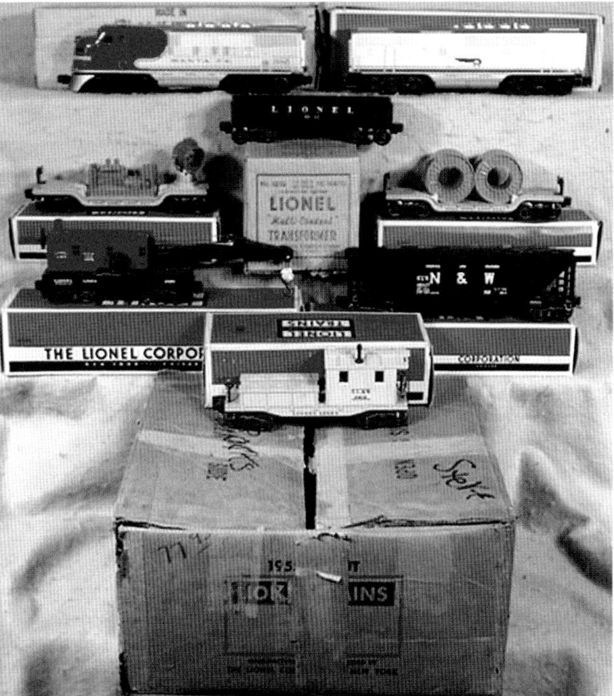

1539W or 513 Five-Car Freight $65 retail

Included: 2243P/2243C Santa Fe A-B F-3 units; 3620 searchlight car; 6446 Norfolk & Western covered hopper; 6561 depressed-center flatcar with cable reels; 6560 crane; 6419 work caboose; eight 1013 curved and five 1018 straight track; 6019 remote control track set; 1033 90-watt transformer; Lockon; lubricant; instructions.

The new single-motor Santa Fe F-3 A-B unit pair was also placed at the head of this outfit. The powered unit was packaged in a tan corrugated carton without a liner. The dummy B-unit was packed in a Middle Traditional box with its stock number on all sides.

In tow behind the twin diesels was an array of rolling stock. The 3620 searchlight car, 6561 depressed center car with reels and the 6419 work caboose all had die-cast chassis and had unpainted gray tool boxes. It came in box 6419-7. The orange cable reels were wrapped with un-insulated aluminum wire. As with the 1954 edition, the searchlight car lacked an on/off switch, however, the molded plastic generator was brighter than it was on the earlier car. The 1955 car also had the additional tab on the coupler flap and a black knuckle pin.

Also included in the outfit were the 6446 Norfolk and Western covered hopper. Both gray and black versions of this car have been reported as components of this outfit.

The crane was redesigned for 1955, no longer having the heavy die-cast frame that had been a feature since 1946. The cab of the crane was modified as well, now including a smokestack—a feature not previously seen on Lionel's Bucyrus-Erie railroad cranes. These cabs are found in molded red with an orange tint, a scarce variation, a painted red variation, which is even harder to find, as well as the common molded pure red. The hand wheels that control the boom and tackle heights featured open spokes, and the redesigned tackle had the hook aligned with the pulley.

Like the remainder of the rolling stock in the set, the crane was packaged in a Middle Traditional box. The outfit box was typical 1955 production.

Excellent	Like New	Scarcity
900	1,500	5

1541WS or 514 Five-Car Freight $69.95 retail

Included: 2065 4-6-4 steam locomotive with operating headlight, smoke and Magne-traction; 2046W streamlined whistle tender; 3494-1 operating New York Central Pacemaker boxcar; 3461X-25 automatic lumber car; 3482 operating milk car; 6415 Sunoco three-dome tank car; 6427 Lionel Lines porthole caboose; eight 1013 curved and five 1018 straight track; 6019 remote control track set; 1033 90-watt transformer; Lockon; lubricant; instructions.

The top of the line 027 outfit in 1955 was truly a first-class train set. At the front was the now familiar but attractive and reliable 2065 steam locomotive, paired with a 2046W Lionel Lines streamlined tender.

In tow behind the steamer were no less than three operating cars, joined by a tanker and caboose. The New York Central operating car was new and was based on the 6464 boxcar body casting. The car was fitted with bar-end trucks with black knuckle pins. The blue figure inside was a 1-5/16-inch tall 3562-62 man with painted face and hands. The nice die-cast log dump car included in the set was painted green and was loaded with stained birch logs. Its receiving bin was packed loose in the 1955-style two-tier outfit carton, and this was indicated by the X marking on the smaller-than-usual box.

The 3482 made its final appearance in an outfit in this set. Perhaps this was to deplete inventory in stock, or perhaps Lionel felt the size of this car was well suited to a 027 outfit, emphasizing that the new 3662 milk car included in O-Gauge sets was much larger. In any event, the correct 3482 for this set is marked with 3482/RT3482—the supply of erroneously marked 3482/RT3472 cars having been long since exhausted.

The 6415 Sunoco triple dome tank car was a run of the mill item, as was the 6427 Lionel Lines porthole caboose. All the rolling stock was packed in Middle Traditional boxes, while the locomotive came in a tan corrugated carton without a liner. The outfit box was, naturally, the new 1955-style two-tier box.

Excellent	Like New	Scarcity
600	1,000	5

O-Gauge

2235W or A-20 Four-Car Freight $39.95 retail

Included: 2338 Milwaukee Road GP-7; 6560-25 crane; 6436-25 Lehigh Valley quad hopper; 6362 railway truck car; 6419 work caboose; eight OC curved and five OS straight track; UCS remote control track; Lockon; lubricant; instructions.

The GP-7, cataloged as 027 in Pennsylvania and Burlington markings, moved to O-Gauge when wearing Milwaukee Road paint—at least for 1955. Like so many of the new-for-1955 locomotives, the 2338 exists in several variations, including a scarce and valuable variation with the orange band extending across the locomotive's cab. However, the version of the 2338 included in this outfit was the most common type, with the locomotive cab painted black.

The crane included in this outfit had a molded red cab, and came in a Middle Traditional box whose markings included the -25 suffix, although the suffix did not appear on the crane itself.

The 6362 railway truck car was new for 1955 and was clearly derived from the 3361 log dump car. The correct truck cargo for this car often is missing and has common trucks. To be correct, the bar-end trucks should exhibit no signs of wear nor have pivot studs installed. Though through the years this car was produced in several variations, the version contained in this outfit has sans-serif lettering.

Also new for 1955, was the 6436-25 large Lehigh Valley hopper in maroon. Created with the covered hopper car tooling, without the roof, this car was much larger than the traditional 6456.

While the 6419 had been produced in prior years, the 1955 version, as included in this set, was slightly different. Rather than being painted, now the toolboxes were unpainted gray plastic. The caboose came in a smaller box than that used in previous years and, rather than having a full wrap-around liner as previously, had only a partial liner. The correct box for 1955 has a -7 inner flap number, rather than the -5 inner flap number of previous years.

The rolling stock all came in Middle Traditional boxes and the outfit box was the standard two-tier 1955 edition.

Excellent	Like New	Scarcity
550	900	3

2237WS or A-21 Three-Car Freight $49.95 retail

Included: 665 4-6-4 steam locomotive with operating headlight, smoke and Magne-traction; 6026W whistle tender; 3562-50 operating barrel car; 6464-275 State of Maine boxcar; 6415 Sunoco three-dome tank car; 6417 Pennsylvania porthole caboose; eight OC curved and five OS straight track; UCS remote control track; Lockon; lubricant; instructions.

During this time in Lionel's history, most of the better freight sets, whether 027 or O-Gauge, included one or more operating cars. Outfit 2237WS was no exception to this. Packed in this outfit was the new 3562-50 yellow operating barrel car. The painted yellow version of this car is known to have been a component of some sets, while others have been reported to have the unpainted version. Some of the earliest of the yellow cars came in 3562-25 boxes, which had been stamped with a "Y" on the end flap to denote the color change. Regardless of painted or unpainted body, the car in this set always had a blue rubber figure and with the hands and face painted in flesh tone.

The 6464 State of Maine boxcar featured molded-in grooves that aided in the masking of the elaborate paint scheme. All reported examples of this outfit contain the multicolor door version of this boxcar.

The 665, the O-Gauge version of the 2065, was numbered in white and was paired with the 6026W whistle tender.

The 6415 triple-dome Sunoco tank car and 6417 Pennsylvania caboose were routine production items and, like all the rolling stock in this outfit, came in Middle Traditional boxes. The locomotive came without a liner in a tan corrugated box and the outfit box itself was the standard 1955 version.

Excellent	Like New	Scarcity
400	750	3

1955

2239W or A-22 Streak-Liner $55 retail

Included: 2363P/2363C Illinois Central A-B F-3 units; 6672 Santa Fe reefer; 6464-125 New York Central Pacemaker boxcar; 6414 Evans auto loader; 6517 bay window caboose; eight OC curved and five OS straight track; UCS remote control track; Lockon; lubricant; instructions.

At the front of this freight train was the new Illinois Central F-3 A-B set. Two variations of this pair of locomotives are known to exist, and either can appear in this set. The "Illinois Central" lettering along the sides of the units can be either brown or black—the brown being earlier, more difficult to properly apply, and consequently harder to find today in collectible condition.

The powered unit came in a tan corrugated carton without a liner, while the B-unit came in its own Middle Traditional box.

Though both the 6672 Santa Fe refrigerator car and the 6464-125 Pacemaker boxcars had been produced previously, the 1955 versions of each included in this outfit differ from the earlier models. Whereas previously the 6672 had been lettered in blue, the car included in this outfit is lettered in black.

Similarly, rather than decorating the NYC Pacemaker with heat stamping as done in 1954, in 1955 rubber stamping was used instead. Many of these rubber-stamped boxcars exhibit a flaw in the stamping, resulting in an extraneous mark beneath the second "s" in "System" in the oval New York Central herald.

The 6414 auto loader with bar end metal trucks was new for this year and came loaded with four 4-5/16-inch long nicely

All Illinois Central A-unit shells were molded in gray, with all the B-unit shells molded in orange. This can aid in identifying repainted and reproduced bodies.

detailed plastic autos. The unpainted red plastic frame of the car was stamped with the number to the right of "LIONEL."

The 6517 bay window caboose was new for 1955 and included in this outfit. The "BLT 12-55 LIONEL" legend was underscored. Like the rest of the rolling stock, it came packed in Middle Traditional boxes with the stock number printed on all sides. The outfit box was typical 1955 issue.

Excellent	Like New	Scarcity
1,800	3,000	5

2241WS or A-23 Freight Snorter $55 retail

Included: 646 4-6-4 steam locomotive with operating headlight, smoke and Magne-traction; 2046W whistle tender; 3359 operating dump car; 6446 Norfolk & Western covered hopper; 3620 searchlight car; 6417 Pennsylvania porthole caboose; eight OC curved and five OS straight track; UCS remote control track; Lockon; lubricant; instructions.

This outfit featured two operating cars: the 3620 searchlight car and the all-new 3359 twin bin dump car. The orange of the 3620's generator was brighter than it had been in 1954, and the knuckle pins were black, changing to silver in 1956. The light housing was gray—most molded that color—though a few were molded in orange and then painted in gray. It is not believed that Lionel shipped any searchlight cars with unpainted orange searchlight housings. A cadmium-plated bracket that featured four ventilating slits supported the searchlight housing.

The twin-bin dump allowed the operator to sequentially dump first one, then the other of the car's two bins. The car came with a 207-1 bag of coal and a 160-2 receiving tray. Inside the included envelope were two OTC-1 lockons with four 2-4-4 rail clips, a 90-1 controller, wiring and instructions. The car, which had black knuckle pins in 1955, came in a Middle Traditional box with the stock number on all sides.

The 6417 was a normal production item, including "New York Zone" lettering beneath "Pennsylvania." Like the rest of the rolling stock in this outfit, it came packaged in a Middle Traditional box.

The large Norfolk and Western covered hopper—referred to by Lionel as a "cement car"—was also included in this outfit. The car could come in either black or gray. Further, it can appear numbered either 546446 or 644625; any of these four cars would be appropriate as a component of this set. Like the rest of the rolling stock in this outfit, the hopper came in a Middle Traditional box, while the outfit box was typical 1955 production.

A medium-sized Hudson was included to power the consist. The 646 was an O-Gauge version of the 2046 and in this outfit it had a trailing truck with plastic side frames.

Excellent	Like New	Scarcity
600	1,000	5

2243W or A-24 Five-car Freight $59.95 retail

Included: 2321 Lackawanna FM Train Master; 6464-300 Rutland boxcar; 3662 operating milk car; 6511 pipe car; 6462-75 gondola; 6417-25 Lionel Lines porthole caboose; eight OC curved and five OS straight track; UCS remote control track; Lockon; lubricant; instructions.

No matter what variations of the various components are included, any example of outfit 2243W is desirable—however, this set has been known to include one of the most desirable and valuable of all postwar freight cars, and potentially a moderately locomotive variation as well.

In most instances, this outfit contained a gray roof version of the twin motor, horn-equipped 2321 Lackawanna FM Trainmaster. However, the more desirable maroon-roof version of this locomotive sometimes is included instead. Regardless of roof color, the locomotive was packed in a tan corrugated carton with a liner.

Among the cars in this outfit was the new-for-1955 6464-300 Rutland boxcar. It is this car that can potentially increase the set value many-fold. Most of these cars have solid yellow doors, rubber-stamped markings and a yellow background of the Rutland shield. A scarce and desirable variation—and unfortunately one that is often forged—instead has green background for the Rutland logo.

The 3662 was new for 1955, and was a larger, better-working version of the earlier 3462-3472-3482 milk car theme. The roof and doors were molded of either red-brown or chocolate brown plastic, and usually match. The milk cans used by this car were plastic with a cadmium-plated bottom weight, whereas the earlier cars had utilized turned aluminum cans with weights installed in the bottom. The 1955 edition of the 3662 had blackened knuckle pins and came in a box with the stock number on all sides.

The 6511, though a continuation of an earlier car, was now unpainted brown plastic with sheet metal rather than die-cast weights. It came with five gray plastic pipes and spring steel posts inside a Middle Traditional box with the stock number printed on every side.

The gondola included in this set was the 6462-75 red New York Central, with the "N" of NYC in the third panel from the car end. It was packaged in a long Middle Traditional box with a 6462-81 inner flap number.

To be proper, all the rolling stock in this set should be in Middle Traditional boxes, with stock numbers on all sides. The set box was the standard 1955 edition.

Excellent	Like New	Scarcity
1,500	2,500	5

2244W or A-25 Three-car Passenger $65 retail

Included: 2367P/2367C Wabash A-B F-3 units; 2530 Railway Express baggage car; 2533 Silver Cloud Pullman; 2531 Silver Dawn observation; eight OC curved and seven OS straight track; UCS remote control track; Lockon; lubricant; instructions.

The new Wabash F-3 units were among the most colorful diesels in Lionel's 1955 lineup. The dual vertical-motor A-unit was paired with a dummy B-unit. This B-unit was nearly identical to the later 2240 B-unit, however they can be distinguished. The white stripe near "Built by Lionel" is only 1/8 in. long, whereas on the 2240 B-unit the stripe is 1/2 in. long. The A-unit came in an unlined tan cardboard carton, while the B-unit came in a Middle Traditional box with a liner.

Behind the locomotive were three extruded aluminum cars: a baggage car, Pullman car and observation car. Most commonly these cars were of the "ribbed channel" variety, although cars made from the "flat channel" extrusions—originally developed to accommodate the color strips of the Congressional and other sets—are sometimes found in this set. Also variable is the method of attaching the "Lionel Lines" and car nameplates on the ribbed-channel cars. Glued or riveted installations have both been found because once the cars were packaged at the factory, it was impossible for those packing sets to know what style of cars were inside, even if they had wanted to match the sets. However, today collectors prefer matched sets, especially of the flat channel cars.

The cars came in Middle Traditional boxes, while the outfit box was the typical 1955-style.

Excellent	Like New	Scarcity
4,000	6,500	6

2245WS or A-26 Five-car Freight $65 retail

Included: 682 6-8-6 steam turbine locomotive with operating headlight, smoke and Magne-traction; 2046WX whistle tender;

3562-25 operating barrel car; 6560 crane; 6561 depressed-center flatcar with cable reels; 6436-25 Lehigh Valley quad hopper; 6419 work caboose; eight OC curved and seven OS straight track; UCS remote control track; Lockon; lubricant; instructions.

The final appearance of the Pennsylvania 20-wheel steam turbine during the postwar era was in this outfit. Despite its recent facelift giving it white striping and a lubricator linkage, the design—futuristic when introduced in 1946—was now dated and, in fact, the locomotives in 2245WS outfits were left over 1954 merchandise. Some of these steamers were paired with tenders with closed rear portholes but lacking integral number boards. Both the locomotive and tender came in Middle Traditional boxes with liners. The tender box was marked "P.R.R."

At the other end of the train was a 6419 work caboose with die-cast frame, also a veteran in Lionel's line. In between were a maroon Lehigh Valley 6436-25 hopper, a die-cast 6561 flatcar loaded with orange cable reels wound with un-insulated aluminum wire, a crane and an operating barrel car.

The barrel car was a gray 3562-25 version with a few changes for 1955. A tab was added near the figure plate in order to secure the plate, preventing inadvertent unloading. The figure had two arms outstretched, and painted face and hands.

Frequently, the crane included in this outfit was the version with the unstamped chassis and orange-red cab. This crane usually comes in a box with an X rubber stamped on the end flap. Like the rest of the rolling stock, the crane came in a Middle Traditional box with the stock number printed on all sides. The outfit box was the standard 1955 version.

Excellent	Like New	Scarcity
800	1,250	5

2247W or A-27 Five-Car Freight $65 retail

Included: 2367P/2367C Wabash A-B F-3 units; 6462-125 gondola; 3662 operating milk car; 6464-150 Missouri Pacific boxcar; 3361X operating log car; 6517 bay window caboose; eight OC curved and seven OS straight track; UCS remote control track; Lockon; lubricant; instructions.

The dual vertical-motor Wabash A-unit was paired with a matching blue, white and gray dummy B-unit. Both had yellow markings. The B-unit was strikingly similar to the 2240 B-unit produced the next year, however, there is a subtle difference. The white stripe near "Built by Lionel" is only 1/8 in. long, whereas on the 2240 B-unit the stripe is 1/2 in. long. The A-unit came in a tan cardboard carton without a liner, while the B-unit came in a Middle Traditional box with a liner.

The big new automatic milk car, the 3662, was included in this set. With the ends and roof as well as its doors molded of either red-brown or chocolate-brown plastic—usually matched—and white sides, the car was more colorful than its all-white predecessors. The milk cans used by this car were plastic with a cadmium-plated bottom weight, whereas the earlier cars had utilized turned aluminum cans with weights installed in the bottom. The 1955 edition of the 3662 had blackened knuckle pins and it came in a box with the stock number on all sides.

The 2247W outfits examined for this volume all contained the sans-serif version of the 3361, although both styles are shown in the catalog and hence are theoretically possible components. One aid to dating 1955 cars is the use of blackened knuckle pins.

The 6464-150 Missouri Pacific boxcar in this outfit had molded-in grooves separating the colors of the striping of the car and it featured blackened knuckle pins.

The red New York Central gondola was stamped with the "N" of "NYC" in the third panel from the end. The car was molded in red plastic, which was left unpainted, and was loaded with six 362 turned wooden barrels.

The new-for-1955 6517 bay window caboose was included in this outfit. The version included had underscoring beneath the "BLT 12-55 LIONEL" legend. Like the rest of the rolling stock in this outfit, it came packed in Middle Traditional boxes with the stock number printed on all sides. The outfit box was typical 1955 issue.

Excellent	Like New	Scarcity
2,500	4,000	5

2249WS or A-28 Five-Car Freight $69.50 retail

Included: 736 2-8-4 Berkshire steam locomotive with operating headlight, smoke and Magne-traction; 2046W whistle tender; 6414 Evans auto loader; 6464-275 State of Maine boxcar; 3562-50 operating barrel car; 3359 operating dump car; 6517 bay window caboose; eight OC curved and seven OS straight track; UCS remote control track; Lockon; lubricant; instructions.

But for the familiar 736 steamer leading the train, this outfit is identical to set 2251W, described later. The 736 in this outfit had white numbers and its trailing truck featured plastic side frames. It was packed in a tan corrugated carton without a liner. The Lionel Lines 2046W tender accompanying it, however, came in a Middle Traditional box without a liner.

The rolling stock was all-typical 1955 production, and all cars have been described earlier in this chapter. Of note is that the painted yellow version of the operating barrel car has been reported in this set, though most seem to have included the unpainted yellow version. Similarly, examples of this set have been reported to contain the 6517 caboose without underscoring, but most reported examples seem to have this characteristic.

All of these cars can be expected to have blackened knuckle pins and are packed in Middle Traditional boxes. The outfit box was typical of 1955.

Excellent	Like New	Scarcity
900	1,500	5

2251W or A-29 Five-car Freight $69.50 retail

Included: 2331 Virginian FM Train Master; 6414 Evans auto loader; 6464-275 State of Maine boxcar; 3562-50 operating barrel car; 3359 operating dump car; 6517 bay window caboose; eight OC curved and seven OS straight track; UCS remote control track; Lockon; lubricant; instructions.

At the front of this train is one of the more desirable postwar diesels, the black and yellow Virginian FM Train Master. The locomotive came packed in a tan corrugated carton with a liner. The body of this locomotive, and all postwar Lionel FMs, was molded slightly long. As a result, the tightening of the body mounting screws at the factory and subsequent handling of the locomotives has lead to many exhibiting hairline cracks near the screw holes at the body ends. Locomotives free from these blemishes command premium prices.

The rolling stock was all-typical 1955 production, and all cars have been described earlier in this chapter. The consist of this set, but for the motive power, duplicates that of outfit 2249W. Of note is that the painted yellow version of the operating barrel car has been reported in this set, though most seem to have included the unpainted yellow version. Similarly, examples of this set have been reported to contain the 6517 caboose without underscoring, but most reported examples seem to have this characteristic.

All of these cars can be expected to have blackened knuckle pins and are packed in Middle Traditional boxes. The outfit box was typical of 1955.

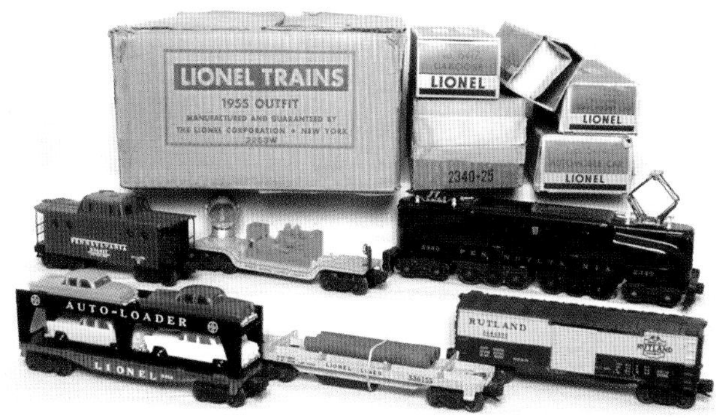

Excellent	Like New	Scarcity
2,500	4,000	5

2253W or A-30 Five-car Freight $75 retail

Included: 2340-25 Pennsylvania GG-1; 6414 Evans auto loader; 6464-300 Rutland boxcar; 3361X operating lumber car; 3620 searchlight car; 6417 Pennsylvania porthole caboose; eight OC curved and seven OS straight track; UCS remote control track; Lockon; lubricant; instructions.

Although all the rolling stock included in this set has been described in detail previously in this chapter, the possibility of the inclusion of a valuable variation of the boxcar warrants the car being addressed again.

The 6464-300 Rutland boxcar was new for 1955. Rubber stamping marked all 1955 production of this car. Usually, this meant that the shield portion of the Rutland herald was unpainted yellow plastic, with the green lettering and shield outline applied. However, a few of these cars were built, and potentially included in this outfit, that had a green Rutland shield with yellow lettering on it. These cars are extremely sought after and valuable, and consequently forgeries exist. An authentic such version of this car is more valuable than the rest of the outfit contents combined. For additional information, see "*The Standard Catalog of® Lionel Trains, 1945-1969.*"

Barring the presence of the scarce boxcar, the star of this outfit is the green 2340-25 GG-1. The GG-1, which had last been cataloged in 1950 as the 2330, returned in 1955 to lead this set, and outfit 2254W, the Congressional. Though given a new number, the green 2340-25 was essentially identical to the 1950 2330, including the five stripes stretching its length. The big electric came in a tan corrugated carton and was protected by a liner.

All the rolling stock in this outfit came in Middle Traditional boxes with numbers on all sides, and had black knuckle pins. Both serif and sans-serif versions of the 3361 log car have been reported as set components, its receiving tray always packed loose in the 1955-style set box.

Excellent	Like New	Scarcity
2,700	4,500	5

2254W or A-31 The Congressional $100 retail

Included: 2340 Tuscan Pennsylvania GG-1; 2541 Alexander Hamilton observation; 2542 Betsy Ross Vista Dome; 2543

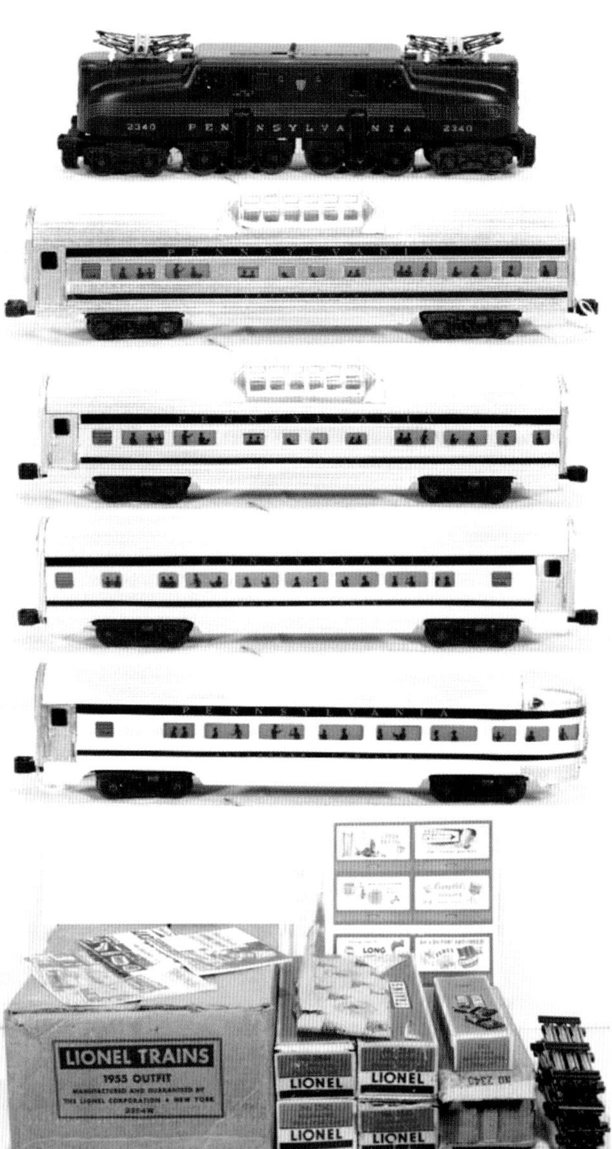

William Penn Pullman; 2544 Molly Pitcher; eight OC curved and 11 OS straight track; UCS remote control track; Lockon; lubricant; instructions.

One of the most desirable of all postwar passenger sets is this one, the Congressional. At $100 retail, it was 33 percent more expensive than the next best set in the 1955 line.

Lionel went to considerable effort to create this set, having the extrusion dies for the aluminum passenger cars retooled in order to create flat channels, one near the top, the other near the bottom, of each side. The channels were formed to accept colored striping, which also included the car and "PENNSYLVANIA" names. The Middle Traditional boxes for these cars included coupler protection flaps and numbers on all sides.

Taking its lead from the actual Pennsylvania Railroad, which had painted six of its GG-1s Tuscan red for Congressional service, Lionel, for the first time, offered its replica in Tuscan as well. It continued to have five stripes and the locomotive itself was numbered 2340. It came in a conventional tan corrugated carton with liner made by St. Joe Paper Co.: "2340" was stamped on one end flap and, often, "55" appears near the box maker's seal. The set box was a standard 1955-type.

Beware that excellent restorations of the GG-1 exist and forgeries of these passenger cars are abundant. As always, the inexperienced are cautioned when contemplating such an expensive purchase to seek the counsel of a trusted, experienced collector.

Excellent	Like New	Scarcity
5,500	9,500	5

Chapter 13

1956

Values for each condition are in U.S. dollars. | **Scarity** = Scale from 1-8 with 8 being the hardest to find.

Lionel continued to add color to its line in 1956, with brightly colored and now very collectible boxcars and diesel locomotives abundant. New designs were introduced as well, including the center-cab switcher, 3530 generator car, 3424 operating brakeman car and 3356 horse car, all of which appeared in sets. Other new items were not included in sets, among them the 3360 Burro crane, 3927 track cleaner and various accessories.

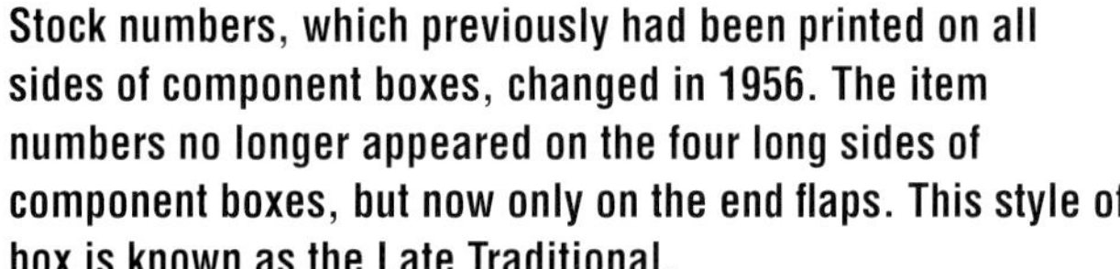

Stock numbers, which previously had been printed on all sides of component boxes, changed in 1956. The item numbers no longer appeared on the four long sides of component boxes, but now only on the end flaps. This style of box is known as the Late Traditional.

A new style of box was introduced in 1956. Known to collectors as the "basket-weave" box, the off-white box was overprinted with blue woven pattern.

Most of the bar-end trucks used in 1956 had the extended tab to aid manual uncoupling. Also, the knuckle pins, which had been blackened in the past, were now shiny, as seen in this photo.

027-Gauge

1542 or 750 Three-Car Freight $19.95 retail

Included: 520 General Electric boxcab electric; 6014 Baby Ruth boxcar; 6012 gondola; 6017 SP-type caboose; eight 1018 curved and one 1013 straight track; 6029 uncoupling section; 1015 45-watt transformer.

This outfit was created specifically to meet a low price point. A new electric-style locomotive was led by the 520. This little locomotive was topped with a plastic pantograph, often broken or missing today. Most locomotives had a black pantograph; a few, now more desirable, locomotives had brass-colored plastic pantographs.

Behind the locomotive was a Baby Ruth 6014 boxcar, the car being a truer red color than previous generations. Also in tow were a black gondola car and a 6017 SP-style caboose. All the cars were equipped with bar-end trucks.

The locomotive, protected by a special insert, and the cars, separated by cardboard dividers, were placed in the outfit box without benefit of component boxes. The set box itself was a two-tier carton, printed with the new basket-weave pattern.

Excellent	Like New	Scarcity
200	375	4

The four least expensive 1956 027 outfits introduced a new packaging technique as shown here. In order to save a few pennies in materials cost and a few more pennies in labor cost, Lionel opted to eliminate the component boxes from the outfit packaging, instead relying on cardboard dividers to protect the items during transit, as seen here.

1543 or 700 Three-Car Freight $25 retail

Included: 627 Lehigh Valley center cab; 6121 flatcar with pipes; 6112 gondola with canisters; 6017 SP-type caboose; eight 1018 curved and one 1013 straight track; 6029 uncoupling section; 1015 45-watt transformer.

The locomotive in this outfit was one of four new center cab diesels introduced in 1956, though one, the 626 Baltimore and Ohio, appeared only in an uncataloged set until the following year. The 627, heading this set, was the only one of the series not to include an operating headlight. Oversized, the locomotive shared trucks with the inexpensive NW-2 switchers, with which it also shared many construction techniques. The 627 Lehigh Valley was packaged in this outfit protected only by a wraparound liner. However, when offered for separate sale, it came in a Late Traditional box.

The rolling stock, all of which had bar-end metal trucks, but none of which had component boxes, was as a rule unremarkable. However, occasional desirable variations surface in this outfit. Among them are red canister loads for the 6112 with black, rather than white, markings. Another possible scarcity involves the caboose, which could be the "LIONEL" only, rather than "LIONEL LINES."

Inside the new single-tier, basket-weave-style box, cardboard dividers separated the various components.

Excellent	Like New	Scarcity
250	400	5

1545 or 701 Four-Car Freight $29.95 retail

Included: 628 Northern Pacific center cab; 6424 flatcar with automobiles; 6014 Baby Ruth boxcar; 6025 Gulf single-dome tank car; 6257 SP-type caboose; eight 1018 curved and three 1013 straight track; 6029 uncoupling section; 1015 45-watt transformer.

The black and yellow Northern Pacific center cab was selected to head this outfit. Once again, Lionel omitted component boxes, even for the locomotive, from the packaging of this

1956

Outfit 1545 was another of the outfits that did not include individual packaging for the components.

outfit. Instead, cardboard dividers separated the components inside the single-tier basket-weave box.

However, the two automobiles that were the cargo for the new 6424 flatcar came inside a protective sleeve, just as they did when shipped with the 6414 Auto-Loader. Also new was the black 6025 Gulf single-dome tank car. The 6014 Baby Ruth boxcar was a true red. All the rolling stock in the outfit rode on bar-end metal trucks.

As a footnote, the 628 occasionally surfaces in a Late Traditional box. Those locomotives were originally sold separately.

Excellent	Like New	Scarcity
300	500	6

1547S or 702 Freight Hauler $33.50 retail

Included: 2018 steam locomotive with headlight and smoke; 6026T square tender; 6121 flatcar with pipes; 6112 gondola with canisters; 6014 Baby Ruth boxcar; 6257-50 SP-type caboose; eight 1018 curved and one 1013 straight track; 6029 uncoupling section; 1015 45-watt transformer.

The final of the 1956 outfits to be packaged without component boxes was the 1547S. Powered by a 2018, which was in essence a 2037 without Magne-traction, the outfit came in a single-tier basket-weave type box.

All the rolling stock was equipped with bar-end metal trucks. The tender not only didn't have a whistle, its body was not even painted. Instead, the Lionel Lines lettering was stamped directly on the unpainted black body.

Also in the outfit was a gray sheet metal flatcar carrying five gray plastic pipes, the new-for-56 6112 black gondolas, which sometimes had black-lettered red canister load, red Baby Ruth boxcar and 6257 caboose. Numerous variations of the caboose are potential components. None of the cars were painted—as they had been in 1955. Instead, they were unpainted red plastic. Unlike earlier models, the 1956 version of the caboose—numbered 6257-50 on the box, but not on the car—does not include brake wheels. Some of the cars include the circle-L Lionel logo, but others do not.

Excellent	Like New	Scarcity
175	300	4

1549 or 703 Three-car Work Train $35 retail

Included: 1615 steam switcher with headlight; 1615T slope-back tender; 6262 flatcar with wheels; 6560-25 crane; 6119-25 work caboose; eight 1018 curved and three 1013 straight track; 6029 uncoupling section; 1015 45-watt transformer.

One of the most interesting 027 outfits of 1956 was this set headed by a switcher. While the diminutive switcher was a pale shadow of those previously offered, it is nevertheless interesting. But it is the cars in this outfit that drive collector interest, and in particular the new flatcar with a wheel load is potentially valuable.

When sold new, this outfit often contained the very collectible red version of the 6262 wheel car, though when sold on the secondary market this car has often been replaced with the more common black version, as in the example shown above. A special note about the 6262: whether black or red, the car was designed to hold more wheel and axle sets than it actually came with when new. Hence, many collectors believe part of the load is missing, and erroneously add two more sets, which often are of the wrong style.

The most desirable version of outfit 1549 included the very sought after red 6262 wheel car, rather than the common black version.

Also of interest is the red-cab crane. The number stamped on the frame now read 656025—at last reflecting the -25 red color code that had appeared on the box alone for years. The crane had open-spoke-style hand wheels. The crane was paired with a new version of the work caboose, the orange 6119-25. The earliest of these cranes came in surplus 1955 Middle Traditional boxes with the -25 suffix rubber stamped on the box. Quickly these boxes were replaced with proper Late Traditional boxes preprinted with the correct number.

But for the possible use of a Middle Traditional box for the caboose, and the locomotive's "56" dated tan corrugated box, all the components of the outfit were packed in Late Traditional boxes. The new two-tier basket-weave type box was selected for the outfit packaging.

Excellent	Like New	Scarcity
800	1,350	5

1551W or 704 Four-Car Freight $39.95 retail

Included: 621 Jersey Central diesel switcher with horn; 6562-25 canister car; 6425 Gulf three-dome tank car; 6362 railway truck car; 6257 SP-type caboose; eight 1018 curved and three 1013 straight track; 6029 uncoupling section; 1053 60-watt transformer.

The two-tier basket-weave box of this outfit contains several new-for-1956 items and one carryover. With the occasional exception of the 6362, all the items, including the locomotive, came in Late Traditional boxes. Because the 6362 was a carryover item, it is theoretically possible that it could appear in this outfit in a Middle Traditional box. The triple-dome tank car wore a new logo in 1956, that of the Gulf Oil Corp.

The familiar New York Central gondola was given a new load—four injection molded plastic canisters rather than six turned wooden barrels—and a new number, 6562, replaced the familiar 6462. The version most often appearing in this outfit is the red one, designated on the box as 6562-25, but some sets have been reported to contain instead the 6562-1, which is gray.

The caboose was molded in red plastic and lacked brake wheels. Over time, two different shades of blue plastic were used to create the bodies of the Jersey Central switcher. Whether royal blue or navy blue, the bodies had a decal with the Jersey Central's Lady Liberty logo applied beneath the cab windows, along with a heat-stamped orange number.

Excellent	Like New	Scarcity
400	700	5

1552 or 705 027 Passenger $39.95 retail

Included: 629 Burlington center cab; 2432 Clifton Vista Dome; 2434 Newark Pullman; 2436 Summit observation; eight 1018 curved and three 1013 straight track; 6029 uncoupling section; 1015 45-watt transformer.

The most desirable of the center-cab diesels is the silver and red unit at the front of this set, the 629 Burlington. Its coloration blended nicely with the red-lettered, 2430-series passenger cars that trailed it. The cars in this outfit can be distinguished from earlier production by their shiny knuckle pins. The cars, as well as the locomotive, were packaged in Late Traditional boxes and the outfit box was a two-tier basket-weave type.

Unfortunately, the silver paint of the locomotive and cars does not wear well, making this outfit difficult to locate in collectible condition.

Excellent	Like New	Scarcity
1,100	1,900	7

This outfit introduced three new cars to Lionel fans: The 6430 flatcar with trailers, commonly called Cooper-Jarrett vans due to their nameplates, was the first of these new cars. The unpainted red car had a metal superstructure, which held the gray vans in place. The metal Cooper-Jarrett

1553W or 706 Five-Car Freight **$49.95 retail**

Included: 2338 Milwaukee Road GP-7; 6464-425 New Haven boxcar; 6430 flatcar with vans; 6462-125 gondola; 6346 Alcoa covered hopper; 6257 SP-type caboose; eight 1018 curved and three 1013 straight track; 6019 Remote Control Track Set; 1053 60-watt transformer.

nameplates came in two styles, with the C-J logo appearing in either orange or copper.

The other new car was an addition to the 6464 series, the -425 New Haven. Through the years, many variations of this car appeared, but the one included in this set has metal trucks and a half-serif "N."

Another component of the set that exists in many variations is the 2338 Milwaukee Road GP-7. However, the variation contained in this set is the most common one, made of opaque orange plastic with a painted black cab. Reportedly, some sets had the locomotive packed in a tan corrugated box, while others had the locomotive, like the cars, packed in a Late Traditional carton.

The third new car was the 6346 Alcoa covered hopper car. This car, too, was produced in three variations, all having to do with the color of the heat-stamped lettering. While red, and to a lesser extent black, lettered cars are very sought after; all reported examples of set 1553W contain the common blue-lettered car.

Also included in the outfit was a 6462-125 unpainted red gondola and a 6257 SP-style caboose. The 6462 box was shorter in 1956 than it had been in 1955. The set was packaged in a two-tier basket-weave box.

Excellent	Like New	Scarcity
700	1,100	5

1555WS or 707 Freight Hauler **$49.95 retail**

Included: 2018 2-6-4 steam locomotive with headlight and smoke; 6026W whistle tender; 6464-400 Baltimore & Ohio Timesaver boxcar; 6462-125 gondola; 3361 operating lumber car; 6257 SP-type caboose; eight 1018 curved and three 1013 straight track; 6019 Remote Control Track Set; 1053 60-watt transformer.

Lionel's economical 2-6-4 was chosen to head this outfit, the Magne-traction-free 2018, which came in a tan corrugated box. The locomotive was accompanied by a whistle-equipped 6026W Lionel Lines tender. Behind the tender were three freight cars and a caboose, including a new boxcar and an operating log dump car. The -400 boxcar was a new member of the 6464 family, and was decorated in a spectacular blue, orange and silver Baltimore and Ohio scheme.

As a rule, the 3361 had serif lettering and silver knuckle pins, although it is possible that some leftover 1955 cars with black knuckle pins and or sans-serif lettering could have been included in these outfits. The number 336155 was stamped to the right of the "LIONEL LINES" lettering.

An unpainted red 6462-125 gondola was included in this outfit, the box for which was shorter than it had been the preceding year. At the rear of the train was a 6257 caboose. All the rolling stock was packed in Late Traditional boxes, and the outfit box was the new two-tier basket-weave type.

Excellent	Like New	Scarcity
350	600	4

1557W or 708 Five-Car Work Train **$49.95 retail**

Included: 621 Jersey Central NW-2 diesel switcher with horn; 6560-25 crane; 6436-25 Lehigh Valley hopper; 6511 pipe car; 3620 searchlight car; 6119-25 work caboose; eight 1018 curved and three 1013 straight track; 6019 Remote Control Track Set; 1053 60-watt transformer.

Like outfit 1551W, set 1557W was headed by the new 621 Jersey Central switcher. However, this outfit included more elaborate rolling stock. A crane with a molded red cab was included, its chassis stamped with the full number 656025. To accompany the crane was the all-orange 6119-25 work caboose, the box variations for which are discussed in the outfit 1549 section.

The 6511 pipe car was the unpainted brown plastic variation, packed in a box with inner flap number 6511-21, unlike in 1955 when the flap number was 6511-19.

The inner flap number of the maroon Lehigh Valley hopper box changed too, from 6436-30 in 1955 to 6436-26 in 1956. The outfit box was the two-tier basket-weave type, while the rolling stock and locomotive usually came in Late Traditional boxes. It is possible, though unreported, that some set components were carried over from 1955 production, and as such would have come in Middle Traditional boxes.

Excellent	Like New	Scarcity
500	950	5

1559W or 709 Five-Car Freight **$49.95 retail**

Included: 2338 Milwaukee Road GP-7; 6414 Evans Auto Loader; 3562-50 operating barrel car; 3494-275 operating State of Maine boxcar; 6362 railway truck car; 6357 illuminated SP-

type caboose; eight 1018 curved and three 1013 straight track; 6019 Remote Control Track Set; 1053 60-watt transformer.

The 2338 Milwaukee Road GP-7 was also chosen to power this outfit, which included two operating cars. The first of these was the yellow 3562-50 operating barrel car. This unpainted yellow car had the molded-in catch to secure the figure swivel plate. On that plate was a blue rubber figure with painted hands and face, and outstretched arms. The knuckle rivets were, as a rule, shiny.

The other operating car was new for 1956: a red, white and blue State of Maine boxcar. This car was offered for three years, so it is important to distinguish the 1956 issue for inclusion in this set. Unlike later year's cars, the 1956 edition did not have a support hole in the coupler drawbar. The blue rubber figure inside had outstretched arms, and its hands and face were painted in flesh tone. The trucks were secured by pushpins rather than the c-clip and stud arrangement used on past operating boxcars. Two different shades of blue were used on the body over the production run of this car. The early, harder to find cars were navy, while the later, more common cars used royal blue.

The orange 6362 was a carryover item that did not have a support hole in the drawbar and likely had silver knuckle rivets, the same held true for the 6414 Auto Loader and the lighted 6357 caboose. Yet again, the version of the locomotive included was the most common with an opaque orange body with painted black cab and decoration. The outfit came in a two-tier basket-weave box.

Excellent	Like New	Scarcity
750	1,200	5

1561WS or 710 Five-Car Freight $59.95 retail

Included: 2065 4-6-4 steam locomotive with headlight, smoke and Magne-traction; 6026W whistle tender; 3424 Wabash operating brakeman; 6430 flatcar with vans; 6262 flatcar with wheels; 6562-25 gondola with canisters; 6257 SP-type caboose; eight 1018 curved and three 1013 straight track; 6019 Remote Control Track Set; 1053 60-watt transformer.

The feedwater heater-equipped 2065 small Hudson powered this 1956 outfit, with a 6026W whistle tender trailing behind. To complete the outfit was a range of new freight cars followed by the familiar 6257 caboose.

Collectors purchasing this outfit based on the catalog illustration are sure to be disappointed, for rather than the scarce red wheel car shown in that publication, instead the common black version was included.

Red was the 6562-25 New York Central gondola with red canister load and the unpainted red 6430 flatcar. This flat was laden with a pair of gray semi-trailers decorated with metal Cooper-Jarrett nameplates. The insignia on these plates can be either copper or orange-colored.

The operating brakeman car included in this outfit almost always has a white figure on its roof and does not have the support hole formed in the coupler head. It is usually wired in black.

All the rolling stock came packed in Late Traditional boxes, while the locomotive came in a tan corrugated carton. The outfit as a whole came in a two-tier basket-weave type box.

Excellent	Like New	Scarcity
575	975	5

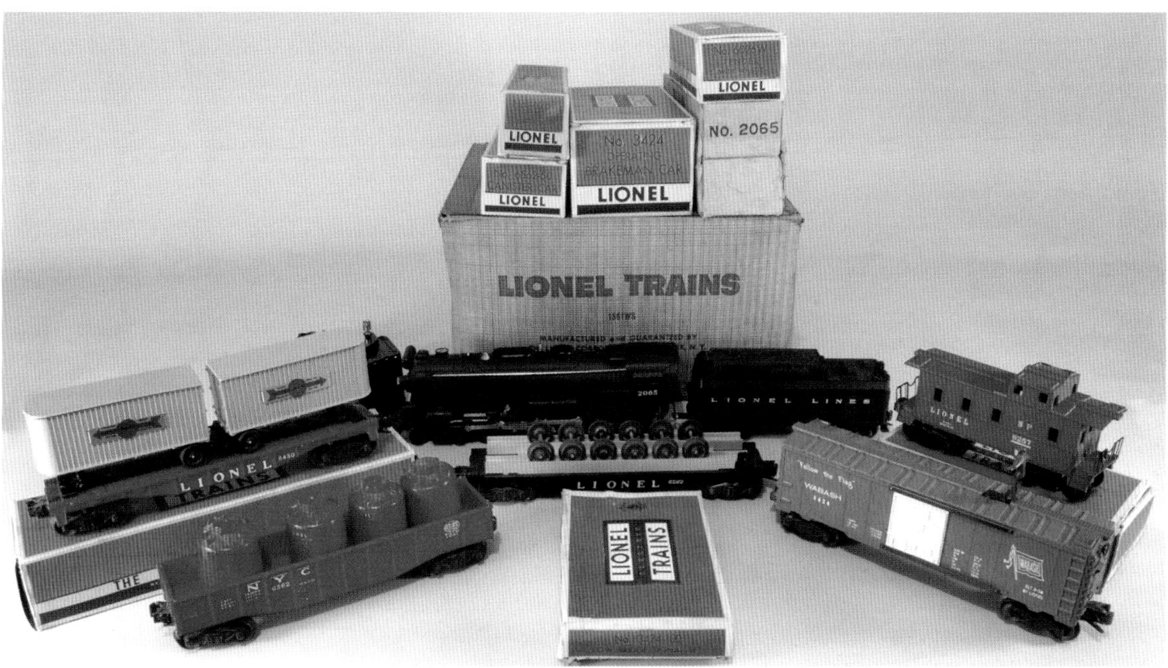

1561WS

1562W or 711 Four-Car Passenger $59.95 retail

Included: 2328 Burlington GP-7; two 2442 Clifton Vista Domes, 2444 Newark Pullman and 2446 Summit observation; eight 1018 curved and three 1013 straight track; 6019 Remote Control Track Set; 1053 60-watt transformer.

As it had been in 1955, the silver 2328 Burlington GP-7 was selected to lead a string of matching passenger cars. This year's outfit was more colorful, and the cars better matched to the locomotive than had been the case in prior years.

The 1956 cars had new numbers and a new paint scheme, a broad red stripe running along the window line of the silver cars, giving them considerably more color than their red letter-only predecessors.

These cars and the matching locomotive, like all of Lionel's silver-painted items, are difficult to find in collectable condition.

All the set components came in Late Traditional boxes, except for the locomotive, which occasionally came in a tan corrugated carton instead. The outfit box was the new two-tier basket-weave type.

Excellent	Like New	Scarcity
1,800	3,000	6

1563W or 712 Five-Car Freight $67.50 retail

Included: 2240P/2240C Wabash F-3 A-B units; 6414 Evans Auto Loader; 3562-50 operating barrel car; 6467 miscellaneous car; 3620 rotating searchlight car; 6357 illuminated SP-type caboose; eight 1018 curved and five 1013 straight track; 6019 Remote Control Track Set; 1033 90-watt transformer.

The 2240 was new for 1956 and a near twin of its 1955 predecessor, the 2367. While external differences are minimal, internally the 2240 had only one motor, whereas the older unit had two. The B-units for the pair are harder to differentiate, the easiest method being to look at the length of the thin white stripe, which is 1/2 in. long on the 2240 B-unit, verses only 1/8 in. on the 2367B. The 2240 B-unit came in a Late Traditional box with liner, while the powered unit came in a tan corrugated carton.

The outfit included a yellow barrel operating barrel car, as described in the 1559W section earlier. The 3620 was a repeat item, but the 1956 edition has bolder lettering and tends to have silver knuckle pins. The 6414 was a carryover item as well, but again silver knuckle pins were the norm for 1956 production. The only new car in the outfit was the 6467, which was produced only in 1956. The unpainted red flatcar had an unpainted black bulkhead attached to either end. On each side were two spring steel 2411-4 posts, although the car did not come with a load.

While it is possible that the carryover cars included in this outfit would surface in Middle Traditional boxes, the bulk of the components of this set were packaged in Late Traditional boxes. The outfit box was naturally of the two-tier basket-weave style.

Excellent	Like New	Scarcity
1,700	2,950	6

1565WS or 713 $69.95 retail

Included: 2065 4-6-4 steam locomotive with headlight, smoke and Magne-traction; 6026W whistle tender; 6414 Evans Auto Loader; 6346 Alcoa covered hopper; 3662 operating milk car; 3650 extension searchlight car; 6357 illuminated SP-type caboose; eight 1018 curved and five 1013 straight track; 6019 Remote Control Track Set; 1033 90-watt transformer.

The interesting 3650 searchlight extension car included in this outfit was new for 1956. It featured a die-cast frame, painted gray, a red plastic reel wound with green wire and a removable gray searchlight head mounted on a red base. A die-cast crank, often missing, was stored on the car when not being used to retract the cable. A small-simulated generator, painted dark gray, was mounted on the end opposite of where the searchlight was stored. Though this car was available through 1959, the 1956 production can be distinguished by the lack of coupler support holes.

The 6346 was also new for 1956 and is described in detail in the outfit 1553 section. The 6414, 6357 and 3662 differed little from the 1955 production, the most obvious change being the frequent use of shiny knuckle pins.

Though as a rule the contents of the two-tier basket-weave box are packed in Late Traditional boxes, it is possible that some of the carry-over items will be found in Middle Traditional boxes.

Excellent	Like New	Scarcity
550	975	6

1567W or 714 Five-Car Freight $75 retail
Included: 2243P/2243C Santa Fe F-3 A-B units; 3424 operating brakeman; 6430 flatcar with vans; 3356 operating horse car; 6672 Santa Fe refrigerator car; 6357 illuminated SP-type caboose; eight 1018 curved and five 1013 straight track; 6019 Remote Control Track Set; 1033 90-watt transformer.

The 3356 operating horse car included in this outfit replaced the 3656 operating cattle car in Lionel's product line. Since the 3356 was produced for many years, it is not surprising that several variations of this car exist. The 1956 edition lacked the support holes in the coupler drawbars, had copper-colored coil windings and the brake wheel was mounted on the right-hand end of the car when facing the operating doors. The car, with its green, white and brown corral, came in a Late Traditional box.

The 6672 refrigerator car was a repeat item, but the version included in this outfit is unusual in that it had black, rather than blue, lettering and lacked the circle "L" logo.

The 3424 most often had a white rubber man and, like the 6430 and caboose, has previously been described in this chapter. All the rolling stock was packaged in Late Traditional boxes.

The dummy B-unit was also packaged in a Late Traditional box, surprisingly with the benefit of a liner. The power unit, which had low profile, molded-in cab ladders, was packaged in a tan corrugated box. The outfit box itself was a two-tier basket-weave style.

Excellent	Like New	Scarcity
975	1,600	6

O-Gauge

1956

2255W or 800 Four-Car Work Train $39.95 retail
Included: 601 Seaboard NW-2 diesel switcher with horn; 3424 Wabash brakeman; 6362 railway truck car; 6560 crane; 6119-50 work caboose; eight TOC curved and three TOS straight track; UCS Remote Control Track Set.

The inexpensive 601 Seaboard switcher was perhaps an unusual choice to head an O-Gauge outfit, but nonetheless was included in this set. While it had Magne-traction and a horn, it did not have an operating headlight.

The 3424 operating brakeman car included in this outfit was mechanically identical to those described as components of 027 sets. However, most reported examples in set 2255W have a blue rubber man, rather than white, which is predominating in the 027 sets.

Another variable in this outfit is the crane car, with either example stamped 6560 or stamped 656025 likely to appear. Most cranes had spoked hand wheels, although some examples with solid hand wheels have been reported as well.

An orange 6362 railway truck car and a brown 6119-50 work caboose completed the consist. To be correct, the cargo of the 6362 should have bar-end trucks without couplers, exhibiting no signs of wear and without mounting stud. It is possible that this car be packed in a Middle Traditional box, but it is more likely that it, like the rest of the components of this set, will be packaged in a Late Traditional box. The outfit box was the new-for-1956 basket-weave carton.

Excellent	Like New	Scarcity
600	1,000	4

2257WS or 801 Five-Car Freight $49.95 retail
Included: 665 4-6-4 steam locomotive with headlight, smoke and Magne-traction; 2046W whistle tender; 6462 red gondola; 6346 Alcoa covered hopper; 3361 operating lumber car; 6467 miscellaneous car; 6427 Lionel Lines porthole caboose; eight TOC curved and three TOS straight track; UCS Remote Control Track Set.

More along the lines of what is normally thought of as an O-Gauge outfit was this set headed by a small Hudson, number 665.

The 6346, 6467 and 3361 have all been previously described in this chapter. Two different versions of the New York Central gondola have been identified as components of this outfit. Some outfits contain 6462-75, red painted car with the "N" in the third panel, while others have the unpainted 6462-125. Note: if the latter car was included, the 1956 box was shorter than it had been in 1955. The Lionel Lines caboose came in a box marked 6427-1. This box, like all the component boxes for this set save the locomotive, was a Late Traditional box. The locomotive came in a tan corrugated box without liner. A basket-weave box was used for the outfit as a whole.

Excellent	Like New	Scarcity
500	750	3

2259W or 802 Five-Car Freight $55 retail

Included: 2350 New Haven EP-5 electric; 6464-425 New Haven boxcar; 6430 flatcar with vans; 3650 searchlight extension car; 6511 pipe car; 6427 Lionel Lines porthole caboose; eight TOC curved and five TOS straight track; UCS Remote Control Track Set.

Lionel selected one of its newly designed locomotives to head this outfit. Lionel called this locomotive an EP-5; although it was supported by the same EMD Bloomberg truck as used on the company's GP-7 diesels (with different pilot details). The actual EP-5 locomotives, built by GE and utilizing mercury-vapor tubes to convert 11,000-volt AC current to 660-volt DC current, rode on six-wheel trucks. As an aside, American Flyer also introduced a replica of the New Haven EP-5 in 1956, and its S-Gauge version had six-wheel trucks. Lionel also compromised on the horn sound of these locomotives, using the same bicycle buzzer horn as used in its diesels. The actual EP-5, like most of the New Haven's electrics, was equipped with a Hancock model 4700-air whistle when delivered.

Lionel's foreshortened representation of the EP-5 was accurately painted in the black, orange and white "McGinnis" paint scheme of the New Haven, which actually owned the real locomotives. The locomotive was packaged in a tan corrugated without liner.

Lionel produced this locomotive in four major variations during 1956. The noses of the locomotives were decorated with either paint or decal, and the "N" and associated lettering on each side could be either white or orange, with the version with decaled nose and white "N" being the most common, and the version presumed included in the pricing below. Collectors should beware that the nose decals are both highly susceptible to wear and have been reproduced. If a locomotive seems to have less wear on its nose than on other areas, it seems probable that the nose decals have been replaced.

All the rolling stock included in this outfit has been described in other outfits listed earlier in this chapter. The outfit box was the two-tier basket-weave type, and Late Traditional boxes were used for the rolling stock.

Excellent	Like New	Scarcity
850	1,400	3

2261WS or 803 Freight Hauler $59.95 retail

Included: 646 4-6-4 steam locomotive with headlight, smoke and Magne-traction; 2046W whistle tender; 6414 Evans Auto Loader; 3562-50 operating barrel car; 6376 circus car; 6436-25 Lehigh Valley quad hopper; 6417 Pennsylvania porthole caboose; eight TOC curved and five TOS straight track; UCS Remote Control Track Set.

The 646 was the O-Gauge version of the popular 027 2046 medium-size Hudson locomotive. The 1956 edition of this locomotive used a trailing truck made of sheet metal and plastic, whereas the 646 used a nicely made trailing truck with die-cast frame. Also, the size of the 1956 cab numbers were reduced compared to the earliest editions. The locomotive came in a tan corrugated box without liner.

The red and white 6376 bi-level circus car was a new item for 1956. Though attractive, the car is notorious for the tendency of the red ink to fade and run when collectors attempt to clean it. This car, being new, naturally came in a Late Traditional box.

The unpainted yellow barrel car, also in a Late Traditional box, came with a blue rubber man, arms outstretched, and with hands and face painted a flesh color. The porthole caboose, strangely a Pennsylvania version rather than a

Lionel Lines version that would have matched the 2046W tender, came in a Late Traditional box with the number "6417-1" stamped on the end flaps.

The big maroon hopper as well as the 6414 Autoloader were both repeat items and, as such, it is theoretically possible that carryover inventory had black knuckle pins and Middle Traditional boxes. However, it is expected that the norm for this outfit would have shiny knuckle pins and be packed in Late Traditional boxes. The outfit box was a two-tier basket-weave style.

Excellent	Like New	Scarcity
575	950	5

2263W or 804 Five-Car Freight $65 retail

Included: 2350 New Haven EP-5 electric; 6414 Evans Auto Loader; 3359 operating dump car; 6468-25 New Haven double-door automobile car; 3662 operating milk car; 6517 bay window caboose; eight TOC curved and seven TOS straight track; UCS Remote Control Track Set.

This was the second 1956 outfit to contain the new 2350 New Haven electric. The locomotive is described in detail in the outfit 2259W segment earlier. In this outfit, like 2259W, the locomotive came packed in a tan corrugated carton without liner.

The rolling stock included in this outfit was all top quality. The 3359 dump car and the 3662 milk car, both returning items, had silver-colored knuckle pins for most, if not all, of the 1956 production.

The 6468-25 automobile boxcar—new for 1956, was fittingly decorated in the orange, black and white McGinnis paint scheme. On most of these cars the large "N" of the "NH" logo was black, and had a half-serif. However, some sets contain double-door cars with the half-serif "N" and associated lettering printed in white.

Known to collectors as the reverse color New Haven, the half-serif "N" in the logo of this car was printed in white and the "H" in black—opposite of the norm for these cars. The 6468-25 New Haven automobile boxcar is also known to exist with brown doors, but these are believed to have been assembled outside the factory, and such cars are not known components of outfit 2263W.

The caboose included in the set was the top of the line 6517 bay window caboose. The variation included in this outfit does not include underscoring beneath the number and "Built 12-55 Lionel."

In most instances, the components of this outfit had shiny knuckle pins and were packed in Late Traditional boxes, although yet again in theory the carry-forward items could truly have been surplus 1955 production with black knuckle pins and Middle Traditional boxes. The outfit box was the basket-weave style.

Excellent	Like New	Scarcity
900	1,500	5

2265WS or 805 Five-Car Freight $69.95 retail

Included: 736 Berkshire steam locomotive with headlight, smoke and Magne-traction; 2046W whistle tender; 3620 rotating searchlight car; 3424 operating brakeman; 6430 flatcar with vans; 6467 miscellaneous car; 6517 bay window caboose; eight TOC curved and seven TOS straight track; UCS Remote Control Track Set.

The tried and true 736 Berkshire provided the motive power for this assortment of operating and high-quality rolling stock. The locomotive in 1956 used a sheet metal and plastic composite trailing truck, rather than the die-cast truck used previously. Its number was heat-stamped in white, rather than rubber stamped as it had been at the dawn of the

1956

decade. It came in a tan corrugated carton without a liner. Behind the locomotive was a 2046W streamlined Lionel Lines tender that came packed in a Late Traditional box.

At the end of the train was a top of the line bay window caboose. The variation included in this outfit did not have underscoring beneath "6517" and "Built 12-55 Lionel."

The lettering of the 3620 in 1956 was stamped a bit bolder than it had been in prior years and the cars had shiny knuckle pins. The 6467 miscellaneous car did not come with a cargo, but did come with four spring-steel 2411-4 posts and a pair of molded black plastic bulkheads.

The Cooper-Jarrett logos on the metal nameplates decorating the gray vans could be either copper or orange-colored. The car itself had a black metal structure to secure the trailers on its red unpainted plastic body.

The operating boxcar, which had a blue body with white doors and Wabash markings, is more frequently reported in this set with a blue rubber figure than white. Included inside each of the cars' Late Traditional boxes in this and the other outfits was a 3424-100 accessory box, which included light orange plastic telltale poles.

With the possible exception of some carry-forward items, all the rolling stock came in Late Traditional boxes, and the outfit box was the basket-weave type.

Excellent	Like New	Scarcity
750	1,200	5

2267W or 806 Five-Car Freight $69.95 retail

Included: 2331 Virginian Train Master; 3562-50 operating barrel car; 6560 crane; 3359 operating dump car; 3361X operating lumber car; 6419-50 work caboose; eight TOC curved and seven TOS straight track; UCS Remote Control Track Set.

Though at first glance one would think that all the rolling stock in this outfit was a carryover item, in reality the caboose had been completely re-engineered. Though it retained its stamped number and a die-cast frame, the method of cab attachment changed. Rather than the tall die-cast stack in use on work cabooses since 1946, the car now used the short stack developed the year prior for the bay window caboose. The caboose came in a Late Traditional box marked 6419-50.

The work caboose accompanied a 6560 crane with red cab. It was usually, but not always, stamped with the full 656025 number on the chassis. The yellow barrel car had an unpainted yellow body, and a blue rubber man with outstretched arms, and painted hands and face.

The 3359 twin bin dump car and 3361 operating car were both repeat items, but the 1956 editions can be distinguished by their shiny knuckle pins and lack of coupler support holes. Both came in Late Traditional boxes, and the log car came in a box numbered 3361X, denoting that the receiving tray was packed loose in the basket-weave outfit box rather than in the box with the car, as it was for separate sale cars.

Of these cars that were high-quality items found in most collections, the star of the outfit was its locomotive, the 2331 blue-and-yellow Virginian Fairbanks-Morse Trainmaster. Most of the locomotives found in 2267W outfits had bodies molded of blue plastic, with only the yellow painted on. However, a few outfits contained a more desirable and harder to find version of the locomotive that had a body molded of gray plastic, with both the blue and the yellow colors painted on. In either instance, it came in a tan corrugated carton with a protective liner. Collectors should beware that repainted and/or reproduction bodies for this locomotive are abundant.

Excellent	Like New	Scarcity
1,600	2,650	5

2269W or 807 Five-Car Freight $75.00 retail

Included: 2368P/2368C Baltimore & Ohio F-3 A-B units; 3356 operating horse car; 6518 double-truck transformer car; 6315 Gulf chemical tank car; 3361X operating log car; 6517 bay window caboose; eight TOC curved and seven TOS straight track; UCS Remote Control Track Set.

This outfit contained what are arguably the most desirable and sought after F-3 diesels Lionel ever made: the 2368 Baltimore & Ohio. The decoration of these locomotives was a combination of rubber-stamped nose striping, painted side striping and heat-stamped lettering. The powered unit came in a tan corrugated carton without a liner, while the B-unit came in a Late Traditional box with a liner.

Because of the high value, desirability and downright good looks of the 2368 reproduction, restored and repainted bodies outnumber authentic items. Fortunately, most of these have been done on the wrong style of body molding, or by using improper decoration techniques. This photo of an original unit can be used for comparison when considering a purchase. Notice there is no evidence of decals or silk-screening found.

While not as spectacular as the locomotive pair, the rolling stock included in the outfit was nevertheless first rate. The 1956 editions of the 3361 and 3356 have already been discussed in depth in this chapter. The 6517 bay window caboose was produced in two major variations, known to collectors as underscored and not underscored—referring to the printing of the catalog number and built dates on the car body. Both versions have been reported as components of this set, with the non-underscored version apparently being the more commonly included.

The nicely detailed single-dome tank was new for 1956. It featured a plastic body, dome, ends and frame, with metal platform, under frame, ladders and handrails. The car, which had Gulf Oil markings, had an unpainted black center section with painted end portions. Several shades of orange/burnt orange were used during the production run of the car and thus far a particular shade has not been associated with this outfit.

The 6518 transformer car came about as a result of Lionel combining, as it so often did, parts of existing product designs to create a new offering. In this case, the simulated transformer load created nine years prior for the 2461 was combined with the 16-wheel railcar introduced in 1955 with a girder cargo, yielding this new car. The insulators, as they are on all of Lionel's transformer cars, are fragile, and reproductions are widespread. The weight of the die-cast car, along with its easily swiveling truck assemblies, frequently has destroyed the large 6518 box. The box had no liner, but did come with two cardboard inserts to protect the transformer insulators.

Excellent	Like New	Scarcity
4,000	6,750	7

2270W or 808 Three-Car Jersey Central Passenger
$75 retail

Included: 2341 Jersey Central Train Master; 2531 Silver Dawn observation, 2532 Silver Range Vista Dome and 2533 Silver Cloud Pullman; eight TOC curved and seven TOS straight track; UCS Remote Control Track Set.

Much like the previous outfit containing the "best" of the postwar F-3 diesels, this outfit contains the "best" of the Fairbanks-Morse Trainmasters: the Jersey Central. As with the 2368 F-3, collectors should beware of repainted/reproduction 2341 bodies mounted on more common FM chassis. The true 2341 chassis has a sticker-type battery plate rather than an etched plate, along with vertical light brackets.

The passenger cars most frequently associated with this set are those with wide flat-channels, however, ribbed-channel cars or a mixture can appear. As a matter of fact, several sets have been reported to contain flat-channel Pullman and dome cars, and ribbed-channel observation cars. Also likely to be mixed were the style of boxes, with both Middle and Late Traditional boxes found in some outfits.

The basket-weave box was used as the outfit package.

Excellent	Like New	Scarcity
5,600	9,000	7

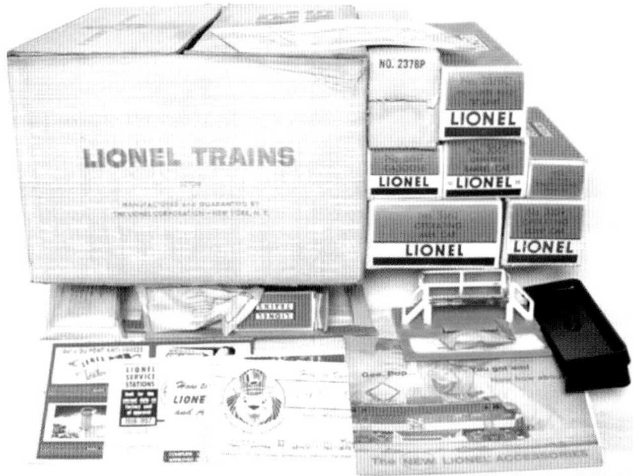

2271W or 809 Five-Car Freight $79.50 retail

Included: 2360-25 green Pennsylvania five-stripe GG-1; 3424 operating brakeman; 3662 operating milk car; 6414 Evans Auto Loader; 6418 double-truck girder car; 6417 Pennsylvania porthole caboose; eight TOC curved and seven TOS straight track; UCS Remote Control Track Set.

Even though the 1950 2330 GG-1 returned in 1955 with no changes and a new number, 2340, the process was repeated again in 1956 with the green GG-1 renumbered as 2360. The official catalog number, which appeared on the box but not the locomotive, was 2360-25. This desirable die-cast, twin-motor locomotive came inside a tan corrugated carton with a liner, made by National.

The Wabash operating brakeman car, 3662 milk car and 6414 Auto Loader were also components of other 1956 sets, and have been previously discussed in this chapter.

The 16-wheel machinery car, number 6418, included in this outfit was laden with a pair of either black or orange girders and had highlighted raised U.S. Steel lettering, as well as the car's number, appearing on the girders. While this car had been introduced in 1955, that year's production had the number "6418" cast in raised numbers on the underside of the car. The raised numbers were removed in 1956 and the knuckle pins changed from black to silver. The box for this car is often found in sad condition, with the double trucks and heavy weight of the car overwhelming the oversized, unlined Late Traditional box.

Fittingly, bringing up the rear of this fabulous outfit was a 6417 Pennsylvania N5C porthole caboose. The car is numbered 536417, while its Late Traditional box is numbered "6417-1."

The outfit is packaged in a basket-weave-type box, which is often found today in damaged condition due to the weight of its contents.

Excellent	Like New	Scarcity
3,000	5,000	5

2273W or 810 Milwaukee Road Diesel Freight $85 retail

Included: 2378P/2378C Milwaukee Road F-3 A-B units; 342 operating culvert loader with 6342 culvert gondola; 3562-50 operating barrel car; 3359 operating dump car; 3662 operating milk car; 6517 bay window caboose; eight TOC curved and seven TOS straight track; UCS Remote Control Track Set.

Another outfit headed by a 1956-only F-3 was this one. The 2378 Milwaukee Road at the front is not as colorful as the 2368 B&O pair in 2269W, but it is still very sought after by collectors. This was the only outfit to contain the A-B Milwaukee Road pair. Though produced in low numbers, the combination nevertheless exists in three different variations. One type, and incidentally the most valuable, has a fine yellow line running along the juncture of the roof and side of both units; the next most desirable as a pair lacks the stripe, while on the third version—the least desirable—the B-unit has the stripe and the A-unit lacks it. Regardless of variation, the large water-slide decal at the front of the A-unit is somewhat fragile and has often been replaced.

The powered A-unit, with its twin motors and battery-operated horn, were packaged in a tan corrugated carton without a liner, while its companion B-unit came in a Late Traditional box with liner.

Another collectable item included in the outfit was the component-boxed culvert loader. The culvert loader, new for 1956, came with a 6342 culvert gondola that did not have its own component box, but rather was held in place inside the loader's box by an insert. This was the first time Lionel had included a large accessory in a set since the 1949 4110WS outfit.

A large water-type decal covers most of the nose of the 2378 A-unit. To find such a unit with the decal in this condition is every collector's dream. Beware, the decal—indeed the entire body for this A-unit has been reproduced. Seen above is an authentic piece, the vents and details of the nose door aiding in its positive identification.

The remainder of the rolling stock in the outfit was run of the mill 1956 items, and is described elsewhere in this chapter. The outfit box was a basket-weave type, albeit a large one in order to accommodate the boxed culvert loader.

Excellent	Like New	Scarcity
4,000	6,500	6

2274W or 811 Congressional **$100 retail**

Included: 2360 Tuscan Pennsylvania GG-1; 2541 Alexander Hamilton observation; 2542 Betsy Ross Vista Dome, 2543 William Penn Pullman, and 2544 Molly Pitcher Pullman; eight TOC curved and eleven TOS straight track; UCS Remote Control Track Set.

The GG1-led Congressional returned for a second year in 1956 with some changes. As with the green version heading the 2271W freight outfit, the Tuscan GG-1 in this set differed from the 1955 version only in its number. The vents on either side of the locomotive were staggered along their top, and five pinstripes ran the length of the engine, tapering to a fine point at each end. The big dual-motor electric came in a tan corrugated carton with a protective liner. The locomotive box was made by National, and included a "56" date beneath the maker's circular seal. The end of the box was stamped "2360."

The cars were virtually identical to the 1955 edition, however a shiny knuckle rivet was used in 1956, rather than the black of the previous year. Also, in 1956 the cars naturally came in Late Traditional boxes. Of course, the 1956 edition of the Congressional came in the new basket-weave-type box.

Inexperienced collectors should beware when contemplating the purchase of a Congressional set, as excellent restorations of the locomotives are available and reproduction/forged cars likely outnumber originals on the market.

Excellent	Like New	Scarcity
5,000	8,500	7

Chapter 14

1957

The big news from Lionel in 1957 was the introduction of a totally new track system known as Super 0. This innovative system featured a narrow center rail made of copper, while the outer running rails had a realistic T-shaped cross section. The rails were joined to a track bed which featured closely spaced molded plastic ties, resulting in the track looking much more authentic than anything previously produced by Lionel. Underneath the plastic ties were three steel ties, which gave the track needed structural integrity.

Also new for the year was one of the most coveted steam locomotives of the postwar era—Lionel's replica of the famed Norfolk and Western class "J" steam locomotive. The Norfolk and Western Railway was the last holdout for mainline steam locomotives in the United States. Situated in the heart of coal country, the N&W had access to plentiful supplies of high-quality, economical coal, and also derived a significant portion of its revenue from the coal industry. To embrace diesel locomotives would alienate a large portion of its customer base. But not only that, N&W was also successful with its steam locomotives, most of which were built in the railroad's own shops in Roanoke. N&W built steam locomotives into the 1950s, by which time they were the only ones building mainline steam engines in this country. This caused dramatic increases in costs of component parts, or made them unavailable, as component suppliers went out of business or raised prices due to lower production. Ultimately, it was this that led N&W to give up on steam.

The Norfolk and Western class "J" 4-8-4 locomotives were powerful (5,200 horsepower), efficient (servicing took merely one hour), and fast (110 mph was recorded) machines designed to pull the road's crack passenger trains. The first, number 600, was built in 1941. The last, number 613, was built in 1950. By October 1959, they had been retired. All but one, the 611—now on display at the Virginia Museum of Transportation in Roanoke—were ultimately scrapped.

New road names appeared on such favorites as the F-3 and GP diesels, and the EP-5 electrics. These locomotives were then chosen to head spectacular new outfits, many of which included new cars such as the 6556 stock car, 3530 Electro-Mobile Power Car, 3444 animated gondola and six new 6464 boxcars.

One outfit of special mention was introduced in 1957, the famous—or infamous—"Lady Lionel." This pastel-colored consist was intended to appeal to fathers seeking to purchase something "special" for their daughters. It was almost complete marketing failure—those daughters unfortunate enough to receive one in 1957 are fortunate indeed today, as the "Girl's Train" has become one of the most sought after and valuable outfits of the postwar era.

More popular at the time, but nevertheless disappointing in terms of quality, were the reintroduced 027 Alco diesels and the new Camtrol uncoupler. The restyling of the Alco paralleled the 1955 redesign of the NW-2 switcher, with the high quality die-cast frame and trucks giving way to stamped sheet metal components. The 1008 Camtrol uncoupler was a manually operated device that was included in the three least expensive 027 outfits in lieu of the previously used 6019 electromagnetic uncoupling/unloading track. Throughout the rest of the 027, the 6019 was replaced by the uncouple-only 6029.

The tan with off-white basket-weave-style box first introduced in 1956 was continued unchanged in 1957 for use with 0 and 027 outfits. The new Super 0 outfits had their own specialized packaging. Lionel continued its policy of offering each set under two numbers: one for the traditional Lionel dealer network, and the other for mass merchants.

A new freight car truck was introduced in 1957. The new featured side frames, bolster, coupler head and drawbar molded as one-piece of plastic. Styled after the Association of American Railroad trucks, the tiny simulated journals on the side frames bore the raised name, "Timken." While this basic truck would remain in production through the end of the postwar era, like so many of Lionel's products, there were many variations. From 1957 through 1961, these trucks used die-cast coupler knuckles, their wheel hubs were flush with the wheel rims, and when the truck was inverted the ends of the axles were not visible.

The die-cast bar-end trucks were changed this year as well. A hole was added to the coupler shank, which would be present throughout the remainder of the trucks' production.

The basket weave box with blue lettering, first produced in 1956, continued to be used for 0 and 027 sets during 1957.

The newly created Super 0 line warranted its own unique packaging, a situation reflecting the top of the line status awarded Super 0. The Super 0 packaging was a dark brown basket weave with pictures of onrushing trains on four sides.

027-Gauge

1569 or 725 Four-Car Diesel Freight $25 retail

Included: 202 Union Pacific Alco A-unit; 6014 Frisco boxcar; (6111) flatcar with logs; 6112 gondola with canisters; 6017 SP-type caboose; eight 1013 curved and two 1018 straight track; 1008 camtrol; 1015 45-watt transformer; Lockon; tube of lubricant; instructions.

This outfit was the first to include the redesigned Alco diesel, and the difference between this unit and those made in 1954 and prior is immediately apparent. Gone was the accompanying dummy A-unit, as well as the heavy die-cast chassis. Instead, a single A-unit with a stamped sheet metal frame and fabricated rather than die-cast trucks was created. As a further nod to the economy pricing of this outfit, the 202 had only single-axle Magne-traction, a two-position E-unit, and lacked a front coupler.

In tow behind the locomotive were three equally economical freight cars. While the cars themselves were not new, they rode on newly designed trucks with one-piece molded side frames, bolster, and coupler head. No individual boxes were included, not even for the locomotive. Instead, the components were placed inside the single-layer basket weave box with cardboard dividers separating them. A wraparound liner offered additional protection for the locomotive—whose paint was and is easily scratched.

Excellent	Like New	Scarcity
300	500	4

Lenny the Lion was Lionel's mascot for much of the postwar period.

1571 or 726 Five-Car Diesel Freight $29.95 retail

Included: 625 Lehigh Valley center cab; 6424 flatcar with autos; 6476 Lehigh Valley hopper; (6121) flatcar with pipes; 6112 gondola with canisters; 6017 SP-type caboose; eight 1013 curved and two 1018 straight track; 1008 camtrol; 1015 45-watt transformer; Lockon; tube of lubricant; instructions.

Lionel's somewhat oversize center cab switcher, wearing a new black and red color scheme, was placed at the head of this train. Once again, low cost was a key factor in the engineering of the locomotive, as this unit lacked operating couplers.

Despite its original low cost, two moderately desirable variations of common cars are known to have been included in this outfit. The first of these is the molded white version of the common 6112 gondola—or as Lionel referred to it, the canister car. The second variation car is the 6424 with AAR trucks riveted to metal truck-mounting plates rather than directly to the car body. The 6017 with AAR trucks was a routine item, and is today one of the most common of all postwar pieces.

The components of this economy-priced outfit did not warrant individual boxes, instead being protected in the set box by special cardboard dividers. .

Excellent	Like New	Scarcity
425	700	5

1573 or 727 Five-Car Steam-type Freight $29.95 retail

Included: 250 2-4-2 steam locomotive with operating headlight; 250T tender; 6464-425 New Haven boxcar; 6112 gondola with canisters; 6476 Lehigh Valley hopper; 6025 Gulf single-dome tank car; 6017 SP-type caboose; eight 1013 curved and four 1018 straight track; 1008 camtrol; 1015 45-watt transformer; Lockon; tube of lubricant; instructions.

After three years of producing die-cast boiler-equipped steam locomotives, a budget-minded plastic-bodied steamer returned to the line. The new 2-4-2 bore a strong resemblance to the earlier Scout locomotives, but was of higher quality. Adding a touch of color, a red stripe adorned the edge of the running board and extended the length of the small streamlined tender, where it was imprinted with the "PENNSYLVANIA" legend.

Behind the locomotive was an interesting array of rolling stock, all riding on the new plastic AAR-type trucks. The nice black 6464-425 NH boxcar was joined by the rather mundane orange 6025 Gulf tank car, and the even more common 6112 gondola, which could be one of a number of colors. Also included, a 6476 Lehigh Valley hopper, with separately applied metal truck mounting plates, which included integral steps. The outfit was packed in a two-tier basket-weave box.

Excellent	Like New	Scarcity
250	400	5

1575 or 728 Five-Car Diesel Freight $37.50 retail

Included: 205P/205T Missouri Pacific Alco A-A units; 6560-25 crane; (6121) flatcar with pipes; 6112 gondola with canisters; (6111) flatcar with logs; 6119-100 work caboose; eight 1013 curved and three 1018 straight track; 6029 uncoupling section; 1015 45-watt transformer; Lockon; tube of lubricant; instructions.

Although still the cheapened Alco, at least in this outfit the Missouri Pacific units were paired powered and dummy. That these locomotives are not harder to find today is purely a result of their sales success, as they were packed without benefit component boxes inside the two-tier outfit carton.

In tow behind the pair of blue diesels were five freight cars. The best of these was the red-cab-equipped 6560-25 crane, the –25 suffix appearing only on the component box. The crane was matched with a work caboose featuring a red cab, gray tool tray and black frame. These were joined in the consist by a pair of sheet metal flat cars loaded with logs and plastic pipe, and a gondola laden with canisters.

Worthy of mention, some of these outfits have been reported to contain Alcos with factory-installed nose supports, painted in blue to go with the blue locos.

Excellent	Like New	Scarcity
350	600	5

1577S or 729 Six-Car Freight with Smoke $37.50 retail

Included: 2018 2-6-4 steam locomotive with operating headlight and smoke; 1130T tender; 6014 Frisco boxcar; 6464-475 Boston and Maine boxcar; (6111) flatcar with logs; (6121) flatcar with pipes; 6112 gondola with canisters; 6017 SP-type caboose; eight 1013 curved and three 1018 straight track; 6029 uncoupling section; 1015 45-watt transformer; Lock-on; tube of lubricant; instructions.

Interestingly, this outfit included both a full-size 6464 boxcar in Boston and Maine livery and a Scout-sized 6014 boxcar in Frisco markings. Additionally, two flat cars were included, one each loaded with logs and pipes. A 6112 gondola with canisters and a 6017 caboose completed the set. All of these cars were equipped with the new plastic AAR-type trucks. To tow these six cars Lionel included a 2018 die-cast steamer with 1130T tender.

While some items in the outfit were individually boxed in Middle Traditional cartons, some pieces relied on cardboard dividers to protect them. The locomotive came in a tan cardboard box without a liner that was dated "57."

Excellent	Like New	Scarcity
250	400	5

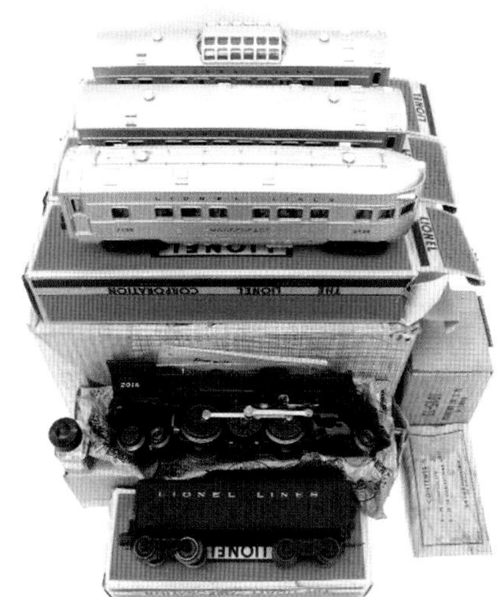

1578S or 730 Passenger with Smoke $43.75 retail

Included: 2018 2-6-4 steam locomotive with operating headlight and smoke; 1130T tender; 2432 Clifton Vista Dome, 2434 Newark Pullman, and 2346 Mooseheart or Summit observation; eight 1013 curved and three 1018 straight track; 6029 uncoupling section; 1015 45-watt transformer; Lockon; tube of lubricant; instructions.

This rather unusual outfit combined the very basic die-cast 2-6-4 2019 with three red-lettered passenger cars that only a few years earlier had been the top of the line items. Even in this year of economy, the passenger cars retained their individual Late Traditional boxes (having stock numbers only on the end flaps). The outfit box was a two-tier basket-weave carton.

Only 4,500 of these outfits were produced, making this one of the more uncommon sets of 1957. Some examples of this outfit have reported to contain the Mooseheart observation car, while others reportedly contain the Summit observation car.

Excellent	Like New	Scarcity
525	925	7

1579S or 731 Seven-Car Freight with Smoke $43.75 retail

Included: 2037 2-6-4 steam locomotive with operating headlight, smoke, and Magne-traction; 1130T tender; 6468-

25 New Haven double-door automobile car; (6121) flatcar with pipes; (6111) flatcar with logs; 6112 gondola with canisters; 6476 Lehigh Valley hopper; 6025 Gulf single-dome tank car; 6017 SP-type caboose; eight 1013 curved and three 1018 straight track; 6029 uncoupling section; 1043 60-watt transformer; Lockon; tube of lubricant; instructions.

Perhaps due to the length of this train, Lionel felt it necessary to include a Magne-traction equipped locomotive in this set. Strangely, however, the 2037 was paired with a non-whistling 1130T tender when placed at the head of the seven-car freight. The largest of these cars, and the only one equipped with bar-end metal trucks, was the 6468-25 New Haven double door automobile boxcar. The remainder of the outfit, including the tender, rode on the new AAR-type plastic trucks.

Excellent	Like New	Scarcity
300	500	5

1581 or 732 Seven-Car Diesel Switcher Freight $43.75 retail

Included: 611 Jersey Central NW-2 diesel switcher; 6464-650 Rio Grande boxcar; 6024 Nabisco boxcar; 6560-25 crane; 6424 flatcar with autos; 6476 Lehigh Valley hopper; 6025 Gulf single-dome tank car; 6119-100 work caboose; eight 1013 curved and three 1018 straight; 6029 uncoupling section; 1043 60-watt transformer; Lockon; tube of lubricant; instructions.

Here again Lionel included the odd pairing of a Scout-sized boxcar, in this case the orange 6024 Nabisco car, with a full-sized 6464 boxcar—the new-for-1957 6464-650 Rio Grande. Other rolling stock included a red-cab-equipped 6560-25 crane, 6476 Lehigh Valley hopper with metal steps, 6025 Gulf tanker, and a 6424 flatcar with two-auto load. This outfit is known to include the 6424 variation with AAR-type trucks attached to metal truck mounting plates. At the rear of the train was the red, gray and black 6119-100 work caboose. While the big Rio Grande boxcar was equipped with bar-end metal trucks, the rest of the cars were equipped with the new plastic trucks.

At the front of this lengthy train was a NW-2 switcher in Jersey Central markings. However, this was not the all-blue unit offered previously, but instead a blue and orange diesel with non-operating couplers.

The outfit was packed in a two-tier basket-weave type carton, with its components a mixture of boxed and unboxed items.

Excellent	Like New	Scarcity
550	975	5

1583WS or 733 Six-Car Freight with Smoke and Whistle $49.95 retail

Included: 2037 2-6-4 steam locomotive with operating headlight, smoke and Magne-traction; 6026W whistle tender; (6121) flatcar with pipes; 6112 gondola with canisters; 6476 Lehigh Valley hopper; 6482 refrigerator car; 6646 stock car; 6017 SP-type caboose; eight 1013 curved and three 1018 straight track; 6029 uncoupling section; 1053 60-watt transformer; Lockon; tube of lubricant; instructions.

The 2037 in charge of six-car freight was equipped not only with smoke and Magne-traction, but its tender had an operating whistle as well. The 6026W Lionel Lines tender rode on bar-end metal trucks and was packed in a Late Traditional box, while the locomotive itself came in a linerless tan corrugated cardboard carton. Strangely, it appears that none of the other trains packed in this two-tier basket-weave outfit box had individual packaging.

All the freight cars were supplied with the new plastic AAR-style trucks, including the two most interesting items in the set, the 6482 and 6646. These two cars were revisions of the long running 6472 refrigerator car and 6656 stock car. While the color of the stock car changed from yellow to orange, a less obvious aspect of the updating of both cars was the deletion of their predecessors' metal trucks in favor of the cheaper plastic-based assemblies. Both of these cars were 1957-only items and are harder to locate today than many collectors realize.

Excellent	Like New	Scarcity
250	400	4

1585W or 734 Nine-Car Freight $49.95 retail

Included: 602 Seaboard NW-2 diesel switcher with horn; 6014 Frisco boxcar; 6024 Nabisco boxcar; 6464-525 Minneapolis & St. Louis boxcar; (6111) flatcar with logs; (6121) flatcar with pipes; 6112 gondola with canisters; 6476 Lehigh Valley hopper; 6025 Gulf single-dome tank car; 6017 SP-type caboose; eight 1013 curved and five 1018 straight track; 6029 uncoupling section; 1053 60-watt transformer; Lockon; tube of lubricant; instructions.

This 027 outfit has the distinction of containing more cars than any other set of the postwar era. In a reasonable interpretation of actual railroad car movements of the era, no less than three boxcars were packed into this set, along with two flat cars, one hopper, gondola and tank car—all trailed of course by a caboose.

The big O-Gauge-sized red 6464-525 boxcar and the orange 6024 Nabisco Scout-type boxcar rode on bar-end metal trucks, while the nearly identical 6014 Frisco boxcar, as well as the rest of the rolling stock, was equipped with plastic AAR-type trucks. Not all the freight cars were individually boxed as some relied on cardboard dividers and careful placement for protection.

To power this lengthy consist, Lionel included a 027 version of 1956's 601 O-Gauge Seaboard NW-2 diesel switcher. Renumbered 602 to reflect its operating coupler-less 027 status, the red and black locomotive retained its operating headlight and horn. It was protected by a Late Traditional box with small cardboard inserts and placed in a two-tier basket-weave outfit box, a die-cut divider separating the layers of set components.

Excellent	Like New	Scarcity
425	700	5

1586 or 735 Three-Car Passenger $49.95 retail

Included: 204P/204T Santa Fe Alco A-A units; two 2432 Clifton Vista Domes; 2436 Summit or Mooseheart observation; eight 1013 curved and five 1018 straight track; 6029 uncoupling section; 1043 50-watt transformer; Lockon; tube of lubricant; instructions.

Two red-lettered Vista Dome cars and a red-lettered observation made up the streamlined consist behind a pair of Alco diesels. The twin F-A units were unique among Lionel's sheet-metal frame equipped economy Alco units in that the dummy, or "T" unit, had an operating headlight. All the other dummy units of this series lacked this feature. Even more bizarre was the color choice for the outfit. Lionel, who by this time had almost 10 years' experience packaging locos painted in Santa Fe's famous red and silver "Warbonnet" passenger scheme with freight cars, now did the opposite: the Santa Fe diesels shipped with the streamlined passenger cars were painted in a variation of Santa Fe's blue and yellow freight scheme!

Both the powered (P) and dummy (T) units were packed in individual tan corrugated cartons, while each of the passenger cars came in a Late Traditional box. The passenger car boxes had the stock numbers only on the ends, the box side numbers having been discontinued the previous year. The outfit box was of course the two-tier basket-weave type.

Either version of the 2436, Summit or Mooseheart, can be found in this outfit.

Excellent	Like New	Scarcity
700	1,200	6

1587S or 736 Lady Lionel $49.95 retail

Included: 2037-500 2-6-4 pink steam locomotive with operating headlight, smoke and Magne-traction; 1130T-500 tender; 6464-510 New York Central Pacemaker boxcar; 6464-515 Missouri-Kansas-Texas boxcar; 6462-500 gondola with canisters; 6436-500 Lehigh Valley quad hopper; 6427-500 Pennsylvania porthole caboose; eight 1013 curved and five 1018 straight track; 6029 uncoupling section; 1043-500 60-watt ivory transformer with ivory cord; Lockon; tube of lubricant; instructions.

Virtually everything in this outfit is unique, including the track and canister load—and though a dud when new, today this is one of the most coveted of all postwar outfits. Unfortunately, this has lead to widespread counterfeiting of the set.

In an ill-advised move to market a train for girls, Lionel created this pastel-colored train. All of the items that were regular production items have their color and markings (a fact that is of benefit to forgers). At the front of the set was a smoke and Magne-traction-equipped 2037 painted pink. The cab was numbered simply "2037" in blue, but the "57" dated tan corrugated loco box was numbered 2037-500. Behind the locomotive was a pink, non-whistling tender. In most cases this was a short streamlined 1130T—though very few rare examples of pink 6026T square tenders are known to exist. In either event, the tenders are marked, "LIONEL LINES" in blue.

Strangely, in a year when Lionel seemed intent on using their new plastic AAR-type trucks throughout the 027 line, all the rolling stock in this outfit was equipped with bar-end metal trucks. Each of the freight cars, as well as the tender, came in their own Late Traditional box, which was preprinted with the unique stock number assigned to each car.

Beware when considering the purchase of a Lady Lionel. Take time to examine each car for signs of sanding or other clues of silk-screen printing—indicative of a forgery. The proper transformer, lockon, tube of lubricant and instructions for this outfit had an ivory-colored case with a white power cord—the plug being marked "LIONEL." Gold-colored screws, binding posts and throttle lever are also characteristic of authentic "Girl's Train" transformer, lockon, tube of lubricant and instructions that came in appropriately numbered 1043-500 tan corrugated boxes.

All the outfit components were packed into a two-tier basket-weave box—however, in keeping with the pastel theme of this set, the base color of this outfit box was mauve.

Excellent	Like New	Scarcity
3,000	5,000	6

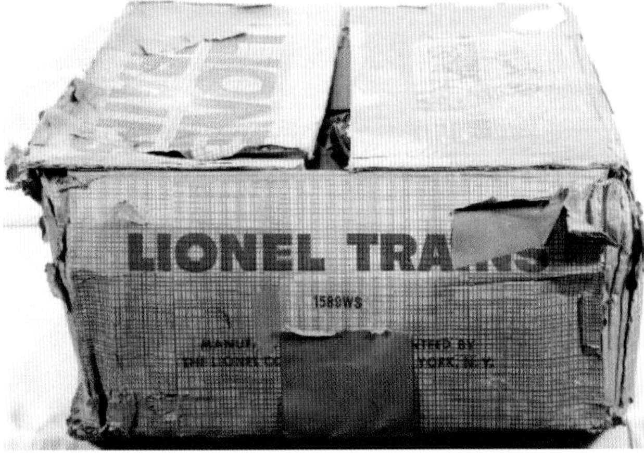

1589WS or 737 Seven-Car Freight $59.95 retail

Included: 2037 2-6-4 steam locomotive with operating headlight, smoke and Magne-traction; 6026W whistle tender; 6464-450 Great Northern boxcar; 6024 Nabisco boxcar; (6111) flatcar with logs; 6424 flatcar with autos; 6112 gondola with canisters; 6025 Gulf single-dome tank car; 6017 SP-type caboose; eight 1013 curved and five 1018 straight track; 6029 uncoupling section; 1044 90-watt transformer; Lockon; tube of lubricant; instructions.

This was the most expensive 027 outfit offered in 1957, though it was not the longest train sold, nor did it include any operating cars. What it did include was a pair of boxcars: the new orange 6024 Nabisco and the previously issued 6464-450 Great Northern, both riding on bar-end metal trucks.

While the orange Gulf tank car as well as the 6112 gondola and 6111 flatcar were equipped with plastic AAR-type trucks, the 6424 flatcar with autos has been reported in this set with either bar-end metal trucks or AAR plastic trucks. In either event the 6424 trucks were attached to sheet metal mounting plates, which in turn were attached to the plastic car body.

The typical production 2037 was included and mated with a 6026W whistle tender mounted on metal trucks. The tender, as well as the freight cars, came in Late Traditional boxes. The locomotive came in a tan corrugated carton without a liner, and all the set components were contained in a two-tier basket-weave box.

Excellent	Like New	Scarcity
500	750	5

O-Gauge

2275W or 815 Four-Car Freight $49.95 retail

Included: 2339 Wabash GP-7; 6464-475 Boston and Maine boxcar; 3444 animated gondola; 6425 Gulf three-dome tank car; 6427 Lionel Lines porthole caboose; eight TOC curved and five TOS straight track; UCS uncoupling/operating section.

The spectacularly decorated GP-7 wore the blue-gray-and-white paint scheme of the Wabash railroad. As an O-Gauge item, the diesel had front and rear operating headlights and couplers, as well an operating horn. It also had the full complement of trim with simulated horns, separately installed cab handrails, and a molded plastic fuel tank. The locomotive was packaged in a Late Traditional box.

Behind the locomotive were four freight cars riding on bar-end metal trucks. A blue 6464 boxcar decorated with black and white Boston and Maine markings debuted in this set—it was to remain a part of the Lionel line for many years. Also included was a triple dome tank car, its sides decorated with the logo of Gulf Oil Corp.—the previous year this car had replaced the 6415 in the product line. The change in decoration resulted in the Gulf car being assigned the new number, 6425.

Also included in the set was the new 3444 animated gondola car—known to some enthusiasts as a cop and hobo car. Centered in this red gondola was a molded tan group of simulated crates, around which a blue vinyl cop chased a gray vinyl hobo. The hobos were suspended from a section of 16mm film and powered by Lionel's reliable vibrator mechanism that was housed in the simulated crates. Black heat-stamped markings decorated the crates—which also contained an off-on switch, the lever of which extended above the car—while the unpainted red plastic car body was decorated with white "ERIE" markings. The earliest of these cars were equipped with a single pickup truck—or "481-1 light coupler truck complete" in company parlance—but in September 1957 this was changed to two pickup roller equipped trucks.

These cars all came in Late Traditional boxes. The outfit box was the two-tier basket-weave type.

Excellent	Like New	Scarcity
750	1,200	3

2276W or 816 1957 Budd RDC Commuter Set $49.95 retail

Included: 404 Budd mail-baggage Rail Diesel Car; two 2559 Budd passenger cars; eight TOC curved and seven TOS straight track; UCS uncoupling/operating section.

Though desirable today, this unusual outfit raised little consumer interest in 1957. No doubt the hope was that this outfit would appeal to Northeastern U.S. commuters—many of who were now relying on real Budd RDC units for their daily travel. To create this outfit Lionel combined their new-for-1957 mail-baggage powered unit, catalog number 404, with two non-powered 2559 passenger cars.

The powered unit was packaged in a conventional tan corrugated carton—which strangely for this late date included a liner. The box was marked with "404" stamping on one end. The non-powered 2559 units each came in their own Late Traditional boxes, and the entire outfit came in a two-tier basket-weave type.

Excellent	Like New	Scarcity
3,000	5,000	5

2277WS or 817 Four-Car Work Train $49.95 retail

Included: 665 4-6-4 steam locomotive with operating headlight, smoke and Magne-traction; 2046W whistle tender; 6560-25 crane; 6446-25 Norfolk & Western covered hopper; 3650 searchlight extension car; 6119-75 work caboose; eight TOC curved and five TOS straight track; UCS uncoupling/operating section.

Lionel powered this set with the 665 4-6-4—the final appearance of this locomotive for almost nine years. It was packed in a tan corrugated carton without a liner. In this outfit it was paired with a 2046W Lionel Lines streamlined tender. Like the rolling stock in this outfit, the tender was equipped with bar-end metal trucks and packaged in a Late Traditional box.

Like the locomotive, all the cars except the caboose had been seen before. The red cab crane box was stamped with a –25 suffix and included a corrugated liner. The searchlight extension car was in its second year of production when it appeared in this set. The variation of the 3650 included in this set was the common light gray and can be distinguished from 1956 production by the hole in the drawbar. The nicely detailed Norfolk and Western 6446-25 covered hopper was the largest car in the outfit. Bringing up the rear of the train was the all-new, all-gray 6119-75 work caboose—its sheet metal frame something of a disappointment given the quality of the rest of the set components. Markings on the caboose's box include the –75 suffix, and the box itself included a cardboard insert. The outfit box was a typical two-tier basket-weave carton.

Excellent	Like New	Scarcity
550	900	5

2279W or 818 Five-Car Freight $55 retail

Included: 2350 New Haven EP-5 electric; 3424 operating brakeman car; 6464-425 New Haven boxcar; 6424 flatcar with autos; 6477 miscellaneous car with pipes; 6427 Lionel Lines porthole caboose; eight TOC curved and seven TOS straight track; UCS uncoupling/operating section.

The New Haven EP-5, introduced in 1956, was included as motive power for this outfit and also included a number of quality cars. The 3434 Wabash, also first produced in 1956, was slightly revised for 1957. In addition to the change in coupler head, which was universal across the product line,

some of the 1957 production of the brakeman car had the pickup roller connected with yellow rather than black wire.

The 6477 was new for 1957 and was an improvement over the 1956 6467 in that the car included a cargo of five gray plastic pipes. The pipes were held on the unpainted red plastic car by black unpainted plastic bulkheads on either end and four spring steel 2411-4 posts (two on each side). An illuminated porthole caboose, the 6427 Lionel Lines, completed the train.

All the cars in this outfit were individually packed in Late Traditional boxes, while the locomotive came in a conventional tan corrugated box without a liner. Though the 2350 was produced in many variations, all the 2279W/818 outfits examined or reported for this volume included the most common version with a nose decal and white "N" and orange "H" side markings. The complete outfit was packaged in a two-tier basket-weave set box.

Excellent	Like New	Scarcity
825	1,300	4

2281W or 819 Five-Car Freight $59.95 retail

Included: 2243P/2243C Santa Fe F-3 A-B-units; 3562-75 operating barrel car; 6464-150 Missouri Pacific boxcar; 6560-25 crane; 3361X operating lumber car; 6119-75 work caboose; eight TOC curved and seven TOS straight track; UCS uncoupling/operating section.

The 3361 log dump car was revised for 1957, with the "336155" being located to the right of the serif "LIONEL LINES" lettering. Though the 1956 production had the numbering to the left of the road name, the 1955 production, like the 1957-61, was to the right of the lettering. However, the 1955 cars lack the hole in the coupler head casting and utilized black knuckle pins. Cars included in outfits were packed in boxes preprinted with the 3361X number. Included in the box with the car were five 7/16-inch-diameter stained-birch logs that were five inches long. The 3-1/2-inch by 8-1/8-inch 160-2 receiving bin was packed loose in the outfit box.

Another operating car included in this outfit was the new-for-1957 orange operating barrel car, number 3562-75. The body of this car was unpainted orange plastic with black heat-stamped lettering. It came with a blue vinyl figure, whose hands and face were painted flesh-tone. Inside its box were also a 160-2 receiving bin, a 90-1 controller, a boxed 362-100 barrel set containing six 362-78 stained barrels and, a 3562-52 packet. The 3562-52 in turn contained a special OTC lockon with two 2-4-4 auxiliary rail clips, two 3562-51 track spacers, a 3562-48 platform extension, wires and instructions.

A third operating car—albeit requiring manual operation—was included in the form of the 6560-25 crane. This crane had an unpainted red-plastic cab, and its boom and hook operating hand wheels were cast with open spokes. To accompany the crane Lionel included all-gray work caboose 6119-75 with sheet metal frame. Both the crane and the work caboose had cardboard inserts inside their Late Traditional boxes.

The 6464-150 Missouri Pacific boxcar had been introduced in 1955 and has the distinction of existing in more variations than any other 6464-series car. The MoPac included in this outfit had a solid yellow door, and it did not have a molded-in groove delineating the color breaks in its sides.

Each car in this set rode on bar-end metal trucks, and each came in its own Late Traditional box. The outfit box itself was a two-tier basket-weave type.

To power this outfit Lionel selected the 2243 Santa Fe F-3. While originally offered as part of the 027 line, the single motor A-B combination provided the company an economical alternative to the more traditional twin motor A-A combination. The units included in this outfit feature low profile molded-in cab ladders—the high profile ladders were 1955-only features. Some of the 1957 locomotives had bodies molded of orange plastic that was then painted. The locomotive came in a dated tan corrugated box without a liner, while the B-unit came in a Late Traditional box.

Excellent	Like New	Scarcity
1,200	2,000	3

2283WS or 820 Five-Car Freight $59.95 retail

Included: 646 steam locomotive with operating headlight, smoke and Magne-traction; 2046W streamlined whistle tender; 6464-525 Minneapolis & St. Louis boxcar; 3424 operating brakeman car; 6562 gondola with canisters; 3361X operating lumber car; 6357 illuminated SP-type caboose; eight TOC curved and seven TOS straight track; UCS uncoupling/operating section.

The O-Gauge version of the medium-sized Hudson was selected to lead this freight train. The locomotive was equipped with a trailing truck that featured plastic side frames as opposed to earlier versions that used a die-cast trailing truck. The locomotive was packaged in a tan corrugated cardboard box without a liner. The steamer was paired with a 2046W Lionel Lines tender, with the 2046W number stamped on the small number boards molded into its sides.

In tow behind the Hudson were two operating cars, one of them being a 3361 log dump car as described above in the outfit 2281W listing. The other operating car was a 3424 Wabash boxcar with operating brakeman as described in the 2279W listing above.

A second boxcar, the 6464-525, was also included in the outfit. The new red Minneapolis & St. Louis car had only the second column of rivets to the right of the door shortened and rode on bar-end metal trucks. When re-introduced in the mid-1960s, both the second and third column of rivets to the right of the door were short, and AAR-style plastic trucks were used.

A 6562 gondola car with four red canisters was included, and both red and black examples have been reported as set components. A 6357 "LIONEL" lighted caboose brought up the rear of the train.

All the rolling stock had bar-end metal trucks and came in Late Traditional boxes. The outfit box was the typical two-tier basket-weave carton.

Excellent	Like New	Scarcity
600	1,000	5

2285W or 821 Five-Car Freight $69.95 retail

Included: 2331 Virginian Train Master; 6414 Evans auto loader; 6418 machinery car; 3662 operating milk car; 6425 Gulf three-dome tank car; 6517 bay window caboose; eight TOC curved and seven TOS straight track; UCS uncoupling/operating section.

Even though nothing new for 1957 was included, this outfit was high quality all the way from its powerful dual motor locomotive to its bay window caboose. As with all postwar bay window cabooses, the one in this outfit rode on passenger car trucks and usually did not have underscored lettering.

The Gulf triple-dome tank car came with a black vertical brake stand installed at one end. With its separately installed metal ladders and handrails, this was an attractive car.

To provide a bit of action, the set included a 3662 automatic milk car. The 1957 production of this long-running action car can be distinguished by its unique combination of a very dull brown roof, copper-colored solenoid windings and a hole in coupler head.

The 16-wheel depressed center flatcar was the largest and most impressive freight car in the outfit. The 1957 version of this car lacked the "6418" cast into the underside of the frame that had been present on previous models, and its cargo of plastic girders had raised "U.S. Steel" lettering rather than "LIONEL." A pair of special silver elastic bands retained the load on the car. As with all the freight cars besides the caboose in this outfit, the 6418 rode on bar-end metal trucks—four of them in this case. The massive, heavy car was packaged in a Late Traditional box, which was nowhere near substantial enough to withstand the box it was to protect.

Pulling this impressive assortment of cars was Lionel's replica of the massive Fairbanks-Morse H24-66 Trainmaster. Equipped with dual motors and a horn, as well as operating headlights at each end, it was truly a top-shelf item. The model was particularly striking in the molded blue and painted yellow markings of the Virginian Railway, as included in this outfit.

The locomotive came in a lined corrugated carton stamped "2331." The remainder of the outfit components utilized Late Traditional boxes, and the outfit box itself was a two-tier basket-weave type.

Excellent	Like New	Scarcity
1,800	3,000	6

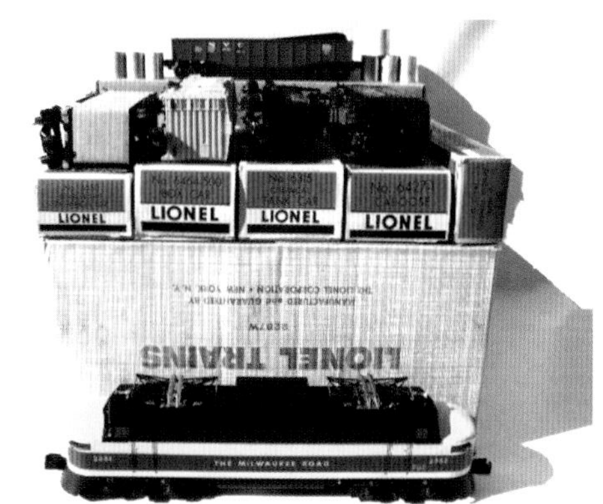

2287W or 822 Five-Car Freight 69.95 retail

Included: 2351 Milwaukee Road EP-5 electric; 342 operating culvert loader with 6342 culvert gondola; 6464-500 Timken boxcar; 3650 searchlight extension car; 6315 Gulf chemical tank car; 6427 Lionel Lines porthole caboose; eight TOC curved and nine TOS straight track; UCS uncoupling/operating section.

Tied with the 2285W as the most expensive O-Gauge set cataloged in 1957 was this outfit headed by a 2351 Milwaukee Road EP-5. Though attractive, this locomotive was in no way realistic. Although the road name was real, the paint scheme was fictitious, and the Milwaukee Road owned no locomotives resembling this one.

The orange and black 6315 Gulf tank car—dubbed a "chemical tank car" by some—was in its second year. The detailed 3650 searchlight extension car included in this outfit was painted light gray, which was typical for this car.

Adding considerable color to the set was the new yellow and white Timken boxcar. The Timken Roller Bearing Co. of Canton, Ohio was, and is, a major supplier to the actual railroad industry and played a major role in the adoption of roller, rather than friction, bearings on locomotives and cars.

At the rear of the train was a lighted 6427 Lionel Lines porthole caboose that once again exhibits the 1957 (and later) characteristic of having a hole in the drawbar.

The fifth car in the set was the unpainted dark red 6342 culvert car that indicates the centerpiece of the outfit. This car was included to accompany the 342 operating culvert loader. A vibrator motor that actuated the mechanical gripper, unloading the metal culvert sections, powered the culvert loader. The 6342 gondola was packed inside a die-cut corrugated liner that in turn was positioned inside the normal 342 corrugated tan boxes that went inside the basket weave set box.

The locomotive came in a corrugated tan carton without a liner, while the remainder of the rolling stock (except for the previously mentioned 6342) came in Late Traditional boxes.

Excellent	Like New	Scarcity
1,800	3,000	6

Super 0

2289WS or 823 Super 0 Five-Car Steam Freight $75 retail

Included: 736 2-8-4 Berkshire steam locomotive with operating headlight, smoke, and Magne-traction; 2046W whistle tender; 3494-275 BAR operating boxcar; 3359 operating dump car; 6430 flatcar with vans; 3361X operating lumber car; 6427 Lionel Lines illuminated porthole caboose; twelve 31 curved, three 32 straight, and one 48 insulated straight track; 39-20 operating packet; bottle of SP smoke pellets; tube of lubricant; instructions.

This outfit served to introduce the new Super 0 track age to the public and was heralded in the catalog as the "first to make the run on Super 0 track." But the track was the only new product in the set; everything else was a repeat item. At the front of the train was the venerable 2-8-4. The version included in this outfit had a sheet metal based trailing truck with plastic side frames, and a single screw as opposed to the two-screw mounting previously used retained the collector roller pickup.

Despite the somewhat dated steam locomotive at the head of the set, as a nod to the future of railroading, the 6430 flatcar with vans was indicative of the importance of inter-modal rail service to the future. The flatcar was laden with two matching vans having die-cast support wheels and metal "Cooper-Jarrett" nameplates. The van bodies and roofs were made of unpainted white or gray plastic. The roofs of these vans were easily lost, and reproduction roofs are abundant.

Matching the Lionel Lines markings on the 2046W tender was a Lionel Lines 6427 porthole caboose with illumination.

The rest of the rolling stock in this outfit were operating cars. Among them was the 3361 operating log car. A complete description of the 1957 version of this car can be found in the 2281W listing.

Arguably the most attractive car in the set was the 3494-275 Bangor and Aroostook "State of Maine" boxcar. This car was home to a blue vinyl man with painted hands and face, whereas the 1956 production of this car had no "extra" holes punched in the frame. In 1957, two additional holes appeared, properly positioned for wiring the trucks—though they were unused on this car. However, it is possible some outfits were assembled using carried-forward inventory from 1956.

The 3359 twin bin ore dump car was also included in this set. As a component of a 1957 set, the proper car should have the new hole in the drawbar. Collectors should not forget however that it is possible that inventory carried-forward from 1956 could have been included in the form of either cars or couplers.

The cars and tender came in Late Traditional boxes, while the locomotive came in a tan corrugated carton without liner. The box was made especially for Super 0 sets. It came in a rust-colored basket-weave outfit box.

Excellent	Like New	Scarcity
750	1,250	5

2291W or 824 Super 0 Five-Car Diesel Freight
$79.95 retail

Included: 2379P/2379C Rio Grande F-3 A-B-units; 3562-75 operating barrel car; 3530 operating generator car; 3444 animated gondola; 6464-525 Minneapolis & St. Louis boxcar; 6657 illuminated Rio Grande SP-type caboose; twelve 31 curved, three 32 straight, and one 48 insulated straight track; Super 0 operating packet.

Bright is a fitting word to describe this outfit. At the front and rear the colorful yellow and silver markings of the Rio Grande decorated the A-B F-3 units and 6657 illuminated caboose. Under the colorful shell of the A-unit lurked twin vertical motors and an operating horn, as well as a working headlight.

The 3444 operating gondola and 6464-525 Minneapolis & St. Louis boxcar have previously been described in this chapter under the 2275W and 2283WS outfits, respectively.

2289WS

A second operating gondola was included in this set, the new-for-1957 3562-75 operating barrel car. Of course the obvious distinguishing characteristic of this car was its unpainted orange plastic body. Many well-intentioned enthusiasts have "upgraded" the condition of these cars by placing the body on the chassis of another variation. To guard against this, be sure the car included in this outfit has silver knuckle pins and drawbars with formed-in holes. It comes packed inside a box printed with the full 3562-75 stock number.

Probably the most interesting car included in the outfit was the 3530 Electro Mobile Power car. This car was a duplicate of an actual series of mobile generator cars built by the Electro-Motive Division of General Motors. When the doors were opened on the miniature car, a light inside the car came on and a simulated fan began to turn. If the car is plugged into the cable extending from the included power pole and leading to a searchlight as intended, then that light illuminates as well.

Lionel produced several variations of the 3530; however, for this set the proper version for this car does not include underscoring below the number, but the white stripe does extend through the simulated ladders on either end of the cars' sides. Its fuel tank, as well as the transformer at the base of the power pole, was blue plastic.

All the rolling stock in this outfit, as well as the B-unit of the locomotive, were packaged in Late Traditional boxes. The A-unit came in a liner-less tan corrugated carton, and the set box itself was the new rust-shaded basket-weave box.

Excellent	Like New	Scarcity
3,000	5,000	6

2292WS or 825 Super 0 Steam Luxury Liner $85 retail

Included: 646 4-6-4 steam locomotive with operating headlight, smoke and Magne-traction; 2046W streamlined whistle tender; 2530 Railway Express Agency baggage car, 2531 Silver Dawn observation, 2532 Silver Range Vista Dome, and 2533 Silver Cloud Pullman extruded-aluminum passenger cars; twelve 31 curved, three 32 straight and one 48 insulated straight track; 39-5 operating packet; bottle of SP smoke pellets; tube of lubricant; instructions.

This outfit included three of the four Lionel Lines extruded aluminum passenger car cataloged at the time, along with a 2530 baggage car. The passenger cars in most cases were flat-channel cars, but in the intervening years many of these cars have been cannibalized to make fraudulent Congressional and Canadian Pacific cars.

To power this gleaming consist, Lionel included a 646 medium-sized Hudson. The locomotive had all it wanted with four of the heavy, poor-rolling passenger cars—which made it smoke very well!

The passenger cars were packaged in Late Traditional boxes, as was the tender. The steam locomotive came in a tan corrugated box without a liner. The outfit box was the Super 0-specific rust-colored basket-weave carton.

Excellent	Like New	Scarcity
1,500	2,500	4

2293W or 826 Five-Car Freight $87.50 retail

Included: 2360 Pennsylvania solid-stripe GG-1; 3662 operating milk car; 3650 searchlight extension car; 6414 Evans auto loader; 6518 double-truck transformer car; 6417 Pennsylvania porthole caboose; twelve 31 curved, three 32 straight and one insulated 48 straight track; 39-20 operating packet.

Looking at this outfit today—and especially considering how the sets were to change over the next few years—it is difficult to imagine that this was not the top of the line set for 1957.

All the rolling stock included were top-quality pieces, and this outfit frequently includes two scarce variation cars. The 3650 searchlight extension car, always a nice piece, in this set is especially hard to find; just as infrequent is the coveted dark gray variation.

Hiding inside the Late Traditional box labeled 6417-1 is often the very desirable "no zone" variation of the 6417 porthole caboose. Whereas most of these cars have "NEW YORK ZONE" beneath the "PENNSYLVANIA" lettering, the zone identification was omitted from the car most often included in this set.

The 6518 16-wheel transformer car is an impressive piece, but its sheer weight, sharp corners and flexible truck mounting all contribute to the destruction of its original box. That, along with the usual discarding of the two special cardboard inserts, often leads to the simulated insulators on top of the transformer being damaged. Inspect this car carefully for signs of reproduction insulators or even entire transformers.

A known component of outfit 2293W is the hard-to-find dark gray version of the 3650 searchlight extension car.

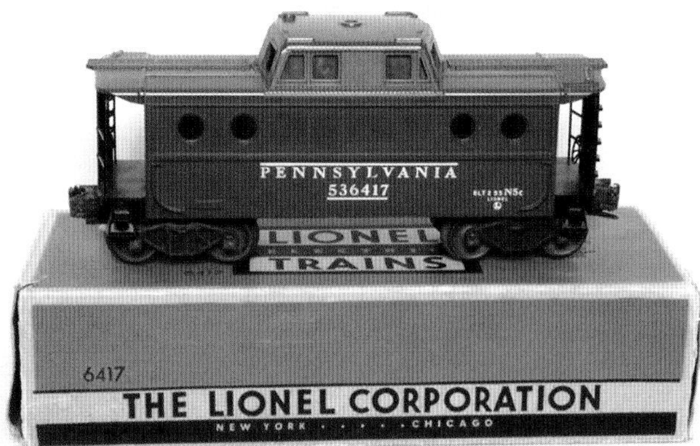

Another known scarce component of this outfit is the sought after "no zone" version of the 6417 caboose. This car lacks the "NEW YORK ZONE" lettering beneath "PENNSYLVANIA" that is typically found on the 6417.

Similarly, collectors should beware of reproduction automobiles on the 6414 Evans Autoloader. The correct autos are 4-5/16 in. long, have chrome-plated bumpers, and came with one each of red, white, yellow and turquoise.

The big 3662 milk car in this outfit was the same variation as described above in outfit 2285W. The milk car with its platform, like the rest of the rolling stock in this outfit, came packed in a Late Traditional box. All of the freight cars were equipped with 1957-style bar-end metal trucks.

But the star of this outfit both in 1957 and today is its locomotive, the magnificent 2360 GG-1. With its die-cast body, twin motors, operating horn and 12-wheel Magne-traction, it could easily handle this freight consist.

The 2360 was slightly redesigned for 1957 with the tops of the simulated ventilators all the same height, whereas previously the top had been staggered. The decoration process was revised for 1957 as well, with a single broad rubber-stamped stripe running the length of the locomotive and an oversized keystone centered on each side above the stamped lettering. The locomotive came in a tan corrugated box with a liner made by National. The date "57" was stamped on the box below the maker's seal.

Typically, this outfit contains the restyled-for-1957 version of the GG-1. The tops of the ventilators are an even height, a single broad stripe runs along either side, and a large "PRR" keystone is located at the center of each side.

Occasionally, the new graphics are found applied to the older body casting, which had staggered height ventilator tops, as shown here. This locomotive variation is very difficult to locate. Regardless of decoration, the big electric came in a box date marked "57."

The set carton was the new rust-brown basket-weave type with Super 0-exclusive graphics.

Excellent	Like New	Scarcity
2,900	4,900	6

2295WS or 827 Five-Car Steam Freight $87.50 retail

Included: 746 4-8-4 Norfolk & Western steam locomotive with operating headlight, smoke and Magne-traction; 746W whistle tender; 342 operating culvert loader with 6342 culvert gondola; 6560-25 crane; 3530 generator car; 3361X operating lumber car; 6419-100 Norfolk & Western work caboose; twelve 31 curved, three 32 straight and one 48 insulated straight track; 39-20 operating packet; bottle smoke fluid; tube of lubricant; instructions.

Truly impressive is perhaps the best way to describe this outfit. At the front of the outfit was the sleek new 746 die-cast 4-8-4 steam locomotive that was new for 1957. Though equipped with conventional Magne-traction—indeed, many of the mechanical components of this locomotive were shared with the proven 736 Berkshire—the smoke unit was a totally new design that used liquid rather than the traditional pill. It was packed in a tan corrugated carton without a liner.

Counter to what was shown in the catalog and what many collectors believe, this outfit, as well as set 2297WS, paired the 746 with the short-stripe version of the 746W tender.

Behind the locomotive was an assortment of top-quality rolling stock. The 3361 log dump car was a reliable operator. The version included in this outfit was marked "336155" to the right of the serif "LIONEL LINES" lettering, and the coupler head had a hole formed in it. The red-cab 6560-25 crane was marked with the abbreviated number "6560" on its chassis and was equipped with open-spoke-style hand wheels.

The 3530 Electro-Mobile power car version included in this set does not include underscoring below the number, but the white stripe does extend through the simulated ladders on either end of the car's sides. The generator car had a blue fuel tank that matched the transformer at the base of the power pole.

At the rear of the train was a die-cast chassis-equipped work caboose. Rather than the D.L.&W. markings of previous 6419 cars, the new 6419-100 was fittingly marked with the Norfolk & Western road name to match the tender. The number stamped on the side of the cab was 576419.

All the rolling stock listed above, including the tender, were packed in Late Traditional boxes. The final car, the 6342, however, did not have a component box in this outfit. Instead, it was packed inside the accessory box for the 342 culvert loader, which in turn was included in the rust-colored basket-weave Super 0 outfit box.

The 342 culvert loader, which was operated by a vibrator-type motor, provided considerable play action for the lucky children receiving this outfit in 1957.

Excellent	Like New	Scarcity
3,000	5,000	7

2296W or 828 Super 0 Diesel Luxury Liner $100 retail

Included: 2373P/2373T Canadian Pacific F-3 A-A-units; 2551 Banff Park observation, three 2552 Skyline 500 Vista Domes; twelve 31 curved, seven 32 straight and one 48 insulated straight track; 39-5 operating packet.

This is one of the most sought after and valuable of all postwar passenger sets. Not surprisingly, this has lead to rampant forging of both locomotives and cars. What is surprising is that there is also considerable confusion about authentic outfits as well.

As originally offered by Lionel, this outfit contained an A-A pair of F-3 diesels, three Vista Dome cars, and an observation—all in Canadian Pacific markings. Offered for separate sale were Pullman numbers 2553 and 2554. Through the years these Pullman cars have been exchanged for two of the Vista Domes in order to create a sequentially numbered set, similar to the Lionel Lines Super Speedliner—but this was not Lionel's intention, or packaging.

With respect to packaging, the tan corrugated 2373P box, number 2373-11, was made by Express, while National made the tan corrugated 2373T box, number 2373-27. This mismatching sometimes raises the suspicions of collectors who are on the lookout for repainted or forged 2373 locomotives.

Authentic 2373 units are painted gray and brown, and have yellow heat-stamped lettering and stripes. The elaborate nose markings are decals, which often have deteriorated. Notice the molded-in "operating" handle on the nose door. This detail was removed from the mold in 1958, and any 2373 without this detail is a repaint.

The passenger cars as well have been subject to duplication. Using an array of stripes ranging from genuine Lionel replacement parts to reproductions in metal, plastic and paper, well-meaning enthusiasts, as well as more larcenous types, have likely created more of these cars than Lionel did!

Examine these cars carefully. The striping on original cars is metallic and often has traces of adhesives showing. The ends of the cars are molded in black plastic and then painted silver. The car number is visible on the window strip—2552 for the dome car, and 2551 for the observation.

Each of the passenger cars came in their own Late Traditional boxes with coupler protection flaps. The outfit box was the rust-colored basket-weave style created just for Super 0 sets.

Excellent	Like New	Scarcity
6,000	10,000	6

2297WS or 829 Five-car Steam Freight with Smoke and Whistle $110 retail

Included: 746 Norfolk & Western steam locomotive with operating headlight, smoke, and Magne-traction; 746W whistle tender; 264 operating forklift with 6264 lumber car; 3356 operating horse car and corral; 3662 operating milk car; 345 operating culvert unloader with 6342 culvert gondola; 6517 bay window caboose; twelve 31 curved, five 32 straight, and one 48 insulated straight track; 39-20 operating packet; bottle smoke fluid; tube of lubricant; instructions.

The top of the line outfit for 1957—and indeed the most expensive set Lionel cataloged during the 1950s—was this set headed by the Norfolk and Western "J" 746. This 4-8-4 is second in desirability to the 773 4-6-4 among postwar steamers.

Every car in the set except the caboose was an operating car or a component of an operating accessory. Activities abounded in this set. The 3662 milk car provided ever-popular animation as the white-clad workman unloaded the cans on its platform. A 3356 operating horse car and corral, considerably more reliable than the old cattle car, exercised black horses in a green, brown and white corral.

When facing the "back" side (opposite of the side through which horses pass) of the horse car, the brake wheel is on the left end of the car in outfit 2297WS. In 1958 the brake wheel was moved to the opposite end. While 1956 cars had the brake wheel in the same position as 1957, the earlier cars lacked the support hole in the coupler drawbar.

The 6517 bay window caboose rode on 2400-series passenger car trucks with magnetic couplers. It did not have underscored lettering.

The milk and cattle car outfits, as well as the tender and caboose, were packaged in Late Traditional boxes.

The 6264 flatcar with lumber load, packed with its new-for-1957 264 forklift platform, and the 6342 culvert gondola, packaged with the equally new 345 culvert unloader, did not come in component boxes. Instead, cardboard liners held them in position within the corrugated accessory boxes.

Except for the previously mentioned caboose, all the cars in this outfit were equipped with bar-end metal trucks.

Excellent	Like New	Scarcity
3,300	5,500	7

Chapter 15

1958

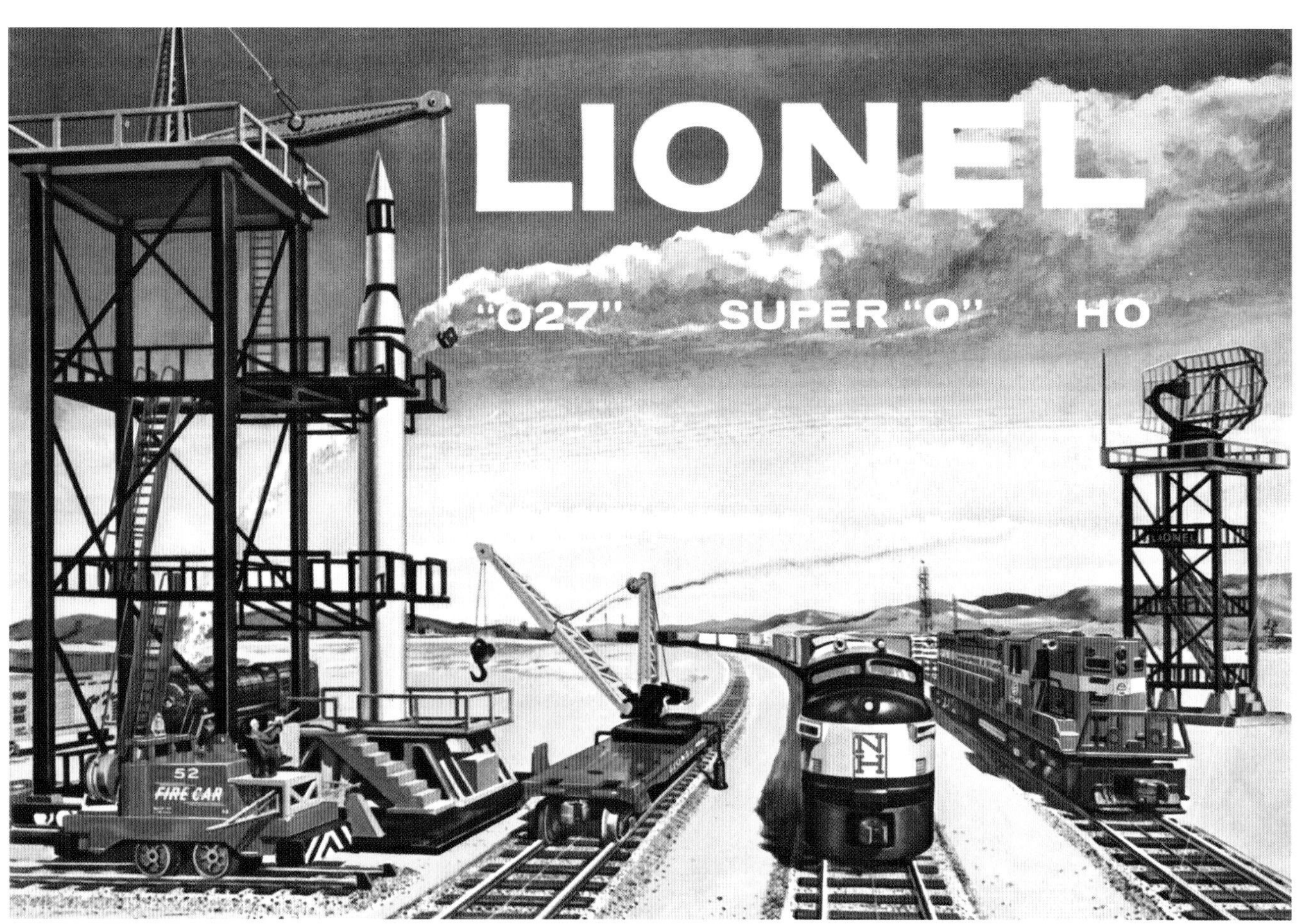

Twenty-nine traditionally-sized outfits were shown in the 1958 catalog—13 of them 027, and notably none of them O-Gauge—as that proven track system was totally eclipsed by Super 0, the new system introduced the previous year. Super 0 track was included in 16 outfits. Also introduced that year, but not featured in this volume, was HO by Lionel—products produced in this year by Rivarossi of Italy. Though only imported and distributed by Lionel, the 1/87 scale trains were packaged and sold as if they were true Lionel products.

As was the case in 1957, the basket-weave box with blue lettering introduced in 1956 was used for 027 outfits in 1958 as well.

GLOSSY: In 1958, a few boxes were made of smooth, glossy, coated cardstock. This box is very uncommon.

The 1958 Super 0 line utilized this dark brown basket-weave box, which had been designed the previous year.

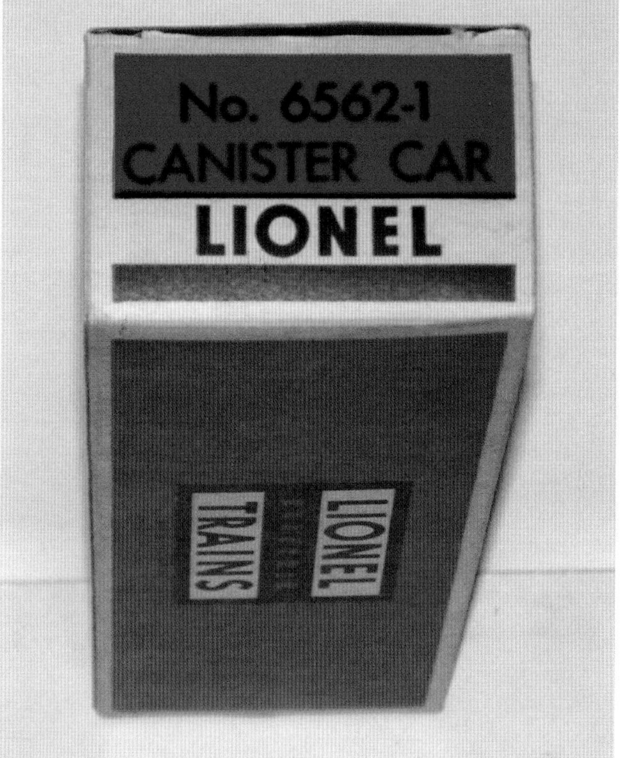

A new component box was introduced in 1958, but was not used universally through the line. Known as the Bold Traditional box, this box is similar to the Late Traditional box, but with a much bolder typeface print on the end flaps.

Most of the 027 freight cars, and even some of the Super 0 product line, rode on the early AAR trucks.

1603WS, 1587S

1587S 📷 **Lady Lionel** **$49.95 retail**

Included: 2037-500 2-6-4 pink steam locomotive with operating headlight, smoke and Magne-traction; 1130T-500 tender; 6464-510 New York Central Pacemaker boxcar; 6464-515 Missouri-Kansas-Texas boxcar; 6462-500 gondola with canisters; 6436-500 Lehigh Valley quad hopper; 6427-500 Pennsylvania porthole caboose; eight 1013 curved and five 1018 straight track; 6029 uncoupling section; 1043-500 60-watt ivory transformer; Lockon; tube of lubricant; instructions with ivory cord.

The lackluster sales of the "Lady Lionel" outfit introduced in 1957 led to Lionel's featuring it once again in the 1958 catalog, in a somewhat futile attempt to spur sales at the retail level. Ultimately, many of these sets—highly collectable today—were repainted into more traditional colors at the time.

Excellent	Like New	Scarcity
3,000	5,000	6

1590 📷 **Four-Car Steam Freight** **$25 retail**

Included: 249 2-4-2 steam locomotive; 250T Pennsylvania tender; 6014 Bosco boxcar; 6151 flatcar with Range Patrol vehicle; 6112 gondola with canisters; 6017 SP-type caboose; eight 1013 curved and two 1018 straight track; 1008 camtrol; 1015 45-watt transformer; CTC Lockon; tube of lubricant; instructions.

The already austere 250 from 1957 was stripped of its operating headlight and a two-position E-unit installed in lieu of a three-position unit in order to become 1958's model 249. It retained its red stripe along its running board, and of course the red-striped 250T Pennsylvania tender.

Behind the diminutive steamer rolled four cars—the most noteworthy of these being the 6151 flatcar with Range Patrol truck. The number "6151" appeared on the component box, but as with all of Lionel's small sheet-metal flatcars the number did not appear on the car itself. The car was marked "Lionel," and the toy truck, which was manufactured by Pyro Plastics, was heat stamped "Lionel Ranch." The car body came in various shades ranging from cream to yellow to orange.

Like all the cars in the outfit, the 6112 rode on AAR-type trucks, but unlike previous years when it was laden with four canisters, in 1958 it came with only three. All the rolling stock, including the tender, was packed in Bold Traditional boxes. The locomotive came in a tan corrugated carton, while the set box was the typical basket-weave-type used for 027 outfits.

Excellent	Like New	Scarcity
300	500	4

1590

1591

1591 U.S. Marine Land & Sea Limited $29.95 retail

Included: 212 U.S. Marine Corps Alco A-unit; 6803 flatcar with military units; 6807 flatcar with DUKW; 6809 flatcar with military units; 6017-50 U.S. Marine Corps SP-type caboose; eight 1013 curved and two 1018 straight track; 1008 camtrol; 1015 45-watt transformer; CTC Lockon; tube of lubricant; instructions.

Back in 1958, this set offered a lot of play value for children. In addition to the train itself, the five military vehicles it carried could be removed and played with separately. This led to many being lost, and the fragility of the toys, plus the rough treatment given to them by youths playing war games, resulted in many of the survivors being damaged, or having missing parts. Thus, as postwar trains came to be viewed as collectibles, these loads, their cars and outfits containing them, became very desirable.

However, the loads themselves were made by Pyro Plastics and not by Lionel. When Pyro folded, the company's molds passed through a succession of hands, resulting in the 1990s "reproductions" of the original loads—and their parts, being produced from the original tooling.

Naturally, these are extremely difficult to distinguish from the 1958-60 vintage items. Accordingly, while many more "complete" flatcars with military loads appeared on the market, their value plummeted due to uncertainty on the part of many buyers as to whether any of these cars are authentic.

Further confusion arises from a couple of other areas. First, Pyro offered similar items, with slightly different coloration or markings as part of their regular product line sold through five and dime stores—many of these have since been placed on flatcars. Secondly, most of the loads are similarly sized and interchangeable on the cars, and Lionel's description is rather vague, leading to cargoes being placed on the wrong flatcar.

The 6803 was properly loaded with two gray USMC vehicles, a tank and a truck with a pair of swiveling loudspeakers. The tank was retained with an elastic band, while the truck was held in place by a black snap-on bracket, which has also been reproduced. This same bracket was used on the 6818 transformer car.

The 6807 carried the load that seems to have the highest survivability rate—a replica of the GMC DUKW amphibious 6 x 6 truck molded in gray with USMC markings. The DUKW was held in place by two elastic bands. Incidentally, DUKW, pronounced "duck," was the GMC model designation, and is decoded as D, first year of production 1942; U, Amphibian Utility body style; K, front-wheel drive; W, two-rear driving axles. A standard GMC military 6 x 6 of the same era as the DUKW was the CCKW. The Pyro/Lionel DUKW was considerably more robust than the balance of the military loads—likely a factor in its relatively common availability today.

The third flatcar with military cargo in this outfit was the 6809. This flatcar carried two trucks, which were held in place by a single black plastic snap-on bracket. One of the trucks, a van, was decorated to represent a medical vehicle, with a caduceus on the side. The other truck was equipped with a representation of a twin 40-mm Bofors anti-aircraft cannon—which in reality would have overwhelmed the chassis of such a truck when fired. Today the cannon-equipped vehicle is often found damaged, as the cannon and its mounting were somewhat fragile.

Pulling the train was a 212 Alco A-unit, painted blue and fittingly marked "United States Marine Corps." At the rear of the outfit was a matching blue SP-style Marine Corps caboose. The locomotive came in a tan corrugated carton made by Star, while the rolling stock were all packaged in Bold Traditional boxes, the caboose box being printed with a -60 suffix. The outfit box was the basket-weave-type introduced in 1956.

Excellent	Like New	Scarcity
1,000	1,850	6

1593 Five-Car UP Diesel Work Train $35 retail

Included: 613 Union Pacific NW-2 diesel switcher; 6660 boom crane car; 6818 flatcar with transformer; 6112 gondola with canisters; 6476 Lehigh Valley hopper; 6119-100 work caboose; eight 1013 curved and two 1018 straight track; 1008 camtrol; 1015 45-watt transformer; CTC Lockon; tube of lubricant; instructions.

While mechanically unremarkable, the yellow and gray Union Pacific NW-2 leading this set is one of the most sought after of the later diesel switchers. The locomotive came in a Bold Traditional box with a pair of inserts to secure it in place.

The only other item in this outfit to arouse collector interest is the 6660, which was produced in 1958 only and was a component of only two cataloged sets. The boom of the crane, which is identical to that used on the 3360 Burro Crane, was fragile, but perhaps even more fragile was the original box. Included originally were two 6660-56 corrugated inserts which both protected the crane and strengthened the box. These bits were often discarded and resultantly the box is often crushed, sometimes damaging the boom assembly.

Another fragile item included in this outfit was the new-for-1958 6818 transformer car. This car was created by mounting a variation of Lionel's tried and true simulated transformer load onto a flatcar, using the mounting bracket most often recognized for its use retaining military vehicle loads. This mounting bracket, the transformer insulators and the transformer itself has all been reproduced.

The 6112 was a returning item, but was now furnished with only three canisters. The 6476 has surfaced in this outfit in both black and red, while the 6119-100 work caboose comes with a red cab and gray tool bin.

The outfit box was the typical 027 basket-weave-type, and most of the rolling stock came in Bold Traditional boxes and featured AAR-type trucks.

Excellent	Like New	Scarcity
550	1,100	5

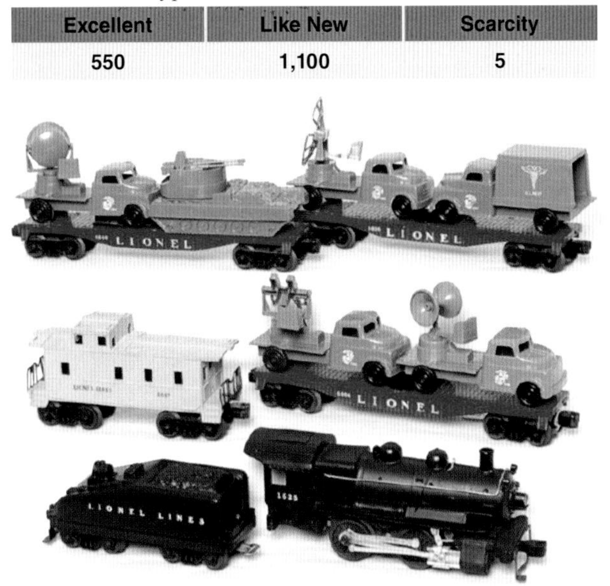

1595 Marine Battlefront Special $37.50 retail

Included: 1625 0-4-0 steam switcher with operating headlight; 1625T slope-back tender; 6804, 6806 and 6808 flatcars with military units; 6017-85 SP-type caboose; eight 1013 curved and one 1018 straight tack; 6029 uncoupling section; 1015 45-watt transformer; CTC Lockon; tube of lubricant; instructions.

Lionel continued the trend of cost-cutting measures (begun a few years ealier) by eliminating the operating front coupler and metal tender trucks from their 0-4-0 switcher. In their stead was a dummy front coupler and AAR-type tender trucks. This resulted in the locomotive being given the new number of 1625 and the tender becoming 1625T.

At the rear of the train was a unique gray Lionel Lines caboose. The SP-style caboose was marked with the name and 6017 number in black; however, its Bold Traditional box was printed with the number 6017-85. Folded tabs secured the body to the frame of the caboose.

Between the tender and caboose were three flatcars carrying gray USMC military vehicles made by Pyro Plastics. For additional information on Pyro's military loads in general, refer to outfit 1591.

The 6804 carried two Marine Corps trucks held in place by a snap-on black plastic clip. One of these trucks was fitted with a pair of swiveling loudspeakers; the other served as a mount for a miniature twin-barrel, 40-mm, Bofors anti-aircraft cannon—both notable for their fragility.

Especially fragile was the rotating radar antenna that was on the rear of one the trucks that the 6806 carried. The other truck on the flatcar was the comparatively solid van-type truck with medical markings. A single black plastic snap-on bracket retained both. The flatcar, like all the flats in this series, had AAR-type trucks.

The third and final flatcar in this outfit was the 6808. This car carried a truck with a rotating, but non-illuminated, searchlight assembly, and was secured to the railcar by a black plastic clip. At the other end of the car, retained by an elastic band, was a replica of an M19 Gun Motor Carriage. This tank-like vehicle with an open-topped turret was used as an anti-aircraft weapon.

The outfit carton was the typical basket-weave-style of the day, while the locomotive was boxed in a tan corrugated carton, and its tender in a Bold Traditional box. The flatcars were packed in Late Traditional boxes.

Excellent	Like New	Scarcity
1,600	2,800	7

1597S Coal King Smoking Freighter $39.95 retail

Included: 2018 2-6-4 steam locomotive with operating headlight and smoke; 1130T tender; 6014 Bosco boxcar; 6818 flatcar with transformer; 6476 Lehigh Valley hopper; 6025 Gulf single-dome tank car; 6112 gondola with canisters; 6017 SP-type caboose; eight 1013 curved and three 1018 straight track; 6029 uncoupling section; 1015 45-watt transformer; CTC Lockon; tube of lubricant; instructions.

Compared to many of the other outfits offered in 1958, this set was rather plain—how ironic that it was nearly identical to what would be the top-of-the-line outfit 11 years later!

A die-cast 2018 steam locomotive led a parade of five freight cars and a caboose. All the cars were repeats, with the singular exception of the 6818 transformer car, described earlier in this chapter. AAR-type trucks were used throughout this set, though the cars were packaged in a mixture of box types. The locomotive came in a tan corrugated carton, and the set in the normal basket-weave-style of the day.

Excellent	Like New	Scarcity
325	600	5

1599 Six-Car Texas Special Freight $39.95 retail

Included: 210P/210T Texas Special Alco A-A units; 6801-50 flatcar with boat; 6014 Frisco boxcar; 6424-60 flatcar with autos; 6112 gondola with canisters; 6465 Gulf double-dome tank car; 6017 SP-type caboose; eight 1013 curved and three 1018 straight track; 6029 uncoupling section; 1015 45-watt transformer; CTC Lockon; tube of lubricant; instructions.

One of the most colorful outfits of the year was this set, headed by a pair of red and white Alcos. The locomotives wore markings reading the Texas Special, but were a far cry from Lionel's F-3s with similar markings. The diesels were packaged in a pair of corrugated cartons made by Express, and were protected by cardboard rings surrounding the couplers.

All of the cars in the outfit rode on AAR-type trucks, and all were repeat items but for the 6465 two-dome tank car, which debuted with Gulf markings. In most instances, the version of this car that was included in this outfit had a gray-painted body.

The 6424 flatcar carried two automobiles, with all documented original sets examined for this volume coming with a yellow and green automobile. The black 6112 gondola came with three red canisters—a minor savings over the four provided in past years. A 6801 flatcar was included, and it carried a yellow-hulled boat with white superstructure. Beware that the boat, its mounting cradle and even the elastic band holding it in place have been reproduced. Authentic yellow hull-boats have Lionel information cast in them, whereas reproductions (as well as authentic boats with brown superstructures) lack these markings. The red boxcar carried Frisco markings, and a utilitarian 6017 Lionel Lines brought up the rear.

All of these cars were packed in a mix of Late and Bold Traditional boxes, and the set box itself was the 027 basket-weave-style.

Excellent	Like New	Scarcity
400	825	4

1600 Burlington Passenger $39.95 retail

Included: 216 Burlington Alco A-unit; 6572 refrigerator car; 2432 Clifton Vista Dome; 2436 Mooseheart observation; eight 1013 curved and three 1018 straight track; 6029 uncoupling section; 1015 45-watt transformer; CTC Lockon; tube of lubricant; instructions.

Attractive in its own right, even more so given the desirability of the silver Burlington Alco A, the occasional presence of a scarce variation of the new REA car make this one of the most sought after of Lionel's 027 passenger outfits.

1958

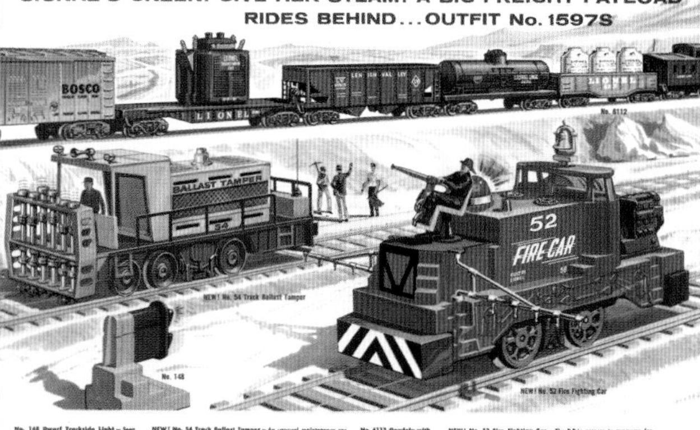

1597S

The 6572 refrigerator car, new for 1958, was a well-detailed car, painted green and decorated in the markings of the Railway Express Agency. Most of these cars—at least of this era—rode on bar-end metal trucks (when reissued in the 1960s, the car was unpainted green plastic and fitted with AAR-type trucks). However, a few of these cars, which are sometimes components of this outfit, instead were equipped with 2400-series passenger car trucks and 480-25 couplers.

The REA car, like the two passenger cars, came packed in a Late Traditional box. Star made the tan corrugated carton that housed the shiny silver Burlington Alco. The fragility of all the later Alcos, combined with the susceptibility of silver paint to damage, have made this one of the most desirable of these small diesels. The outfit box itself was the normal 027-style, basket-weave carton of the time.

Excellent	Like New	Scarcity
950	1,700	7

1601W Five-Car Diesel Freight $49.95 retail

Included: 2337 Wabash GP-7; 6800 flatcar with airplane; 6801-50 flatcar with boat; 6810 flatcar with van; 6464-425 New Haven boxcar; 6017 SP-type caboose; eight 1013 curved and three 1018 straight track; 6029 uncoupling section; 1053 60-watt transformer; CTC Lockon; tube of lubricant; instructions.

There was very little in the way of innovation in this outfit. The 2337 was essentially a duplicate of 1957's 2339, only stripped of its operating couplers. Now equipped with dummy couplers and placed in the 027 product line, the handsome blue, white and gray GP-7 was given the new catalog number of 2337.

In tow behind, the General Purpose diesel was a caboose, a boxcar and three flatcars—all riding on AAR-type trucks. The sole component of the outfit, which was new, was the 6810 flatcar with van. Unlike the earlier trailer on flatcar items Lionel had produced, which used a sheet metal bracket to hold two trailers in place, the 6810 carried only a single white van, held in place with an elastic band. The van was decorated with a Cooper-Jarrett nameplate.

The 6801 flatcar, which, when loaded with a yellow-hulled boat as in this set, was assigned product number 6801-50, has been described previously in this chapter. The black and yellow airplane riding on the 6800 had each of its wing halves assembled using three rivets, and bore raised markings on its underside reading "THE LIONEL CORPORATION, NEW YORK, NEW YORK."

Packaging for this outfit included a basket-weave-outfit box, Late and Bold Traditional boxes for the rolling stock, and a Bold Traditional box for the locomotive.

Excellent	Like New	Scarcity
900	1,600	5

1603WS Whistling Mountain Climber Steam Freight $49.95 retail

Included: 2037 2-6-4 steam locomotive with operating headlight, smoke and Magne-traction; 6026W tender; 6014 Bosco or Frisco boxcar; 6424-60 flatcar with autos; 6818 flatcar with transformer; 6112 gondola with canisters; 6017 SP-type caboose; eight 1013 curved and three 1018 straight track; 6029 uncoupling section; 1053 60-watt transformer; CTC Lockon; tube of lubricant; instructions.

The proven 2037 steam locomotive was in charge of this set. All the components of this outfit have already been discussed, but for the Bosco 6014 boxcar which occasionally surfaces in the set. When molded in red, the Bosco is one of the most common boxcars of this style, the white version of the Bosco is more difficult to find in collectible condition than most enthusiasts realize. The prices listed below presume either the red Bosco or a Frisco boxcar.

The die-cast steamer was trailed by a 6026W tender riding on bar-end metal trucks, while the rest of the rolling stock featured AAR-type plastic trucks. The tender came in a Late Traditional box, while the cars were packed in a mix of Late and Bold Traditional boxes. The locomotive itself came in a "58" dated tan corrugated carton, and the outfit as a whole was shipped in a basket-weave-type box.

Excellent	Like New	Scarcity
400	750	5

1605W Six-Car Santa Fe Diesel Freight $55 retail

Included: 208P/208T Santa Fe Alco A-A units with horn; 6800 flatcar with airplane; 6464-425 New Haven boxcar; 6801 flatcar with boat; 6477 miscellaneous car with pipes; 6802 flatcar with girders; 6017 SP-type caboose; eight 1013 curved and three 1018 straight track; 6029 uncoupling section; 1053 60-watt transformer; CTC Lockon; tube of lubricant; instructions.

While most of these outfits came with a flatcar loaded with a yellow boat with white superstructures as seen here, some sets have been reported to contain a blue-hulled boat.

The outfit was headed by the new for 1958 208 P and T Alco FA units. These locomotives were decorated in a blue and yellow paint scheme, representing the Santa Fe Railway's freight Diesel colors. In tow behind the pair of Diesels was an array of common but nice freight cars. The 6802 flatcar with two girders was the only new car, but the 6800 flatcar with airplane is the car that arouses the most collector interest. The packaging of the outfit was the typical 1957 basket-weave type.

Excellent	Like New	Scarcity
900	1,600	5

1607WS Trouble Shooter Work Set $59.95 retail

Included: 2037 2-6-4 steam locomotive with operating headlight, smoke, and Magne-traction; 6026W tender; 6464-425 New Haven boxcar; 6660 boom crane car; 6112-85 canister car; 6818 flatcar with transformer; 6465 Gulf double-dome tank car; 6119-100 work caboose; eight 1013 curved and five 1018 straight track; 6029 uncoupling section; 1044 90-watt transformer; CTC Lockon; tube of lubricant; instructions.

The top of the line 027 freight set was this outfit, headed by the reliable and common 2037 2-6-4 steam locomotive. Its tender rode on bar-end metal trucks and usually had an unpainted body. The locomotive was packed in a "58"-dated, tan corrugated box, while the tender came in a Late Traditional box, as did the 6818 flatcar with transformer and 6464-425 New Haven boxcar.

The remainder of the rolling stock was packaged in Bold Traditional boxes. Those items included the 6465-60 Gulf tank car, 6112-85 blue gondola, 6119-100 and the new 6660 boom car, described earlier in this chapter. The Gulf tank car was shown as orange in the catalog, although all examples of outfit 1607WS examined while researching this volume included gray tank cars. Some have reported black Gulf two-dome tanks as components of this set.

As with the other 1958 027 outfits, the set came in an off-white basket weave set carton.

Excellent	Like New	Scarcity
325	700	5

1608W Merchants Limited Diesel Passenger $65 retail

Included: 209P/209T New Haven Alco A-A units with horn; two 2432 Clifton Vista Domes, 2434 Newark Pullman and 2436 Mooseheart observation; eight 1013 curved and five 1018 straight track; 6029 uncoupling section; 1053 60-watt transformer; CTC Lockon; tube of lubricant; instructions.

This outfit, elusive today, was the best 027 passenger outfit offered in 1958. While the Clifton, Newark and Mooseheart are common streamlined plastic passenger cars and came in Late Traditional boxes, the locomotives are what make the outfit special. The paired Alcos, painted in New Haven Railroad livery known to buffs as the "McGinnis" scheme, came only in this outfit. Each of the locomotives had their

Railroad livery known to buffs as the "McGinnis" scheme, came only in this outfit. Each of the locomotives had their own corrugated tan carton made by Star and were packed with two cardboard coupler protection rings. Naturally, the outfit box was the off-white basket-weave-style.

Excellent	Like New	Scarcity
1,500	2,700	7

The locomotive was packed in a corrugated tan carton made by Star, while the rolling stock was packed in a mix of Late and Bold Traditional boxes. All this was then packed in a 1957-style brown basket weave Super 0 set box.

Excellent	Like New	Scarcity
750	1,400	5

Super 0

2501W Super 0 Work Train $49.95 retail

Included: 2348 Minneapolis & St. Louis GP-9; 6464-525 Minneapolis & St. Louis boxcar; 6560-25 crane; 6802 flatcar with girders; 6119-100 work caboose; 12 31 curved, three 32 straight and one 48 insulated straight track; 39-5 operating packet.

This work train was Lionel's basic Super 0 offering in 1958. The train was pulled by a very attractive red, white and blue Minneapolis & St. Louis diesel. Lionel added a dynamic brake housing to their GP-7, and then referred to it as a GP-9 fantasy, but of course the whole miniature empire they built was based on fantasy! While the caboose at the rear of the train somewhat strangely had D.L.&W. markings, at least the consist did include an M & St. L. boxcar, the 6464-525.

The 6802 flatcar was a new addition to the catalog and was created by marrying Lionel's basic 6511-type mold with the girders used by the 214 bridge. This car, like most of the ones in this set, rode on AAR-type trucks.

2502W Super 0 Rail-Diesel Commuter $59.95 retail

Included: 400 Budd Rail Diesel Car; 2550 Budd mail-baggage car; 2559 Budd passenger car; twelve 31 curved, three 32 straight and one 48 insulated straight track; 39-5 operating packet.

With only 600 of these outfits packaged, this set was likely produced in lower numbers than any other regularly cataloged set of the postwar era—hence, its extreme scarcity today. Such low production is probably a result of the somewhat limited appeal of the Budd RDC units, familiar to only a small portion of the public in 1958. Today, this same lack of appeal persists, somewhat limiting the value of this set, despite its scarcity.

Die-hard Lionel enthusiasts covet not only the outfit as a whole, but if the set is unavailable, the dummy Budd cars, numbers 2550 and 2559 are sought, particularly the former, which is the scarcest of all the RDC cars.

2503WS

The powered unit was packed in a tan corrugated carton, while the dummies used Late Traditional boxes. The outfit box was the brown basket-weave-style.

Excellent	Like New	Scarcity
2,000	4,000	8

2503WS **$59.95 retail**

Included: 665 4-6-4 steam locomotive with operating headlight, smoke and Magne-traction; 2046W tender; 6801 flatcar with boat; 6536 Minneapolis & St. Louis hopper; 3361 operating lumber car; 6434 poultry car; 6357 illuminated SP-type caboose; twelve 31 curved, three 32 straight and one 48 insulated straight track; 39-20 operating packet.

Routine—that is perhaps the best way to describe outfit 2503WS. The 665 locomotive, 3361 operating log car, 6801 flatcar with boat and 6357 lighted caboose were all familiar items. New were the 6536 Minneapolis & St. Louis boxcar and the 6434 poultry car.

The bright red 6434 poultry car was the same size and proportion as the 3356 boxcar. The illuminated car had translucent side panels imprinted with color images of poultry. The 6536 was another of the large hoppers that traced their origins to Lionel's covered hopper cars. The car included a steel spreader bar, and the version most often reported in this outfit rode on bar-end metal trucks.

Bar-end metal trucks were used on all the rolling stock in this outfit except for the 6801, which was equipped with AAR-type trucks. Boxes were less uniform, with both Late and Bold traditional boxes used for the rolling stock and a tan corrugated carton made by Star housing the locomotive. The outfit box of course was the brown basket-weave-type.

Excellent	Like New	Scarcity
550	1,000	5

2505W Super O Five-Car Freight **$59.95 retail**

Included: 2329 Virginian rectifier electric; 6805 atomic energy disposal car; 6519 Allis-Chalmers car; 6800 flatcar with airplane; 6464-500 Timken boxcar; 6357 illuminated SP-type caboose; twelve 31 curved, three 32 straight and one 48 insulated straight track; 39-5 operating packet.

Though attractively painted, the odd-looking rectifier at the front of this outfit was not widely recognized by the American public or even toy train enthusiasts in 1958. This no doubt hampered sales and that in turn has lead to a relative scarcity of this outfit today. Adding to today's collectability of the outfit is the fragility of three of the included cars; the 6519 Allis-Chalmers heat exchanger car, 6800 flatcar with airplane and the 6805 atomic waste disposal car.

The brake wheels of the 6519 and their mounting tabs are often found missing or repaired. Like all of Lionel's aircraft cargo, the Beechcraft riding on the 6800 was fragile and easily broken—and it has also been well reproduced—some of these reproductions even include all the Lionel Corp. molded-in markings of the original. As an aside, the proper 6800 flatcar for this outfit is equipped with AAR-type trucks.

The new-for-1958 6805 on the other hand rode on bar-end metal trucks to facilitate the electrical connection needed to power the flashing radioactive waste containers. These containers are somewhat fragile, and when knocked free tend to wind up with cracked handles or corners. Lionel has re-issued this car numerous times during the Modern era, and Lionel made replacement radioactive waste canisters available at those times. The car came packaged in a Late Traditional box.

While these outfits universally come packaged in the dark brown basket-weave-type Super 0 box, the component boxes inside were far from uniform. The locomotive came in a Star-made tan corrugated carton, while the cars came in a mix of Late and Bold Traditional boxes.

Excellent	Like New	Scarcity
1,500	2,750	5

2507W Super O Five-Car Diesel Freight **$65 retail**

Included: 2242P/2242C New Haven A-B F-3 units; 3444 animated gondola; 6464-425 New Haven boxcar; 6468-25 New Haven double-door automobile car; 6424-85 flatcar with autos; 6357 illuminated SP-type caboose; twelve 31 curved, three 32 straight and one 48 insulated straight track; 39-5 operating packet.

This outfit represents one of the few times during the postwar era that Lionel almost provided a matching road name throughout a freight set. New Haven markings adorned a conventional boxcar, a double-door automobile type boxcar and the new F-3 A-B diesels.

1958

The F-3 body mold tooling was modified with the introduction of the 2242. The molded-in nose door had its molded-in simulated handle eliminated to aid the heat stamping of the white "NH" on the nose door.

The powered unit was packaged in a tan corrugated carton, but the non-powered B-unit was packed in a Late Traditional box with liner. Unfortunately, too often these boxes did not do an adequate job of protecting the elaborate, and easily scratched and soiled the orange, white and silver paint scheme. As with all of the postwar F-3s, repaints, reproductions and even outright forgeries exist. Authentic New Haven units have heat-stamped orange markings, whereas most non-Lionel units have silk-screened markings.

Although the locomotives were new, all the cars behind were returning items. The flatcar, which carried a red and white automobile, rode on AAR-type trucks, as did the black New Haven boxcar. The double-door boxcar, however, as well as the caboose and animated gondola car, was equipped with bar-end metal trucks. Animated gondola cars produced in 1958 were fitted with a metal washer above the pulley nearest the off-on switch.

Excellent	Like New	Scarcity
2,000	3,200	6

2509WS The Owl Five-Car Freight $65 retail

Included: 665 4-6-4 steam locomotive with operating headlight, smoke and Magne-traction; 2046W tender; 6805 atomic energy disposal car; 6414 Evans Auto Loader; 6464-475 Boston and Maine boxcar; 3650 extension searchlight car; 6357 illuminated SP-type caboose; twelve 31 curved, three 32 straight, and one 48 insulated straight track; 39-5 operating packet.

The locomotive style, known as the "baby Hudson," led this outfit. Behind the steamer was one of the new atomic energy disposal cars described earlier in this chapter, and an array of returning cars. Unlike earlier editions, the 6414 Auto Loader included in this set was equipped with AAR-type trucks, and had the number stamped to the left of "LIONEL." The Boston and Maine boxcar also used AAR-type plastic trucks, while the rest of the cars were fitted with bar-end metal trucks.

Both Late and Bold Traditional boxes were used for the rolling stock in this outfit, while the locomotive was packed in a Star-produced tan corrugated carton. The outfit box was of course the dark brown basket weave Super 0 version.

Excellent	Like New	Scarcity
800	1,300	5

2511W, 2518W

2511W **Super 0 Five-Car Electric Work Train** **$69.95 retail**

Included: 2352 Pennsylvania EP-5 electric; 3562-75 operating barrel car; 3424 operating brakeman; 6560-25 crane; 3361 operating lumber car; 6119-100 work caboose; twelve 31 curved, three 32 straight and one 48 insulated straight track; 39-10 operating packet.

Lionel reused the tooling that created their abbreviated version of the New Haven EP-5 rectifier to create a Pennsylvania edition, which was then placed in front of this train. The Pennsylvania never actually owned an EP-5, but ultimately the Pennsylvania, New Haven and New York Central merged to form the Penn Central, which then assumed ownership of the actual EP-5. So, in a convoluted manner this outfit foretold the future.

All the cars in this set had been issued in prior years, and hence not surprisingly the component boxes were a mix of Late and Bold Traditional boxes. The correct 3424 for this outfit—the only Super 0 outfit it was ever packaged with—had a support hole at the top of the drawbar, and sometimes used a pale yellow wire for the power lead. It also came with zinc-plated support bases.

The orange barrel car was included in this outfit and came with a figure with outstretched arms. This car naturally had bar-end metal trucks, as did the log and operating brakeman cars. The crane and its companion, the 6119-100 work caboose, rode on AAR trucks.

The outfit was packed in the then-standard brown basket-weave carton and uniquely included packet 39-10 which contained the 38-95 adapter track needed by the operating brakeman car.

Excellent	Like New	Scarcity
1,200	2,100	6

2513W **Super 0 Six-Car Freight Train** **$69.95 retail**

Included: 2329 Virginian rectifier electric; 6414 Evans Auto Loader; 6434 poultry car; 6556 Missouri-Kansas-Texas stock car; 6425 Gulf triple-dome tank car; 3359 operating dump car; 6427-60 Virginian porthole caboose; twelve 31 curved, three 32 straight and one 48 insulated straight track; 39-20 operating packet.

The odd-looking Virginian rectifier also led this set, which contains two cars that were unique to the outfit and highly collectable today. The locomotive itself was packaged inside a tan corrugated carton made by Star. Reproduction frames and pantographs have been produced, and purchasers should examine these components carefully.

While the Evans Auto Loader with AAR-type trucks and the new 6434 poultry car are interesting, and the 6425 Gulf triple-dome tanker and 3359 operating dump car are quality pieces—none of these are what today's collectors lust after.

The same cannot be said for the 6556 Katy stock car and the 6427-60 Virginian caboose. Both of these cars were new for 1958, and were available only in this set.

The brilliant red paint of the 6556 is particularly susceptible to damage during cleaning, which is a process that this writer strongly recommends enthusiasts leave to professionals.

The blue 6427 caboose came in a 6427-1 box that was over-stamped with the "1" being obliterated, and a "60" stamped beside the newly stamped block of ink. Forgeries of this car are rampant, and are usually identifiable by sanding marks and silk-screen printing.

The outfit was packed into a brown basket weave Super 0 box, and the rolling stock in both Late and Bold Traditional boxes.

Excellent	Like New	Scarcity
2,000	3,700	7

2515WS **Mainliner Steam Freight** **$75 retail**

Included: 646 4-6-4 steam locomotive with operating headlight, smoke and Magne-traction; 2046W tender; 6800 flatcar with airplane; 6424 flatcar with autos; 3444 animated gondola; 3662 operating milk car; 6427 Lionel Lines porthole caboose; twelve 31 curved, three 32 straight and one 48 insulated straight track; 39-20 operating packet.

This outfit was the swan song for Lionel's medium-sized Hudson. For its final appearance, the 646 was packed in a tan corrugated carton and matched to a 2046W streamlined whistle tender.

Behind the big steamer was a selection of top-quality freight cars, all like the locomotive repeats of previous issues. The big milk car had a flat brown roof, and inside was a coil with red windings and a figure with painted face and hands. Beneath the car was a pair of bar-end metal trucks.

Metal trucks were also found on the 3444 animated gondola, which has been described earlier in this chapter, as well as the caboose. The airplane and automobile cars, also described elsewhere in this chapter, rode on plastic AAR-type trucks. Both Late and Bold Traditional boxes were used on the components of this outfit.

In addition to reproduction boiler fronts for the steam locomotive, reproduction milk cans, milk platform, milk car doors, platform deck, 3444 figures, automobiles, automobile wheels and bumpers, airplanes, and propellers exist.

Excellent	Like New	Scarcity
800	1,500	5

2517W Super O Five-Car Diesel Freight $75 retail

Included: 2379P/2379C Rio Grande A-B F-3 units; 6519 Allis-Chalmers car; 6805 atomic energy disposal car; 6434 poultry car; 6800 flatcar with airplane; 6657 Rio Grande SP-type caboose; twelve 31 curved, three 32 straight and one 48 insulated straight track; 39-5 operating packet.

The Rio Grande locomotives and caboose at either end of this train had been seen in 1957, but made them no less attractive the second time around. Their striking paint jobs continue to attract collectors, though from the relative scarcity of this outfit not many buyers in 1958 were attracted.

The 6800 flatcar with a black and yellow airplane rode on AAR-type plastic trucks, as did the 6519 heat exchanger car. The brake stands of the Allis-Chalmers car, as well as their mounting tabs, are particularly fragile, and are often found broken, missing or repaired. The airplane was fragile as well, particularly its propeller, which always matched the lower surface of the fuselage. Reproduction propellers and indeed entire airplanes exist, and are not always marked as reproduction.

The atomic energy car and poultry car were both new for 1958 and have been described in detail earlier in this chapter. Both rode on bar-end metal trucks, as did the 6657 Rio Grande illuminated caboose.

Whether the 1957 or 1958 release, the 2379 is a desirable locomotive. Unfortunately the nose decoration, done by decal, is somewhat fragile. Examples with pristine decals, as above, command a premium. Excellent reproduction decals exist, as do restored, repainted and non-original cabs. Lettering on originals was heat stamped, a process not used by others.

Both Late and Bold Traditional boxes were used packing the rolling stock of this outfit, while the B-unit came in a Late Traditional box with liner. The A-unit came in a tan corrugated carton; the outfit box itself was the standard brown basket-weave-type.

Excellent	Like New	Scarcity
2,400	4,100	7

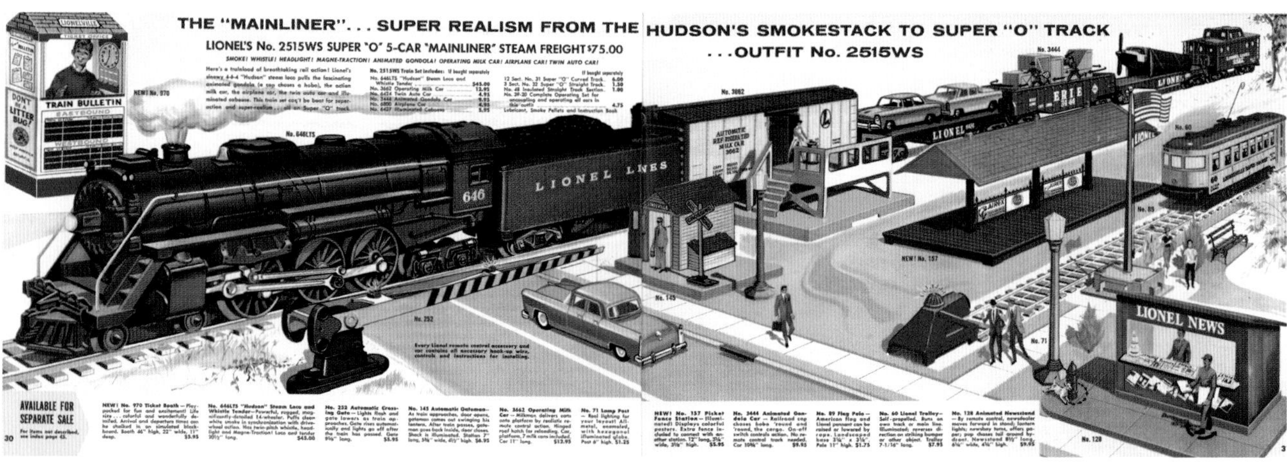

2515WS

2518W Super O Three-car Passenger $75 retail

Included: 2352 Pennsylvania EP-5 electric; 2533 Silver Cloud Pullman; 2534 Silver Bluff Pullman passenger cars; 2531 Silver Dawn observation; twelve 31 curved, three 32 straight and one 48 insulated straight track; 39-5 operating packet.

The Pennsylvania EP-5 described under set 2511W was also placed at the head end of this three-car aluminum passenger consist. The moderately scarce flat-channel cars of this outfit came in Late Traditional boxes while the locomotive came in a tan corrugated box. Of note is the fact that this was the only outfit to contain the flat-channel version of the Silver Bluff.

Excellent	Like New	Scarcity
1,500	2,600	7

2519W Super O Six-Car Diesel Freight $79.95 retail

Included: 2331 Virginian Train Master; 6414 Evans Auto Loader; 6464-275 State of Maine boxcar; 6434 poultry car; 3530 operating generator car; 6801-50 flatcar with boat; 6557 SP-type smoking caboose; twelve 31 curved, three 32 straight and one 48 insulated straight track; 39-5 operating packet.

The big Virginian Train Master was a repeat item, as was much of the rolling stock included in this set—not that this is a factor in the outfit's desirability to collectors.

The locomotive came in a tan corrugated carton with liner, while the rolling stock was packed in both Late and Bold Traditional boxes. The outfit box was the then-standard brown basket weave Super 0 type.

The 6414 had its number stamped to the left of Lionel, and rode on AAR-type plastic trucks, as did the State of Maine boxcar and the 6801 flatcar with boat. Beware that the boat, its cradle and the automobiles have been reproduced.

The 3530 Electro-Motive power car was a returning item, which had been produced in several variations. The version most likely to surface in this set had support holes in the coupler drawbars, a maroon pole, matching fuel tank and transformer base, and stripe extending the full length of the car.

The 6434 was a new car in 1958 and has been described earlier in this chapter. The other new car in the outfit was the 6557, and this caboose had a feature separating it from all the rest of Lionel's cabooses—it smoked! Like the 6434 and 3530, it rode on bar-end metal trucks.

Excellent	Like New	Scarcity
2,000	3,200	5

2521WS Super O Six-Car Freight $89.95 retail

Included: 746 4-8-4 Norfolk & Western steam locomotive with operating headlight, smoke and Magne-traction; 746W tender; 6805 atomic energy disposal car; 6424 flatcar with autos; 6430 flatcar with vans; 3356 operating horse car; 3361 operating lumber car; 6557 SP-type smoking caboose; twelve 31 curved, three 32 straight and one 48 insulated straight track; smoke fluid; 39-15 operating packet.

This lengthy train showcased many of Lionel's better items in 1958. The 746, introduced the year before, was the top-of-the-line Lionel steamer, and was paired with the short-stripe version of the 746W whistle tender—despite catalog illustrations showing a longer stripe.

In tow, behind the class "J," was the new atomic energy disposal car and smoking caboose, both fitted with bar-end metal trucks. The returning 3356 operating horse car also rode on metal trucks, and its brake wheel was on the left-hand end of the car when facing the side with the horse chutes. It most frequently appears in this set packed in a Bold Traditional box. The familiar 3361 lumber car was included in the outfit, with its number stamped to the right of the serif "Lionel Lines" lettering. As with all 3361 cars, metal trucks were used, this time with the coupler support hole formed in the drawbar.

AAR-type plastic trucks were used on the 6424 and 6430 flatcars. Both cars had their numbers stamped to the right of the "LIONEL" markings. The red and white automobiles of the 6424, as well as the roofs for the white vans on the 6430, have been reproduced. Also reproduced is the die-cast "landing gear"—support legs—for the trailers, as well as their Cooper-Jarrett nameplates.

The locomotive was packaged in a tan corrugated carton, while the tender and rolling stock were packed in a mixture of Late and Bold Traditional boxes. The outfit box was the brown basket-weave Super 0 type. A unique inclusion in the outfit was the 39-15 operating packet needed to actuate the log and horse cars.

Excellent	Like New	Scarcity
2,500	4,200	6

2523W Super 0 Super Chief Freight $95 retail

Included: 2383P/2383T Santa Fe A-A F-3 units; 264 operating forklift with 6264 lumber car; 6800 flatcar with airplane; 3662 operating milk car; 6434 poultry car; 6517 bay window caboose; twelve 31 curved, three 32 straight and one 48 insulated straight track; 39-20 operating packet.

The classic double A-unit Santa Fe roared back into the Lionel catalog in 1958 to head this freight set, as well as the 2526W passenger set. The train stretching back behind the dual-motor units was comprised entirely of repeat or carryover rolling stock save for the poultry car. The 6424 poultry car rode on bar-end metal trucks to facilitate its illumination, showing off the colorful illustrations of its feathered cargo.

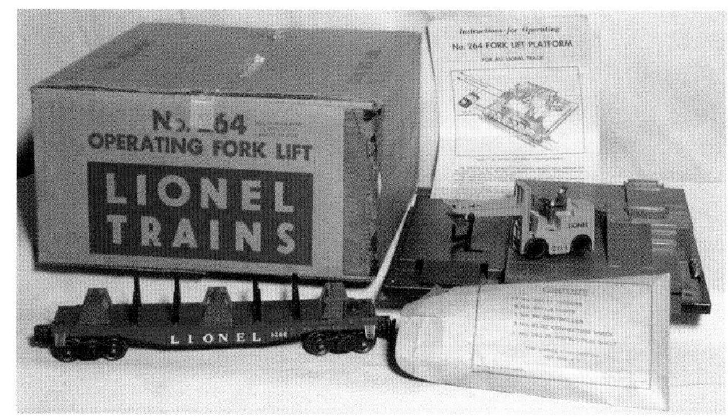

The 6800 airplane car and the 3662 milk car, and the potential pitfalls of both, have been discussed earlier in this chapter. The 6517, as included in this outfit, did not have underscoring beneath the "Built by Lionel" or the date, but did continue to ride on 2400-series passenger car trucks.

The centerpiece for the outfit was the 264 operating forklift platform, which naturally came packed with a 6264 flatcar. Because it was packed with the forklift platform, this car did not have an individual component box in this set. Each of the other rolling stock items were packed in their own boxes, of either the Late or Bold Traditional styles.

The locomotives came in tan corrugated boxes made by Star, which were unique to 1958 production. The outfit carton was the standard brown basket weave Super 0 type.

Excellent	Like New	Scarcity
1,800	3,000	6

2525WS Super 0 Six-Car Work Train $100 retail

Included: 746 4-8-4 Norfolk & Western steam locomotive with operating headlight, smoke and Magne-traction; 746W tender; 342 operating culvert loader with 6342 culvert gondola; 345 operating culvert unloader with 6342 culvert gondola; 6519 Allis-Chalmers car; 6518 double-truck transformer car; 6560-25 crane; 6419-100 N & W work caboose; twelve 31 curved, five 32 straight and one 48 insulated straight track; smoke fluid; 39-5 operating packet.

This accessory-laden outfit is one of the most desirable of the postwar era. In addition to the top-quality 746 steamer, the set included the desirable 6419-100 N & W work caboose, two sought-after culvert accessories and a variety of rolling stock.

The long, die-cast base 6518 16-wheel transformer car was a returning item. It is difficult to locate in a pristine original box because the heavy and cumbersome car often

destroyed the Late Traditional box, especially if the two special cardboard inserts had been discarded, as they often were. When that was the case, the transformer insulators were often damaged or broken—beware of replacements, or even entire reproduction transformer loads.

As told earlier in this chapter, the 6519 was fragile as well. The 6560 crane, which came in a 6560-25 box, was somewhat more robust, but reproduction booms are plentiful. Its companion 6419-100 work caboose came in a box printed with the –100 suffix, even though the cab was numbered 576419. Reproduction cabs and toolboxes have been made for this car.

Two 6342 culvert gondolas were included in the outfit, but neither came with a component box. Instead, one was packed inside the 342 box, and the other with the 345. Reproduction culverts exist, as does reproductions of the bridge spanning the two accessories and the magnet for the culvert unloader.

The locomotive was furnished with the short-stripe version of the 746W tender, the tender coming in a Late Traditional box, and the locomotive in a tan corrugated carton. The outfit box was massive in order to accommodate the two accessories, which came in their own corrugated boxes inside the brown basket-weave set box.

Excellent	Like New	Scarcity
3,000	5,000	4

2526W Super Chief Passenger $100 retail

Included: 2383P/2383T Santa Fe A-A F-3 units; 2530 Railway Express Agency baggage car; two 2532 Silver Range Vista Domes; 2531 Silver Dawn observation; twelve 31 curved, seven 32 straight and one 48 insulated straight track; 39-5 operating packet.

Reprising a role they began in 1952, once again dual motor Santa Fe F-3s lead the Lionel Lines extruded aluminum passenger set. The passenger cars were the flat-channel version and, like the baggage car, were packed in Late Traditional boxes.

The 1958 edition of the 2383 P&T, whether in outfit 2526W or 2523W, came in tan corrugated cartons made by the Star Container Co., as seen here. In later years the boxes were perforated, or made by other box manufacturers.

The twin diesels were packed individually in tan corrugated boxes made by Star. These non-perforated boxes were unique to 1958. The outfit as a whole came in the standard brown basket weave Super 0 box.

Excellent	Like New	Scarcity
1,800	3,000	4

Chapter 16
1959

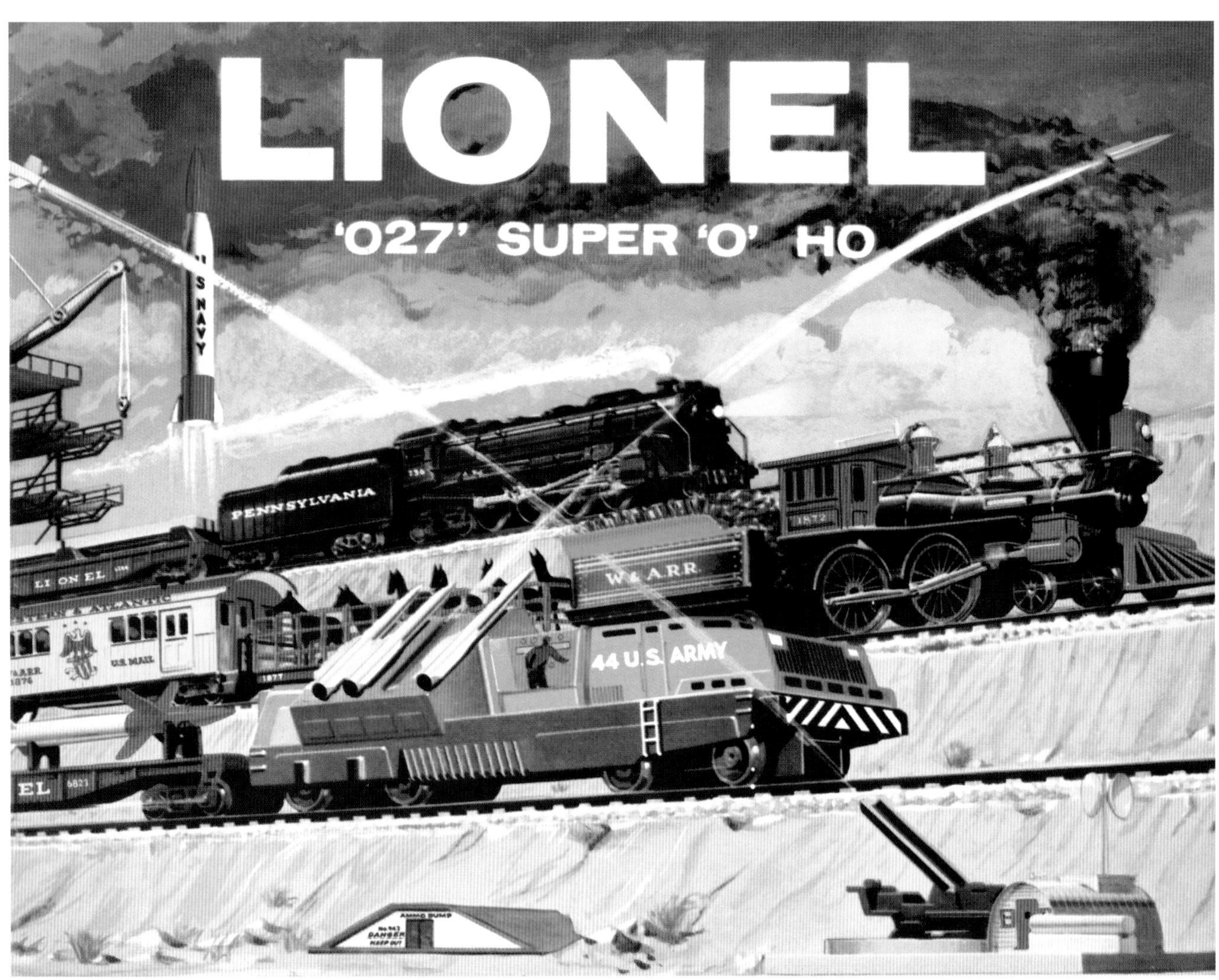

The 1959 offerings, while attractive, were not as spectacular as they had been four years earlier. The most heavily promoted new locomotive for the year was the plastic-bodied General 4-4-0 steamer, though the 2358 Great Northern electric is far more desirable to collectors today.

By 1959, merchandising trends had moved toward consumer self-service, and Lionel's products had an increasing presence in discount chains. This resulted in a total change in Lionel's packaging. The new box was made of orange-coated stock and featured a tear-out perforated front panel that allowed the contents to be displayed. This box was introduced in 1959 and used through 1960 and is referred to in this text as the "Perforated box."

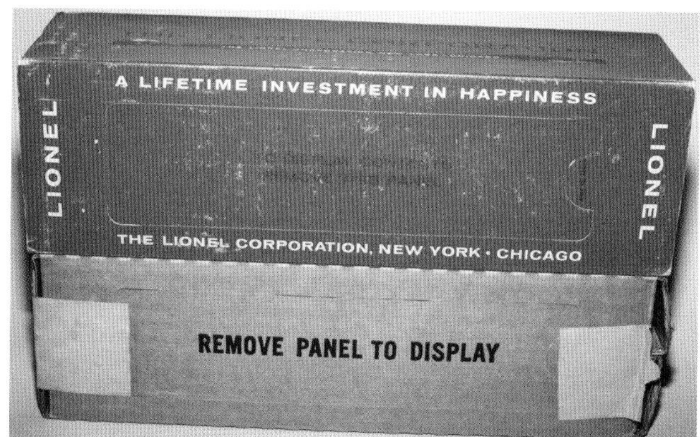

Similar packaging was used for many of the locomotives, with the heavy corrugated carton also being perforated. An orange slipover sleeve was used with many of these boxes as seen here.

This colorful box was new for 1959 and was used for the more elaborate Super O outfits.

Packaging was extensively revamped in 1959. A new component box, referred to here as the "Perforated box," was introduced. As one would gather, a large part of the front panel of the glossy, solid orange box was perforated allowing its removal. This innovation was no doubt a response to the merchandising needs of large chain

Frequently found containing 027 outfits, new flat display boxes were also introduced in 1959. Some, like this one however, were used with the simpler Super O outfits.

Sometimes the new flat display boxes contained individually boxed components—usually in their own Perforated boxes.

Some of the flat display boxes used a die-cut insert as shown here to hold the components in place. Others used cardboard dividers to create separate compartments for each of the outfit components. Outfits packed in either of these style cartons did not include component boxes.

New for 1959 was the arch-bar-style truck. Originally created for the "General" series rolling stock, for which it was prototypical. In the coming decade, Lionel would mount this inexpensive truck on a broad array of items, regardless of era represented.

stores, which were becoming increasingly important to Lionel's business. Perforated packaging was even extended to corrugated locomotive boxes. An orange slipover sleeve was used with many of these boxes.

The Perforated boxes were not as robust as their predecessors, making them harder to find today, particularly with the perforated panel still in place.

The set boxes were extensively revamped as well, once again with a nod towards display. Many outfits came in flat boxes with an attached perforated lid, which could be folded to both display the contents and create a marketing aid. Some of these outfit boxes housed individually boxed components, others had unboxed contents housed in a "tray" which consisted of folded pasteboard dividers, and still other outfit cartons included a die-cut liner, which held the unboxed components in place.

Arch-bar trucks were introduced in 1959 to equip the new line of 19th-century-style trains pulled by the "General" steam locomotive inspired by Disney's "Great Locomotive Chase" movie. These trucks, like the AAR trucks, were molded plastic and, though very different cosmetically from the AAR-trucks, were almost identical from the manufacturing standpoint. The trucks themselves had either no coupler, as used on tender fronts and passenger cars (which had separate body-mounted couplers), or non-operating couplers, as used on tender rears and the General set flatcar. In the later desperate years of Lionel's production, these trucks came to be used across the product line, regardless of whether they were correct for the period of the prototype railcar.

Of minor interest was a change in track made during the course of the year. Previously, all Super 0, as well as the recently produced 027 track, used blued steel for the crossties (in the case of 027) or under-tie support structure (in the case of Super 0). The new style track utilized metal with a gray finish for these components.

027-Gauge

1105 **No retail**

Included: 1055 Texas Special Alco A-unit; 6045 Lionel Lines two-dome tank car; 6044 Airex boxcar; 6042 or 6112 gondola with canisters; 6047 SP-type caboose; eight 1013 curved and two 1018 straight track; 1026 25-watt transformer; CTC Lockon; tube of lubricant; instruction sheet.

Though this outfit does not appear in the 1959 consumer catalog, it is listed here because it was included in the 1959 advance catalog, which also meant it was widely available through Lionel's traditional distribution network.

All the rolling stock in this outfit was produced with economy in mind, with arch-bar trucks with fixed couplers being the norm. The locomotive, though a stripped down version at the time, had many features that only appeared on better units, including a ballast weight and decorative horn. However, the 1055 did lack a front coupler.

The set came packaged in a display-type outfit box, printed in blue and orange on a white background. The set was dubbed "THE TEXAS SPECIAL"—the name taken from the decoration of the locomotive.

Occasionally this set surfaces containing a hard-to-find variation of the 6044 Airex boxcar. The common car is blue, while the scarce car is purple. The values listed below presume this car is blue.

Excellent	Like New	Scarcity
100	250	6

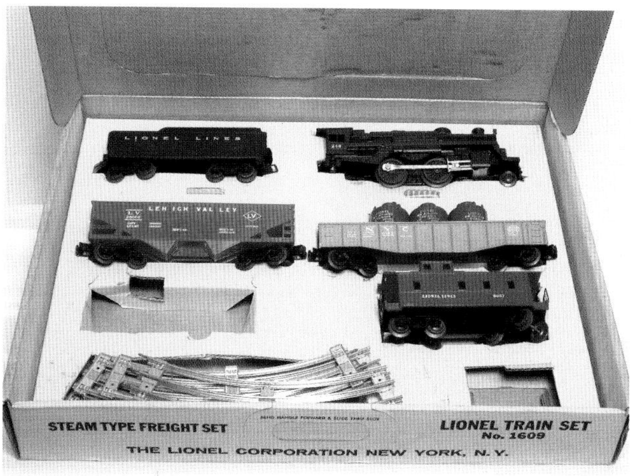

1609 **Three-Car Steam Freight** **$19.95 retail**

Included: 246 steam locomotive with headlight and Magne-traction; 1130T tender; 6162-25 blue gondola with canisters; 6476 red Lehigh Valley hopper; 6057 SP-type caboose; eight 1013 curved and two 1018 straight track; 1008 camtrol; 1016 35-watt transformer; CTC Lockon; tube of lubricant; instruction sheet.

This set was unassuming and inexpensive; it nevertheless was sold in large numbers, resulting in several packaging variations. In fact, for many collectors the packaging is more interesting than the contents! Some came in tan conventional cardboard boxes. Others came in yellow display boxes, but, more interestingly, all three versions of this box were used; those housing individual boxes, those with integral dividers, and those using a die-cut insert.

All the rolling stock, like the locomotive in this outfit, was relatively plain and is common today. The exception to this is the occasional inclusion of a painted version of the 6057 in lieu of the common unpainted red plastic version.

Tan conventional box:

Excellent	Like New	Scarcity
200	450	4

Display box with dividers:

Excellent	Like New	Scarcity
125	200	2

Display box with die-cut filler:

Excellent	Like New	Scarcity
150	225	2

Display box with individual component boxes:

Excellent	Like New	Scarcity
150	250	3

1959

Values for each condition are in U.S. dollars. | **Scarity** = Scale from 1-8 with 8 being the hardest to find.

Most of the 1611 Alaska outfits were packaged like this—in a display box with a die-cut insert holding the components in place.

As was the case with many of the 1959 outfits, a few of the 1611 sets came in conventional tan corrugated cartons, as seen here.

1611 Four-Car Alaskan Freight $25 retail

Included: 614 Alaska NW-2 diesel switcher; 6825 flatcar with trestle; 6162-60 Alaska gondola with canisters; 6465 Lionel Lines two-dome tank car; 6027 Alaska SP-type caboose; eight 1013 curved and two 1018 straight track; 1008 camtrol; 1016 35-watt transformer; CTC Lockon; tube of lubricant; instruction sheet.

AAR trucks were utilized on the rolling stock in this outfit, which contains several moderately desirable cars. However, it is the locomotive itself that garners the most attention from collectors. Especially those included in a few outfits which include a yellow outline on the "BUILT BY LIONEL" markings on some locomotives. Be aware that the distinctive air brake tank and dynamic brake housing on top of the locomotive is often missing and has been reproduced.

This is another of the outfits that came utilized with at least two different styles of set boxes. Some came in a tan single-tier conventional outfit box, while most came in a yellow display-style box with die-cut insert. Although difficult to locate, due to the tan outfit box, there are existent individual perforated boxes for the gondola and caboose, counter to what many collectors believe.

Display box:

Excellent	Like New	Scarcity
575	950	4

Tan conventional box:

Excellent	Like New	Scarcity
650	1,400	6

1612 The General Old-Timer Outfit $29.95 retail

Included: 1862 4-4-0 General with headlight; 1862T tender; 1866 mail-baggage car; 1865 passenger car; eight 1013 curved and two 1018 straight track; 1015 45-watt transformer; CTC Lockon; smoke fluid; tube of lubricant; instruction sheet.

No doubt inspired by the 1956 Disney movie "The Great Locomotive Chase," and the then-current interest in the Old West (fed by TV shows), Lionel introduced two versions of the 19th-Century steamer the "General." One version was 027; the other was Super 0.

The 027 version had a gray boiler and matching gray stack. The 1959 version can be distinguished from later models by the lack of small holes in the boiler, which were used to install the trim bands on the later-produced 1872. Reportedly, the earliest of the 1862 locomotives had red headlight housing, however, the bulk of these steamers had a black housing. A delicate simulated whistle was mounted atop the locomotive.

The passenger cars, as well as the tender, rode on the new arch-bar trucks, which had been developed specifically for the General-series cars. The cars were not illuminated, nor did they have operating couplers—although the couplers were at least die-cast. The green plastic tender featured a brown rubber woodpile.

1613S

As with most 1959 outfits, set 1612 frequently came in a yellow display-type box with a die-cut insert holding the components in position. However, some sets were shipped in conventional tan set cartons, with individually boxed components. In these instances, the rolling stock was packaged in Orange Perforated boxes and the locomotive came in a perforated front corrugated box with display sleeve and special insert to protect the whistle.

Display box:

Excellent	Like New	Scarcity
350	600	1

Tan conventional box:

Excellent	Like New	Scarcity
450	900	4

1613S Four-Car B&O Steam Freight $29.95 retail

Included: 247 blue-striped steam locomotive with headlight and smoke; 247T Baltimore & Ohio blue-striped small streamlined tender; 6826 flatcar with Christmas trees; 6819 flatcar with helicopter; 6821 flatcar with crates; 6017 SP-type caboose; eight 1013 curved and two 1018 straight track; 1008 camtrol; 1015 45-watt transformer; CTC Lockon; smoke fluid; tube of lubricant; instruction sheet.

The little steamer at the front of this outfit was trimmed with a blue stripe, which also extended along the side of its tender—no doubt part of Lionel's promised "more color" campaign. The locomotive and tender are desirable, more collectors seem to covet the three new flatcars that followed it. The 6826 flatcar loaded with Christmas trees has long been a favorite with collectors, while the 6819 flatcar with non-operating helicopter appeals to military fans. The third car carried a cargo of "crates" which Lionel derived from the crate load centered in the 3444 Erie operating gondola car. Both the Christmas trees and the helicopter have been reproduced in great detail—unfortunately these re-pros are sometimes passed off as originals. Also, beware that the proper crate cargo does not have any markings, nor does it have the slot cut out for the 3444's off-on switch. Sometimes the slightly shorter HO version of this load is found on this car, but it is believed that this is a post-factory substitution. All three flatcars, as well as the tender and caboose, rode on AAR-type trucks.

All the cars came in Orange Perforated boxes, while the locomotive was packaged in a tan corrugated carton with an orange slipover sleeve. The components were then packed in a yellow display-type box.

Excellent	Like New	Scarcity
300	500	5

1615 Five-Car Boston & Maine Diesel Freight $39.95 retail

Included: 217P/217C Boston and Maine Alco A-B units; 6464-475 Boston and Maine boxcar; 6800 flatcar with airplane; 6812 track maintenance car; 6825 flatcar with trestle; 6017-100 Boston and Maine SP-type caboose; eight 1013 curved and five 1018 straight track; 6029 uncoupling section; 1015 45-watt transformer; CTC Lockon; tube of lubricant; instruction sheet.

This moderately desirable set was headed by a new-for-1959 black and blue Boston and Maine Alco F-A set. Numbered 217P and 217C, the powered unit featured a three-position E-unit, operating headlight and Magne-traction on both axles. Perhaps more noteworthy was the 217C, which was the first Alco B-unit produced by Lionel. The powered unit came in an orange-sleeved tan carton, while the B-unit came in an Orange Perforated box.

Trailing the two-unit diesel was a matching 6464-475 B&M boxcar as well as a matching 6017-100 Boston and Maine caboose. Also included was the somewhat collectable 6800 flatcar with a yellow and black airplane. Beware, reproductions—both marked and unmarked—of the aircraft are plentiful.

Also included was the new-for-1959 6812 track maintenance car. The cars included in this outfit always had all-yellow superstructures and, although the shade could vary from light to dark yellow, all three components (base, platform and crank) matched.

The third flatcar included was the 6825 flatcar with trestle. The cargo of this car was a black bridge that was molded using the tooling created for the HO line. The true HO trestles, which are sometimes found on these cars and likely placed there by unknowing dealers or collectors, are gray, rather than the black properly used on these cars.

As a rule, the airplane car, with AAR trucks, was packaged in a Late Traditional box while the rest of the rolling stock came in Perforated boxes. A few 6800 airplane cars came in the Perforated box, but that is unusual. A limited number of these outfits were packed in tan corrugated boxes, while the bulk of the sets came in the new yellow display box.

Display box:

Excellent	Like New	Scarcity
575	975	5

Tan box:

Excellent	Like New	Scarcity
675	1,150	6

1617S Five-Car Busy Beaver Steam Work Train $39.95 retail

Included: 2018 2-6-4 steam locomotive with headlight and smoke; 1130T tender; 6670 boom crane car; 6816 flatcar with bulldozer; 6536 Minneapolis & St. Louis hopper; 6812 track maintenance car; 6119-100 work caboose; eight 1013 curved and three 1018 straight track; 6029 uncoupling section; 1015 45-watt transformer; CTC Lockon; bottle of SP smoke pellets; tube of lubricant; instruction sheet.

While the 2018 was a nice die-cast steamer, it is the rolling stock that makes this outfit. For collectors, the star of the set is the 6816 flatcar with bulldozer.

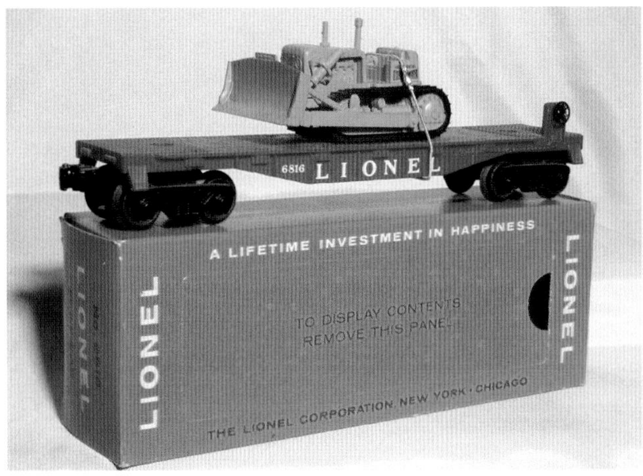

The flatcar with bulldozer is the most desirable component of the set. Beware, however, of broken or damaged hydraulic cylinders, exhaust and air intake stacks.

Not as sought after, but nevertheless an uncommon piece is the 6670 boom crane car. The more common version has the number "6670" stamped to the left of "Lionel," while a somewhat scarce version has the number stamped to the right of "Lionel." Often this car was packaged in the Bold Traditional box created for the 6660, only over stamped with the 6670 number.

The track maintenance car has an all-yellow upper works mounted on a red flatcar body. The 6536, like the rest of the rolling stock, rode on AAR trucks, however, it came in a Late Traditional box. Except as otherwise noted, the remainder of the rolling stock was packaged in perforated boxes. The locomotive was packaged in a tan corrugated carton with orange sleeve. The outfit box was the yellow display type.

Excellent	Like New	Scarcity
850	1,500	5

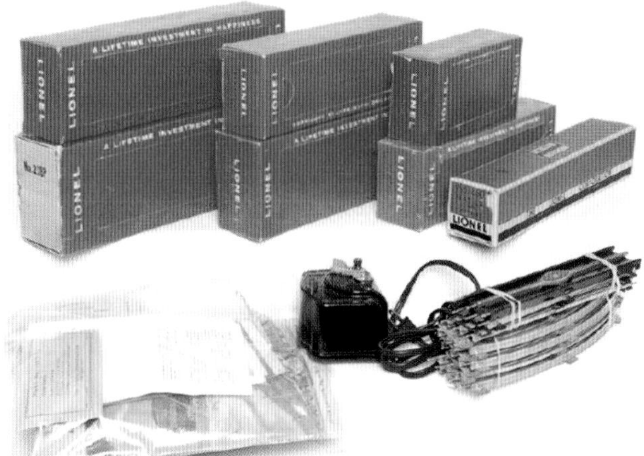

1619W Five-Car Santa Fe Diesel Freight $49.95 retail

Included: 218P/218T Santa Fe Alco A-A units with horn; 6519 Allis-Chalmers car; 6801 flatcar with boat; 6802 flatcar with girder; 6819 flatcar with helicopter; 6017-185 Santa Fe SP-type caboose; eight 1013 curved and three 1018 straight track; 6029 uncoupling section; 1053 60-watt transformer; CTC Lockon; tube of lubricant; instruction sheet.

As with so many of the late-1950s, early-1960s outfits, key to the value of this outfit is the presence and condition of the loads carried by the various cars included. As discussed previously in this volume, the boatload borne by the 6801 has been reproduced, as has the helicopter cargo of the 6819 and the heat exchanger transported by the 6519. The vertically mounted brake wheels, and more specifically the tiny tabs that

they mount to, are particularly fragile and are often found missing or repaired. All the cars rode on AAR-type trucks.

Santa Fe decoration was applied to the 6017-185 caboose as well as the A-A Alco diesels powering the set. Lionel chose to apply Santa Fe's traditional red and silver "warbonnet" scheme to these units—despite the fact that the real railroad used this scheme (at that time) for passenger service, and this was clearly a freight set. However, the powered unit was furnished with a three-position E-unit, two-axle Magne-traction and an operating horn. It was packed in a tan corrugated carton with an orange sleeve, while the dummy unit was packaged in a perforated box, as was the rolling stock of this outfit.

The outfit as a whole typically came in a yellow display-type box, although a few came in a tan corrugated set box.

Excellent	Like New	Scarcity
450	900	4

1621WS Five-Car Construction Special Steam Freight $49.95 retail

Included: 2037 2-6-4 steam locomotive with headlight, smoke, and Magne-traction; 6026W square whistle tender; 6519 Allis-Chalmers car; 6464-475 Boston and Maine boxcar; 6825 flatcar with trestle; 6062 gondola with cable reels; 6017 SP-type caboose; eight 1013 curved and three 1018 straight track; 6029 uncoupling section; 1053 60-watt transformer; CTC Lockon; bottle of SP smoke pellets; tube of lubricant; instruction sheet.

All the items in this outfit are common—hence it arouses little collector interest. As with all sets containing them, beware of missing or damaged brake wheels at each end of the 6519 and gray trestle bridges replacing the black one on the 6825. All the rolling stock rode on AAR-type trucks, and was packed in Perforated boxes. The only item of note, but even yet of little value, is the inclusion in some sets of the earliest version of the 6062, which had a metal underframe, rather than the usual all-plastic version. The locomotive was packed in a tan corrugated box with an orange sleeve. The outfit itself came in a yellow display-type box.

Excellent	Like New	Scarcity
300	525	4

1623W Five-Car NP Diesel Freight $59.95 retail

Included: 2349 Northern Pacific GP-9; 3512 operating fireman and ladder car; 3435 aquarium car; 6424 flatcar with autos; 6062 gondola with cable reels; 6017 SP-type caboose; eight 1013 curved and three 1018 straight track; 6029 uncoupling section; 1053 60-watt transformer; CTC Lockon; tube of lubricant; instruction sheet.

The attractive, and now desirable, 2349 Northern Pacific GP-9 was introduced at the front of this set. It was packaged in a tan corrugated carton with an orange sleeve.

Behind the new diesel was an interesting array of rolling stock. The most sought after one of these today was the new-for-1959 Aquarium Car. Its body was molded of clear plastic, which was masked, leaving four large windows, and then painted green. A filmstrip was installed inside that had images of fish printed on it. This filmstrip was driven by a vibrator motor that was controlled by an on-off lever extending through the bottom of the car. When backlit by the interior illumination, the movement simulated fish swimming. This car rode on AAR-type trucks with operating couplers. At least four variations of this car—varying widely in values—were produced, and conclusive evidence as to which versions may have come in this set has not yet surfaced.

3435 AQUARIUM CAR (Type I): The most desirable, and perhaps earliest version, of the Traveling Aquarium had the circle surrounding the molded-in "L" side logo picked out in gold. The heat-stamped lettering on the car was done in gold, and included "TANK No. 1" and "TANK No. 2" markings beneath the windows.

1623W

3435 AQUARIUM CAR (Type II): Almost as hard to find and desirable is a version identical to Type I, but lacking the gold circle around the "L" logo.

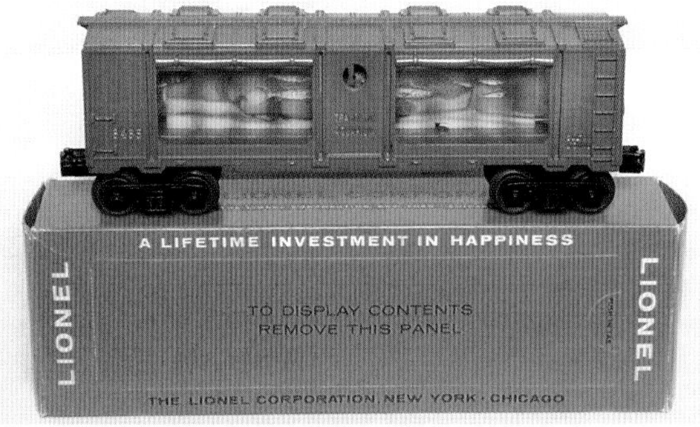

3435 AQUARIUM CAR (Type III): Some cars were made with gold heat-stamped lettering, but omitted not only the gold circle, but also the "TANK No. 1" and "TANK No. 2" designations.

3435 AQUARIUM CAR (Type IV): The bulk of the aquarium cars had yellow rather than gold markings, and these were rubber stamped rather than heat stamped. The rubber-stamped cars had neither the tank labels nor the "L" encircled.

The other car in this outfit to garner collector interest is the 3512 operating fireman and ladder car. While always difficult to find in unbroken condition with all its original accessories—two decorative ladders and three nozzles—the variation with a silver extension ladder is particularly coveted.

The operating fireman and ladder car, a component of outfit 1623W, is sometimes found with a silver rather than black extension ladder. The silver ladder variation is more desirable than the black, but all are sought after in complete, unbroken condition.

All the rolling stock in this outfit came with AAR trucks and was packed in Perforated boxes. The outfit box itself was a yellow display-style set box.

Excellent	Like New	Scarcity
1,200	2,100	7

1625WS Five-Car Action King Steam Freight

$59.95 retail

Included: 2037 2-6-4 steam locomotive with headlight, smoke and Magne-traction; 6026W whistle tender; 6470 exploding boxcar; 3512 operating fireman and ladder car; 6650 flatcar with IRBM launcher; 6636 Alaska quad hopper; 6017 SP-type caboose; eight 1013 curved and five 1018 straight track; 6029 uncoupling section; 1053 60-watt transformer; SP smoke pellets; CTC Lockon; tube of lubricant; instruction sheet.

Indicative of the cold war tensions of the time, this outfit included the new-for-1959 6650 missile-launching flatcar. Its unpainted red 6511-type plastic body was heat-stamped "6650 LIONEL" in typical Lionel white serif letters. On

the bed of the car was mounted a pivoting unpainted blue plastic launcher base with a black plastic launch rail. The cocking of both the launch and elevating mechanisms were done manually. A rubber diaphragm dampened the spring-driven elevation of the launch rail. The car fired a 6650-8 missile, which was either white and red or red and white, all tipped with a blue rubber nose cone.

Naturally, for play value such a miniature weapon had to have a suitable target. Thus Lionel's engineers created the 6470 explosives boxcar. The ends of this ill-fated car were screwed to the sheet-metal frame of the car, while a series of tabs and slots retained the roof and sides. When struck, a mousetrap-like mechanism hurled the sides and roof from the car. A locking pin, 497-51, with its own rubber retainer, was provided to prevent accidental activation of the car—both are frequently missing today.

The remainder of the outfit has been previously described in this and preceding chapters. All the cars, as well as the tender, were equipped with AAR-type trucks and packaged in Perforated boxes. The locomotive came in a Perforated-front tan corrugated carton with orange sleeve. The outfit box itself was a yellow two-tier conventional carton.

Excellent	Like New	Scarcity
325	700	5

1626W Four-Car Santa Fe Diesel Passenger

$65 retail

Included: 208P/208T Santa Fe Alco A-A units with horn; 3428 operating U.S. Mail boxcar; two 2412 Vista Domes and 2416 observation with blue-striped Santa Fe markings; eight 1013 curved and five 1018 straight track; 6029 uncoupling section; 1053 60-watt transformer; CTC Lockon; tube of lubricant; instruction sheet.

Strangely enough, outfit freight 1619W was headed by a pair of Santa Fe diesels painted in passenger colors, while Lionel chose to head this Santa Fe passenger set with Alcos painted in the A.T. & S.F.'s blue and yellow freight scheme!

Nevertheless, this was the top-of-the-line 027 outfit for 1959, and as such is somewhat sought after today. The 2400-series plastic passenger cars were given yet another face lift and new numbers for inclusion in this set. The cars bore a broad blue stripe through their window line and featured interior illumination. Adding color to the outfit, while attempting to replicate the mail service on which real railroads so depended for passenger-service subsidizing revenue, was the new 3428 boxcar. This red, white and blue operating boxcar included a blue or gray vinyl figure, which upon activation opened the car door and seemingly hurled a vinyl mailbag of the opposite color from the train. The boxcar rode on plastic AAR-type trucks. Like the passenger cars, the boxcar came in a Perforated box.

The locomotives were packaged in a pair of corrugated tan boxes, and came with two cardboard rings for coupler protection.

Excellent	Like New	Scarcity
550	1,100	5

1959

Gift Pack

1800 The General Frontier Pack $25 retail

Included: 1862 4-4-0 General with headlight; 1862T tender; 1866 mail-baggage car; 1865 passenger car; 1877 flatcar with horses; the "General" story book.

Lionel developed the Gift Pack concept to target customers who already owned a set or entire miniature railroad. The gift pack allowed these customers to add an entire train of similar-theme items in a single purchase, rather than buying items individually. The 1959 General Frontier Pack came in a display-type box with a die-cut insert securing the trains.

Excellent	Like New	Scarcity
400	725	3

Super O

2527 Super O Missile Launching Outfit $39.95 retail

Included: 44 U.S. Army missile launcher; 3419 flatcar with operating helicopter; 6823 flatcar with IRBM missiles; 6844 flatcar with missiles; 6814 medical caboose; 943 exploding ammo dump; twelve 31 curved, one 32 straight and one 48 insulated straight track; 39-25 operating packet.

This outfit was new for 1959 and reflected Lionel's increasing interest in military-themed trains. All the cars were equipped with AAR-type plastic trucks and only the locomotive and caboose were painted.

The blue 44 locomotive had no real-life counterpart and featured a launcher that would fire four missiles in sequence. The companion 6844—usually black, although a scarce red version does exist—carried additional missiles that would fit the launcher. The locomotive came in a tan corrugated carton with orange sleeve.

A royal blue 3419 with two-inch spool and two-blade helicopter was also included in the set. The helicopter, its components, as well as the spool and tail rest, have all been reproduced, so utilize caution when purchasing this item.

So too, have been reproduced the various accessories that complete the 6814 caboose, which came with a special insert for its tool bin, as well as tiny stretchers and oxygen tanks. Its white body and tool bin were mounted on a gray sheet-metal frame. Like the rest of the rolling stock in this outfit, it was packaged in a Perforated box.

The scarce red-bodied version of the 6844 is believed to be a sometimes component of outfit 2527. Beware of reproduction components, including missiles and mounting racks, on these cars.

The 6823 flatcar with missiles is an outstanding example of Lionel's adaptive reuse of existing tooling. The missiles were created to serve as ammunition for the 6650 launcher, while their storage racks and elastic retainers had been developed to secure the more civil boats of the 6801 flatcar. Note that the missiles, racks and bands have all been reproduced.

As with so many of the 1959 outfits, two styles of set packaging were used during the run of the 2527. Most sets came in a yellow display box, but the outfit occasionally surfaces in a tan two-tier conventional set box as well.

Display box:

Excellent	Like New	Scarcity
700	1,200	4

Tan conventional box:

Excellent	Like New	Scarcity
825	1,350	5

2528WS Five-Star Frontier Special Outfit $49.95 retail

Included: 1872 4-4-0 General with headlight, smoke and Magne-traction; 1872T tender; 1877 flatcar with horses; 1876 illuminated mail-baggage car; 1875W illuminated passenger car with whistle; twelve 31 curved, one 32 straight and one 48 insulated straight track; smoke fluid; 39-25 operating packet.

The 19th-Century-styled 4-4-0 steamer was also offered in Super 0, in the form of the 1872. Like the 1862, it bore the markings of the Western and Atlantic Railroad's General, although the color scheme and level of detail differed from the 027 version.

The smokestack of the 1872, which housed an operating liquid-type smoke unit, was painted black. Behind the locomotive was the 1877 flatcar with six Bachman Bros. horses secured by a maroon fence. Also included was an 1876 passenger car and an 1875W baggage-mail car, which, due to space considerations in the small 1872T tender, housed the outfit's whistle. Like the 1876, the 1875W was illuminated. All the rolling stock rolled on arch-bar trucks and had operating couplers.

Two of the carton types for the 2528WS included individual perforated orange boxes for the rolling stock and a perforated-front tan corrugated locomotive box. While the third, the display box with die-cut filler did not include individual component boxes.

Tan conventional box:

Excellent	Like New	Scarcity
900	1,600	4

Display box with die-cut filler:

Excellent	Like New	Scarcity
750	1,350	3

Display box with individual component boxes:

Excellent	Like New	Scarcity
825	1,475	3

2529W Five-Car Virginian Rectifier Work Train $59.95 retail

Included: 2329 Virginian rectifier; 6560 crane; 3512 operating fireman and ladder car; 6819 flatcar with helicopter; 6812 track maintenance car; 6119-25 or 6119-100 work caboose; twelve 31 curved, three 32 straight and one 48 insulated straight track; 39-25 operating packet.

The colorful blue and yellow 2329 Virginian rectifier led an unusual assortment of rolling stock in this outfit. Two other operating cars; the venerable 6560 red-cabbed crane and the new-for-1959 3512 joined the new 6812 track maintenance car, with an all-yellow superstructure. Both the 3512 and the 6812 have been described in detail earlier in this chapter.

Also in the set were two non-operating cars, the 6819 flatcar with helicopter and a work caboose. The 6819 was also a new car for 1959, and it was intended to carry a non-operating version of the Lionel helicopter. However, examples have been reported by original owners loaded with an operating helicopter—likely a result of shortages of the non-operating version during assembly. Beware that both the operating and non-operating helicopter, as well as their component parts, have been reproduced.

But for the work caboose, all the rolling stock in this outfit was equipped with AAR-type plastic trucks. The crane was frequently packed in a Late Traditional box—perhaps indicative that obsolete inventory was being exhausted through this set.

This is almost certainly the case for the work caboose. Though cataloged with the 6119-100 work caboose, this set has been known to contain an all-orange 6119-25 with bar-end trucks—an item that dated from 1956. The outfit box itself was somewhat archaic—being a relabeled brown basket-weave box in the 1958 style.

Excellent	Like New	Scarcity
1,250	2,100	5

2531WS Five-Car Steam Freight $59.95 retail

Included: 637 2-6-4 steam locomotive with headlight, smoke, and Magne-traction; 2046W tender; 3435 aquarium car; 6636 Alaska hopper; 6817 flatcar with earth scraper; 6825 flatcar with trestle; 6119-100 work caboose; twelve 31 curved, three 32 straight and one 48 insulated straight track; SP smoke pellets; 39-25 operating packet.

Although the locomotive in this outfit arouses little collector interest, being merely a 2037 marked with a three-digit number to denote its promotion of the Super 0; the same cannot be said for the cars trailing it.

The aquarium car, as well as the Alaska hopper and flatcar with trestle, has been discussed earlier in this chapter—the first two being desirable collectors items. However, of the cars in this outfit, the one arousing the greatest collector interest is the 6817 flatcar with scraper.

This car had as its cargo an orange articulated Allis-Chalmers scraper retained with a 6418-9 elastic band. AAR-type plastic trucks with operating couplers were riveted directly to the body of this car. The markings on this car consisted of a white heat-stamped "6817" just to the left of white heat-stamped "LIONEL."

Two versions of the unpainted orange plastic scraper load were produced. The earliest Type I version had a windshield frame made of wire installed and had "ALLIS CHALMERS" heat-stamped in white on the scraper frame, and the raised "ALLIS CHALMERS" on the tractor hood picked out in black.

The later Type II version lacked the wire windshield frame and had no colorful markings. The grille molding was modified as well. This version is much more abundant than the early version.

The scraper was fragile and is often found broken. The usual victims are the exhaust stack, the pin that couples the tractor to the scraper (this is often repaired with an insulating track pin), or again as with the bulldozer, the hydraulic cylinders.

The most common and earliest flatcar was unpainted red plastic. It is shown here with the Type I scraper.

Shown here is the most common version of the 6817, an unpainted red flatcar with a windshield-less (Type II) scraper. It is this version that is assumed to be included in the values for this set—for other variations the outfit value should be increased accordingly.

A scarce variation was built using an unpainted black flatcar body. Though shown here with a Type I scraper, the black flatcar is so valuable—around $4,000 in top condition—that the scraper type in this instance is virtually irrelevant.

The locomotive came in a tan, Perforated-front cardboard carton with an orange sleeve. The rolling stock, with the sometimes exception of the tender and work caboose, came in Perforated boxes. The outfit box itself was the new Super 0 yellow two-tier box.

Excellent	Like New	Scarcity
1,250	2,100	6

2533W **Five-Car Great Northern Electric Freight**
$65 retail

Included: 2538 Great Northern EP-5 electric; 6414 Evans Auto Loader; 6470 exploding boxcar; 6650 flatcar with IRBM launcher; 3444 animated gondola; 6357 illuminated SP-type caboose; twelve 31 curved, three 32 straight and one 48 insulated straight track; 39-25 operating packet.

This set seems to represent the collision of two eras at Lionel. The Auto Loader, animated gondola, caboose, and even the EP-5 locomotive, which wore a new paint scheme, were all traditionalist items from Lionel's past. On the other hand, the 6650 missile-launching flatcar and 6470 exploding boxcar were indicative of the new Lionel—increasing reliance on plastics, military and space.

The correct variation of the 3444 for this outfit has two roller pickups and an embossed frame. It and the caboose were packaged in Late Traditional boxes. And like the 3444, the caboose had metal trucks. Whereas the remainder of the rolling stock was equipped with plastic AAR-type trucks and packaged in Perforated boxes.

The 2358 was the final version of the EP-5 to be produced by Lionel and is the most sought after. Though not prototypical, the locomotive is attractive.

The decals on the nose of the 2358 are fragile and have often deteriorated with age. Collectors dream of finding outstanding original examples as shown here, but are often disappointed to find either damaged or reproduction decals instead.

The decals adorning both noses of the locomotive are notable for their fragility and have often been replaced.

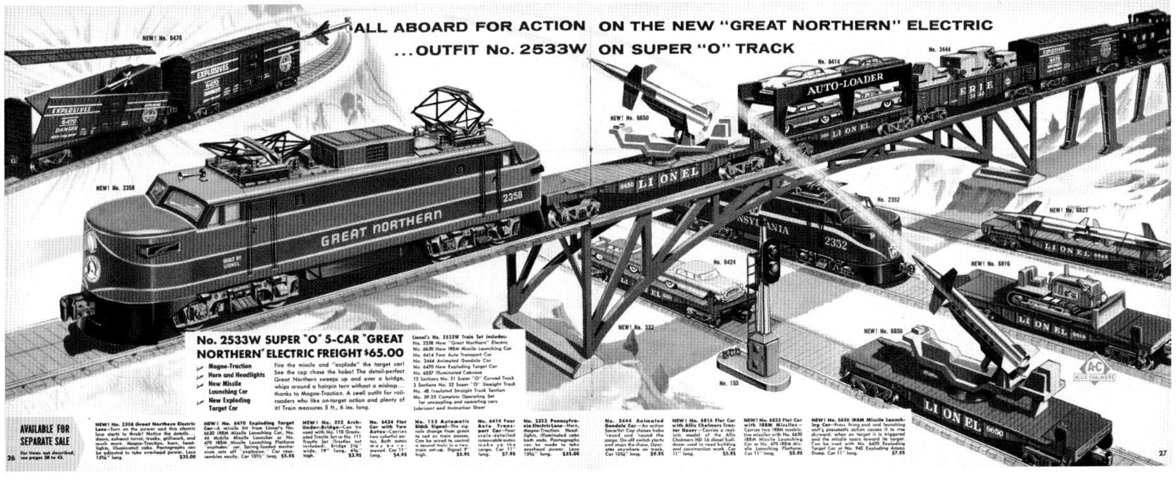

2533W

Reproductions have been produced in both the original water-slide style as well as self-adhesive. The 2358 Great Northern was packaged in a Perforated-front tan corrugated carton.

The set as a whole came in the new 1959 yellow two-tier Super 0 carton.

Excellent	Like New	Scarcity
1,800	3,100	7

2535WS Five-Car Hudson Steam Freight $69.95 retail

Included: 665 steam locomotive with headlight, smoke and Magne-traction; 2046W tender; 3434 chicken sweeper car; 6823 flatcar with IRBM missiles; 3672 operating Bosco car; 6812 track maintenance car; 6357 illuminated SP-type caboose; twelve 31 curved, three 32 straight and one 48 insulated straight track; SP smoke pellets; 39-35 operating packet.

While the locomotive and caboose at the ends of this set were old standbys, everything in between was new for 1959. This included two highly sought after operating cars.

The first of these was a revision of the venerable operating milk car. New Bosco graphics and brown and yellow colors made the car much more attractive. A new number, 3672, was assigned as well, and the car was packed in a unique box. The car rode on metal bar-end trucks.

The sides of this car were molded as one plastic part, while the roof and ends were molded separately of brown plastic that was left unpainted. The roof hatch and side doors were also molded from brown plastic, and the markings of the car were heat-stamped in brown. Of note is that the presence of this car required this outfit to include a 39-35 operating packet, rather than the more common 39-25 operating packet, which lacked the number 36 remote control set with 90 controller needed to operate the milk car.

The second new operating car was the somewhat whimsical operating chicken sweeper car. This interesting operating car featured a spring-loaded man that was also suspended from a spring. Releasing the mechanism by means of an electromagnet caused the car door to open and the figure to gyrate, as if sweeping out the inside of the car. The stock car-type body was painted brown and was imprinted with white heat-stamped lettering. Its doors were unpainted gray plastic with black heat-stamped lettering.

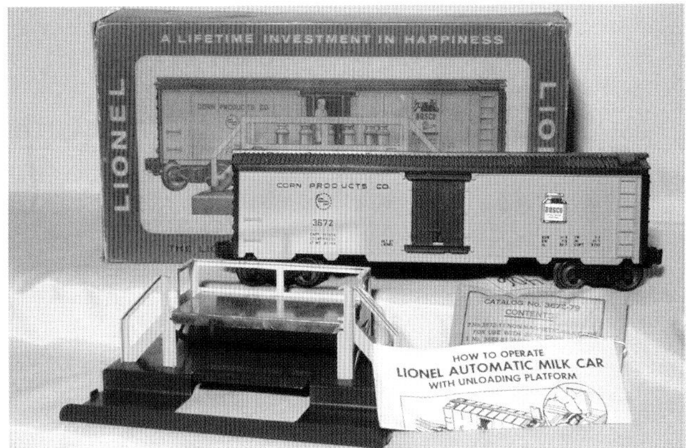

To be complete, the car must have with it its specific yellow and brown platform and seven yellow milk cans rubber-stamped "BOSCO" in red, and the listings below assume the presence of these items. The box for this car was not Perforated, which would have been futile considering the liner, but instead featured an illustration of the Bosco car.

Two bulbs illuminated the interior of the 3434 chicken sweeper car, and the light shown out through "windows"

printed with colorful chickens. The sweeper figure was made of blue rubber with painted face and hands, or gray with or without painted face and hands. The 1959 edition of this car, as well as the 1960 version, rode on bar-end metal trucks.

Less substantial, or desirable, were the other two new cars included in this set, the 6823 and 6812, both of which are discussed in the 027 portion of this chapter. As can be seen from the outfit photo, an array of packaging was used for the components of this outfit. The set box was the new yellow two-tier 1959 carton.

Excellent	Like New	Scarcity
1,000	1,700	5

2537W Five-Car New Haven Diesel Freight $75 retail

Included: 2242P/2242C New Haven A-B F-3 units; 3435 aquarium car; 6464-275 State of Maine boxcar; 6819 flatcar with helicopter; 3650 searchlight extension car; 6427 Lionel Lines porthole caboose; twelve 31 curved, three 32 straight and one insulated track; 39-25 operating packet.

Decorated in a stylized version of the New Haven's McGinnis scheme, the 2242 returned for a second year, heading a different freight lineup than the prior year. The aquarium car as well as the flatcar with non-operating helicopter was new for 1959, and are discussed, along with their packaging, earlier in this chapter. As documented, the aquarium car came in numerous variations, but the values listed below assume the most common variant is included.

The red, white and blue State of Maine boxcar, while not new, got a minor revision by being equipped with plastic AAR-type trucks. In fact, but for the searchlight car and caboose, all the rolling stock in this outfit rolled on AAR-style trucks.

The 3650 searchlight extension car, introduced in 1956, made its final appearance in this set. Since the car is packaged in a Late Traditional box, as was the caboose, it is likely that these cars were left over from previous years' production. The proper variation for this outfit includes a coupler support hole, and between "New York" and "Chicago" on both box sides were four dots (differing numbers appeared on earlier boxes).

Outfit packaging was the new yellow two-tier Super 0 box.

Excellent	Like New	Scarcity
2,500	4,200	7

2539WS Five-Car Hudson Steam Freight $79.95 retail

Included: 665 steam locomotive with headlight, smoke and Magne-traction; 2046W whistle tender; 3361 operating log car; 6464-825 Alaska boxcar; 3512 operating fireman and ladder car; 6812 track maintenance car; 6357 illuminated SP-type caboose; 464 operating sawmill; twelve 31 curved, three 32 straight and one 48 insulated straight track; SP smoke pellets; 39-35 operating packet.

Youngsters receiving this outfit in 1959 were no doubt thrilled, and enthusiasts finding this set in collectible condition today are no less excited. While the Alaska boxcar is the only single item in the outfit that is notably sought after by itself, the set as a whole was composed of a mixture of new and numerous surplus 1958 items, including a 464 sawmill! The large sawmill required that the set's yellow Super 0 outfit box be oversized.

One of Lionel's better operating vibrator-powered items, the 464 was offered for separate sale from 1956 through 1960, but was only included in one outfit; the 2539WS. The operation of this reliable accessory simulated the rough sawing of logs into lumber. It was used in conjunction with the 3361 log dump car and was also included in the outfit. This car deposited logs onto one side of the center building. From there, a hidden conveyor made from movie film pulls logs inside where they were deposited into a hidden compartment. From the other side of the building emerge planks, which amazingly were larger than the logs! Though not illuminated, the front of the building was a large window, and a red dust-collecting cyclone was mounted on the roof. Also packed in the 464 carton with a 364C controller are logs and lumber.

The 6464-825 Alaska boxcar had a painted blue body and yellow-painted stripe near the top of its sides. The blue areas of the body were marked with yellow heat-stamped markings, while lettering on the yellow stripe was done with navy blue heat-stamped lettering. Cars with white markings or stripes are fraudulent.

The body mold of the car in this outfit had three full columns of rivets to the right of the door. To the left of the door, the second rivet column was short, having only five rivets (three at the top and two at the bottom). The interior of the roof was ribbed. This version of the car was produced using bodies molded of either gray or blue plastic. Lionel always produced this car with blue-painted doors. Examples with doors of other colors are plentiful and were assembled outside of the factory, most likely by Madison Hardware.

2537W

The track maintenance and fire fighting cars, which rode on AAR-type trucks and were packed in Perforated boxes, were new for 1959 and are described earlier in this chapter.

The locomotive, tender, caboose and log car were all carry-over items and came in 1958 packaging. The log car's "336155" marking was stamped to the right of the serif-type "Lionel Lines" lettering. The presence of the log car in the outfit required a 39-35 operating packet be included in the set rather than the more common 39-25, which lacked the control rails and push button found in the former.

Excellent	Like New	Scarcity
1,500	2,600	6

2541W Five-Car Super Chief Freight $89.95 retail

Included: 2383P/2383T Santa Fe A-A F-3 units; 6519 Allis-Chalmers heat exchanger car; 6816 flatcar with bulldozer; 3356 operating horse car; 3512 operating fireman and ladder car; 6427 Lionel Lines porthole caboose; twelve 31 curved, three 32 straight and one 48 insulated straight track; 39-25 operating packet.

The famed red and silver Santa Fe F-3 A-A diesels were placed at the front of this outfit. The ever-popular dual-motor locomotives made easy work of towing the four freight cars and caboose included in the set.

During 1959 and 1960, the 2383 Santa Fe locomotives were packaged in perforated-front tan corrugated cartons. Unfortunately, the carton was not really substantial enough to protect the heavy locomotives, resulting in many of the boxes being damaged as here, if not totally destroyed.

Allis-Chalmers was well represented in this outfit, which included the 6519 heat exchanger car as well as the new-for-1959 6816 flatcar with Allis-Chalmers bulldozer. The latter is the most desirable single component of the outfit, in large part due to the fragility of the load. During the two-year production run of this car, no less than six versions of the load and two versions of the rail car were produced—although the second version of the rail car, which was black rather than red, has not been reported as a component of this set.

The earliest version (Type I) is believed to have been molded in dark orange plastic. "ALLIS-CHALMERS" was heat stamped on the back of the seat in white, while the "TORQUE CONVERTER" emblem was heat stamped in black on each side of the seat. The raised "ALLIS-CHALMERS" molded alongside the hood was picked out in black.

Lionel soon discontinued the black highlighting of the lettering on the hood, resulting in the first variation in the design. We will call this the Type II tractor.

The next variation (Type III) came about when "HD 16 DIESEL" began to be stamped in black above the torque converter emblem on the seat sides.

The Type IV was identical to the Type III, except the rear drawbar was shortened and its holes filled in.

When production of the Type V tractor began the seat back lettering was changed to black.

The final version (Type VI) was made of a considerably lighter orange plastic than the other vehicles.

The plastic bulldozer was tempting to play with, but was much too delicate for this use. It is often found today with either the simulated hydraulic blade control cylinders missing, or their rams broken. Similarly, both the exhaust stack and air intake was easily damaged. Beware that Lionel Trains Inc. has reproduced this item as part of their Postwar Celebration series.

The other new and collectable car in this set was the 3512 operating fireman car. It too was somewhat fragile and included separate parts, making it difficult to find complete today. This car is discussed in greater detail earlier in this chapter.

The version of the 3356 included in this set rode on bar-end metal trucks. Also, beginning in 1958, the brake wheel was mounted on the left end of the car when viewed from the operating door side, so naturally it is this style of car found in this outfit. The car was packaged in a Bold Traditional box. The 3356-79 envelope was revised to include a 36-7 Super 0 blade and screw.

The 6427 Lionel Lines porthole caboose came in a Late Traditional box and featured interior illumination. The outfit not surprisingly came in the new 1959-style Super 0 outfit box.

Excellent	Like New	Scarcity
2,300	3,900	6

2543WS Six-Car Berkshire Steam Freight $95 retail

Included: 736 2-8-4 Berkshire steam locomotive with headlight, smoke and Magne-traction; 2046W whistle tender; 264 operating fork lift with 6264 lumber car; 3435 aquarium car; 6823 flatcar with IRBM missiles; 6434 poultry car; 6812 track maintenance car; 6557 SP-type smoking caboose; twelve 31 curved, three 32 straight and one 48 insulated straight track; SP smoke pellets; 39-25 operating packet.

Looking back, it is hard to imagine that this spectacular set was NOT the top-of-the-line offering in 1959. The massive and venerable Berkshire provided the motive power for a mixed freight consist. The cars included three new-for-1959 items, 3435 aquarium car, 6812 track maintenance car, and the 6823 flatcar with missiles, all discussed in detail elsewhere in this chapter, and all packed in Perforated boxes. Also included were three returning older pieces of rolling stock, the 6434 poultry car, 6557 smoking caboose, and 6264 lumber car.

The 6434 was unchanged from the 1958 production. In fact, it may not have been produced in 1959 at all. Rather, these cars may have merely been left over from the previous year. However, variations in the 6434 box exist, with examples being found in both Late Traditional boxes as well as the much harder to find Bold Traditional box.

The 6557, like the 6434, rode on bar-end metal trucks, and seems to have been unchanged from the 1958 edition. The 6264 included in this outfit was an unusual version, equipped with AAR-type plastic trucks, and featuring the number stamped to the left of "LIONEL," rather than the more common metal trucks and right side numbering. This car was not packed in its own box for inclusion in this set, rather it was packed inside the box of the 264 forklift platform, which was then packed in the oversized yellow outfit box.

Excellent	Like New	Scarcity
2,000	3,500	7

The 1959 edition of this outfit is known to have come in the new yellow Super 0 set box seen here. However, examples have also been reported in the brown basket weave Super 0 outfit box, re-marked appropriately.

2541W, 2544W

Perforated-front boxes were used to package the 2383 P and T in 1959 and 1960, including those in this outfit. This style of packaging is much less common than the typical tan carton used in other years.

2544W Four-Car Super Chief Streamliner $100 retail

Included: 2383P/2383T Santa Fe A-A F-3 units; 2530 Railway Express Agency baggage car; 2561 Vista Valley observation; 2562 Regal Pass Vista Dome, and 2563 Indian Falls Pullman; twelve 31 curved, five 32 straight and one 48 insulated straight track; 39-25 operating packet.

The top-of-the-line passenger outfit for 1959 was this stylish streamliner. For the first time the extruded aluminum cars carried Santa Fe markings in order to match the red and silver F-3 units with which they had so often been paired.

As they did in freight outfit 2541W, the diesels in this set came in tan Perforated front boxes. The passenger cars were manufactured with the flat-channel extrusions introduced previously—only now the channels bore red striping with the individual car names as well as the "Santa Fe" lettering. Two sizes of Santa Fe type are known to have been used on these cars, and while both are correct, collectors prefer matched sets. Beware that reproduction striping exists. While at one time these cars were so common that they were routinely re-striped as more desirable road names, notably Canadian Pacific, today the Santa Fe's are very collectible in their own right.

Perhaps the most unusual passenger car in this set is not a passenger car at all, but rather the 2530 baggage car. The version included in this outfit is much shinier than previous editions.

Excellent	Like New	Scarcity
4,000	6,500	6

2545WS Six-Car N&W Space-Freight $100 retail

Included: 746 4-8-4 Norfolk & Western steam locomotive with headlight, smoke, and Magne-traction; 746W N & W whistle

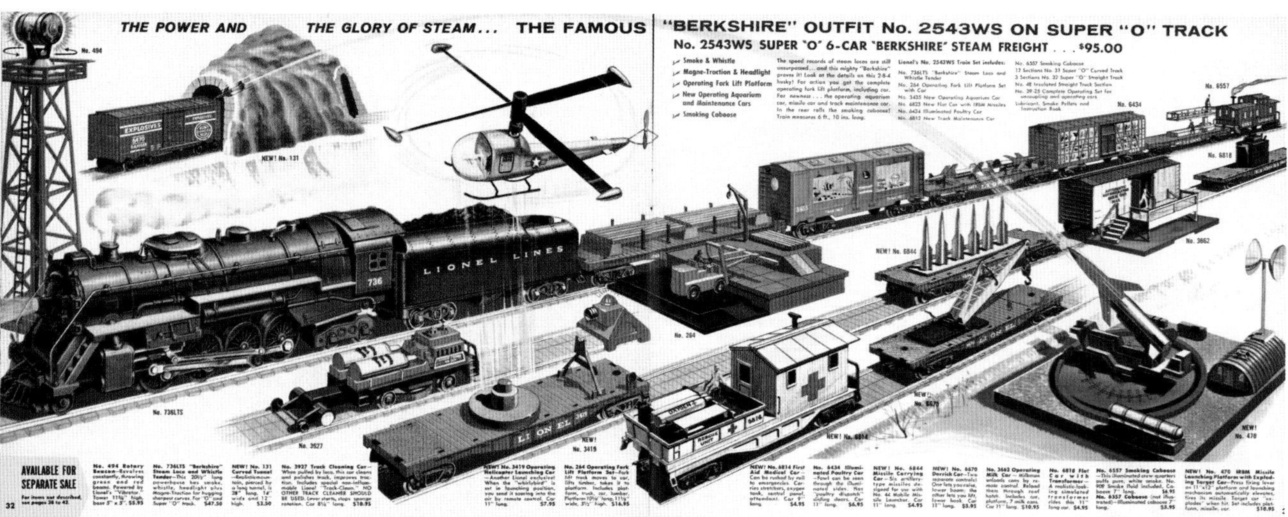

2543WS

tender; 6175 flatcar with rocket; 6470 exploding boxcar; 3419 flatcar with operating helicopter; 6650 flatcar with IRBM launcher; 3540 radar scanning car; 6517 bay window caboose; 175 operating rocket launcher; twelve 31 curved, three 32 straight and one 48 insulated straight track; smoke fluid; 39-25 operating packet.

With this set, the mighty Norfolk and Western class "J" bid adieu to Lionel cataloged sets. However, for its swan song the locomotive was often equipped with a scarce and desirable tender—the celebrated "long-stripe" version of the 746W. This final production run of the tender lacked the number stamping on its sides, but the red and yellow stripes extended all the way to the ends of the body.

Somewhat symbolizing the changing times, the big steamer pulled a train consist entirely of aviation and military-theme cars. Only the deluxe bay window caboose, itself like the locomotive a carry-over item, and the tender had metal trucks and came in Late Classic boxes. The balance of the new space-age rolling stock utilized the comparatively new and inexpensive AAR-type trucks, and was packed in Perforated boxes.

The 175 rocket launcher and its companion 6175 flatcar were carryover items. The rocket propelled by the launcher and transported by the car is often found in deteriorated condition, but reproductions are widely available. When considering purchase of this outfit, examine the launcher carefully—it is both complex and fragile, and hence is often found damaged or repaired.

The 3540 is a desirable and fragile car. The rotating antenna, as well as the two-dish fixed array are both fragile, and as of this writing only the fixed antenna and their post have been reproduced.

The perforated front box for this car came with a die-cut corrugated insert to protect the fragile radar array.

The outfit box was an oversized version of the new yellow 1959 Super 0 carton.

Excellent	Like New	Scarcity
3,000	5,000	6

Chapter 17

1960

There were few substantive changes to the product line in 1960. One improvement was made to the inexpensive 1015 and 1016 transformers. A binding post was modified to act as a reversing control. However, it was during this year that the postwar set; the most difficult to find in collectable condition, was made. The combined HO and Super 0 "Over & Under Twin Railroad Empire," also known as the Father and Son set, was produced. While only the illuminated 6357-50 Santa Fe caboose is difficult to find, the complete outfit packaging for the two sets in one is truly rare, with only a handful of surviving examples known.

Lionel used this box for most of the 027 outfits shown in the catalog. Most used dividers to hold unboxed outfit components in place, although some had a die-cut insert that displayed the rolling stock and loco. Counter to this, a few sets were shipped in tan conventional corrugated boxes.

In 1961, the "Santa Fe" freight-type tender was given a new number, 243W, indicative of the change to AAR-type trucks. An operating coupler was mounted on the rear truck.

This new box was introduced for Super 0 outfits in 1960. The train illustrations were the same as used previously, but the vivid orange box was very different from the yellow used previously.

Late in the year this tender began to be used. The new tender utilized plastic AAR-type trucks. Numbered 736W, the tender was lettered "PENNSYLVANIA" in white, but its number boards were blank. The back lights' portholes were molded shut on this tender body. It remained in the product line through 1968.

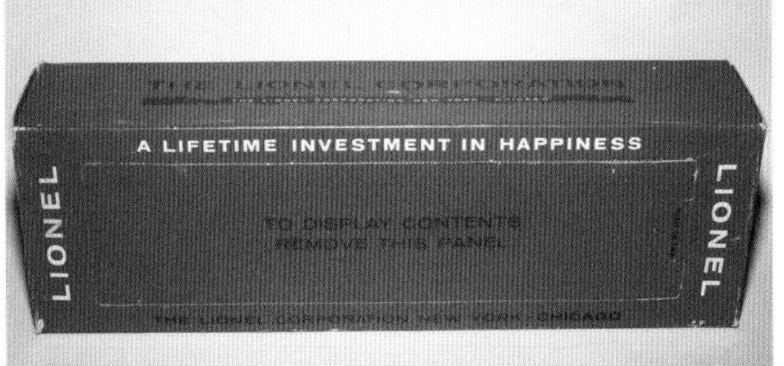

The new Perforated box with tear-out perforated front panel introduced in 1959 continued its use for rolling stock. This style packaging is referred to in this text as the "Perforated box."

027-Gauge

1107 — Advance catalog, no retail

Included: 1055 Texas Special Alco A-unit; 6044 Airex boxcar; 6042 or 6112 gondola with canisters; 6047 caboose; eight 1013 curved and two 1018 straight track; 1026 25-watt transformer; CTC Lockon; tube of lubricant; instructions.

This outfit came packed inside one of the "racing trains" set boxes typically used for such inexpensive trains. At the front of the set was a solid-red 1055 Alco A-unit wearing "The Texas Special" markings. And that name also appeared on the front of the outfit box.

Lacking a front coupler, the pilot of the Alco was molded closed. A decorative plastic fuel tank was screwed to the underside of the frame, and a headlight was installed in the nose. A ballast weight was riveted on the inside of the rear wall of the body. Two different moldings were used to make the 1055 bodies—some with and some without the reinforcing ledge at the bottom of the pilot. There is no difference in value.

All the rolling stock came equipped with arch-bar trucks, and none had operating couplers. Observant readers will note that this set is identical to 1959 outfit 1105 and in fact is sometimes a relabeled example of the previous year's set.

Excellent	Like New	Scarcity
100	250	6

1109 — Advance catalog, no retail

Included: 1060 2-4-2 steam locomotive with operating headlight; 1060T tender; 6404 flatcar with auto with gray bumpers; 3386 giraffe car; 6047 caboose; eight 1013 curved and two 1018 straight track; 1026 25-watt transformer; CTC Lockon; tube of lubricant; instructions.

Another of the very low cost outfits offered to dealers through the advance catalog, but not shown in the consumer catalog, was this steam outfit. To power this budget-minded set Lionel chose forward-only steam locomotive with operating headlight. Numbered 1060, the boiler of this steamer was based on that of the 1001 from 12 years earlier. The locomotive was paired with a small streamlined tender riding on arch-bar trucks, with a non-operating rear coupler.

The rolling stock also came with arch-bar trucks with non-operating couplers. The 3386 giraffe car was a 1960-only item and was found in many non-cataloged sets. While the car itself is common, when found in an original separate-sale box it is a rare item indeed.

The car in this set that typically is of interest to collectors is the lowly 6404 General-type flatcar with automobile. The automobile, which had gray bumpers, could either be yellow or brown—with brown being more desirable.

The outfit came in two different styles of set carton. One was a single-tier tan corrugated carton. The other was the display-type box, labeled "THE 2-4-2 STEAM FREIGHTER." Regardless of set carton type, the components were not individually boxed.

Excellent	Like New	Scarcity
150	400	6

1609 — Three-Car Steam Freight — $19.95 retail

Included: 246 2-4-2 steam locomotive with operating headlight and Magne-traction; 1130T tender; 6162-25 blue gondola with canisters; 6476 red Lehigh Valley hopper; 6057 SP-type caboose; eight 1013 curved and two 1018 straight track; 1008 camtrol; 1016 35-watt transformer; CTC Lockon; tube of lubricant; instruction sheet.

This inexpensive, very basic outfit was first offered in 1959 and then returned in 1960. The difference between the two years' production was the transformer, which had a binding post-based directional control during the second year's production.

Tan conventional box:

Excellent	Like New	Scarcity
200	450	4

Display box with dividers:

Excellent	Like New	Scarcity
125	200	2

Display box with die-cut filler:

Excellent	Like New	Scarcity
150	225	2

Display box with individual component boxes:

Excellent	Like New	Scarcity
150	250	3

1612, 1629

1612 **The General Old-Timer Outfit** **$29.95 retail**

Included: 1862 4-4-0 General with operating headlight; 1862T tender; 1866 mail-baggage car; 1865 passenger car; eight 1013 curved and two 1018 straight track; 1015 45-watt transformer; CTC Lockon; smoke fluid; tube of lubricant; instruction sheet.

The 027 General outfit was catalog for a second year, unchanged from its 1959 edition.

Display box:

Excellent	Like New	Scarcity
350	600	1

Tan conventional box:

Excellent	Like New	Scarcity
450	900	4

1627S **Three-Car Steam Freight** **$25 retail**

Included: 244 2-4-2 steam locomotive with operating headlight and smoke; 244T tender; 6825 flatcar with trestle; 6062 gondola with cable reels; 6017 caboose; eight 1013 curved and two 1018 straight track; 1008 camtrol; 1015 45-watt transformer; CTC Lockon; tube of lubricant; instructions.

None of this outfit's components are sought after or scarce. In fact, even the set when boxed in the normal yellow display box is common. Only when packaged in a single-tier tan conventional outfit box is any premium at all placed on the set. All the rolling stock, which was unboxed, rode on AAR-type trucks and had operating couplers. The tender, a slope-back model, also had an operating coupler and AAR-type trucks, and was lettered "LIONEL LINES." A plastic-bodied Scout-type 2-4-2 steamer with operating headlight and smoke towed it.

Excellent	Like New	Scarcity
90	150	1

1629 **Four-Car C&O Diesel Freight** **$29.95 retail**

Included: 225 Chesapeake & Ohio Alco A-unit; 6470 exploding boxcar; 6819 flatcar with helicopter; 6650 flatcar with IRBM launcher; 6219 C&O work caboose; eight 1013 curved and two 1018 straight track; 1008 camtrol; 1015 45-watt transformer; CTC Lockon; tube of lubricant; instructions.

This outfit featured a new-for-1960 matching diesel locomotive and work caboose combination. The 6819 and 6650, which both had AAR-type trucks with operating couplers, were returning items that have been detailed elsewhere in this volume. Beware of reproduction missiles, helicopters and helicopter components.

The components of this set were placed without individual boxes inside a yellow display-style set carton.

Excellent	Like New	Scarcity
300	500	1

1631WS **Four-Car Industrial Steam Freight** **$39.95 retail**

Included: 243 2-4-2 steam locomotive with operating headlight and smoke; 243W tender; 6519 Allis-Chalmers car; 6465 Cities Service double-dome tank car; 6812 track maintenance car; 6017 caboose; eight 1013 curved and four 1018 straight track; 1008 camtrol; 1053 60-watt transformer; CTC Lockon; tubes of lubricant and smoke; instructions.

1627S

1631WS

The green 6465 Cities Service two-dome tank car was the only new freight car included in this set. It was equipped with AAR-type trucks with operating couplers. The 6519 was unchanged from 1959—and perhaps was merely carry over inventory. While the 6812 was changed from previous editions in that its superstructure and platform were black and gray, or gray and black, respectively. Both color combinations were produced in equal numbers. In any event, the crank handle matched the platform.

The locomotive and tender however were new for 1960. The locomotive had a plastic body, with a metal motor mounted inside. It had a two-position reverse unit and a liquid-type smoke unit. Paired with the locomotive was Lionel's newest incarnation of the 6026W, now equipped with AAR-type trucks and numbered 243W. An operating coupler was at the rear of the tender.

Outfit packaging came in two versions. One was a reused surplus 1617S, with a new label applied printed with the proper 1631WS number. The other was merely a standard yellow display-style outfit carton. In both cases the outfit components were unboxed.

Excellent	Like New	Scarcity
300	500	2

1633

1633 Land-Sea-Air Two-Unit Diesel Freight

$39.95 retail

Included: 224P/224C U.S. Navy Alco A-B units; 6820 flatcar with helicopter and missiles; 6830 flatcar with submarine; 6544 missile firing car; 6017-200 U.S. Navy caboose; eight 1013 curved and three 1018 straight track; 6029 uncoupling section; 1015 45-watt transformer; CTC Lockon; tube of lubricant; instructions.

This highly sought after outfit was one of the relatively few sets from the postwar era that featured all-new components. The all-blue train was decorated with U.S. Navy markings.

The body mold created for the 6519 heat exchanger car was reused to create the 6544 missile-firing car. The car was molded in blue, with white heat-stamped lettering, like the 6519, the 6544 had metal brake stands mounted on fragile plastic tabs at each end of the car. These are often found broken today. The Lionel Service Manual mentioned this problem and states that some cars were produced without brake wheels to prevent this breakage. AAR-type plastic trucks with operating couplers were riveted directly to the body of these cars. In the center of the car was installed an unpainted gray plastic rocket-launching station. The car came with two small envelopes, each containing four 44-40 rockets. Four could be loaded on the launch rails, and the remaining four stored on a rack separating the launch rails from the simulated control panel. The control panel of the version of this car packed in this outfit has white heat-stamped markings.

The 6830 was a medium blue molded flatcar with heat-stamped lettering. Probably as an economy move, this flatcar carried a non-operating version of the familiar Lionel submarine. It was identical to the 3830 operating submarine, except for its black heat-stamped number and, of course, the omission of various internal parts. The car body was heat stamped "LIONEL" and

"6830" in white. As with the other submarine cars, two special wire clips held the submarine to the car.

Lionel's helicopter was equipped with two huge, non-firing missiles—similar to those used by the 6544—for use with the 6820 flatcar. The car body was painted semi-gloss medium blue with heat-stamped lettering including "6820" to the left of "LIONEL," in white serif letters. AAR-type trucks with operating couplers were used on this car.

Beware that the helicopters, its components, the submarine, control panel and missiles have all been reproduced.

The 224 A-B Alco F-A locomotive pair leading the set matched the 6017-200 SP-style caboose at the rear. In most instances, this outfit came in an orange-and-white display box, with its components unboxed. However, some sets were packed in a tan two-tier conventional carton.

Excellent	Like New	Scarcity
900	1,600	4

1635WS Five-Car Heavy-Duty Special Steam Freight

$49.95 retail

Included: 2037 2-6-4 steam locomotive with operating headlight, smoke and Magne-traction; 243W tender; 6821 flatcar with crates; 6826 flatcar with Christmas trees; 6636 Alaska hopper; 6361 timber transport; 6017 caboose; eight 1013 curved and three 1018 straight track; 6029 uncoupling section; SP smoke pellets; 1053 60-watt transformer; CTC Lockon; tube of lubricant; instructions.

The 2037, first produced in 1953, was placed at the lead of this set. Behind it, the newly introduced 243W tender, riding on AAR-type trucks, an operating coupler at the rear. Following the motive power were four freight cars and a caboose. The 6636 Alaska hopper, as well as the 6826 flatcar with Christmas trees, was a carry-forward item from the previous year, yet are still sought-after pieces. Caution should be used however, as reproduction Christmas tree loads are commonplace.

The 6361 timber transport car was based on the body created originally for the 3361 operating lumber car. This handsome car was to be cataloged throughout most of the rest of the postwar era. Its unpainted dark green body was attached to a blued-steel under frame, which also had a pair of AAR-type trucks with operating couplers installed on it. Its cargo, secured with two lengths of chain (a spring held tension on the chains) consisted of three actual tree limbs, including bark. During this, its first year of production, the metal under frame of the car was solid, and the lettering was rubber-stamped in dull white. The chains securing the load were black-oxide coated. In subsequent years the under frame stamping was modified to accommodate the operating mechanism required by the 3362.

The set was packed inside a orange display-style carton, with each component having its own component box. Some sets were packages in a tan two-tier boxes as well.The locomotive came in a tan corrugated carton, while Orange Perforated boxes were used for the remainder of the items.

Excellent	Like New	Scarcity
450	850	5

1637W Five-Car Twin Unit Diesel Freight

$49.95 retail

Included: 218P/218T Santa Fe Alco A-A units with horn; 6464-475 Boston and Maine boxcar; 6175 flatcar with rocket; 6801 flatcar with boat or 6424-110 flatcar with autos; 6475 pickle vat car; 6017-185 Santa Fe caboose; eight 1013 curved and three 1018 straight track; 6029 uncoupling section; 1053 60-watt transformer; CTC Lockon; tube of lubricant; instructions.

The only new item in this outfit was the 6475 vat car. The version of this car that is found in this outfit had an unpainted tan body, while the roof could be painted one of a number of various shades of brown. The meager lettering on the body was heat stamped in green and a separate metal brake wheel was fitted. Its four vats were unpainted yellow plastic with "Pickles" heat stamped in red on them. The vats were further decorated with black rubber stampings to represent staves and hoops. The car rode on AAR-type trucks with operating couplers.

The remainder of the components of this outfit was as described earlier in this volume. The rolling stock used AAR-type trucks with operating couplers. Though cataloged with the 6801 flatcar with boat—which should be in an Orange Perforated box—a common factory substitution replaced this car with a 6424-110 flatcar with automobiles.

Outfit components in their individual boxes were packed inside the new orange-and-white display-style set carton for distribution.

Excellent	Like New	Scarcity
500	950	5

1639WS Six-Car Power House Special Steam Freight
$59.95 retail

Included: 2037 2-6-4 steam locomotive with operating headlight, smoke and Magne-traction; 243W tender; 6560-25 crane; 6530 firefighting instruction car; 6816 flatcar with bulldozer; 6817 flatcar with earth scraper; 6812 track maintenance car; 6119-100 work caboose; eight 1013 curved and three 1018 straight track; 6029 uncoupling section; 1053 60-watt transformer; SP smoke pellets; CTC Lockon; tube of lubricant; instructions.

Though the 2037 at the front of this set was lackluster, two of the cars included, even though repeat items, are extremely desirable. The 6816 and 6817 flatcars with bulldozers and earth scrapers are extremely desirable, and sadly the cargoes very fragile. These cars are discussed in detail in the 1959 chapter of this book.

New for 1960, and included in this outfit, was the 6530 firefighting instruction car.

This car was based on the tooling created to produce the 3530 Electromobile Power Car. It had an unpainted red plastic body and unpainted white plastic opening doors. The white markings were applied by heat stamp. Like the rest of the rolling stock in this set, it had AAR-type trucks with operating couplers and a blackened metal brake wheel.

The individually boxed components of this set—locomotive in tan perforated-front corrugated carton and tender and rolling stock in Orange Perforated boxes—were packed in an orange-and-white display-type set box.

Excellent	Like New	Scarcity
1,750	2,800	7

1640W Five-Car Presidential Campaign Special
$65 retail

Included: 218P/218T Santa Fe Alco A-A units with horn; 3428 operating U.S. Mail boxcar; two 2412 Vista Domes and 2416 observation; 1640-100 Presidential whistle-stop kit; eight

1013 curved and three 1018 straight track; 6029 uncoupling section; 1053 60-watt transformer; CTC Lockon; tube of lubricant; instructions.

While most Santa Fe Alco-led passenger sets meet with little enthusiasms from collectors, this outfit is an exception to the rule. The key to this set is contained in a small orange box—the 1640-100 Presidential Special accessory set.

This unassuming little box contained the decals and figures that differentiate outfit 1640W from other 027 Santa Fe passenger sets, and is key to its value.

The powered unit was packaged in a perforated front tan corrugated carton. The matching dummy unit, as well as the mail and passenger cars utilized Orange Perforated boxes. The outfit box was an orange-and-white display-type set box.

Excellent	Like New	Scarcity
650	1,000	4

Gift Pack

1800 The General Frontier Pack $25 retail

Included: 1862 4-4-0 General with operating headlight; 1862T tender; 1866 mail-baggage car; 1865 passenger car; 1877 flatcar with horses; the General story book.

The 1800 Gift Pack, first cataloged in 1959, returned again. While some of those shipped during 1960 were merely unsold 1959 inventory, as evidenced by their yellow display-style packaging, others were freshly packaged in 1960, as disclosed by their appearance in orange and white display boxes.

Excellent	Like New	Scarcity
400	675	3

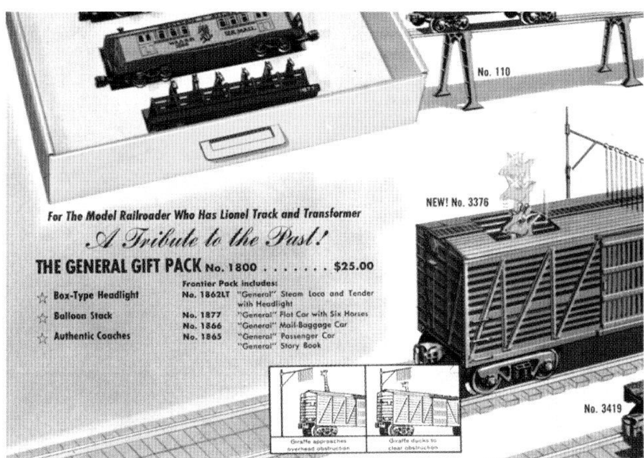

1800

1805 Land-Sea and Air Gift Pack $35 retail

Included: 45 U.S. Marine Corps missile launcher; 3429 U.S. Marine Corps flatcar with operating helicopter; 6640 U.S. Marine Corps flatcar with IRBM launcher; 3820 U.S. Marine Corps flatcar with operating submarine; and 6824 medical caboose.

Highly sought by collectors is the all-olive drab outfit led by the U.S.M.C. missile launcher. While this locomotive/missile launcher does not arouse much collector interest, all the trailing cars are heavily sought after.

The 3429 was created specially for inclusion in this Gift Pack. Fittingly, the car was painted olive drab and heat stamped "BUILT BY/LIONEL U. S. M. C. 3429" in white on both sides of the body. The car was equipped with AAR-type trucks with operating couplers. The car is difficult to locate, but is of nominal value unless it has the correct, unique load—an original single-rotor operating helicopter with a gray body with "USMC" heat stamped on the tail boom. A separate pale yellow tail rotor was installed on the tail.

Missile launching car 6640 also had a plastic body that was painted olive drab and was heat stamped "U.S.M.C. 6640" in white. On the bed of the car was mounted a pivoting unpainted olive drab plastic launcher base with a black plastic launch rail. The cocking of both the launch and elevating mechanisms were done manually. A rubber diaphragm dampened the spring-driven elevation of the launch rail. The car fired a 6650-8, which was either white over red or, more commonly, red over white, all tipped with a blue rubber nose cone. This car also was equipped with AAR-type trucks with operating couplers.

The scarce 3820 flatcar with submarine was produced from 1960 through 1962 expressly for inclusion in the Land-Sea and Air Gift Pack, but later appeared as well in sets 1810 and 13028. The body of this car was painted olive drab and featured white heat-stamped sans-serif lettering. The car was equipped with AAR-type trucks with operating couplers. Its cargo was the conventional factory-assembled gray "U.S. NAVY 3830" submarine.

The 6824 U.S.M.C work-type caboose was created to complete this train and in fact came only in this gift pack. The cab, tool compartment, tool compartment insert and frame were all painted olive drab. The markings were all done in white: "U.S.M.C." rubber stamped on the sheet-metal frame and "RESCUE UNIT," "6824" and two crosses heat stamped on the plastic components. The First-Aid Medical Car had a short black die-cast smokejack, a blue rubber figure with painted hands and face, a white plastic air tank, and two white plastic stretchers with Red Cross markings. It was equipped with AAR trucks and the front truck had an operating coupler.

Because of the many fragile cargoes of these cars, numerous reproduction items have been offered. Among these are control panels, crewmen and missiles for the 45, reproduction helicopters and helicopter components for the 3429, and the numerous small details of the 6824. Be aware that in addition to reproduction 3830 submarines, forgeries stamped "U.S.M.C. 3820" also exist.

Outfit packaging for this gift pack consisted of an orange-and-white display box with die-cut insert holding the unboxed components in place. The box was printed with "LAND-SEA and AIR GIFT PACK" on the lid.

Excellent	Like New	Scarcity
1,750	3,000	5

Super 0

2527 Super 0 Missile Launcher Outfit $39.95 retail

Included: 44 U.S. Army missile launcher; 3419 flatcar with operating helicopter; 6823 flatcar with IRBM missiles; 6844 flatcar with missiles; 6814 medical caboose; 943 exploding ammo dump; twelve 31 curved, one 32 straight and one 48 insulated straight track; 39-25 operating packet.

This was a repeat of the same outfit cataloged in 1959. Most came in the same yellow outfit box used the year before, while a few came in the new-style orange and white display box. Comprehensive information about this set can be found in the 1959 chapter.

Yellow display box:

Excellent	Like New	Scarcity
700	1,200	4

Orange and white display box:

Excellent	Like New	Scarcity
750	1,300	4

Tan conventional box:

Excellent	Like New	Scarcity
825	1,350	5

2528WS Five-Star Frontier Special Outfit $49.95 retail

Included: 1872 4-4-0 General with operating headlight, smoke and Magne-traction; 1872T tender; 1877 flatcar with horses; 1876 illuminated mail-baggage car; 1875W illuminated passenger car with whistle; twelve 31 curved, one 32 straight and one 48 insulated straight track; smoke fluid; 39-25 operating packet.

Another outfit repeated from 1959 was the Five-Star General. Although the lanterns on locomotives in known 1960-sold outfits are black rather than red of 1959, no 1960-style orange and white display boxes have yet surfaced. This possibly indicates that sales in 1959 did not meet expectations—expectations for which many boxes had ordered.

Tan conventional box:

Excellent	Like New	Scarcity
900	1,600	4

Display box with die-cut filler:

Excellent	Like New	Scarcity
750	1,350	3

Display box with individual component boxes:

Excellent	Like New	Scarcity
825	1,475	3

2544W Four-Car Super Chief Streamliner $100 retail

Included: 2383P/2383T Santa Fe A-A F-3 units; 2530 Railway Express Agency baggage car; 2561 Vista Valley observation; 2562 Regal Pass Vista Dome, and 2563 Indian Falls Pullman; twelve 31 curved, five 32 straight and one 48 insulated straight track; 39-25 operating packet.

Although this outfit is identical to one of the same number offered in 1959, its packaging was the new 1960-style Super 0 set box. For a detailed description of the trains in this outfit, refer to the 1959 chapter.

Excellent	Like New	Scarcity
4,000	6,500	6

2547WS Four-Car Variety Special Steam Freight $49.95 retail

Included: 637 2-6-4 steam locomotive with operating headlight, smoke and Magne-traction; 2046W tender; 3330 flatcar with submarine kit; 6475 pickle vat car; 6361 timber transport; 6357 illuminated caboose; twelve 31 curved, one 32 straight and one 48 insulated straight track; 39-25 operating packet; SP smoke pellets; tube of lubricant; instructions.

This outfit was probably packaged early in the year, as evidenced by the tender. The 637 steam locomotive was paired with a bar-end metal truck-equipped 2046W tender. All the rest of the rolling stock in the set, which were all new cars for 1960, rode on AAR-type trucks and had two operating couplers each.

The body of the submarine car was unpainted medium blue plastic with white "3330" heat stamped to the left of "LIONEL" in serif lettering. The car was equipped with AAR-type trucks with operating couplers. The cargo provided with the car was an unassembled, gray plastic rubber band—powered submarine. Except for the two halves of the hull, all the kit parts, including a small container of glue, were packaged in a clear plastic bag. That plastic bag was placed inside the hull halves and along with the 3330-107 instruction sheet, was then placed inside the standard (for the time) Orange Perforated box. The correct submarine for this car is lettered "U.S. NAVY 3830" in black heat-stamped sans-serif lettering, today collectors dream of finding this car with its submarine unassembled, still in its bag. Note, submarines lettered 3330 are forgeries.

The remainder of the rolling stock has been discussed earlier in this volume, and came in Orange Perforated boxes. The locomotive came in a tan corrugated box with perforated front. Two styles of set packaging were used for this outfit. Most came in an orange-and-white display-type box, but a few came in conventional tan two-tier set boxes.

Excellent	Like New	Scarcity
600	1,000	5

2549W

2549W A Mighty Military Diesel Outfit $59.95 retail

Included: 2349 Northern Pacific GP-9; 6470 exploding boxcar; 6819 flatcar with helicopter; 6650 flatcar with IRBM launcher; 3540 radar scanning car; 3535 security car; eighteen 31 curved, two 32 straight, five 34 half-straight and one 48 insulated straight track; 90-degree crossing; 39-25 operating packet; tube of lubricant; instructions.

The only new item in this outfit was the 3535 operating security car with rotating searchlight. A prime example of Lionel's adapting of existing tools and parts, this car was both unusual and interesting. On the roof of the offset unpainted red superstructure, which itself was derived from the 520 electric body, was a twin 40mm Bofors anti-aircraft cannon borrowed from the Pyro military loads found on the 6804 and 6809. Mounted on the other end of the unpainted black plastic flatcar base was a small blued-steel deck with a vibrator-operated rotating searchlight installed. There was no lettering on the base, but the superstructure was heat stamped "AEC" "SECURITY CAR" and "3535" in white.

This car, like the rest of the rolling stock in this outfit, came with AAR-type trucks with operating couplers, and again like the rest of the cars in the set, was packed in an Orange Perforated box.

The locomotive, though a repeat from 1959, was nonetheless one of the most attractive GP-diesels produced in the postwar era—its gold markings having a metallic sheen. The locomotive came in an orange-sleeved tan corrugated carton with Perforated front. The outfit box was the orange two-tier Super 0 box introduced this year.

Excellent	Like New	Scarcity
1,200	2,000	3

2551W Six-Car Great Northern Diesel Freight $75 retail

Included: 2358 Great Northern EP-5 electric; 3512 fireman and ladder car; 6827 flatcar with Harnischfeger power shovel; 6828 flatcar with Harnischfeger crane; 6736 Detroit & Mackinac hopper; 6812 track maintenance car; 6427 Lionel Lines porthole caboose; twenty four 31 curved, thirteen 32 straight, and one 48 insulated straight track; 110 graduated trestle set; 39-25 operating packet; tube of lubricant; instructions.

What enthusiast would not want this impressive, collectible-laden outfit to grace their collection? The locomotive was the colorful 2358 Great Northern EP-5. Introduced the previous year, this was the last reuse of the EP-5 tooling in the postwar era. While not prototypical, this was nevertheless a handsome locomotive with its orange and green "Empire Builder"-inspired paint scheme set off with three small yellow stripes. "Great Northern" was heat stamped on the sides in yellow, but the end markings, number and "BLT BY LIONEL" were done with a single large decal on each end. This decal is somewhat fragile, and is prone to flake with age. Many of these locomotives are found today with these decals damaged or replaced by excellent reproductions. The locomotive came packed in a Perforated-front tan corrugated carton.

The 6827 and 6828 both were black flatcars, whose cargo of construction equipment came as unassembled kits, packed in their own black, yellow and white boxes. These boxes were then placed atop the flatcars, and in turn slid into their Orange Perforated boxes. The loads were attractive, but fragile, and are today often missing parts. Lionel continued to produce versions of these cargoes into the MPC-era. Hence collectors should be wary of modern-era parts on postwar cars.

The 6427 porthole caboose was leftover circa 1958 inventory and was the only component of the set to come with bar-end metal trucks. It was also the only car in the set to come in a Late Traditional box rather than an Orange Perforated box. The fireman and ladder car was a repeat from 1959, and is described in detail in that chapter. In contrast to the caboose and fireman cars, the Detroit & Mackinac hopper was new for 1960.

The outfit, which included a 110 trestle set, came packaged in the new for 1960-style Super 0 set carton.

Excellent	Like New	Scarcity
2,100	3,500	6

2553WS The Majestic Berkshire Five-Car Freight $100 retail

Included: 736 2-8-4 Berkshire steam locomotive with operating headlight, smoke and Magne-traction; 2046W tender; 3435 traveling aquarium car; 3672 operating Bosco car; 3830 flatcar with operating submarine; 3419 flatcar with operating helicopter; 6357 caboose; eighteen 31 curved, seven 32 straight, two 33 half-curved, six 34 half-straight and one 48 insulated straight track; 120 90-degree crossing; 142LH left-hand manual turnout; SP smoke pellets; 260 bumper; 39-35 operating packet; tube of lubricant; instructions.

Action-packed is one way to describe this outfit. Every car in the set, except for the caboose, which was illuminated, was an operating car. Two, the 3435 traveling aquarium and 3672 operating Bosco car, were high-quality traditional-type items. The other two, the 3830 and 3419, were more modern, more military, and more plastic. The set even included a turnout and bumper, allowing a siding to be added to the figure-eight track layout.

All Bosco cars are desirable, but some of these outfits include the painted yellow version of the car, which is particularly sought after. Also highly collectable is the 3435 aquarium car, the version of which that was included in this outfit had yellow rubber-stamped markings.

The 3830 had an unpainted blue plastic body was heat stamped "3830 LIONEL" in white on both sides. The car was equipped with AAR-type trucks with operating couplers. The cargo provided with the car was a fully assembled, gray plastic rubber band-powered submarine. The correct submarine for this car is lettered "U.S. NAVY 3830" in black heat-stamped sans-serif lettering.

The 3419 appeared for the second year, but differed substantially from its predecessor. The winding spool, formerly two-inches in diameter, was now only 1-3/8-inches in diameter.

Outfit packaging is an unusual assortment. The locomotive came in a Perforated-front tan corrugated carton. The Bosco car came in a special box, with a detailed image of its contents on the front. The aquarium, submarine, helicopter cars all came in Orange Perforated boxes. An orange 1960-style Super 0 box housed it all.

Excellent	Like New	Scarcity
1,500	2,500	5

2553WS

Super 0 and HO-Gauge

2555W 📷 **Over & Under Twin Railroad Empire**

$150 retail

Super 0 components Included: 2383P/2383T Santa Fe F-3 A-A units; 6414 Evans Auto Loader; 6464-900 New York Central boxcar; 3434 operating chicken sweeper car; 3366 operating circus car; 6357-50 illuminated Santa Fe caboose; twelve 31 curved, three 32 straight and one 48 insulated straight track; 111-50 set of twenty 110A elevated trestle piers; 39-25 operating packet; tube of lubricant; instructions; 1044 90-watt transformer.

The HO components Included: 0565/0595 Santa Fe F3 A-A units; 0814 Evans Auto Loader; 0864-900 New York Central boxcar; 0834 illuminated poultry car; 0866-200 circus car; 0817-150 illuminated Santa Fe caboose; twelve 0989 curved, two 0909 straight and one 0925 straight terminal track; two 0905 1-1/2-inch straight track; one 0919 uncoupler/rerailer track; 0101 power pack; 0114 engine house with horn; instructions.

Thee most valuable of all postwar outfits is this twin HO and Super 0 set, which was featured on the cover of the 1960 consumer and accessory catalogs. All the components, except for the special 110A elevated trestle set and the 6357-50 Santa Fe illuminated caboose, are easily found individually. The true keys to the astronomical value of this set are two set boxes that contained it.

The HO components, each in individual boxes, were all packed in a two-tier tan conventional box stamped 5555W. This box was then placed, along with the component-boxed Super 0 items, inside a large tan two-tier corrugated carton stamped 2555W.

When set up, the HO outfit ran directly beneath the Super 0 set, its track laid between the uprights of the special 110A piers, which lack the cross braces of normal 110 piers, and stand on small matching gray elevating blocks.

The two boxes, and to a lesser extent, the special pier set described are so pivotal to the value of the set, the trains themselves and their packaging are almost irrelevant. The Super F-units came in tan Perforated-front corrugated cartons, the 3366 in its own unique picture-type box, and the rest of the Super 0 components in Orange Perforated boxes.

The HO components of this set, which is known alternately as the "Father and Son" or "Over and Under" set, came in typical HO window boxes.

Excellent	Like New	Scarcity
8,500	40,000	8

A TRULY GREAT MODEL RAILROADING ACHIEVEMENT

IDENTICAL SUPER "O" and HO TWIN RAILROAD EMPIRE No. 2555W. $150.00

☆ Matching Locos and Cars ☆ Two level layout ☆ Complete with Transformer and Power Pack

SUPER "O" TRAIN OUTFIT:

No. 2383 Santa Fe GM F3 Type Twin "A" Unit Diesel with Two Motors, Horn, Magne-Traction, Headlight
No. 3434 Operating Chicken Car with Sweeper
No. 3366 Operating Circus Car
No. 6414 Four Auto Transport Car
No. 6464-900 New "New York Central" Box Car
No. 6357-50 Illuminated Santa Fe Caboose
12 Sections **No. 31** Super "O" Curved Track
3 Sections **No. 32** Super "O" Straight Track
No. 48 Insulated Straight Track Section
20 Pieces **No. 110A** Elevated Trestle Piers
No. 39-25 Complete Operating Set for uncoupling and operating cars
No. 1044 90-Watt Transformer
Lubricant and Instruction Book

HO TRAIN OUTFIT:

No. 0565 Santa Fe Powered "A" Unit w/Headlight
No. 0595 Santa Fe Dummy "A" Unit
No. 0834 Illuminated Poultry Car
No. 0866-200 Circus Car
No. 0814 Four Auto Transport Car
No. 0864-900 New "New York Central" Box Car
No. 0817-150 Santa Fe Caboose
12 Sections **No. 0989** 18" Rad. Curved Track 9" Long
2 Sections **No. 0909** Straight Track 9" Long
1 Section **No. 0925** Straight Term. Track 9" Long
2 Sections **No. 0905** Straight Track 1½" Long
1 Section **No. 0919** Uncoupler Re-Railer 9" Long
No. 0101 1¼ Amp. Power Pack
No. 0114 Engine House with Horn
Wires and Instruction Sheet

31

2555W

CHAPTER 18

1961

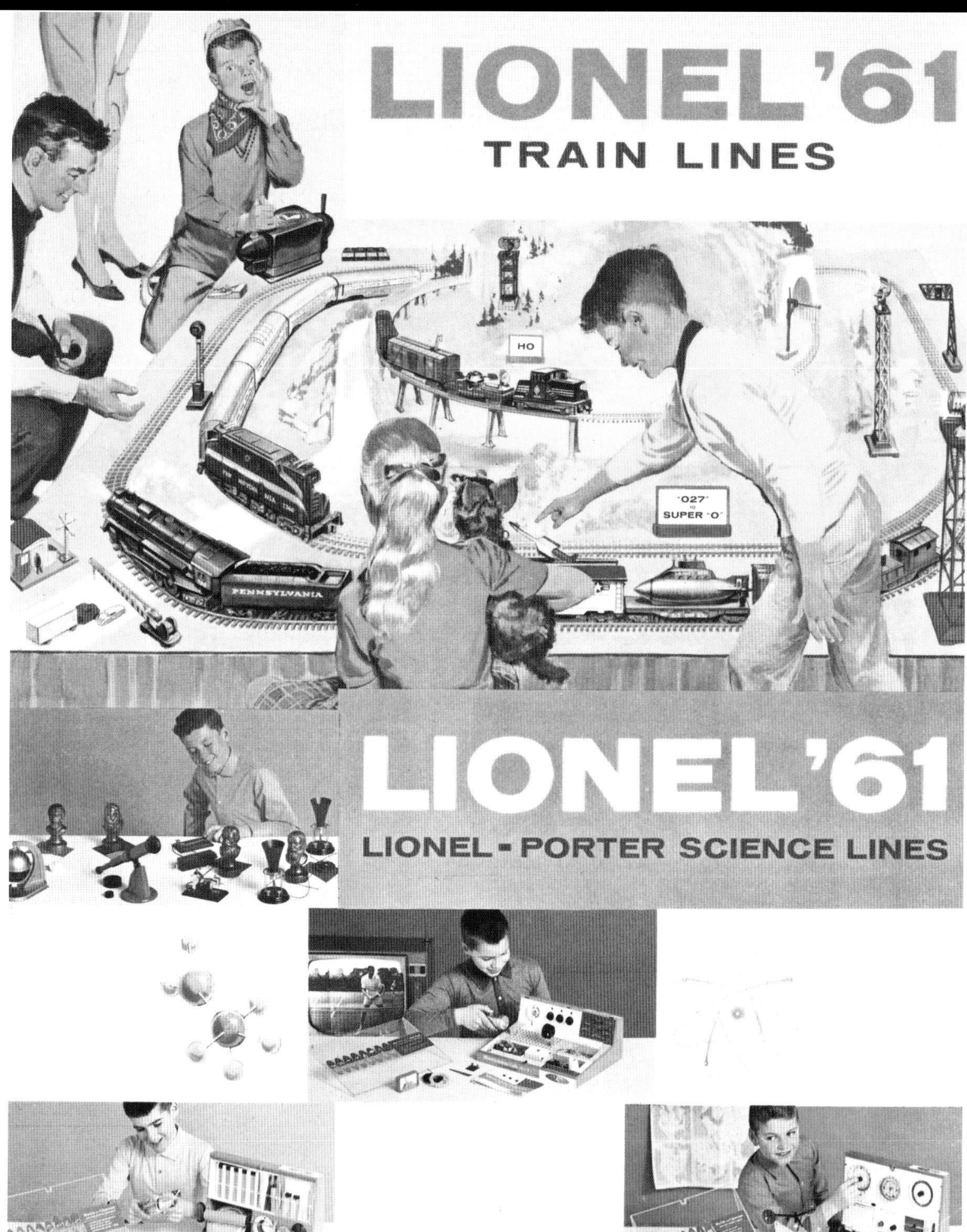

Lionel continued its campaign to lower manufacturing costs during the year. Metal trucks were eliminated from virtually all the rolling stock, including tenders and cabooses. Even the plastic AAR-type trucks were subject to cost reduction because by the end of the year the metal knuckle previously used was replaced with a plastic knuckle, but still installed with a shiny rivet. When viewed from the bottom, the ends of the axles of these trucks could not be seen.

Both of Lionel's better tenders, the streamlined Pennsylvania-style and the rectangular "freight" tender, were given new numbers this year, reflecting the shift from metal to plastic trucks. The streamlined tender was now known as the 736W, while the freight tender became 233W with operating coupler and 234W without.

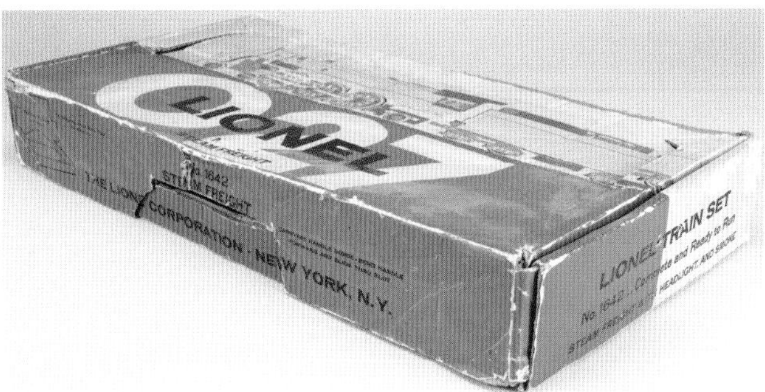

Lionel used this box, first introduced in 1960, for most of the 027 outfits shown in the 1961 catalog. Most used dividers to hold unboxed outfit components in place, although some had a die-cut insert that displayed the rolling stock and loco. This type of box included a pasteboard suite case-style handle that often rips. Counter to this, a few sets were shipped in tan conventional corrugated boxes.

This style box, referred to as the Orange Picture box, was made of glossy orange cardstock and had a white panel with an illustration of a steam and diesel locomotive on the front. The city names "NEW YORK" and "CHICAGO" appeared on the box, as did the corporate name "THE LIONEL CORPORATION." This is the box that was in use from 1961 through 1964.

The most inexpensive outfits of 1961, whether listed in the consumer catalog or only in the advance catalog, came in this box with locomotives racing across its top.

This shiny overall orange outfit box was used for Super O sets as well as the better 027 outfits.

The final version of the streamlined tender under the aegis of the Lionel Corp. utilized plastic AAR-type trucks. Numbered 736W, the tender was lettered "PENNSYLVANIA" in white, but its number boards were blank. The back lights' portholes were molded shut on this tender body. It remained in the product line through 1968.

027-Gauge

1123 Advance catalog No retail

Included: 1060 2-4-2 steam locomotive with operating headlight; 1050T tender; 6406 flatcar with auto; 6042 gondola with canisters; 6067 caboose; eight 1013 curved and two 1018 straight track; 1026 25-watt transformer; CTC Lockon; tube of lubricant; instructions.

This was the first of three inexpensive outfits shown in the advance catalog, but not in the consumer catalog. Most of these outfits came in a display-type box with racing Santa Fe F-3 diesels and baby Hudson steam locomotives printed on the hinged lid. A cardboard insert protected the unboxed components of the set. Some outfits came in tan two-tier conventional outfit boxes, again with unboxed components.

The inexpensive steam locomotive at the lead was paired with the 1050T slope-back tender, which rode on arch-bar trucks, and like the rest of the cars in this outfit, had a fixed coupler. The payload for the locomotive-tender combination consisted of an undecorated maroon General-style flatcar carrying a yellow automobile with gray bumpers, a blue "LIONEL" gondola with red canisters and an undecorated caboose. The red body of the caboose was attached to its end-rail equipped black frame with tabs. None of the cars had operating couplers.

Excellent	Like New	Scarcity
125	300	5

1124 The Hawk advance catalog, no retail

Included: 1060 2-4-2 steam locomotive with operating headlight; 1060T small streamlined tender; 3409 flatcar with helicopter; 6076 Lehigh Valley hopper; 6067 caboose; eight 1013 curved and two 1018 straight track; 1026 25-watt transformer; CTC Lockon; tube of lubricant; instructions.

The outfit box and locomotive were the same as those described in outfit 1123 above; however, the steamer was now paired with a small streamlined 1060T tender with arch-bar trucks.

The unmarked red caboose was also identical to the one found in set 1123, while the 3409 was unique to this outfit only and is hence very difficult to locate. The Lehigh Valley hopper was run of the mill and, like all the other cars in this set, came with fixed coupler, arch-bar trucks.

Excellent	Like New	Scarcity
175	500	5

1125 Advance catalog No retail

Included: 1065 Union Pacific Alco A-unit; 6630 flatcar with IRBM launcher; 6480 exploding boxcar; 6120 work caboose; eight 1013 curved and two 1018 straight track; 1026 25-watt transformer; CTC Lockon; tube of lubricant; instructions.

Yet again Lionel utilized the box described under the outfit 1123 heading to package an advance catalog set—in this case numbered 1125. While the Alco is a no-frills inexpensive unit of little interest to collectors, the missile launcher and undecorated yellow work caboose are somewhat desirable. Arch-bar trucks with non-operating couplers were used throughout this set.

Excellent	Like New	Scarcity
200	450	5

1641 📷 Three-car Headliner Steam Freighter $25 retail

Included: 246 2-4-2 steam locomotive with operating headlight and Magne-traction; 244T tender; 3362 helium tank unloading car; 6162 gondola with canisters; 6057 caboose; eight 1013 curved and two 1018 straight track; 1008 camtrol; 1010 35-watt transformer; CTC Lockon; tube of lubricant; instructions.

This outfit was packed in the 1960-style orange-and-white display box that was shown at the introduction to this chapter. The steam loco at the front of the set was equipped with Magne-traction and was paired with a 244T Lionel Lines slope-back tender. For shoppers of the day, probably the most attractive feature of the set, beyond its low price,

1961

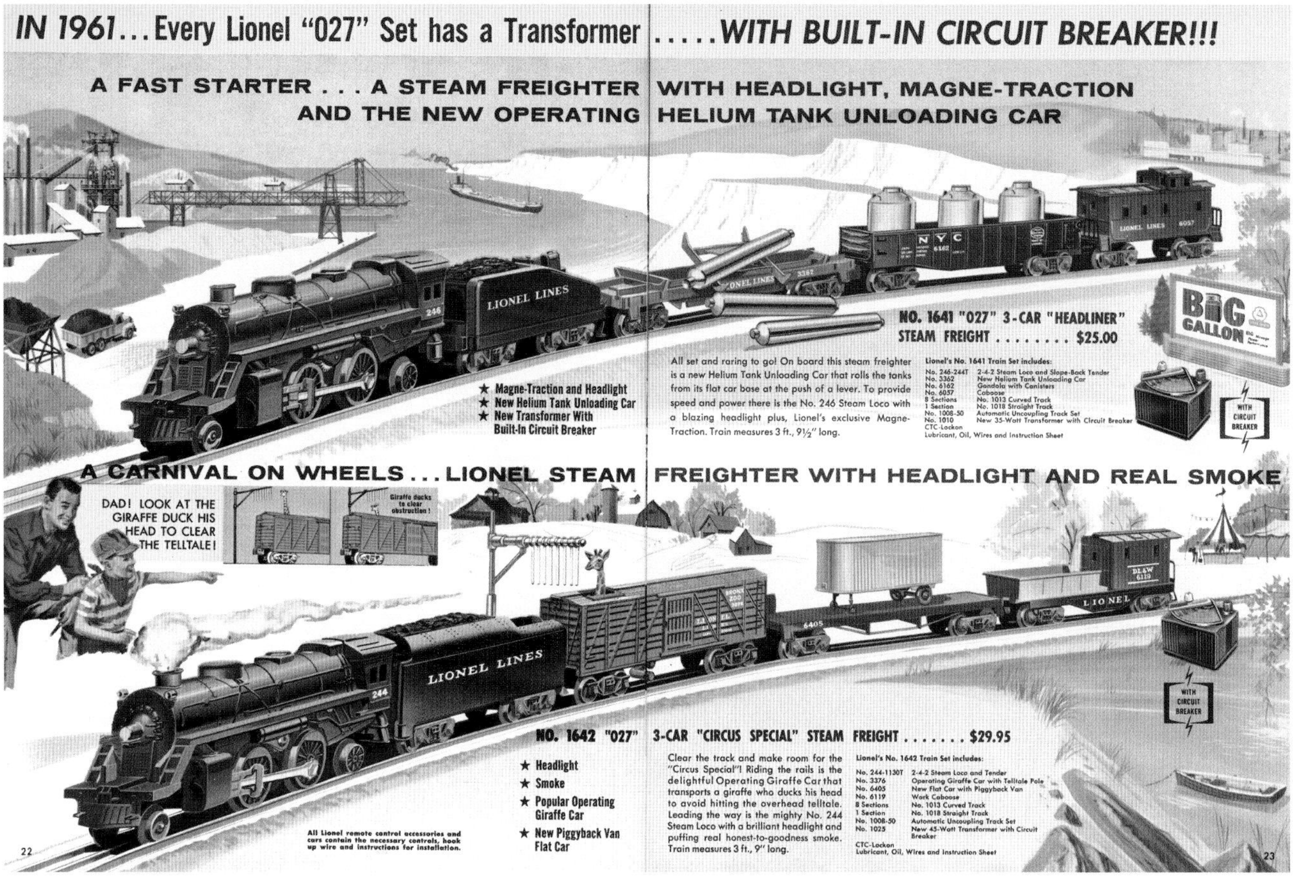

IN 1961... Every Lionel "027" Set has a Transformer ..... WITH BUILT-IN CIRCUIT BREAKER!!!

A FAST STARTER . . . A STEAM FREIGHTER WITH HEADLIGHT, MAGNE-TRACTION AND THE NEW OPERATING HELIUM TANK UNLOADING CAR

★ Magne-Traction and Headlight
★ New Helium Tank Unloading Car
★ New Transformer With Built-In Circuit Breaker

NO. 1641 "027" 3-CAR "HEADLINER" STEAM FREIGHT $25.00

All set and raring to go! On board this steam freighter is a new Helium Tank Unloading Car that rolls the tanks from its flat car base at the push of a lever. To provide speed and power there is the No. 246 Steam Loco with a blazing headlight plus, Lionel's exclusive Magne-Traction. Train measures 3 ft., 9½" long.

Lionel's No. 1641 Train Set includes:

No. 246-244T 2-4-2 Steam Loco and Slope-Back Tender
No. 3362 New Helium Tank Unloading Car
No. 6162 Gondola with Canisters
No. 6057 Caboose
8 Sections No. 1013 Curved Track
1 Section No. 1018 Straight Track
No. 1008-50 Automatic Uncoupling Track Set
No. 1010 New 35-Watt Transformer with Circuit Breaker
CTC-Lockon
Lubricant, Oil, Wires and Instruction Sheet

WITH CIRCUIT BREAKER

A CARNIVAL ON WHEELS . . . LIONEL STEAM FREIGHTER WITH HEADLIGHT AND REAL SMOKE

DAD! LOOK AT THE GIRAFFE DUCK HIS HEAD TO CLEAR THE TELLTALE!

NO. 1642 "027" 3-CAR "CIRCUS SPECIAL" STEAM FREIGHT $29.95

★ Headlight
★ Smoke
★ Popular Operating Giraffe Car
★ New Piggyback Van Flat Car

Clear the track and make room for the "Circus Special"! Riding the rails is the delightful Operating Giraffe Car that transports a giraffe who ducks his head to avoid hitting the overhead telltale. Leading the way is the mighty No. 244 Steam Loco with a brilliant headlight and puffing real honest-to-goodness smoke. Train measures 3 ft., 9" long.

Lionel's No. 1642 Train Set includes:

No. 244-1130T 2-4-2 Steam Loco and Tender
No. 3376 Operating Giraffe Car with Telltale Pole
No. 6405 New Flat Car with Piggyback Van
No. 6119 Work Caboose
8 Sections No. 1013 Curved Track
1 Section No. 1018 Straight Track
No. 1008-50 Automatic Uncoupling Track Set
No. 1025 New 45-Watt Transformer with Circuit Breaker
CTC-Lockon
Lubricant, Oil, Wires and Instruction Sheet

All Lionel remote control accessories and cars contain the necessary controls, hook up wire and instructions for installation.

WITH CIRCUIT BREAKER

22 23

1641, 1642

was the inclusion of the new 3362 dumping car, which added play value to the small outfit. Since no remote control track was packed in this outfit, the 1008 camtrol uncoupler was also used to activate the dumping mechanism.

Excellent	Like New	Scarcity
90	175	3

1642 Circus Special Steam Freight $29.95 retail

Included: 244 2-4-2 steam locomotive with operating headlight and smoke; 1130T tender; 6405 flatcar with van; 3376 giraffe car; 6119 work caboose; eight 1013 curved and two 1018 straight track; 1008 camtrol; 1025 45-watt transformer; CTC Lockon; tube of lubricant; instructions.

A smoking 2-4-2 steam locomotive with ballast weights was paired with a small streamlined tender to head this outfit. The contents of this set that are of greatest interest to collectors individually are the 6405 flatcar with yellow van and the 3376 giraffe car.

The correct version of the giraffe car for this outfit rides on early-style AAR-type trucks and its roof does not have the faint impressions of the 3370 roof openings that are characteristic of giraffe cars produced later in the year.

An undecorated yellow van was held by an elastic band on a maroon General-style flatcar. This combination comprised the 6405 that bore its catalog number in heat stamping on the side of the flatcar body.

The outfit came in an orange-white 1960-style-display outfit box.

Excellent	Like New	Scarcity
175	300	3

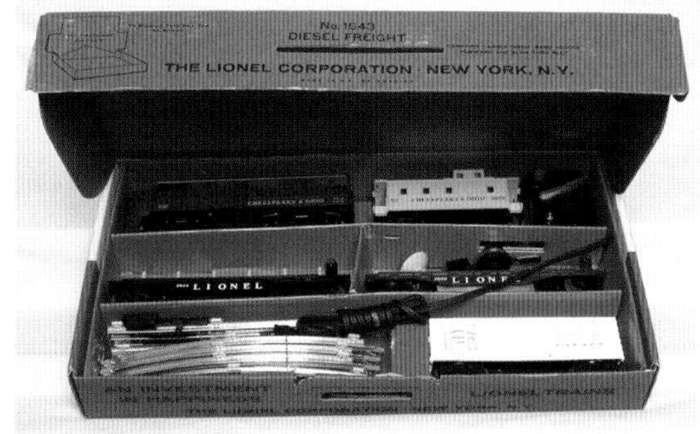

1643 Four-Car Sky-Scout Diesel Freight $29.95 retail

Included: 230 Chesapeake & Ohio Alco A-unit; 6050 savings bank boxcar; 6175 flatcar with rocket; 3509 satellite launching car; 6058 C&O caboose; eight 1013 curved and two 1018 straight track; 1008 camtrol; 1025 45-watt transformer; CTC Lockon; tube of lubricant; instructions.

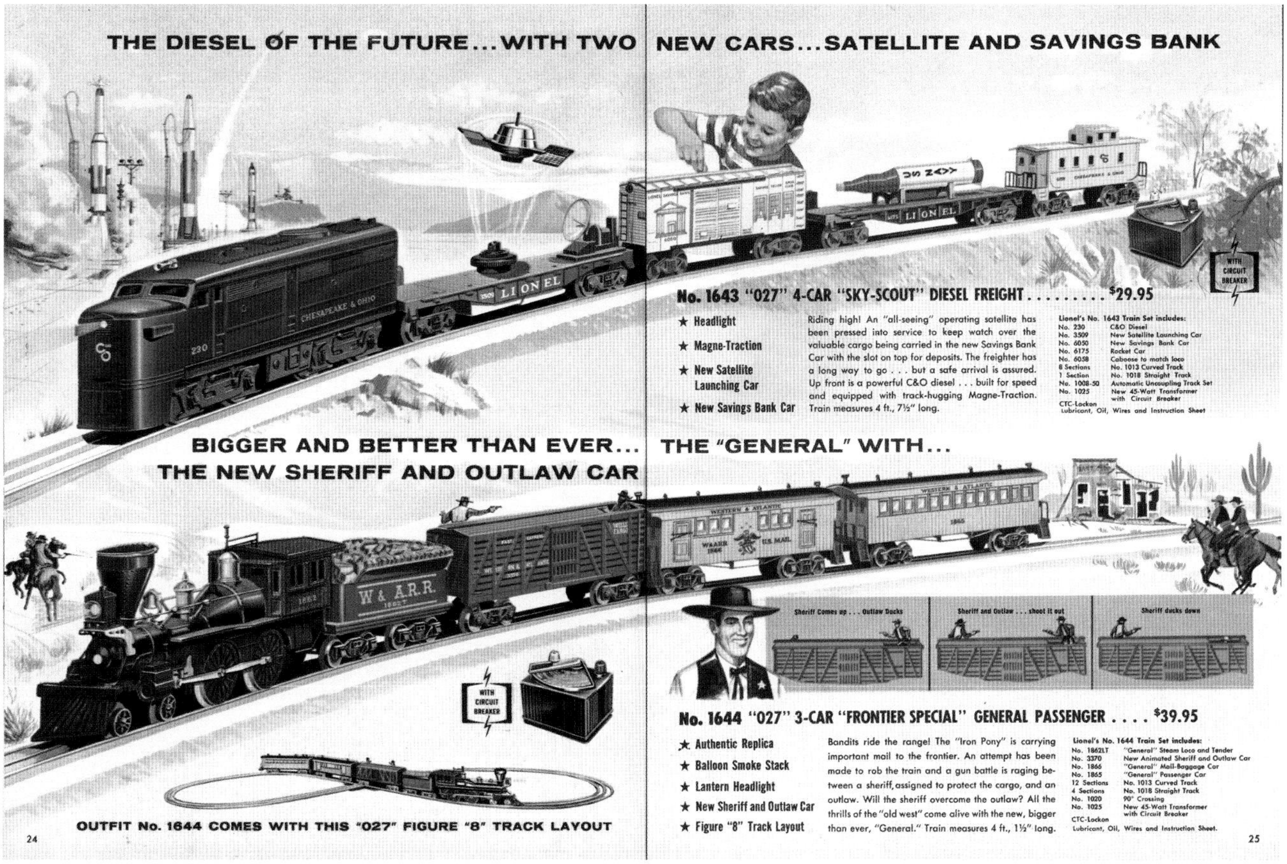

THE DIESEL OF THE FUTURE... WITH TWO NEW CARS... SATELLITE AND SAVINGS BANK

No. 1643 "027" 4-CAR "SKY-SCOUT" DIESEL FREIGHT $29.95

★ Headlight
★ Magne-Traction
★ New Satellite Launching Car
★ New Savings Bank Car

Riding high! An "all-seeing" operating satellite has been pressed into service to keep watch over the valuable cargo being carried in the new Savings Bank Car with the slot on top for deposits. The freighter has a long way to go . . . but a safe arrival is assured. Up front is a powerful C&O diesel . . . built for speed and equipped with track-hugging Magne-Traction. Train measures 4 ft., 7½" long.

Lionel's No. 1643 Train Set includes:
No. 230 C&O Diesel
No. 3509 New Satellite Launching Car
No. 6050 New Savings Bank Car
No. 6175 Rocket Car
No. 6058 Caboose to match loco
8 Sections No. 1013 Curved Track
1 Section No. 1018 Straight Track
No. 1008-50 Automatic Uncoupling Track Set
No. 1025 New 45-Watt Transformer with Circuit Breaker
CTC-Lockon
Lubricant, Oil, Wires and Instruction Sheet

BIGGER AND BETTER THAN EVER... THE NEW SHERIFF AND OUTLAW CAR THE "GENERAL" WITH...

Sheriff Comes up . . . Outlaw Ducks
Sheriff and Outlaw . . . shoot it out
Sheriff ducks down

No. 1644 "027" 3-CAR "FRONTIER SPECIAL" GENERAL PASSENGER $39.95

★ Authentic Replica
★ Balloon Smoke Stack
★ Lantern Headlight
★ New Sheriff and Outlaw Car
★ Figure "8" Track Layout

Bandits ride the range! The "Iron Pony" is carrying important mail to the frontier. An attempt has been made to rob the train and a gun battle is raging between a sheriff, assigned to protect the cargo, and an outlaw. Will the sheriff overcome the outlaw? All the thrills of the "old west" come alive with the new, bigger than ever, "General." Train measures 4 ft., 1½" long.

Lionel's No. 1644 Train Set includes:
No. 1862LT "General" Steam Loco and Tender
No. 3370 New Animated Sheriff and Outlaw Car
No. 1866 "General" Mail-Baggage Car
No. 1865 "General" Passenger Car
12 Sections No. 1013 Curved Track
4 Sections No. 1018 Straight Track
No. 1020 90° Crossing
No. 1025 New 45-Watt Transformer with Circuit Breaker
CTC-Lockon
Lubricant, Oil, Wires and Instruction Sheet.

OUTFIT No. 1644 COMES WITH THIS "027" FIGURE "8" TRACK LAYOUT

24 25

1643, 1644

Matching Chesapeake and Ohio locomotives and cabooses are found in these outfits. While the C&O was not a new road name for the Alco, the 230 number that lacked a front coupler was new.

The black 6175 flatcar with rocket was a returning item, while the 6050 savings bank boxcar and hard-to-find 3509 manual-release satellite launching car were new for 1961. Although the latter is shown in the catalog as blue, it was actually produced only in green. Collectors should beware that reproduction satellites have been produced; these have simulated solar panels that are flat, whereas originals have the shape of an arc. Reproduced also are the rocket and its cradle for the 6175.

This outfit has been found in no less than three styles of boxes; the orange-and-white 1960-style packaging, yellow 1959-style display packaging, or a mundane tan corrugated two-tier set box. In any case, the outfit components were placed unboxed in the set package.

Excellent	Like New	Scarcity
275	475	3

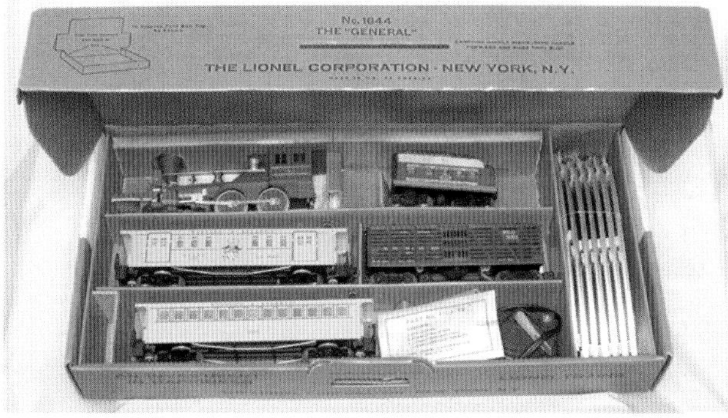

No. 1644 THE "GENERAL"
THE LIONEL CORPORATION · NEW YORK, N.Y.

1644 Frontier Special General Passenger

$39.95 retail

Included: 1862 4-4-0 General with operating headlight; 1862T tender; 3370 sheriff and outlaw car; 1866 mail-baggage car; 1865 passenger car; 12 1013 curved and four 1018 straight track; 90-degree crossing; 1025 45-watt transformer; CTC Lockon; tube of lubricant; instructions.

Sales of the General-series outfits were lagging. In an effort to boost these outfits, Lionel packaged them with a figure-eight track assortment. They then replaced the somewhat dull flatcar with horses with an action car—the new 3370

1961

animated sheriff and outlaw car. The green body molding for this car was created by modifying the tooling used to create the bodies for the 3376 giraffe car. Although this car was also produced with AAR-type trucks, those packed in this set rode on arch-bar trucks so as to match the era of the passenger cars and locomotive.

The components of this outfit, without individual boxes, were packed in an orange-and-white 1960-style display set box.

Excellent	Like New	Scarcity
475	700	3

1645 Four-Car Diesel Freight $39.95 retail

Included: 229 Minneapolis & St. Louis Alco A-unit with horn; 3410 flatcar with helicopter; 6465-110 Cities Service double-dome tank car; 6825 flatcar with trestle; 6059 Minneapolis & St. Louis caboose; eight 1013 curved and four 1018 straight track; 1008 camtrol; 1073 60-watt transformer; 147 horn controller.

While in 1962 the 229 Minneapolis & St. Louis Alco A was paired with a B-unit, during 1961 it came as a single A-unit only, just as in this set. While the locomotive had an operating horn and single-axle Magne-traction, it was equipped with only a two-position E-unit.

A green Cities Service tanker added a splash of color to the set, while the 3410 manually operated helicopter car provided action. The 3410 is an uncommon car, produced only two years, and the cars differed by year. The correct car for this outfit does not have the extra hole in the housing unit for the trigger mechanism. This car most often came with a Navy helicopter, but has been reported with all-yellow helicopters as well. Be advised that reproduction helicopters, helicopter parts, launching reels and tail supports are common.

All the outfit components came unboxed in an orange-and-white 1960-style set display box.

Excellent	Like New	Scarcity
240	400	4

1646 Four-Car Utility Steam Freight $39.95 retail

Included: 233 2-4-2 steam locomotive with operating headlight, smoke and Magne-traction; 233W tender; 6343 barrel ramp car; 6162 gondola with canisters; 6476 Lehigh Valley hopper; 6017 SP-type caboose; eight 1013 curved and four 1018 straight track; 1008 camtrol; 1073 60-watt transformer; 147 whistle controller.

Though as humble-looking as any Scout-type locomotive, the 233 at the front of this set was rather unusual. The locomotive was equipped with Magne-traction and smoke, and was paired with a whistle tender. The freight-type tender had an operating coupler and was numbered 233W. In an unusual move for sets of this time and of this quality, Lionel chose to pack both the locomotive and tender in their own boxes, the loco in a Perforated-front tan corrugated box and the tender in an overstamped Perforated box.

The 6343 barrel ramp car was a new item, and bore the same type of barrels that were furnished with the 3562. The blue gondola was a returning item and came with a load of white canisters.

A MIGHTY NEW DIESEL...THE MINNEAPOLIS AND ST. LOUIS...WITH RAIL-GRIPPING MAGNE-TRACTION AND DEEP-THROATED HORN
B-E-E-E-E-E-P
CITIES SERVICE
LIONEL
WITH CIRCUIT BREAKER
No. 1645 "027" 4-CAR "MINNEAPOLIS & ST. LOUIS" DIESEL FREIGHT....$39.95
★ New Diesel Unit
★ Horn
★ Headlight
★ Magne-Traction
★ Helicopter Launching Car
The diesel with full power! Oil for industry and steel for construction make up the cargo of this high-powered freighter. In addition...a flying helicopter has been assigned to serve as an aerial reconnaissance unit. This "pride of the midwest" diesel comes well equipped for the job with...piercing headlight, track-gripping Magne-Traction and a deep throated horn. Train measures 4 ft., 2" long.
Lionel's No. 1645 Train Set includes:
No. 229 New M. St. Louis Diesel
No. 3410 Helicopter Launching Car
No. 6465 Two Dome Cities Service Tank Car
No. 6825 Flat Car with Arch Trestle Bridge
No. 6059 Caboose to match loco
8 Sections No. 1013 Curved Track
3 Sections No. 1018 Straight Track
No. 1008-50 Automatic Uncoupling Track Set
No. 1073 60-Watt Transformer with Circuit Breaker
No. 147 Horn Controller
CTC-Lockon
Lubricant, Oil, Wires and Instruction Sheet
A NEW FEATURE-PACKED MAGNE-TRACTION AND STEAMER...WITH REAL SMOKE, AUTHENTIC SOUNDING WHISTLE
OH BOY!
WHAT A HONEY OF A SET.
IT'S GOT EVERYTHING
THAT A REAL TRAIN HAS!
LIONEL LINES
LIONEL
LEHIGH VALLEY
No. 1646 "027" 4-CAR "UTILITY" STEAM FREIGHT.....$39.95
★ New Steam Loco
★ Smoke and Headlight
★ Magne-Traction
★ Whistle
★ New Barrel Ramp Car
A hard-at-work freight train! When a job has to be done this is the steamer that will do it. Barreling down the track at top speed is the new No. 233 loco equipped with real smoke, blazing headlight, high pitched whistle and track-gripping Magne-Traction, followed by an array of unique cargo cars. It all adds up to many happy hours of model railroading pleasure. Train measures 4 ft., 8¼" long.
Lionel's No. 1646 Train Set includes:
No. 233LTS New Steam Loco and Whistle Tender
No. 6162 Gondola with Canisters
No. 6343 New Barrel Ramp Car
No. 6476 Hopper Car
No. 6017 Caboose
8 Sections No. 1013 Curved Track
3 Sections No. 1018 Straight Track
No. 1008-50 Automatic Uncoupling Track Set
No. 1073 60-Watt Transformer with Circuit Breaker
No. 147 Whistle Controller
CTC-Lockon
Lubricant, Oil, Wires and Instruction Sheet
WITH CIRCUIT BREAKER
All Lionel remote control accessories and cars contain the necessary controls, hook up wire and instructions for installation.
26
27

1645, 1646

1647, 1648

Two styles of packaging were used during the production of this outfit. Some sets came in a factory-fresh, especially made yellow display box, while others came in yellow 1631WS boxes that had been remarked.

Excellent	Like New	Scarcity
350	600	2

1647 Freedom Fighter Missile Launcher Outfit

$49.95 retail

Included: 45 U.S. Marines missile launcher; 6448 exploding boxcar; 6830 flatcar with submarine; 3665 Minuteman car; 3519 satellite launching car; 6814 medical caboose; eight 1013 curved and three 1018 straight track; 6019 uncoupling/operating section; 1073 60-watt transformer; CTC Lockon; tube of lubricant; instructions.

The set was military from one end to the other and every component either operated or carried separate cargo. Of course, this means that there are plenty of pieces that can be lost or broken—many of which have now been reproduced.

Three of the items—the satellite and Minuteman launching cars and the exploding boxcar—were new for 1961 and were of course then packed in Orange Picture boxes. Reproduction parts are available today for all three of these cars.

The green 3519 was mechanically similar to the 3419 helicopter launching car, but rather than a helicopter, this car spun a chrome-topped satellite into the air. Near the end of the car opposite the launching mechanism was a small gray plastic superstructure that held the same yellow microwave dish that was found on the dispatching station. This dish, as well as the satellite, has been reproduced. Reproduction satellites lack the arc found in the solar panels of the originals.

The 3665 was created by heavily modifying the tooling of the 3530 Electro-Motive power car. The car debuted in 1961 and remained in the product line through 1964. The correct car for inclusion in this and other 1961 outfits projects a red over white missile. The roof halves were dark blue, bordering on purple. The bodies lacked the small holes on the sides that were introduced as a result of the 1962 debut of the 3619 reconnaissance car that shared the body tooling.

The blue-painted 6830 flatcar carried a non-operating submarine numbered 6830 as well. This car, like the 6814 medical caboose, was a carry-over item and came in a Perforated box. This car had a pure white body and tray mounted on a black-lettered gray pressed-steel frame. The body and tray were heat stamped in red. Inside the tray, attached to a special white insert, rode the same blue man as used by the 50 gang car. Also placed inside the tray were a plastic oxygen tank and a pair of white plastic stretchers with red crosses stamped on. All these small items have been reproduced.

The olive drab Marine Corps mobile missile launcher also had a blue rubber crewman, which, like its control panel and missiles, has also been reproduced. The powered unit came in a tan corrugated carton. The presence of this locomotive necessitated the inclusion of a 6019 track section in the orange two-tier set box.

Excellent	Like New	Scarcity
900	1,475	6

1648 Five-Car Supply Line Steam Freight $49.95 retail

Included: 2037 2-6-4 steam locomotive with operating headlight, smoke and Magne-traction; 233W tender; 6519 Allis-Chalmers car; 6062 gondola with cable reels; 6465-110 Cities Service double-dome tank car; 6476 Lehigh Valley hopper; 6017 caboose; eight 1013 curved and four 1018 straight track; 1008 camtrol; 1063 75-watt transformer; CTC Lockon; tube of lubricant; instructions.

With the singular exception of the tender, from one end to the other this entire outfit was comprised of repeat items. Because of this, the cars in this outfit were packed in a combination of Perforated and Orange Picture boxes. The proper box for the Cities Service tank car is stamped 6465-110.

This outfit came in the new solid orange conventional two-tier set carton with the contents individually boxed.

Excellent	Like New	Scarcity
250	400	3

1649 Five-Car Two Unit Diesel Freight $49.95 retail

Included: 218P/218C Santa Fe Alco A-B units with horn; 6343 barrel ramp car; 6445 Fort Knox car; 6405 flatcar with yellow van; 6475 pickle vat car; 6017 caboose; eight 1013 curved and four 1018 straight track; 1008 camtrol; 1063 75-watt transformer; CTC Lockon; tube of lubricant; instructions.

All the freight cars in this outfit have been discussed earlier in this chapter, except for the Fort Knox bullion car. This car was created by inserting a newly tooled simulated gold bullion load inside a body based on that of the 3435 aquarium car. But for the large windows the aquarium car body was painted green, silver was used on similar areas of the Fort Knox car. The Knox car also had a slot in the roof so that it could serve as a bank. Lionel's silver paint is notoriously vulnerable and the large clear windows are subject to crazing. The car came inside an Orange Picture box.

The 218C B-unit, with the box itself being very uncommon, also used an Orange Picture box. The Alco A-unit was packaged in a tan corrugated carton. Some sets reportedly have the Santa Fe units replaced with 226 Boston and Maine A-B combinations. Two-tier orange set boxes were used for these outfits, with the B&M set cartons being stamped as 1649NE.

Excellent	Like New	Scarcity
525	900	6

1650 Five-Car Guardian Steam Freight $59.95 retail

Included: 2037 2-6-4 steam locomotive with operating headlight, smoke and Magne-traction; 233W tender; 6470 exploding boxcar; 3330 flatcar with submarine kit; 3419 flatcar with operating helicopter; 6544 missile firing car; 6017 caboose; eight 1013 curved and three 1018 straight track; 6029 uncoupling section; 1063 75-watt transformer; CTC Lockon; tube of lubricant; instructions.

This steam powered set was another outfit comprised totally of returning items, once again with the singular exception of the tender that had AAR-type trucks and an operating coupler.

Collectors dream of finding the 3330 flatcar with its submarine still in its cellophane bag unassembled, but this is rarely the case. The halves of the submarine incidentally are stamped 3830, with the tops of the threes flat.

The 6544 used a body derived from the 6519 Allis-Chalmers heat exchanger car. Like the Allis-Chalmers car, it has notably fragile brake stands, hence caution should be used when evaluating this outfit to insure that both brake

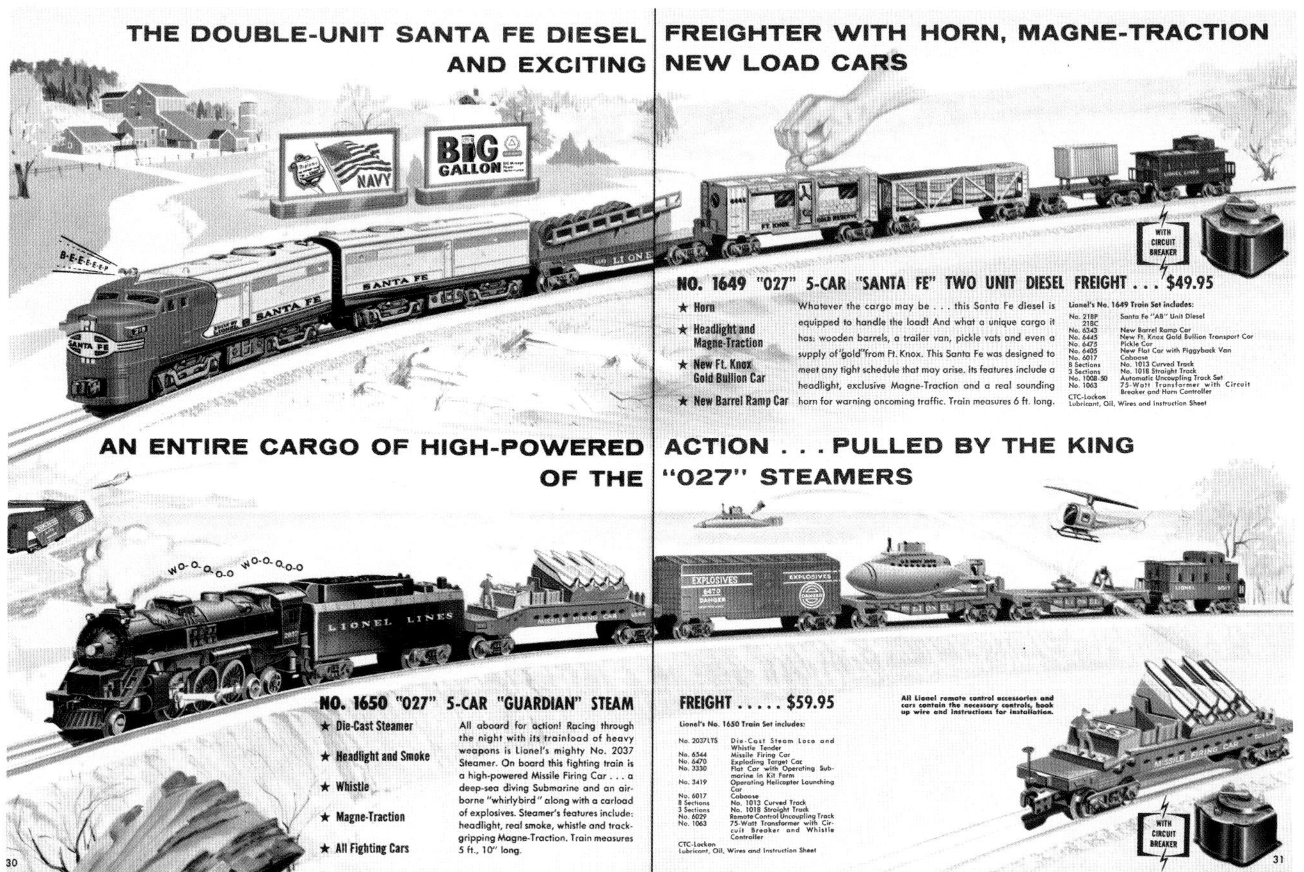

THE DOUBLE-UNIT SANTA FE DIESEL FREIGHTER WITH HORN, MAGNE-TRACTION
AND EXCITING NEW LOAD CARS
BIG GALLON
NAVY
SANTA FE
WITH CIRCUIT BREAKER
NO. 1649 "027" 5-CAR "SANTA FE" TWO UNIT DIESEL FREIGHT . . . $49.95
★ Horn
★ Headlight and Magne-Traction
★ New Ft. Knox Gold Bullion Car
★ New Barrel Ramp Car
Whatever the cargo may be . . . this Santa Fe diesel is equipped to handle the load! And what a unique cargo it has: wooden barrels, a trailer van, pickle vats and even a supply of "gold" from Ft. Knox. This Santa Fe was designed to meet any tight schedule that may arise. Its features include a headlight, exclusive Magne-Traction and a real sounding horn for warning oncoming traffic. Train measures 6 ft. long.
Lionel's No. 1649 Train Set includes:
No. 218P 218C Santa Fe "AB" Unit Diesel
No. 6343 New Barrel Ramp Car
No. 6445 New Ft. Knox Gold Bullion Transport Car
No. 6475 Pickle Car
No. 6405 New Flat Car with Piggyback Van
No. 6017 Caboose
8 Sections No. 1013 Curved Track
3 Sections No. 1018 Straight Track
No. 1008-50 Automatic Uncoupling Track Set
No. 1063 75-Watt Transformer with Circuit Breaker and Horn Controller
CTC-Lockon
Lubricant, Oil, Wires and Instruction Sheet
AN ENTIRE CARGO OF HIGH-POWERED ACTION . . . PULLED BY THE KING
OF THE "027" STEAMERS
WO-O-O-O-O WO-O-O-O-O
LIONEL LINES
EXPLOSIVES
NO. 1650 "027" 5-CAR "GUARDIAN" STEAM FREIGHT $59.95
★ Die-Cast Steamer
★ Headlight and Smoke
★ Whistle
★ Magne-Traction
★ All Fighting Cars
All aboard for action! Racing through the night with its trainload of heavy weapons is Lionel's mighty No. 2037 Steamer. On board this fighting train is a high-powered Missile Firing Car . . . a deep-sea diving Submarine and an air-borne "whirlybird" along with a carload of explosives. Steamer's features include: headlight, real smoke, whistle and track-gripping Magne-Traction. Train measures 5 ft., 10" long.
Lionel's No. 1650 Train Set includes:
No. 2037LTS Die-Cast Steam Loco and Whistle Tender
No. 6544 Missile Firing Car
No. 6470 Exploding Target Car
No. 3330 Flat Car with Operating Submarine in Kit Form
No. 3419 Operating Helicopter Launching Car
No. 6017 Caboose
8 Sections No. 1013 Curved Track
3 Sections No. 1018 Straight Track
No. 6029 Remote Control Uncoupling Track
No. 1063 75-Watt Transformer with Circuit Breaker and Whistle Controller
CTC-Lockon
Lubricant, Oil, Wires and Instruction Sheet
All Lionel remote control accessories and cars contain the necessary controls, hook up wire and instructions for installation.
MISSILE FIRING CAR
WITH CIRCUIT BREAKER
30
31

1649, 1650

stands on the 6544 are present, undamaged and not repaired. The various components of the outfit were packed in a combination of Perforated and Orange Picture boxes, except for the loco which came in a tan corrugated carton and the tender that came in an Orange Picture box.

Excellent	Like New	Scarcity
450	800	6

1651 Four-Car All Passenger Diesel $69.95 retail

Included: 218P/218T or 220T Santa Fe Alco A-A units with horn; two 2412 Vista Domes; 2414 Pullman and 2416 observation; eight 1013 curved and three 1018 straight track; 6029 uncoupling section; 1063 75-watt transformer; CTC Lockon; tube of lubricant; instructions.

This attractive blue-striped passenger set was the top-of-the-027-line for 1961. Because the cars were carry-over items they could come in either Perforated or Orange Picture boxes. At the front of streamliner was a pair of Santa Fe warbonnet Alcos. The 218P came in a tan corrugated carton, while the dummy unit, which could be either the 218T or 220T, was packed in an Orange Picture box.

Excellent	Like New	Scarcity
750	1,200	4

Gift pack

1809 The Western Gift Pack $29.95 retail

Included: 244 2-4-2 steam locomotive with operating headlight and smoke; 1130T tender; 3370 sheriff and outlaw car; 3376 giraffe car; 1877 flatcar with horses; 6017 caboose.

Lionel continued their program of gift packs—which offered customers with existing railroads the ability to add another entire train to their empire—with two packs in 1961. The first of these was this Western Gift Pack. All the items in this outfit have been described previously in this chapter except for the 1877 flatcar, which is described in the 1959 chapter. Packaging for the gift pack was in an orange-and-white display box, but the outfit components themselves were unboxed.

Excellent	Like New	Scarcity
300	500	3

THE PRIDE OF THE "027" STREAMLINERS .... LIONEL'S "DOUBLE ENDER" SANTA FE PASSENGER WITH HORN

★ Headlight
★ Horn
★ Magne-Traction
★ All Illuminated Cars

No. 1651 "027" 4-CAR "ALL PASSENGER" DIESEL.... $69.95

WITH CIRCUIT BREAKER

The diesel giant that roams the west! While passengers are relaxing and enjoying the surrounding countryside . . . this sleek streamliner is racing to meet its schedule. Although the journey is long, with rivers to cross and mountains to climb . . . a comfortable ride is assured. This "double-ender" comes equipped with headlight, horn and track-gripping Magne-Traction. Train measures 5 ft., 9½" long.

Lionel's No. 1651 Train Set includes:

No. 218 Alco Santa Fe Twin "A" Unit Diesel
No. 2414 Illuminated Santa Fe Pullman
No. 2412 Illuminated Santa Fe Vista-Dome
No. 2412 Illuminated Santa Fe Vista-Dome
No. 2416 Illuminated Santa Fe Observation
8 Sections No. 1013 Curved Track
3 Sections No. 1018 Straight Track
No. 6029 Remote Control Uncoupling Track
No. 1063 75-Watt Transformer with Circuit Breaker and Horn Controller
CTC-Lockon
Lubricant, Oil, Wires and Instruction Sheet

FOR THE MODEL RAILROADER WHO HAS LIONEL TRACK AND TRANSFORMER ...... A SECOND TRAIN FOR A TWO-TRAIN LAYOUT

Tomorrow's Weapon Carrier...Today!!

No. 1810 THE "SPACE AGE" GIFT PACK... $35.00

★ New Rock Island Diesel ★ Headlight
★ Magne-Traction ★ Three Operating Cars

Roof separates – launcher rises – missile blasts off!
Satellite gracefully rises!
Submarine moves under water!

Space Age Gift Pack includes:

No. 231 New Rock Island Diesel with Headlight and Magne-Traction
No. 3665 New Minuteman Missile Launching Car
No. 3519 New Satellite Launching Car
No. 3820 Operating Submarine Car
No. 6017 Caboose

From out of the West...
The Sheriff and Outlaw!!

No. 1809 THE "WESTERN" GIFT PACK.. $29.95

★ Headlight ★ Popular Operating Giraffe Car
★ Smoke ★ New Animated Sheriff & Outlaw Car

Sheriff and Outlaw – shoot it out!
Giraffe ducks to clear obstruction!

Western Gift Pack includes:

No. 244-1130T Steam Loco and Tender with Headlight and Smoke
No. 3370 New Animated Sheriff and Outlaw Car
No. 3376 Operating Giraffe Car
No. 1877 Horse Transport Car
No. 6017 Caboose

32 33

1809, 1651, 1810

1810 The Space Age Gift Pack $35 retail

Included: 231 Rock Island Alco A-unit; 3820 U.S. Marine Corps flatcar with operating submarine; 3665 Minuteman car; 3519 satellite launching car; 6017 caboose.

The second gift pack of 1961 was far removed from the old-west style assortment above, incorporating an array of space, military and rocket-related items. The 231 Alco at the front of this outfit was new for 1961, as was the satellite launching and Minuteman cars—which are described earlier in this chapter. The USMC flatcar with submarine, however, represented unused 1960 inventory. None of these items were component boxed before being placed inside the Gift Pack's orange-and-white display box.

Excellent	Like New	Scarcity
550	975	3

Super O

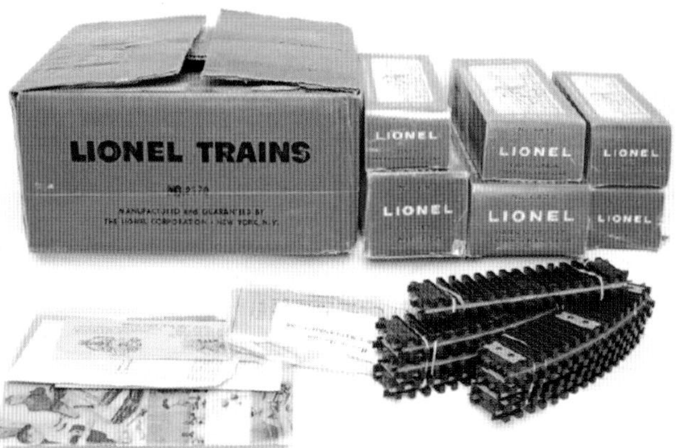

2528WS Five-Star Frontier Special Outfit $49.95 retail
Included: 1872 4-4-0 General with headlight, smoke and Magne-traction; 1872T tender; 1877 flatcar with horses; 1876 illuminated mail-baggage car; 1875W illuminated passenger car with whistle; twelve 31 curved, one 32 straight and one 48 insulated straight track; smoke fluid; 39-25 operating packet.

Sales of this General outfit, first cataloged in 1959, were disappointing. So much so that it was shown in the 1960 and 1961 catalogs just to help move unsold inventory in Lionel's warehouse. A detailed description of this outfit is in the 1959 chapter.

Tan conventional box:

Excellent	Like New	Scarcity
900	1,600	4

Display box with die-cut filler:

Excellent	Like New	Scarcity
750	1,350	3

Display box with individual component boxes:

Excellent	Like New	Scarcity
825	1,475	3

2570 Five-Car Husky Diesel Freight $49.95 retail
Included: 616 Santa Fe NW-2 diesel switcher with horn; 6828 flatcar with Harnischfeger crane; 6736 Detroit & Mackinac hopper; 6822 searchlight car; 6812 track maintenance car; 6130 Santa Fe work caboose; twelve 31 curved and two 32 straight track; 39-25 operating packet; tube of lubricant; instructions.

In contrast to the many Space or Wild West oriented trains offered in 1961 was this set, whose Santa Fe diesel switcher pulled an assortment of relatively normal freight and maintenance-of-way cars.

The 616 Santa Fe NW-2 was offered in 1961-62. It was painted black with white safety stripes, referred to as zebra stripes, which were painted on. The lettering and Santa Fe logo was applied with heat stamping. The model was an unusual mix with almost no trim, but with many deluxe operating features. It had no ornamental bell or horn, and had only plastic non-operating couplers, yet it had a lever-down three-position E-unit, an operating horn and headlight, and two-axle Magne-traction. A simulated fuel tank was attached to the bottom of the frame, and the headlight housing even had a lens in it—unusual for a low-cost locomotive. In this outfit cardboard inserts held the locomotive in place inside an Orange Picture box.

It's believed that Perforated boxes have been used for some of the 6736 hoppers and 6812 track maintenance cars, the latter of which had a black-and-gray superstructure.

A new searchlight car, based on a red plastic 6511-type flatcar, appeared in this outfit. Atop the flatcar was a black plastic superstructure, which in turn supported a gray plastic searchlight housing, held in place by a metal bracket. The searchlight was constantly illuminated, but manually aimed. A blue rubber crewman, with one arm outstretched, rode on the car. As with all Lionel searchlight cars, the lamp housing and lens have been reproduced, as has the crewman. The car was packed in an Orange Picture box.

An Orange Picture box was used as well for the outer package for the 6828. Inside was a black flatcar, and a second box, this time yellow, black and white, containing the assembly kit for the 6828 crane itself. Be advised that the crane was also produced during the MPC era, so prospective purchasers should examine these carefully to ensure consistent coloring of all the parts.

At the rear of the train was a new version of the work caboose. Sporting a red cab and tool tray, which was sometimes painted, the car had a blacked pressed steel frame.

The work caboose came in an Orange Picture box that, with the remainder of the outfit components, was packed inside an orange two-tier set carton.

Excellent	Like New	Scarcity
550	900	4

2571 Fort Knox Special Steam Freight $49.95 retail

Included: 637 2-6-4 steam locomotive with operating headlight, smoke and Magne-traction; 736W tender; 3419 flatcar with operating helicopter; 6445 Fort Knox car; 6361 timber transport; 6119-100 work caboose; twelve 31 curved and two 32 straight track; 39-25 operating packet; tube of lubricant; instructions.

Lionel placed their 637 steam locomotive—actually a 2037 assigned a new number indicative of its Super 0 status—at the front of this outfit. The loco was paired with a streamlined Pennsylvania tender, newly given AAR-type trucks and renumbered 736W.

The timber transport car, which used blackened miniature chains to secure its load, utilized a sheet-metal frame. The 1961 and later frames differed from their earlier counterparts by incorporating changes required by the operating mechanism of the 3362 dump car, which used the same basic frame stamping.

The 3419 helicopter launching car came with a 1-3/8-inch diameter winding spool and 1-3/8-inch-tall tail support. Close examination of helicopter flatcar bodies molded in this and subsequent years reveals the faint impression of the 3509 satellite car characteristics. The actuating mechanism was also modified in 1961, reflecting the adaptation of the parts for use on a manually operated helicopter launching car.

The Fort Knox bullion transport car was new for 1961, and has been discussed earlier in the chapter. Bringing up the rear of the train was a red, gray and black D. L. & W. 6119-100 work caboose.

The component-boxed contents of this outfit were packed inside a solid orange two-tier set box numbered 2571.

Excellent	Like New	Scarcity
600	1,000	5

2572 Five-Car Space Age Diesel Freighter

$59.95 retail

Included: 2359 Boston and Maine GP-9; 6448 exploding boxcar; 3830 flatcar with operating submarine; 6544 missile firing car; 3519 satellite launching car; 3535 security car; twelve 31 curved and four 32 straight track; 39-25 operating packet; tube of lubricant; instructions.

The 3830 flatcar with submarine, as well as the 3535 security car, were returning items from the previous year. The remaining cars found in this outfit were new for 1961, as was the locomotive.

The 2359 Boston and Maine diesel had a black plastic body painted blue, a cab painted black, white heat-stamped lettering and a black-and-white heat stamped "BM" on each side of the long hood. It had a sheet-metal frame painted white, Magne-traction, three-position lever-down E-unit, operating headlight at each end, operating horn, and two operating couplers. It came packaged in a tan corrugated carton—some reportedly with a perforated front.

On the roof of the offset unpainted red superstructure of the 3535 was a twin 40mm Bofors anti-aircraft cannon borrowed from the Pyro military loads. Mounted opposite of the superstructure, which was based on the cab of the 520 electric locomotive, was a small blued-steel deck with a vibrator-operated rotating searchlight installed. There was no lettering on the black flatcar itself, but the superstructure was heat-stamped "AEC" "SECURITY CAR" and "3535" in white. This car was packaged in an Orange Picture box. Beware that the searchlight housing, lens, anti-aircraft gun and mount have all been reproduced.

The 6448 came either with red roof and white sides, or with a white roof and red sides. It was furnished with a 497 lock pin and rubber stop, which are often missing—but have been reproduced—today.

A solid orange two-tier set box was used for this outfit, whose components were boxed in a mixture of Perforated and Orange Picture boxes.

Excellent	Like New	Scarcity
800	1,350	4

2573 Five-Car TV Special Steam Freight $75 retail

Included: 736 2-8-4 Berkshire steam locomotive with operating headlight, smoke and Magne-traction; 736W tender; 6416 Boat Loader; 6440 flatcar with vans; 6475 pickle vat car; 3545 operating TV monitor car; 6357 illuminated caboose; twelve 31 curved and four 32 straight track; 39-25 operating packet; tube of lubricant; instructions.

The old favorite, the 736 Berkshire towed a variety of cars, including three new designs in this five-car freight outfit. The locomotive came in a tan corrugated box, while the streamlined Pennsylvania tender—newly fitted with AAR-type trucks and renumbered 736W—came in an Orange Picture box. Orange Picture boxes were used for the remainder of the set components, except for the lighted caboose. The SP-style 6357 crummy was a carry-over item that was packed in a Perforated box.

The desirable 6416 Boat Loader was created using the tooling that was built to manufacture the 6414 Auto Loader. Its unpainted red plastic body was heat stamped "6416 LIONEL" in standard white serif letters. The sheet-metal superstructure was painted black and rubber-stamped "BOAT-LOADER" in white serif lettering. The car was equipped with AAR-type trucks with operating couplers. Its cargo was four HO cabin cruisers built by Athearn, a prominent maker of HO-Gauge trains. The only proper color combination of boat for this car has a hull painted white, blue-painted cabin, and brown-painted interior. Athearn did and continues to build the same boats in a variety of other colors, but they are not accurate for this car.

The 6440 flatcar with trailers illustrates the subtle changes Lionel was making to lower costs. At first glance, it looks like the earlier 6430, but it rides on AAR-type trucks, has no metal trailer retaining rack, and the trailers themselves are more austere. They were unpainted gray plastic with only single rear wheels and no decoration whatsoever.

The 3545 operating TV monitor car, based on the 3540 radar car designs, had an unpainted black plastic body with an unpainted blue superstructure. Atop the superstructure was a simulated light array mounted at one end. A simulated TV camera was mounted at the other end. The TV camera revolved as the train rolled along the track, driven via a rubber band from an axle on the car. Two rubber figures rode the car, one manning the camera, the other monitoring the huge display showing a moving locomotive. The box for this car seems to be unusually delicate.

The 6475 pickle car was, like the caboose, a returning item. It was packed in an Orange Picture box and placed with the rest of the set components in a solid orange two-tier-outfit carton.

Excellent	Like New	Scarcity
1,200	2,000	5

2574 Five-Car Defender Diesel Freight $89.95 retail

Included: 2383P/2383T Santa Fe A-A F-3 units; 3419 flatcar with operating helicopter; 3830 flatcar with operating submarine; 3665 Minuteman car; 448 missile firing range set with 6448 exploding boxcar; 6437 Pennsylvania caboose; twelve 31 curved, three 32 straight and one half-32 straight track; 109 trestle set; 943 exploding ammo dump; 39-25 operating packet; tube of lubricant; instructions.

1961

The classic Santa Fe F-3 diesels, in the form of the 2383 version, were given charge of this military express. Though most of the components of this outfit have already been discussed in this volume, a few key items are worthy of mention here.

The 6437 Pennsylvania porthole caboose—an ironic inclusion considering the Santa Fe locomotives—was a new item in that it had AAR-type trucks, which resulted in the new number being assigned.

The 448 was a new item for 1961. Its launcher was based on the mechanism of the 6544 flatcar and even fired the same rockets. However, the control panel for the 448 was blank, unlike the printed panel of the 6544. Packed inside this accessory's special Orange Picture box—which itself is incredibly fragile—was a cellophane bag of lichen "bushes," presumably for camouflage, and a 6448 Target Range Car with red sides and white lettering, roof, and ends. The car rode on Timken trucks with operating couplers.

The 109 12-piece trestle set amounted to the lower portion of the classic 110 trestle set.

Another partial set of 12 piers was packaged, this time in 1961. These piers were gray, and the packaging amounted to adhering them to two strips of waxy cardboard, then placing them inside a re-marked 1044 transformer box. The trestle set came with its own special manila envelope of hardware.

The locomotives in this outfit each had its own tan corrugated carton, and the red of the locomotive's paint scheme had a distinctly orange tint to it, in contrast to the strong red color used earlier. The rolling stock all came in Orange Picture boxes, while the outfit box was the solid orange two-tier type.

Excellent	Like New	Scarcity
1,800	3,000	5

Values for each condition are in U.S. dollars. | **Scarity** = Scale from 1-8 with 8 being the hardest to find.

2575 📷 **Seven-Car Dynamo Electric Freight $100 retail**

Included: 2360 Pennsylvania GG-1; 6530 fire prevention car; 6828 flatcar with Harnischfeger crane; 6464-900 New York Central boxcar; 6827 flatcar with Harnischfeger power shovel; 6736 Detroit & Mackinac hopper; 6560 crane; 6437 Pennsylvania caboose; twelve 31 curved and six 32 straight track; 39-25 operating packet; tube of lubricant; instructions.

The only new item in this outfit was the 6437 Pennsylvania caboose discussed in the outfit 2574 listing. However, collector interest lies in the locomotive to which the caboose was perfectly matched—the spectacular Pennsylvania GG-1.

Returning after a two-year absence, during which the tooling was changed so that the ventilator heights were even, the big electric continued to wear a single broad stripe on each side. On some 1961 locomotives this stripe was rubber stamped, and on others it was heat stamped. The large keystone emblems were decals. The locomotive came in a tan corrugated carton with liner produced by Mead.

Because the rolling stock consisted of returning items, a mix of Perforated and Orange Picture boxes is not unexpected. The construction equipment kits came in their own black, yellow and white boxes, which were then placed with their black flatcars inside the orange component boxes. These loads are fragile and as mentioned earlier often have had parts replaced with MPC-produced pieces. The set box was a solid orange two-tier type.

Excellent	Like New	Scarcity
3,000	5,000	7

2576 Four-Car Super Chief Streamline $100 retail

Included: 2383P/2383T Santa Fe A-A F-3 units; two 2562 Regal Pass Vista Domes; 2563 Indian Falls Pullman; 2561 Vista Valley observation; twelve 31 curved and six 32 straight track; 39-25 operating packet; tube of lubricant; instructions.

The red-striped Santa Fe extruded-aluminum passenger cars were once again fittingly combined with a pair of F-3 diesels of the same road name to create this outfit. All the components had been previously produced and came in Perforated-front boxes, including the locomotives. The outfit box was a tan two-tier corrugated carton. As always, beware of replacement stripes and windows on the passenger cars.

Excellent	Like New	Scarcity
4,000	6,500	6

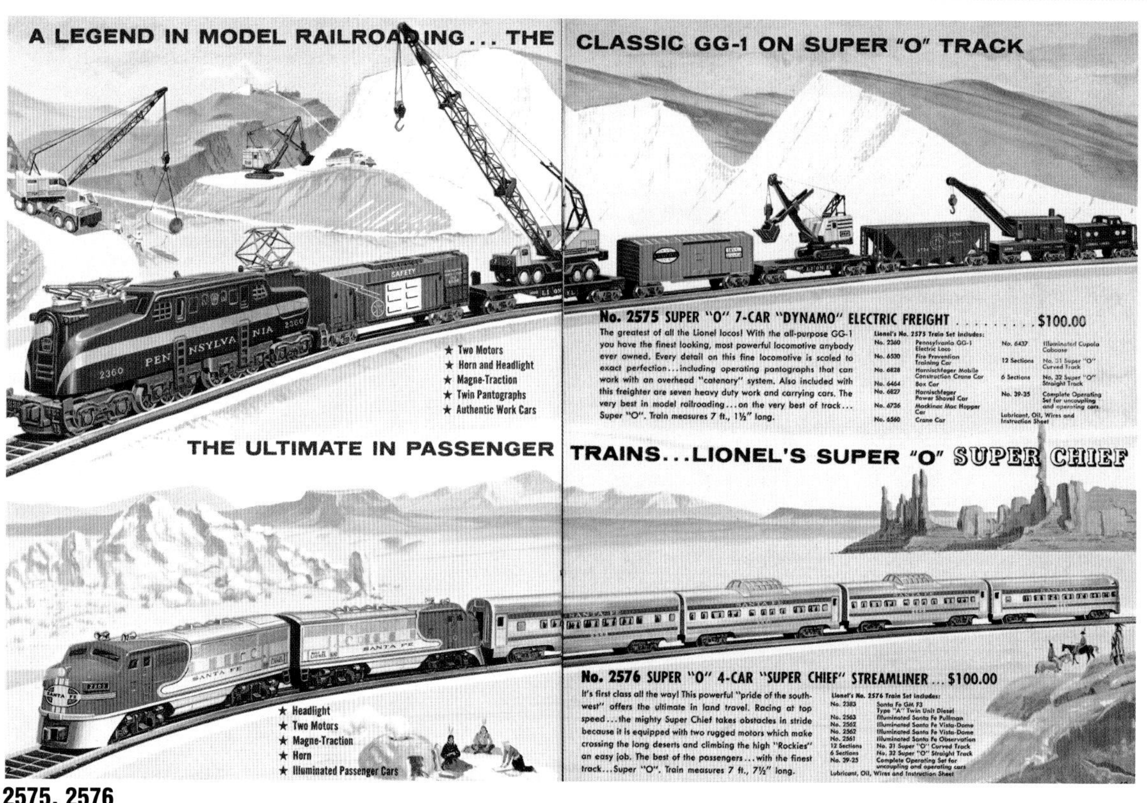

2575, 2576

CHAPTER 19

1962

LIONEL
1962

Lionel continued their subtle campaign of reducing manufacturing costs during this year, involving many minor changes. The tiny pads previously found on the inner surfaces of the AAR-type truck side frames were removed, resulting in a smooth surface. The chrome plating previously used on the 6414 automobile bumpers was deleted. Also, half-sections of track replaced one of the straight sections of Super 0 previously included in those outfits.

Packaging was essentially unchanged from the previous year, as were most set components. Many of the new items were space related.

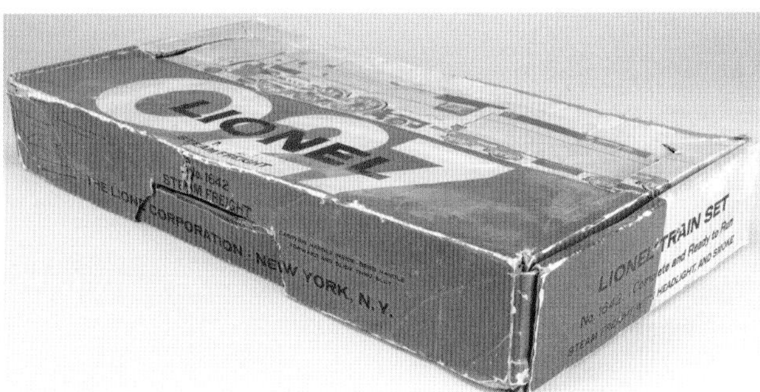

Lionel used this box, first introduced in 1960, for most of the 027 outfits shown in the 1961 catalog. In 1962, dividers were used to hold the unboxed outfit components in place. This type of box included a pasteboard suite case-style handle that often rips. Further, a few sets were shipped in tan conventional corrugated boxes.

This style box, referred to as the Orange Picture box, was made of glossy orange cardstock and had a white panel with an illustration of a steam and diesel locomotive on the front. The city names "NEW YORK" and "CHICAGO" appeared on the box, as did the corporate name "THE LIONEL CORPORATION." This is the box that was in use from 1961 through 1964.

The most inexpensive outfits of 1962 came in this box with locomotives racing across its top.

This shiny overall orange outfit box was used for Super 0 sets, as well as the better 027 outfits.

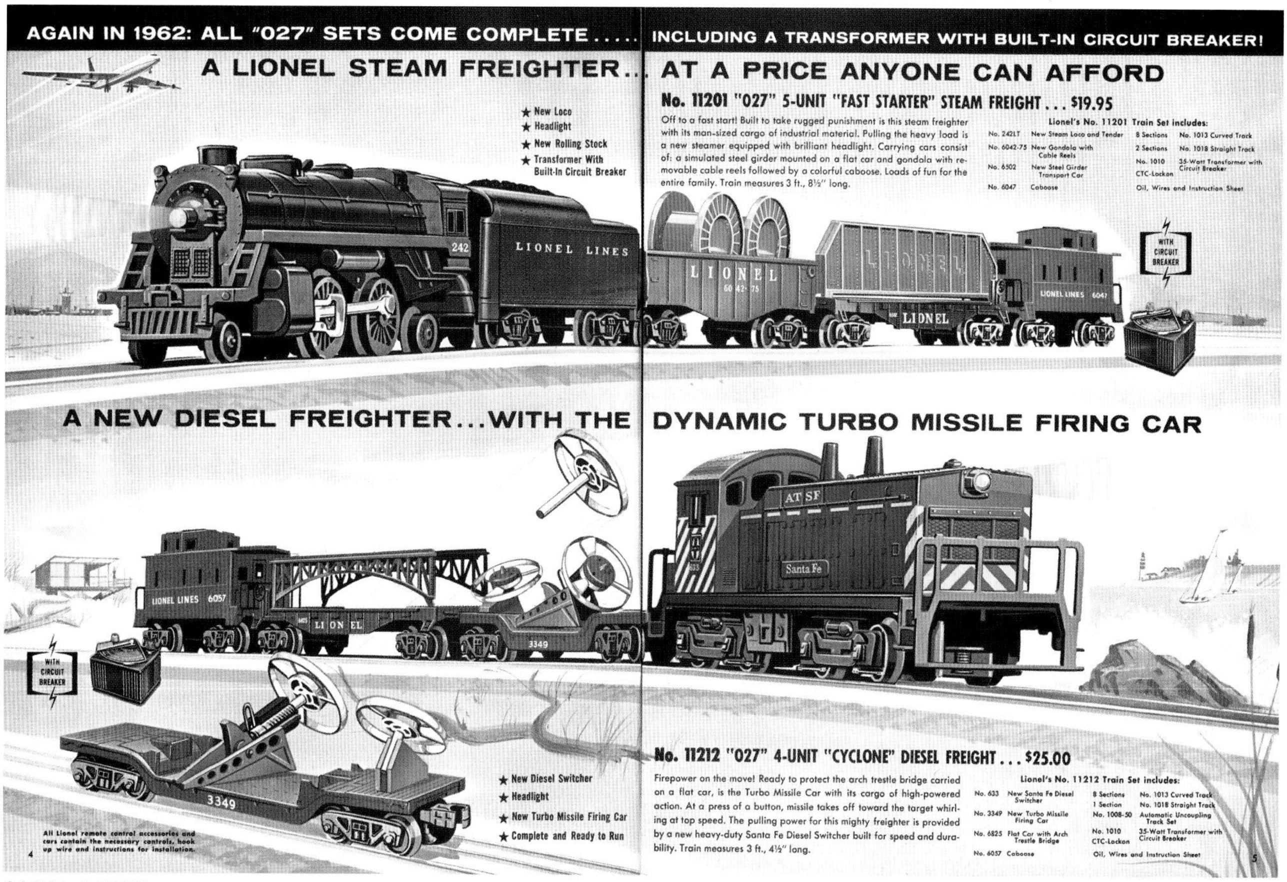

AGAIN IN 1962: ALL "027" SETS COME COMPLETE..... INCLUDING A TRANSFORMER WITH BUILT-IN CIRCUIT BREAKER!

A LIONEL STEAM FREIGHTER... AT A PRICE ANYONE CAN AFFORD

★ New Loco
★ Headlight
★ New Rolling Stock
★ Transformer With Built-In Circuit Breaker

No. 11201 "027" 5-UNIT "FAST STARTER" STEAM FREIGHT... $19.95

Off to a fast start! Built to take rugged punishment is this steam freighter with its man-sized cargo of industrial material. Pulling the heavy load is a new steamer equipped with brilliant headlight. Carrying cars consist of: a simulated steel girder mounted on a flat car and gondola with removable cable reels followed by a colorful caboose. Loads of fun for the entire family. Train measures 3 ft., 8½" long.

Lionel's No. 11201 Train Set includes:

No. 242LT New Steam Loco and Tender
No. 6042-75 New Gondola with Cable Reels
No. 6502 New Steel Girder Transport Car
No. 6047 Caboose
8 Sections No. 1013 Curved Track
2 Sections No. 1018 Straight Track
No. 1010 35-Watt Transformer with Circuit Breaker
CTC-Lockon
Oil, Wires and Instruction Sheet

WITH CIRCUIT BREAKER

A NEW DIESEL FREIGHTER... WITH THE DYNAMIC TURBO MISSILE FIRING CAR

WITH CIRCUIT BREAKER

★ New Diesel Switcher
★ Headlight
★ New Turbo Missile Firing Car
★ Complete and Ready to Run

All Lionel remote control accessories and cars contain the necessary controls, hook up wire and instructions for installation.

4

No. 11212 "027" 4-UNIT "CYCLONE" DIESEL FREIGHT... $25.00

Firepower on the move! Ready to protect the arch trestle bridge carried on a flat car, is the Turbo Missile Car with its cargo of high-powered action. At a press of a button, missile takes off toward the target whirling at top speed. The pulling power for this mighty freighter is provided by a new heavy-duty Santa Fe Diesel Switcher built for speed and durability. Train measures 3 ft., 4½" long.

Lionel's No. 11212 Train Set includes:

No. 633 New Santa Fe Diesel Switcher
No. 3349 New Turbo Missile Firing Car
No. 6825 Flat Car with Arch Trestle Bridge
No. 6057 Caboose
8 Sections No. 1013 Curved Track
1 Section No. 1018 Straight Track
No. 1008-50 Automatic Uncoupling Track Set
No. 1010 35-Watt Transformer with Circuit Breaker
CTC-Lockon
Oil, Wires and Instruction Sheet

5

11201, 11212

027-Gauge

11001 **Advance catalog, no retail**

Included: 1060 steam locomotive with operating headlight; 1060T tender; 6402 flatcar with cable reels; 6042 gondola with canisters; 6067 caboose; eight 1013 curved and two 1018 straight track; 1026 25-watt transformer; CTC Lockon; tube of lubricant; instructions.

This economy-minded outfit was not shown in the consumer catalog, but it was shown in the 1961 dealer advance catalog. Minimal expense was the driving concern in the production of the components of this set. Non-operating couplers mounted on arch-bar trucks were used throughout the set, and neither the caboose nor the flatcar had any paint or stamping applied. The General-style flatcar was produced in both maroon and gray. The only superfluous items in the outfit were the canisters riding in the gondola and the cable reels held to the flatcar with an elastic band.

Packaging for this outfit could be either the display type or tan two-tier set box.

Excellent	Like New	Scarcity
75	150	3

11011 **Advance catalog, no retail**

Included: 222 Rio Grande Alco A-unit; 6076 Lehigh Valley hopper; 3510 satellite launching car; 6120 work caboose; eight 1013 curved and two 1018 straight track; 1026 25-watt transformer; CTC Lockon; tube of lubricant; instructions.

While hardly spectacular, this outfit does contain some moderately collectable items. Chief among these is the unnumbered red 3510 satellite launching car. Also sought after is the undecorated yellow work caboose with black stamped-steel frame and the yellow Rio Grande Alco. The work caboose, hopper and satellite car all came with arch-bar trucks and non-operating couplers. The set came in a display box.

Excellent	Like New	Scarcity
200	450	X

11201 **Fast Starter Steam Freight** **$19.95 retail**

Included: 242 steam locomotive with operating headlight; 1060T tender; 6042-75 gondola with cable reels; 6502 flatcar with girder; 6047 caboose; eight 1013 curved and two 1018 straight track; 1010 35-watt transformer; CTC Lockon; tube of lubricant; instructions.

THE DELIGHTFUL NEW COP & HOBO CAR...IN A STEAM FREIGHTER THAT FEATURES HEADLIGHT, SMOKE AND EXCLUSIVE MAGNE-TRACTION
HOBO LEAPS OFF... AS COP LEAPS ON
No. 11222 "027" 5-UNIT "VAGABOND" STEAM FREIGHT...$29.95
★ Headlight
★ Smoke
★ Exclusive Magne-Traction
★ New Cop and Hobo Car
Get set for real fun! Barreling down the track at top speed is Lionel's mighty No. 236 steamer, complete with real smoke, blazing headlight and track-gripping Magne-Traction. But what's this . . . there's a policeman chasing a hobo. As the policeman leaps from the train to the trestle, the hobo evades him by jumping from the trestle to the train. Will the policeman catch the hobo? Train measures 3 ft., 9", long.
Lionel's No. 11222 Train Set includes:
No. 236-1050T Steam Loco and Slope Back Tender
No. 3357 New Cop and Hobo Car
No. 6343 Barrel Ramp Car
No. 6119 Work Caboose
8 Sections No. 1013 Curved Track
1 Section No. 1018 Straight Track
No. 1008-50 Automatic Uncoupling Track Set
No. 1025 45-Watt Transformer with Circuit Breaker
CTC-Lockon
Oil, Wires and Instruction Sheet
236
LIONEL LINES
LIONEL LINES 3357
HYDRAULIC PLATFORM MAINTENANCE CAR
LIONEL
DL&W 6119
WITH CIRCUIT BREAKER
A MIGHTY NEW HAVEN DIESEL FREIGHTER... COMPLETE WITH MAGNE-TRACTION, HEADLIGHT AND NEW MERCURY CAPSULE CARRYING CAR
NEW HAVEN
N H
232
LIONEL
NYC
MERCURY PROJECT CAPE CANAVERAL
LIONEL LINES 6057
WITH CIRCUIT BREAKER
No. 11232 "027" 5-UNIT "NEW HAVEN" DIESEL FREIGHT...$29.95
★ New Diesel Unit
★ Headlight and Magne-Traction
★ Helicopter Launching Car
★ New Mercury Capsule Carrying Car
On its way to the missile site! There's a missile launching to be made and this freighter has been chosen to carry the valuable mercury capsules. A helicopter has been assigned to serve as an aerial reconnaissance unit to protect the cargo. The rugged "pride of the northeast" New Haven diesel is supplying the pulling power and comes well equipped with blazing headlight and track-gripping Magne-Traction. Train measures 4 ft., 2½" long.
Lionel's No. 11232 Train Set includes:
No. 232 New! New Haven Diesel
No. 3410 Helicopter Launching Car
No. 6062 Gondola with Cable Reels
No. 6413 New Mercury Capsule Carrying Car
No. 6057-50 Caboose to match loco
8 Sections No. 1013 Curved Track
1 Section No. 1018 Straight Track
No. 1008-50 Automatic Uncoupling Track Set
No. 1025 45-Watt Transformer with Circuit Breaker
CTC-Lockon
Oil, Wires and Instruction Sheet
6
7

11222, 11232

A new Scout-type steam locomotive with traction tire and operating headlight powered this short freight set. To hold costs down, all the rolling stock in this outfit was fitted with arch-bar trucks and non-operating couplers. Likely indicative of its low price point, the set came packaged in the same style display box as did the advance catalog sets—a box that featured a steam and diesel locomotive racing across the front.

The flatcar did not have its number stamped on it, although it was lettered "LIONEL" in white. If the flatcar was black, it carried a single orange girder, while the red version was loaded with a black girder. The blue gondola bore a pair of orange cable reels.

Two non-descript freight cars complete the set. A long plastic flatcar lettered simply "Lionel," which hauled an orange girder, and a small blue gondola. Lionel internally numbered this car 6042-75, which specified the car was laden with cable reels, but only a white "6042" was stamped on the car sides.

Excellent	Like New	Scarcity
90	175	1

11212 📷 Four-Unit Cyclone Diesel Freight $25 retail

Included: 633 Santa Fe NW-2 diesel switcher; 3349 turbo missile launcher; 6825 flatcar with trestle bridge; 6057 SP-type caboose; eight 1013 curved and two 1018 straight track; 1008 camtrol; 1010 35-watt transformer; CTC Lockon; tube of lubricant; instructions.

The 3349 turbo missile launching car was new for 1962. It can be distinguished from the almost identical 3309 by virtue of the 3349's two operating couplers. Strangely, the locomotive, however, had only one coupler attached at the rear. These components, along with the previously described flatcar with trestle bridge and the SP-style caboose, were packed most often in a display-type box, although some sets have surfaced in tan two-tier boxes.

Excellent	Like New	Scarcity
225	375	2

11222 📷 Five-Unit Vaga-Bond Steam Freight $29.95 retail

Included: 236 steam locomotive with operating headlight, smoke and Magne-traction; 1050T tender; 6343 barrel ramp car; 3357 cop and hobo car; 6119-100 work caboose; eight 1013 curved and two 1018 straight track; 1008 camtrol; 1025 45-watt transformer; CTC Lockon; tube of lubricant; instructions.

The Scout-type steam locomotive included in this set had many of the features normally reserved for much larger steamers—smoke, operating headlight and Magne-traction. However, it was paired with a rather disappointing slope-back tender with arch-bar trucks.

Behind the locomotive were the returning barrel ramp car and red, gray and black work caboose, and these cars were joined by the new 3357 cop and hobo car. This car, based on the 6014-type boxcar, rode on AAR-type trucks in this outfit. The version in this set can be distinguished by two full rows of rivets to the left of the doors. The trestle components came packed in a tan cardboard box, which was positioned in the outfit's orange-and-white display box.

Excellent	Like New	Scarcity
125	200	3

11232 Five-Unit Diesel Freight $29.95 retail

Included: 232 New Haven Alco A-unit; 3410 flatcar with helicopter; 6062 gondola with cable reels; 6413 Mercury capsule carrier; 6057-50 caboose; eight 1013 curved and two 1018 straight track; 1008 camtrol; 1025 45-watt transformer; CTC Lockon; tube of lubricant; instructions.

The 232 New Haven was a new item for 1962, and this was the only set to contain the new Alco. The 3410 manually operated helicopter-launching car was a returning item from 1961. Beware of reproduction helicopters, helicopter components, launching spools and tail supports.

The body of the new 6413 Mercury Capsule carrying car was molded from the tooling used to create the Allis-Chalmers heat exchanger car. The steel plates and Mercury capsules with their combination wire and elastic retainers are unique to this car, and have all been reproduced. The version of the Mercury Capsule car found in this set had two operating couplers.

The orange 6057-50 caboose nicely complemented the New Haven Alco at the other end of the train. Outfit packaging consisted of the orange-and-white display box.

Excellent	Like New	Scarcity
425	700	6

11252 Seven-Unit Diesel Freight $39.95 retail

Included: 211P/211T Texas Special Alco A-A units; 6448 exploding boxcar; 3509 satellite launching car; 3349 turbo missile launcher; 6463 rocket fuel tank car; 6057 caboose; eight 1013 curved and four 1018 straight track; 1008 camtrol; 1025 45-watt transformer; CTC Lockon; tube of lubricant; instructions.

The double-A Texas Special locomotive at the front of this set was new for 1962 and was striking in its red and white paint scheme. The 3349 turbo missile launching car came with operating couplers on each end while the 3509, in its second year, was a manually operated version of the satellite launching car. Collectors are advised to beware of reproduction turbo missiles, satellites and launcher components.

The white with red lettering tank car is difficult to find in pristine condition. The outfit was packaged in an orange and white display-type box, without component boxes.

Excellent	Like New	Scarcity
400	850	5

1962

11242 Trail Blazer Steam Freight $39.95 retail

Included: 233 steam locomotive with operating headlight, smoke and Magne-traction; 233W tender; 6162 gondola with canisters; 6476 Lehigh Valley hopper; 6465-110 Cities Service double-dome tank car; 6017 caboose; eight 1013 curved and four 1018 straight track; 1008 camtrol; 1073 60-watt transformer; 147 whistle controller.

The locomotive, whistle tender, as well as the other components of this outfit had all been introduced in prior years and thus are described elsewhere in this volume. An orange-and-white display box housed the outfit.

Excellent	Like New	Scarcity
80	125	2

11268 Six-Unit Diesel Freight $49.95 retail

Included: 2365 Chesapeake & Ohio GP-7; 3470 aerial target launcher; 6501 flatcar with jet motorboat; 3619 reconnaissance copter car; 3349 turbo missile launcher; 6017 caboose; eight 1013 curved and three 1018 straight track; 6029 uncoupling section; 1073 60-watt transformer; CTC Lockon; tube of lubricant; instructions.

Lionel applied new paint and graphics to their GP-7 in 1962 to create the attractive 2365 Chesapeake & Ohio locomotive included in this set. This locomotive was packaged in a tan corrugated carton. The rolling stock in the outfit was packaged in Orange Picture boxes. Notably, inside the 3470 box was a small envelope containing the balloons that served as targets, while a foil envelope was packed in the 6501 box. This foil envelope contained baking soda, which was used as propellant for the "jet boat" that the unnumbered flat car transported.

The 6501 included in this outfit offered the bizarre opportunity to play with part of your electric train set in water. A small plastic boat was the cargo for this car and its design was such that it was propelled through the water by a reaction motor. Pellets of baking soda, supplied with the car, along with warm water, were put in a compartment in the boat hull. The ensuing reaction would push the boat about 10 feet through the water. The deck of the boat was brown; its hull was white and had a jet nozzle protruding from it.

The yellow-bodied 3619 had black roof halves and rode on AAR-type trucks with operating couplers. It launched a red HO-sized helicopter. Both the helicopter and the roofs for the car have been expertly reproduced.

All the components, in their individual boxes, were packed in a shiny orange two-tier outfit box.

Excellent	Like New	Scarcity
900	1,500	4

11278 Seven-Unit Plainsman Steam Freight $49.95 retail

Included: 2037 2-6-4 steam locomotive with operating headlight, smoke and Magne-traction; 233W tender; 6825 flatcar with trestle bridge; 6162 gondola with canisters; 6473 rodeo car; 6050-110 Swift savings bank car; 6017 SP-type caboose; eight 1013 curved and four 1018 straight track; 1008 camtrol; 1073 60-watt transformer; 147 whistle controller.

The reliable but common 2037 powered this consist of freight cars. The box and rodeo cars were new for 1962, while the remainder of the outfit contained repeat items.

The red-stamped 6473 rode on AAR-type trucks with operating couplers. A tiny flaw in the mold resulted in one of the slots being partially filled in near the upper right corner of one side of the car throughout 1960. The boxcar had a slot in its roofwalk, allowing it to serve as a coin bank. Its Orange Picture box was numbered 6050-110. Orange picture boxes were used for all the contents of the outfit except the locomotive, which came in a tan corrugated carton. The outfit box was a glossy solid-orange two-tier style.

Excellent	Like New	Scarcity
250	450	4

11288 Seven-Unit Orbiter Diesel Freight $49.95 retail

Included: 229P/229C Minneapolis & St. Louis Alco A-B units; 6512 cherry picker car; 3413 Mercury capsule launcher; 6413 Mercury capsule carrier; 6463 rocket fuel tank car; 6059 Minneapolis & St. Louis caboose; eight 1013 curved and four 1018 straight track; 1008 camtrol; 1073 60-watt transformer; 147 horn controller.

This outfit revolves around the Mercury Space program, and though this set contains many desirable and collectable items, but for many enthusiasts the Orange Picture box containing the red-painted M&St.L. caboose is the challenging item to locate.

This outfit contained both the 3413 Mercury capsule launcher and the 6512 cherry picture car, which were designed to operate in tandem.

The 3413 had an unpainted red plastic chassis with a gray plastic superstructure mounted on it. "LIONEL" was heat stamped in white serif letters on both sides of the body, but the catalog number was not found anywhere on the car. The rocket launcher contained a coil spring, which was compressed during the manual cocking action. An electromagnetic uncoupling track section was used to release the spring tension. The idea was that the spring would hurl the rocket upward. The white booster was tied to the railing of the superstructure with a string, causing it to stop traveling while inertia carried the parachute-equipped gray plastic capsule further upward. Its red parachute then opened, allowing it to gently float down. In reality, the spring-loaded mechanism often released with the car still in the carton, destroying the box, and the force of the spring was such that when the slack came out of the string during launching it often broke the handrail it was tied to.

This car was built using various shades of red and gray plastic components, and in this outfit the car had two operating couplers. The rocket, capsule and parachute have all been reproduced.

As a companion to the 3413 Mercury capsule launching car, this outfit included a 6512 cherry picker car. Its body was unpainted black plastic and the only markings on it were "LIONEL" heat stamped in white on both sides of the car. AAR-type plastic trucks with operating couplers were riveted directly to the body of these cars. The operating mechanism was adapted from the 3512 fireman and ladder car. At the end of the extension ladder was a newly designed orange plastic cage containing a diminutive astronaut figure. Upon contact with the capsule the figure appeared, seeming to enter the space ship. Much of the operating mechanism of this car has been reproduced, so caution should be used.

The body of the 6413 Mercury Capsule carrying car was molded from the tooling used to create the Allis-Chalmers heat exchanger car. The steel plates and Mercury capsules with their combination wire and elastic retainers are unique to this car, and have all been reproduced. The version of this car found in this set is blue, and has two operating couplers.

The powered A-unit came in a tan corrugated carton, while the new for 1962 matching B-unit came in an Orange Picture box, as did the rest of the set components. The outfit box was the glossy two-tier solid orange style box.

Excellent	Like New	Scarcity
750	1,200	5

11298 Seven-Unit Vigilant Steam Freight $59.95 retail
Included: 2037 2-6-4 steam locomotive with operating headlight, smoke and Magne-traction; 233W tender; 6448 exploding boxcar; 3330 flatcar with submarine kit; 3419 flatcar with operating helicopter; 6544 missile firing car; 6017 caboose; eight 1013 curved and three 1018 straight track; 6029 uncoupling section; 1063 75-watt transformer; CTC Lockon; tube of lubricant; instructions.

Though none of the military items that make up this outfit are scarce, they can be hard to find in all-original, undamaged condition. This is particularly the case with the 6544 missile firing car, which often has its brake stands damaged or, as is usually the case with the control panel and missiles, missing altogether.

The submarine, itself not hard to find, is truly scarce in complete unassembled condition in its original cellophane bag. The submarine, as well as its components, has been reproduced quite convincingly.

The 3419 helicopter car had plastic knuckles in both its operating couplers. The fixed portion of the launching mechanism, when viewed from the bottom, lacks the large hole found on 1963 up cars. This car could have either the gray Navy helicopter with single-blade rotor or the solid yellow helicopter normally associated with the 419 heliport. Beware of reproduction helicopters, copter components, launching spools and tail supports.

All the components of this set were individually boxed before being packed in the solid-orange two-tier outfit box.

Excellent	Like New	Scarcity
400	750	5

11308 Six-Unit Diesel Passenger $69.95 retail
Included: 218P/218T Santa Fe Alco A-A units with horn; two 2412 Vista Domes; 2414 Pullman; 2416 observation; eight 1013 curved and three 1018 straight track; 6029 uncoupling section; 1063 75-watt transformer; CTC Lockon; tube of lubricant; instructions.

Blue-striped Santa Fe passenger cars were paired with Santa Fe Alco A-units wearing the classic ATSF "Warbonnet" paint scheme. The dummy A-unit, as well as the passenger cars were all packed in Orange Picture boxes, while the powered unit relied on a tan corrugated carton for protection. Passenger sets have limited play value, essentially just trundling along in an oval, hence have lower sales than do freight sets, but likewise tend to suffer less damage.

Excellent	Like New	Scarcity
600	1,000	4

1962

Gift Pack

12502 Prairie-Rider Gift Pack $35 retail
Included: 1862 4-4-0 General with operating headlight; 1862T tender; 3376 giraffe car; 1877 flatcar with horses or 6473 rodeo car; 1866 mail-baggage car; 1865 passenger car.

With sales of General outfits seemingly never meeting Lionel's expectations, the company chose turn to the "Gift Pack" to help exhaust the inventory of these products. Gift Packs lack track and transformers and were intended to supplement existing miniature railroad empires. Dubbed the "PRAIRIE-RIDER," this outfit came in an orange-and-white display-style outfit box.

Excellent	Like New	Scarcity
600	1,100	5

12512 Enforcer Gift Pack $39.95 retail

Included: 45 U.S. Marine Corps mobile missile launcher; 3470 aerial target launcher; 3413 Mercury capsule launcher; 3619 reconnaissance copter car; 3349 turbo missile launcher; 6017 caboose.

Strangely, this set, one of the most desirable of all 027 space and military sets isn't a set at all in the traditional sense of the word. The Enforcer, like the Prairie Rider, was a gift set, packed without track or transformer in an orange-and-white display-style outfit box.

The 45, which doubled as both a missile launcher and a locomotive, had been introduced two years previously. Beware of reproduction missiles, crewmen and control panels on this piece. The remainder of the set components was new in 1962 and has been discussed earlier in this chapter. A die-cut insert held the unboxed components in place in the set box.

Excellent	Like New	Scarcity
900	1,800	5

Super 0

13008 Six-Unit Champion Steam Freight $49.95 retail

Included: 637 2-6-4 steam locomotive with operating headlight, smoke and Magne-traction; 736W tender; 6448 exploding boxcar; 6501 flatcar with jet motorboat; 3349 turbo missile launcher; 6119-100 work caboose; twelve 31 curved, one 32 straight and one 34 half-straight track; 39-25 operating packet; tube of lubricant; instructions.

But for the track, little distinguished this outfit from the numerous 027 military sets offered in 1962. All the rolling stock in this set also appeared in 027 outfits and are described above, while the locomotive, the 637 was merely the reliable 027 2037 stamped with a three digit O-Gauge number—637.

The locomotive came in an appropriately numbered tan corrugated carton, while Orange Picture boxes were used by the tender and rolling stock. The outfit box was a two-tier orange container.

Excellent	Like New	Scarcity
400	750	5

13018 Six-Unit Starfire Diesel Freight $49.95 retail

Included: 616 Santa Fe NW-2 diesel switcher with horn; 6448 exploding boxcar; 6500 flatcar with airplane; 6650 flatcar with IRBM launcher; 3519 satellite launching car; 6017-235 Santa Fe caboose; twelve 31 curved, one 32 straight and one 34 half-straight track; 39-25 operating packet; tube of lubricant; instructions.

Another of the military-themed Super 0 sets from 1962 was this outfit, which featured matching Santa Fe locomotive and caboose. The carry-over black diesel switcher had white "Zebra" safety stripes applied to its cab, while the red 6017-235 caboose—moderately collectable in its own right—should not be confused with the very scarce 6357-50 illuminated Santa Fe caboose from 1960.

Though still very desirable, the more common version of the airplane has white lettering on red upper wings and fuselage. The lower fuselage half and propeller were white.

A less common, and hence more collectable, version of the airplane had a reversed color scheme. It had white upper surfaces, red lower surfaces and a red propeller.

The most desirable car in this outfit and the only one not already discussed in this book is the 6500 flatcar with airplane. The car itself was the rather plain black flatcar lettered "LIONEL," but the desirable part was the red and white airplane it carried. The red and white Bonanza single-engine airplane had folding wings held together by four rivets and was secured to the car using a 6418-9 rubber band. The airplane had more markings than the car, being heat stamped with "BONANZA" on each side and the FAA registration number N2742B on one wing. The more common version of the airplane, the 6500-10, has white lettering on red upper wings and fuselage with white lower fuselage half and propeller. A less common airplane, the 6500-26, had a reversed color scheme. It had white upper surfaces, red lower surfaces and a red propeller. Beware; both marked and unmarked reproductions of this airplane exist. Also available are reproduction repair parts, including the oft-broken propeller.

This car, like the rest of the outfit components, including the locomotive, came packaged in an Orange Picture box.

Excellent	Like New	Scarcity
1,200	2,000	6

13028 Six-Unit Defender Diesel Freight $59.95 retail

Included: 2359 Boston and Maine GP-9; 3470 aerial target launcher; 3820 U.S. Marine Corps flatcar with operating submarine; 3665 Minuteman car; 3349 turbo missile launcher; 6017-100 Boston and Maine caboose; 943 exploding ammo dump; twelve 31 curved, one 32 straight and one 34 half-straight track; 39-25 operating packet; tube of lubricant; instructions.

The Boston and Maine GP-9 returned for a second time to lead a space and military outfit. While this blue, black and white locomotive is attractive and desirable to enthusiasts, the set component collectors truly covet is the 3820 Marine Corps flatcar with operating submarine. Originally produced for the "Land-Sea and Air Gift Pack" of the previous year, surplus cars were used in this outfit, as well as uncataloged sets of 1963. This car not only came with a submarine stamped "3830" (all 3820-stamped submarines are fakes), it even came in a relabeled 3830 component box.

The caboose in this outfit, 6017-100, wore Boston and Maine markings, thus matching the locomotive. The remainder of the outfit components has been previously discussed. Orange Picture boxes were used for all outfit components save the locomotive, which came in a tan corrugated carton. The outfit itself came in a solid orange two-tier set box.

Excellent	Like New	Scarcity
900	1,500	3

13036 Six-Unit Plainsman Steam Outfit $59.95 retail

Included: 1872 4-4-0 General with operating headlight, smoke and Magne-traction; 1872T tender; 1876 illuminated mail-baggage car; 1875W illuminated passenger car with whistle; 6445 Fort Knox car; 3370 sheriff and outlaw car; twelve 31 curved, one 32 straight and one 34 half-straight track; 39-25 operating packet; tube of lubricant; instructions.

Lionel made yet another effort to move its Super 0 Generals by creating this outfit, which came in a solid orange two-tier outfit box, with a mixture of both boxed and unboxed set components.

For the first time, Lionel included the 6445 Fort Knox car with a General outfit, as well as the animated 3370 operating Sheriff and Outlaw car. The 6445 is discussed elsewhere in this volume. The 3370 included in this outfit had trucks with one-piece Delrin knuckles in both operating couplers.

The lighted passenger cars, locomotive and tender were unchanged from the previous year.

Excellent	Like New	Scarcity
900	1,650	4

13048 Seven-Unit Steam Freight $75 retail

Included: 736 Berkshire steam locomotive with operating headlight, smoke and Magne-traction; 736W tender; 6414

Evans Auto Loader; 6440 flatcar with vans; 3362 helium tank unloading car; 6822 searchlight car; 6437 Pennsylvania caboose; twelve 31 curved, one 32 straight and one 34 half-straight track; 39-25 operating packet; tube of lubricant; instructions.

This set was comprised of high-quality traditionally themed components. However, comparing this set to similar outfits from only a few years before, one can see cost-cutting measures.

The 736W tender was equipped with plastic AAR-type trucks—as was all the rolling stock of this outfit. The 6414 came with four pale yellow automobiles that did not have chrome-plated bumpers—cheaper for Lionel to make—but today more desirable than the four-color assortment of autos with chrome trim that originally rode on these cars.

The vans riding on the 6440 did not have metal nameplates and had only single rear wheels, and the car lacked the pressed steel center-mounted retaining rack found on the earlier 6430 and 3460 versions.

The 3362 helium tank unloading car was a simplified version of the 3361 log dump, using a spring-loaded dump mechanism rather than the solenoid-operated mechanism of the 3361. The version of the 3362 found in this set had AAR-type trucks with die-cast coupler knuckles retained by rivets.

Fortunately, the Pennsylvania markings on the porthole caboose at rear matched the name on the flanks of the tender.

The locomotive came in a tan corrugated box, the balance of the set components being packaged in Orange Picture boxes that were then placed inside a solid-orange two-tier set carton.

Excellent	Like New	Scarcity
800	1,500	3

13058 Seven-Unit Vanguard Diesel Freight $89.95 retail

Included: 2383P/2383T Santa Fe A-A F-3 units; 6512 cherry picker car; 3413 Mercury capsule launcher; 3619 reconnaissance helicopter car; 470 missile launching platform with 6470 exploding boxcar; 6437 Pennsylvania caboose; twelve 31 curved, three 32 straight and one 34 half-straight track; 39-25 operating packet; tube of lubricant; instructions.

This outfit in many ways was a conflict of marketing strategies. The classic A-A F-3 diesels, wearing Santa Fe's timeless warbonnet passenger paint scheme, pulled an array of futuristic and often toy-like space-themed cars, followed by a Pennsylvania porthole caboose!

All the space-related cars in this set have already been discussed in the 027 portion of this chapter. Lionel likely included the 470, which was new in 1959, in this set merely to rid itself of otherwise dead inventory—the accessory was not cataloged in subsequent years. The launcher in this outfit could come in a brown box, or more commonly in a yellow box. In some instances, the 6470 exploding boxcar, which was component boxed inside the 470 box, was packed in an over-stamped 6448 box.

The locomotives each came in their own tan corrugated cartons made by Mead, and the rolling stock was packaged in Orange Picture boxes before being placed in an oversized solid orange two-tier outfit box.

Excellent	Like New	Scarcity
1,600	2,700	4

13068 Eight-Unit Goliath Electric Freight $100 retail

Included: 2360 Pennsylvania solid-stripe GG-1; 6416 Boat Loader; 6464-725 New Haven boxcar; 6530 fire prevention car; 6828 flatcar with Harnischfeger crane; 6827 flatcar with Harnischfeger power shovel; 6475 pickle vat car; 6437 Pennsylvania porthole caboose; twelve 31 curved, five 32 straight and one 34 half-straight track; 39-35 operating packet; tube of lubricant; instructions.

This was the top-of-the-line freight outfit for 1962, and even today most collectors would find it top of the line. Although only the 6464-725 boxcar was new for 1961, all the cars in this outfit, except the ubiquitous 6437 Pennsylvania porthole caboose (which did at least match the locomotive) are sought after collector's items.

The orange with black door New Haven boxcar came in a box labeled "6464-735." The remainder of the rolling stock has been discussed previously in this book and for this outfit was packaged in Orange Picture boxes. The unassembled steam shovel and construction crane kits came in their own black, yellow and white boxes, which along with the cars, were then packed in the orange Lionel boxes.

In 1962, the final variation of the 2360 emerged. While at a glance it appears identical to the previously issued stamped-stripe version, closer examination reveals that the letters and numbers were applied with decals, rather than being stamped on. Regardless of marking method used, the GG-1 in this outfit had even-height ventilators and came in a liner-equipped tan carton made by Mead. The outfit box was the orange two-tier carton.

Excellent	Like New	Scarcity
3,000	5,000	7

13078 Five-Unit Presidential Passenger $125 retail

Included: 2360 Pennsylvania solid-stripe GG-1; two 2522 President Harrison Vista Domes; 2523 President Garfield Pullman; 2521 President McKinley observation; twelve 31 curved, five 32 straight and one 34 half-straight track; 39-35 operating packet; tube of lubricant; instructions.

Though not shown in the consumer catalog, this outfit is included here because it was listed in the 1962 dealer advance catalog. This was likely an effort by Lionel to move unsold 1961 inventory on the shelves of the factory and wholesalers. Readers should refer to the 1961 chapter for details of this outfit.

Excellent	Like New	Scarcity
3,600	6,500	6

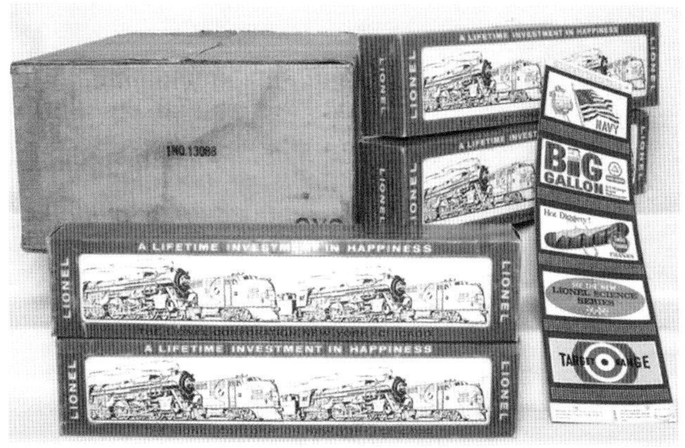

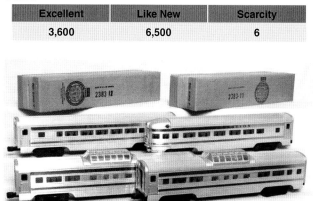

13088 Six-Unit Presidential Passenger $120 retail

Included: 2383P/2383T Santa Fe A-A F-3 units; two 2522 President Harrison Vista Domes; 2523 President Garfield Pullman; 2521 President McKinley observation; twelve 31 curved, five 32 straight and one 34 half-straight track; 39-25 operating packet; tube of lubricant; instructions.

While all extruded aluminum passenger outfits led by Santa Fe F-3's are attractive, many are common. Though valuable, even the Presidential sets are not that difficult to find. What makes this version collectable is the boxes the extruded aluminum passenger cars came in—the rare Perforated Picture box. These boxes combined the traits of both the newer Orange Picture box with the cardstock of the Perforated box.

The twin diesels came in tan corrugated boxes made my Mead and the set carton was the tan conventional two-tier style.

Excellent	Like New	Scarcity
2,500	4,200	5

Values for each condition are in U.S. dollars. | **Scarcity** = Scale from 1-8 with 8 being the hardest to find.

Chapter 20

1963

LIONEL
1963
"027" Super "O" HO Trains
Standard & HO Motor Racing
LIONEL LINES
The Leader in Model Railroading...The Pioneer in Model Racing

As was the case throughout the late 1950s and into the 1960s, Lionel tried to lower costs. Unfortunately, this often translated into lower quality. As every piece of rolling stock had two trucks, and most of these had operating couplers, any savings in this area, no matter how minor, multiplied by the huge production quantities could result in sizeable savings. Hence, Lionel sought to improve the AAR-type truck they first introduced in 1957. Accordingly, a new plastic knuckle was introduced with integral plastic spring and pivot points. This eliminated not only the metal knuckle and pin, but also the assembly step of rolling the rivet.

Some cars further reduced costs by removing the operating coupler completely, substituting a fixed coupler molded as one piece with the truck frame. Late in the year both the operating coupler and non-operating coupler trucks were further redesigned. When viewed from the bottom, on the new design the ends of the axles were visible in the journal boxes.

In the same vein, the frames of inexpensive tenders and cabooses were now galvanized rather than painted or blackened and the bodies of these items were held in place by tabs instead of screws.

While components of Super 0 sets were packed in Orange Picture boxes, components of 027 outfits lacked individual boxes. Those outfits were packed in display boxes with cardboard dividers.

027-Gauge

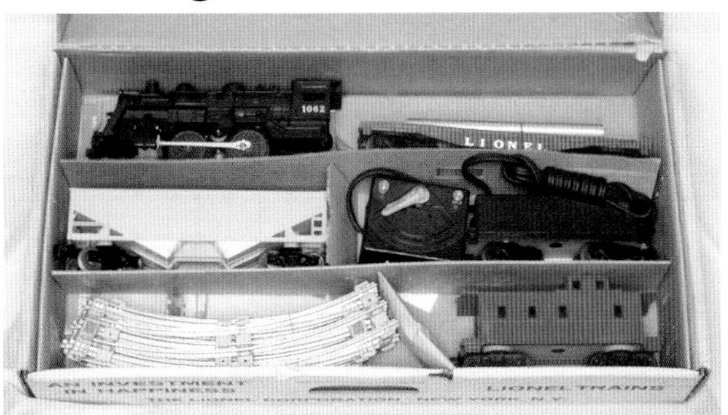

11311 Value Packed Steam Freight $14.95 retail

Included: 1062 steam locomotive with operating headlight; 1061T tender; 6409-25 flatcar with pipes; hopper; 6167-25 caboose; eight 1013 curved track; 1026 25-watt transformer; CTC Lockon; tube of lubricant; instructions.

Lionel's bargain-basement steam engine was one of the few items that was upgraded in 1963. For the first time the loco featured a two-position E-unit and operating headlight. In contrast to this, the slope-back tender body was devoid of stamping and had a non-operating coupler. AAR-type trucks were also used on the unstamped red caboose, which had only one coupler, and it was also fixed.

The undecorated gray hopper car rode on arch-bar trucks, with one each operating and non-operating coupler. The new full-sized, plastic bodied flatcar had AAR-type trucks with non-operating couplers. The number of the car was not stamped on its sides, but "LIONEL" was. It was loaded with three plastic pipes, held in place with an elastic band.

The new style display box was used as packaging for this outfit.

Excellent	Like New	Scarcity
90	150	2

11321 Five-Unit Diesel Freighter $16.95 retail

Included: 221 Rio Grande Alco A-unit; 6076-75 Lehigh Valley hopper; 6042-75 gondola with cable reels; 3309 turbo missile launcher; 6167-50 caboose; eight 1013 curved and two 1018 straight track; 1026 25-watt transformer; CTC Lockon; tube of lubricant; instructions.

New for 1963 was this low-cost ALCO A-unit. Its unpainted yellow body was trimmed only with a black stripe along the roofline and three narrow black stripes along the lower body. "Rio Grande" lettering was heat stamped on the lower rear body panel. The ornamental horn, which had been a feature of every ALCO up to this point, was eliminated, as was the simulated fuel tank, which had been screwed to the bottom of the frame. There was no front coupler and the unit had a closed pilot with reinforcing ledge. The headlight found on earlier units was gone, as was Magne-traction, with traction tires substituted for the latter. Austerity went so far as to eliminate one of the geared axles, resulting in the locomotive having only single-axle drive. A two-position E-unit controlled its direction.

The rolling stock of this outfit was similarly bland. The black Lehigh Valley hopper came with arch-bar trucks with fixed couplers, as did the 3309 turbo missile car. The unmarked 3309 turbo missile car and the nearly identical 3349 turbo missile car confuse many collectors. However, distinguishing the two is really very simple. If the car has operating couplers on each end, it is a 3349. All other variants are 3309.

The blue gondola with cable reel load, as well as the unmarked yellow caboose rode on AAR-type trucks. Both of these cars had non-operating couplers.

Excellent	Like New	Scarcity
250	400	3

11331 Outdoorsman Steam Freight $19.95 retail

Included: 242 2-4-2 steam locomotive with operating headlight; 1060T tender; 6142 gondola with canisters; 6476-25 Lehigh Valley hopper; 6473 rodeo car; 6059-50 Minneapolis & St. Louis SP-type caboose; eight 1013 curved and one 1018 straight track; 6139 uncoupling section; 1010 35-watt transformer; CTC Lockon; tube of lubricant; instructions.

Little of this outfit is of interest to collectors. The steam locomotive was furnished with a 1060T tender, which had a non-operating coupler—usually attached to arch-bar trucks, though occasionally surfacing with AAR-type trucks.

Included in the set was a red hopper with AAR-type trucks and operating couplers. The red-lettered rodeo car from 1963 can be identified by the filled-in slot beside the center door on one side of the car. It had one operating and one non-operating coupler, and rode on AAR-type trucks.

Excellent	Like New	Scarcity
125	200	2

11341 Space-Prober Diesel Freight $25 retail

Included: 634 Santa Fe NW-2 diesel switcher; 6014-325 Frisco boxcar; 3410 helicopter flatcar; 6407 flatcar with rocket; 6463 rocket fuel tank car; 6059-50 Minneapolis & St. Louis SP-type caboose; eight 1013 curved and one 1018 straight track; 6139 uncoupling section; 1010 35-watt transformer; CTC Lockon; tube of lubricant; instructions.

Though from the standpoint of the quality of the items in this set, this outfit was unremarkable, from the collector's standpoint the opposite is true as it contains some of the most desirable items produced in 1963.

Foremost in desirability is the 6407 flatcar with missile. The body of the car was heat stamped "LIONEL," but the number did not appear on the body or the load. It is the load that generates the interest in this car. A large missile with removable Mercury capsule was transported resting in a 6801-64 cradle. The missile was produced by Sterling Plastics, which had developed it as a pencil case as part of their regular product line. The standard Sterling missile included a pencil sharpener in the base of the capsule, a feature omitted on the missiles produced specifically for Lionel. The Sterling Plastics name was always molded into the base of the capsules; reproductions, made from the original tooling, lack this imprint. The car was equipped with AAR-type trucks, with one fixed and one operating coupler.

Also sought after is the 3410 flatcar with helicopter. This car was cataloged only in lower-priced sets such as this one, but not as a separate-sale item. Its body was unpainted light blue plastic with "3410" heat stamped in white to the left of "LIONEL" in serif letters on both sides of the body. The 1963 version of this car had one operating and one non-operating coupler on AAR-type trucks and carried a solid yellow helicopter with an integral tail. The car was designed so that the helicopter could be launched by manually actuating the release, but unlike the similar 3419 there was no provision for triggering the mechanism with an uncoupling track.

Even the lowly white Frisco boxcar is frequently present in this outfit in a scarce variation, with a slot in its roofwalk allowing it to be used as a bank. The two-dome rocket fuel tank car is not uncommon, but to find one with an unmarred snow white finish is—and its red markings make cleaning difficult without risking damage. AAR-type trucks, one with an operating coupler and the other with a fixed coupler, were used in pairs on the rolling stock throughout this set.

The blue Santa Fe switcher even had non-operating couplers, die-cast at the rear and plastic at the front. Those units produced in 1963 had yellow safety stripes painted on the sides of the cab. Later models did not have these stripes. The Santa Fe lettering, number and logo were all heat stamped in yellow. The 634 had no separately installed trim at all and was mounted on the late-style stamped sheet-metal frame with integral fuel tank sides. Typical of later NW-2 production, the 634 was equipped with trucks with plastic side frames. The rear truck had the collector assembly attached, while traction tire-equipped motor powered the front truck. A two-position E-unit controlled the direction and a headlight showed the way down the track. Beginning in 1965, a ballast weight was screwed to the inside of the hood, which is absent from the 1963 model included in this outfit.

Typical of the day, none of the components were individually boxed, instead placed loose inside the new style display set box.

Excellent	Like New	Scarcity
950	1,600	6

11351 Land Rover Steam Freight $29.95 retail

Included: 237 2-4-2 steam locomotive with operating headlight and smoke; 1060T tender; 6050-100 Swift boxcar; 6408 flatcar with pipes; 6162 gondola with canisters; 6465-150 Lionel Lines double-dome tank car; 6119-110 work caboose; eight 1013 curved and one 1018 straight track; 6139 uncoupling section; 1025 45-watt transformer; CTC Lockon; tube of lubricant; instructions.

Little of this outfit arouses collector interest on an individual basis. The most interesting of the cars likely is the unnumbered 6408 flatcar with pipe load. Though the number was not stamped on the red car, it was proudly lettered "LIONEL," and carried a load of five plastic pipes, held in place by an elastic band. It rode on AAR-type trucks and had one operating and non-operating coupler.

The boxcar had a slot in its roofwalk, allowing it to serve as it was labeled—as a Savings Bank. The tank car had an unpainted orange body with unpainted black ends.

The 237 locomotive was available for a number of years, but the 1963 model differs from later production. For the first year of the steamers production run, 1963, the boiler was cast in a tool originally intended for die-casting, and hence had thick running boards. Subsequent years used a plastic-specific mold, which had notably thinner running boards. The tender rode on AAR-type trucks and had a non-operating coupler.

Excellent	Like New	Scarcity
200	350	3

11361 Shooting Star Diesel Freight $35 retail

Included: 211P/211T Texas Special Alco A-A units; 6470 exploding boxcar; 3413-150 Mercury capsule launcher; 6413 Mercury capsule carrier; 3665-100 Minuteman car; 6257-100 caboose with stack; eight 1013 curved and three 1018 straight track; 6139 uncoupling section; 1025 45-watt transformer; CTC Lockon; tube of lubricant; instructions.

The twin unit Texas Special diesels and the unpainted 6257-100 SP-type caboose, which strangely featured a die-cast smokejack, were the only conventional railroad items included in this futuristic (for the time) set. Although the 211 had been equipped with single-axle Magne-traction in 1962, the 1963 and later issues lacked this feature.

The body of the 6413 Mercury Capsule carrying car, which had been introduced the year prior, was molded from the tooling used to create the Allis-Chalmers heat exchanger car. The steel plates and Mercury capsules with their combination wire and elastic retainers are unique to this car, and have all been reproduced. The version of this car found in this set most often has one operating and one fixed coupler, and is usually blue, although some collectors report finding the aquamarine version in this outfit.

The 3413 had an unpainted red plastic chassis with a gray plastic superstructure mounted on it. "LIONEL" was heat stamped in white serif letters on both sides of the body, but the catalog number was not. In fact, it did not appear anywhere on the car. The rocket launcher contained a coil spring, which was compressed during the manual cocking action. An electromagnetic uncoupling track section was used to release the spring tension. The idea was that the spring would hurl the rocket upward. The white booster was tied to the railing of the superstructure with a string, causing it to stop traveling while inertia carried the parachute-equipped gray plastic capsule further upward. Its red parachute then opened, allowing it to gently return to Lionelville. In reality, the spring-loaded mechanism often released with the car still in the carton, destroying the box, and the force of the spring was such that when the slack came out of the string during launching it often broke the handrail it was tied to.

This car was built using various shades of red-and-gray plastic components, and in this outfit the car had one operating and one non-operating coupler. The rocket, capsule and parachute have all been reproduced.

The operating Minuteman missile-launching car included in this set is most often a unique and desirable variation. The tooling to create the body had been modified to produce the 3619 helicopter launching car the previous year. As a result of this, 1963 and later production Minuteman cars have a small hole molded in the side near the top, this hole serving to mount a hinge pin when the molding was used for the helicopter car. The Minuteman found in this outfit can be further distinguished by have one fixed and one operating coupler, and frequently has light blue roof panels. These roof panels, as well as the missile itself, have been reproduced, so use caution when evaluating this outfit.

The 6470 exploding boxcar found in this set is usually the late production type that did not have the unsightly open slots in the sides found prior to 1962. Most often this car had one dummy and one operating coupler, although some sets have been reported with cars with two operating couplers. In any event, for this outfit the proper car has early-style, closed-journal AAR-type trucks.

Most examples of this outfit come in the newly redesigned display packaging, but some were packaged in tan corrugated two-tier boxes numbered "11361-500."

Excellent	Like New	Scarcity
750	1,250	6

1963

11375 Cargomaster Steam Freight $39.95 retail

Included: 238 2-4-2 steam locomotive with operating headlight and smoke; 234W tender; 6414-150 Evans Auto Loader; 6162 gondola with canisters; 6476-75 Lehigh Valley hopper; 6822-50 searchlight car; 6465-150 Lionel Lines double-dome tank car; 6257-100 caboose with stack; eight 1013 curved and three 1018 straight; 6139 uncoupling section; 1073 60-watt transformer; CTC Lockon; tube of lubricant; instructions; 147 whistle controller.

Another of the wholly unremarkable outfits but for a single component was this 1963 offering. The small steam locomotive with thick running boards was paired, as the 238 always was with a 234W whistle tender. This tender had AAR-type trucks and a non-operating coupler.

The 6257-100 unpainted red caboose with die-cast stack is fairly hard to find, but no one seems to care. What collectors do care about in this set is the 6414 Auto Loader. While some outfits contain Auto Loaders laden with deluxe cars with gray bumpers, this outfit normally contains the 6414-150, a very desirable variation. This car, which bares the number 6414 on its side, carries four of Lionel's least expensive autos, two each red and yellow. These cars have no bumpers or windshield, and even the wheels are molded as part of the body.

The searchlight car, like the other cars in this outfit, had one operating and one fixed coupler. Its lamp housing was black, while the supporting superstructure was gray. The car itself was red. The hopper car was black and the tank car orange with black ends. All had early closed-journal AAR-type trucks.

This outfit came in a tan corrugated two-tier set box.

Excellent	Like New	Scarcity
650	1,100	5

11385 Space Conqueror Diesel Freight $49.95 retail

Included: 223P/218C Santa Fe Alco A-B units with horn; 3830-75 flatcar with operating submarine; 6407 flatcar with rocket; 3619-100 reconnaissance copter car; 3470-100 aerial target launcher; 3349-100 turbo missile launcher; 6257-100 caboose or 6017-235 Santa Fe caboose; eight 1013 curved and three 1018 straight track; 6139 uncoupling section; 1073 60-watt transformer; CTC Lockon; tube of lubricant; instructions; 147 horn controller.

This outfit is one of the most desirable 027 space and military outfits ever produced, containing many desirable cars, often in scarce variations.

Among these were the 6407 flatcar with rocket, described earlier in this chapter, the 3470-100 target car and the 3619-100 helicopter-launching boxcar. The helicopter-launching car in this outfit, at least in theory, had one operating and one non-operating coupler. More than theory, the body of the car in this outfit was often the dark yellow variation. The correct helicopter for this car was red and included a small window just aft of the side windows. Reproduction helicopters, as well as roof doors, have been produced for this car.

The battery-powered 3470-100 aerial target launcher in this outfit had one operating and one non-operating coupler and, more notably, used a light blue molded plastic flatcar body. The "basket" as well as the red switch at the top of the car, as well as the balloon targets used by this car have all been reproduced.

The 3349-100 turbo missile launching car had one operating and one non-operating coupler. The turbo missiles it launched have been reproduced.

The 3830-75 was essentially the same car as the previously cataloged 3830, with a non-operating coupler replacing one of the operating couplers used on the standard car. The submarine cargo, as well as all its components, has been reproduced.

The reproduction subs came in two variations, one more difficult to detect than the other. Early reproduction submarines use the wrong shape for the numeral "3" in the stamping, giving the number a round top rather than the proper flat top. Also, the propeller was too pure a black color, whereas originals have a brownish tint.

Early reproduction submarines were stamped such that the top of the "3" was rounded just like the "8".

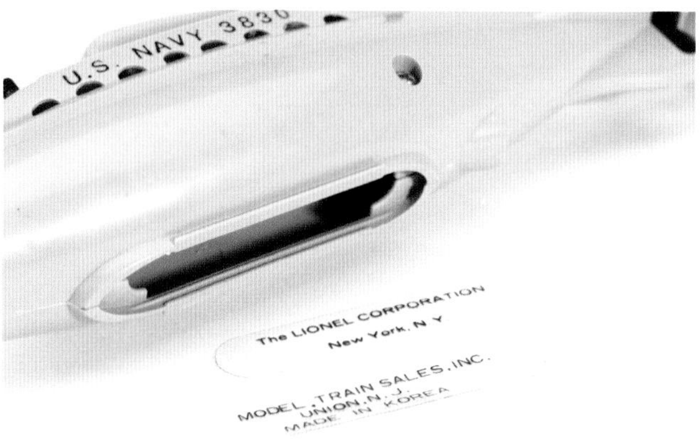

Reproduction bottom plates with "The Lionel Corporation" markings are often substituted for reproduction bottom plates.

Original submarines, like the one above, are naturally the most sought after and can be identified by close examination of details.

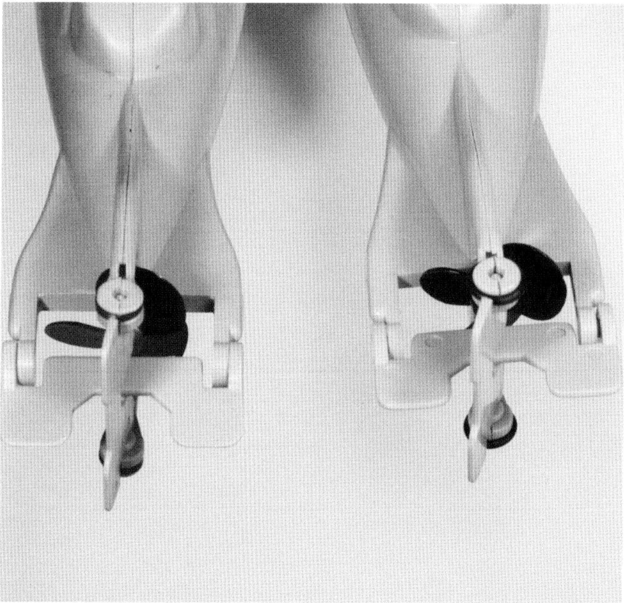

Compare the brownish-black tint of the original propeller (left) with the pure black of the reproduction (right). Also, the O-rings holding the rear of the sub together are noticeably thicker than those orginally used.

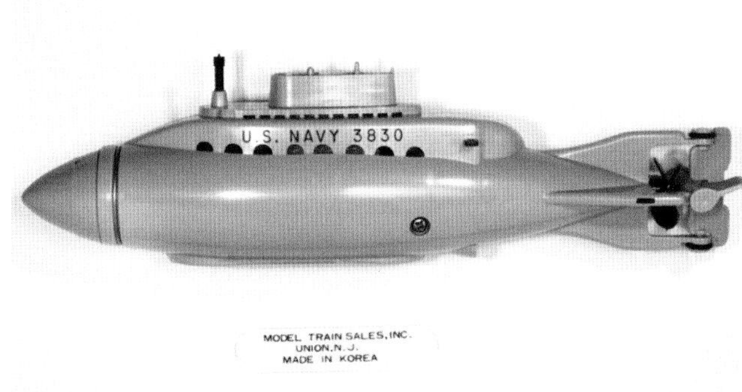

Later reproductions corrected the shape of the "3" stamping, but the propeller continues to be too pure of a black color.

The beginning and end of this outfit is subject to variation. Most sets come in a tan corrugated two-tier box numbered "11385" and contain the advertised 223P and 218C Santa Fe Alco A-B pair, and a 6257-100 Lionel caboose with smokejack. However, sometimes a 6017-235 Santa Fe caboose has been substituted. Similarly, outfits boxed in solid orange two-tier cartons numbered 11385-500 contain 212P-212T Santa Fe A-A units. Components were both boxed and unboxed.

Excellent	Like New	Scarcity
1,800	3,000	6

11395 Muscleman Steam Freight $59.95 retail

Included: 2037 2-6-4 steam locomotive with operating headlight, smoke and Magne-traction; 233W or 234W tender; 6464-725 New Haven boxcar; 6560-50 crane; 6440-50 flatcar with vans; 6536 Minneapolis & St. Louis hopper; 6469-50 liquefied gas car; 6119-100 work caboose; eight 1013 curved and three 1018 straight track; 6029 uncoupling section; 1073 60-watt transformer; CTC Lockon; tube of lubricant; instructions; 147 whistle controller.

Utilizing both boxed and unboxed items; this set contained a variety of traditional-type items. At the front was the die-cast 2037 steam locomotive paired with a whistle tender. At the rear was a 6119-100 red, gray and black work caboose, and between the two was a boxcar, hopper, crane car and two flatcars, one of which was rather unusual.

The crane, red-painted hopper, liquefied gas car and flatcar with vans all had one operating and one non-operating coupler. The flatcar with vans did not include a metal retaining rack found on most such cars, rather relying on two elastic bands to hold the car in place.

The 6469, which was unboxed in this outfit, has been subject to considerable reproduction. The black plastic bulkheads have been reproduced, as has the pasteboard tube that makes up the car body. Reproduction tubes exist as both marked reproductions and unmarked frauds. The fakes are 8 7/8 inches long which is slightly shorter than originals aiding in identification.

The orange New Haven boxcar was the only car in the outfit to intentionally have two operating couplers. Like the rest of the rolling stock, it was fitted with early style AAR-type trucks.

The liquefied gas car, crane and hopper cars were placed unboxed inside the tan two-tier outfit carton. The other components came in individual boxes.

Excellent	Like New	Scarcity
600	1,000	5

11405 Six-Unit Diesel Passenger $69.95 retail

Included: 218P/218T Santa Fe Alco A-A units with horn; 2414 Pullman; two 2412 Vista Domes; 2416 observation; eight 1013 curved and three 1018 straight track; 6029 uncoupling section; 1073 60-watt transformer; CTC Lockon; tube of lubricant; instructions; 147 horn controller.

This outfit was the final appearance of both the blue-striped Santa Fe passenger cars and the 218 A-A Alcos pulling them. The locomotives were placed unboxed in the bottom of the tan corrugated two-tier set box, while the passenger cars came in Orange Picture boxes.

Excellent	Like New	Scarcity
700	1,125	4

11415 **No retail, advance catalog**

Included: 1061 steam locomotive; 1061T tender; 6502 flatcar with girder; 6167-25 caboose; eight 1013 curved track; 1026 25-watt transformer; CTC Lockon; tube of lubricant; instructions.

Whereas in most cases, low-cost outfits appearing in the advance catalog were numbered sequentially lower than the rest of the line, the opposite is the case in this instance. Only the locomotive had any stamping—its catalog number. The tender, blue flatcar with unpainted orange girder and red caboose were all unpainted plastic and rode on early AAR-type trucks. No operating couplers were used on any of the set components.

Galvanized, tab-mounted frames were used for both the caboose and tender, the latter lacking an electrical ground found on better versions of the slope-back tender.

The outfit components were placed unboxed in a small conventional two-tier corrugated set box.

Super 0

13098 **Goliath Steam Freight** **$49.95 retail**

Included: 637 2-6-4 steam locomotive with operating headlight, smoke and Magne-traction; 736W tender; 6414 Evans Auto Loader; 6464-900 New York Central boxcar; 6469 liquefied gas car; 6446 Norfolk & Western covered hopper; 6447 non-illuminated Pennsylvania caboose; twelve 31 curved, one 32 straight and one 34 half-straight track; 39-25 operating packet; tube of lubricant; instructions.

The caboose at the rear of this outfit is usually the single most desirable item in the set. The non-illuminated Pennsy caboose, which had only one operating coupler, was unique to this set, making it one of the scarcest, if not the scarcest of the porthole cabooses.

The locomotive was a 2037, renumbered 637 in order to move it into the 0 and Super 0 range. Its Pennsylvania tender, numbered 736W, rode on early AAR-type trucks and had an operating coupler at the rear.

The Auto Loader mostly carried four yellow automobiles with gray bumpers, but some collectors report their set includes four Kelly green autos with gray bumpers—in which case this car eclipses the caboose in desirability. The values assigned below assume the presence of yellow cars; green cars (which, like the yellow ones, have been reproduced) would dramatically increase the values.

Green is also the color of the 6464-900 New York Central boxcar and, like the rest of the freight cars in this set, had operating couplers on both ends. The 6469, when a part of this set, was like the rest of the rolling stock of the outfit—individually packed in an Orange Picture box. The locomotive came in a tan corrugated carton and the set box itself was an orange two-tier box.

Excellent	Like New	Scarcity
2,000	3,600	6

13108 **Seven-Unit Diesel Freight** **$49.95 retail**

Included: 617 Santa Fe NW-2 diesel switcher with horn; 3665 Minuteman car; 3419 flatcar with operating helicopter; 6448 exploding boxcar; 3830 flatcar with operating submarine; 3470 aerial target launcher; 6119-100 work caboose; twelve 31 curved, one 32 straight and one 34 half-straight track; 39-25 operating packet; tube of lubricant; instructions.

Perhaps because it was being issued in the premium Super 0 line, the locomotive in this outfit is a rare instance where the level of detail was increased over that of earlier similar products.

The black-and-white Santa Fe zebra-striped NW-2 had all the trim items: black ornamental bell, silver ornamental horn and headlight lens. It even had marker light lenses and a round radio antenna, both features that had not been seen since 1955! Mechanically, the 617 had an operating horn, three-position lever-down E-unit, operating headlight and two-axle Magne-traction, although its couplers were non-operating. The black body color and white stripes were both applied by painting, while the Santa Fe logo and lettering were heat stamped. The 617 was produced with two distinctly different style frames.

The early production used the same sheet-metal frame that had been used since 1955. This frame had separate steps and platform railings that were riveted in place and the simulated fuel tank was a plastic molding that was screwed on. Later production used a new sheet-metal frame assembly. The steps, platform railings and fuel tank sides were integral with the basic frame stamping. The locomotive came packed in an Orange Picture box.

The 3665 missile launching boxcar included in this outfit had a body molded from the tool used to create the 3619 helicopter launching boxcar—hence it had a small hole cast in the side near the top.

As evidenced by the lack of suffixes assigned to the product numbers, Lionel chose to include their better products in this Super 0 outfit. Hence each piece of rolling stock typically had operating couplers on both of their AAR-type trucks. The cars were individually boxed in Orange Picture boxes that in turn were placed inside a two-tier orange set carton.

Excellent	Like New	Scarcity
900	1,500	5

13118 Eight-Unit Steam Freight $75 retail

Included: 736 2-8-4 Berkshire steam locomotive with operating headlight, smoke and Magne-traction; 736W tender; 6560 crane; 6827 flatcar with Harnischfeger power shovel; 3362 helium tank unloading car; 6446-60 Lehigh Valley hopper; 6315-60 Lionel Lines tank car; 6429 work caboose; twelve 31 curved, one 32 straight and one 34 half-straight track; 39-25 operating packet; tube of lubricant; instructions.

While much of this outfit looks routine at a glance, a closer inspection reveals a couple of real treasures lurking within. Foremost of these was the seemingly ubiquitous die-cast frame D. L. & W. work caboose. However, this car differed from its predecessors in ways beyond just the number stamped on the sides. The new car rode on early AAR-type trucks. It had unpainted light gray toolboxes and a painted-gray die-cast frame. Both the tooling for the frame and the cab were modified to allow the cab to mount with tabs, rather than the four screws previously used. The cab itself was unpainted with black heat-stamped lettering, while the frame was marked "Lionel Lines" in black heat-stamped lettering. The car used the short die-cast smokejack and had two 2419-23 brake stands, wire handrails, blued-steel steps and a ladder. The toolboxes as well as the cab of this caboose have been reproduced.

The other scarce car included in this set is the large Lehigh Valley hopper with cover. It was assigned catalog number 6446-60, but the number on the car itself, however, was 6436. The body was painted red, but the roof and hatches were left unpainted. The white heat-stamped markings included "NEW 3-55" centered on the car sides. Holes for the spreader bar were present in the body, but the bar itself was not installed, the roof providing the needed support.

The flatcar with crane is a desirable piece, but is not in the same league with the cars listed above. The helium tank unloading car had operating couplers on each of its early-style AAR-type trucks and utilized an all-plastic coupler knuckle installed with a rivet. It carried three silver simulated helium tanks made of wood. The unpainted orange tank car was lettered "Lionel Lines."

But for the locomotive, which came in a tan corrugated carton, the components of this outfit were packaged in Orange Picture boxes. The outfit box itself was a two-tier orange carton.

Excellent	Like New	Scarcity
1,500	2,500	5

13128 Seven-Unit Diesel Freight $89.95 retail

Included: 2383P/2383T Santa Fe A-A F-3 units; 6512 cherry picker car; 3619 reconnaissance copter car; 3413 Mercury capsule launcher; 448 missile firing range set with 6448 exploding boxcar; 6437 Pennsylvania porthole caboose; twelve 31 curved, three 32 straight and one 34 half-straight track; 39-25 operating packet; tube of lubricant; instructions.

In 1962, Lionel had a sales success with outfit 13058, so that set was given a minor facelift for 1963. The earlier set's 470 accessory with 6470 boxcar gave way to the new 448 with 6448 boxcar. In addition to these two new items, the outfit contained the 3413 Mercury capsule launching car. This car was identical to the 3413-150 packed in outfit 11361 except in this set it had two operating couplers and was packed in an Orange Picture box—which is often found damaged today by an errant firing of the car.

As a companion to the 3413 Mercury capsule launching car, this outfit included a 6512 cherry picker car. Its body was unpainted black plastic and the only markings on it were "LIONEL" heat stamped in white on both sides of the car. AAR-type plastic trucks with operating couplers were riveted directly to the body of these cars. The operating mechanism was adapted from the 3512 fireman and ladder car. At the end of the extension ladder was a newly designed orange plastic cage containing a diminutive astronaut figure. This figure seemed to be made to enter the waiting capsule when the lever on the side of the cage contacts the capsule, forcing the man into view. Much of the operating mechanism of this car has been reproduced, so caution should be used.

All the rolling stock in this outfit was equipped with two operating couplers, but for the tender and caboose which each had one. The locomotives each came in their own Tan Corrugated box made by Mead. The 6448 was packed in an Orange Picture box, which was then packed inside the 448 box, which was also an Orange Picture box. This style of box was utilized for the remaining rolling stock in the outfit as well. The set box was a solid orange two-tier carton.

Excellent	Like New	Scarcity
1,800	3,000	6

13138 Majestic Electric Freight $100 retail

Included: 2360 Pennsylvania solid-stripe GG1; 6416 Boat Loader; 6464-725 New Haven boxcar; 6828 flatcar with Harnischfeger crane; 6827 flatcar with Harnischfeger power shovel; 6315-60 Lionel Lines tank car; 6436-110 Lehigh Valley hopper; 6437 caboose; twelve 31 curved, five 32 straight and one 34 half-straight track; 39-25 operating packet; tube of lubricant; instructions.

Amazingly, this fantastic set was NOT the top-of-the-line outfit for 1963, although it was the best freight set, and it contains many collectible items. Among the desirable components in this set is the 6416 Boat Loader.

1963

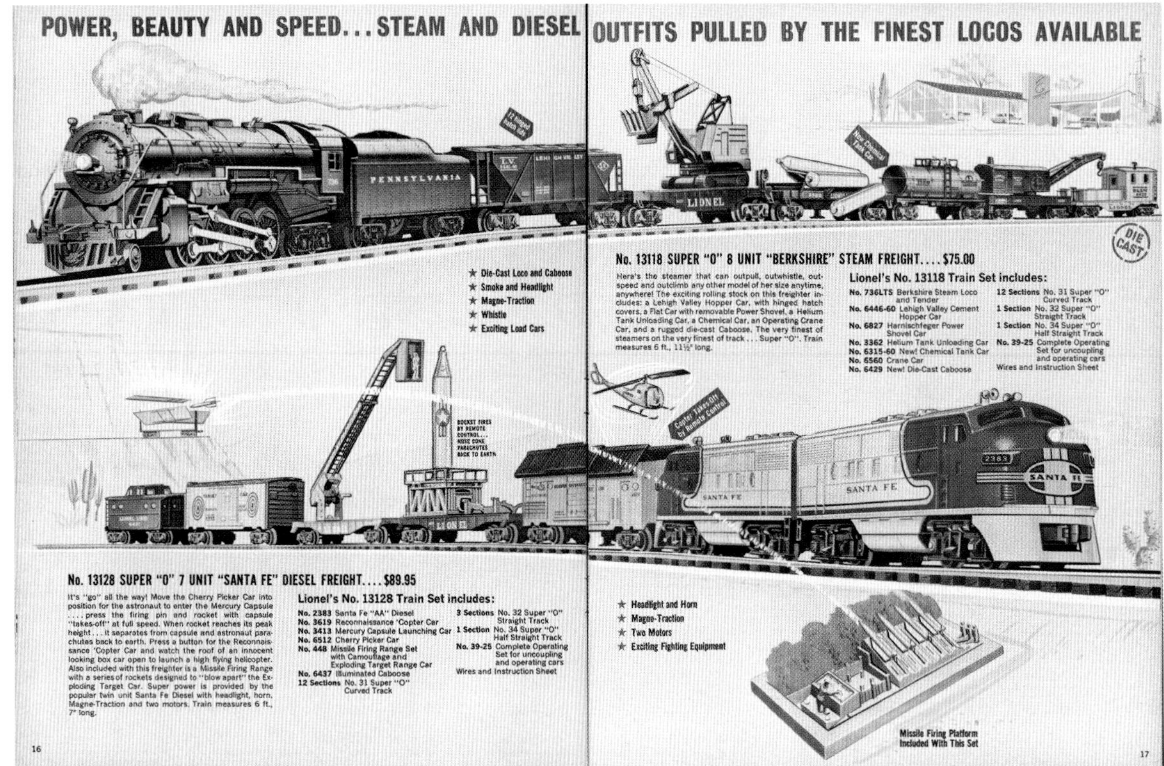
POWER, BEAUTY AND SPEED... STEAM AND DIESEL OUTFITS PULLED BY THE FINEST LOCOS AVAILABLE

★ Die-Cast Loco and Caboose
★ Smoke and Headlight
★ Magne-Traction
★ Whistle
★ Exciting Load Cars

No. 13118 SUPER "O" 8 UNIT "BERKSHIRE" STEAM FREIGHT.... $75.00

Here's the steamer that can outpull, outwhistle, outspeed and outclimb any other model of her size anytime, anywhere! The exciting rolling stock on this freighter includes: a Lehigh Valley Hopper Car, with hinged hatch covers, a Flat Car with removable Power Shovel, a Helium Tank Unloading Car, a Chemical Car, an Operating Crane Car, and a rugged die-cast Caboose. The very finest of steamers on the very finest of track . . . Super "O". Train measures 6 ft., 11½" long.

Lionel's No. 13118 Train Set includes:

No. 736LTS Berkshire Steam Loco and Tender
No. 6446-60 Lehigh Valley Cement Hopper Car
No. 6827 Harnischfeger Power Shovel Car
No. 3362 Helium Tank Unloading Car
No. 6315-60 New! Chemical Tank Car
No. 6560 Crane Car
No. 6429 New! Die-Cast Caboose
12 Sections No. 31 Super "O" Curved Track
1 Section No. 32 Super "O" Straight Track
1 Section No. 34 Super "O" Half Straight Track
No. 39-25 Complete Operating Set for uncoupling and operating cars
Wires and Instruction Sheet

DIE CAST

Copter Takes Off by Remote Control

ROCKET FIRES BY REMOTE CONTROL... NOSE CONE

★ Headlight and Horn
★ Magne-Traction
★ Two Motors
★ Exciting Fighting Equipment

No. 13128 SUPER "O" 7 UNIT "SANTA FE" DIESEL FREIGHT.... $89.95

It's "go" all the way! Move the Cherry Picker Car into position for the astronaut to enter the Mercury Capsule .... press the firing pin and rocket with capsule "takes-off" at full speed. When rocket reaches its peak height ... it separates from capsule and astronaut parachutes back to earth. Press a button for the Reconnaissance 'Copter Car and watch the roof of an innocent looking box car open to launch a high flying helicopter. Also included with this freighter is a Missile Firing Range with a series of rockets designed to "blow apart" the Exploding Target Car. Super power is provided by the popular twin unit Santa Fe Diesel with headlight, horn, Magne-Traction and two motors. Train measures 6 ft., 7" long.

Lionel's No. 13128 Train Set includes:

No. 2383 Santa Fe "AA" Diesel
No. 3619 Reconnaissance 'Copter Car
No. 3413 Mercury Capsule Launching Car
No. 6512 Cherry Picker Car
No. 448 Missile Firing Range Set with Camouflage and Exploding Target Range Car
No. 6437 Illuminated Caboose
12 Sections No. 31 Super "O" Curved Track
3 Sections No. 32 Super "O" Straight Track
1 Section No. 34 Super "O" Half Straight Track
No. 39-25 Complete Operating Set for uncoupling and operating cars
Wires and Instruction Sheet

Missile Firing Platform Included With This Set

16 17

13118, 13128

This car was created using the tooling that was built to manufacture the 6414 Auto Loader. Its unpainted red plastic body was heat stamped "6416 LIONEL" in standard white serif letters. The sheet-metal superstructure was painted black and rubber stamped "BOAT - LOADER" in white serif lettering. The car was equipped with AAR-type trucks with operating couplers. Its cargo was four HO cabin cruisers built by Athearn, a prominent maker of HO-Gauge trains. The only proper color combination of boat for this car has a hull painted white, blue-painted cabin and brown-painted interior. Athearn did and continues to build the same boats in a variety of other colors, but they are not accurate for this car.

The black flatcars carried construction equipment, which were intricate assembly kits, and hence today are often missing parts. Both the crane and the power shovel came in their own black and yellow boxes, which were placed on the flatcars and slid inside the Orange Picture box of the rail cars. Lionel continued to produce the crane and power shovel into the MPC era, so beware of replacement parts, especially those molded in black.

The orange tank car was marked in Lionel Lines graphics, a change from the Gulf markings used earlier. The big hopper, which was not covered, was painted red and, like the rest of the cars in this set, rode on AAR-type trucks. Each piece of rolling stock was packed in its own Orange Picture box.

The boxcar and caboose were routine issue items, as was the GG-1. But all GG-1's garner collector attention, and this one is no exception. The locomotive, which came in a lined tan corrugated carton made by Mead, had stamped stripes and utilized decals for the numbers and lettering. It had a single broad stripe and large keystone on each side.

The outfit, which came in a solid orange two-tier carton, included a 39-25 operating packet. This packet strangely did not contain the items necessary to actuate the coil couplers of the GG-1.

Excellent	Like New	Scarcity
3,000	5,000	6

13148 Super Chief Passenger $120 retail

Included: 2383P/2383T Santa Fe A-A F-3 units; 2522 President Harrison Vista Dome; two 2523 President Garfield Pullmans; 2521 President McKinley observation; twelve 31 curved, five 32 straight and one 34 half-straight track; 39-25 operating packet; tube of lubricant; instructions.

Packed in a tan two-tier box, this outfit contained a Vista Dome, two Pullmans and an observation car, each packed in their own Orange Picture box. A pair of 2383 Santa Fe diesels, which each had its own tan corrugated carton made by Mead, provided the motive power. The red paint on these locos had a distinct orange cast, common to all these units made between 1961 and 1963.

Excellent	Like New	Scarcity
2,300	4,200	5

Chapter 21

1964

In 1964, it seems that Lionel was still trying to find its position in the market place. The catalog was a rather austere black-and-white rendition and the trains inside were too.

In 027, Magne-traction was dropped, as was the illumination in 027 passenger cars. Counter to this, however, not only did O-Gauge outfits return, but so did a single Super 0 outfit!

The standard component box, for those outfits so equipped, was once again the Orange Picture box. Three styles of outfit boxes were used; outfit 13150, the Super 0 set, came in a tan corrugated carton, as did some versions of some 027 outfits; the O-Gauge offerings were packed in white two-tier boxes with orange printing; and the 027 sets came in a display box without component boxes once again, but it was restyled. While the illustration on the cover was the same as the previous editions, now the lid lifted off rather than being hinged.

Trucks were the AAR-type, and a mixture of both the early style, and the "new" style introduced in 1963 that featured axle ends that were visible when viewed from beneath. Most often the later trucks have knuckles that were not riveted in place, but rather had knuckle pivot points molded as part of the knuckle.

Examples of two O-Gauge outfits, numbers 12750 and 12770 have never been located, although they were cataloged. These sets, as shown in the catalog, differed little from other sets listed.

A new style of display box was unveiled in 1963. This box, used extensively in the 027 line, combined the graphics of the old set cartons with a new lift-off lid.

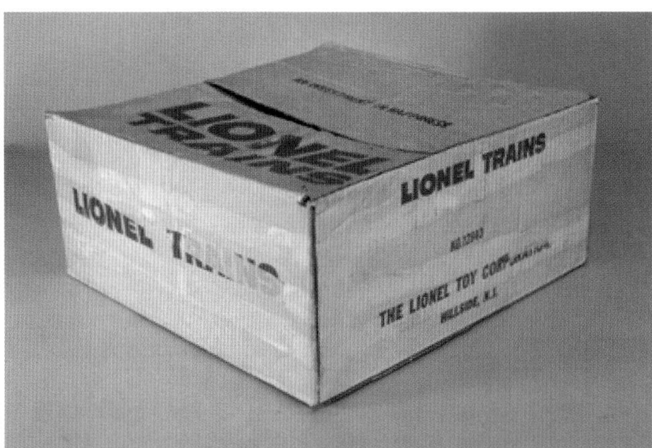

While a few O-Gauge outfits came in orange two-tier boxes likely carried over from the year before, or even more uncommonly, a plain tan corrugated carton, most came in this new box. Also corrugated, but white with orange printing, this box would be the new standard for O-Gauge sets.

The Orange Picture box, introduced in 1961, continued to be the standard component box during 1963. Made of glossy orange cardstock, it had a white panel with an illustration of a steam and diesel locomotive on the front. The city names "NEW YORK" and "CHICAGO" appeared on the box, as did the corporate name "THE LIONEL CORPORATION."

027-Gauge

11420 Four-Unit Steam Freight $11.95 retail

Contents: 1061 steam locomotive; 1061T slope-back tender; 6042-250 gondola; 6167-25 SP-type caboose; eight 1013 curved track; 1026 25-watt transformer.

At under $12, this was the least expensive outfit to appear in the consumer catalog during the postwar era. One way that Lionel was able to achieve this low price point was by eliminating all decoration—save for the locomotive number—from the set. None of the cars were stamped and all were molded in their final colors. The gondola was blue and the caboose fittingly red.

Further cost savings were achieved by removing any form of reversing mechanism from the locomotive, which thus ran forward only. The sets were packages in tan two-tier boxes.

Excellent	Like New	Scarcity
75	125	2

11430 Five-Unit Steam Freight $14.95 retail

Contents: 1062 0-4-0 steam locomotive with operating headlight; 1061T slope-back tender; 6142 unstamped gondola; 6176 unstamped hopper; 6167-125 unstamped SP-type caboose; eight 1013 curved and one 1018 straight track; 6149 uncoupling section; 1026 25-watt transformer.

Almost as inexpensive, both in terms of retail and cost, was this outfit. Once again the cars were all unpainted and denude of markings. The outfit in this set, however, did at least include a two-position reversing unit. However, because of the locomotive's wheel arrangement and the lack of a ground connection on the tender, the reversing ability could cause trouble. Oftentimes an excited new owner would be dismayed to find the loco had a tendency to reverse while crossing these sections.

The unstamped yellow hopper and the sometimes-included unstamped translucent green gondola are moderately desirable. All the rolling stock in this set came with new-style AAR-type trucks and had one operating and one non-operating coupler.

Excellent	Like New	Scarcity
90	150	2

11440 Five-Unit Diesel Freight $17.95 retail

Contents: 221 Rio Grande Alco A-unit; 6142-125 gondola; 6176-50 Lehigh Valley hopper; 3309 turbo missile launcher; 6167-100 SP-type caboose; eight 1013 curved and one 1018 straight track; 6149 uncoupling section; 1026 25-watt transformer.

In earlier years, Lionel would have likely carried over outfit 11321 from 1963. But in 1964 every penny counted, so Lionel stripped the outfit of the load for its gondola and each of the cars had only one operating coupler.

This outfit had a red "LIONEL LINES" caboose with operating coupler and also included a black hopper car.

The unmarked 3309 turbo missile car and the nearly identical 3349 turbo missile car confuse many collectors. However, distinguishing the two is really very simple; if the car has operating couplers on each end, it is a 3349—all other variants are 3309.

Excellent	Like New	Scarcity
200	350	2

11450 Six-Unit Steam Freight $19.95 retail

Contents: 242 2-4-2 steam locomotive with operating headlight; 1060T tender; 6473 rodeo car; 6142-75 gondola with canisters;

Values for each condition are in U.S. dollars. | **Scarity** = Scale from 1-8 with 8 being the hardest to find.

1964

6176-50 Lehigh Valley hopper; 6059-50 Minneapolis & St. Louis SP-type caboose; eight 1013 curved and one 1018 straight track; 6149 uncoupling section; 1010 35-watt transformer.

AAR-type trucks were installed on all the rolling stock in this outfit, with one operating coupler on each freight car. The blue gondola was laden with two canisters. The tender did not have grounding provisions, nor did it have an operating coupler.

The proper variation of the rodeo car for this outfit was lettered in red and even more telling was the molded-in cadmium-yellow plastic with flawed tooling. The tooling damage resulted in one of the slots to the right of the center door on one side of the car being partially filled in.

The Lehigh Valley hopper car, a mainstay of postwar sets for a decade at this point, was unpainted black plastic in this outfit. Set packaging was the newly restyled display box.

Excellent	Like New	Scarcity
150	250	2

11460 Seven-Unit Steam Freight $34.95 retail

Contents: 238 2-4-2 steam locomotive with operating headlight and smoke; 234W tender; 6014-325 Frisco boxcar; 6142-100 gondola with canisters; 6176-75 Lehigh Valley hopper; 6465-150 Lionel Lines double-dome tank car; 6119-110 work caboose; eight 1013 curved and one 1018 straight track; 6149 uncoupling section; 1073 60-watt transformer; 147 whistle controller.

At first glance, no part of this outfit would raise much collector interest. However, some of these sets contain variations worthy of closer inspection. The locomotive in this outfit was molded using tooling created for die-casting earlier Scout-type locomotives. Later years' production used a new tool made specifically for injection molding and those shells have notably thinner running boards.

Sometimes the bank version of the Frisco boxcar is found in this set. This car has a slot in the roof walk that will accept coins. Also, occasionally a painted-cab variation of the work caboose is found in this set.

Excellent	Like New	Scarcity
125	200	3

11470 Seven-Unit Steam Freight $29.95 retail

Contents: 237 2-4-2 steam locomotive with operating headlight and smoke; 1060T tender; 6014-325 Frisco boxcar; 6142-100 gondola with canisters; 6176-75 Lehigh Valley hopper; 6465-150 Lionel Lines double-dome tank car; 6119-110 work caboose; eight 1013 curved and one 1018 straight track; 6149 uncoupling section; 1025 45-watt transformer.

This outfit was essentially an 11460 stripped of its whistle components. At the time, Lionel felt this warranted a change in loco number, which was 237 for those paired with non-whistling tenders. This loco was made in two variations, the early one, included in this outfit, had thick running boards, a result of being molded in tooling originally intended for die-casting.

Excellent	Like New	Scarcity
180	300	5

11480 Seven-Unit Diesel Freight $34.95 retail

Contents: 213P/213T Minneapolis & St. Louis Alco A-A units; 6014-325 Frisco boxcar; 6142-150 gondola with cable reels; 6176-50 Lehigh Valley hopper; 6473 rodeo car; 6257-100 SP-type caboose with stack or 6059 Minneapolis & St. Louis SP-type caboose; twelve 1013 curved and three 1018 straight track; 6149 uncoupling section; 90-degree crossing; 1025 45-watt transformer.

Although the number of the locomotive in this set was new, the Minneapolis and St. Louis road name was not. The Alco diesel, included as a powered-dummy combination in this set, lacked Magne-traction, instead using a traction tire. It featured a two-position E-unit. Though its lack of a horn meant that none of these have suffered battery damage, the bar beneath the front coupler was fragile on these units, as they were on all sheet-metal framed Alcos.

Behind the locos stretched a string of cars, most of which have been previously discussed in this chapter. The blue gondola hauled a pair of empty cable reels and the hopper was the rather drab black version. All the freight cars in this set had AAR-type trucks and one operating coupler. The Lionel Lines caboose was somewhat strangely equipped with a die-cast smokejack.

Excellent	Like New	Scarcity
600	1,000	5

11490 Five-Unit Diesel Passenger $49.95 retail

Contents: 212P/212T Santa Fe Alco A-A units with horn; 2404 Vista Dome; 2405 Pullman; 2406 observation with Santa Fe markings in blue letters; eight 1013 curved and three 1018 straight track; 6149 uncoupling section; 1073 60-watt transformer; 147 horn controller.

The ever-popular red-and-silver Santa Fe "warbonnet" paint scheme adorned the A-A Alco pair at the front of this passenger train. The diesels had no Magne-traction and only had a simple two-position E-unit, but they were not the only part of the set to fall short of earlier standards.

GREATER THAN EVER . . .
COLOSSAL LIONEL STEAM
AND DIESEL OUTFITS
"027" TRAIN OUTFITS
Set No. 11500 With Die-Cast Steamer with Whistle and Smoke $44.95
Set No. 11510 With Die-Cast Steamer with Smoke $39.95
Set No. 11490 With Horn $49.95
Set No. 11480 With Figure "8" Track Layout $34.95
Set No. 11460 With Smoke and Whistle $34.95
Set No. 11470 With Smoke $29.95
Set No. 11450 $19.95
No. 11450 6-Unit Steam Freight . . . $19.95
No. 11460 7-Unit Steam Freight . . . $34.95
No. 11470 7-Unit Steam Freight . . . $29.95
No. 11480
7-Unit Diesel Freight . . . $34.95
No. 11490
5-Unit Diesel Passenger . . . $49.95
No. 11500
7-Unit Steam Freight . . . $44.95
No. 11510
7-Unit Steam Freight . . . $39.95

11450, 11460, 11470, 11480, 11490, 11500, 11510

The plastic-bodied passenger cars trailing them had lacked not only illumination, but were even devoid of window glazing! The unboxed set components were packed in the new-style display box.

Excellent	Like New	Scarcity
600	1,000	4

11500 Seven-Unit Steam Freight $44.95 retail

Contents: 2029 2-6-4 steam locomotive with operating headlight and smoke; 234W tender; 6014-325 Frisco boxcar; 6402-50 flatcar with cable reels; 6176-75 Lehigh Valley hopper; 6465-150 Lionel Lines double-dome tank car; 6257-100 SP-type caboose with stack or 6059 Minneapolis & St. Louis SP-type caboose; eight 1013 curved and three 1018 straight track; 6149 uncoupling section; 1073 60-watt transformer; 147 whistle controller.

When Magne-traction was dropped from 027 locomotives, the long-running 2037 became history. In its place was introduced the similar-appearing 2029. Key differences between the two models were the use of a traction tire rather than Magne-traction and a reverse unit having only two-positions rather than three.

Behind the steamer rolled a 234W whistle tender and an assortment of freight cars, most of which were common to other outfits of the year. AAR-type trucks were used on all the rolling stock—even the unlettered gray 6402-50 flatcar, which was molded in tooling created for the General set. This car was laden with cable reels held in place by an elastic band.

These sets have surfaced in both display and tan two-tier packaging.

Excellent	Like New	Scarcity
250	400	4

11510 Seven-Unit Steam Freight $39.95 retail

Contents: 2029 2-6-4 steam locomotive with operating headlight and smoke; 1060T tender; 6014-325 Frisco boxcar; 6402-50 flatcar with cable reels; 6176-75 Lehigh Valley hopper; 6465-150 Lionel Lines double-dome tank car; 6257-100 SP-type caboose with stack or 6059 Minneapolis & St. Louis SP-type caboose; eight 1013 curved and three 1018 straight track; 6149 uncoupling section; 1025 45-watt transformer.

This outfit was a stripped-down, whistle-less version of the 11500. Perhaps because there was only a relatively meager $5 retail savings achieved by this, today this set is harder to find than its whistling counterpart.

Excellent	Like New	Scarcity
275	450	5

O-Gauge

12700 Seven-Unit Steam Freight $59.95 retail

Contents: 736 2-8-4 Berkshire steam locomotive with operating headlight, smoke and Magne-traction; 736W tender; 6414-75 Evans Auto Loader; 6464-725 New Haven boxcar; 6162-100 gondola with canisters; 6476-125 Lehigh Valley hopper; 6437 Pennsylvania caboose; eight TOC curved and five TOS straight track; UCS uncoupling/operating section.

Just as the venerable Berkshire was heralded as the first to run on Super 0 in 1957, it was also chosen to lead the re-introduction of O-Gauge outfits seven years later. Behind the steamer was a 736W Pennsylvania whistling tender and a variety of interesting freight cars, all riding on AAR-type trucks—most frequently of the latest style with open-bottom journals. Operating couplers were on each end of all the cars.

The Auto Loader normally carried four red sedans with gray bumpers, but some outfits reportedly contain cars laden with four cheap autos with molded-in wheels. The orange New Haven boxcar came packed in a box stamped 6464-735—even though the number on the car is 6464-725. This error is even more comical given that the catalog listed this car as a 646-750!

The unpainted blue gondola carried three white canisters. The correct box for the yellow hopper is numbered 6476—despite car being stamped 6176. The 6476 was Lionel's designation for the car with couplers on each end.

The locomotive came in an unlined tan corrugated carton, while all the rolling stock was packed in Orange Picture boxes. Most outfits were packed in the new white box with orange printing, but some have been reported in apparently surplus orange 1963 Super 0-style boxes. As was traditionally the case for O-Gauge outfits, no transformer was included in this set.

Excellent	Like New	Scarcity
900	1,500	5

12710 Seven-Unit Steam Freight $75 retail

Contents: 736 2-8-4 Berkshire steam locomotive with operating headlight, smoke and Magne-traction; 736W tender; 6414-75 Evans Auto Loader; 6464-725 New Haven boxcar; 6162-100 gondola with canisters; 6476-125 Lehigh Valley hopper; 6437 Pennsylvania caboose; eight TOC curved and five TOS straight track; LW 125-watt transformer; UCS uncoupling/operating section.

This outfit was identical to set 12700 but for the inclusion of an additional component—an LW transformer. The outfit box was the new white with orange printing two-tier carton.

Excellent	Like New	Scarcity
925	1,550	5

12720 Seven-Unit Diesel Freight $65 retail

Contents: 2383 Santa Fe F-3 A-A; 6414-75 Evans Auto Loader; 6464-725 New Haven boxcar; 6162-100 gondola with canisters; 6476-125 Lehigh Valley hopper; 6437 Pennsylvania caboose; eight TOC curved and five TOS straight track; UCS uncoupling/operating section.

This outfit was identical to set 12700, but the big steam locomotive and its tender were replaced by a pair of 2383 Santa Fe F-3 A-A units. The diesels were packed in tan corrugated cartons made by Mead. As with the 12700, it has been reported in both the new two-tier white box and the two-tier orange carton normally associated with 1963 Super 0 production.

Excellent	Like New	Scarcity
1,500	2,500	5

12730 Seven-Unit Diesel Freight $79.95 retail

Contents: 2383 Santa Fe F-3 A-A; 6414-75 Evans Auto Loader; 6464-725 New Haven boxcar; 6162-100 gondola with canisters; 6476-125 Lehigh Valley hopper; 6437 Pennsylvania caboose; eight TOC curved and five TOS straight track; LW 125-watt transformer; UCS uncoupling/operating section.

As with the steam-powered sets, the F-3 powered outfit was also offered with an included transformer. The transformer-equipped sets are substantially easier to locate than their transformer-less brothers are. This outfit was packed in a two-tier white carton with orange printing.

Excellent	Like New	Scarcity
1,500	2,500	5

12740 Nine-Unit Diesel Freight $79.95 retail

Contents: 2383P/2383T Santa Fe A-A F-3 units; 6464-525 Minneapolis & St. Louis boxcar; 6436-110 Lehigh Valley hopper; 3662 operating milk car; 6822 searchlight car; 6361 timber transport; 6315-60 Lionel Lines tank car; 6437 Pennsylvania caboose; eight TOC curved and five TOS straight track; UCS uncoupling/operating section.

The old favorite operating milk car returned in this set after a three-year absence from the catalog. This car rode on AAR-type trucks and lacked the "New 4-55" found on earlier editions of this car. The platform was changed too, no longer having the stamped-in information that had been present since the platform's inception in 1947.

The searchlight car had a black lamp housing and a gray superstructure and, like all the cars in this set except the caboose, had two operating couplers.

Orange Picture boxes were used for the freight cars and caboose, and the diesels were packed in tan corrugated cartons made by Mead. The outfit box was a white two-tier carton with orange printing.

Excellent	Like New	Scarcity
1,500	2,500	6

12760 Nine-Unit Steam Freight $75 retail

Contents: 736 2-8-4 Berkshire steam locomotive with operating headlight, smoke and Magne-traction; 736W tender; 6464-525 Minneapolis & St. Louis boxcar; 6436-110 Lehigh Valley hopper; 3662 operating milk car; 6822 searchlight car; 6361 timber transport; 6315-60 Lionel Lines tank car; 6437 Pennsylvania caboose; eight TOC curved and five TOS straight track; UCS uncoupling/operating section.

As was the case with the O-Gauge outfits listed above, this was merely a repeat of set 12740, with the 736 steamer replacing the Santa Fe F-3 units.

Excellent	Like New	Scarcity
1,500	2,500	6

12780 Six-Unit Diesel Passenger $120 retail

Contents: 2383P/2383T Santa Fe A-A F-3 units; 2522 President Harrison Vista Dome; two 2523 President Garfield Pullmans; 2521 President McKinley observation; eight TOC curved and five TOS straight track; UCS uncoupling/operating section.

With this outfit, the Presidential streamliner moved down from Super 0 to 0, where it would remain through 1966. The twin diesels were packed in tan corrugated cartons made by Mead, while Orange Picture boxes were used for the extruded aluminum passenger cars. As with all of the flat channel-type extruded cars, beware of reproduction striping.

Two types of outfit boxes were utilized for this set in 1964. While most came in the new two-tier white carton with orange printing, some outfits were packed in a tan two-tier corrugated carton made by the Bobbins Container Corp.

Excellent	Like New	Scarcity
3,300	5,500	5

1964

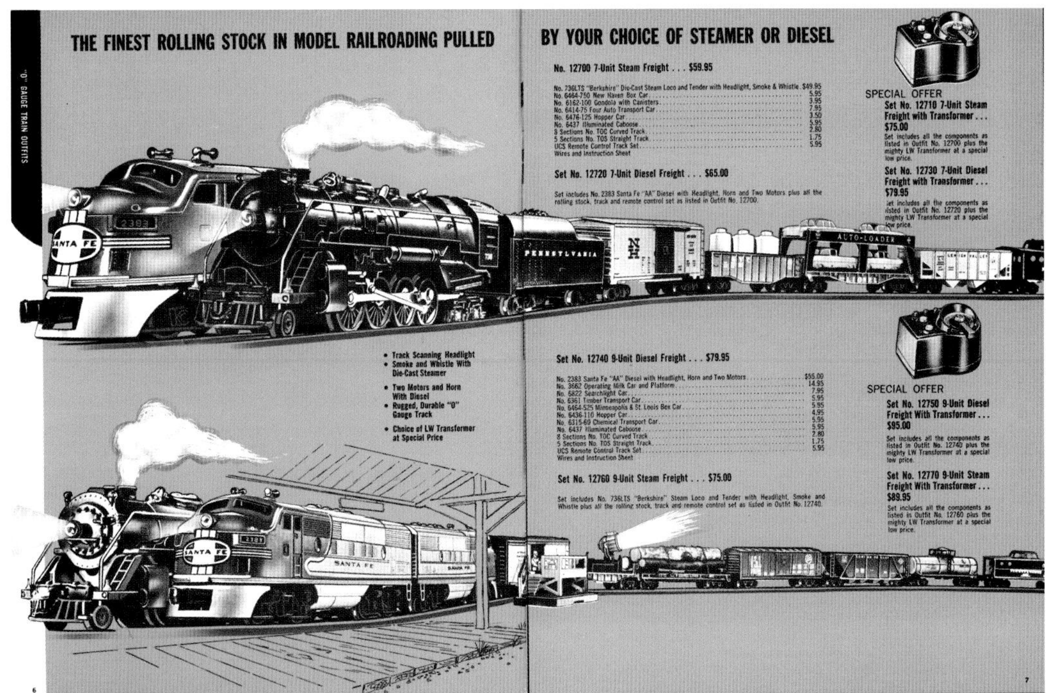

THE FINEST ROLLING STOCK IN MODEL RAILROADING PULLED BY YOUR CHOICE OF STEAMER OR DIESEL

"O" GAUGE TRAIN OUTFITS

No. 12700 7-Unit Steam Freight . . . $59.95

No. 736LTS "Berkshire" Die-Cast Steam Loco and Tender with Headlight, Smoke & Whistle	$49.95
No. 6464-750 New Haven Box Car	5.95
No. 6162-100 Gondola with Canisters	3.95
No. 6414-75 Four Auto Transport Car	7.95
No. 6476-125 Hopper Car	3.50
No. 6437 Illuminated Caboose	5.95
8 Sections No. TOC Curved Track	2.80
5 Sections No. TOS Straight Track	1.75
UCS Remote Control Track Set	5.95
Wires and Instruction Sheet	

SPECIAL OFFER

Set No. 12710 7-Unit Steam Freight with Transformer . . . $75.00

Set includes all the components as listed in Outfit No. 12700 plus the mighty LW Transformer at a special low price.

Set No. 12720 7-Unit Diesel Freight . . . $65.00

Set includes No. 2383 Santa Fe "AA" Diesel with Headlight, Horn and Two Motors plus all the rolling stock, track and remote control set as listed in Outfit No. 12700.

Set No. 12730 7-Unit Diesel Freight with Transformer . . . $79.95

Set includes all the components as listed in Outfit No. 12720 plus the mighty LW Transformer at a special low price.

- Track Scanning Headlight
- Smoke and Whistle With Die-Cast Steamer
- Two Motors and Horn With Diesel
- Rugged, Durable "O" Gauge Track
- Choice of LW Transformer at Special Price

Set No. 12740 9-Unit Diesel Freight . . . $79.95

No. 2383 Santa Fe "AA" Diesel with Headlight, Horn and Two Motors	$55.00
No. 3662 Operating Milk Car and Platform	14.95
No. 6822 Searchlight Car	7.95
No. 6361 Timber Transport Car	5.95
No. 6464-525 Minneapolis & St. Louis Box Car	5.95
No. 6436-110 Hopper Car	4.95
No. 6315-60 Chemical Transport Car	5.95
No. 6437 Illuminated Caboose	5.95
8 Sections No. TOC Curved Track	2.80
5 Sections No. TOS Straight Track	1.75
UCS Remote Control Track Set	5.95
Wires and Instruction Sheet	

SPECIAL OFFER

Set No. 12750 9-Unit Diesel Freight With Transformer . . . $95.00

Set includes all the components as listed in Outfit No. 12740 plus the mighty LW Transformer at a special low price.

Set No. 12760 9-Unit Steam Freight . . . $75.00

Set includes No. 736LTS "Berkshire" Steam Loco and Tender with Headlight, Smoke and Whistle plus all the rolling stock, track and remote control set as listed in Outfit No. 12740.

Set No. 12770 9-Unit Steam Freight With Transformer . . . $89.95

Set includes all the components as listed in Outfit No. 12760 plus the mighty LW Transformer at a special low price.

12700, 12720, 12740, 12760

Super 0

13150 Nine-Unit Steam Freight $225 retail

Included: 773 4-6-4 Hudson steam locomotive with headlight, smoke and Magne-traction; 736W tender; 3434 chicken sweeper car; 3356 operating horse car; 6436-110 Lehigh Valley hopper; 3662 operating milk car; 6415 Sunoco three-dome tank car; 6361 timber transport; 6437 Pennsylvania caboose; sixteen 31 curved, nineteen 32 straight and four 34 half-straight track; 112 pair remote-control switches; two 39-25 operating packets; 275-watt ZW transformer; SP smoke pellets; lubricant; instructions.

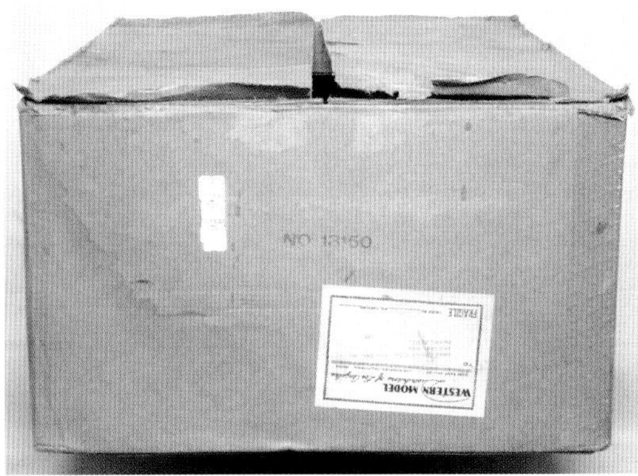

The top-of-the-line outfit in 1964—as well as the next two successive years—was this Hudson-led Super 0 set. Strangely, Lionel chose to pair the impressive and mighty New York Central Hudson replica with a streamlined tender lettered "Pennsylvania." While Lionel would correct this situation in later production, they persisted in finishing the train with a 6437 Pennsylvania porthole caboose.

The variation of the milk car included in this set has been described earlier in this chapter. The operating horse car rode on AAR-type trucks and after November was devoid of the "Blt 5-56 By Lionel" found on earlier editions of the car. It came with nine black horses, which were packed in their own white box inside operating horse car and corral outfit.

Continuing the 'only the best' theme of this outfit was the inclusion of the massive ZW transformer, which came in its own white box inside the outfit's huge tan carton.

The locomotive came inside a lined tan corrugated carton with red printing that included the date "1964." The rolling stock all came in Orange Picture boxes.

Excellent	Like New	Scarcity
2,800	4,850	7

Chapter 22

1965

LIONEL

Toys for 1965

Lionel changed very little in their offerings for 1965. The total number of sets offered in O-Gauge was reduced, but pleasantly outfits headed by the fabulous Virginian FM Train Master and Boston and Maine Geep returned. Five new outfits debuted in the 027 line, while the sole Super 0 offering was merely a re-cataloging of the 13150 of the year prior.

A new-style outfit box was introduced in 1965. On the front of the box was now a full-cover scene of a 2037-led freight train steaming through the countryside. The lid, which was not attached to the base, lifted off to expose the unboxed components. This style box was used almost exclusively for 027 outfits.

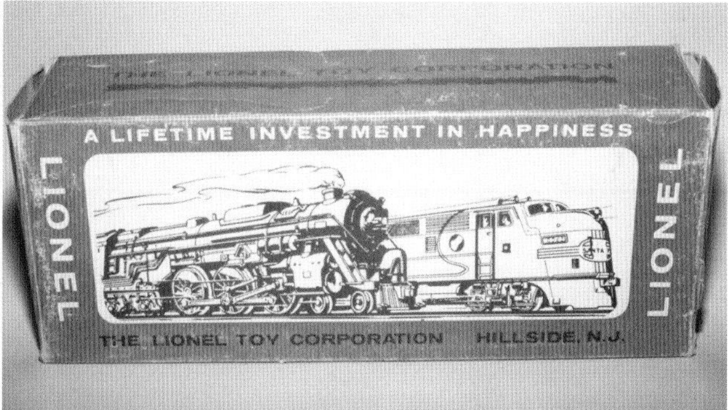

The Hillside picture box, introduced this year, was essentially the same as the earlier Orange Picture box, but rather than the showroom locations of New York and Chicago, the box sides bore "HILLSIDE, N.J." (the location of Lionel's factory) and bore the new corporate name "THE LIONEL TOY CORPORATION." This box was used for part of 1965.

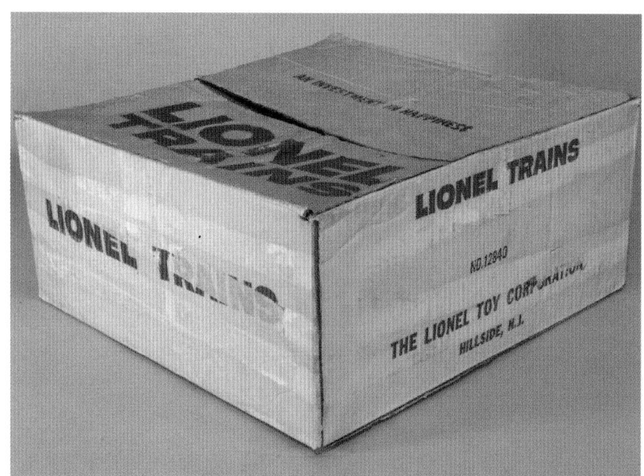

But for a single exception—outfit 12800 which came in the new 027 outfit box described above—1965 O-Gauge outfits came in this solid white box with orange lettering which had been introduced the year previously.

The late-style AAR-type trucks with open journals, first seen in 1963 were now used throughout the line. The 1965 trucks with operating couplers had knuckle pivot points that were molded integral with the knuckle, eliminating the knuckle rivet and its installation.

027-Gauge

11490 Five-Unit Diesel Passenger $55 retail

Included: 212P/212T Santa Fe Alco A-A units with horn; 2404 Vista Dome; 2405 Pullman; 2406 observation; eight 1013 curved and three 1018 straight track; 6149 uncoupling section; 1073 60-watt transformer; CTC Lockon; lubricant; instructions; 147 horn controller.

The 027 Santa Fe passenger outfit from 1964 returned in 1965. Some of these outfits were very likely produced and packaged in 1964. However, the appearance of these sets in the new-for-1965 outfit box is indicative that other sets were at least packaged, if not wholly produced in 1965.

Excellent	Like New	Scarcity
600	1,000	4

11500 Seven-Unit Steam Freight $50 retail

Included: 2029 steam locomotive with headlight and smoke; 234W tender; 6014-325 Frisco boxcar; 6402-50 flatcar with cable reels; 6176-75 Lehigh Valley hopper; 6465-150 Lionel Lines double-dome tank car; 6257-100 SP-type caboose with stack or 6059 Minneapolis & St. Louis SP-type caboose; eight 1013 curved and three 1018 straight track; 6149 uncoupling section; 1073 60-watt transformer; CTC Lockon; lubricant; instructions; 147 whistle controller.

Outfit 11500, like 11490, had been cataloged in 1964. However, the freight outfit was clearly returning due to positive sales, and there were clear differences between the two years' production. While the new box styling was a distinct change, less obvious was updated components. The improved AAR-truck design was used throughout the set, and the hopper car was now black, rather than yellow. The hopper number changed as well from 6176 to 6076.

Excellent	Like New	Scarcity
250	400	4

11520 Six-Unit Steam Freight $20 retail

Included: 242 2-4-2 steam locomotive with headlight; 1062T tender; 6176 Lehigh Valley hopper; 3364 log unloading car; 6142 gondola with canisters; 6059 Minneapolis & St. Louis SP-type caboose; eight 1013 curved and one 1018 straight track; 6149 uncoupling section; 1010 35-watt transformer; CTC Lockon; lubricant; instructions.

This was the least expensive outfit cataloged in 1965, yet it still contained an operating car—the log-unloading car. Despite being assigned product number 3364, the dark green car was actually stamped with the same number as its predecessor the 3362. This difference between the two cars was the cargo. The 3362 hauled helium tanks, while the 3364 was laden with three six-inch long, 5/8-inch diameter brown-stained logs. The car, like the others normally found in this outfit, had an operating coupler on one end, and a dummy coupler on the other.

The outfit included the 1062T Lionel Lines tender, which included grounding provisions, improving the performance of the locomotive, especially on uncoupling sections, turnouts and crossovers.

Excellent	Like New	Scarcity
100	175	2

11530 **$25 retail**

Included: 634 Santa Fe NW-2 diesel switcher; 6014 Frisco boxcar; 6142 gondola with canisters; 6402 flatcar with cable reels; 6130 Santa Fe work caboose; eight 1013 curved and one 1018 straight track; 6149 uncoupling section; 1010 35-watt transformer; CTC Lockon; lubricant; instructions.

Although the catalog showed the switcher at the front of this outfit to have safety stripes on its cab, most examples lack these stripes. Those switchers that do have the stripes are likely surplus 1963 production. In tow behind the switcher were cars in a rainbow of colors; a white boxcar, painted red caboose, gray flatcar, and either a blue or green—usually the latter—gondola.

The outfit box was normally the display type with artist's rendering on the cover, but some sets are known to have come in two-tier tan corrugated cartons. Regardless of set box type, the components were unboxed.

Excellent	Like New	Scarcity
175	300	2

11540 **$30 retail**

Included: 239 2-4-2 steam locomotive with headlight and smoke; 242T tender; 6176 Lehigh Valley hopper; 6473 rodeo car; 6465 Lionel Lines double-dome tank car; 6119-100 work caboose; eight 1013 curved and one 1018 straight track; 6149 uncoupling section; 1025 45-watt transformer; CTC Lockon; lubricant; instructions.

This was another of the outfits that included the rodeo car. The variation included in this outfit had no damaged slats (as described above), used the new "open journal"-type AAR trucks, and could be lettered in either red or maroon.

The heat-stamped die-cast Scout-type 239 was mated with a small streamlined Lionel Lines tender. However, unlike the earlier tenders of this style, this fixed-coupler tender, which rode on the new-style AAR trucks, was equipped with an electrical ground.

The two-dome tank car was unpainted orange plastic with unpainted black ends. The work caboose had a red cab and gray tool bin.

Excellent	Like New	Scarcity
175	300	5

11550 **$40 retail**

Included: 239 2-4-2 steam locomotive with headlight and smoke; 234W tender; 6176 Lehigh Valley hopper; 6473 rodeo car; 6465 Lionel Lines double-dome tank car; 6119-100 work caboose; eight 1013 curved and one 1018 straight track; 6149 uncoupling section; 1073 60-watt transformer; CTC Lockon; lubricant; instructions; 147 whistle controller.

This was another of the many 1965 sets that used two styles of packaging—either the display-type or the two-tier tan corrugated carton. Regardless of style of the outfit box, the components were not individually boxed—nor were they exciting.

The two-dome tank car was unpainted orange with black ends. The hopper could be yellow or black, but is more commonly the latter. The rodeo car used in 1965 has been described earlier in this chapter, as has the locomotive and caboose. The tender was the 234W, a whistle tender with non-operating coupler.

Excellent	Like New	Scarcity
225	375	4

11560 **$37.50 retail**

Included: 211P/211T Texas Special Alco A-A units; 6142 gondola with canisters; 6076 Lehigh Valley hopper; 6465 Lionel Lines double-dome tank car; 6473 rodeo car; 6059 Minneapolis & St. Louis SP-type caboose; twelve 1013 curved and three 1018 straight track; 90-degree crossing; 6149 uncoupling section; 1025 45-watt transformer; CTC Lockon; lubricant; instructions.

Paired red and white Texas Special Alco A-units lead this outfit, and the locos were the most interesting of the set components, which was all run of the mill. None of the components were individually boxed and the rolling stock each had one operating and one non-operating coupler. A black hopper and blue gondola were typically included in this set. But yellow hoppers and green gondolas have been known to surface with the outfit. The outfit was packed in the new-style set box.

Excellent	Like New	Scarcity
250	400	2

O-Gauge

12710 Seven-Unit Steam Freight **$80 retail**

Included: 736 2-8-4 Berkshire steam locomotive with headlight, smoke and Magne-traction; 736W tender; 6414-75 Evans Auto Loader; 6464-725 New Haven boxcar; 6162-100 gondola with canisters; 6476-125 Lehigh Valley hopper; 6437 Pennsylvania porthole caboose; eight OC curved and five OS straight track; UCS uncoupling/operating section; LW transformer; SP smoke pellets; CTC Lockon; lubricant; instructions.

This impressive steam outfit was a repeat of an outfit with the same number cataloged the year previously. However, this was not merely an effort to deplete the carry-over outfit, rather, it was an effort to continue the previous years' success. Evidence of this comes in the form of reports of this outfit containing Hillside Picture component boxes.

Excellent	Like New	Scarcity
925	1,550	5

12730 Seven-Unit Diesel Freight **$85 retail**

Included: 2383 Santa Fe A-A F-3 units; 6414-75 Evans Auto Loader; 6464-725 New Haven boxcar; 6162-100 gondola with canisters; 6476-125 Lehigh Valley hopper; 6437 Pennsylvania porthole caboose; eight OC curved and five OS straight track; UCS uncoupling/operating section; LW transformer; CTC Lockon; lubricant; instructions.

Another returning, successful outfit was this Santa Fe F3-led freight set. Other than the locomotive, it was identical to the Berkshire-equipped 12710. Once again, further 1965 packaging can be confirmed by the appearance of Hillside Picture boxes.

Excellent	Like New	Scarcity
1,500	2,500	5

12780 Six-Unit Diesel Passenger **$125 retail**

Included: 2383P/2383T Santa Fe A-A F-3 units; 2522 President Harrison Vista Dome; two 2523 President Garfield Pullmans; 2521 President McKinley observation; eight OC curved and five OS straight track; UCS uncoupling/operating section.

A Santa Fe powered passenger train continued to be offered; now cataloged as 12780. The dual-motor F-3 was placed in front of two President Garfield Pullmans, a President Harrison dome and a President McKinley observation. The passenger cars in this outfit came in Hillside Picture boxes, unlike previous editions. The outfit box was the two-tier white set carton.

Excellent	Like New	Scarcity
3,300	5,500	5

12800 **$60 retail**

Included: 2346 Boston and Maine GP-9; 6464-475 Boston and Maine boxcar; 6428 U.S. Mail boxcar; 6436 Lehigh Valley hopper; 6415 Sunoco three-dome tank car; 6017-100 Boston and Maine SP-type caboose; eight curved and five straight track; UCS uncoupling/operating section.

Unlike the other O-Gauge outfits, which came in white two-tier cartons, this set came in the same new type of display box used by 027 outfits. Of course, this meant the new 2346 Boston and Maine diesel, as well as the rest of the components, did not have individual boxes. Unlike so many of Lionel's sets, the caboose of this outfit actually matched the locomotive. Not only that, but so did one of the set's two boxcars! Sometimes this Boston and Maine boxcar surfaces with a deep blue color, which is somewhat difficult to locate.

Both boxcars, as did the rest of the rolling stock, came with late, open-journal AAR-type trucks. These trucks all had operating couplers.

Excellent	Like New	Scarcity
600	1,000	3

12820 **$100 retail**

Included: 2322 Virginian Train Master; 6464-725 New Haven boxcar; 6436 Lehigh Valley hopper; 3662 operating milk car; 6822 searchlight car; 6361 timber transport; 6315 Lionel Lines tank car; 6437 Pennsylvania caboose; eight curved and five straight track; UCS uncoupling/operating section; 125-watt LW transformer.

The blue-and-yellow Virginian Train Master made a surprising return this year after a seven-year absence. This is one of the most common FMs, and often the chassis from these locomotives are placed inside earlier, more desirable bodies, whose original chassis may have been damaged by leaking batteries. The 1960s era FMs have green or orange windings on their motors and E-unit coils. The proper box for the locomotive in this outfit was made by United Container, and is stamped with a "65" date, and includes a liner.

Green wire was also used to wind the coil of the 3662 operating milk car. This car rode on the newer, open-journal type AAR trucks, and the roofs and other cast brown components had a deep hue.

The 6822 included in this set also was equipped with the open-journal type trucks. The searchlight housing was black and the car superstructure was unpainted gray plastic. The logs of the 6361 timber transport were held in place by black-oxide coated chains. A Lionel Lines deluxe tank car and 6437 Pennsylvania porthole caboose completed the rolling stock.

The rolling stock was packed in a combination of Orange Picture and Hillside Picture boxes. The outfit box itself was the typical white set carton with orange printing.

Excellent	Like New	Scarcity
1,500	2,500	5

Super O

13150 Nine-Unit Steam Freight **$225 retail**

Included: 773 4-6-4 Hudson steam locomotive with headlight, smoke and Magne-traction; 773W tender; 6436-110 Lehigh Valley hopper; 3434 chicken sweeper car; 3356 operating horse car; 3662 operating milk car; 6415 Sunoco tank car; 6361 timber transport; 6437 Pennsylvania porthole caboose; sixteen 31 curved, nineteen 32 straight and four 34 half-straight track; 112 pair remote-control switches; two 39-25 operating packets; 275-watt ZW transformer; SP smoke pellets; lubricant; instructions.

This incredible outfit returned for the second year, possibly merely to sell off carry-over merchandise. Research in preparing this volume did not uncover any of these outfits unquestionably produced or packaged in 1965. This would include green coil windings on the milk car, and green or red windings on the horse car's coil.

Excellent	Like New	Scarcity
3,000	5,000	7

Chapter 23

1966

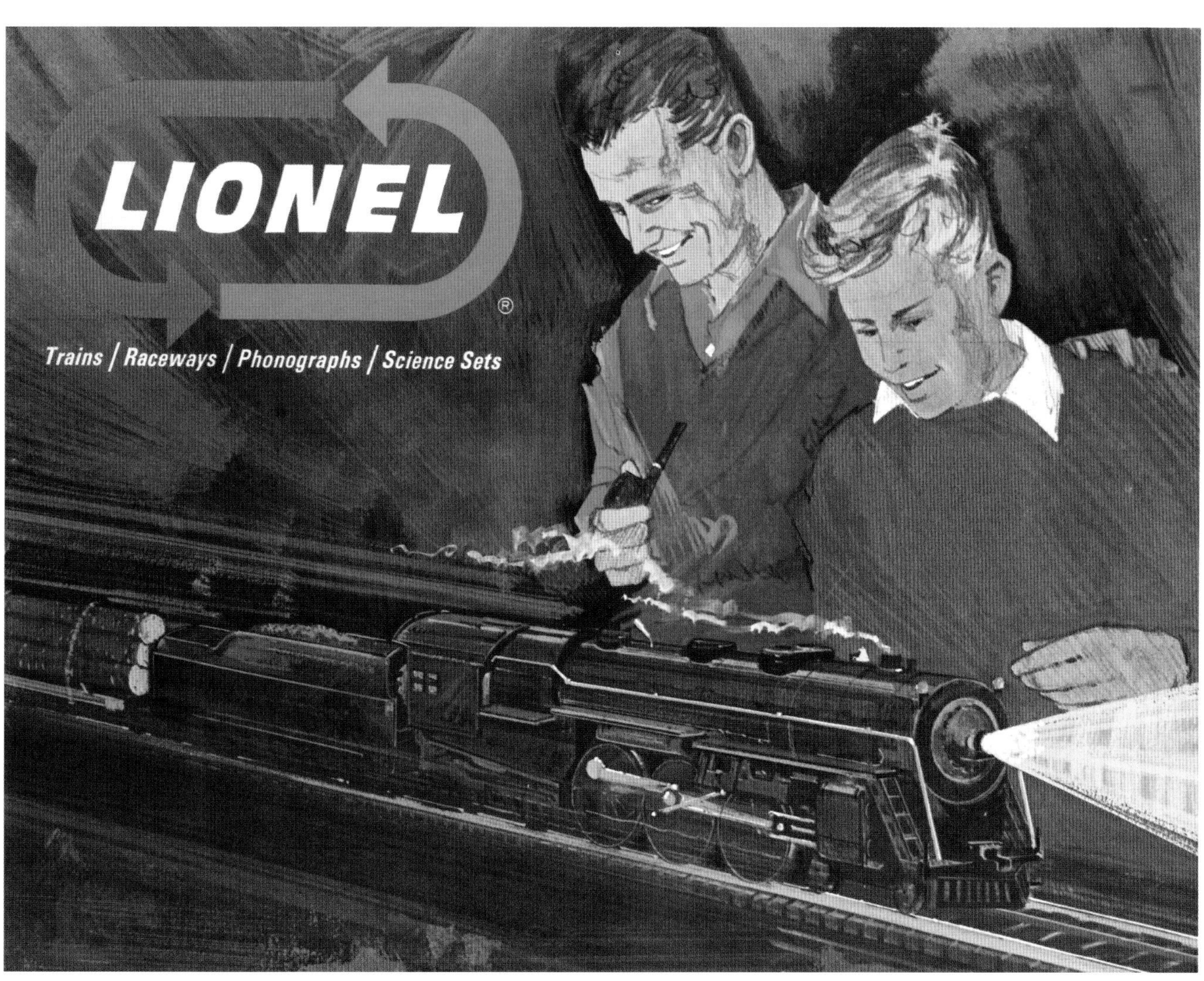

Although the catalog had a totally new look this year, for the first time relying totally on color photographs, the bulk of the trains looked very familiar. Almost all of the outfits, as well as separate sale items, were repeats from the previous two years. Only one Super 0 outfit was offered—the fabulous 13150 led the massive 773 Hudson steam locomotive. This was to be the final year for both Super 0 and O-Gauge.

Outfit packaging, as a rule, was a repeat of the 1965 flat packaging with an artist's rendering on the front. Component packaging was changed, with the new box having a transparent front. The boxes were more generic than their predecessors, with the stock number being rubber stamped according to contents, rather than being machine printed during the box's manufacturing process.

For the second year Lionel packed 027 outfits in this flat box, with colorful artists rendering of a train on the front.

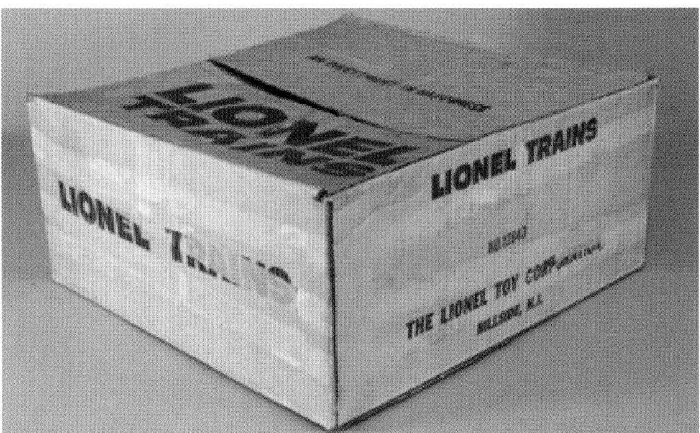

This rather plain white box with orange lettering was used for O-Gauge outfits during 1966.

Furthering the idea introduced with 1958's Perforated box, in 1966, Lionel introduced the Window box. With this box the contents were still visible through a cellophane window in the front of the box, but yet were protected from shop wear and dust. Today this box is often found with cellophane loose or missing.

11500

11500 **Seven-Unit Steam Freight** **$50 retail**
Included: 2029 2-6-4 steam locomotive with headlight and smoke; 234W tender; 6014-325 Frisco boxcar; 6402-50 flatcar with cable reels; 6176 Lehigh Valley hopper; 6465-150 Lionel Lines double-dome tank car; 6257-100 SP-type caboose with stack or 6059 Minneapolis & St. Louis SP-type caboose; eight 1013 curved and three 1018 straight track; 6149 uncoupling section; 1073 60-watt transformer; CTC Lockon; lubricant; instructions; 147 whistle controller.

For the third year the die-cast 2029 returned at the lead of this outfit. The set was unchanged from previous issues except for the Lehigh Valley hopper, which was now yellow rather than black.

Excellent	Like New	Scarcity
250	400	4

11520 **Six-Unit Steam Freight** **$22.50 retail**
Included: 242 2-4-2 steam locomotive with headlight; 1062T slope-back tender; 6176 Lehigh Valley hopper; 3362/3364 operating log car; 6142 gondola with canisters; 6059 Minneapolis & St. Louis SP-type caboose; eight 1013 curved and one 1018 straight track; 6149 uncoupling section; 1010 35-watt transformer; CTC Lockon; lubricant; instructions.

This outfit was a repeat of an identical set, with the same number, issued the previous year. This was to be the case with several outfits in 1966.

Excellent	Like New	Scarcity
100	175	2

11530 **Five-Unit Diesel Freight** **$25 retail**
Included: 634 Santa Fe NW-2 diesel switcher; 6014 Frisco boxcar; 6142 gondola with canisters; (6402) General-type flatcar with cable reels; 6130 Santa Fe work caboose; eight 1013 curved and one 1018 straight track; 6149 uncoupling section; 1010 35-watt transformer; CTC Lockon; lubricant; instructions.

This outfit was also a repeat of an outfit with the same number offered the previous year. In addition to the display box, some of these sets were packaged in brown two-tier outfit boxes with cardboard dividers.

Excellent	Like New	Scarcity
175	300	2

11540 **Six-Unit Steam Freight** **$31.50 retail**
Included: 239 2-4-2 steam locomotive with headlight and smoke; 242T tender; 6473 rodeo car; 6465 Lionel Lines double-dome tank car; 6176 Lehigh Valley hopper; 6119-100 work caboose; eight 1013 curved and one 1018 straight track; 6149 uncoupling section; 1073 60-watt transformer; CTC Lockon; lubricant; instructions; 147 whistle controller.

This outfit was a more economically priced version of set 11550. The $10 retail savings was achieved by deleting the whistle and associated components. The 1073 transformer; CTC Lockon; lubricant; instructions and 147 controller found in 11550 were replaced with a 1025, and at the same time the 234W tender was replaced by the whistle-less 242T.

Excellent	Like New	Scarcity
175	300	5

11550 **Six-Unit Steam Freight** **$41.50 retail**
Included: 239 2-4-2 steam locomotive with headlight and smoke; 234W square whistle tender; 6473 rodeo car; 6465 Lionel Lines double-dome tank car; 6176 Lehigh Valley hopper; 6119-100 work caboose; eight 1013 curved and one 1018 straight track; 6149 uncoupling section; 1073 60-watt transformer; CTC Lockon; lubricant; instructions; 147 whistle controller.

Outfit 11550 first appeared in 1965, with sufficient sales to warrant being cataloged again in 1966. Not only that, evidence indicates additional production occurred in 1966 as well. The new edition of the outfit contains a rubber-stamped version of the die-cast steamer, whereas 1965-dated outfits have a rubber-stamped version of the loco. Further, the work caboose found in 1966 sets is frequently the relatively hard-to-find version with a builder's plate stamped "BUILT BY LIONEL." The black hopper car of the 1965 set was replaced with a yellow version in 1966.

The 1966 version of the outfit has been reported in two different types of packaging. While most came in the flat package, some also were packaged in a two-tier tan corrugated carton. Regardless of package style, a label was pasted on the carton, which featured a photograph of the outfit inside.

Excellent	Like New	Scarcity
225	375	4

11560 Seven-Unit Diesel Freight $37.50 retail

Included: 211P/211T Texas Special Alco A-A units; 6473 rodeo car; 6076 Lehigh Valley hopper; 6142 gondola with canisters; 6465 Lionel Lines double-dome tank car; 6059 Minneapolis & St. Louis SP-type caboose; twelve 1013 curved and three 1018 straight track; 90-degree crossing; 6149 uncoupling section; 1025 45-watt transformer; CTC Lockon; lubricant; instructions.

Another of the many repeated sets offered in 1966 was this outfit led by a pair of Texas Special Alcos.

Excellent	Like New	Scarcity
250	400	2

11590 Five-Unit Illuminated Passenger $60 retail

Included: 212P/212T Santa Fe Alco A-A units with horn; 2408 Vista Dome; 2409 Pullman; 2410 observation; eight 1013 curved and three 1018 straight track; 6149 uncoupling section; 1073 60-watt transformer; CTC Lockon; lubricant; instructions; 147 horn controller.

Evidently Lionel regretted their earlier decision to strip their 027 passenger cars of illumination, as lighting returned in this outfit. The new blue-striped cars included in this set also had windows with silhouettes, a feature that had been deleted previously with the illumination. The outfit was packed in the 1965-style flat box with formed dividers.

Excellent	Like New	Scarcity
700	1,100	4

O-Gauge

12710 Seven-Unit Steam Freight $85 retail

Included: 736 2-8-4 Berkshire steam locomotive with headlight, smoke and Magne-traction; 736W tender; 6414-75 Evans Auto Loader; 6464-725 New Haven boxcar; 6162-100 gondola with canisters; 6476-125 Lehigh Valley hopper; 6437 Pennsylvania porthole caboose; eight OC curved and five OS straight track; UCS uncoupling/operating section; LW transformer; SP smoke pellets; CTC Lockon; lubricant; instructions.

This Berkshire-led set returned for the third and final time in 1966—indeed, this would be the final time the venerable Berkshire was placed at the front of a cataloged outfit. Although the set was indeed a repeat, all of them were not carry-forward merchandise, as evidenced by some outfits containing Window boxes.

Excellent	Like New	Scarcity
925	1,650	5

12730 Seven-Unit Diesel Freight $90 retail

Included: 2383 Santa Fe A-A F-3 units; 6414-75 Evans Auto Loader; 6464-725 New Haven boxcar; 6162-100 gondola with canisters; 6476-125 Lehigh Valley hopper; 6437 Pennsylvania porthole caboose; eight OC curved and five OS straight track; UCS uncoupling/operating section; LW transformer; CTC Lockon; lubricant; instructions.

As was the case for the 12720, this set made its third and final appearance in 1966. And, as with the Berkshire of 12720, the classic Santa Fe F-3 diesels would vanish with this, and its passenger sister 12780. Once again, presence of Window boxes in some outfits indicates they were packaged during 1966, although some were also likely carry-over merchandise from 1965.

Excellent	Like New	Scarcity
1,500	2,500	5

12780 Six-Unit Diesel Passenger $125 retail

Included: 2383P/2383T Santa Fe A-A F-3 units; 2522 President Harrison Vista Dome; two 2523 President Garfield Pullmans; 2521 President McKinley observation; eight OC curved and five OS straight track; UCS uncoupling/operating section.

This outfit was also making its third appearance—four if one considers the identical but for the number outfit from 1963. This was also the swan song for Santa Fe F-3-powered streamliners and the Santa Fe F-3s period. While some of these may have been carry-forward merchandise from 1965, Window boxes found in some sets indicate that they were packed in 1966. Two sizes of white outfit boxes were used during the packaging of this outfit.

Excellent	Like New	Scarcity
3,300	5,500	5

12800 Six-Unit Diesel Freight $60 retail

Included: 2346 Boston and Maine GP-9; 6428 U.S. Mail boxcar; 6464-475 Boston and Maine boxcar; 6436 Lehigh Valley hopper; 6415 Sunoco three-dome tank car; 6017-100 Boston and Maine SP-type caboose; eight OC curved and five OS straight track; UCS uncoupling/operating section.

Yet another returning outfit was this Boston and Maine set, first cataloged in 1965. No changes were made between the years, and today this outfit is relatively easily found in collectable condition, no doubt due in no small part to the outfit's availability until the very end of Madison Hardware.

Excellent	Like New	Scarcity
600	1,000	3

12840 Seven-Unit Steam Freight $80 retail

Included: 665 4-6-4 steam locomotive with headlight, smoke and Magne-traction; 736W tender; 6464-375 Central of Georgia; 6464-450 Great Northern boxcars; 6431 flatcar with vans and Midge toy tractor; 6415 Sunoco three-dome tank car; 6437 Pennsylvania porthole caboose; eight OC curved and five OS straight track; UCS uncoupling/operating section; 125-watt LW transformer; SP smoke pellets or smoke fluid; CTC Lockon; lubricant; instructions.

Amazingly, considering the trend of the times at Lionel, the 665 baby Hudson returned to the line in 1966. This, the final edition, can be distinguished by the green or orange wire used to wind the motor and E-units this year. Interestingly, some of these locomotives were equipped with fluid-type smoke generators rather than the normal pill-type. The locomotive was packed in a tan corrugated carton made by Consolidated Container Corp.

Those collectors comparing their outfits to the catalog photo will be surprised at the differences. The catalog illustration shows bar-end metal trucks on the tender. In fact AAR-type plastic trucks were used. The molding used on the 6464 boxcars differed slightly from what was shown in the catalog. Finally, the vans in the photo have Cooper-Jarrett plates, which were not in fact installed on the trailers in the set.

Among set components, it is the 6431 flatcar with vans and Midge toy tractor that is of greatest singular interest to collectors. The flatcar itself was stamped "6430" to the left of "LIONEL"—the number 6431 appearing only on the box. That number denoted the flat and vans came with a red die-cast Midge toy tractor, which was held in the oversized Window box by a special folded insert. Like the other components of this set, the flatcar was equipped with AAR-type trucks.

The individual components of this set, but for the locomotive, came in Window boxes. The outfit box itself was the white corrugated carton with orange lettering introduced the previous year.

Excellent	Like New	Scarcity
900	1,600	5

12850 Eight-Unit Diesel Freight $135 retail

Included: 2322 Virginian Train Master; 6464-725 New Haven boxcar; 6436 Lehigh Valley hopper; 3662 operating milk car; 6822 searchlight car; 6315 Lionel Lines tank car; 6361 timber transport; 6437 Pennsylvania porthole caboose; pair 022 turnouts; 10 OC curved and 14 OS straight track; UCS uncoupling/operating section; 125-watt LW transformer; CTC Lockon; lubricant; instructions.

This outfit was nearly a duplicate of the 1965-vintage 12820, only with additional track and a pair of switches. Looking into the large white outfit box it looks like Lionel was cleaning out the warehouse—which is likely what was happening—as components were packed in Orange Picture, Hillside Picture and Window boxes.

Excellent	Like New	Scarcity
1,500	2,500	5

Super 0

13150 Nine-Unit Steam Freight $225 retail

Included: 773 4-6-4 Hudson steam locomotive with headlight, smoke and Magne-traction; 773W tender; 3434 chicken sweeper car; 3356 operating horse car; 6436-110 Lehigh Valley hopper; 3662 operating milk car; 6415 Sunoco three-dome tank car; 6361 timber transport; 6437 Pennsylvania porthole caboose; sixteen 31 curved, nineteen 32 straight and four 34 half-straight track; 112 pair remote-control switches; two 39-25 operating packets; 275-watt ZW transformer; SP smoke pellets; lubricant; instructions.

The mighty Hudson, as well as Super 0 outfits bid farewell with this, the third appearance of outfit 13150. As with the two previous editions, it is very difficult to find this outfit with its original set box because that box was so large, and hence flimsy. Window boxes have been found in this set, proving that some of these sets were at least packaged in 1966, even though the trains themselves may have been produced in prior years.

Excellent	Like New	Scarcity
3,500	11,000	7

Chapter 24

1967

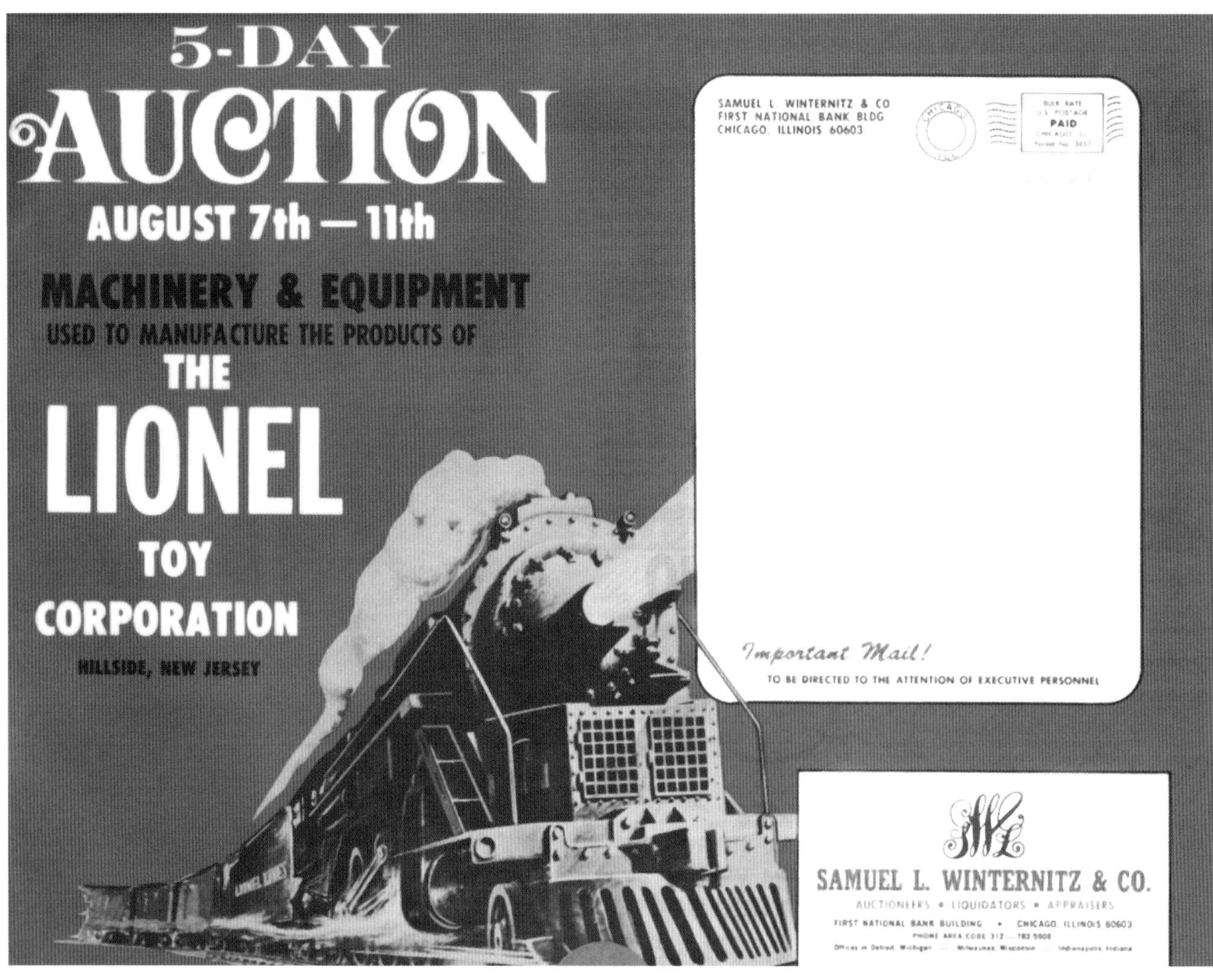

The most somber year of the postwar era for Lionel enthusiasts was 1967. But for 1943-44, when the company produced war material exclusively, this was the only year that a catalog was not issued since 1900. Perhaps even more indicative of the company's troubled position, no trains were produced during 1967 either—the company, relying heavily on its electronics and defense business—sold only carry-over merchandise—some of which had been languishing in the massive warehouse since the 1950s. Some uncataloged sets were packaged for select accounts, drawing entirely on the stock in hand for the components.

During this time the company sat out to vacate the massive Hillside plant, moving operations to the smaller Hagerstown, Md. facility of its Porter subsidiary. This led to a catalog being issued, but not *by* Lionel, instead, told volumes *about* Lionel. This was the auction catalog issued by Samuel L. Winternitz & Co. of Chicago. This 23-page catalog promoted the auction, by Winternitz, of the equipment and machinery housed at Hillside. Though Lionel announced their intentions to stay in the train business—at least the 027 train business—the disposal of equipment and facilities amassed over two-thirds of a century was not seen as a commitment to further train production by hobbyists.

For Lionel buffs, the most dismal catalog in the company's history—and it wasn't even issued by the company!

CHAPTER 25

1968

1968
TRAINS
AND
ACCESSORIES

THE LEADER IN MODEL RAILROADING

At any other point in the company history, the 1968 catalog would have been considered disastrous. However, since not only was there no catalog issued in 1967, but the company went so far as to liquidate the production equipment housed in the Hillside plant, any catalog, no matter how thin, was an improvement. Joy over the issuance of the catalog was tempered though by the listing of but a single train set—the 027-Gauge.

HAGERSTOWN CHECKERBOARD: In 1968, the separate sale boxes were revised yet again and featured a bold white and orange checkerboard pattern. Yet again, the city imprint changed as well, this time to "HAGERSTOWN, MARYLAND," reflecting Lionel's 1967 relocation of manufacturing operations to the Hagerstown facility of its Porter science subsidiary.

11600 **No retail**

Included: 2029 steam locomotive with headlight and smoke; 234W tender; 6014 Frisco boxcar; 6560 crane; 6476 Lehigh Valley hopper; 6315 Lionel Lines tank car; 6130 Santa Fe work caboose; remote-control left-hand switch; 260 black plastic illuminated bumper; twelve 1013 curved and six 1018 straight track; 90-degree crossing; 6149 uncoupling section; 1044 90-watt transformer; CTC Lockon; SP pellets; instruction sheet.

Almost every item in this outfit looked familiar, yet was strangely different from anything preceding it. The display box looked familiar from the front, but the blue sides of the package were unique. Also unique was the placement of the track, turnout and crossing beneath a false bottom, which supported the train itself. Similarly, the 2029 was a returning number, but was now made in Japan, and its nameplate read "Lionel, Hagerstown, Md., rather than "New York, New York."

The venerable 6560 crane was included in the outfit, but now rather than black, dark blue plastic was used for the frame and boom. Its companion, the 6130 work caboose, also had odd characteristics. Specifically, the frame was chemically treated, rather than painted, which resulted in it having an odd golden-black color. The same coloration is found on the hand wheels and hook on the crane. The unpainted red cab of the caboose featured a molded-in, but unused, builder's plate.

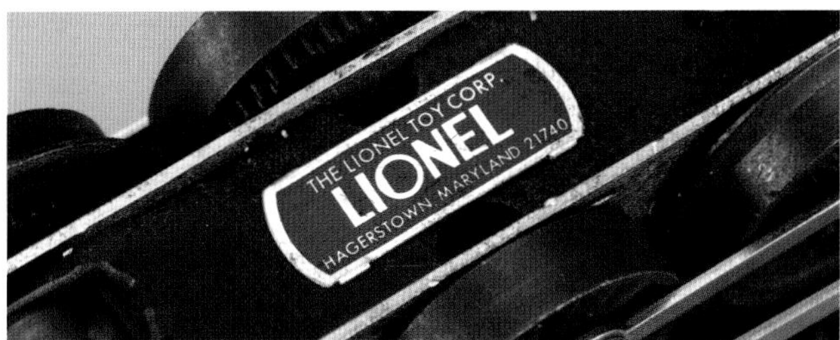

The nameplate of the 2029 included in this outfit listed Hagerstown, Md. as Lionel's base of operations.

Despite Hagerstown on the nameplate, the locomotive's true origins are revealed by the "Japan" on the trailing truck.

The yellow hopper car was listed as a 6476, yet the car itself—if it had any number stamped on it at all—bore the number 6176. At least it, like the rest of the rolling stock in this outfit, had couplers on both of its AAR-type trucks.

A Hagerstown Checkerboard box housed the black plastic 260 bumper that was included in the outfit. It was intended that this bumper, used in conjunction with the turnout, would allow increased play value from this set.

Excellent	Like New	Scarcity
750	1,250	6

CHAPTER 26

1969

With six outfits listed, the 1969 catalog was a considerable expansion over the 1968 edition. But so few sets, all only 027, made the selection a far cry from those of a decade earlier. Things were not well for Lionel, and a look through the catalog revealed it. Before the year ended, the Lionel Corp. had inked a deal with General Mills. In exchange for the modest sum of $650,000, Lionel ceded thousands of tools, and, in return for a royalty payment, General Mills gained the rights to the vaunted Lionel name in the toy train market.

Conventional two-tier outfit boxes returned in 1969, but now they were white and listed "Hillside, N.J." as the corporate home. An identifying label pasted on one end and on the label was a photo of the set inside—an excellent merchandising technique, but too late. Cardboard dividers inside protected the components, which lacked individual boxes.

A new outfit box was introduced in 1969. The clean white box and bright label with the full-color photo of the trains inside was a great merchandising move, but would last only one year.

No new designs were offered this year and any new color schemes introduced were the result of using different marking colors with existing heat-stamp tooling. Arch-bar and AAR-type trucks were used in the outfits, with little consistency with regard to style, or coupler type. One item that was consistent throughout the sets was the instruction sheet, as only a single style was printed and it was included with each outfit.

11710 **No retail**

Included: 1061 2-4-2 steam locomotive; 1061T or 1062T slope-back tender; 6402 flatcar with cable reels; 6142 gondola with canisters; 6059 Minneapolis & St. Louis caboose; eight 1013 curved and two 1018 straight track; 1025 45-watt transformer; CTC Lockon; instruction sheet.

Other than the outfit as a whole, there is little in most of these sets to interest collectors. However, there is one notable exception—some of these outfits include a scarce variation of the 1061 which was not decorated with heat stamping, but rather by a pasted-on black paper label with the white "1061" printed on it. This variation of the locomotive, in top condition, is easily worth twice as much as the entire outfit with the standard locomotive.

The rolling stock was wholly inexpensive, although most cars were equipped with a working coupler on one end, and a fixed coupler on the other. The gondola, which was usually green, was laden with only two canisters. When the car body was introduced more than a decade earlier, it came with four canisters. That the load would be reduced, despite being so inexpensive to begin with, was indicative of the strained situation at Lionel.

Some examples of outfit 11710 have been known to contain this scarce variation of the 1061. Rather than having heat-stamped lettering, a simple paper label with the locomotive number was pasted beneath the cab window.

The flatcar included in the outfit was molded in gray plastic from the tooling created to produce the flatcar for the "General" steam sets 10 years earlier. This mold, which had seen little use, was in good shape and required little plastic to fill—holding costs down. In this outfit the car bore two cable reels, without wire.

The Minneapolis and St. Louis caboose was unpainted with white heat-stamped markings. All the components were placed unboxed inside the new-for-1969 outfit box.

Excellent	Like New	Scarcity
100	225	3

11720 **No retail**

Included: 2024 Chesapeake & Ohio Alco A-unit; 6402 flatcar with cable reels; 6142 gondola with canisters; 6176 Lehigh Valley hopper; 6057 unstamped SP-type caboose; eight 1013 curved and three 1018 straight track; 6149 uncoupling section; 1025 45-watt transformer; CTC Lockon; instruction sheet.

1969

A single Alco A-unit powered this freight outfit. The unpainted blue diesel body was decorated in Chesapeake & Ohio markings and was numbered 2024.

Stretching behind the diesel was a caboose and three inexpensive freight cars. It was intended that each car come with one fixed and one operating coupler, but some cars have been reported with operating couplers on each end. Once again the green gondola carried only two canisters, and the caboose was even devoid of markings—both efforts to save pennies, or fractions of a penny, on each item. The 6402 flatcar, which was to be a mainstay of sets this year, carried two empty cable reels.

Excellent	Like New	Scarcity
200	350	5

11730 **No retail**

Included: 645 Union Pacific NW-2 diesel switcher; 6014-85 Frisco boxcar; 6176 6402 flatcar with boat; 6142 gondola with canisters; Lehigh Valley hopper; 6167-85 Union Pacific SP-type caboose; eight 1013 curved and five 1018 straight track; 6149 uncoupling section; 1025 45-watt transformer; CTC Lockon; instruction sheet.

The Union Pacific NW2 switcher was matched with a 6167-85 Union Pacific caboose in this outfit, making it one of the few sets, particularly of the 1960s, that had matching road names on the locomotive and caboose. However, this was more a result of serendipity than design. The caboose body was first produced in 1963 and was cataloged through 1966. It is likely that those incorporated into this outfit were merely a surplus of earlier productions.

Of the remaining cars, the one that garners the most attention from collectors is the 6402 flatcar. Although this car was included in other 1969 outfits carrying cable reels, in this set its cargo was a blue-hulled 6801-75 boat.

Also included was an orange Frisco boxcar and a black Lehigh Valley hopper, which was cataloged as a 6176, but did not actually have that, or any other number stamped on it. The set components were packed into the new-style two-tier set box, where cardboard dividers separated the unboxed locomotive and cars.

Excellent	Like New	Scarcity
300	500	4

11740 **No retail**

Included: 2041P/2041T Rock Island Alco A-A units; 6014-410 Frisco boxcar; 6142 gondola with canisters; 6476 Lehigh Valley hopper; 6315 tank car; 6057 unstamped SP-type caboose or 6059 Minneapolis & St. Louis SP-type caboose; eight 1013 curved and seven 1018 straight track; 6149 uncoupling section; 1025 45-watt transformer; CTC Lockon; instruction sheet.

An A-A pair of Alcos led this set, which was the top of the line diesel outfit for 1969. Because this was considered a "better" set, the cars included typically had operating couplers on each end. The outfit also included a returning, and revamped O-Gauge-sized single dome tank car. Overall orange and wearing Gulf livery, the returning car is known to sometimes be the hard-to-find version with "BLT 1-56" stamped near the ladder. Most of these cars, including those produced the year previously for separate sale, lacked this date marking.

In tow behind the locos were a white Frisco boxcar, yellow Lehigh Valley hopper and green gondola. Bringing up the rear of the train was typically an unpainted maroon Minneapolis & St. Louis caboose—ironic given the Rock Island locos in front.

Excellent	Like New	Scarcity
325	550	5

11750 **No retail**

Included: 2029 2-6-4 steam locomotive with operating headlight and smoke; 234T tender; 6014-85 Frisco boxcar; 6476 Lehigh Valley hopper; 6473 rodeo car; 6315 tank car; 6130 Santa Fe work caboose; seven 1013 curved and seven 1018 straight track; 6149 uncoupling section; 1025 45-watt transformer; CTC Lockon; instruction sheet.

A die-cast steamer was included in this, and the top-of-the-line 11760 outfit. The locomotive in question was the 2029, which was in itself rather uninteresting. However, accompanying the locomotive was a 234T non-whistling tender. Despite its lack of a whistle, Lionel persisted in using the same tender shell for both this and the whistle-equipped 234W, which meant its lettering read "234W." Even more interesting was the fact that some of these were stamped "Pennsylvania" rather than Lionel Lines. Beware, this highly collectible tender shell has been reproduced, and the reproductions are of high quality.

Behind the steamer was an unnumbered 6476 black Lehigh Valley hopper, an orange 6014-85 Frisco boxcar, a 6315 Gulf tank car, as well as a 6130 caboose and 6473 rodeo car. The caboose was built on a chemically-treated, unpainted frame, and featured an unpainted red cab with unmarked builder's plate—just as found in the 1968 11600 outfit. Apparently, however, a short additional assembly run of the caboose was required to fill outfit orders, as some of these cabooses turn up with gray rather than red tool bins.

The 6473 rodeo car was produced in numerous variations through the years, but the version included in this set is identifiable. The car has two operating couplers, red heat-stamped markings and has an unpainted body molded of cadmium-yellow plastic.

The entire outfit was naturally packaged in the new-style set carton and none of the components were individually boxed.

Excellent	Like New	Scarcity
500	800	6

11760 **No retail**

Included: 2029 2-6-4 steam locomotive with operating headlight and smoke; 234W whistle tender; 6014-410 Frisco boxcar; 3376 giraffe car; 6476 Lehigh Valley hopper; 6315 tank car; 6119 work caboose; seven 1013 curved and seven 1018 straight track; 6149 uncoupling section; 1044 90-watt transformer; CTC Lockon; instruction sheet.

The 2029 made its final appearance in this outfit—indeed the final outfit of the postwar era. Just as with the set listed above, sometimes the 234W tender included was lettered "PENNSYLVANIA" rather than Lionel Lines. The Pennsylvania version of this tender frequently did not have an operating coupler.

The cars in the outfit, however, usually had two operating couplers. Among the cars in the set were the 6315, 6014-410 and 6476 described earlier in this chapter. More desirable than these was the 3376 giraffe car, especially when it was the 3376-160 green version, or the even more elusive yellow-lettered blue car. To properly identify 1969-produced giraffe cars, look for giraffes without spots, open journal boxes on the AAR-type trucks, and sometimes a brass coupler armature pin. The values listed below presume that the 3376 included is the common blue with white lettering.

Somewhat sought after by collectors is this green version of the giraffe car.

Although shown here packaged for separate sale in a component box, this scarce yellow-lettered version of the blue 3376 is sometimes a component of outfit 11760—though sans individual box.

The work caboose was a bit of a contradiction. It used the unpainted red plastic cab of the 6130, yet it had the gray tool bin of the 6119, mounted on an unpainted and unlettered frame—hence it was numbered 6119.

Once again, all the components were packed sans individual boxes in a 1969-style outfit box.

Excellent	Like New	Scarcity
300	550	4

CROSS-REFERENCE

Catalog to "Special" Numbers

A-20	2338	2235W
A-21	665	2237WS
A-22	2363	2239W
A-23	646	2241WS
A-24	2321	2243W
A-25	2367	2244W
A-26	682	2245WS
A-27	2367	2247W
A-28	736	2249WS
A-29	2331	2251W
A-30	2340-25	2253W
A-31	2340	2254W
500	600	1525
501	610	1001
502	1615	1527
503	2028	1529
504	2037	1513S
505	2328	1531W
506	2016	1000W
507	2055	1533WS
508	2328	1534W
509	2243	1535W
510	2245	1536W
511	2065	1537WS
512	2065	1538WS
513	2243	1539W
514	2065	1541WS
700	627	1543
701	628	1545
702	2018	1547S
703	1615	1549
704	621	1551W
705	629	1552
706	2338	1553W
707	2018	1555WS
708	621	1557W
709	2338	1559W
710	2065	1561WS
711	2328	1562W
712	2240	1563W
713	2065	1565WS
714	2243	1567W
725	202	1569
726	625	1571
727	250	1573
728	205	1575
729	2018	1577S
730	2018	1587S
731	2037	1579S
732	611	1581
733	2037	1583WS
734	602	1585W
735	204	1586
736	2037-500	1587S
737	2037	1589WS
750	520	1542
800	601	2255W
801	665	2257WS
802	2350	2259W
803	646	2261WS
804	2350	2263W
805	736	2265WS
806	2331	2267W
807	2368	2269W
808	2341	2270W
809	2360-25	2271W
810	2378	2273W
811	2360	2274W
815	2339	2275W
816	404	2276W
817	665	2277WS
818	2350	2279W
819	2243	2281W
820	646	2283WS
821	2231	2285W
822	2351	2287W
823	736	2289WS
824	2379	2291W
825	646	2292WS
826	2360	2293W
827	746	2296WS
828	2373	2296W
829	746	2297WS

Outfit Locomotive Years

463W	224	1945
1000W	2016	1955
1001	610	1955
1105	1055	1959 advance
1107	1055	1960 advance
1109	1060	1960 advance
1111	1001	1948
1112	1001 or 1101	1948
1113	1120	1950
1115	1110	1949
1117	1110	1949
1119	1110	1951-52
1123	1060	1961 advance
1124	1060	1961 advance
1125	1065	1961 advance
1400	221	1946
1400W	221	1946
1401	1654	1946
1401W	1654	1946
1402	1666	1946
1402W	1666	1946
1403	221	1946
1403W	221	1946
1405	1666	1946
1405W	1666	1946
1407B	1665	1946
1409	1666	1946
1409W	1666	1946
1411W	1666	1946
1413WS	2020	1946
1415WS	2020	1946
1417WS	2020	1946
1419WS	2020	1946
1421WS	2020	1946
1423W	1655	1948-49
1425W	1656	1948-49
1426WS	2026	1948-49
1427WS	2026	1948
1429WS	2026	1948
1430WS	2025	1948-49
1431	1654	1947
1431W	1654	1947
1432	221	1947
1432W	221	1947
1433	221	1947
1433W	221	1947
1434WS	2025	1947
1435WS	2025	1947
1437WS	2025	1947
1439WS	2025	1947
1441WS	2020	1947
1443WS	2020	1947
1445WS	2025	1948
1447WS	2020	1948-49
1449WS	2020	1948
1451WS	2026	1949
1453WS	2026	1949
1455WS	2025	1949
1457B	6220	1949-50
1459WS	2020	1949
1461S	6110	1950
1463W	2036	1950
1463WS	2026	1951
1464W	2023	1950-51
1464W	2033	1952-53
1465	2034	1952
1467W	2023	1950-51
1467W	2032	1952-53
1469WS	2035	1950-51
1471WS	2035	1950-51
1473WS	2046	1950
1475WS	2046	1950
1477S	2026	1951-52
1479WS	2056	1952
1481WS	2035	1951
1483WS	2056	1952
1484WS	2056	1952
1485WS	2025	1952
1500	1130	1953-54
1501S	2026	1953
1502WS	2055	1953
1503WS	2055	1953-54
1505WS	2046	1953
1507WS	2046	1953
1509WS	2046	1953
1511S	2037	1953
1513S	2037	1954-55
1515WS	2065	1954
1516WS	2065	1954
1517W	2245	1954
1519WS	2065	1954
1520W	2245	1954
1521WS	2065	1954
1523	6250	1954
1525	600	1955
1527	1615	1955
1529	2028	1955
1531W	2328	1955
1533WS	2055	1955
1534W	2328	1955
1535W	2243	1955
1536W	2245	1955
1537WS	2065	1955
1538WS	2065	1955
1539W	2243	1955
1541WS	2065	1955
1542	520	1956
1543	627	1956
1545	628	1956
1547S	2018	1956
1549	1615	1956
1551W	621	1956
1552	629	1956
1553W	2338	1956
1555WS	2018	1956
1557W	621	1956
1559W	2338	1956
1561WS	2065	1956
1562W	2328	1956
1563W	2240	1956
1565WS	2065	1956
1567W	2243	1956
1569	202	1957
1571	625	1957
1573	250	1957
1575	205	1957
1577S	2018	1957
1578S	2018	1957
1579S	2037	1957
1581	611	1957
1583WS	2037	1957
1585W	602	1957
1586	204	1957
1587S	2037-500	1957-58
1589WS	2037	1957
1590	249	1958
1591	212 Marine	1958
1593	613	1958
1595	1625	1958
1597S	2018	1958
1599	210	1958
1600	216	1958
1601W	2337	1958
1603WS	2037	1958
1605W	208	1958
1607WS	2037	1958
1608W	209	1958

1609	246	1959-60
1611	614	1959
1612	1862	1959-60
1613S	247	1959
1615	217	1959
1617S	2018	1959
1619W	218	1959
1621WS	2037	1959
1623W	2349	1959
1625WS	2037	1959
1626W	208	1959
1627S	244	1960
1629	225	1960
1631WS	243	1960
1633	224	1960
1635WS	2037	1960
1637W	218	1960
1639WS	2037	1960
1640W	218	1960
1641	246	1961
1642	244	1961
1643	230	1961
1644	1862	1961
1645	229	1961
1646	233	1961
1647	45	1961
1648	2037	1961
1649	218	1961
1650	2037	1961
1651	218	1961
1800	1862	1959-60
1805	45	1960
1809	244	1961
1810	231	1961
2100	224	1946
2100W	224	1946
2101	224	1946
2101W	224	1946
2103W	224	1946
2105WS	671	1946
2110WS	671	1946
2111WS	671	1946
2113WS	726	1946
2114WS	726	1946
2115WS	726	1946
2120S	675	1947
2120WS	675	1947
2121S	675	1947
2121WS	675	1947
2123WS	675	1947
2124W	2332	1947
2125WS	671	1947
2126WS	671	1947
2127WS	671	1947
2129WS	726	1947
2131WS	726	1947
2133W	2333	1948
2135WS	675	1948-49
2136WS	675	1948-49
2137WS	675	1948
2139W	2332	1948-49
2140WS	671	1948-49
2141WS	671	1948-49
2143WS	671	1948
2144W	2332	1948-49
2145WS	726	1948
2146WS	726	1948-49
2147WS	675	1949
2148WS	773	1950
2149B	622	1949
2150WS	681	1950
2151W	2333	1949
2153WS	671	1949
2155WS	726	1949
2159W	2330	1950
2161W	2343	1950
2163WS	736	1950-51
2165WS	736	1950
2167WS	681	1950-51
2169WS	773	1950
2171W	2344	1950
2173WS	681	1950-51
2175W	2343	1950-51
2177WS	675	1952
2179WS	671	1952
2183WS	726	1952
2185W	2344	1950-51
2187WS	671	1952
2189WS	726	1952
2190W	2343	1952
2190W	2353	1953
2191W	2343	1952
2193W	2344	1952
2201WS	685	1953
2201WS	665	1954
2203WS	681	1953
2205WS	736	1953
2207W	2353	1953
2209W	2354	1953
2211WS	681	1953
2213WS	736	1953
2217WS	682	1954
2219W	2321	1954
2221WS	646	1954
2222WS	646	1954
2223W	2321	1954
2225WS	736	1954
2227W	2353	1954
2229W	2354	1954
2231W	2356	1954
2234W	2353	1954
2235W	2338	1955
2237WS	665	1955
2239W	2363	1955
2241WS	646	1955
2243W	2321	1955
2244W	2367	1955
2245WS	682	1955
2247W	2367	1955
2249WS	736	1955
2251W	2331	1955
2253W	2340-25	1955
2254W	2340	1955
2255W	601	1956
2257WS	665	1956
2259W	2350	1956
2261WS	646	1956
2263W	2350	1956
2265WS	736	1956
2267W	2331	1956
2269W	2368	1956
2270W	2341	1956
2271W	2360-25	1956
2273W	2378	1956
2274W	2360	1956
2275W	2339	1957
2276W	404	1957
2277WS	665	1957
2279W	2350	1957
2281W	2243	1957
2283WS	646	1957
2285W	2331	1957
2287W	2351	1957
2289WS	736	1957
2291W	2379	1957
2292WS	646	1957
2293W	2360	1957
2295WS	746	1957
2296W	2373	1957
2297WS	746	1957
2501W	2348	1958
2502W	400	1958
2503WS	665	1958
2505W	2329	1958
2507W	2242	1958
2509WS	665	1958
2511W	2352	1958
2513W	2329	1958
2515WS	646	1958
2517W	2379	1958
2518W	2352	1958
2519W	2331	1958
2521WS	746	1958
2523W	2383	1958
2525WS	746	1958
2526W	2383	1958
2527	44	1959-60
2528WS	1872	1959-61
2529W	2329	1959
2531WS	637	1959
2533W	2358	1959
2535WS	665	1959
2537W	2242	1959
2539WS	665	1959
2541W	2383	1959
2543WS	736	1959
2544W	2383	1959-60
2545WS	746	1959
2547WS	637	1960
2549W	2349	1960
2551W	2358	1960
2553WS	736	1960
2555W	2383	1960
2570	616	1961
2571	637	1961
2572	2359	1961
2573	736	1961
2574	2383	1961
2575	2360	1961
2576	2383	1961
3105W	1666	1947 advance
4109WS	671R	1946-47
4110WS	671R	1948-49
11001	1060	1962 advance
11011	222	1962 advance
11201	242	1962
11212	633	1962
11222	236	1962
11232	232	1962
11242	233	1962
11252	211	1962
11268	2365	1962
11278	2037	1962
11288	229	1962
11298	2037	1962
11308	218	1962
11311	1062	1963
11321	221	1963
11331	242	1963
11341	634	1963
11351	237	1963
11361	211	1963
11375	238	1963
11385	223	1963
11395	2037	1963
11405	218	1963
11415	1061	1963 advance
11420	1061	1964
11430	1062	1964
11440	221	1964
11450	242	1964
11460	238	1964
11470	237	1964
11480	213	1964
11490	212	1964-65
11500	2029	1964-66
11510	2029	1964
11520	242	1965-66
11530	634	1965-66
11540	239	1965-66
11550	239	1965-66
11560	211	1965-66
11590	212	1966
11600	2029	1968
11710	1061	1969
11720	2024	1969
11730	645	1969
11740	2041	1969
11750	2029	1969
11760	2029	1969
12502	1862	1962
12512	45	1962
12700	736	1964
12710	736	1964-66
12720	2383	1964
12730	2383	1964-66
12740	2383	1964
12750	2383	1964
12760	736	1964
12770	736	1964
12780	2383	1964-66
12800	2346	1965-66
12820	2322	1965
12840	665	1966
12850	2322	1966
13008	637	1962
13018	616	1962
13028	2359	1962
13036	1872	1962
13048	736	1962
13058	2383	1962
13068	2360	1962
13078	2360	1962
13088	2383	1962
13098	637	1963
13108	617	1963
13118	736	1963
13128	2383	1963
13138	2360	1963
13148	2383	1963
13150	773	1964-66

Numeric By Locomotive Number, With Outfit Number and Catalog Year

44: 2527 (1959-60)
45: 1805 (1960), 1647 (1961), 12512 (1962)
202: 1569 or 725 (1957)
204: 1586 or 735 (1957)
205: 1575 or 728(1957)
208: 1605W (1958), 1626W (1959)
209:1608W (1958)
210: 1599 (1958)
211: 11252 (1962), 11361 (1963), 11560 (1965-66)
212 (USMC): 1591 (1958)
212 (Santa Fe): 11490 (1964-65), 11590 (1966)
213: 11480 (1964)
216: 1600 (1958)
217: 1615 (1959)
218: 1619W (1959), 1637W (1960), 1640W (1960), 1649 (1961), 1651 (1961), 11308 (1962), 11405 (1963)
221 (steam): 1400 and 1400W (1946), 1403 and 1403W (1946), 1432 and 1432W (1947), 1433 and 1433W (1947)
221 (diesel): 11321 (1963), 11440 (1964)
222: 11011 (1962 advance)
223: 11385 (1963)
224 (steam): 463W (1945), 2100 and 2100W (1946), 2101 and 2101W (1946), 2103W (1946)
224 (diesel): 1633 (1960)
225: 1629 (1960)
229: 1645 (1961), 11288 (1962)
230: 1643 (1961)
231: 1810 (1961)
232: 11232(1962)
233: 1646 (1961), 11242 (1962)
236:11222 (1962)
237: 11351 (1963), 11470 (1964)
238: 11375 (1963), 11460 (1964)
239: 11540 (1965-66), 11550 (1965-66)
242: 11201 (1962), 11331 (1963), 11450 (1964), 11520 (1965-66)
243: 1631WS (1960)
244: 1627S (1960), 1642 (1961), 1809 (1961)
246: 1609 (1959-60), 1641 (1961)
247: 1613S (1959)
249: 1590(1958)
250: 1573 or 727(1957)
400: 2502W(1958)
404: 2276W or 816 (1957)
520: 1542 or 750 (1956)
600: 1525 or 500 (1955)
601: 2255W or 800 (1956)
602: 1585W or 734 (1957)
610: 1001 or 501(1955)
611: 1581 or 732(1957)
613: 1593 (1958)
614: 1611 (1959)
616: 2570 (1961), 13018(1962)
617: 13108 (1963)
621: 1551W or 704 (1956), 1557W or 708 (1956)
622: 2149B (1949)
625: 1571 or 726 (1957)
627: 1543 or 700(1956)
628: 1545 or 701(1956)
629: 1552 or 705(1956)
633: 11212 (1962)
634: 11341 (1963), 11530 (1965-66)
637: 2531WS (1959), 2547WS (1960), 2571 (1961), 13008 (1962), 13098 (1963)
645: 11730 (1969)
646: 2221WS (1954), 2222WS (1954), 2241WS orA-23 (1955), 2261WS or 803 (1956), 2283WS or 820 (1957), 2292WS or 825 (1957), 2515WS (1958)
665: 2201WS (1954), 2237WS or A-21 (1955), 2257WS or 801 (1956), 2277WS or 817 (1957), 2503WS (1958), 2509WS (1958), 2535WS (1959), 2539WS (1959), 12840 (1966)
671: 2105WS (1946), 2110WS (1946), 2111WS (1946), 2125WS (1947), 2126WS (1947), 2127WS (1947), 2140WS (1948-49), 2141WS (1948-49), 2143WS (1948), 2153WS (1949), 2179WS (1952), 2187WS (1952)
671R: 4109WS (1946-47), 4110WS (1948-49)
675: 2120S and 2120WS (1947), 2121S and 2121WS (1947), 2123WS (1947), 2135WS (1948-49), 2136WS (1948-49), 2137WS (1948), 2147WS (1949), 2177WS (1952)
681: 2150WS (1950), 2167WS (1950-51), 2173WS (1950-51), 2203WS (1953), 2211WS (1953)
682: 2217WS (1954), 2245WS or A-26 (1955)
685: 2201WS (1953)
726: 2113WS (1946), 2114WS (1946), 2115WS (1946), 2129WS (1947), 2131WS (1947), 2145WS (1948), 2146WS (1948-49), 2155WS (1949), 2183WS (1952), 2189WS (1952)
736: 2163WS (1950-51), 2165WS (1950), 2205WS (1953), 2213WS (1953), 2225WS (1954), 2249WS orA-28 (1955), 2265WS or 805 (1956), 2289WS or 823 (1957), 2543WS (1959), 2553WS (1960), 2573 (1961), 13048 (1962), 13118 (1963), 12700 (1964), 12710 (1964-66), 12760 (1964), 12770 (1964)
746: 2295WS or 827 (1957), 2297WS or 829 (1957), 2521WS (1958), 2525WS (1958), 2545WS (1959)
773: 2148WS (1950), 2169WS (1950), 13150 (1964-66)
1001: 1111 (1948), 1112 (1948)
1055: 1105 (1959 advance), 1107 (1960 advance)
1060: 1109 (1960 advance), 1123 (1961 advance), 1124 (1961 advance), 11001 (1962 advance)
1061: 11415 (1963 advance), 11420 (1964 consumer), 11710 (1969)
1062: 11311 (1963), 11430 (1964)
1065: 1125 (1961 advance)
1101: 1112 (1948)
1110: 1115 (1949), 1117 (1949), 1119 (1951-52)
1120: 1113 (1950)
1130: 1500 (1953-54)
1615: 1527 or 502 (1955), 1549 or 703 (1956)
1625: 1595 (1958)
1654: 1401 and 1401W (1946), 1431 and 1431W (1947)
1655: 1423W(1948-49)
1656: 1425B (1948-49)
1665: 1407B (1946)
1666: 1402 and 1402W (1946), 1405 and 1405W (1946), 1409 and 1409W (1946), 1411W (1946), 3105W (1947 advance)
1862: 1800 (1959-60), 1612 (1959-60), 1644 (1961), 12502 (1962)
1872: 2528WS (1959-61), 13036 (1962)
2016: 1000W or 506 (1955)
2018: 1547S or 702 (1956), 1555WS or 707 (1956), 1577S or 729 (1957), 1578S or 730 (1957), 1597S (1958), 1617S (1959)
2020: 1413WS (1946), 1415WS (1946), 1417WS (1946), 1419WS (1946), 1421WS (1946), 1441WS (1947), 1443WS (1947), 1447WS (1948-49), 1449WS (1948), 1459WS (1949)
2023: 1464W (1950 yellow, 1951 silver), 1467W (1950 yellow, 1951 silver)
2024: 11720(1969)
2025: 1434WS (1947), 1435WS (1947), 1437WS (1947), 1439WS (1947), 1430WS (1948-49), 1445WS (1948), 1455WS (1949), 1485WS (1952)
2026: 1426WS (1948-49), 1427WS (1948), 1429WS (1948), 1451WS (1949), 1453WS (1949), 1463WS (1951), 1477S (1951-52), 1501S (1953)
2028: 1529 or 503 (1955)
2029: 11500 (1964-66), 11510 (1964), 11600 (1968), 11750 (1969), 11760 (1969)
2032: 1467W (1952-53)
2033: 1464W (1952-53)
2034: 1465 (1952)
2035: 1469WS (1950-51), 1471WS (1950-51), 1481WS (1951)
2036: 1463W (1950)
2037: 1511S (1953), 1513S (1954), 1513S or 504 (1955), 1579S or 731 (1957), 1583WS or 733 (1957), 1589WS or 737 (1957), 1603WS (1958), 1607WS (1958), 1621WS (1959), 1625WS (1959), 1635WS (1960), 1639WS (1960), 1648 (1961), 1650 (1961), 11278 (1962), 11298 (1962), 11395 (1963)
2037-500: 1587S or 736 (1957-58)
2041: 11740 (1969)
2046: 1473WS (1950), 1475WS (1950), 1505WS (1953), 1507WS (1953), 1509WS (1953)
2055: 1502WS (1953), 1503WS (1953-54), 1533WS or 507 (1955)
2056: 1479WS (1952), 1483WS (1952), 1484WS (1952)
2065: 1515WS (1954), 1516WS (1954), 1519WS (1954), 1521WS (1954), 1537WS or 511 (1955), 1538WS or 512 (1955), 1541WS or 514 (1955), 1561WS or 710 (1956), 1565WS or 713 (1956)
2240: 1563W or 712 (1956)
2242: 2507W (1958), 2537W (1959)
2243: 1535W or 509 (1955), 1539W or 513 (1955), 1567W or 714 (1956), 2281W or 819 (1957)
2245: 1517W (1954), 1520W (1954), 1536W or 510 (1955)
2321: 2219W (1954), 2223W (1954), 2243W or A-24 (1955)
2322: 12820 (1965), 12850 (1966)
2328: 1531W or 505 (1955), 1534W or 508 (1955), 1562W or 711(1956)
2329: 2505W (1958), 2513W (1958), 2529W (1959)
2330: 2159W (1950)
2331: 2251W or A-29 (1955), 2267W or 806 (1956), 2285W or 821 (1957), 2519W (1958)
2332: 2124W (1947), 2139W (1948-49), 2144W (1948-49)
2333: Santa Fe or New York Central 2133W (1948), 2151W (1949)
2337: 1601W(1958)
2338: 2235W or A-20 (1955), 1553W or 706 (1956), 1559W or 709(1956)
2339: 2275W or 815 (1957)
2340: 2254W or A-31 (1955)
2340-25: 2253W or A-30 (1955)
2341: 2270W or 808 (1956)
2343: 2161W (1950), 2175W (1950-51), 2190W (1952), 2191W(1952)
2344: 2171W (1950), 2185W (1950-51), 2193W (1952)
2346:12800(1965-66)
2348: 2501W(1958)
2349: 1623W (1959), 2549W (1960)
2350: 2259W or 802 (1956), 2263W or 804 (1956), 2279W or 818(1957)
2351: 2287W or 822 (1957)
2352: 2511WC1958), 2518 (1958)
2353: 2190W (1953), 2207W (1953), 2227W (1954), 2234W (1954)
2354: 2209W (1953), 2229W (1954)
2356: 2231W(1954)
2358: 2533W (1959), 2551W (1960)
2359: 2572 (1961), 13028 (1962)
2360: 2274W or 811 (1956), 2293W or 826 (1957), 2575 (1961), 13068 (1962), 13078 (1962), 13138 (1963)
2360-25: 2271W or 809 (1956)
2363: 2239W or A-22 (1955)
2365: 11268 (1962)
2367: 2244W or A-25 (1955), 2247W or A-27 (1955)
2368: 2269W or 807 (1956)
2373: 2296W or 828 (1957)
2378: 2273W or 810 (1956)
2379: 2291W or 824 (1957), 2517W (1958)
2383: 2523W (1958), 2526W (1958), 2541W (1959), 2544W (1959-60), 2555W (1960), 2574 (1961), 2576 (1961), 13058 (1962), 13088 (1962), 13128 (1963), 13148 (1963), 12720 (1964), 12730 (1964-66), 12740 (1964), 12750 (1964), 12780 (1964-66)
6110: 1461S (1950)
6220: 1457B (1949-50)
6250: 1523 (1954)